AUDITORY DISORDERS IN SCHOOL CHILDREN

SECOND EDITION

WITHDRAWN

Date Due

D1710752

AUDITORY DISORDERS IN SCHOOL CHILDREN

Identification • Remediation

SECOND EDITION

Roeser, Ph.D.

Ross J. Roeser, Ph.D.
Chief of Audiology and Professor
Callier Center for Communication Disorders
University of Texas at Dallas
Dallas, Texas

Marion P. Downs, M.A., D.H.S.
Professor Emeritus, Department of Otolaryngology
Division of Audiology
University of Colorado
Health Sciences Center
Denver, Colorado

1988
Thieme Medical Publishers, Inc.
Georg Thieme Verlag • Stuttgart • New York

Thieme Medical Publishers, Inc.
381 Park Avenue South
New York, New York 10016

AUDITORY DISORDERS IN SCHOOL CHILDREN
Second Edition
Ross J. Roeser and Marion P. Downs

Library of Congress Cataloging in Publication Data
Auditory disorders in school children: identification, remediation
[edited by] Ross J. Roeser, Marion P. Downs.   p.   cm.
   Includes index.
      1. Hearing disorders in children.   2. School children—Diseases.
3. Physically handicapped children—Rehabilitation.   I. Roeser,
Ross J.   II. Downs, Marion P.
   [DNLM: 1. Education, Special—United States.   2. Hearing
Disorders—in infancy & childhood.   3. Hearing Disorders—therapy.
4. Remedial Teaching.   WV 271 A912]
   RF291.5.C45A85   1988   362.1'98920978—dc19
   DNLM/DLC   87-27809

Printed in the United States of America.

TMP ISBN 0-86577-270-3
GTV ISBN 3-13-599802-9

CONTENTS

PREFACE
TO THE
SECOND EDITION

The first edition of *Auditory Disorders in School Children* was written as a result of the then recent changes in educational placement of handicapped children that were mandated in PL 94-142. This law was labeled a "civil rights act for the handicapped," and has had a profound effect on educational institutions and the personnel serving handicapped children in the schools. It was our goal in the first edition to attack the question of what is best for the school child with an auditory disorder as it related to the Law, to Identification, and to Management and Remediation. Our goal was to put forth ideas, ideals, and procedures for identification and remediation that would allow each child to achieve his or her maximum educational potential.

In this second edition, we have made significant modifications and provide innovative and new challenging concepts. Most educators and school administrators are now familiar with the laws that govern handicapped children; these laws change more quickly than the typical life expectancy of a textbook. Consequently, we have eliminated the section we included in the first edition on the Law. Instead, readers will find relevant material on legal issues relating to state and federal guidelines and mainstreaming in a more practical format in the section covering Remediation.

Eliminating the section on the Law has allowed us to concentrate on Identification and Remediation. In this second edition we present unique materials related to:

• Advances in immittance and auditory screening
• New concepts in medical management
• New strategies in identifying and providing remediation for central auditory disorders
• Assistive listening devices as they relate to school-age children
• Providing assistance to deaf students with cochlear implants and tactile aids
• A thorough listing of resource materials for use with hearing impaired students

This text brings together a group of experts who present innovative ideas on how to help the individual child with hearing loss in the schools in the best possible way. Knowledge of the material presented in this text is mandatory for students who are planning careers in the schools. All practicing school clinicians should be aware of the contents of this book so that children with auditory disorders will be served appropriately and reach their maximum educational potential.

Ross J. Roeser
Marion P. Downs

ACKNOWLEDGMENTS

We wish to thank our authors for their diligence in meeting our tight schedule and hasty deadlines. We also thank Jackie L. Clark, M.S. for her help in reviewing and editing manuscripts.

Ross J. Roeser
Marion P. Downs

CONTRIBUTORS

CAROL AMON, M.A.
    Consultant, Colorado Department of Education, Special Education Services, Denver, Colorado
    Remediation Within and Beyond State and Federal Guidelines

R. RAY BATTIN, Ph.D.
    Director, The Battin Clinic, Houston, Texas
    Psycho-Educational Assessment of Children with Auditory Language Learning Problems

LaVONNE BERGSTROM, M.D., F.A.C.S.
    Professor of Surgery, Division of Head and Neck Surgery, U.C.L.A., Los Angeles, California
    Medical Problems and Their Management

VIRGINIA S. BERRY, M.S.
    State Consultant, Educational Audiology, Arkansas School for the Deaf, Little Rock, Arkansas
    Classroom Intervention Strategies and Resource Materials for the Auditorily Handicapped Child

MARION P. DOWNS, M.A., D.H.S.
    Professor Emeritus, Department of Otolaryngology, Division of Audiology, University of Colorado Health Sciences Center, Denver, Colorado
    Contribution of Mild Hearing Loss to Auditory Language Learning Problems

DIANE FOMBY, M.S. Ed.
    Teacher, Southwest School for the Hearing Impaired, Los Angeles, California
    Mainstreaming as a Remedial Strategy

TERESE FINITZO, Ph.D.
    Associate Professor, Callier Center for Communication Disorders, University of Texas at Dallas, Dallas, Texas
    Classroom Acoustics

GLORIA H. HOVERSTEN, M.A.
    Audiologist, Southwest School for the Hearing Impaired
    Mainstreaming as a Remedial Strategy

ROBERT W. KEITH, Ph.D.
>   Professor and Director, Division of Audiology and Speech Pathology,
>   University of Cincinnati Medical Center, Cincinnati, Ohio
>   Tests of Central Auditory Function

ROBERT E. KRETSCHMER, Ph.D.
>   Associate Professor, Department of Special Education, Teachers College,
>   Columbia University, New York, New York
>   Psycho-Educational Assessment of Hearing Impaired Children

LYNDA MILLER, Ph.D.
>   Director, The Language and Learning Institute, Chicago, Illinois
>   Remediation of Children with Auditory Language Learning Disorders

CAROLYN J. MITCHELL, Ph.D.
>   Clinical Psychologist, Private Practice, Dallas, Texas
>   Counseling for the Parent

CAROLYN H. MUSKET, M.A.
>   Coordinator, Graduate Practicum in Audiology, University of Texas at
>   Dallas, Callier Center for Communication Disorders, Dallas, Texas
>   Maintenance of Personal Hearing Aids
>   Assistive Listening Devices and Systems for the Hearing Impaired Student

ETHEL F. MUSSEN, Ph.D.
>   Clinical Audiologist, Private Practice, Berkeley, California
>   Techniques and Concepts in Auditory Training and Speechreading

JERRY L. NORTHERN, Ph.D.
>   Professor, Department of Otolaryngology, Head of Audiology Division,
>   University of Colorado Health Sciences Center, Denver, Colorado
>   Screening for Hearing Loss and Middle Ear Disorders

RICHARD G. PIMENTEL, B.A.
>   Vice President, Sales and Marketing, Phonic Ear, Inc., Mill Valley, California
>   Classroom Amplification Systems for the Partially Hearing Student

STEPHEN P. QUIGLEY, Ph.D.
>   Professor of Education and Speech Hearing Science, University of Illinois,
>   Champaign, Illinois
>   Psycho-Educational Assessment of Hearing Impaired Children

ROSS J. ROESER, Ph.D.
>   Chief of Audiology and Professor, Callier Center for Communication Disor-
>   ders, University of Texas at Dallas, Dallas, Texas
>   Audiometric and Immittance Measures: Principles and Interpretation
>   Screening for Hearing Loss and Middle Ear Disorders
>   Cochlear Implants and Tactile Aids for the Profoundly Deaf Student

Identification | I

INTRODUCTION

The quest for the most appropriate test to identify hearing loss in school children began as early as 1927, at which time the Western Electric 4-C Group Speech Test was introduced as a screening technique. Following this early effort, procedures for hearing screening in the schools emphasized group tests and for 30 to 35 years such tests were in vogue. However, this trend changed with the discovery of the many pitfalls that exist in group tests, and at present virtually all of the emphasis is placed on individual tests.

The emphasis on individual testing and the gradual collection of data on hearing loss in school children has given a new direction to school hearing conservation programs. It is now well established that middle ear disorders, even those that are transient, can have a significant effect on speech and language development. This fact, coupled with the introduction of new technology making it possible to conduct reliable, valid, and cost-effective screening for middle ear disorders, has changed many of the traditional approaches in school auditory screening programs.

There is some controversy regarding the place of immittance testing for mass screening of middle ear function. This controversy has recently resulted in a position statement from the American Academy of Pediatrics (AAP), Committee on School Health, against the use of immittance measures in school screening.[1] While there may be pragmatic reasons why immittance measures can be questioned, the AAP position statement does not appear to be in the best interest of the individual child; if the program is designed in the best possible interest of the individual child, there would be no question that auditory screening programs will include appropriate screening of middle ear function along with audiometric screening for hearing loss.

With sophistication of equipment and advancement of screening techniques comes the requirement that the personnel involved in auditory screening programs have greater skills. Also is the requirement that they have concern for the total program, so that the individual needs of each child be met. No longer should school personnel be content with simply identifying the child with hearing losses. School personnel *must* be concerned about: identifying those children with all types of auditory disorders, including minimal hearing loss and middle ear disorders; referring those children failing the screening for appropriate medical follow-up; and providing remedial educational programs for those children who have sustained hearing loss. All facets of the process must be established and carried out on each child for the program to be effective.

This part of our text covers information on the identification process. It is imperative that those involved in audiometric and immittance screening have a thorough understanding of the principles underlying the measurements obtained and be able to interpret the data collected from the screening tests and from additional diagnostic testing. This information is covered in Chapter 1. The physician plays a key role in the diagnosis and management of auditory disorders in school children. Chapter 2 covers medical aspects of hearing loss that must be known by the school personnel involved in the identification program.

Far too often, school personnel involved in the screening do not have a general overview of the purpose of screening and the philosophies underlying the screening process. Moreover, there are numerous sets of guidelines that have been published on screening for hearing loss and middle ear disorders. In Chapter 3, the screening process is reviewed and guidelines are presented which summarize an effective program. Chapter 4 covers the difficult area of central auditory testing; practical guidelines are given on how to identify and assess this most perplexing population of children. In Chapters 5 and 6, psycho-educational assessment of children with hearing impairment and language learning problems are covered respectively.

In this part of our book we bring together all of the knowledge and expertise one should have in developing and carrying out an effective hearing conservation program, and in assessing the child with auditory impairment in the schools.—RJR, MPD

REFERENCE

1. American Academy of Pediatrics, Committee on School Health, Impedance bridge (tympanometer) as a screening device in schools. *Pediatrics*, 79 (1987), 472.

1

AUDIOMETRIC AND IMMITTANCE MEASURES: PRINCIPLES AND INTERPRETATION*

Ross J. Roeser

INTRODUCTION

The overall purpose of this chapter is to provide the necessary information for school personnel to procure and maintain equipment for school programs and to help them interpret audiometric data from the screening program and diagnostic test results from follow-up testing. Information is also given on purchasing and maintaining equipment used in audiometric and immittance screening programs.

THE PHYSICAL BASES OF HEARING

Sound

Most people are aware that the human ear responds to sound, but few are familiar with the technical aspects of sound and the terms used to describe its physical characteristics. Both the technical aspects and physical characteristics of sound must be understood by those dealing with hearing loss to have a working knowledge of the range of difficulty that a particular loss of hearing may present.

All definitions of sound contain two primary concepts necessary to its understanding. The first is that sound is created by the movement or vibration of molecules in the air. Vibration refers to back-and-forth movement or oscillation of molecular particles. To give rise to a

---

*Originally, the term *impedance* was used to describe this clinical procedure. However, because the procedure is electronically/electroacoustically based on the measurement of impedance or admittance, the term *immittance*[1] was created to encompass both techniques. The term immittance is now widely accepted, although some clinicians and manufacturers have not chosen to adopt the new terminology.

sound wave, an object, or vibrator, must be set into motion by a force causing molecular displacement or disruption of air particles.

The second basic element necessary to understand sound is that vibrations are propagated in an elastic medium. The elastic medium propagating sound in our environment is air. This implies that if a vibrator was set into motion in a vacuum, the sensation of hearing would not occur, because no medium exists to transmit the vibrations.

With the above three factors (vibrator, force, and medium), sound should be created. However, simply causing the physical conditions needed for sound may not be enough. Some people say that to create sound, it is also necessary to have an ear to perceive sound. Thus, if a vibrator were set into motion and air particles were carried by a medium but no one perceived the vibrations, these people would say that the sound in actuality did not occur.

Figure 1-1 is a summary of the concepts presented above. In this figure, the four elements necessary for sound are presented: a force, a vibrator, a medium, and an ear.

Frequency and Intensity

Two parameters of sound that define its basic characteristics are frequency and intensity.

Frequency. The physical measurement of what is psychologically perceived as pitch is frequency. Frequency specifies the number of back-and-forth oscillations or cycles produced by a vibrator in a given time as a sound is created. The term used to describe frequency is *Hertz*, abbreviated Hz, and this term specifies the number of cycles that occur in one second. For example, if a vibrator were set into motion and completed 1000 back-and-forth cycles in one second, it would have a frequency of 1000 Hz. Frequency and pitch are related in

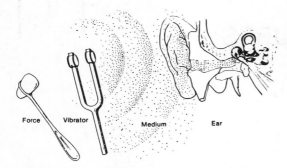

Figure 1-1. The four elements necessary for the production of sound.

that as the frequency of a sound increases, the listener perceives a tone of a higher and higher pitch.

A sound can be made up of only one frequency or, as in most instances, of many different frequencies. The simplest form of sound occurs if only one frequency is present; this form of sound is called a *pure* tone. In the example given above, the 1000 Hz vibrator was generating a pure tone, because only one frequency occurred.

Pure tones are used primarily because they are the simplest form of sound to generate, the easiest to control, and they differentially test the specific effects of lesions in the auditory system. However, pure tones do not exist in our everyday environment. Most sounds we encounter are *complex sounds*, which contain many different frequencies.

The human ear responds to frequencies between 20 and 20,000 Hz. Frequencies that are below this range are *infrasonic* and those above this range, *ultrasonic*. For example, a sound with a frequency of 10 Hz is infrasonic and would not be perceived by the normal ear, and a sound with a frequency of 30,000 Hz is ultrasonic and would also not be perceived.

Even though the ear responds to frequencies ranging from 20 to 20,000 Hz, only those frequencies between 300 to 3000 Hz are actually critical for the perception of speech. This means that it would be possible for an individual to have essentially no hearing above 3000 Hz and have only marginal difficulty in hearing speech in a quiet environment. In audiometric testing the frequencies evaluated range from 125 or 250 Hz through 8000 Hz. These frequencies are generally the most audible to the human ear and provide the audiologist with guidelines as to how well the individual is able to perceive speech, since the speech frequencies fall within this range.

As part of a standard audiometric evaluation, frequencies are tested at octave intervals. Thus, the typical audiogram is obtained at the frequencies 250, 500, 1000, 2000, 4000, and 8000 Hz, and in many instances, the half-octave frequencies of 750, 1500, 3000, and 6000 Hz are included.

Intensity. The physical measurement of what is psychologically perceived as loudness is intensity. Specifically, the intensity of a sound is determined by the amount of movement or displacement of air particles that occurs as a sound is created. The greater the amount of displacement, the more intense, or louder the sound. Intensity is measured in units called decibels, abbreviated dB, a term which literally means one-tenth of a Bell (named after Alexander Graham Bell). Technically the decibel is defined as the logarithmic ratio between two magnitudes of pressure or power.

As indicated by the technical definition, intensity is far more complicated than frequency, and to fully understand the decibel requires knowledge of advanced mathematical functions. The decibel is based on logarithmic function because the ear responds to a very large range of pressure changes and logarithms allow these changes to be expressed by smaller numbers than would be required for a linear function. There are excellent references that the interested reader may consult for additional information on how to compute decibels using logarithms (e.g., Berlin[2]).

Although the concepts underlying the decibel are somewhat complicated and will not be covered in this chapter, a less difficult concept is that the decibel is a relative unit of measurement. This means that simply saying, for example, 10 dB or 20 dB has no specific meaning without specifying the reference for the measure. There are two dB reference levels most often used in audiometric testing: *sound pressure level* (SPL) and *hearing level* (HL). These two reference levels are described as follows:

dB SPL. Sound pressure level refers to the absolute pressure reference level for the decibel. The pressure reference used to determine dB SPL is .000204 dynes/cm², so 0 dB SPL is equal to a pressure force of .000204 dynes/cm² and 10 dB or 20 dB SPL equals 10 or 20 dB above the .000204 dynes/cm² force. Because dB SPL is a physical measure, it is not affected by the frequencies present in sound.

dB HL. The reference for the decibel used to express deviation from normal hearing sensitivity is dB HL. As will be pointed out below, the ear is not sensitive to all frequencies at the same intensity. Hearing sensitivity changes as a function of the frequency of the sound. Therefore, 0 dB HL represents an intensity equal to the threshold sensitivity of the normal ear at each frequency. Audiometers are calibrated in dB HL, so that any decibel value above 0 dB HL represents a deviation from normal hearing levels. For example, 25 dB HL is 25 decibels above the normal hearing threshold for that frequency.

Over the past 30 years, three different standards have been used to define the absolute (SPL) levels at which the normal ear responds as a function of frequency. The three standards are: the American Standards Association (ASA), adopted in 1951[3]; the International Standards Organization (ISO),[4] adopted in 1961; and the American National Standards Institute (ANSI), adopted in 1969.[5] At present, all audiometers should conform to the ANSI 1969 standard.

In some instances, dB *hearing threshold level* (HTL) will also be used. When dB HTL is used, it implies that the decibel value given was a measured threshold from a patient; that is, the value was an actual level obtained from a given patient.

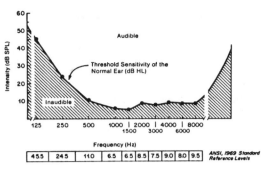

Figure 1-2. The threshold sensitivity of the normal ear as a function of frequency. The numbers at the bottom are the 1969 ANSI dB SPL values required to reach normal threshold sensitivity at each frequency.

THE AUDIOMETER AND AUDIOMETRY

The Audiometer

An audiometer is technically defined as an electronic device that generates signals used to assess hearing. There are various types of audiometers presently available from numerous manufacturers. The types of audiometers commercially available vary from simple screening models to very complex clinical instruments, and the signals generated range from simple pure tones to more complex stimuli, which are used in comprehensive testing.

Frequency and Intensity Function of the Human Ear

As stated earlier, the ear responds to different frequencies at different absolute intensities, or different SPLs. Stated in another way, it takes a different SPL to reach the level at which the normal ear will perceive the sound (threshold level) at different frequencies. Figure 1-2 illustrates the threshold sensitivity function of the normal ear and gives the 1969 ANSI levels required to reach threshold sensitivity at each frequency for normal ears (0 dB HL).

As shown in this figure, the ear is most sensitive in the midfrequencies, around 1000 to 1500 Hz. Since audiometers are calibrated in dB HL, it is not necessary to know the absolute dB SPL/HL difference at each frequency. The audiometer automatically corrects for the dB SPL/HL difference as the frequency is changed.

Basic Functions

Audiometers were first designed to generate the same frequencies as those produced by tuning forks; for example 256, 512, 1024, etc. However, audiometer manufacturers have now standardized their instruments on a scale based on even thousands of Hertz. Therefore, audiometers today generate at least all the following test frequencies: 125, 250, 500, 750, 1000, 1500, 2000, 2500, 3000, 4000, 6000, and 8000 Hz.

Several models of audiometers with limited versatility have been recommended for screening. Screening audiometers generally provide a choice of several discrete frequency pure tones as well as a method of precisely controlling the intensity of the tones. These audiometers range in price from about $400 to $600.

Diagnostic audiometers provide, in addition to pure tones, a speech circuit, and are designed so that many special diagnostic (site-of-lesion) auditory tests may be performed. The cost of this type instrument can be as high as $10,000 to $12,000, and its use requires a commercially built, sound-treated room. Diagnostic audiometers are generally found in clinical or medical settings and are not usually available in the school setting.

Regardless of the make or model, pure-tone audiometers have certain basic controls and switches in common. These components may vary in appearance and location according to different designs; however, they perform the same basic functions. To show the diversity that can be found in audiometers, Figure 1-3 illustrates two different commercially available audiometers with the external controls and parts of the instruments appropriately labeled. The correct way that the audiometer and tester should be situated in relation to the child when screening is shown in Figure 1-3B. As shown in this figure, the child should be readily observable to the tester, but the tester should be out of the child's peripheral vision.

The following describes the function of each major control shown in Figure 1-3.

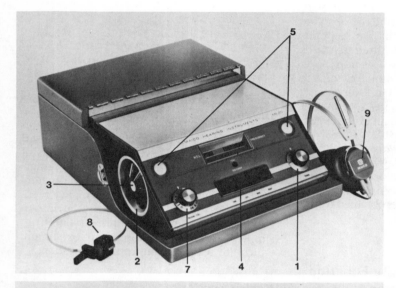

Figure 1-3. Components of two commercially available audiometers (see text for description) (*Top, courtesy of* Maico Hearing Instruments; *Bottom,* Beltone Electronics).

Power Supply (not shown). Some portable screening audiometers are battery powered. Battery-powered instruments are desirable because they can be used when power outlets are unavailable. However, the use of battery-powered audiometers is discouraged because the battery current may vary with usage, resulting in large variability in the output of the test stimuli.

On-Off or Power Switch (1 in Fig. 1-3). After the audiometer has been plugged in, it should be turned on and allowed to "warm up" for approximately 10 minutes prior to testing. This procedure assures that the proper current has reached all parts of the instrument for optimal functioning. The audiometer should remain in the "on" position for the remainder of the day when additional testing is to be performed, as there is less wear on the electrical components to leave it on all day than to turn it on and off several times during the day.

Attenuator or Hearing Level (HL) Dial (2 in Fig. 1-3). The intensity of the stimuli is controlled by the *attenuator* or *hearing level (HL) dial*. The attenuator is actually a group of resistors built into the output circuit to control the intensity in small steps. Most attenuators are designed to operate in 5 dB steps, although some operate in steps of 1 or 2 dB.

The attenuator dial has a range of 0 to 110 dB HL for air conduction testing, with 0 dB HL at each frequency being the threshold sensitivity for normal listeners. Not all of the test stimuli are capable of being presented at intensities of 110 dB HL. In most cases, 125, 250, and 8000 Hz have limited outputs, and the maximum output for each frequency is specified on the frequency selector dial. Bone conduction testing is limited to 0 to 40 or 0 to 60 or 65 dB HL, depending on the frequency.

Frequency Selector Dial (3 in Fig. 1-3B). The frequency selector dial allows stimuli to be varied in discrete steps from 125 to 8000 Hz in octave and half-octave intervals. As mentioned above, the frequency selector dial also shows, by use of smaller numerals on the dial, the maximum output (dB HL or dB HTL) that the audiometer is capable of producing at each test frequency.

Output Selector Switch (4 in Fig. 1-3). Test signals may be delivered to the right earphone, left earphone, or bone conduction oscillator. The output selector switch determines which of these devices is activated. Some audiometers may also have a "group" position on the output selector switch. This position is used when the audiometer activates multiple earphones for group testing. Because group tests are very seldom employed in school screening (see Chapter 3), the group output selector position is rarely, if ever, used.

Tone Interrupter (5 in Fig. 1-3) and *Tone Reverse Switch* (6 in Fig. 1-3B). The *tone interrupter* is a button, bar, or lever used either to present or interrupt the test stimuli, depending on the position of the *tone reverse switch*. The tone reverse switch allows for the tone to be "normally on" or "normally off." In the "normally on" position, the tone is turned off by depressing the tone interrupter. In the "normally off" position, the tone is presented by depressing the tone interrupter.

In audiometric testing the tone reverse switch should *always* be in the "normally off" position. Serious errors can result if the tone reverse switch is in the "normally on" position. The "normally on" position is used only during calibration, and for special audiometric tests not performed as part of screening.

Masking Dial (7 in Fig. 1-3A). In some instances, a masking sound must be applied to the non-test ear to ensure that crossover of the test signal is not occurring. The *masking dial* controls the level of the masking signal noise. Masking is a complicated procedure to understand and is not employed in screening programs.

Bone Conduction Oscillator (8 in Fig. 1-3A). The *bone conduction oscillator* is used to obtain threshold measures of bone conduction sensitivity. Bone conduction testing is a diagnostic procedure and should not be performed as part of routine screening unless specifically designed and supervised by an audiologist.[6] The capability to perform bone conduction tests is not necessary in audiometers used in screening programs.

Earphones (9 in Fig. 1-3). The earphones are secured in a standard headband, and transmit test tones to each ear individually according to a standardized color code: red for the right ear and blue for the left ear. Important points regarding earphones are: (*1*) earphones are calibrated to one specific audiometer and should always be considered an integral part of that particular instrument; (*2*) earphones should never be interchanged between audiometers unless the equipment is recalibrated;

and (3) the tension of the headband and re-siliency of the earphone cushions are impor-tant factors for reliable test results.

The standard audiometer earphone is made up of a driver mounted in a supra-aural (MX-41/AR) cushion (see example in Fig. 1-3). Al-though supra-aural cushions are standard equip-ment on audiometers, noise-excluding ear-phone cushions have been suggested for use in screening, because they reduce (attenuate) ambient noise more effectively than the stan-dard MX-41/AR cushion. This feature implies that accurate tests may be performed in the presence of higher background noise levels.

Figure 1-4 shows a diagram of the supra-aural cushion and two types of noise-exclud-ing cushions, the circumaural cushion, and the combined (circumaural/supra-aural) cushion. Although noise-excluding cushions do attenu-ate ambient noise more effectively than the standard cushion, research has shown that there is no advantage for using the circumaural cushion in audiometry, due to the excessive volume created by incomplete coupling of the driver to the pinna.[7,8] The use of the *combina-tion-type* cushion does provide both proper coupling and superior attenuation of ambient noise, which allows for accurate testing to be conducted in test environments having exces-sive noise.[9] However, the size and complexity of noise-excluding earphones make them more difficult to use and they have not been en-dorsed for use in hearing screening in the schools.

Calibration of Audiometers

All audiometers, whether they are used for screening or diagnostic purposes, must meet minimum requirements set by ANSI.[5] The standard can be obtained for a small fee by writing to the American National Standards Institute at 1430 Broadway, New York, NY 10018, or the Acoustical Society of America at 335 East 45th St., New York, NY 10017. While it is not mandatory to have the standard, it may be helpful to have it if the school system has the basic equipment necessary for calibration.

Studies have documented the unfortunate finding that audiometers used for school hear-ing screenings tend to go out of calibration frequently.[10] For example, Walton and Wil-son[11] found that 82% of the 50 audiometers used in a school hearing conservation pro-gram that were routinely serviced had one or more calibration problems that could have interfered with test results. Problems with me-chanical conditions, internal noise, intensity, use time, attenuator linearity, and frequency accounted for the major errors. Some manu-facturers have updated their equipment and are using more modern electronic compo-nents such as digital electronics and integrated circuits, which should increase the reliability and durability of screening audiometers. How-ever, field studies have not yet been reported.

The user of the audiometer is responsible for checking the equipment and providing for the regular calibration. Calibration is neces-

A = Electro-Acoustic Driver
B = Supra-Aural Cushion (MX-41/AR)
C = Resilient Cushion
D = Circumaural Dome
E = Foam Filled Cavity
F = Enclosed Volume of Air

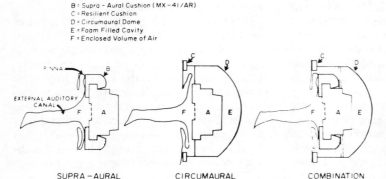

SUPRA-AURAL   CIRCUMAURAL   COMBINATION

Figure 1-4. Schematic showing the components of a supra-aural earphone cushion, a circumaural cushion, and a combination (cir-cumaural/supra-aural) cushion (from Musket and Roeser[9]).

sary to insure that the audiometer is producing a pure tone at the specific frequency and intensity, that the stimulus is present only in the earphone to which it is directed, and that the stimulus is free from unwanted noise, interference, and distortion.

There are four types of calibration schedules. These include a daily listening check, a monthly biological check, a periodic check (yearly), and an exhaustive check (every five years).

Daily Listening Check. Each morning following an appropriate warm-up time (10 minutes), the tester should listen to the signal emitted from the audiometer at various intensities and at all frequencies for transient clicks or distortions of the signal. The tester should also determine that the signal is in the correct earphone. It is far better to discover a malfunction in the equipment at the beginning of testing than to face inappropriate referrals.

Biological Calibration. Each month that the audiometer is in use, a biological calibration check is required on at least one subject whose hearing threshold is known. The procedure involves obtaining baseline threshold measurements on three to five normal-hearing individuals who will be available for comparison testing throughout the year. If on the monthly check, a threshold difference greater than 5 dB HL is found for one of the individuals for any test frequency between 500 and 6000 Hz, then the other subjects should be checked. If a shift greater than 5 dB in the same direction is confirmed by the additional biological checks, an electronic calibration of the audiometer is required. The results from each monthly biological calibration check should be recorded on a form that is kept in a calibration file maintained for each audiometer.

Periodic Electronic Calibration. At least once a year, every audiometer should have an electronic calibration to ensure that it meets the minimum standards defined by ANSI.[5] This service is provided by electronic or acoustic firms using specialized equipment. If it is necessary to ship the audiometer to another location for calibration, it should be packed carefully so that the instrument will be protected from damage in transit. As soon as the audiometer is returned from calibration or repair, the user should perform a biological check in order to re-establish new baseline threshold records on subjects as described above.

Exhaustive Electronic Calibration. Every five years, each audiometer must have an exhaustive electronic calibration. This calibration is more comprehensive than the periodic electronic calibration and includes the testing of all settings on the frequency and intensity (HL/HTL) dials, as well as replacing switches, cords, and earphone drivers and cushions.

BASIC AUDIOMETRIC TESTS

Pure tone and speech stimuli are employed in routine audiometry. Pure tone stimuli are used to obtain *air conduction* and *bone conduction thresholds* and results are displayed on a *pure-tone audiogram*. The term *threshold* is used to define the *lowest* or least intense level at which the individual being tested responds to the signal presented in a given number of trials. Standard psychophysical procedures have been developed for use in threshold assessment.[12] Speech stimuli are used in obtaining *speech reception thresholds* (SRT), also referred to as *spondee thresholds* (ST), and *speech* or *word discrimination* scores. Results from speech testing are typically recorded in a table next to the pure tone audiogram.

Pure Tone Audiometry

Pure Tone Air Conduction Audiometry. This type of testing involves the measurement of auditory sensitivity using specific pure tones presented to the listener through earphones mounted in a headset and placed over the ears. Pure tones provide information regarding the differential effects of lesions in the auditory system.

Pure Tone Bone Conduction Audiometry. Bone conduction testing is part of diagnostic audiometric testing. In bone conduction testing, thresholds are established in much the same manner as air conduction thresholds. However, instead of using earphones, a single bone conduction oscillator, secured in a standard headband (see Fig. 1-3A, #8) is placed behind the ear on the mastoid bone. The signal from the bone conduction oscillator sets the bones of the entire skull into motion, thus stimulating both inner ears (cochleas). Because both cochleas are stimulated, the response obtained may reflect the auditory sensitivity of the better cochlea. Thus, in bone conduction testing, it may become necessary to mask the ear not being tested when a hearing loss is present.

Speech Audiometry

Many individuals first become aware that they have a hearing loss when their ability to understand speech becomes impaired. Pure tone measurements only give limited information concerning communication difficulties. To quantify communication difficulty, it is necessary to assess the individual's ability to detect and understand speech material.

In speech audiometry, words are spoken into a microphone or delivered using a tape or record with the output signal regulated by the audiometer. The listener wears earphones, is instructed to repeat the test words or write them down, and one ear is tested at a time. With children, several standardized tests have also been developed using picture-pointing responses, rather than written and/or spoken responses.

Using these basic procedures, the threshold for speech and speech or word discrimination scores are obtained. The measure of the threshold for speech was first referred to as the *speech reception threshold* (SRT) and many clinics still use this terminology. However, the term *spondee threshold* (ST) was recently recommended as a replacement for the term SRT.[13]

Spondee Threshold.   The ST is a measure of auditory threshold sensitivity for speech. The standard procedure in obtaining the ST is to use spondee words. Spondee words are compound or bisyllabic words such as *railroad, toothbrush,* and *outside,* presented with equal stress on both syllables. The main function of the ST is to confirm the pure tone thresholds; in addition it serves as a reference for the level at which word discrimination testing is performed.

The primary frequencies used to discriminate speech sounds are between 300 and 3000 Hz. Thus, the ST should be in agreement with the thresholds that fall within this region. The three octave frequencies tested within the 300 to 3000 Hz range are 500, 1000, and 2000 Hz. Together these three frequencies are used to calculate the *pure tone average* (PTA). For example, if thresholds are 60, 75, and 80 dB HL at 500, 1000, and 2000 Hz, the PTA would be 72 dB HL. The ST and PTA should agree to within −8

to +6 dB[14]; in the above example, the ST should be 64 to 78 dB HL.

In some cases, when there is a large difference in one of the three frequencies, only two frequencies are used to calculate the PTA.[15] If the PTA and ST are not in close agreement, it suggests that the listener may not be fully cooperating with the testing (functional hearing loss) or may not understand the task.

When hearing loss is in the severe to profound range, and/or word discrimination is very poor, a reception threshold to spondee words may not be obtainable. In such cases a *speech awareness threshold* (SAT) is obtained. Rather than a measure of speech reception, the SAT simply quantifies the lowest level at which speech is detected. The SAT will agree with the pure tone audiogram, in that it will be within 5 to 10 dB of the best (lowest) threshold in the 250 to 3000 Hz range. The SAT may also be influenced by the threshold at 125 Hz, and although this frequency is not routinely tested, it should be tested when an SAT is obtained.

Word Discrimination.   This type of test was first referred to as a test of speech discrimination, but word discrimination more accurately describes the test. Word discrimination tests provide an index of the patient's ability to understand spoken words presented at a level ideal for maximum intelligibility, typically at 30 to 40 dB above the listener's ST. Word discrimination ability is tested using standardized, phonetically balanced lists of single syllable (monosyllabic) words. Phonetically balanced indicates that the distribution of phonetic elements in the lists approximates the distribution found in everyday conversation.

Word discrimination scores are calculated in percentage correct, 100%, meaning that all speech stimuli were discriminated correctly. The following is a general guide for interpreting most standard word discrimination test scores.[16]

90 to 100%—within the range of normal
75 to 90%—slight difficulty
60 to 75%—moderate difficulty
50 to 60%—poor discrimination
       50%—very poor discrimination

The Audiogram

The audiogram is a graph or grid on which audiometric data are displayed. Many clinics use audiograms to record their data, but some prefer to use a tabular form to record audiometric results. Figure 1-5 compares the same pure tone findings on a standard audiogram and a tabular form.

A wide variety of symbols and symbol systems have been used by different clinics to record results on audiograms. In this diversity is the potential for confusion and misinterpretation, especially when records are exchanged between clinics.[17] Because of the potential for misinterpretation, the American Speech and Hearing Association (ASHA)* has developed a standard audiogram format and symbol system for audiograms.[18] It is recommended that in constructing an audiogram, one octave on the frequency scale should be equivalent in span to 20 dB on the HL (hearing level) scale. In addition, grid lines of equal darkness and thickness should appear at octave intervals on the frequency scale and at 10 dB intervals on the intensity scale.

The symbol system recommended by ASHA is illustrated in Figure 1-6. An important criterion used in developing the recommended symbol system was that it not be necessary to use different colors to differentiate between ears, as some symbol systems do. As shown, the symbols "O" and "X" are used to represent unmasked air conduction thresholds, while arrows pointing to the left and right are used to

*The American Speech and Hearing Association changed its name to the American Speech-Language-Hearing Association in 1980, but kept the acronym ASHA.

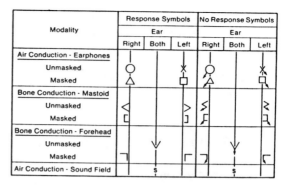

Figure 1-6. Symbol system for audiograms recommended by ASHA.[17]

represent unmasked bone conduction thresholds for the right and left ears, respectively. When masking is used, a triangle and square are used for right and left air conduction thresholds and brackets with the open end facing the right and left are used for bone conduction thresholds for the right and left ears respectively. The symbol "S" is used to represent sound field testing. Sound field tests utilize one or two loudspeakers rather than earphones, and when unilateral hearing loss is present, thresholds represent the sensitivity of the better ear. The ASHA guidelines also recommend that when no response is obtained at the maximum output of the audiometer, an arrow be attached to the lower outside corner of the appropriate symbol about 45 degrees outward from the frequency axis, pointing to the right for left ear symbols and to the left for right ear symbols.

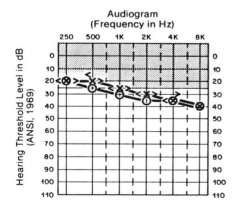

Figure 1-5. Comparison of audiometric findings on a standard audiogram form (*left*) and grid-type form (*right*).

Freq.	RIGHT EAR				LEFT EAR				Sound Field
	AC	Mask	BC	Mask	AC	Mask	BC	Mask	
250	20		20		20		20		
500	25		15		20		20		
750									
1000	30		25		25		25		
1500									
2000	35		30		30		30		
3000									
4000	35		35		35		30		
6000									
8000	40				40				

Because of the potential confusion that can occur as a result of using different symbol systems, audiograms should follow the ASHA guidelines. It is also important that the symbol system used, and an explanation of any other notations used, appear in a legend on the audiogram.

Audiometric Interpretation

Types of Hearing Loss

The type of hearing loss determined through audiometric testing identifies that part of the auditory mechanism with impairment. Through audiometric tests, three types of hearing loss can be identified: *conductive, sensorineural*, and *mixed*. Figure 1-7 illustrates the difference between these types of hearing loss on the basis of the anatomic site involved. In addition, functional or nonorganic hearing loss, also referred to as pseudohypacusis, may be found.

Conductive Hearing Loss.   Conductive hearing loss is by far the most common type of hearing loss found in school children. Conductive hearing loss literally means that part or all of the mechanical conducting components of the auditory mechanism are inefficient. The mechanical components of the auditory mechanism include the pinna, external ear canal, eardrum, middle ear ossicles and muscles, and the middle ear cavity (see Fig. 1-7). A purely conductive hearing impairment assumes no disorder of the inner ear or cochlea and/or the auditory nerve.

Congenital anomalies of the outer ear may cause conductive hearing loss, but most conductive loss is acquired. The most common cause of an acquired conductive impairment in children is serous otitis media, an inflammation of the middle ear cavity accompanied by fluid.[19] Impacted ear wax (cerumen), perforated eardrum, and otosclerosis, a spongy-like growth originating on the footplate of the stapes, are some of the other common factors causing conductive hearing loss.

Figure 1-8 presents the audiometric pattern for conductive loss. As shown, the pure tone audiometric pattern for conductive hearing loss is normal bone conduction thresholds and abnormal air conduction thresholds. In addition, with conductive loss, impedance measures (described later) are most likely abnormal. Two behavioral symptoms separate those persons with conductive hearing loss from those with sensorineural hearing loss. Individuals with conductive hearing loss will demonstrate normal word discrimination ability when the signal is made sufficiently loud. Moreover, the individual's own speech may be softly spoken, because he hears his own voice

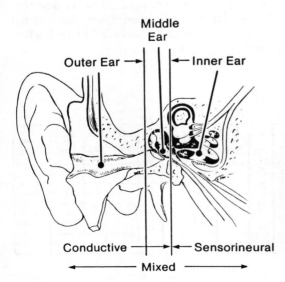

Figure 1-7.   The three types of hearing loss classified according to anatomic site involved.

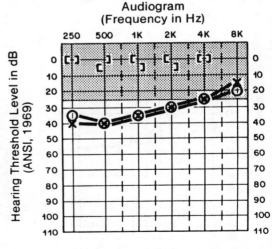

Figure 1-8.   Pure tone air and bone conduction pattern for conductive hearing loss.

louder than normally, due to an "occlusion effect" resulting from the conductive hearing loss. Fortunately with a conductive hearing loss, spontaneous recovery is frequent, or the loss can be reversed through medical and/or surgical treatment.

Sensorineural Hearing Loss. A hearing loss due to pathology in the inner ear, or along the nerve pathway from the inner ear to the brainstem, is referred to as a sensorineural hearing impairment. The inner ear contains the cochlea and sensory receptors or hair cells located on the basilar membrane, a structure within the cochlea.

The hair cells transmit information to nerve fibers and the information is then fed to the temporal lobe of the brain via the VIII cranial nerve and auditory pathway. A pure sensorineural impairment exists when the sound conducting mechanism (outer and middle ear) is normal in every respect, but a disorder is present in the cochlea and/or auditory nerve.

The pure tone audiometric pattern for sensorineural hearing loss is shown in Figure 1-9. With sensorineural hearing loss, air and bone conduction thresholds are both elevated and within 10 dB of each other. The immittance measures of the tympanogram and static compliance, described later, are normal, and acoustic reflexes may be present, elevated, or absent.

Causes of sensorineural hearing impair-

ment can be congenital (prior to or at birth) or acquired after birth. Congenital sensorineural hearing loss may result from hereditary factors, which can cause underdevelopment or early degeneration of the auditory nerve, in utero viral infections, or birth trauma. Acquired sensorineural loss may be caused by factors such as noise exposure, acoustic tumor, head injury, or the toxic effect of certain drugs. In virtually all cases, sensorineural hearing loss is not amenable to medical and/or surgical treatment.

Several symptoms characteristic of sensorineural hearing loss are shouting or talking in a loud voice, poor word discrimination ability, and recruitment. Shouting or speaking in a loud voice may occur with sensorineural loss because the impaired person does not have normal hearing by bone conduction. Hence, he does not hear his own voice or other voices normally and may have difficulty regulating the intensity level of his voice. Not all people with sensorineural hearing loss speak loudly and not all with conductive loss speak softly; many learn to regulate their voice levels appropriately.

The frequent decrease in word discrimination associated with sensorineural hearing loss is due to distortion of the speech signal caused by nerve fiber loss. The typical sensorineural hearing loss is characterized by better hearing in the low frequencies than in the high frequencies. Consonants contain high-frequency information while vowels are predominantly low in frequency. Therefore, consonant sounds may be easily confused or not heard at all. Shouting at the individual with sensorineural loss may result only in agitation rather than improved comprehension because the person may hear voices, but not be able to understand them.

The third symptom of sensorineural hearing impairment, recruitment, refers to an abnormal, rapid growth in loudness once the threshold of hearing has been crossed. After the signal is intense enough to be perceived, any further increase in intensity may cause a disproportionate increase in the sensation of loudness. Because of recruitment and word discrimination difficulty, individuals with sensorineural hearing loss experience greater difficulty in noisy surroundings than those with normal hearing or conductive hearing loss.

Mixed Hearing Loss. With a mixed hearing loss, a significant conductive impairment is

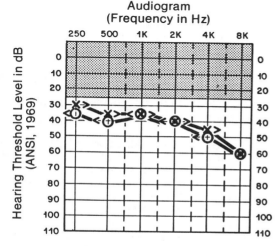

Figure 1-9. Pure tone air and bone conduction pattern for sensorineural hearing loss.

superimposed on a sensorineural hearing loss. Causes of mixed hearing loss may be any combination of the causes described previously for conductive and sensorineural hearing loss. The conductive component of the mixed hearing loss may be amenable to medical treatment, but the sensorineural component is not reversible. Figure 1-10 shows audiometric data depicting a mixed hearing loss.

Functional Hearing Loss. The diagnosis of functional hearing loss is made when an individual claims to have a hearing loss, but discrepancies in audiometric test findings and/or behavior suggest that the loss does not exist at all, or does not exist to the degree that is indicated by voluntary test results. Functional hearing loss is also referred to as *nonorganic hearing loss, psychogenic hearing loss,* or *pseudohypacusis.*

Several factors may explain causes for functional hearing loss. Some feel that emotional stress may lead an individual to unconsciously develop a "hearing loss" as a protective device or an escape from what seems to be an intolerable situation. Another motive for functional loss may be pecuniary, and the individual may be well aware of the true status of auditory sensitivity. Whenever functional loss is found in children, referral to a professional family counselor should be made to investigate the motives behind the need for feigning the loss of hearing.

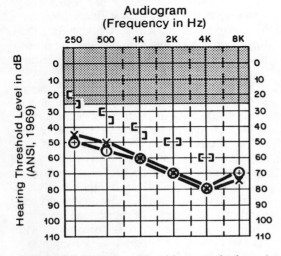

Figure 1-10. Pure tone air and bone conduction pattern for mixed hearing loss.

Degree of Hearing Loss

Once a hearing loss has been identified, it becomes necessary to classify it according to the degree of difficulty it presents to the individual. The term *deaf* is sometimes used by nonprofessionals to refer to all persons who have a hearing impairment. However, the term *deaf* is technically reserved for the hearing-impaired individual whose auditory mechanism is so severely impaired that only a few of the prosodic and phonetic elements of speech can be recognized. The individual who is deaf must rely mainly or entirely upon speech reading or other forms of visual receptive communication for the perception of language.[20] Few individuals with hearing loss would be classified as being deaf under this definition.

On the other hand, the term *hard-of-hearing* refers to a hearing-impaired individual who can identify enough of the distinguishing features of speech through hearing alone to permit at least partial recognition of spoken language. With the addition of the visual system, the hard-of-hearing individual may understand even more language, provided the vocabulary and syntax are within the person's linguistic code.

Although it is difficult to draw firm boundaries between individuals who are deaf and those who are hard-of-hearing on the basis of the loss demonstrated by pure tone findings only, the following classification, based on the PTA (500, 1000, and 2000 Hz) is a general guide to the degree of hearing loss as it relates to children.[21]

```
 15 to 30   dB HL—mild
 31 to 50   dB HL—moderate
 51 to 80   dB HL—severe
 81 to 100 dB HL—profound
      100 dB HL+—anacusis or total hearing loss
```

The classification used with adult populations is as follows[22]:

```
 −10 to 26 dB HL—within normal limits
  27 to 40 dB HL—mild loss
  41 to 55 dB HL—moderate loss
  56 to 70 dB HL—moderate-to-severe loss
  71 to 90 dB HL—severe loss
        91+—profound loss
```

The relationship between the degree of hearing loss (PTA) and the amount of handicap it presents is provided in Table 1-1.

Table 1-1   Degree of Communication Difficulty as a Function of Hearing Loss
(Adapted from Goodman[23])

Communication Difficulty	Level of Hearing Loss (Pure Tone Average 500, 1000, and 2000 Hz)	Degree of Hearing Loss
Demonstrates difficulty understanding soft-spoken speech; needs preferential seating and may benefit from speech reading training; good candidate for a hearing aid.	25–40	Mild
Demonstrates an understanding of speech at 3–5 feet; requires amplification, preferential seating, speech reading training, and speech therapy.	40–55	Moderate
Speech must be loud for auditory reception; difficulty in group and classroom discussion; may require special classes for hearing-impaired; plus all of the above needs.	55–70	Moderate to Severe
Loud speech may be understood at 1 ft from ear; may distinguish vowels but not consonants; requires classroom for hearing-impaired and mainstreaming at a later date.	70–90	Severe
Does not rely on audition as primary modality for communication; may work well with a total communication approach; may eventually be mainstreamed at higher grade levels.	90	Profound

In addition to the degree of loss, a complete description of an individual's hearing impairment should include whether one ear (unilateral) or both ears (bilateral) are involved, and a statement regarding the type of loss. Besides the degree of loss through the speech frequencies, the overall effect of the hearing loss will depend on whether it involves one ear, both ears equally, or one ear to a lesser degree. For example, the child with a profound hearing loss in one ear and normal hearing in the other may function quite well in most listening situations.

AUDIOMETRIC TESTS IN CHILDREN

Chapter 3 describes methods that can be used in screening younger children. When such methods are not successful, procedures using behavioral methods for the difficult-to-test child and the child that is impossible to test are available. This section describes advanced tests used with children. These tests would not be used in school screening programs, but are presented to explain the types of tests that are available in diagnostic settings.

The Difficult-to-Test Child

Difficult children can many times be tested using *behavioral observation audiometry* (BOA), *conditioned orientation reflex* (COR), *audiometry* or *visual reinforcement audiometry* (VRA). The use of these techniques requires a calibrated sound field system and diagnostic audiometer, and these tests are administered by an audiologist. The procedure with all three tests involves placing the child in the sound-treated room, presenting stimuli in the sound field through the calibrated speakers, and observing the child's behavior for expected reactions. Depending on the technique used, the child can be reinforced for responding to the sound. Although these are gross tests of hearing, valuable information can be obtained through BOA, COR, and/or VRA with the difficult-to-test child.

Tests using speech stimuli are sometimes more successfully used with difficult-to-test children, because speech is more meaningful than pure tones, and the child will respond more readily. A common procedure for the audiologist is to present the stimulus either through earphones or in sound field and to observe the child, or when possible, to have the child respond by pointing to pictures. However, even if responses to speech are within normal limits, pure tone testing is required because speech stimuli do not test the high frequencies, and significant hearing loss could still be present.

The Impossible-to-Test Child

When behavioral tests are unreliable or cannot be used, valid but limited information on hearing sensitivity can be obtained through the use of *auditory brainstem response* (ABR) audiometry. ABR has also been called *brainstem-evoked response* audiometry (BSER), but ABR is the widely accepted term. ABR has proven to be highly successful in evaluating those children who are impossible to test with behavioral procedures, including infants only a few hours old.

The procedure used to obtain ABR results involves placing small electrodes on the head and the mastoids of the individual being tested. Auditory stimuli—usually a rapid succession of clicks presented at a rate of about 10 per second—are delivered to the relaxed, preferably sleeping patient. The electrodes pick up the minute electrical activity emanating from the brain and this activity is fed into a computer averager. The computer extracts the auditory signal from the ongoing *electroencephalographic* (EEG) activity of the brain.

The electrical signal extracted from the EEG activity reflects the sound-induced neuronal activity of the auditory nerve and brainstem pathways. The resulting response has three distinct peaks (total of seven) and the amplitude of the peaks and the time required for these peaks to appear is measured. The threshold of the ABR is used along with the time (latency) and amplitude of the peaks to determine whether hearing loss is present and the functional status of the auditory system.

The primary advantages of the ABR technique are that it is an objective procedure used for evaluating auditory sensitivity that does not require voluntary participation on the part of the patient, and it is noninvasive. As long as the patient can be maintained in a relaxed state, it is possible to obtain information on auditory sensitivity. Many clinics use sedation to test their patients.

Although the technique is highly valuable for the impossible-to-test patient, a major limitation is that the test only evaluates high frequencies in the 1000 to 4000 Hz range. Thus, only partial information is obtained regarding hearing sensitivity. In addition, ABR tests auditory sensitivity only and not "hearing" (i.e., cognitive interpretation of sounds such as in speech audiometry). As such, ABR provides no clue of how the patient will interpret sounds, even if results are normal. These two limitations make long-term monitoring of the child necessary until behavioral tests can be performed and more complete audiometric information obtained.

Although the above limitations do affect the generalizations from the ABR test, the technique has proven useful for those children who are impossible to test with behavioral methods. Galambos and Hecox[24] provide a more complete overview of the ABR procedures and interpretations.

THE IMMITTANCE INSTRUMENT AND IMPEDANCE MEASURES

Up to this point, the material presented in this chapter has been directed toward the assessment of hearing. Routine immittance measures do not assess hearing, but provide objective information on the mechanical transfer function of sound in the outer and middle ear. That is, routine immittance measures assess the functional state of the conductive mechanism of the ear. Through such assessment, it is possible to detect and define disorders in the outer and middle ear system objectively.

One distinct advantage of immittance measurement is that successful testing does not rely on a behavioral response from the individual being tested. The measures can be obtained on a semicooperative child usually in less than one minute per ear with little difficulty. With the uncooperative child, more time is usually required and there are a few children who cannot be tested without major variations in the testing protocol.

Because little cooperation is required, the testing can be performed on younger children, as well as difficult-to-test and impossible-to-test children. The advantage of being able to apply immittance to untestable populations successfully has tempted many to use routine immittance measures in an effort to assess hearing sensitivity. While there is a relationship between audiometric results and immittance measures, the use of immittance measures does not eliminate the need for audiometric testing. A child can have perfectly normal findings on routine immittance tests and still manifest a significant bilateral sensorineural hearing loss.

Although the procedures used to administer immittance tests are relatively simple and can be learned in a matter of hours, the difficulty with the immittance testing lies in interpretation. To interpret the diagnostic value of the results from the immittance test battery, a thorough understanding of the auditory system and the principles of immittance are required. Such understanding includes a comprehensive knowledge of the acoustic and physiologic principles underlying the immittance technique and auditory system, as well as the various pathologic conditions that may affect the auditory system. This section presents the basics of the immittance technique as they apply to immittance screening and interpretation of results. Chapter 3 details the screening tests to be used and their interpretation.

Principles of Immittance Measurement

There are actually two types of immittance instruments; one is based on impedance and the other upon admittance. Both measures rely on similar functions, but the principles on which they operate differ. Specifically, acoustic impedance refers to the *opposition* to transfer of the acoustic signal through the mechanical system of the ear to the cochlea or inner ear, while acoustic admittance refers to the ease with which acoustic energy is *transmitted* by the mechanical system of the ear. This difference, although not grossly affecting results from routine tests, has caused some terminologic confusion. To encompass both electroacoustic techniques, the term *immittance* was proposed by ASHA 1 to describe this clinical procedure; most clinicians and manufacturers have adopted this new terminology.

Most commercial instruments base their measurement principle on the impedance characteristics of the ear. Thus, this section will only discuss immittance. However, the reader should be aware that some instruments mea-

sure admittance and other concepts may apply. For the interested reader, Wiley and Block[29] review the principles of admittance measures.

The total or complex immittance of the ear is based on a number of physical characteristics, including mass, stiffness, and friction. For the serious student of immittance measurement, these factors and the relationship between them must be known.* However, because the ear is a stiffness-dominated system, immittance can be explained simplistically by considering stiffness only.

The clinical measurement of immittance is based on the principle that when a known quantity of sound (acoustic energy) is applied to the ear, a certain amount of measured energy is reflected back; the amount of reflected energy will vary depending on the stiffness (immobility) or flaccidity (mobility) of the system. The stiffer or less flaccid or less compliant (mobile) the system, the greater the amount of energy that will be reflected back. Conversely, the less stiff, more flaccid, or more compliant (mobile) the system, the smaller the amount of energy that will be reflected back. Note that stiffness and compliance are reciprocally related. As one increases, the other decreases.

Various disorders in the outer and middle ear affect the stiffness of the system, which concomitantly affects compliance. When the reflected energy varies from a known normal range, many disorders affecting the outer and middle ear can be detected. This principle can be understood better by reviewing the mechanics of the immittance instrument itself.

The Immittance Instrument

The immittance instrument is sometimes called an "immittance audiometer" or an "immittance bridge," but neither of these terms is technically appropriate. An audiometer is a device used to assess hearing. Since immittance measures do not assess hearing, it is misleading to refer to the immittance instrument as an audiometer. The term "immittance bridge" was adopted because the instrument incorporates an electronic component called a Wheatstone bridge. Because this is only one component of a more complex system, the terminology is also not accurate.

*The reader seeking more detailed information should consult Northern and Grimes.[25]

Presently ANSI standards have not been adopted for immittance instruments as they have been for audiometers. However, ASHA has suggested minimum requirements for such instruments.[1] These minimum requirements indicate that the instrument should have the capability for tympanometry and for eliciting and monitoring an acoustic reflex. In addition, it should contain an automatic recording and pump system that produces a permanent record of the test results. Included as minimum requirements are: a 2 cc coupler for calibration, a minimum air pressure range from +100 to −300 daPa, probe tone frequency between 220 and 660 Hz, and a reflex—eliciting stimulus of 100 dB HL and 105 dB HL for contralateral and ipsilateral stimulation, respectively. The audiometer section of the instrument must meet the minimum ANSI 1969 requirements.[5]

Although these are the minimum recommended requirements, they are recent and many instruments do not meet the minimum. However, these guidelines should be considered by those purchasing new impedance instruments.

Basic Functions

Figure 1-11 shows two different types of immittance instruments with their respective parts labeled. Figure 1-11A is an instrument with a digital-type meter read-out for compliance; Figure 1-11B has an analog-type meter read-out for compliance. Both types of instruments provide the same information, but the digital meter reads compliance in absolute units, whereas the analog meter reads compliance in relative units. Presently, virtually all manufacturers have chosen to use digital-type read-outs, and compliance measures are reported in absolute units.

The function of each major component is as follows.

Air Pump and Manometer System (1 in Fig. 1-11). The air pump is used to increase and decrease the air pressure in the external auditory canal during tympanometry. The manometer measures the pressure change as it occurs. The range of pressures available in most impedance instruments is from +200 to −400 or −600 decaPascals (daPa). Originally, immittance units measured pressure in millimeters of water pressure (mm/H_2O), and older

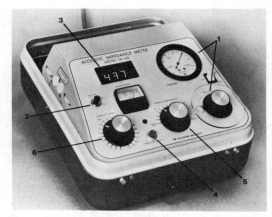

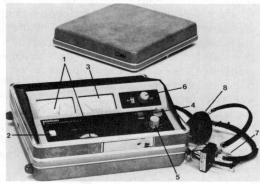

Figure 1-11. Examples of immittance instruments. The instrument at the top (A) uses a digital compliance meter and the bottom (B) an analog compliance meter (*Top, courtesy of* Teledyne Avionics; *Bottom,* Madsen Electronics).

equipment will express pressure in this terminology. Since daPa and mm/H_2O are virtually the same in the pressure ranges used to perform immittance measures on the ear (97.8 daPa = 100 mm/H_2O), the two measures can be considered equivalent.

Pressure Release (2 in Fig. 1-11). The pressure release valve is used to equalize the pressure in the external auditory canal after the probe tip has been inserted. Prior to performing any measurements, the pressure release button should be pressed after inserting the probe into the external ear canal.

Compliance Meter (3 in Fig. 1-11). The compliance meter provides a measure of equivalent volume in milliliters (ml), as well as monitors the change in the reflected energy from the probe tone when it occurs for various parts of the immittance test battery. Older immittance units measured compliance in cubic centimeters (cc), but the recent trend is to use ml. For all practical purposes, the two measures are equivalent (100 cc = 100 ml), so they can be interchanged. As stated earlier, older immittance units measured compliance with an analog meter in relative units, but the newer units measure compliance with a digital display in absolute units (ml). The compliance meter is used to plot the tympanogram, measure static compliance, and monitor acoustic reflexes.

Tone Interrupter (4 in Fig. 1-11). The tone interrupter is used to present the reflex-eliciting stimulus for the acoustic reflex test. Since the immittance instrument can also be used as an audiometer, the tone interrupter can also be used in conjunction with the attenuator dial (6) to present stimuli during audiometric tests.

Frequency Selector Dial (5 in Fig. 1-11). The frequency selector dial specifies the type of stimulus and the frequency of the stimulus to be used to elicit the acoustic reflex or in audiometric testing. Most instruments include frequencies between 250 to 6000 to 8000 Hz in octave and some half-octave intervals. In addition, many instruments also include high-pass, low-pass, and wide band noises. The use of the noise bands is for more advanced diagnostic procedures not typically used in the standard test battery.

Attenuator or Hearing Level (HL) Dial (6 in Fig. 1-11). The HL dial controls the intensity of the signal in the reflex-eliciting earphone. The intensities of the HL dial range from 0 dB to 110 dB HL. Many programs use the immittance instrument to perform both impedance and hearing screening. Thus, hearing screening would be performed at lower intensities of 20 or 25 dB HL, and the reflex-eliciting stimulus would be presented in the 100 to 105 dB HL range.

Probe (7 in Fig. 1-11B). The probe is inserted into the external auditory canal, and the ear into which the probe is inserted is the ear from which the impedance is actually being measured. Not shown are the various sized probe tips that are placed at the end of the probe. These plastic or rubber tips allow the probe to be inserted into the external auditory canal so that a hermetic (airtight) seal can be obtained during tympanometric measures.

Contralateral Reflex-Eliciting Earphone (8 in Fig. 1-11B). The contralateral reflex-eliciting earphone is placed over the ear opposite (contralateral to) the probe ear. The reflex-

eliciting earphone is used to present a signal to the ear to determine the presence or absence of an acoustic reflex. In addition, the reflex-eliciting earphone can be used for audiometric tests.

Figure 1-12 shows how the probe is placed in the ear canal (*top*) and how the headset of the immittance instrument is placed on an individual for testing (*bottom*).

When the headset is on one position during basic immittance testing, information on immittance is being obtained for one ear (the probe ear), and the contralateral reflex-eliciting tone is being delivered to the opposite ear (reflex-eliciting ear). In Figure 1-12, the immittance of the right ear can be measured, and the contralateral acoustic reflex-eliciting signal can be delivered to the left ear. After the measures are obtained, the headset is reversed and additional measures recorded. When describ-

Figure 1-12. Placement of the probe into the external auditory canal (*top*), and the headset of the immittance instrument (*bottom*). With this placement, the probe ear is the right ear and the reflex-eliciting earphone is over the left ear.

ing immittance results, it is helpful to describe them in reference to the probe ear. In this way, no confusion will exist about the ear being described.

Figure 1-13 is a schematic representation of the principles used to determine the immittance in the probe ear. The diagram illustrates the closed cavity between the probe tip of the immittance instrument and the external ear canal to the tympanic membrane. As shown in Figure 1-13, the probe tip is connected to three basic components in the immittance instrument: a loudspeaker (2a), an air pump and manometer (4a), and a microphone (5a). The immittance probe apparatus measures the stiffness or compliance of the middle ear system in the following way: a 220 Hz (sometimes 660 Hz) probe tone from the loudspeaker (2a) is introduced into the external ear canal through a hole in the probe tip (2b). Depending on the state of the ear canal and middle ear, some energy is absorbed and transmitted to the inner ear and some energy is reflected. The reflected energy is picked up through a second hole in the probe tip (5b) and delivered to the microphone (5a), and the system analyzer (6) compares the input signal to the reflected energy.

As described above, the immittance instrument acts like a small sound pressure measuring device in determining the state of the middle ear. The amount of reflected energy picked up by the microphone from the probe tone determines the functional state of the ear. A high amount of reflected energy means that the system is more stiff or less compliant than normal, and vice versa. Conditions such as otitis media and ossicular chain fixation result in high stiffness or low compliance; in such cases the reflected energy would be higher than normal. Conversely, low stiffness or high compliance would be caused by conditions such as disarticulation of the ossicular chain or a scarred, flaccid tympanic membrane. Under these conditions, more energy would pass through than normally, so the amount reflected would be less than normal.

The third hole in the probe tip (4b) is connected to an air pump and manometer (4a). The air pump and manometer act together to increase and decrease and measure the air pressure in the outer ear. This system is used in obtaining the tympanogram (described below).

Immittance Measures

In the routine immittance test battery, three measures are obtained: the tympanogram (tympanometry), static compliance, and acoustic reflex. Although each test provides significant information by itself, the tests are not performed or interpreted in isolation. Diagnostic capabilities are strengthened when the results of all three test procedures are considered together.

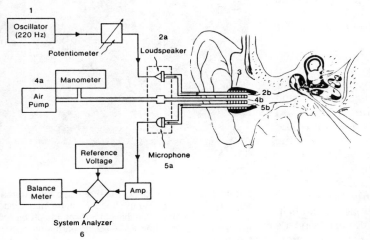

Figure 1-13. Principles of immittance measurement in the probe ear (see text for description).

Tympanometry

Tympanometry is an objective measurement of tympanic membrane compliance or mobility as a function of mechanically varying the air pressure in a hermetically sealed external ear canal. The compliance or mobility of the eardrum at specific air pressures is recorded on a graph referred to as a tympanogram. The tympanogram is plotted by introducing positive and negative air pressure into the probe ear, and recording the compliance of the ear, based on the amount of reflected energy.

To understand how varying the air pressure in the external auditory canal affects the amount of reflected energy from the tympanic membrane, one must understand the pressure compliance principle. Figure 1-14 demonstrates this principle in a normal ear. Recall that stiffness and compliance are reciprocally related, and that by measuring one of these characteristics, the other can be derived.

In Figure 1-14, the amount of reflected energy is at its lowest point when the pressure in the external auditory canal is at atmospheric pressure (0 daPa). Under this condition, in the normal ear, there is equal pressure between the external and middle ear cavities, the amount of energy absorbed by the tympanic membrane and middle ear structures from the probe tone is at the greatest level, the amount of reflected energy from the probe tone is at its lowest level, and the compliance is at its highest point. However, when either a positive or negative pressure is introduced into the exter-

nal ear canal, the force exerted on the normal tympanic membrane stretches and stiffens it and other middle ear structures. The increase in stiffness, with a concomitant decrease in compliance, increases the amount of reflected energy. In Figure 1-14, the amount of reflected energy is highest at +200 and −300 daPa, which indicates that compliance is at its lowest point at these two pressures for this ear.

A tympanogram is manually plotted in the manner shown in Figure 1-15 and described in this paragraph. In Figure 1-15, results on the left are for a digital-type immittance instrument measuring absolute compliance and the results on the right for an analog-type instrument measuring relative compliance. Air pressure is introduced into the ear canal at +200 daPa. This +200 pressure establishes a stiff system with low compliance, and the amount of reflected energy is greater than at atmospheric pressure. At this point, the first reading (1 in Fig. 1-15) is noted from the compliance change balance meter (component 3 in Fig. 1-11). Under this condition, the compliance of the normal ear is low (note that when measuring relative compliance, most instruments use high numbers to represent low compliance, while low numbers represent high compliance). The air pressure is then gradually reduced from +200 daPa until it reaches the point where the amount of reflected energy is the lowest, and the compliance is the highest. This point is termed the point of maximum compliance, and indicates when air pressure is equal between the external ear canal and middle ear cavity. At this point, the second reading (2 in Fig. 1-15) is noted on the tympanogram. In the normal ear, the point of maximum compliance is at or near atmospheric pressure (0 daPa). Finally, a third reading (3 in Figure 1-15) is made at a more negative point, about −200 daPa less pressure than the point of maximum compliance, to complete the tympanometric configuration. When the three points are connected, a pattern results that can be classified according to normal or various abnormal middle ear conditions. In plotting the tympanogram manually, the standard notation of "O" and "X" is used to represent the right and left ears respectively.

Although the above general procedure is followed for plotting tympanograms manually, with one configuration, the flat or type B curve, no point of maximum compliance is found. When this occurs, only the +200 daPa

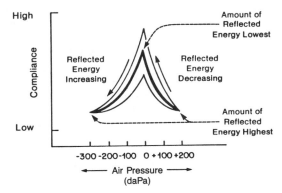

Figure 1-14. Schematic representation of how varying air pressure in the external ear canal affects reflected energy from the probe tone (see text for description).

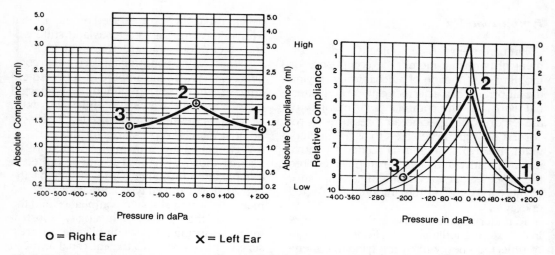

Figure 1-15. Examples of manually plotted tympanograms. The tympanogram at the left is plotted using an immittance instrument with a digital-type (Absolute) compliance meter, and the right an analog-type (relative) compliance meter (see text for description). New immittance instruments use digital-type displays.

point, and a point at −300 or −400 daPa need be noted on the tympanogram, and a horizontal line connects them. It should also be noted that recording devices are available that plot the tympanogram automatically. For large screening programs, automatic recording devices should be considered, as they expedite testing.[1]

Tympanograms are classified according to the A, B, C system shown in Figure 1-16 and described in Table 1-2. The three type A classifications represent normal middle ear pressure, whereas the type C classification represents abnormal negative pressure in the middle ear. Initially, the normal pressure range was defined as ±50 daPa and significant abnormal ranges were felt to be more positive than +50 daPa and more negative than −100 daPa. However, most of the present guidelines do not consider pressure abnormal until it is more positive than +50 daPa and more negative than −200 daPa (see Chapter 7). The type B classification represents little or no compliance in the conductive system, regardless of the air pressure in the external ear. This is the most abnormal tympanogram that can be found.

Correct classification of the tympanogram depends on the location and shape of the tympanogram peak and the absolute compliance of the system. With either type of immittance instruments previously described, the absolute or static compliance can be determined

and must be known to properly classify the tympanogram.

Static Compliance

Whereas measurement of the tympanogram depends on the pressure/compliance principle of the ear, static compliance depends on the volume principle. The volume principle states that the absolute size of a cavity of known physical characteristics can be determined by knowing the amount of reflected energy from an input signal of known intensity. Figure 1-17 illustrates this concept.

Figure 1-17A shows a fixed volume cavity with an input acoustic signal and a reflected SPL value, which is high compared to 1-17B and 1-17C. In Figure 1-17B, the same input acoustic signal is used, but the output SPL is reduced due to the increased volume in the larger cavity; with a larger cavity, there is less resistance and therefore less reflection of energy. In Figure 1-17C, the same input acoustic signal is also used, but the output again is reduced due to an even larger cavity. Based on this simple principle, the absolute size of any cavity can be determined as long as the physical characteristics of the cavity are specified.

The volume principle may be applied to measurement of the volumes in the ear. If a positive pressure is introduced into the exter-

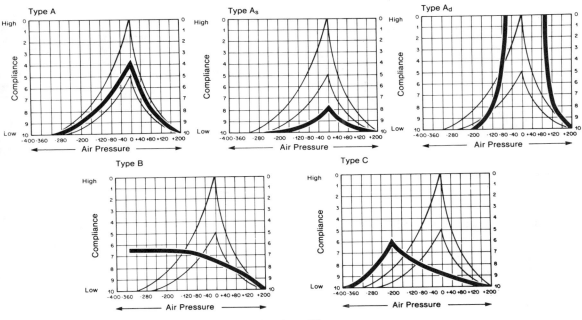

Figure 1-16. Classifications of tympanograms (after Jerger[26]).

Table 1-2 Description of Tympanogram Types*

Type A—represents normal middle ear function. The peak (point of maximum compliance) occurs within normal static compliance limits and at pressures between +50 to −100 daPa.

Type A$_d$—represents a flaccid tympanic membrane resulting from scar tissue or a possible disarticulation of the middle ear ossicles. Compliance measures are abnormally high.

Type A$_s$—represents abnormal stiffness in the middle ear system resulting in a fixation of the ossicular chain as in otosclerosis. Compliance measures are abnormally low.

Type B—represents restricted tympanic membrane mobility, and would indicate that some pathologic condition exists in the middle ear. Static compliance measures are abnormally low.

Type C—represents significant negative pressure in the middle ear cavity (considered significant when more negative than −200 daPa). This finding means that the ambient air pressure in the external ear canal is greater than the middle ear air pressure. This may indicate a precursory state of otitis media or the resolution of an ear infection. Compliance measures are usually within normal limits.

*See Figure 1-16 (after Jerger[26]).

nal auditory canal of a normal ear, the stiffness of the tympanic membrane sets up an artificial acoustical "wall." Under this condition, the volume of the cavity from the probe tip of the impedance instrument to the eardrum can be measured in units equivalent to a cavity of known physical characteristics. If the pressure is then removed and the tympanic membrane returns to its natural resting place, the artificial acoustical wall will no longer be present. Under this condition, the cavity from the probe tip, including the external canal and middle ear space, can be measured in equivalent units. Note that in each case the term equivalent units is used, because the physical characteristics of each ear canal will vary, and the reflected energy must be used in comparison to a standard cavity (a hard-wall cavity) of known physical characteristics.

The procedure used to obtain static compliance measures is to place the probe tip into the external ear canal and introduce a pressure of +200 daPa with the probe tone on. The positive air pressure serves to stretch and stiffen the tympanic membrane, resulting in a large amount of reflected energy. A compliance reading is obtained, which gives an equivalent volume in milliliters (ml) of compliance at this

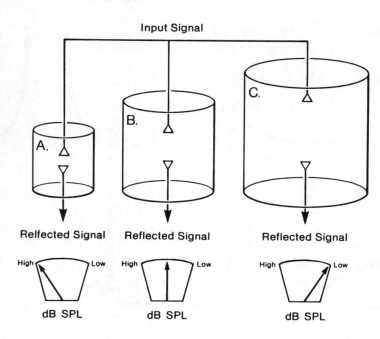

Input Signal

Reflected Signal   Reflected Signal   Reflected Signal

High   Low   High   Low   High   Low

dB SPL   dB SPL   dB SPL

Figure 1-17. The effects of volume change on the input/output function of an acoustic signal for: (A) a small cavity, (B) a medium cavity, and (C) a large cavity.

positive air pressure setting. This reading is the *equivalent* volume of the external ear canal and is referred to as the C_1 reading. The air pressure is then adjusted from +200 daPa to find the point of maximum compliance (at or near 0 daPa in the normal ear) and a second reading is made. This reading is the *equivalent* volume of the total outer and middle ear system and is referred to as the C_2 reading. Static compliance is calculated by subtracting the value obtained at the C_1 point from the C_2 point. This derived value represents the *equivalent* volume of the middle ear system.

In clinical use, static compliance values within the range of 0.28 to 2.50 ml are normal.[25] This means that abnormally low static compliance values are less than 0.28 ml and abnormally high values are above 2.50 ml. Thus, for a tympanogram to be classified as type A, the static compliance has to be in the 0.28 to 2.50 ml range. Type A_s or B tympanograms would require static compliance values less than 0.28 ml, and type A_d greater than 2.50 ml. Type C tympanograms typically have static compliance within the normal range of 0.28 to 2.50 ml.

Static compliance measures parallel tympanometric measures, and in this sense, they are redundant. In fact, when a digital-type immittance instrument is used, the static compli-

ance can be calculated directly from the tympanogram. With an analog-type instrument, a separate step must be taken to record the C_1 and C_2 values. If the compliance of the tympanogram is obviously within the normal range, there is no specific need to calculate the static compliance, except for possible diagnostic purposes. However, when the relative compliance of the tympanogram is questionable, the static compliance provides for accurate classification.

In some cases, static compliance measures can be very important in the detection and diagnosis of pathologic states of the ear. This additional information is made available by the *physical volume test* (PVT).[25] With the PVT, a perforation in the tympanic membrane not visible through pneumatic otoscopy can be detected. This measure can also aid in determining whether ventilating tubes (discussed in Chapter 6) are unobstructed (patent) or obstructed, and/or if the eustachian tube is functioning when a ventilating tube is present and patent.

The PVT is accomplished by introducing positive air pressure into the external auditory canal and obtaining a C_1 reading. If this reading is unusually high, often exceeding 4.0 to 5.0 ml in adults, it indicates that a perforation is present or that the ventilating tube is patent.

Although the size and shape of the probe tip will influence the C_1 reading, in an average adult with an intact tympanic membrane the value will be between 1.0 to 1.5 ml and in a child 0.6 to 0.8 ml.[25]

By introducing a positive pressure in the external ear canal with an open ventilating tube in the tympanic membrane, the pressure may suddenly release. This finding would indicate that the eustachian tube is functioning. When ventilating tubes are present and C_1 readings are normal or below normal, the ventilating tube may be blocked.

Acoustic Reflexes

The acoustic reflex occurs when a small muscle in the middle ear, the stapedius muscle, contracts. When a high intensity stimulus is delivered to a normal ear, this reflex should occur in both ears (bilateral). The fact that the acoustic reflex is bilateral means that a signal directed to one ear can elicit a recordable reflex in the opposite (contralateral) ear.

The effect of middle ear muscle contraction in the normal ear is a stiffening of the tympanic membrane. This stiffening of the tympanic membrane during contraction is detected by the immittance instrument by a change in the reflected energy from the probe tone. The change is monitored by the system analyzer and projected to the balance (compliance) meter.

Contralateral measurement of the acoustic reflex is achieved by presenting different signals through the reflex-eliciting earphone to one ear and measuring the change in stiffness that results due to the muscle contraction in the probe ear. This test should be performed with the middle ear system at the point of maximum compliance. If the reflex is not measured at the point of maximum compliance, it may be obliterated due to the pressure imbalance between the ear canal and the middle ear cavity.

Ipsilateral measurement of the acoustic reflex is possible with some instruments. Ipsilateral reflex measurement is achieved by stimulating and measuring the reflex in the same probe ear. The advantages of ipsilateral reflex measurement in diagnostic testing are reviewed by Jerger.[26]

Acoustic reflexes can be assessed by obtaining the threshold at which the reflex occurs, or screened by presenting the reflex-eliciting tone at a fixed intensity (100 or 105 dB HL) to see if the reflex is present. In the normal ear, the median threshold at which the acoustic reflex is elicited is 85 dB HL.[28] Once threshold is established, the level is recorded. Other frequencies can be tested. However, in immittance screening only one frequency is usually screened (see Chapter 3).

The presence of reflexes within normal limits at all frequencies is consistent with normal auditory sensitivity. However, acoustic reflexes may occur at all frequencies when mild or moderate-to-severe sensorineural hearing loss is present. For this reason, acoustic reflexes *cannot* be used as an index of hearing threshold sensitivity.

If reflexes are absent, some form of middle-ear pathology may be indicated, such as fixation of the ossicular chain or the presence of fluid in the middle ear space. Absent reflexes may also indicate a moderate-to-severe sensorineural hearing loss without recruitment, a paralysis of the VII cranial nerve in the presence of normal hearing and no middle ear pathology, or a possible lesion in the central auditory pathway. Absent reflexes have also occasionally been observed in individuals with normal hearing. Therefore, it should be emphasized that the acoustic reflex should not be used as an index of hearing sensitivity.

Partial or elevated reflexes may be recorded. Partial means that a reflex is present at some frequencies tested and absent at others, and elevated refers to reflexes that are present at a hearing level exceeding 100 dB. Partial or elevated reflexes may indicate the presence of a hearing loss at those frequencies where they occur. However, to stress the point again, some individuals with normal auditory sensitivity may also demonstrate partial or elevated acoustic reflexes.

Table 1-3 summarizes the findings that may occur from the three standard immittance measures and shows the relationship between them. This table points out that the tympanogram type is determined by the location of the pressure peak, its overall shape and its static compliance. Reflexes can be present at normal levels, partial, elevated, or absent for each tympanometric shape, although for the type B tympanogram, the presence of reflexes is unusual. Together with audiometric data, these measures provide diagnostic information on the ear, as well as on the extent, type, and nature of hearing loss when it is present.

Table 1-3   Summary of Immittance Results

Tympanogram	Location of Pressure Peak	Static Compliance	Acoustic Reflex
A	Normal (+50 to −100 daPa)	Normal (0.28–2.50 ml)	Present at normal levels Partial, elevated, or absent
A$_d$	Normal (+50 to −100 daPa)	Abnormally high (greater than 2.50 ml)	Present at normal levels Partial, elevated, or absent
A$_s$	Normal (+50 to −100 daPa)	Abnormally low (less than 0.28 ml)	Present at normal levels Partial, elevated, or absent
B	No Peak (Flat or Rounded)	Abnormally low (less than 0.28 ml)	Present at normal levels* Partial, elevated, or absent
C	Abnormally Negative (more negative than −100 daPa)	Normal (0.28–2.50 cc), or Low (less than 0.28 ml)	Present at normal levels Partial, elevated, or absent

*The presence of reflexes with type B tympanograms is an unlikely finding.

Automatic (Microprocessor) Immittance Units

Recently, several manufacturers have introduced automatic immittance screening units. This type of equipment is designed to be used in situations where rapid assessment of middle-ear function is required, such as in large-scale screening programs and with the pediatric population, where the child typically will not remain quiet for more than a few seconds. Figure 1-18 shows an automatic immittance unit in use. The primary advantages of using this type of equipment is that obtaining an airtight seal requires only that it be held over the entrance of the ear canal, simplifying the procedure; and only about 5 to 10 seconds is required to perform tympanometry, static compliance, and ipsilateral acoustic reflex measures for each ear. Following the data collection, the information is displayed on an LED screen and/or can be printed out on hard copy. Figure 1-19 is an example of typical data that are derived from this type of instrument.

Automatic immittance screening units are effective in mass middle ear screening programs, and when screening for middle ear pathology in special populations (see Chapter 3). The equipment cost ranges from about $2900 to $3500. These units do not provide diagnostic test results, so when abnormal findings are obtained, comprehensive middle ear analysis should be performed on a clinical immittance unit.

Application of Audiometric and Immittance Principles

The following four cases will be used to integrate and clarify the audiometric principles discussed to this point.

Figure 1-20 shows findings for normal hearing and normal middle ear function. On the audiogram, thresholds were no poorer than 5 dB HL at any test frequency. Speech data revealed normal SRT, agreeing with the PTA, and word discrimination scores within the normal range (90 to 100%). Tympanograms were type A, with static compliance in the range of normal limits. Acoustic reflex thresholds were within the normal range of 80 to 100 dB HL.

Figure 1-21 shows findings for a mild-to-severe bilateral sensorineural hearing loss. Thresholds were within the range of normal limits at 250 and 500 Hz. In addition, the loss would be described as sloping and high frequency because above 1000 Hz, threshold sensitivity decreased as frequency increased. Thresholds at 4000 and 8000 Hz are in the severe range. ST were within normal limits and agreed with the two-frequency PTA at 500 and 1000 Hz. In this case, because of the large difference between thresholds at 1000 and 2000 Hz, only 500 and 1000 Hz were used to calculate the PTA. Word discrimination scores were reduced bilaterally, with a poorer score in the left ear (70%) than in the right (82%).

Immittance findings were within normal limits (tympanograms type A with normal

Figure 1-18. Example of an automatic immittance unit being used in a school screening program.

static compliance bilaterally), with the exception of acoustic reflexes which were partially present and elevated. The finding that immittance was within normal limits is consistent with the sensorineural hearing loss found by pure tone air and bone conduction testing. That is, immittance findings would rule out any abnormal condition of the outer and middle ear and indicate that the loss was in the inner ear.

Individuals with audiometric findings like those shown in Figure 1-21 would be difficult to identify without audiometric tests. Such individuals will usually respond to speech within normal limits, because of the good thresholds in the 250 to 1000 Hz range. However, such individuals will have considerable difficulty in discriminating speech, especially in the presence of background noise; and this difficulty may not be readily apparent to others. In addition, a subtly abnormal speech pattern may be present, in that the high frequency fricative and sibilant sounds would be distorted. Only through audiometric screening would individuals with audiometric results like those shown in Figure 1-21 be detected.

The results in Figure 1-22 show a moderate-to-mild left ear conductive hearing loss with normal hearing in the right ear. ST are in agreement with the PTA for both ears and support the degree of hearing loss in the left ear. Word discrimination scores were within normal limits bilaterally.

Immittance findings support the presence of the conductive hearing loss in the left ear, in that a flat (type B) tympanogram with low static compliance is demonstrated. For the right ear, the tympanogram was normal (type A), with static compliance within the normal range. With unilateral conductive hearing loss, contralateral acoustic reflexes will be absent in the probe ear with the hearing loss due to conduc-

TA-7A Automatic Impedance Meter

Name_____

Date_____

COMPL   ml 0.7
         daPa -220

VOLUME   ml 0.9
REFLEX   dB   95

LEFT / RIGHT

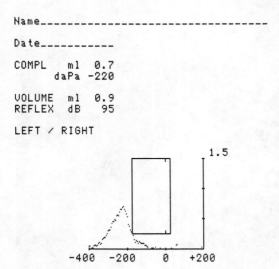

Figure 1-19. Example of the read-out obtained from an automatic immittance unit. Results indicate abnormal middle-ear pressure, static compliance within the range of normal limits, and the ipsilateral acoustic reflex present at 95 dB. All three measures were obtained in less than 20 seconds.

tive pathology, and absent or elevated in the probe ear with normal hearing due to the decrease in hearing in the reflex-eliciting ear (the ear with the conductive hearing loss). In such cases ipsilateral reflex measurement, described earlier, is a very helpful procedure.

Figure 1-23 shows audiometric results for a hearing loss in the severe-to-profound range bilaterally. Thresholds between 250 and 500 Hz ranged from 65 dB HL to no response at 110 dB HL. ST and word discrimination scores could not be obtained due to the severity of the loss. Note that even though ST could not be measured, speech awareness thresholds (SAT) were obtained and agreed with thresholds in the 125 to 250 Hz region. Response by bone conduction was obtained at 250 Hz at maximum limits of the audiometer (40 dB HL) for each ear, but no responses were obtained above this frequency. Because bone conduction threshold responses were present only at 250 Hz at equipment limits, they were consid-

ered tactile rather than auditory; the child felt them rather than heard them.

Immittance findings were abnormal bilaterally. For the right ear, the tympanogram was flat (type B) with low static compliance. For the left ear abnormal negative pressure (type C) was found, with static compliance in the normal range. As expected, acoustic reflexes were absent bilaterally at the limits of the audiometer (110 dB HL).

The data in Figure 1-23 point out the value of impedance measures when severe to profound hearing loss is present. Due to the output limitations of bone conduction testing, it is impossible to detect conductive hearing loss when air conduction thresholds exceed 70 dB HL. Therefore, the only means available to detect conductive disorders with this severe a loss is through the use of immittance testing. The results in Figure 1-23 suggest the presence of a significant conductive disorder and the child should be referred for medical examination.

POINTS TO REMEMBER

Care and Maintenance of Equipment

The cost of modern audiometric and immittance equipment, the expense of annual calibration services, and the necessity for reliability in test results, emphasize the importance of handling instrumentation with the utmost care. Guidelines for the proper care and maintenance of equipment at the standards at which it was manufactured are summarized in this discussion.

Care of Equipment

Audiometric and immittance equipment should not be handled roughly or dropped at any time. This equipment is delicate and expensive, and should be protected from extremes in temperature and humidity. The life of an audiometer is much shorter in coastal cities if the audiometer is not properly cared for.

When transporting instruments in a car or on an airplane, keep them in a passenger compartment, protected from freezing or hot temperatures and abusive handling. Having the

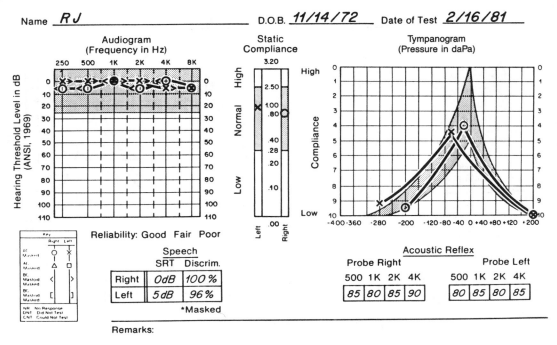

Figure 1-20. Audiometric and immittance findings within normal limits.

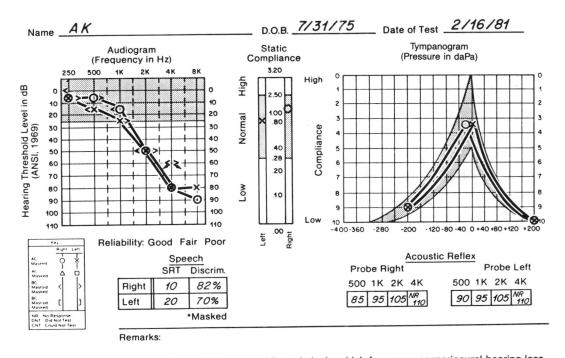

Figure 1-21. Typical findings for a mild-to-severe, bilateral-sloping, high-frequency sensorineural hearing loss.

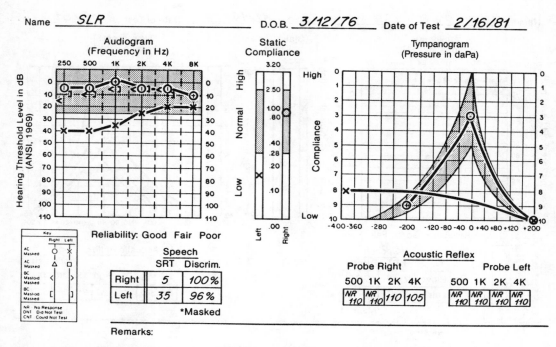

Figure 1-22.   Moderate-to-mild left ear rising conductive hearing loss with normal hearing in the right ear.

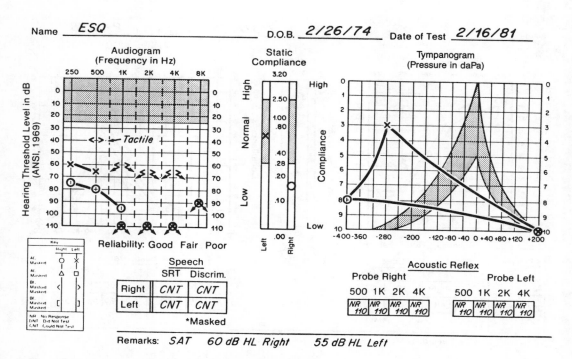

Figure 1-23.   Severe-to-profound bilateral hearing loss with abnormal immittance findings.

equipment x-ray screened at the airport should not damage it. On hot days, never allow it to remain in a closed, unventilated vehicle for long periods of time. Summer temperatures in a closed car may well reach over 100°F within a few minutes.

When not in use, instruments should be stored off the floor, under a protective cover in an area of relatively even temperature. Dusty and salty conditions may rapidly affect the calibration and operation of the equipment. The storage compartment, available on most equipment, should be reserved for storing *that* instrument's earphones and cords. Never interchange earphones between machines.

The earphones are the most delicate part of the equipment and are the most likely component to go out of calibration as a result of being dropped or of some other form of misuse. The cushions may be cleaned with a mild solution of soap and water. Never use alcohol on the cushions, as it tends to dry them out and make them hard, resulting in frequent replacement. Also, guard the receiver inside the cushion from getting wet. The diaphragms of the earphones should be protected from liquids and sharp objects that can enter the perforations in the grid protecting the diaphragm.

Earphone cushions should never be pressed down on a flat surface or packed cushion-to-cushion without a separating pad, such as foam rubber, which helps keep a vacuum from forming and prevents destruction due to percussion blows. The earphone cords should not be twisted or knotted and should be packed loosely in the storage compartment. Plugs or cords that do not have to be regularly removed from the earphone jacks may have a corrosive-type film form between the plug and the jack. This film can be broken up by periodically pulling the plugs in and out several times. However, when doing this always be careful to replace plugs in their proper output jacks and see that they are pushed in all the way.

Purchasing Equipment for School Screening

A pure tone screening audiometer should have:

(*1*) AC voltage line. Do not purchase a battery-operated instrument.
(*2*) Two standard earphones and cushions.

(*3*) At least these six frequencies: 250, 500, 1000, 2000, 4000, and 6000 Hz.
(*4*) The capability for pure tone air conduction screening only—diagnostic instruments having bone conduction, masking, and speech capabilities are not cost-effective for school use.
(*5*) Been calibrated to ANSI, 1969 specifications for audiometers.

A screening immittance instrument should have:

(*1*) The capability of measuring tympanograms, static compliance, and contralateral reflexes at least at 1000 Hz at 100 to 105 dB HL.
(*2*) The capability of presenting test stimuli in 5 dB increments between 0 and 110 dB HL.
(*3*) A wide variety of hard and soft plastic or rubber probe tips.

Using the Audiometer or Immittance Instrument

The following points should be kept in mind when using this equipment:

(*1*) Be sure the instrument is properly grounded, using a three-wire power cord. A properly grounded two-prong adapter can be used if a three-prong receptacle is not available.
(*2*) Allow the instrument to warm up for 10 minutes prior to use and leave it in the "on" position for the entire period of testing.
(*3*) Store it in a cool, dry place.
(*4*) Do not drop, shake, or abuse the instruments. They are very delicate and easily abused.
(*5*) Be entirely familiar with the operator's manual.
(*6*) Keep the operator's manual with the equipment for trouble-shooting in the field.
(*7*) Keep all wires untwisted and unkinked at all times to prevent them from breaking.

Using the Audiometer

These points should be remembered specifically for use of the audiometer:

(*1*) Always keep the tone reverse switch in the "normally off" position.
(*2*) Use the interrupter switch rather than turning the instrument on and off for tone presentation.
(*3*) Listen to the tones every day prior to testing.
(*4*) Be sure to follow the calibration schedule (daily, monthly, yearly, and five-year exhaustive).
(*5*) Give clear instructions.

Using the Immittance Instrument

When using the immittance instrument, remember to:

(*1*) Keep the following spare parts with the equipment: a new set of tubing, alcohol swabs to clean the probe tips, a small wire to clean cerumen (ear wax) from the probe, and extra probe tips.
(*2*) Check for leaks in the pressure system.

REFERENCES

1. American Speech and Hearing Association (ASHA) Committee on Audiometric Evaluation, Guidelines for acoustic immittance screening of middle ear function. *ASHA*, 21, No. 4 (1979), 283–288.
2. Berlin CI: Programmed instruction in the decibel, in Northern JL, ed: *Hearing Disorders* (Boston: Little, Brown & Co., 1976).
3. Specification of the council on physical medicine and rehabilitation of the American Medical Association. *JAMA*, 146 (1951), 255–257.
4. Standard Reference zero for calibration of pure-tone audiometers. ISD recommendation R389 (New York: American National Standards Institute, 1964).
5. Specifications for audiometers. ANSI S3.6-1969. (New York: American National Standards Institute, 1970).
6. Kelly BR, Denneston GL: Unoccluded bone conduction screening as an alternative to impedance screening. *J Amer Aud Soc*, 2, No. 3 (1976), 83–87.
7. Roeser RJ, Glorig A: Pure tone audiometry in noise with auraldomes. *Audiology*, 14 (1975), 144–151.
8. Roeser RJ, Seidel J, Glorig A: Performance of earphone enclosures for threshold audiometry. *Sound and Vibration* 10, No. 9 (1975), 22–25.
9. Musket CH, Roeser RJ: Using circumaural enclosures with children. *J Speech Hear Res* 20 (1977), 325–333.
10. American Speech and Hearing Association (ASHA) Committee on Audiometric Evaluation, Guidelines for identification audiometry. *ASHA*, 17 (1975), 94–99.
11. Walton WK, Wilson WR: Stability of routinely serviced portable audiometers. *Lang Sp and Hearing Serv Schools*, 3 (1972), 36–43.
12. Carhart R, Jerger J: Preferred method for clinical determination of pure tone thresholds. *J Speech Hear Disord*, 24 (1959), 330–345.
13. Byers V: Revision of spondaic word list. *ASHA*, 20 (1978), 487–488.
14. Hopkinson NT: Speech Reception Threshold, in Katz J, ed: *Handbook of Clinical Audiology*, ed 2 (Baltimore: Williams and Wilkins Co., 1978).
15. Fletcher H: A method of calculating hearing loss for speech from an audiogram. *J Acoust Soc Am*, 22 (1950), 1–5.
16. Goetzinger CP: Word Discrimination Testing, in Katz, J, ed: *Handbook of Clinical Audiology*, ed 2 (Baltimore: Williams and Wilkins Co., 1978).
17. Martin FN, Kopra LL: Symbols in pure tone audiometry. *ASHA* 12 (1970), 182–185.
18. American Speech and Hearing Association (ASHA), Guidelines for Audiometric Symbols. *ASHA*, 16 (1974), 260–264.
19. Northern JL: Clinical applications of impedance audiometry, in Northern JL, ed: *Hearing Disorders* (Boston: Little, Brown & Co., 1976).
20. Berg FS: Definition and incidence, in Berg FS, Fletcher SG, eds: *The Hard of Hearing Child* (New York: Grune and Stratton, 1970).
21. Northern JL, Downs MP: *Hearing in Children*, ed 2 (Baltimore: Williams and Wilkins Co., 1978).
22. Green DS: Pure tone air conduction testing, in Katz J, ed: *Handbook of Clinical Audiology* (Baltimore: Williams and Wilkins, Co., 1978).
23. Goodman A: Reference zero levels for pure tone audiometers. *ASHA*, 7 (1965), 262–263.
24. Galambos R, Hecox K: Clinical application of the auditory brainstem response. *Otolaryngol Clin North Amer*, 11 (1978), 709–722.
25. Northern JL, Grimes AM: Introduction to acoustic impedance, in Katz J, ed: *Handbook of Clinical Audiology* (Baltimore: Williams and Wilkins Co., 1978).
26. Jerger J: Clinical experience with impedance audiometry. *Arch Otolaryngol* 92 (1970), 311–324.
27. Jerger J: Diagnostic use of impedance measures, in Jerger J, ed: *Handbook of Clinical Impedance Audiometry* (Acton, MA: American Electromedics Co., 1975).
28. Feldman AS: Acoustic impedance—Admittance battery, in Katz J, ed: *Handbook of Clinical Audiology* (Baltimore: Williams and Wilkins Co., 1978).
29. Wiley TL, Block MG: Overview and basic principles of acoustic immittance measures, in Katz J, ed: *Handbook of Clinical Audiology* (Baltimore: Williams and Wilkins Co., 1985).

2

MEDICAL PROBLEMS AND THEIR MANAGEMENT

LaVonne Bergstrom

INTRODUCTION

Medical problems play three significant roles in auditory problems. First, they *cause* hearing loss either primarily, as in middle ear infections, or secondarily, as in instances where meningitis may destroy the inner ear. Second, they may create additional problems, as in the multihandicapped child whose mother had rubella (German measles) during the first few weeks of pregnancy. Such additional handicaps may include heart defects, congenital eye disorders (the most common of which is cataract), microcephaly (small head), and associated mental retardation. When the child has rubella, the virus may persist in body fluids and tissues for many months, contributing to the progression or worsening of some conditions. During the time of persistent virus infection, the child is potentially infectious to others, including pregnant women. A small minority of rubella-handicapped children develop progressive neurologic symptoms and mental deterioration in late childhood or early adolescence.

The third role that medical problems play is that they may develop from related genetic factors when a child has a genetic (hereditary) type of hearing loss. Medical problems caused by genetic factors related to genetic hearing loss may not appear until late childhood or adolescence. For example, progressive loss of vision and equilibrium may occur. However, examples of this type of relation between medical and auditory problems are extremely rare.

The school teacher, nurse, and other school personnel may be critically important in recognizing children who might not otherwise be identified as needing medical care for middle ear infections and hearing loss, as in Case History 1.

TYPES OF DEAFNESS

Genetic Hearing Loss

The term *genetic hearing loss* generally refers to loss that is inherited. A very small number of hearing losses that are not inherited may still be considered genetic because the chromosomes and probably the genes have been disarranged. Many of the children who survive infancy with chromosome disorders are profoundly retarded, multihandicapped, and institutionalized. However, others are trainable, educable, or even of normal intelligence. Children with Down's syndrome (mongolism, trisomy 21, or mosaic Down's) have a high incidence of congenital (present at birth) or acquired hearing loss, and are in the educational system.[1] Figure 2-1 illustrates various genetic birth defect syndromes with associated hearing loss.[2]

Four types of genetic hearing loss are hereditary: autosomal dominant, autosomal recessive, sex- or x-linked, and chromosomal.

Autosomal Dominant Hearing Loss

This type of genetic hearing loss is the easiest to understand and to diagnose. *Autosomal* signifies that the trait is carried on one of the 44 non-sex chromosomes. Affected individuals can be found in each generation of a family, once a trait such as deafness appears. However, not all individuals are affected. Genes descend from one generation in a family in an entirely random fashion, similar to the outcome in rolling dice. However, in genetics, there is a pair of dice for each trait; whether it is for blue eyes or for deafness, the mother has one die, the father has the other. Both parents may have all nor-

Case history #1. A public school teacher in a small town became convinced that a 9-year-old girl who was doing poorly academically had a hearing loss, although the child had passed school hearing screening tests performed by an itinerant public health nurse who used a portable audiometer. The teacher finally persuaded the nurse and parents to obtain further consultation through local services. Diagnostic testing confirmed the teacher's suspicions. The child was found to have a severe hearing loss in the upper speech frequencies and in higher frequencies in both ears. This type of loss was undetected because it only interfered with consonant perception. It is likely that the loss had been present since birth. Furthermore, the child had escaped earlier detection because she had above-average intelligence, had developed speech, and had probably used extra-auditory cues to "fake" a normal audiogram in the particular school testing environment.

mal genes on their dice. Or the die of one parent may contain half-normal and half-abnormal genes. A dominant gene apparently can override a normal gene coming from the other parent.

Each time the genetic dice are thrown at conception, a dominant abnormal gene has a 50% chance of appearing if it is present. Producing a number of children with the abnormal trait is possible, but would be considered an unlucky series of dice throws. The more children with the abnormal trait, the rarer such bad luck would be. With great good luck, these parents could have all normal children, and the trait could "fade out" with that generation. The continuation of the abnormal trait is not dependent on the percentage of affected individuals, but on the appearance in each generation of the abnormal trait in an individual in direct lineage.

In a family in which dominant hearing loss occurs, one parent will have the trait *to some degree*. If the pattern of hearing loss in a family happens to be limited in severity or in the audiometric frequencies involved, it may not be evident to the casual observer. However, the loss will be detectable by complete audiometric testing, just as certain hidden medical problems may be found by complete physical examination and appropriate laboratory tests. If the hearing loss tends to be severe in another family, affected individuals generally will be evident to the untrained observer. However, it must be stressed that there are influences on *dominantly inherited* conditions that may make an affected individual appear to be normal; thus, it may seem that an inherited condition has "skipped a generation."

One influence is that of *diminished penetrance*. In this circumstance, for some poorly understood reason, the abnormal gene is present but fails to exert its full effect. Thus, an apparently normal person who is the offspring of a dominantly deaf parent and has produced two or more affected children may be found to have a partial hearing loss limited to only part of the audiometric range.

Another influence is that of *variable expressivity*. This is most easily explained in the context of a *syndrome*. A *syndrome* refers to any medical condition that contains several features occurring together fairly consistently. One syndrome in which dominant hearing loss occurs is Waardenburg's syndrome (see Fig. 2-1). One constant feature of this syndrome is the displacement of the tiny ligament that attaches the eyelids to the side of the nose, so that the eyes appear somewhat far apart (although technically they are not). Other features may include a central white forelock of the scalp hair, variegated eye color (e.g., one blue and one brown eye), broad nasal bridge, eyebrows meeting over the nasal bridge, a narrow lower part of the nose, obstructed tear ducts, and incompletely pigmented skin areas, often in inconspicuous locations of the body. To the casual observer, these persons may be strikingly good-looking—but not necessarily abnormal in appearance. Only one of five affected persons has hearing loss; yet *each* person minimally affected is capable of passing on to his/her offspring all of the characteristics of the syndrome, so that a parent with normal hearing could have a deaf child.[3]

Dominant hearing loss appears in a number of forms, varying in time of onset, degree and

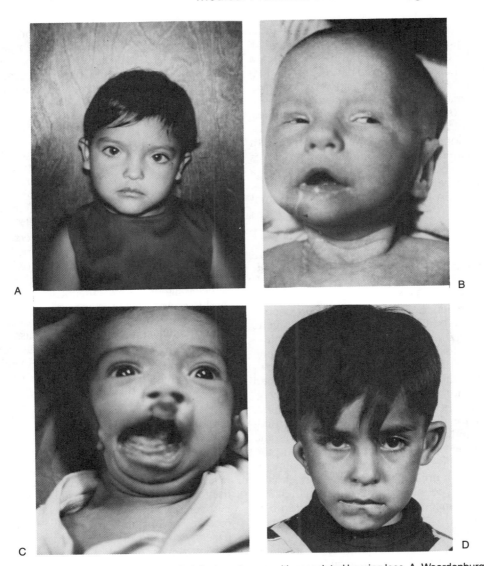

Figure 2-1.   Examples of genetic birth defect syndromes with associated hearing loss. A. Waardenburg syndromes. This patient does not have a white forelock; she has the increased medial intercanthal distance, severe hearing loss, and brilliant blue eyes. B. Rubella syndrome. This infant had microcephaly, microphthalmia, carp-shaped mouth, large abnormal ears, a bulbous nasal tip, and a fixed stapes. C. Treacher-Collins syndrome with severe facial malformations, a very small mandible which caused the tongue to obstruct the airway which caused his death. Temporal bone pathology showed a malformed monopod stapes, and the facial nerve exited directly from the side of the skull. D. Microtia-atresia. Both the malformed right ear and the normal-appearing left ear had conductive losses. The left ear hearing loss was due to stapes fixation. (Figure 2-1 B reprinted with permission from Hemenway,[26] Figure 2-1 C reprinted with permission from Sando et al.,[27] Figure 2-1 D reprinted with permission from Bergstrom.[2])

type of loss, and tendency to worsen with time. For example, some losses may be congenital, as in the case in Waardenburg's syndrome. In others, the gene effect is delayed, and the loss does not appear until the second or third decade. It may stabilize at some point or worsen steadily over the years. In still other families, the hearing loss may be limited in severity or scope. Sometimes it involves only one ear. In some families, only the middle ear structures are involved in the congenital defect, with a resultant conductive hearing loss. In others, the inner ear is affected, giving a sensorineural loss.

Autosomal Recessive Hearing Loss

This type of loss seldom appears in more than one generation of a family. The reason is that this type of hearing loss requires a gene from *each parent* for the abnormal trait—hearing loss—to appear. A recessive gene from one parent is not strong enough alone to produce the trait, as its effect is overwhelmed by the normal gene from the other parent. Since genes for hearing loss are not common, and since the two genes must be matching genes and not dissimilar recessive genes, the likelihood of prospective parents having the same rare recessive gene is indeed slim. In fact, it is so unlikely that even if congenitally deaf young people marry each other, their statistical chance of having all deaf children is only about 15% greater than that of the normal-hearing population at large.[4]

However, should each parent have a matching recessive gene, the statistical likelihood of their having an affected child is one in four, since this is the likelihood of the genetic throw of dice resulting in matching genes. Again, with bad luck, four of four children could be affected, or with good luck, none of four. All affected individuals could pass on the trait if they mate with a carrier, since half of the non-affected persons may be carriers. The offspring of affected individuals of the next generation will be affected only if history repeats itself, in that the parents bear the same gene. In the extremely rare instances of affected parents being *affected* with matching genes, their genes will all be abnormal for deafness and all offspring will be deaf. If only one parent is a carrier, half of the offspring will be deaf—

speaking, of course, in statistical probability. Consanguinity, or marriage between persons who are related to each other, may increase the likelihood of offspring having deafness or other traits of autosomal recessive inheritance.

Sex- or X-Linked Hearing Loss

This type of loss is carried by the mother on one of her X chromosomes. In the recessive mode, the mother passes on the carrier capability to a theoretic 50% of her daughters, and they will not display hearing loss. On the other hand, 50% of her sons theoretically will receive the abnormal gene and be affected with hearing loss, since they have only one X chromosome, which they can receive only from their mother. In the dominant mode, when an affected father has a dominant abnormal gene on his only X chromosome, all his daughters are affected, but none of his sons. Theoretically, the affected daughters then pass on the trait to 50% of their children. In either autosomal or X-linked recessive traits, the likelihood of producing affected offspring increases if the parents are blood relatives.

Chromosomal Hearing Loss

The fourth type of genetic defect is seldom hereditary. A number of disorders that involve hearing loss are characterized by a defect in the form or number of chromosomes. Chromosomes are normally paired, with one chromosome of the pair being received from each parent. In some instances, there are three chromosomes instead of two at one location. Such a condition is called trisomy. In one form of Down's syndrome, the defect occurs at the site of the 21st chromosomes, and the scientific term for this condition is *trisomy 21.*[1] In a more rare form of Down's syndrome, some of the chromosomal material is displaced to one of the 21st chromosomes in the patient. This condition is called partial trisomy.

In partial trisomy, no obvious defect is present in the parents, but when parental chromosomes are examined, a balanced transfer or exchange of a part of chromosomal material is found to have occurred between two chromosomes. Chromosomal symmetry is preserved, and thus no symptoms result, but the parents are at some risk for having an affected child with each pregnancy.

In other instances, some chromosomal material seems to be entirely missing, resulting in what is called a deletion. In the 18-deletion syndrome, one of those features is atresia of the bony external auditory canal, and the trait may be passed to offspring of an affected individual. In other syndromes, the sex chromosomes may be similarly affected, so that there may be extra X (female) chromosomes or extra Y (male) chromosomes.

Hearing loss occurs in a few of these entities. In Turner's syndrome, an affected female has only one normal X chromosome in most cells—a condition called monosomy. Technically, in this particular disorder, the defect is termed an XO chromosome disorder. The causes of chromosomal disorders are multiple. Some may be related to relatively advanced parental age; others to mutations that may be induced by x-rays, viruses, or drugs. Many are of unknown origin.

Associated Genetic Defects

As has already been implied, genetic deafness may occur alone or with other characteristics or defects. Associated defects are varied, and may be single or multiple. They may occur in the head and neck region only, apparently unrelated defects may occur widely scattered throughout the body; or defects may occur whose embryologic origin is from one type of tissue. Abnormalities of the head and neck region alone are more frequently associated with middle ear defects than inner ear defects. This is because middle ear structures are adaptations of the primitive gill apparatus, which also forms the structures of the face, jaw, mouth, throat, and neck.[5] Multiple defects that are apparently unrelated may be of chromosomal origin or may represent gene mutations.

Examples of defects of organs arising from similar embryologic tissue are those of inner ear, eye, central nervous system, and skin and its appendages (hair, nails, and teeth). All of these structures originate from an embryologic tissue layer called ectoderm. The involvement of the hearing apparatus in an inherited generalized bone or cartilage abnormality is another instance that involves embryologic tissue. The ear is preformed in cartilage; later, its middle ear structures and the protective layers around the inner ear and its nerve canals become bone. Neural crest cells, which are of neuroectodermal origin, also contribute to the development of the ossicles.[5] Thus, an abnormality of these processes could affect form and function of the ear. When these structures are affected, the audiometric patterns and time of onset of hearing loss vary widely, but are fairly consistent within a family tree.

Congenital hearing loss occurs in about 1 in 800 live births.[6] Genetic hearing loss accounts, on the average, for about 35% of all congenital hearing loss. Autosomal recessive hearing loss is believed to be the most frequent, autosomal dominant the next, and the X-linked and chromosomal disorders are quite rare.

Acquired Hearing Loss

Prelinguistic hearing loss may also be due to factors acquired during prenatal life or during the time surrounding birth. On the average, acquired causes account for another 35% of congenital hearing losses; and in the remaining 30%, the cause is unknown.[7]

Hearing Loss Acquired During the Prenatal and Perinatal Period

During the prenatal and perinatal period, potential causes of hearing loss include: (1) infections such as cytomegalovirus, rubella and syphilis; (2) drugs toxic to the inner ear (ototoxic antibiotics or diuretics), or toxic to the entire young organism (e.g., thalidomide, cortisone-type steroids, certain hormones, and some anticonvulsant medications); (3) toxic chemicals to which the mother might be exposed during pregnancy (lead, mercury); (4) lack of oxyen supply to the fetus or baby; (5) maternal illnesses (toxemia, eclampsia, or diabetes); and (6) severe incompatibility between mother and baby of the Rh factors in their blood. After the baby is born, severe prematurity, perinatal infection (e.g., meningitis), neurologic abnormality or injury, and prolonged or severe respiratory distress of the newborn may cause hearing loss and other deficits if the infant survives.[7] The rate of congenital hearing loss among infants in the newborn intensive care unit may be as high as 1 in 60.[6]

Hearing Loss Acquired Later

Once the risks of birth are safely past, which fortunately is true for about 95% of live-born infants, other factors intervene. Each year a small percentage of children are deafened by one of the following six factors:

(1) *Infection other than otitis media.*   Such infections include: mumps and other viral infections, many of which cause sudden hearing loss; meningitis that may be a complication of sinus or middle ear infections or that may secondarily invade the inner ear from primary meningeal infection; congenital syphilis; and tuberculosis.

(2) *Injury.*   The injury might occur to the ear itself by accidental eardrum perforation with a sharp instrument, by a blunt blow to the ear, or during diving because of abrupt pressure changes. Or the injury might be to the bone of the middle and inner ear when the base of the skull fractures, often as a result of severe falls or vehicular accidents. School teachers and nurses may be all too aware that the battered child is often the victim of blows to the head, to the point of skull fractures and severe brain injury.

(3) *Ototoxic medications.*   These medications, usually given only for severe, life-threatening infections, may—if prolonged, repeated, or combined with other medications—cause hearing loss or injury to the inner ear balance mechanism.

(4) *Acoustic trauma.*   This is a problem for older grade school children who are exposed to the noise of farm machinery or who go hunting. Teenagers may also suffer the effects of exposure to loud, live, amplified music, especially as performers, or they may be exposed to noise in industrial arts or to industrial noise during holidays and summers (see Chapter 3).

(5) *Medical diseases.*   Children who are frequently hospitalized for treatment of severe, recurrent infections or malignancies, or who have chronic kidney disease that requires the use of an artificial kidney (dialysis) machine or one or more kidney transplant operations, are at special risk for losing hearing, either as a result of their illness or as a result of the treatments and medications they receive.[8]

(6) *Sudden hearing loss.*   This is often due to viral infection or injury, but inner ear membrane ruptures, blood clot closure of blood vessels supplying the inner ear, and the spread of cancer (the second leading killer of children) to the middle or inner ear are other causes.[9]

Middle Ear Disorders

Middle ear infection (otitis media), either in its acute (severe) or chronic (long-lasting) form, is the leading cause of hearing loss in children, perhaps accounting for 15 to 20% of childhood hearing loss.[10] The type of loss caused is usually conductive in nature (see Chapter 1), due to middle ear involvement; but chronic otitis media is also the leading cause of sensorineural hearing loss in children.

Middle ear infections or middle ear fluid, if prolonged or frequent in occurrence, may also have a significant effect on language development and speech, especially if these episodes occur during the first two years of life. During that time, the infant first hears speech sounds, later imitates them, and finally initiates speech. The normal development of speech and language apparently requires consistent input in quantity, as well as a delicate integration of the end-organ (ear), its nerve fiber, relay centers, and the brain, perhaps in concert with other types of input.

Although the disease itself is fairly easy to diagnose, the damaging aspect of otitis media is that its effects on language development are subtle and insidious (see Chapter 9). However, until recently, the need for intervention with children whose episodes of otitis media may have already passed, perhaps undiagnosed, before they entered school has gone largely unrecognized. These children may show a significant gap between verbal and performance levels on appropriate psychometric testing (see Chapter 5). They may also show defects in auditory perceptual and auditory memory tests; therefore, they may be thought to have perceptual or central auditory problems. Hearing tests and medical examination of the ears after resolution of otitis media are likely to be normal.[11-15]

Otitis media is classified into acute suppurative otitis, chronic suppurative otitis, and serous or secretory otitis media. The first two are characterized by signs of infection and bacteria; serous otitis and secretory otitis are characterized by sterile fluid in the middle ear, which perhaps generally results from abnormal function or structure of the middle ear and eustachian tube.

Acute Suppurative Otitis Media. This type of middle ear disorder is usually preceded by a cold or sore throat, and is associated with fever, pain, a throbbing sound, and a clogged sensation in the ear. A school-aged child will probably be able to describe hearing loss in the ear. There is pus in the middle ear, earache, and there may be ear drainage; sometimes the ear drainage is associated with dramatic relief of the earache. Drainage may be so scanty that it is not readily visible, but the ear may have a foul odor. Symptoms usually regress with antibiotic treatment, but hearing loss and eardrum abnormalities may persist for weeks or even months after acute otitis media.[16-18] A child who has had frequent episodes of otitis media may not complain of hearing loss, perhaps because the child has grown accustomed to it.

Chronic Suppurative Otitis Media. Children with chronic otitis media may have a continual perforation in the eardrum. When the child has a cold or gets water in the ear, it may be mildly painful and drain pus, but the hearing remains at a slightly depressed level both between and during episodes. The amount of hearing loss depends mainly on the amount of middle ear damage and very little on the perforation itself. In a few instances, the ear has a constant foul odor. In other instances, the ear has not drained for years and the eardrum, although it shows signs of previous otitis, is intact. The main symptoms of chronic otitis media are hearing loss and perhaps some difficulty in equalizing middle ear pressure and atmospheric pressure during altitude changes, if the tympanic membrane is intact.

Serous or Secretory Otitis Media. This type of otitis media is without apparent symptoms in the preverbal child, and is often nonsymptomatic even in the school-aged child, who may have suffered from the disorder since infancy. Unlike acute and chronic suppurative otitis media, which usually affect only one ear during an episode, serous or secretory otitis media nearly always involves both ears. Early in its course, serous otitis media may be characterized by thin fluid behind the eardrum in the middle ear. However, unfortunately, serous otitis in young children may be an incidental finding during a routine physical examination. By the time it is discovered, the fluid is usually thick and tenacious. This condition is called "glue ear" by physicians—a term that connotes how hearing is impaired when the middle ear is full of this material. Serous and perhaps secretory otitis media seem to be consequences of an obstructed eustachian or auditory tube.

Eustachian Tube Malfunction. The eustachian tube connects the front or anterior part of the middle ear space and the nasopharynx, which is that part of the upper throat behind the fleshy part of the roof of the mouth (soft palate) and the nose (Fig. 2-2). The nasopharynx contains the adenoids. The eustachian tube is normally closed except during swallowing, yawning, chewing, or forcing of air through the tube. The eustachian tube opens through the action of a branch of the V cranial nerve (trigeminal nerve) and of a branch of the IX cranial nerve (glossopharyngeal), which stimulate two muscles—both small muscles of the soft palate. A common cause of nonfunction of the eustachian tube opening is a cleft palate,[19] but neurologic deficit probably causes some eustachian tube malfunction. The opening of the eustachian tube may be obstructed; in children, a common cause of this is abnormally enlarged adenoids.

Adenoids, tonsils, and other lymphoid tissue help to manufacture antibodies that build up immunity and the body's defenses against infection during the early years. To build this immunologic defense system, these structures grow in size until the child reaches about 8 years of age, after which they normally shrink, until in adults they may be barely visible. However, in some children, adenoids are repeatedly infected, and enlarge to an abnormal size; they remain enlarged, resulting in chronic eustachian tube and even posterior nasal obstruction.

A very common cause of eustachian tube obstruction is persistent swelling of the mucous lining of this very narrow structure. Swelling may result from frequent colds, from nasal allergies, or perhaps from irritants. When the eustachian tube remains obstructed, the air in the middle ear is reabsorbed into the bloodstream, and a partial vacuum ensues in the middle ear. This exerts a force that causes

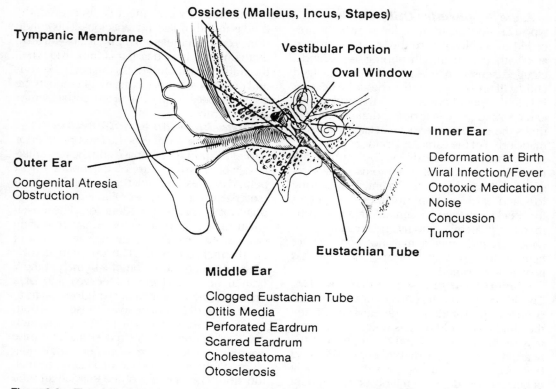

Ossicles (Malleus, Incus, Stapes)

Tympanic Membrane

Vestibular Portion

Oval Window

Inner Ear

Deformation at Birth
Viral Infection/Fever
Ototoxic Medication
Noise
Concussion
Tumor

Outer Ear

Congenital Atresia
Obstruction

Eustachian Tube

Middle Ear

Clogged Eustachian Tube
Otitis Media
Perforated Eardrum
Scarred Eardrum
Cholesteatoma
Otosclerosis

Figure 2-2. The major anatomic landmarks of the ear, with common childhood disorders of hearing in the outer ear, middle ear, and inner ear.

serous fluid to exit from the capillary blood vessels of the lining of the middle ear. It is possible that increased mucus may be produced from the mucus cells of the anterior part of the middle ear space; or that in the course of time, the lining of the middle ear may change, so that a larger area contains mucus-producing cells.

This thicker mucus may then be more difficult to propel down the eustachian tube into the throat, thus setting up a vicious cycle. In some ears where eustachian tube obstruction and infections have combined, the blood supply of the middle ear may diminish, resulting in scar tissue and damage to the middle ear bones (ossicles), which amplify and transmit sound to the inner ear. In other instances, chronic middle ear vacuum or an eardrum perforation may allow outer ear canal skin to grow into the middle ear, forming a cyst that is infected and filled with dead skin. These cysts, called *cholesteatomas* (also called *keratomas*), produce chemicals capable of eating away

bone, and mark a dangerous stage of middle ear disease. Cholesteatomas have the potential to destroy the middle ear, and to invade the inner ear, the membrane surrounding the brain, and even the brain itself.

The prevalence of otitis media varies by ethnic and socioeconomic factors. Among American Indians and Eskimos, it has an incidence of 15 to 60%. The poor, especially those living in crowded, unsanitary circumstances, are believed to have the above-average incidence. The highest incidence is in children under 10 years of age; males have a higher rate of infection than females. Children under four years of age have an average prevalence rate of 8 to 20%; children up to 10 to 12 years of age, 5 to 22%. Certain infants may be at risk for otitis media: sick or premature infants who stayed in the newborn intensive care unit for a long time or infants having a defective immune system. These babies will have recurrent otitis media before 6 months of age. There is less incidence of acute otitis media now than in the preantibiotic era.[20,21] However, definitive statistical studies of this population have yet to be performed in the United States.

THE ANATOMY OF DEAFNESS

The Outer Ear

Figure 2-2 shows a diagram of the ear and lists the common causes of hearing loss in children. A number of abnormalities of the outer ear have been described that may be *associated* with hearing loss. However, only one anatomic defect of the outer ear *causes* hearing loss. The defect is atresia of the outer ear canal, in which the canal is either closed or has failed to form. The resultant hearing loss is *conductive* in nature, in that sound cannot be transmitted to the eardrum and middle ear structures that conduct sound to the inner ear.

The Middle Ear

The human eardrum (*tympanic membrane*) alone is incapable of efficiently transmitting sound to the inner ear, because they are separated by the middle ear space. An ingenious system of tiny bones (*ossicles*), which are normally flexibly linked to each other by joints, not only assist in this process but help to amplify sound, so that it will carry from the normally air-filled middle ear to the fluid-filled inner ear (*labyrinth*) with a minimal loss of energy. The first of the ossicles, the hammer bone (*malleus*), is attached to the tympanic membrane. The malleus is linked by a joint to the anvil bone (*incus*), which in turn touches the stirrup bone (*stapes*). The stapes footplate fits snugly, but not rigidly, into the tiny *oval window*, which abuts directly on a fluid space of the inner ear.

The Inner Ear

The Auditory Portion

As shown in Figure 2-3, the inner ear consists of several compartments containing fluid. The largest contains *perilymph*, which is a thin fluid with about the same concentrations of sodium, potassium, protein, and other chemi-

cals as blood serum or cerebrospinal fluid. The *cochlea*, which is the acoustic part of the inner ear, has two large compartments containing perilymph. One is the *scala vestibuli*, which begins just beyond the oval window and ends at the apical turn of the cochlea where the *scala tympani* begins. It ends at the *round window*. The round window is covered by a membrane called the *round window membrane*. It separates the fluid-filled inner ear from the normally air-containing space of the middle ear.

The second largest space of the inner ear is filled with *endolymph*, and is named the *scala media*. This space is partitioned off from the scala vestibuli and scala tympani by two important membranes. The *vestibular membrane*, more commonly called *Reissner's membrane*, separates the endolymphatic portion of the cochlea from the scala vestibuli. The *basilar membrane*, on which the organ of hearing (*Corti's organ*) rests, adjoins the scala tympani. Endolymph is a viscous fluid whose chemical composition is more like that found inside cells, in that it is high in potassium and relatively low in sodium, while these ratios are reversed in perilymph. In the cochlea, the endolymph chemical composition and the metabolism of Corti's organ are probably maintained by the *stria vascularis*, which is a structure containing many blood vessels.

Corti's organ contains three rows of outer hair cells, each of which has protruding from it an array of stiff hairs (*stereocilia*) and one row of inner hair cells, which also contain a group of cilia. The stereocilia of the outer hair cells indent into and are loosely adherent to a ribbon-like structure called the *tectorial membrane*. These sensory cells are surrounded by a variety of supporting cells.

Within Corti's organ are two tiny fluid spaces. One, called *Corti's canal*, is triangular in shape and bounded by the basilar membrane and two stiff structures called the *pillars of Corti*. This space lies between the rows of outer hair cells and the single row of inner hair cells. *Nuel's space* is between the outermost pillar cells and the outer hair cells. Some investigators believe that this space of the inner ear contains a fluid identical in composition to perilymph, or perhaps perilymph itself, because there may be microscopic spaces connecting the scala tympani and Corti's canal. Nerve fiber endings are attached to the inner and outer half cells, with each fiber coming

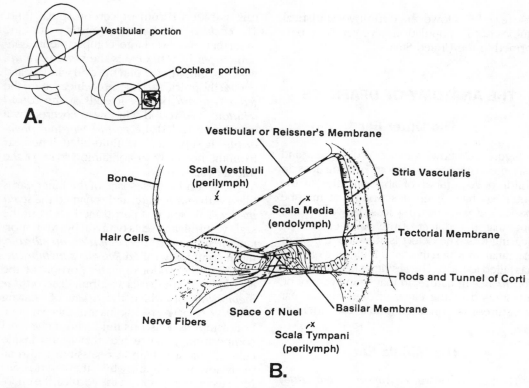

Figure 2-3. Diagram of the inner ear, showing: A. The cochlear and vestibular portions of the inner ear. B. The structures in a cross-section of the cochlear portion of the inner ear.

from the acoustic or auditory branch of the VIII cranial nerve.

The sound wave set up in the scala vestibuli by the rocking motions of the stapes footplate spreads throughout the perilymphatic spaces of the cochlea. This fluid movement causes undulating and shearing motions of delicate inner ear membranes, which in turn exert mechanical forces on Corti's organ. This mechanical stimulation, and probably associated chemical events within the cells of this organ, in turn excite the nerve fibers that attach to the sensory cells of Corti's organ. The nerve impulses then go through various relay points called *ganglia* and *nuclei* to the brain centers for hearing and decoding what we hear.

The Vestibular Portion

The balance (*vestibular*) portion of the ear contains fluids identical in composition to the fluids in the cochlea, and its sensory cells and nerve fibers are similar. However, they do not respond to sound, but instead to body movements (e.g., turning, rotation, and bending over), to gravity, and to linear acceleration, for example. The superior and inferior vestibular nerves and facial nerve accompany the auditory nerve through the *internal auditory canal* to the brainstem, where they go through their own relay points to the brain and cerebellum.

DISORDERS OF HEARING

External and Middle Ear

Beginning with the external canal, which leads from the ear to the eardrum, anything that obstructs the canal may prevent sound waves from reaching the inner ear in full force (see Fig. 2-2). A familiar example is the reduction in hearing that occurs when the ear canal is clogged with earwax (cerumen). Another example that has been mentioned previously is that the ear canal may fail to form (congenital atresia), which is a defect often associated with gross deformity of the outer ear. Also, the ear canal may scar shut as a result of injury or severe canal infection.

A perforated eardrum contributes relatively little by itself to hearing loss. A thick, scarred eardrum perhaps affects hearing a bit more. Fluid, pus, or blood may impede the movement of the eardrum; if the fluid is sufficiently thick, it dampens movement of the ossicles to an additional degree. As described in the preceding section, such fluid results mostly from otitis media, which in children is often due to eustachian tube malfunction.

Heavy deposits of inflammatory scar tissue, which may even be calcified, or bony fusion of the ossicles to each other or to surrounding structures, will greatly impede ossicular motion. Inflammatory tissue is an aftereffect of repeated or chronic otitis media. Bony fusion of ossicles may be congenital or degenerative in nature.

A degenerative condition rarely seen in persons of school age is otosclerosis—an inherited disease in which abnormal bone forms and fixes the stapes footplate to the adjacent bone so that the stapes cannot move. A congenital disorder in which fixation may occur is osteogenesis imperfecta (fragile bone disease). In this disease, frequent fractures occur; and fracture or extreme thinning of the stapes may also occur, resulting in separation of the stapes arch from the footplate and loosening of the contact between the ossicles.

Anything that prevents the ossicles from contacting the eardrum or the oval window will impair hearing. Infection or cholesteatoma (defined earlier) may cause tiny but vital areas of ossicular bony tissue to be lost. Vital connecting areas may also fail to form, creating an ossicular defect. Injury may fracture or dislocate the ossicles and tear or perforate the eardrum. The ossicles or oval window may be congenitally absent or so poorly formed that they do not function at all. In extreme cases, the entire middle ear may fail to form or be very small.

Inner Ear

In the inner ear, Corti's organ may lose sensory cells as a result of virus infection of the inner ear itself, of ototoxic medication, of severe noise injury or severe concussion, or of degeneration. Membranes of the inner ear may be displaced, deformed, or absent. In the most severe cases, Corti's organ may be absent or degenerated in part or all of the cochlea. These abnormalities may be seen in both congenital and hereditary deafness. In some instances, hearing (auditory) nerve degeneration will also be seen.

In some rare conditions, the cochlea and/or balance (vestibular) parts of the inner ear may be grossly malformed or absent. In the latter instance, the space where the inner ear should have been may be solid bone. The inner ear may also become filled with solid bone, as a long-term aftereffect of meningitis or bacterial inner ear infection (suppurative labyrinthitis).

In extremely rare cases, a child or adolescent may develop a tumor on the VIII nerve in the internal auditory canal—the so-called acoustic neuroma, which is more properly called a vestibular schwannoma. This is a noncancerous tumor that creates noticeable progressive loss of hearing, noise in the ear (tinnitus), and insidious, nonsymptomatic disturbance of the inner ear balance function.

Central Pathways

Much basic information needs to be learned regarding the abnormalities that occur as a result of problems in the central hearing pathways. The normal anatomy has been worked out well. However, some new and startling information regarding abnormal states is beginning to appear.

It has been known for a few years that certain diseases causing congenital hearing loss are associated with primary abnormalities in the relay centers located in the brainstem (cochlear nuclei). The nerve cells within these areas are significantly diminished in numbers and shrunken. The changes that occur in the brainstem have been described thus far only in children who have had severe lack of oxygen around the time of birth, or who had severe jaundice postnatally.[22] It has been assumed, but not as yet proven, that various rare causes of hearing loss in the inner ear might be responsible for changes or degeneration in higher centers in the brain. It had never been theorized that middle ear disease or pathology could induce changes beyond the middle ear unless, of course, the inner ear was secondarily involved by direct extension from the middle ear.

Recent animal experimental work on mice has shown that closing the ear canal at a very early time of life causes no injury to the inner ear. However, cells in the cochlear nucleus were diminished in number and size to a significant degree.[23] This is significant information, because it at least suggests that the cochlear nuclei may not develop and function properly if they are not stimulated during some critical period of life, probably during the early periods of language acquisition. Closure of the external ear canal causes a conductive hearing loss similar in degree to that seen in the more severe forms of otitis media, and in traumatic and congenital defects of the middle ear or ear canal. Researchers who have studied language deficits in children with an early history of recurrent otitis media have found that there are some abnormalities of higher centers similar to those seen in experimental mice.[23] These abnormalities might account in part for the problems that otitis-prone children experience.

RELATIONSHIP BETWEEN ANATOMY AND FUNCTION

Humans vary greatly in their adaptations to deprivation and adversity, but a few correlations between anatomic abnormalities and hearing behavior may be cautiously advanced. Perhaps the simplest concept to defend is that total lack of a hearing mechanism permits no sound sensations to reach the brain, and therefore no true hearing response can be expected. Responses seen may be to tactile sensation, as in the child who feels a heavy truck drive by the house, or who "hears" through a powerful ear-level hearing aid that may be stimulating the sense of touch as it oscillates near or in contact with the skull. Likewise, responses may be to visual stimuli, as in the totally deaf child who "hears" her mother speaking to her when she has really seen out of the corner of her eye the mother's shadow or movement as she approaches. The child then turns to see who or what is sneaking up on her. It is, of course, natural to believe that it is the mother's voice to which the child is responding.

Children who are severely to profoundly hard-of-hearing may not show many signs of responding to normal or even fairly loud sounds unless they are stimulated with strong vibratory signals. However, children who are otherwise normal will usually respond when sound is sufficiently amplified above threshold. These children have some residual hearing, which is made possible from usable remnants of inner ear anatomic structures that transmit impulses to the brain when stimulated.

Self-monitoring of voice quality and pitch requires the inner ear to have some residual function. The more severely disrupted inner ear function is, the less often the individual can control pitch, quality, and loudness of the voice, since the individual can barely hear it. Also, the background noise over which one's voice must be projected may not be able to be heard.

The auditory behavior of persons with less severe degrees of hearing loss is less easy to predict. Children with long-standing, unrecognized hearing loss may be thought of as inattentive or of dull intelligence because they may not respond at all, respond inappropriately, or say "huh?"—a response guaranteed to irritate anyone over 30 years. Some children with significant losses may give virtually no signs of their hearing loss, as they compensate well by lip-reading, catching contextual cues, and generally scrambling to get the maximum from all channels of input.

The child with static conductive hearing loss usually has less trouble than a similar child with a sensorineural hearing loss of a comparable decibel level, because with a conductive hearing loss, the inner ear apparatus and nerves are intact, and distortion, ear noises (tinnitus), and tolerance problems for louder sounds are seldom present. Conductive hearing losses may be more flat or involve low frequencies, sparing the higher frequencies where soft unvoiced consonants occur. Such sounds are so critical in distinguishing words with identical vowel components.

Many conductive hearing losses easily lend themselves to use of a hearing aid. Hearing aids can virtually always be worn at the more natural ear level, which is an advantage in simulating the natural condition, since the sound is not only directed into the ear canal but is picked up by the receiver at ear level rather than at chest level for an instrument on the body.

There are special physical requirements for fitting children with aids. Children born with very minimal, or absent bilateral external ears cannot wear air conduction hearing aids, but instead must wear a special bone conduction aid applied snugly to the bone over the mastoid process. Newer aids of this type provide less distortion than formerly, so that the acoustics are more optimum. Bone conduction aids are noted for their high distortion, and this poses problems in providing the optimum acoustics.

The child who has a peculiarly shaped external ear or very narrow canal may be difficult to fit with an instrument that will stay in place and not give off a type of whistling feedback into his ear. It should be remembered that all children's ears grow, and feedback may occur as a result of a mold that fits poorly.

The child who has sensorineural hearing loss may not only suffer from sound and human speech deprivation, but may also experience ear noises, distortion of sounds, inability to tolerate large increases in loudness, plugged sensation in the ear, fluctuating hearing loss, and vertigo and equilibrium problems. A certain number of children who have severe-to-profound congenital losses become dizzy with loud sounds. An infant with a severe malformation of the balance organs of the inner ear, and of the hearing organs, may be quite delayed in motor development. The inner ear acts as a captain of the balance system, especially in early life. Consequences of absence or mal-function of the inner ear balance organs can be rather dramatic, as shown in Case History 2.

It has been believed that children who have vestibular disorders have learning disabilities as a consequence. This may be a dangerous conclusion to draw, unless hearing loss has been ruled out.

It has also been believed that children with serous otitis media have a high incidence of vestibular problems. In a personal series of 26 patients with serous otitis media who had had complete pediatric assessments, 15 had normal-to-advanced motor development without evidence of vestibular dysfunction. Three had histories or physical findings that suggested true vestibular involvement. Of the other patients, one had had a traumatic birth and had neurologic deficits believed to be secondary to otitis media. Three others had prior skull fractures and were believed in retrospect to be battered children. The symptoms of one were attributed to a rare type of migraine and epilepsy. Three others were children with various birth defects.

Forty-one autopsied cases in which serous otitis media was found were also surveyed. Two had abnormalities in the balance organs that conceivably could have been related to serous otitis. It does not seem that this issue is as yet fully resolved.

All children with hearing loss share, to some degree, the stigma of being thought of as dull, inattentive, unfriendly, stubborn, or simply "different." If their language and educational deficiencies persist, they will of course suffer economically in the job market, and perhaps some will suffer from health consequences of their ear disease. They may suffer some social isolation, or those whose hearing impairment is severe and congenital may be sequestered,

Case history #2. Twin girls were put up for adoption at 4 months of age. At 11 months, when it was near time to finalize their adoption, the prospective adoptive parents sought medical consultation because the twins still could not hold up their heads. The consultant concluded that they were profoundly retarded and recommended against adoption. Instead, the parents went through with the adoption process. Slowly, the girls began to progress through the stages of motor development until at three years of age they finally walked, but still did not talk. At 3.5 years, they were found to be profoundly deaf. Later, x-rays showed gross malformations of the balance portions of the inner ears of both children. Their subsequent language and school progress has been excellent, and they are physically very active.

to some degree, as adults in the "deaf community."

For those children who have multiple handicaps in addition to hearing disability, life may seem to be an endless round of visits to the physicians, hospitalizations, tests, and surgeries. Some children with orthopedic or neurologic problems may have great difficulty inserting and operating their own hearing aids or communicating in sign language. Children with cerebral palsy who have motor, coordination, and speech problems may find both oral and manual communication difficult. Children with obvious facial, external ear, or cranial defects that contribute to hearing loss usually also will have severe problems with their image and self-esteem, especially as they approach adolescence. This is well exemplified in Case History 3.

Therapists and teachers must see the child holistically. Hopefully, the preceding overview of the various aberrations of ear structure and function will give some insight into why some children function relatively well and why others do poorly. Many other familial, socioeconomic, medical, and personal factors complete the equation. One important variable is how promptly hearing loss is detected and treated. A number of studies demonstrate that early intervention seems to improve the congenitally deafened child's linguistic and educational prospects. There is still great progress to be made. One study of 100 profoundly deaf children showed that, on the average, the children were suspected to have a hearing loss at 11 months of age, but were not diagnosed until 21 months, and not provided with a hearing aid until 27 months. This represents a loss of many months of valuable time that could have been spent with the child involved in some type of language stimulation program with amplification.[7]

These dismal statistics can be contrasted with those attained in a study of multihandicapped children under 3 years of age in an experimental school for early intervention. A pilot study revealed that multihandicapped infants were suspected by their parents to be hearing impaired (on the average) at 17 months of age. A study was launched to see if the staff, which closely observed the children—using bells and noisemakers and also exposing them to oral and sign language—could identify earlier children who needed examination by the consulting otologist. Multihandicapped hearing-impaired children were aided by 20 months of age, which is a remarkable attainment, since the youngest entered the school between 12 and 14 months of age.[24]

Teachers and therapists treating a hearing-handicapped student who is not doing well should consider that perhaps some important problem has been overlooked. Perhaps hearing has worsened—progressive losses and catastrophic additional losses do occur. Perhaps serous fluid has accumulated, adding a conductive loss to an underlying sensorineural loss. Perhaps wax build-up is clogging the hearing aid insert (see Chapter 10). Perhaps a genetically programmed, additional health problem, such as a visual or kidney problem, is beginning to manifest itself. Perhaps the true nature of the child's hearing status has never been adequately diagnosed. Case History 4 is such an example.

Another important consideration relates to the child who has one severely deformed ear and an absent external ear canal. It is often assumed that the opposite ear, which appears normal, has normal hearing. However, in about

---

Case history #3.   A 5-year-old child underwent her first audiogram and was found to have moderately severe hearing loss. She had visible mild defects of the craniofacial area, had been slow in motor development and learning, was clumsy and hyperactive, but had developed speech that was poorly intelligible. Prior to the audiogram, she had multiple pediatric, neurologic, ophthalmologic, orthopedic, psychological, and physical rehabilitation assessments, with various prescription applied. The audiogram was obtained at the parents' insistence. A hearing aid was fitted, and speech and language are improving as her other problems are being addressed.

Case history #4.   An 8-year-old child had a hearing aid since age 3, and had faithfully attended speech and language therapy sessions and special classes for the hearing handicapped, but had never developed a single intelligible word, nor had she ever seemed to understand anything said to her. However, the family felt she heard some sounds. She had had no medical specialty ear diagnostic work-up. An ear specialist was consulted. Audiometry showed no responses to the loudest sounds the equipment could generate. X-rays showed total absence of both inner ears.

20% of these cases, the opposite ear is also found to have a significant hearing loss.[19] Because sound can cross from one ear to the other through the skull bone, such children require expert hearing testing.

Children who have unilateral hearing loss have been thought to function well in the classroom as long as they had preferential seating and/or a CROS hearing aid (see Chapter 10). A recent study by Bess et al looked at a variety of factors: grades failed, school achievement, teacher ratings, academic and social status, and cognitive measures. They have made recommendations for audiologic intervention in the school.[25]

PRACTICAL CLINICAL FACTS

Health history as taken from the parents by the school nurse, using a health questionnaire, can be an important means of identifying students who may be at risk for hearing loss and who are undiagnosed when they enter the school system. If the nurse has the opportunity or authority to modify an existing health questionnaire, certain items would be useful if they are not already on the questionnaire. The following questions should be included on the health questionnaire:

(1) Is there a family history of hearing loss?
(2) Did the child's mother have German measles during pregnancy? Were there complications during pregnancy?
(3) Was the child premature? If so, what was his birth weight?
(4) Did the child have breathing problems at the time of birth?
(5) Was the child severely jaundiced after birth? Did the child require transfusions or other special treatment?

In addition to these questions, when the nurse first sees the child, certain abnormalities should alert her, such as cleft palate, abnormal external ear, or abnormal facial, cranial, or jaw configuration. These conditions are frequently associated with far more than the average incidence of otitis media or with congenital hearing problems.[19]

Certain symptoms are important—ear pain or pressure, clogged sensation in the ear, pulsation or noises in the ear, ear drainage, and severe itching, bleeding, or foul odor to the ear. Vertigo in conjunction with any of these symptoms is a potentially ominous sign. Frequent absences from school for ear infection should prompt a check to see if hearing has been tested, and the child should be put on the priority list for hearing testing if the school offers this service. Otherwise, the school nurse or other school personnel may be able to help with referral to a qualified ear specialist and an audiologist.

The child who has severe nasal obstruction, sinus infections, or severe allergies also may have middle ear infections or fluid. A student who has contracted mumps, measles (rubeola), severe flu, infectious mononucleosis, or other acute viral infections, and who complains afterward of poor hearing should be taken seriously. An ear may become severely deafened from these infections.

The student who returns to school after a head injury should also be observed for possible hearing loss. Students who do not wear ear protection when they participate in rock music groups, school rifle teams, and other noisy activities are at risk for developing hearing loss. Both they and their parents should be so counseled, if possible. Students with preexisting sensorineural hearing losses should, if possible, be counseled into other extracurricular activities.

MEDICAL AND SURGICAL MANAGEMENT OF AUDITORY IMPAIRMENT

Every hard-of-hearing child deserves a complete work-up by an audiologist and ear specialist. Ear specialists certified for Crippled Children's Services may have special interest and expertise. Specialty services are available in the private setting, in some community speech and hearing clinics, and in teaching hospital outpatient departments. In the more rural areas, the state health department or regional centers may provide traveling otology and audiology clinics to which referral may be made. Subsequent or concurrent referral may be needed for children who are multihandicapped or who have concomitant defects. In some areas, clinics sponsored by the Easter Seal Society or the March of Dimes may provide a single center for assessing a child who has multiple needs. Some centers also offer specialized speech, language, and educational consultation. Large metropolitan school systems may have special diagnostic resources available as well. Family counseling for emotional support and for help with paperwork and bureaucracies, and genetic counseling for families of congenitally hard-of-hearing children, are offered in centers such as those cited above (see Chapter 18).

Medical treatment of otitis media includes antibiotics, ear cleaning, and perhaps additional medications such as decongestants. A child may usually attend school while on medication. Doses may need to be given during the day while the child is in school; and the school, in cooperation with the parents and the physician, can make this possible. Students with perforated eardrums or with tubes in their ears are usually instructed not to get water in their ears. They can protect the ear during showering after gym classes or team sports by plugging it with dry cotton smeared with Vaseline or by the use of special ear plugs.

When ear disease is present, swimming is forbidden by many physicians, but may be permitted, where tubes are in place, if the student has well-fitted ear plugs. Diving is usually strictly forbidden. Students who have had recent major ear surgery usually must avoid entirely getting water in the ear and are generally restricted from contact sports until the ear is healed. Each physician has personal preferences; these are common precautions. If a student who has had tubes or major ear surgery develops ear pain, drainage, or bleeding, the student should be referred back to the ear surgeon promptly.

Middle Ear Ventilation Tubes

What are tubes and what is their purpose? Tubes come in various colors, styles, sizes, and materials. They generally are made of some type of plastic or silicone material. The tubes are tiny, measuring perhaps 2 mm in size; and they have some type of flange and a lumen or opening in the center. Tubes are designed to ventilate the middle ear when eustachian tube function is inadequate. The tube is placed in the eardrum by making a small incision just off the center of the eardrum under local or general anesthesia, and any fluid present is suctioned from the middle ear. The tube is then inserted. One end is in the middle ear, and one is just outside the eardrum. Air pressure is equalized between the middle ear and the outside world through the hole in the middle of the tube. Eventually the tube, being an object foreign to the ear, works its way out of the eardrum and falls out of the ear canal, and the eardrum usually heals. Some children need tubes placed repeatedly, if medical treatment fails to clear fluid from the ear. Children with cleft palates are especially prone to repeated placement of tubes, due to their chronic middle ear problems.

Major Ear Surgeries

More major types of ear surgery may have as their primary purpose the removal of middle ear disease (chronic infection) that has not been cleared by the use of medicines and other conservative measures. Reconstruction of the middle ear hearing mechanism is a secondary consideration, except in congenital defects of the middle ear, where it is the primary purpose of surgery. Occasionally, radical mastoid surgery is required for the complications of otitis media. Since the use of antibiotics, emergency mastoid surgery is rarely required to drain an abscess. Reconstructive plastic surgery may also be done to reshape a deformed ear or modify a severely malformed ear. In some of the latter instances, an artificial or prosthetic ear is preferred because it looks more normal. Prosthetic ears are attached to the head with adhesives, but may be detached during rough and tumble play. The detachment may create a sensation, but does no physical harm.

Conservation of Hearing

Preventive measures for otitis media probably consist mainly of providing good nutrition, good sanitation, good health, and an uncrowded, concerned home. It also consists of recognizing and treating early the otitis-prone child, who may even benefit from a mild gain hearing aid until the tendency to infection is outgrown. The hearing aid may do much to prevent or mitigate language disruptions.

For sensorineural hearing losses, hearing conservation measures are indicated to avoid preventable causes of additional hearing loss. Patients or their parents should be instructed to get treatment for ear symptoms promptly, to avoid exposure to loud noise or to drugs or medications potentially toxic to the ear, and to have hearing tests annually or more often if necessary. Immunizations against mumps and flu should be advocated to prevent the rare cases of sudden deafness that may complicate these illnesses. However, the pediatrician or family physician should decide whether flu vaccine is advisable for the individual young child.

Surgery is the treatment of choice for benign tumors of the VIII nerve, but it is fruitless for cancer that has spread from elsewhere in the body to the VIII nerve or to the bone surrounding the structures of the ear.

EDUCATIONAL AND OTOLOGIC COOPERATION

School teachers, school nurses, and other school personnel have an opportunity to see hearing-handicapped children daily in the school setting. Ear specialists (otologists) see children relatively briefly, periodically, or sometimes only once in a setting that most children dislike or unwillingly tolerate: the physician's office or clinic. Hopefully, children like the school setting better than they like the physician's office.

The teacher, school nurse, or school speech pathologist should try to work with the parents to find out when the student is going to the physician for a scheduled visit. A brief report of observations, school progress, or language progress can be quite helpful to the otologist, even if it is a photocopy from school records or reports to the parents (with the parents' written consent, of course). In the author's experience, routine requests are made to the otologist for medical and audiologic information many times with no exchange of information. For example, the otologist or the audiologist

---

Case history #5. A 5-year-old Spanish-speaking child underwent radical mastoid surgery for cholesteatoma. The ear remained somewhat moist and mildly inflamed. The opposite ear had a dry perforation, and a hearing aid was fitted to that ear. A report had been sent to the school explaining the surgery and the reasons for the fitting. The operated ear was nearly dry when on an office visit, the mother, who spoke only Spanish, reported to the otologist that the school audiologist had referred the child to a hearing aid dealer for a new mold and had switched the aid to the operated ear, over the mother's vigorous protestations. It was only then that the otologist learned, fortunately before making a heated phone call, that the child was being bussed to a new school that did not have her otologic records.

who fitted a hearing aid might be quite cha-
grined to learn that the student has lost his aid,
no longer uses it, or seems to derive no benefit
from it even thou_ ' _ raithfully wears it for
his annual visits. In return, the school audiologist might learn that there is a very significant
reason why the hearing aid was fitted to a
particular ear, as shown in Case History 5.
Communication is the most significant factor
in the follow-up of the hearing-impaired child.

REFERENCES

1. Balkany TJ, et al: Ossicular abnormalities in
   Down's syndrome. *Otolaryngol Head Neck
   Surg*, 87 (1979), 372–384.
2. Bergstrom L: Congenital deafness, in English
   GM, ed: *Otolaryngology Loose Leaf Series*, Vol. 1
   (Philadelphia: Harper & Row, 1982), pp. 6, 8.
3. Waardenburg PJ: A new syndrome combining
   developmental anomalies of the eyelids, eyebrows and nose root with pigmentary defects of
   the iris and head hair and with congenital deafness. *Amer J Hum Genet*, 3 (1951), 195–253.
4. Brown KS: The genetics of childhood deafness,
   in McConnell F, Ward PH: *Deafness in Childhood* (Nasville: Vanderbilt University Press,
   1967), p 177.
5. Van De Water TR, Maderson PFA, Jaskoll TF: The
   morphogenesis of the middle and external ear,
   in Gorlin RJ, ed. *Morphogenesis and Malformation of the Ear* (New York: Alan R. Liss, Inc.,
   1980), pp 147–180.
6. Simmons FB: Identification of hearing loss in
   infants and young children. *Otolaryngol Clin
   North Amer*, 11 (1978), 19–28.
7. Bergstrom L, Hemenway WG, Downs MP: A
   high risk registry to find congenital deafness.
   Otolaryngol Clin North Amer, 4 (1971), 369–
   399.
8. Bergstrom L, Thompson P, Wood RP II: New
   patterns in genetic and congenital otonephrop-
   athies. *Laryngoscope*, 89 (1979), 177–194.
9. Mattox DE, Simmons FB: Natural history of sudden sensorineural hearing loss: *Ann Otol Rhinol Laryngol*, 86 (1977), 463–480.
10. Eagles EL, Wishik SM, Doerfler LG: Hearing sen-
    sitivity and ear disease in children: A prospec-
    tive study. *Laryngoscope* (monograph) (1967),
    1–274.
11. Eisen NH: Some effects of early sensory depri-
    vation on later behavior: The quondam hard-of-

12. Holm VA, Kunze LH: Effect of chronic otitis
    media on language and speech development.
    Pediatrics, 43 (1969), 833–838.
13. Howie VM, Ploussard JH, Sloyer JL: Natural his-
    tory of otitis media. *Ann Otol Rhinol Laryngol*,
    suppl 25 (1976), 18.
14. Lewis N: Otitis media and linguistic incompe-
    tence. *Arch Otolaryngol*, 102 (1976), 387–390.
15. Needleman H: Effects of hearing loss from early
    recurrent otitis media on speech and language
    development, in Jaffe B, ed: *Hearing Loss in
    Children* (Baltimore: University Park Press,
    1977), p 640.
16. Lowe JF, Bamforth JS, Pracy R: Acute otitis media:
    One year in a general practice. *Lancet*, 2 (1963),
    1129–1132.
17. Neil JF, Harrison SH, Morby RD, et al: Deafness
    in acute otitis media. *Br Med J*, 1 (1966), 75–77.
18. Olmstead RW, Alvarez MC, Morony RD et al: The
    pattern of hearing following acute otitis media. *J
    Pediatr*, 65 (1964), 252–255.
19. Bergstrom L: Congenital and acquired deafness
    in clefting and craniofacial syndromes. *Cleft Pal
    J*, 15 (1978), 254–261.
20. Giebink GS: Epidemiology and natural history
    of otitis media, in Lim D, Bluestone C, Klein J,
    Nelson JD, eds: *Recent Advances in Otitis Media
    with Effusion* (Philadelphia: BD Decker, Inc.
    1984), pp 5–9.
21. Casselbrant M, Okeowo PA, Flaherty MR, et al:
    Prevalence and incidence of otitis media in a
    group of preschool children in the United
    States. (Ibid) pp 16–19.
22. Dublin WB: *Fundamentals of Sensorineural
    Auditory Pathology* (Springfield: Charles C.
    Thomas, 1976), pp 108, 190.
23. Webster DB, Webster M: Neonatal sound depri-
    vation affects brain stem auditory nuclei. *Arch
    Otolaryngol*, 103 (1977), 392–396.
24. Bergstrom L, Tessier A: Early childhood educa-
    tion: a means to early diagnosis of hearing im-
    pairment in the multihandicapped. *Int'l J Ped
    Otorhinolaryngol*, 5 (1983), 167–172.
25. Selected papers by Bess FH, et al: in *Ear and
    Hearing*, 7 (1986), 3–54.
26. Hemenway WG, Sardo I, McChesney D: Tempo-
    ral bone pathology following maternal rubella.
    Arch Klin Exp Ohren Nasen Kehlkopfheilkd, 193
    (1969), 287–300.
27. Sando I, Hemenway WG, Morgan RW: Histo-
    pathology of the temporal bones in mandibulo-
    facial dysostosis. *Trans Am Acad Opthalmol
    Otolaryngol*, 72 (1968), 913–924.

hearing child. J Abnorm Soc Psychol, 65 (1962),
338–342.

SCREENING FOR HEARING LOSS AND MIDDLE EAR DISORDERS

3

Ross J. Roeser and Jerry L. Northern

INTRODUCTION

Paramount to all other considerations in the implementation of a hearing conservation program in the schools is the definition of the primary goal or goals of the program. The operational definition determines critical aspects of the program, including the selection of procedures to be used, necessary equipment, personnel to be employed, and other such pragmatic factors.

The foremost purpose of any hearing conservation program is to identify the children in the population who have hearing impairment that will interfere with their educational development.[1] Any significant loss in hearing sensitivity or auditory function will influence the overall educational process of the involved child.

A school system could implement a program of "identification audiometry" with the sole purpose of locating those children with hearing impairment. However, this limited program could not be considered adequate because the actual identification of hearing-impaired children is only the initial step in the development of a school hearing conservation program. More than identification of hearing loss is needed to meet the special educational needs of those children found to have significant hearing loss.

Experience suggests that few hearing conservation programs are comprehensive in their scope. The vast majority of school programs have acceptable identification procedures, but fall short in providing adequate follow-up services. Once a child is found to have significant hearing impairment, it is imperative that provisions be made for proper medical diagnosis and treatment, if prescribed; for appropriate amplification when indicated; and, in all cases, for special educational intervention. Without provisions for these comprehensive follow-up services, children with significant hearing loss will continue to be sensorially deprived and will not attain their maximum educational potential.

Anderson[2] points out that hearing conservation programs lacking requisite comprehensive follow-up services actually are worse than programs not providing screening at all. The inadequate screening programs delude those being served by them into assuming that an effective program exists when it does not. It cannot be stressed enough that all aspects—identification, audiologic and medical referral/follow-up, and special educational considerations—must be included in any school hearing conservation program.

A major question in defining the overall purpose of a hearing conservation program in the schools is deciding whether to attempt to identify only those children with significant auditory impairment or to have the dual purpose of identifying children with auditory impairment and middle ear disorders. Traditionally, hearing screening programs have used air conduction hearing tests to identify children with peripheral hearing impairments. Such tests have proven to be effective in identifying significant hearing loss, but it is now well established that there are serious limitations with air conduction tests in identifying middle ear pathology. A number of studies have pointed out that audiometric screening alone will fail to detect about one-half of the children with confirmed middle ear pathology.[3–6]

Prior to 1970, there were no practical means for routine screening for middle ear disorders, especially in school children. The only valid procedure was to have a highly sophisticated professional examine the ear with an otoscope. However, with the emergence of immittance* measures of the ear (described in Chapter 1), a feasible method of identifying ear disorders in school children is available now and many school systems have implemented acoustic immittance screening programs. From a theoretic point of view, few audiologists and other health professionals would argue that immittance is a valuable part of school hearing conservation and belongs in every program. Such a statement is based on the validity and reliability of immittance tests and the relative ease with which immittance measurements are performed. However, several pragmatic factors should be considered before any school system implements an immittance screening program. These factors will be outlined later in this chapter.

When a school system elects to perform immittance screening, the one point that must be stressed emphatically is that immittance measures provide screening for middle ear disorders; immittance measurements *do not* provide direct information on screening for hearing sensitivity. That is, even if a child has normal results on immittance measures, it is still necessary to perform some type of behavioral or electrophysiologic test (ABR audiometry) to assess hearing sensitivity. By providing immittance screening, the school system is expanding its hearing conservation program to include detection of middle ear disorders; it is not replacing the procedures used in the hearing screening program. However, because of the high incidence of middle ear disorders in school children (especially in the primary grades; see Chapter 9) and its effects on educational achievement, immittance screening must be considered as an integral part of all elementary school hearing conservation programs.

This chapter reviews basic principles underlying screening. In addition, considerations and procedures for hearing and immittance screening programs for school children are presented. Guidelines are also presented that

*Originally, the term *impedance* was used to describe this procedure. However, because the procedure was electronically based on the measurement of impedance or admittance,[7] the term *immittance* was adopted to encompass both procedures. The term immittance is now widely accepted to describe this technique.

will allow for the implementation of an effective program to identify hearing loss and middle ear disorders in school children. Readers who are not completely familiar with audiometric and immittance principles should review them in Chapter 1 before reading this chapter.

PRINCIPLES OF SCREENING

The Concept of "Pass" and "Fail"

The purpose of screening is to identify those individuals having a defined disorder as early as possible, who would have otherwise not been identified, and to administer treatment at a time when it will either remediate the disorder or retard its rate of development.[8] Screening can be viewed as the general process by which groups of people are separated into those who manifest some defined trait, or those who do not. In this sense, it is a binary process—either passing the individual who is considered a likely candidate not to have the disorder, or failing the individual who is considered a likely candidate to have the disorder.

Although screening is an "either/or" process, disorders may exist on a continuum from "not present at all" to "present in the most severe form." Based on this principle, it is incorrect to think that those individuals who pass the screening are completely free from the disorder for which the screening is being conducted. Instead, one should view those who pass the screening as individuals who do not manifest the disorder for which the screening is being conducted in a form severe enough to warrant consideration for additional testing.

The above information is especially relevant for the screening of auditory disorders in school children, because of the constraints that typically are put on such screening programs. As will be pointed out in later sections of this chapter, the procedures used for identifying auditory disorders in school children are limited, due to the nature of the tests themselves and the environment in which they are performed. Therefore, if a child successfully passes a school auditory screening test, it is not appropriate to think that the child's auditory system is completely within normal limits, because the child may, in fact, have some auditory impairment. However, if the criteria are appropriate and the child passes the school screening, one can say that the child's auditory system is not impaired to the extent that it would interfere with educational achievement, and if hearing loss does exist, it is not significant enough to warrant additional audiologic testing.

To illustrate, a child is screened at 500, 1000, 2000, and 4000 Hz at a level of 20 dB HL, and the pass-fail criterion is failure to respond to two frequencies in the same ear. If the child does not respond at 4000 Hz in either ear, she/he will pass the screening and most likely will not have significant auditory problems in the classroom as a result of the loss at 4000 Hz. Although it has been estimated by the school's screening criteria that the child's hearing loss will not cause significant educational problems, the child still does have hearing loss; hearing is not "normal." This concept of "pass" and "fail" must be maintained throughout the development and implementation of all hearing conservation programs, especially those in the schools.

Reliability and Validity

Four related terms are used to describe the general effectiveness of any type of screening test: reliability and validity, and sensitivity and specificity. Reliability deals with the consistency of the test. That is, if the test is administered and then repeated by the same tester at a different time, will the test results be the same (test-retest or intraexaminer reliability); or, if two examiners perform the same test on the same individual, will the results be the same (interexaminer reliability). Without a high degree of reliability, the screening tool is ineffective, because the results of the test will vary from test session to test session and from tester to tester.

The consequences of poor reliability can easily be seen. However, just because a screening test is reliable, it still may not be an effective test if it fails to identify the problem for which the screening is being conducted. To illustrate, one could use the color of children's hair as a screening test for deafness, and in all probability this measure would have a high degree of test-retest and interexaminer reliability. However, hair color is a very poor index of deafness, because this measure is not a *valid* test for deafness. Another more realistic example would be the use of pure tone screening tests to identify middle ear disorders. As has already been stressed, pure tone testing fails to identify about one-half of the children with middle ear disorders. Therefore, pure tone testing is not a valid measure to assess the state of the middle ear, and should not be used for identifying middle ear problems.

The validity of a screening test, then, is the degree to which results are consistent with the actual presence or absence of the disorder. In other words, validity determines whether the test is actually measuring the trait for which the screening is being conducted. It is important to realize that newly developed screening procedures must be validated in some way before they are put into widespread use. Such assessment would involve calculating the percentage of false-positive and false-negative identification, and the sensitivity and specificity of the test.

False-Positive and False-Negative Identifications

It would be ideal if a screening test was 100% accurate in its classification; if all those with and without the disorder were correctly identified. However, this situation is rarely if ever the case, and there are always an expected number of false-positive and false-negative identifications. These two conditions are illustrated in the tetrachordic table in Figure 3-1.

As shown in this figure, diagnostic test results indicate whether the disorder is actually present or not present. For example, in assessing hearing loss, the diagnostic test would be the pure tone threshold test performed in a sound-treated room. Results from the screening test, shown along the side of the figure, can either be positive, indicating failure on the test, or negative, indicating that the test was passed. These cells represent all possible outcomes once the results of both the screening and diagnostic tests are known. The results can range from correct identification of the abnormal and normal subjects (cells A and D), to false-positive (cell B) and false-negative (cell C) identifications. As illustrated, a false-positive identification occurs when an individual fails the screening test, but actually does not have the disorder. A false-negative identification occurs when an individual passes the screening test and has the disorder. The formulas in Figure 3-1 show how the percentage

SCREENING TEST RESULTS	DIAGNOSTIC TEST RESULTS: Disorder Present	DIAGNOSTIC TEST RESULTS: Disorder not Present
POSITIVE (Fail)	A Correct Identification of Abnormal Subjects	B False Positive
NEGATIVE (Pass)	C False Negative	D Correct Identification of Normal Subjects

$$\text{Percent of False Positive} = \frac{B}{B + D} \times 100$$

$$\text{Percent of False Negative} = \frac{C}{A + C} \times 100$$

Figure 3-1. Tetrachordic table classifying results into correct identifications (cells A & D), false-positive identifications (cell B), and false-negative identifications (cell C).

of false-positive and false-negative identifications can be calculated. Examples of how the formulas are used are presented below.

Neither false-positive nor false-negative identifications are desirable in screening programs and represent a liability or "cost" to the screening process. The cost can be the actual dollars that are spent as a result of the screening, or the needless expenditure of time, effort, or any other resource. Frankenberg[8] lists the following as costs of false-positive identifications: (*1*) the cost associated with retrieving the child for further evaluations; (*2*) the cost of additional screening and/or diagnostic tests that will fail to confirm the disorder; (*3*) mental anguish of the parents and/or the child; and (*4*) the cost and danger of unnecessary treatment, if the absence of the disease is not detected by diagnostic tests.

False-positives are most likely to interfere with the overall acceptance of the screening program in the community it serves. This especially is true for hearing screening, because the cost of false-positive identifications may be high. An office visit to an otolaryngologist and/or audiologist can be expensive, and it is quite disconcerting for a parent to be told for such a fee that his child is normal. Only a few parents voicing their dissatisfaction over this unnecessary visit would be needed before false-positive identifications would ultimately jeopardize acceptance of the program. Thus, from the perspective of the administrator of the screening program, false-positive identifications must be avoided.

The costs of false-negative identifications are: (*1*) the loss of the benefits associated with early identifications and diagnosis; and (*2*) false reassurance, which will delay correct identification of the child's problem, even when symptoms persist. In the case of hearing impairment, time lost in providing the necessary educational and possibly medical intervention is detrimental to the child; if this delay is too great, the child may be deprived of full educational potential.

Sensitivity and Specificity

Sensitivity and specificity are used to measure the validity of a screening test. The sensitivity of a test is its accuracy in correctly identifying the disordered subjects. Specificity is the test's accuracy in correctly identifying the nondisordered subjects. Figure 3-2 is an extension of Figure 3-1, and illustrates how these two terms are applied. Cell A represents those subjects who failed the screening test and actually had the disorder. Data from cell A are used to calculate the sensitivity of the test. Cell D represents subjects who passed the screening and did not have the disorder. Data from this cell are used to calculate the specificity of a given

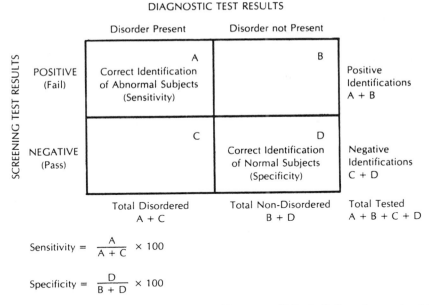

Figure 3-2. Correct identification of abnormal subjects—sensitivity (cell A) and normal subjects—specificity (cell D) for a screening test.

screening test. The sensitivity and specificity of a given test are computed using the formulas provided at the bottom of Figure 3-2.

Figure 3-3 presents data showing how the false-positive, false-negative, sensitivity, and specificity of a screening test can be calculated using hypothetic data from a hearing screening test on 1000 children. Of these 1000 children, diagnostic test results showed that 92 actually had hearing loss (cells A + C), and 908 actually were free from hearing loss (cells B + D). The screening test identified 96 children with hearing loss (cells A + B), and 904 children without hearing loss (cells C + D). Based on the data presented in Figure 3-3, the sensitivity of this test is calculated to be 95.7% and the specificity 99.1%. Stated differently, the screening test correctly identified 95.7% of those subjects who actually had hearing loss and 99.1% of the subjects who were free from hearing loss. The false-negative and false-positive rates were calculated to be 4.3% and 0.9%, respectively.

The hypothetic data in Figure 3-3 would strongly support the validity of the screening test being used to detect hearing loss, because both the sensitivity and specificity were high, and the false-positive and false-negative rates low. This is a desired result that one attempts to achieve in any screening program.

In designing a screening test, the sensitivity and specificity must be considered together because they are related, and they directly influence the false-positive and false-negative rates. The overall goal is to maintain a balance between the factors that determine the validity of the test, so that the sensitivity and specificity, as well as the related false-positive and false-negative rates, are within a predetermined acceptable range for the screening that is being conducted. An extreme example is the case where the screening test fails all those screened (cells A or B). Such a test will produce 100% sensitivity. However, the false-positive rate would also be 100%, and the specificity and false-negative rates each 0%, making the test worthless. Conversely, redesigning the same test so that all those screened would pass the test, results in 100% specificity. However, in this case the false-negative rate would be 100% and the sensitivity and false-positive rates 0%, also providing a worthless test.

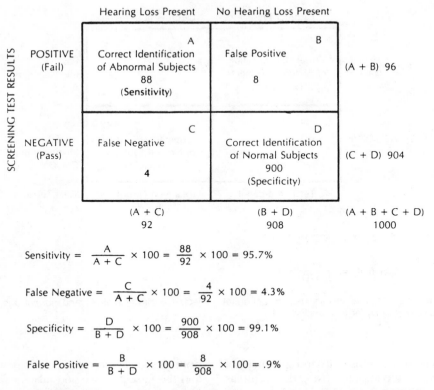

Figure 3-3. Calculating the sensitivity, false-negative rate, specificity, and false-positive rate for a screening test administered on 1000 subjects.

Co-Positivity and Co-Negativity

It is possible to compare two different types of screening tests that are screening for the same disorder and/or to evaluate the performance of a given tester by comparing the test results with those obtained by an expert. In either case, for the results obtained, the co-positivity and co-negativity can be determined. The co-positivity is the extent to which the two tests agree in identifying those with the disorder (the positives), and the co-negativity is the agreement in identifying those without the disorder (the negatives). An example of two different audiometric tests would be the comparison of results from a test using speech signals to those using pure tones presented at a fixed intensity. To compare tester performance, results that are obtained by the tester would be compared directly to those obtained from the same subjects by a certified audiologist.

The co-positivity and co-negativity of a test are calculated using the same formulas for calculating sensitivity and specificity, respectively. However, unlike sensitivity and specificity, measures of co-positivity and co-negativity, while providing valuable information on the reliability of a screening test, do not measure the test's validity.

Program Evaluation

Program evaluation should be an integral part of any screening process, and can occur at a number of levels, from evaluation of the equipment to evaluation of the procedures and personnel used in the program. Of course routine calibration checks of the equipment are mandatory (see Chapter 1). With the information previously given, it is possible to conduct a methodologic evaluation of the screening procedures and personnel, provided one of two steps is added to the screening process—either the reliability of the procedures can be evaluated by comparing test results from those individuals who perform routine screening with those obtained by an audiologist (co-positivity and co-negativity), or the validity of the procedures can be evaluated by comparing screening results with diagnostic findings (sensitivity and specificity).

Co-positivity and Co-negativity An example of evaluating the reliability of the program by calculating its co-positivity and co-negativity follows: Two audiometric support personnel screen 868 children and the school's audiologist immediately rescreens the children. Figure 3-4 shows the data after they have been categorized into a tetrachordic table. The co-positivity and co-negativity for Support Person #1 were 76% and 94%, respectively, with commensurate false-negative and false-positive rates of 24% and 6%, respectively. However, for Support Person #2 the respective values were 97% and 99.3% for co-positivity and co-negativity and 3% and 0.7% for the false-negative and false-positive rates.

The data in Figure 3-4 would indicate that for some reason, the results of the screenings performed by Support Person #1 are inferior to those obtained by Support Person #2, when compared to the audiologist's results. In fact, these hypothetic data would be alarming if they were actually obtained through program evaluation, because of the high false-negative rates found for Support Person #1. To check Support Person #1, the equipment being used would be examined to ensure that it is in proper calibration and there are no malfunctions, and the actual test procedures used in the screening would be evaluated. If findings similar to those in Figure 3-4 were revealed through program evaluation, careful scrutiny of the performance of Support Person #1 should be made until it is within limits similar to those for Support Person #2.

Sensitivity and Specificity. Whenever results from a screening test can be compared to results from a diagnostic test, the sensitivity and specificity of the screening test can be calculated to determine the validity of the results. Such an evaluation can be performed retrospectively after the results have been obtained and reported; or it can be planned prospectively by including a diagnostic test with the screening test. An example of retrospective

evaluation is as follows: Wilson and Walton[9] evaluated a recommended fixed-intensity pure tone screening technique, and as part of their study screened 1168 children and also performed threshold tests on these children in a sound-treated room. Interestingly, they report that the overall accuracy of the screening test was 94.7%; the results from both screening and threshold tests would pass the subjects 91.4% of the time and fail the subjects 3.3% of the time. The false-positive and false-negative rates were stated to be 3.2% and 2.0%, respectively, producing an "inaccuracy" rate of 5.2%. From these data, they concluded that the screening procedures used were highly accurate in identifying hearing loss. However, they failed to recognize the importance of the sensitivity and specificity of the test, as described above.

Figure 3-5 presents Wilson and Walton's data calculated in the manner described in Figure 3-3. As shown in Figure 3-5, the respective sensitivity and specificity of the screening test was 63% and 97%, and the false-positive and false-negative rates, 3% and 37%. These data mean that 97% of the children with normal hearing were correctly identified, producing an overreferral rate of 3%. This rate is well within acceptable limits. However, a discouraging result was that only 63% of the children with hearing loss were correctly identified, leaving 37% improperly classified as having no significant loss. When viewed in these terms, the results from this screening survey do not support the use of the screening test that Wilson and Walton were evaluating under the conditions that it was used, because of the low sensitivity and high false-negative rates. For a screening test for hearing loss to be acceptable, the sensitivity should be within the 90 to 95% range and the corresponding false-negative rate 5 to 10%. These ranges appear to be reasonable as goals, given the present state of knowledge in the area of hearing screening.

It is unfortunate that most school hearing conservation programs do not routinely evaluate the reliability and validity of their procedures. Program evaluation does require extra time on the part of the personnel in the program, which ultimately translates into added dollars. But without appropriate evaluation, the basic issue of the program's reliability and validity will always be subject to question. Although the examples given in this section have only used tests of hearing sensitivity, similar

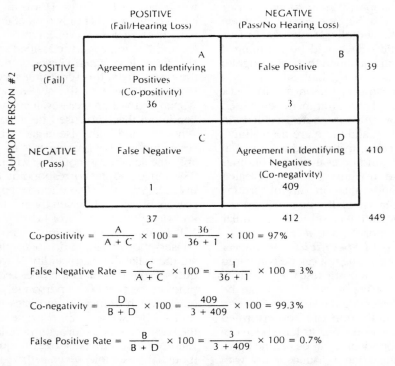

AUDIOLOGIST'S RESULTS

	POSITIVE (Fail/Hearing Loss)	NEGATIVE (Pass/No Hearing Loss)	
POSITIVE (Fail)	A Agreement in Identifying Positives (Co-positivity) 16	B False Positive 22	38
NEGATIVE (Pass)	C False Negative 5	D Agreement in Identifying Negatives (Co-negativity) 376	381
	21	398	419

(SUPPORT PERSON #1)

Co-positivity = $\dfrac{A}{A + C}$ × 100 = $\dfrac{16}{16 + 5}$ = 76%

False Negative Rate = $\dfrac{C}{A + C}$ × 100 = $\dfrac{5}{16 + 5}$ × 100 = 24%

Co-negativity = $\dfrac{D}{B + D}$ × 100 = $\dfrac{376}{22 + 376}$ × 100 = 94%

False Positive Rate = $\dfrac{B}{B + D}$ × 100 = $\dfrac{22}{22 + 376}$ × 100 = 6%

AUDIOLOGIST'S RESULTS

	POSITIVE (Fail/Hearing Loss)	NEGATIVE (Pass/No Hearing Loss)	
POSITIVE (Fail)	A Agreement in Identifying Positives (Co-positivity) 36	B False Positive 3	39
NEGATIVE (Pass)	C False Negative 1	D Agreement in Identifying Negatives (Co-negativity) 409	410
	37	412	449

(SUPPORT PERSON #2)

Co-positivity = $\dfrac{A}{A + C}$ × 100 = $\dfrac{36}{36 + 1}$ × 100 = 97%

False Negative Rate = $\dfrac{C}{A + C}$ × 100 = $\dfrac{1}{36 + 1}$ × 100 = 3%

Co-negativity = $\dfrac{D}{B + D}$ × 100 = $\dfrac{409}{3 + 409}$ × 100 = 99.3%

False Positive Rate = $\dfrac{B}{B + D}$ × 100 = $\dfrac{3}{3 + 409}$ × 100 = 0.7%

Figure 3-4. Calculating co-positivity and co-negativity of a screening test for two support personnel.

THRESHOLD TEST

	Disordered (Fail) (Hearing Loss)	Non-Disordered (Pass) (No Hearing Loss)	Total
POSITIVE (Fail)	A 3.3% (39)	B 3.2% (38)	(A + B) 77
NEGATIVE (Pass)	C 2.0% (23)	D 91.4% (1068)	(C + D) 1091
	(A + C) 62	(B + D) 1106	(A + B + C + D) 1168

SCREENING TEST RESULTS

$$\text{Sensitivity} = \frac{A}{A + C} \times 100 = \frac{39}{39 + 23} \times 100 = 63\%$$

$$\text{False Negative} = \frac{C}{A + C} \times 100 = \frac{23}{39 + 23} \times 100 = 37\%$$

$$\text{Specificity} = \frac{D}{B + D} \times 100 = \frac{1068}{38 + 1068} \times 100 = 97\%$$

$$\text{False Positive} = \frac{B}{B + D} \times 100 = \frac{38}{38 \times 1068} \times 100 = 3\%$$

Figure 3-5. Retrospective analysis of hearing screening data reported by Wilson and Walton.[9]

evaluations can and should be performed for impedance measures used in screening.

THE PREVALENCE OF HEARING LOSS AND MIDDLE EAR DISORDERS IN CHILDREN

Frasier[10] and Stewart[11] estimate that congenital profound hearing loss occurs in 1 in 1000 births worldwide. These reports only represent severe hearing loss, so the true incidence of all hearing loss in infants and children would be significantly greater. Northern and Downs[12] indicate that there are 42,000 severely hearing-impaired children attending special schools or classes for the hearing-impaired in the United States at the present time. Berg[13] estimates that there are another 950,000 hard-of-hearing children having losses in the 26 to 55 dB HL range, who will require assistance in the classroom.

Data from studies on screening for ear disease in school children suggest that the preva-lence of ear disease is much greater than that of hearing loss. Based on a survey of 3197 children between the ages of 0 to 5 years, Klein[14] estimates that the occurrence of middle ear disease ranges between 8.3% and 25.3%. Jerger[15] recently stated that estimates of the prevalence of otitis media with fluid, the primary middle ear disorder that causes hearing loss in children, range up to 30%, and have seldom been less than 15%. By conservative estimates, this prevalence rate implies that there are some 2,500,000 children between the ages of 0 to 6 years in this country affected by middle ear disease. Furthermore, Jerger states that as many as 8,000,000 to 9,000,000 children in the 0 to 6 age range have experienced at least one bout of otitis media with fluid. Brooks[16] has pointed out that undetected (and therefore untreated) middle ear disease can lead to numerous possible serious complications that require surgery and/or cause permanent hearing loss.

The above data clearly document the need for hearing conservation programs and screening for middle ear disorders in the schools. However, these estimates do not address questions regarding the number of children expected to fail a given audiometric screening test or a screening test for middle ear disorders. Answers to these questions are important to school personnel in the overall planning of the program.

With respect to hearing loss, Anderson[2] states that a referral rate of between 5 to 10% is reasonable. This estimate is the range typically quoted in virtually all of the recent literature. For example, Silverman, Lane, and Calvert[17] state that, "Our best estimate . . . is that 5 percent of school-age children have hearing loss, in one ear at least." Results from the Pittsburgh study[18] also support the 5% incidence figure. However, is this range realistic? Should about 5% of the children screened in the program fail the test? Moreover, if the 5% figure is representative, by how much can the rate vary before there is concern about the false-positive and false-negative identifications?

Connor[19] reviewed 31 separate studies conducted between 1926 and 1960. Depending on the particular study, he found that the incidence of hearing loss ranged from 0.5 to 21%. Although this survey is almost 20 years old, more recent surveys on the incidence of hearing disorders demonstrate the same inconsistencies. Melnick et al[3] screened 860 children and failed 135 (15.7%) of the population. Fay et al,[20] on the other hand, failed 90 of 336 children, representing a failure rate of 26.7%. However Robinson et al[21] reported a failure rate of only 3.5%.

The discrepancies in findings of these studies can be related to variables such as the types of tests used, the instruments used to perform the screening, the training of the tester, environmental noise present during the hearing screening, and the pass-fail criteria. However, even when these factors are controlled as closely as possible, variability still exists. For example, Table 3-1 presents results from audiometric screening of 54,370 children in the Dallas public schools during the 1978 school year. Six different testers were used in the program, but the procedures, equipment, and pass-fail criteria were identical, and all testers had the same training. Despite this continuity in the program, the percentage of failures ranged from 0.9 to 3.4%; all of the values were lower than the nominal 5% value suggested by most other reports. What then can account for the variability? This question can be answered

Table 3-1   Screening Data from 1978–1979 School Year for Dallas Independent School District

Tester	No. of Children Screened	Percent Failing Test (%)
1	10,129	1.0
2	8525	3.4
3	9680	1.4
4	7997	2.1
5	9351	1.2
6	8688	.9
Total	54,370	$\bar{X}$ 1.7

on the basis of data gathered from epidemiologic studies of auditory disorders in children.

Epidemiology is technically defined as the study of frequencies and distributions of disorders, and the relationship between the various factors that contribute to their occurrence.[22] When an epidemiologic study is conducted, all of the factors that relate to a particular disease process are considered, including age, sex, social and cultural characteristics, climate, and so on. Once an epidemiologic study is completed it is possible to assess how the factors studied affect the incidence of the disorder and its severity.

The generalizations we are able to make now about auditory disorders include: hearing loss and ear disease are more prevalent in younger children and in certain populations, such as American Indians[23] and Eskimo children[24]; low socioeconomic status may increase the incidence of hearing loss and ear disease[20]; the incidence of hearing loss and ear disease changes with climate and specific seasons of the year[25]; and high frequency sensorineural hearing loss is more prevalent in older males in the grades 9 to 12.[26,27] A summary of literature dealing with screening in special populations has recently been published by Northern.[28] These factors make it impossible to estimate the expected incidence of hearing loss or ear disease in a population of school age children on an *a priori* basis, no matter what screening techniques are used.

HEARING SCREENING IN THE SCHOOLS—IDENTIFICATION OF HEARING LOSS

General considerations for any hearing conservation program, whether it be designed for preschool or school age children, include the test environment; the personnel supervising and administering the testing; the equipment; the contributions of school personnel, such as the teacher and/or school administrator; the periodicity of testing; the tests to use; and the pass-fail criteria and follow-up.

Test Environment

The test environment chosen to perform the audiometric tests should be well lighted, adequate in size to accommodate the tester and equipment, well ventilated, and have low ambient noise levels. One of the most critical requirements of the test environment is the ambient noise level, because serious problems can occur in hearing screening if the background noise levels are too high. The most desirable space for hearing screening in any school is located as far away as possible from heating units, air conditioners, and other mechanical equipment, and from the cafeteria, shop areas, music room, rest rooms, and other high traffic areas. The best areas for hearing screening in the schools typically include the auditorium stage with the curtains drawn, the nurse's office, or the teachers' lounge. But the exact location depends entirely on the school building itself and the schedule of daily activities.

The problem with testing in environments having high ambient noise levels is that the noise in the environment has the potential to mask or block out the test stimulus itself. High ambient noise levels have a limiting effect on the frequencies and intensity at which hearing screening can be performed, and are the reason for imposing many of the recommended guidelines for hearing screening. Most noise found in a typical school environment will have its main energy concentrated in the frequencies below 1000 Hz. This one factor is the primary reason why guidelines for school screening programs have recommended testing at 1000 Hz and above, even though some important data can be obtained at 500 and 250 Hz. Moreover, screening tests performed at intensities of 10 to 15 dB HL can be severely affected by noise, even though these intensities are more sensitive to marginal hearing loss.

It has been reasoned by some that if the background noise level is too high, simply increasing the intensity level of the test stimuli will solve the problem. However, this solution is not acceptable, because by increasing the intensity level, the sensitivity of the screening test is reduced and those children who actually have hearing loss at the screening level optimally chosen may pass at the higher level. In no case should the levels of the test stimuli be increased above those specified by the screening program, and an alternate test site should be selected.

One solution to resolve the problem of ambient noise is the use of sound-isolated rooms. The National Conference on Identification Audiometry recommended that all schools purchase and install commercial sound-treated booths.[29] This recommendation is ideal, because it would insure that acceptable background noise levels would be present all of the time. However, with the constant demands and limitations on school finances, such equipment is beyond the scope of most school budgets. Mobile test vans or trailers are commercially available with sound-isolating booths installed, and do provide adequate test environments. However, mobile test vans also represent a sizeable financial investment in both purchase and maintenance.

Small, portable hearing test booths have been developed, which are economical and can be effective in reducing ambient noise levels. In a recent study, Fisher[30] has shown that the use of a portable sound room can provide significant benefit in school hearing conservation programs. In this study, data obtained from the portable rooms were compared with those obtained in an open environment and in an audiometric sound-treated booth. Results from the portable sound-treated enclosure correctly identified a significantly larger percentage of students with and without hearing impairment than the open environment. The major advantage of using the portable sound room appears to be that the number of false-positive* identifications is reduced sig-

---

*This study incorrectly states that false-negative identifications are reduced by the use of portable sound rooms, rather than false-positive identifications.

nificantly, saving a considerable amount of time and money in retesting. The use of the portable sound rooms in school screening is not widespread at this time, but results from Fisher's study indicate that their use definitely deserves additional consideration.

A final solution for eliminating unwanted background noise is the use of noise-excluding earphone enclosures (described in Chapter 1). Certain types of these enclosures are generally more effective in reducing background noise than the standard headsets.[31–33] Furthermore, laboratory and field studies on their use with children have proven their overall effectiveness.[34,35] Despite these studies supporting their use, noise-excluding headsets do present inherent problems, such as earphone placement. Thus, they should be utilized only by highly experienced examiners who are aware of the difficulties that may occur with their use. Noise-excluding headsets should not be used routinely in hearing conservation programs.

With or without noise-excluding equipment, a simple biological check should always be made to assess the appropriateness of the test environment before any testing is performed. The biological check is performed by screening one or preferably two subjects with proven normal hearing sensitivity. Obviously, if both of these individuals fail to perceive the test stimuli at the same frequency, the environment most likely is not satisfactory, providing of course that the equipment is known to be in good calibration. Table 3-2 provides allowable dB (SPL) levels for conducting screening.

Personnel

Two levels of personnel may be utilized in school hearing conservation programs, one supervisory and one technical.[29,36] The super-visor of the program should be an audiologist holding the Certificate of Clinical Competence from the American Speech-Language-Hearing Association (ASHA).* As the supervisor of the program, the audiologist is responsible for selecting the screening procedures to be used, training and monitoring the technical staff, ensuring proper equipment calibration, referring certain children for comprehensive audiologic testing, discussing test results with medical personnel, and generally carrying out the higher administrative functions of the program.

Resources may not be available in smaller school systems to have a full-time audiologist to supervise the hearing conservation program. In such cases, it is possible in most areas of the country to have a part-time audiologist consultant who will monitor the activities listed above. The consultant's primary role is to set up the program and train the technical staff as thoroughly as possible. Only when the special problems arise is the consultant required to be available in the school system itself.

The technical or support personnel perform the actual screening tests and carry out the day-to-day activities of the program, such as performing daily calibration checks and filling out statistical reports. Many school systems use nurses or speech-language pathologists in this role. Because of their training, such professionals are effective, but still should be provided with in-service training to re-familiarize them with the general area of hearing, hearing disorders, and audiometric testing. Such sessions should be held for no less than one full

*The American Speech and Hearing Association became the American Speech-Language-Hearing Association in 1980. However, the acronym ASHA is still used.

Table 3-2   Approximate Octave Band Levels Allowable for Screening at 20–25 dB Level Recommended by the ASHA Committee on Audiometric Evaluations (dB SPL)[36]

	Test Frequency	500	1000	2000	4000
	Octave Band Cut-off	300	600	1200	2400
	Frequencies	600	1200	2400	4800
Allowable ambient noise for threshold at Zero HL (re: ANSI-1969)		26	30	38	51
Plus ASHA screening level (re: ANSI-1969)		20	20	20	25
Resultant maximum ambient noise allowable for ASHA screening		46	50	58	76

day before the individual begins to perform in the program. We have found that a very helpful way to avoid any confusion in the program and to keep it uniform is to develop a manual describing the screening program and procedures used, to guide each technical and support person in the program.

When paraprofessionals or professionals with no training in auditory disorders and screening are used for technical support, additional training is mandatory. The National Conference on Identification Audiometry recommended that for such persons, the training course be conducted over a two to six week period, with at least one-half of the time devoted to supervised practice in testing.[29] Since the success of the entire hearing conservation program rests on the support personnel, the need for adequate training of these individuals cannot be stressed enough. The absolute minimum training period for the paraprofessionals should be no less than five days, with one-half of the time in supervised practicum. As a guide, topics that should be included in the training program are listed in Table 3-3.

Three organizations that currently have training manuals for audiometric technicians are listed in Table 3-4. Although these manuals were not designed specifically for school hearing conservation programs, they can be adapted for use in training school personnel.

Speech vs Pure Tones

Two choices of test stimuli are available for assessing hearing. Speech has the advantage of being less abstract than pure tones, so tests using speech can generally be administered more successfully to younger children. Based on this one principle, several tests using speech

Table 3-4   Organizations That Have Training Manuals for Audiometric Technicians

1. Council for Accreditation in Occupational Hearing Conservation
   1619 Chestnut Avenue
   Haddon Heights, NJ 08035
2. Audiometric Assistant Trainee's Workbook
   US Department of Health, Education and Welfare
   US Office of Education
   Division of Manpower Development and Training
   Washington, DC
3. American Association of Industrial Nurses
   79 Madison Avenue
   New York, NY 10016

stimuli were developed and are still in use today in some school systems.

The Verbal Auditory Screening for Children (VASC) test is one of the more popular hearing screening procedures using speech.[37] While there is some variability in the procedures used in the VASC test,[38] in the classic test four recorded randomized lists of 12 spondaic (bisyllabic) words, such as "cowboy" and "airplane," are used as stimuli. The initial level of presentation is 51 dB HL, and each stimulus decreases in intensity 4 dB. During the test, the child points to a picture representing the stimulus after each presentation.

Early reports on the VASC screening procedure were encouraging, suggesting a very low rate of false-positive identifications.[37] However, the major limitation of using speech as a stimuli for any hearing screening procedure is that it is not sensitive to mild and/or high-frequency hearing impairment, causing the false-negative rate to be unacceptably high. Studies that have compared both speech and pure tone tests have reported false-negative rates between 50 to 58% for speech tests, primarily because they were not sensitive enough to detect mild and high frequency hearing losses.[39–41] Mencher and McCullock[42] state that the high false-negative results occur with speech stimuli due to the high intensity cues in speech, which provide clues to the child, resulting in positive responses. Because of their insensitivity, the use of speech stimuli alone in school screening programs must be considered inadequate, and at least with children in grades one and above, the use of tests utilizing pure tones is recommended.

Table 3-3   Topics to Be Included in Paraprofessional Training Programs for Auditory Screening in Schools

1. Basic physical principles of sound.
2. Anatomy and physiology of the auditory system.
3. Disorders of the ear and types of hearing loss.
4. Use, care, maintenance, and calibration of audiometers.
5. Screening procedures.
6. Threshold measurement and referral procedures.
7. Record keeping.

Group vs Individual Testing Procedures

Group hearing screening procedures were developed primarily as a means of saving time. In group tests, several children, as many as 40 at a time, are screened with each administration of the examination. Following the initial group screening, children who fail are seen for either a second group test or an individual test.

Newhart[48] identified several inherent problems with group tests that use speech stimuli, and points out that the only advantage of group tests over individual tests is that approximately two or three times as many children can be screened per unit time. In a report from Michigan, it is estimated that individual screening tests cost between 25 to 35 cents per capita, while group screening costs only 15 to 17 cents.[12]

Because of their time-saving potential, group tests were frequently used in the early years of school hearing screening, and there is a wealth of literature describing their use. Table 3-5 summarizes the most popular group hearing screening procedures that have been advocated throughout the years.

Even though studies have documented the efficacy of group tests as a means of saving time, when other considerations are taken into account, group tests are less desirable overall than individual tests and their use is discouraged. From a practical point of view, limiting factors include the calibration and maintenance problems of multiple earphones, finding an appropriate test environment, increased set-up time, and the level of training of the personnel administering the test. Because of these factors, individual screening tests have been recommended over the use of group tests.[29,36] The use of group tests in hearing screening programs is discouraged by virtually all audiologists.

The Individual Pure Tone Sweep-Check Test

The most widely preferred individual pure tone test is the sweep-check screening test,[20] originally described by Newhart.[49] The pure tone sweep-check test is the screening procedure recommended by the ASHA Committee on Audiometric Evaluation.

In this procedure, stimuli at predetermined frequencies are presented at fixed intensity levels, and the child is instructed to respond by raising a hand, raising a finger, or responding in some other manner. Earphones are placed over both ears of the child and a practice tone is presented at a level above the test tone (i.e.,

Table 3-5 Summary of Group Hearing Screening Tests

Literature Reference	Name of Test	Stimuli	Method of Response	Maximum No. of Children Tested Per Session
Fowler & Fletcher[42]	Fading Numbers Test or Western Electric 4-A Phonographic Recording Test	Recordings of spoken single or paired digits	Written	40
Reger & Newby[43]	Pulse Tone Test	Pure tones (250, 1000, 2000, & 4000 Hz)	Written (record the number of pulses heard)	40
Johnson[44]	Massachusetts Test	Pure tones (500, 4000, & 8000 Hz)	Written (circle "yes" or "no")	40
Bennett[45]	Bennett Test	Phonetically similar words	Pointing	*
Johnston[46]	Johnston Group Screening Test	Pure tones	Hand raise	10
DiCarlo & Gardner[47]	Modified Massachusetts Test	Pure tones (500, 1000, 2000, & 8000 Hz)	Written (circle "yes" or "no")	40

*NOTE: Maximum number not specifically stated.

40 dB HL) to acquaint the child with the type of signal to be heard. All of the test stimuli are first presented to one ear and then the other, and a record is made as to the presence or absence of a response at each frequency; no attempt is made to alter the attenuator dial to determine the threshold level when the child fails to respond. The sweep-check procedure can be successfully administered to both school-age and preschool children in about 2 minutes per child.[50]

Frequencies and Intensities. Controversy exists over the specific frequencies and intensities to test in the individual pure tone sweep-check test. In general, the frequencies recommended have been in the 500 to 6000 Hz range. Tones *below* 500 Hz typically are not recommended because they are more easily masked by room noise and do not provide significant information to the testing procedure. These two problems also occur at 500 Hz, and most recent guidelines do not recommend using this frequency.[36] The use of 6000 Hz in screening has also been questioned due to its variability.[50]

At one time, it was believed that limiting the test frequency to one or two tones would significantly reduce the time required for the individual sweep-check test without affecting the overall test results. House and Glorig[52] first suggested screening only at 4000 Hz. This recommendation was made after careful examination of 5000 records and observing that 98 to 99% of the subjects with hearing loss at lower frequencies had the same or greater loss at 4000 Hz. Although the test was initially suggested as a screening tool for industrial workers, it was felt to be suitable for screening in the schools. Other investigators suggested screening with two tones, using 2000 and 4000 Hz[53]; 500 and 4000 Hz[54]; and 1000 and 4000 Hz.[55]

Although data are available to support limited frequency screening,[56] conclusive data suggest that limited frequency screening procedures are not as effective as the pure tone sweep-check test. Siegenthaler and Sommer[54] evaluated the audiometric test results of more than 19,500 children and estimated that 35% of those failing the sweep-check test did not demonstrate losses at 4000 Hz. Stevens and Davidson[57] report similar observations on 1784 audiograms. These findings suggest that limiting the screening to a single frequency, or even to two frequencies, significantly reduces the sensitivity of hearing screening, at least in school

children. In light of these data, it is apparent that screening should be performed at three or four frequencies.

The recommended intensity or intensities at which screening should occur has generally varied between 20 to 30 dB HL (ANSI, 1969). In selecting the screening level, two factors should be considered. First is the effect of the background noise and second is the sensitivity of the test in detecting even slight hearing loss. Background noise was discussed previously in this chapter. Needless to say, as the screening level decreases, the ambient noise will have a greater effect on the test signal. This one factor has prevented schools from screening at and below 15 to 20 dB HL.

By decreasing the level at which the test is performed, the sensitivity of the test can be increased and children with even slight hearing loss can be identified. Since audiologists feel that even slight hearing losses affect the development of speech and language the goal of many programs is to reduce the screening level to identify these children. However, we are forced into accepting screening levels of 20 to 25 dB HL because of the conditions under which most screening is performed. It is unfortunate, but reduction of the screening level to 10 or 15 dB HL would significantly increase the number of overreferrals because of false-positive identification due to background noise.

Pass-Fail Criteria. The specific pass-fail criteria used in the program will depend entirely on the frequencies and intensities at which the screening is performed. However, results from several studies make it quite clear that referral should be based on failure of two screening tests given several hours apart on the same day or several days apart. In this procedure, the child is referred for follow-up only if he fails the second screening test. The reason for requiring the second test is that temporary factors, such as noise in the test environment, nervousness, and transient conductive hearing loss can be allowed to abate, thus reducing the number of overreferrals. Melnick, Eagles, and Levine[3] found that the inclusion of a second screening reduced the number of overreferrals by 23%. Wilson and Walton[9] rescreened 411 children in grades K to 5 who failed an initial screening test and found that slightly more than 50% passed the rescreening. Results from these two studies certainly support the need for rescreening before referral.

Table 3-6 summarizes six recommended

Table 3-6   Comparison of Recommended Test Frequencies, Intensity Levels, and Pass-Fail Criteria for School Hearing Screening

Source	Test Frequencies	Intensity Level (ANSI, 1969)	Pass-Fail Criteria
National Conference on Identification Audiometry[29]	1000, 2000, 4000, and 6000 Hz	20 dB at 1000, 2000, and 6000 Hz 30 dB at 4000 Hz	Fail to hear any signals at these levels in either ear.
State of Illinois Department of Public Health[58]	500, 1000, 2000, and 4000 Hz	25 or 35 dB	Fail to respond to 1 tone at 35 dB in either ear or respond to any 2 tones at 25 dB in the same ear.
American Speech and Hearing Association Committee on Identification Audiometry[36]	1000, 2000, and 4000 Hz	20 dB at 1000 and 2000 Hz 25 dB at 4000 Hz	Fail to respond at any frequency in either ear.
Northern & Downs[12]	1000, 2000, 3000, and/or 4000 and 6000 Hz	25 dB	Fail to respond to 1 tone at 1000 or 2000 Hz; or Fail to respond to 2 out of 3 tones at 3000, 4000, and 6000 Hz.
Anderson[2]	1000, 2000, and 4000 Hz	20 dB	Fail to respond to any 1 signal in any ear.
Downs[59]	1000, 2000, 4000, and 6000 or 8000 Hz	15 dB	Fail to respond to either 1000 or 2000 Hz or to both 4000 and 6000–8000 Hz in either ear.

procedures. Although these six protocols in no way exhaust the possible screening guidelines that have been suggested, they represent the wide range of screening procedures employed in the schools. We support the procedures outlined by the American Speech-Language-Hearing Association[36] because they represent the most acceptable screening procedures available to date.

It should be recognized that although the ASHA procedures will detect those children with educationally significant hearing loss, these guidelines are not exclusive to the identification of educationally significant hearing loss. Specifically, those who fail at 4000 Hz only should not experience significant auditory problems in the classroom, unless the loss is in the severe range and also affects 3000 Hz, because 4000 Hz falls outside of the speech range (see Chapter 1). However, those children with hearing loss at 4000 Hz need to be identified so that comprehensive audiologic testing can be performed and appropriate action (medical follow-up or counseling) initiated to prevent any further decrease in hearing. Moreover, the ASHA guidelines do not detect minimal hear-

ing loss (see Chapter 9). Thus, they should be used with immittance measures, since minimal hearing loss is virtually always conductive and associated with a middle ear disorder.

Screening Preschool Children and Special Populations

The standard pure tone sweep-check test can be successfully administered to most children in kindergarten and above, but some difficulty will often be experienced with younger children and with children in special education, such as those in Trainable Mental Retarded and Educatable Mentally Retarded classes. With these children, special techniques must be used in both the hearing screening program and in the comprehensive audiologic evaluation. Two of the techniques frequently used in the screening program include play conditioning and test training.

Play Conditioning.   This technique uses a form of operant conditioning, in which the child is trained to perform a motor response, such as dropping a block in a box, putting a peg in its place, or stacking blocks when a stimulus is heard. Either tangible reinforcement (cereal or a small piece of candy) or social reinforcement (praise) is given upon successful completion of the response. In addition, because the response involves a type of play activity, performing the behavior provides some intrinsic reinforcement for the child. Play conditioning is a relatively simple technique to teach and use, and the personnel performing the routine screening can be taught the procedure with only minimal additional training.

A technique that is most helpful in play audiometry is *play audiometry reinforcement using a flashlight* (PARF). We have found PARF to be efficient with very young children, as young as 2 to 2.5 years of age, as well as older, difficult-to-test children. PARF is used to initiate the test by teaching the child the correct task to be performed in response to light, and then replacing the visual stimulus with the pure tone auditory stimulus.

The steps employed in the procedure using ring stacking are illustrated in Figure 3-6 and are as follows. With the flashlight in the examiner's hand, the child holds a ring to the light (Fig. 3-6A). Once the light is flashed on and off briefly (one to two seconds), the examiner takes the child's hand and moves it to the stack and helps the child to place the ring on the stack (Fig. 3-6B). Usually, after two or three trials, the child knows the response and the flashlight is put completely out of sight.

Earphones are then placed on the child's ears and the examiner takes the child's hand, which has a ring in it, and places it to the child's cheek (Fig. 3-6C). A tone is presented at 1000 Hz at 50 dB HL, and the examiner guides the child's hand to the stack and helps him to place the ring on the stack. If the child does not appear to respond at 50 dB HL, the tone is increased in intensity. After the child learns the correct response, usually after three or four trials, the intensity is lowered to 20 dB HL, and the child is given the opportunity to respond. If the child responds appropriately, the testing is continued at 2000 and 4000 Hz at 20 and 25 dB HL, and then the other ear is screened.

Play conditioning can be used successfully with younger children. Matkin[60] states that play conditioning is limited when children are less than 30 months of age. but can be used with good results on children above this age.

Test Training. Test training is used with

Figure 3-6. Play audiometry reinforcement using a flashlight (PARF). A. Conditioning the child to respond to the light. B. Teaching the correct response. C. Transferring to the auditory-only stimulus.

children who cannot be conditioned in one or two sessions using play techniques. The procedure involves teaching the child over a series of sessions to respond by block dropping, inserting pegs into a board, or performing some other overt behavior to the presentation of an auditory stimulus. The purpose of the training is to establish a behavior that can be used in screening or testing.

The procedures used in test training are essentially the same as those described for play conditioning, but the training occurs over several, and sometimes numerous, sessions. The number of sessions required to train a child will vary with each child; sometimes only five to six sessions are required and sometimes many more. It is important to keep sessions brief (10 to 15 minutes) and frequent (once or twice per school day).

The speech pathologist, whose schedule permits frequent, short contacts, often is the most likely person to do the actual training. It is advisable to set up the test training program under the direction of the audiologist because children who are in this difficult-to-test category should be tested by an audiologist after the child's behavior has been shaped.

A formal means of providing test training is *tangible reinforcement operant conditioning audiometry* (TROCA). With this procedure, primary reinforcement, such as sugar-coated cereal, is given after each appropriate response. The procedure should only be used by the experienced audiologist, and its success depends heavily on the use of a carefully defined conditioning paradigm. Bricker and Bricker[61] provide an excellent approach using the TROCA technique.

PARF can also be used in test training. In fact, a clinical observation that we have made repeatedly is that if a child will not condition to the visual stimulus with PARF, it is highly unlikely that he will condition to an auditory stimulus. This is probably because the auditory stimulus is less concrete than the visual stimulus used with PARF.

Pitfalls to Avoid in Hearing Screening

The following factors often are found in hearing screening programs and can have a detrimental effect on the results of the screening and should be avoided at all costs.

(1) Child observing dials. This should be avoided at all times, because children will respond to the visual cues. The appropriate position to seat the child is at an oblique angle, so the tester and audiometer are out of the child's peripheral vision.
(2) Examiner giving visual cues (facial expression, eye or head movements, etc.).
(3) Incorrect adjustment of the headband and earphone placement. Care must be taken to place the earphones carefully over the ears so that the

protective screen mesh of the earphone diaphragm is directly over the entrance of the external auditory canal. Misplacement of the earphone by only one inch can cause as great as a 30 to 35 dB threshold shift.
(4) Vague instructions.
(5) Noise in the test area.
(6) Overlong test sessions. The screening should require only three to five minutes. If a child requires significantly more time than this, the routine screening should be discontinued and a short rest taken. If the child continues to be difficult to test, play conditioning should be used.
(7) Too long or too short a presentation of the test tone. The test stimulus should be presented for one to two seconds. If the stimulus is for a shorter or longer time than this, inaccurate responses may be obtained.

IMMITTANCE SCREENING IN THE SCHOOLS—IDENTIFICATION OF MIDDLE EAR DISORDERS

The literature is now replete with studies showing why screening for middle ear disorders in school children is needed. The most notable finding is unanimous documentation that pure tone screening tests are not sensitive to middle ear disorders. Moreover, these studies have shown that immittance measures increase the overall accuracy of the screening program, reduce the number of children who must be retested prior to referral, and increase the likelihood that all children who are referred for medical examination have valid otologic problems.[62] In addition to these factors, there is compelling evidence now that significant delays in speech and language development and educational retardation are related to chronic ear disease in children, especially during the early years.

In the classic study of Holm and Kunze,[63] the performance of two groups of 16 children each, an experimental group with documented histories of otitis media and a matched normal control group, ages 5 to 9 years, was evaluated using standardized tests of language and speech. Findings revealed the experimental group was significantly delayed when compared to the control group in all language skills requiring auditory reception or speech production, but no significant differences were observed on tests of visual or motor skills. This study provided the first formal documentation on the detrimental effects of middle ear disorders on the development of speech and language. Numerous parallel studies have been conducted since with similar findings.[62]

Although the research data support the use of immittance screening to detect middle ear disorders in school children, the extreme sensitivity of the test has caused high false-positive rates for a large number of programs. This factor, combined with the lack of definitive research on the specific referral criteria and benefits of immittance measures and the sometimes transient nature of middle ear disorders,[64] has significantly affected the widespread use of immittance in screening programs. In fact, recommendations from an International Conference on Impedence Screening, held in 1977 in Nashville, Tennessee, did not favor universal mass screening with immittance on a routine basis for the detection of middle ear disorders.[65] However, it should be emphasized that the recommendations from the Nashville conference did not discourage screening with immittance, just *mass* screening. Moreover, the Conference recommended that immittance screening be performed routinely on special populations of children, such as Native Americans and those with sensorineural hearing loss, developmental delay and mental impairment, and craniofacial anomalies, including cleft palate and Down's syndrome.

Test Environment

Unlike screening for hearing loss, there are no background noise level requirements needed to perform immittance screening, because the test stimuli used are presented well above normal threshold sensitivity. This factor has prompted many to state that sound-treated environments are not necessary when immittance is used.[7] This statement is technically valid, and when immittance screening is performed alone, background noise levels can be ignored. However, as emphasized earlier, immittance screening must be performed in conjunction with hearing screening if the identification program is to be effective. Therefore, when hearing and immittance screening are performed in the same testing area, it is necessary to have background levels that meet the minimum requirements necessary for hearing screening.

Otoscopic Inspection

Otoscopy is the process by which the ear canal and tympanic membrane are inspected by an examiner, using an instrument called an otoscope (see Fig. 3-7). The purpose of the inspection is to assess the overall condition of the outer ear and tympanic membrane. In immittance testing, two areas of controversy exist with respect to otoscopic inspection of the ear. These two areas center around the preimmittance test otoscopic inspection and postimmittance test agreement.

Should the ear canal be inspected prior to performing immittance measures? There are those who feel that this procedure is not necessary because any significant abnormality such as wax impaction will show up in the immittance test results. But other conditions, such as a foreign object in the ear canal and infection in the outer ear, will not necessarily be detected by the immittance measures. Thus, otoscopic inspection should be performed as part of the test battery. Musket and Dworaczyk[66] state that otoscopic inspection can be frightening to school children, especially preschoolers. They describe a modification of an otoscope in which it is disguised as a puppet, so it will be acceptable to younger children. Figure 3-8 shows this innovative modification.

What if an examiner feels that an abnormal amount of cerumen is present in the ear canal in the pretest otoscopic inspection—a condition that occurs frequently. Depending on the exact condition of the ear, most would suggest that the immittance test be performed even if excessive ear wax is present. If the immittance results are normal, should the child be referred to have his ears cleaned? There is no

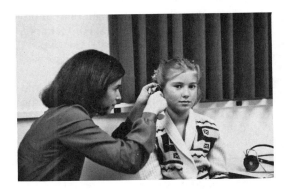

Figure 3-7. Otoscopic inspection of the external ear.

Figure 3-8. Modification of an otoscope to disguise it as a puppet (after Musket and Dworaczyk[66]).

simple answer to this often encountered condition. If there is an extreme amount of cerumen present, it is advisable to make a referral to have it removed. If there is simply an abnormal amount, this finding should be brought to the attention of the parents so that it can be checked by the managing physician during routine health visits. Under no circumstances should the examiner remove cerumen or any other material from the ear canal, unless under the direct supervision and with the approval of a physician.

Controversy on post-test agreement centers around discrepancies found between the immittance test results and the otoscopic examination. In the past, the otoscopic examination by the physician has provided the final criteria by which ear disease has been diagnosed, and many physicians continue to rely solely on this method to make their diagnoses. However, clinical studies have shown that otoscopic inspection, even when using highly trained examiners with pneumatic otoscopes, is not as sensitive to alterations in the state of the middle ear as immittance measures. For example, negative pressure in the middle ear (type C tympanogram) cannot be accurately assessed with the otoscopic inspection.[67]

Otoscopy is subjective, and the training and orientation of the examiner, cooperation of the child, and other similar factors affect the otoscopic results. Immittance measures are based on more objective procedures, and are highly sensitive to small variations from normality. Thus, many ears found to have abnormal immittance results may be judged normal by otoscopic examination. Until physicians recog-

nize the value of immittance measures and use them along with their otoscopic examination, discrepancies will be found in classifying children with normal and abnormal middle ear function.

Personnel

The personnel used in the hearing screening program should be those used in the immittance screening program, but more extensive training is necessary. The technical personnel must be thoroughly familiar with the mechanics of the instrumentation used in the program, the proper use of the instrumentation, and the problems that can be encountered with the instrument and how to trouble-shoot such problems. They must also be familiar with interpretation of test results and thoroughly knowledgeable about disorders of the ear.

Training seminars have been developed that cover the basic procedures used in immittance screening in one or two days. This type of seminar is appropriate for those who have had exposure and experience with hearing loss and screening procedures (speech pathologists and school nurses), but does not meet the necessary requirements for those who have had no past training in this area. There are no guidelines for training paraprofessionals in the use of immittance. However, it is felt that two or three days of specific training in immittance, beyond the training in hearing screening is required. As with hearing screening, an emphasis on supervised practicum is needed. Because the addition of immittance screening requires more technical expertise, there is a far greater need for a certified audiologist to be available to the program.

Pass-Fail Criteria and Follow-Up

Several sets of guidelines have been established for immittance screening. The two most notable are the Nashville guidelines[66] and the guidelines from the American Speech-Language-Hearing Association.[7] Tables 3-7 and 3-8 summarize the respective recommended procedures from these two sources.

Both guidelines recommend that the tympanogram and contralateral acoustic reflex be used in the immittance screening battery. The

Table 3-7   Summary of Nashville Symposium Guidelines for Immittance Screening[65]

Classification	Initial Screen	Retest	Subject Outcome
1	Tympanogram: Normal* and Acoustic reflex: Present†	Not required	Cleared
2	Tympanogram: Abnormal‡ and/or Acoustic reflex: Absent†	Tympanogram: Abnormal‡ and/or Acoustic reflex: Absent†	Referred
3	Tympanogram: Abnormal‡ and/or Acoustic reflex: Absent†	Tympanogram: Normal* and Acoustic reflex: Present†	At risk Recheck at a later date

*Clear peak between +50 and −200 daPa.
†Contralateral or ipsilateral tone 1000 Hz at 105 dB HL.
‡Flat or rounded, or negative pressure equivalent beyond −200 daPa.

Table 3-8   Summary of ASHA Recommendation for Immittance Screening[7]

Classification		Initial Screen	Disposition
I. Pass	Tympanogram:	Normal* or Mildly positive/negative†	Clear; no return
	Acoustic reflex:	Present‡	
II. At Risk	Tympanogram: and	Abnormal§	Retest 3–5 wk a) If results fall into class I, pass
	Acoustic reflex: or	Present‡	b) If results fall into class II, fail and refer
	Tympanogram:	Normal* or Mildly positive/negative†	
	Acoustic reflex:	Absent‡	
III. Fail	Tympanogram:	Abnormal§	
	Acoustic reflex:	Absent‡	Refer

*Peak at ±50 daPa.
†+50 to +100 daPa or −50 to −200 daPa.
‡Contralateral tone 1000 Hz at 100 dB HL or ipsilateral tone at 105 dB HL.
§Pressure peak more than +100 daPa or more negative than −200 daPa.

Nashville guidelines recommend the use of 1000 Hz pure tone at 105 dB HL for screening reflexes and provide tympanometric criteria for both rounded (flat type B) and negative pressure (type C) curves. The ASHA guidelines suggest that a 1000 Hz contralateral tone at 105 dB HL ipsilateral be used for the reflex, and that tympanometric criteria be based on peak pressure only. Basing tympanometric findings solely on peak pressure is confusing, as it does not take into account rounded or flat (type B) tympanograms. However, it is assumed that such a tympanogram would be considered abnormal by the ASHA guidelines.

Although procedural factors of the Nashville and ASHA guidelines are similar, there are considerable philosophical differences between the two with regard to follow-up. First, the Nashville guidelines recommend retest in two to six weeks of all those failing the first screening before referral is made. This procedure assumes that some of those screened may recover spontaneously from their abnormal middle ear condition. However, the ASHA guidelines suggest direct referral on the first screening for one group (category III). The second philosophical difference is that the child with an abnormal tympanogram and an acoustic reflex present on the second screening is considered "at risk" and retested by the Nashville guidelines, but the ASHA guidelines would fail and refer.

By comparison, it can easily be seen that the Nashville guidelines are more conservative than the ASHA guidelines, and are based on the pragmatic factors involved in immittance screening. On the other hand, the ASHA guidelines represent concerns about the educational, social, and psychological sequelae of otitis media. Those who favor the ASHA recommendations feel that the detrimental effects of otitis media are too severe to delay any possible treatment.

From our clinical experience, the use of the ASHA recommendations may lead to an abnormally high rate of false-positive referrals. This is due to the sensitivity of immittance in detecting middle ear disorders compared to otoscopic examination discussed earlier, and the spontaneous recovery of middle ear disorders. Tos,[64] for example, performed immittance screening on 2-year-old children at three-month intervals. Of 51 ears found to have flat (type B) tympanograms initially, 27 (53%) improved spontaneously during the first three months, and spontaneous improvement was found in 45 (84%) within nine months. This finding not only raises the question of when to refer following the immittance screening, but also questions the nature and course of medical treatment when abnormal results are found.

IDENTIFYING HEARING LOSS AND MIDDLE EAR DISORDERS— A RECOMMENDED PROGRAM

A very clear limitation of both of the above guidelines for immittance screening is the fact that neither considers the results from the hearing screening in formulating follow-up recommendations. Follow-up for a child with abnormal findings on the immittance screening *and* the presence of hearing loss should be considered more critical than when hearing loss is not found. The recommended program we outline in Table 3-9 combines the results from both hearing screening and immittance tests.

Table 3-9 is a summary of guidelines that we have found to be valid and reliable in identifying both hearing loss and middle ear disorders

in school screening programs. Although some have recommended the use of only one tone in the hearing screening when immittance is used,[6] the audiometric procedures we recommend follow those recommended by ASHA.[36] As outlined in Table 3-6, this procedure utilizes the frequencies 1000, 2000, and 4000 Hz presented at 20 dB, 20 dB, and 25 dB HL, respectively. The child fails the test if he does not respond to any one of the tones in either ear. The reason we include additional frequencies in our program is twofold. First, as discussed earlier, limited frequency hearing screening can fail to identify some individuals with significant losses, and second, the inclusion of two additional frequencies adds an insignificant amount of time to the screening process (as little as 10 to 15 seconds per ear) while significantly increasing the sensitivity of the test.

The immittance screening procedure we recommend uses the tympanogram and acoustic reflex elicited using a 1000 Hz contralateral tone at 100 dB HL. Tympanogram findings are classified into those with peaks within the range of +50 to −200 daPa (peak normal), those with no peaks or rounded peaks (flat), and those with abnormal peaks (greater than +50 daPa or more negative than −200 daPa). The procedures combine the Nashville and ASHA guidelines, depending on the results from hearing screening tests, in that some immittance categories are considered at risk and retesting is recommended (those classified II or III) and some categories (those classified IV) are referred immediately.

As shown in Table 3-9, a total of 12 possible outcomes can occur on the initial screening test when using the three measures. These 12 outcomes are categorized into severity types, ranging from type I, which represents normal findings on both hearing and immittance measures, to type IV, which represents grossly abnormal findings on immittance and failure on hearing tests. Table 3-10 summarizes the characteristics and follow-up procedures for the four severity types. Type I would pass and no follow-up would be recommended. Type II occurs when marginally abnormal results are found on the immittance testing, but no loss is found on the hearing screening. A marginally abnormal result on immittance includes abnormal middle ear pressure with or without acoustic reflexes, and the absence of reflexes with normal middle ear pressure. Such conditions can lead to a high number of false-

Table 3-9   Recommended Guidelines Combining Results from Hearing Screening and Immittance Measures

Possible Outcome (See explanation below)		Severity Type	Follow-Up	Disposition After Follow-Up
1	T[(1)]: Peak normal[(4)] R[(2)]: Present[(5)] H[(3)]: Pass[(6)]	I	None-Pass	
2	T: Peak normal R: Absent H: Pass	II	Retest[(8)]	A. Change to type I—pass B. No change or other type II—at risk—retest C. type III—refer for audiologic testing D. type IV—medical referral
3	T: Peak normal R: Absent H: Fail	III	Retest	A. Change to type I—pass B. Change to type II—at risk—retest C. No change or other type III—refer for audiologic testing D. Change to type IV—medical referral
4	T: Peak normal R: Present H: Fail	III	Retest	A. Change to type I—pass B. Change to type II—at risk—retest C. No change or other type III—refer for audiologic testing D. Change to type IV—medical referral
5	T: No peak or rounded R: Present H: Pass	II	(Not a likely finding—check equipment) Retest if confirmed	A. Change to type I—pass B. No change or other type II—at risk—retest C. Change to type III—refer for audiological testing D. Change to type IV—medical referral
6	T: No peak or rounded R: Absent H: Pass	IV	Immediate medical referral	
7	T: No peak or rounded R: Absent H: Fail	IV	Immediate medical referral	
8	T: No peak or rounded R: Present H: Fail	IV	(Not a likely finding—check equipment) Immediate medical referral if confirmed	
9	T: Abnormal peak[(7)] R: Present H: Pass	II	Retest	A. Change to type I—pass B. No change or other type II—at risk—retest C. Change to type III—refer for audiological testing D. Change to type IV—medical referral

Continued

(1) T = Tympanogram. (2) R = Reflex. (3) H = Hearing Screening. (4) +50 to −200 daPa. (5) 1000 Hz contralateral Tone at 1000 dB HL. (6) Failure to respond to 1000 or 2000 Hz at 20 dB HL or 4000 Hz at 25 dB HL in either ear. (7) Greater than +50 daPa or more negative than −200 daPa. (8) Retest in 2–6 weeks.

Table 3-9 Continued

Possible Outcome (See explanation below)		Severity Type	Follow-Up	Disposition After Follow-Up
10	T: Abnormal peak R: Absent H: Pass	II	Retest	A. Change to type I—pass B. No change or other type II—at risk—retest C. Change to type III—refer for audiological testing D. Change to type IV—medical referral
11	T: Abnormal peak R: Absent H: Fail	III	Retest	A. Change to type I—pass B. Change to type II—at risk—retest C. No change or other type III—refer for audiologic testing D. Change to type IV—medical referral
12	T: Abnormal peak R: Present H: Fail	III	Retest	A. Change to type I—pass B. Change to type II—at risk—retest C. No change or other type III—refer for audiologic testing D. Change to type IV—medical referral

(1) T = Tympanogram. (2) R = Reflex. (3) H = Hearing Screening. (4) +50 to −200 daPa. (5) 1000 Hz contralateral Tone at 1000 dB HL. (6) Failure to respond to 1000 or 2000 Hz at 20 dB HL or 4000 Hz at 25 dB HL in either ear. (7) Greater than +50 daPa or more negative than −200 daPa. (8) Retest in 2–6 weeks.

Table 3-10 Characteristics of Severity Types Used With Recommended Screening Procedures

Severity Type	Characteristics	Follow-Up
I	Normal	None-Pass
II	Marginally abnormal immittance findings with pass on hearing screening	At risk—retest
III	Normal or marginally abnormal immittance findings with fail on hearing screening	Refer for audiometric threshold testing
IV	Grossly abnormal immittance findings *and* pass or fail hearing screening	Medical referral

positive referrals unless hearing loss is present. If hearing loss is present, the severity would be classified as type III and audiologic referral made. Type III occurs when there is failure on the hearing screening with normal or marginally abnormal findings on the immittance testing. Children falling into the type III category would be suspect of hearing loss and in need of more detailed audiometric testing.

Finally, Type IV occurs when immittance results indicate the presence of a significant ear disorder with or without hearing loss present, indicating a need for immediate medical attention.

Using these criteria, a retest is scheduled for type II and type III outcomes in two to six weeks, and the follow-up disposition depends on the results from the second screening. The specific follow-up dispositions are listed for each of the eight possible outcomes where retests are recommended. For type II findings, if no change occurs, children are considered at risk and retesting at regular intervals is scheduled until there is a change to another type. If type II results change to type I, the child passes; if they change to another type II, retesting is scheduled; or if they change to type IV, medical referral is made. It is possible for a child to remain in the type II category for an extended period of time. After the first retest children remaining in the type II category should continue to be monitored, but less frequently at increasingly greater intervals.

Type III findings that do not change or are reclassified into another type III category are referred for audiometric threshold testing. However, if type III findings change to a type II, the child is considered at risk and retested at scheduled intervals. On the other hand, if the findings change to type IV, medical referral is made.

Type IV findings represent the most significant involvement in that all three measures support the presence of auditory impairment. For this reason, referral is made immediately after the first screening, or whenever this finding occurs in the retesting.

Table 3-9 demonstrates the complexity of a screening program relying on three measures to make a referral decision. In addition, the table points out that effective procedures will involve closely monitored follow-up, possibly for an extended period, until the child is clear of the abnormal condition or the screening findings become severe enough to warrant referral. Although seemingly complicated at first, these procedures can be implemented and used most effectively in identifying both hearing loss and middle ear disorders in school children with relative ease.

Pitfalls to Avoid in Immittance Screening

The following factors often are found in immittance screening programs and can have a detrimental effect on results from the screening.

(1) Clogged probe and probe tip. The probe and probe tips must be kept free from earwax.
(2) Probe tip too large or too small. Each ear canal is different and may require a different-sized probe tip. Utilization of the correct size for each child will avoid possible errors.
(3) Head movement, swallowing, or eye blinks. The child should be kept still during testing, as a sudden abnormal movement during testing may be interpreted as a reflex.
(4) Probe tip against ear canal wall. The probe tip must be inserted directly into the ear canal and when the canal is not straight, the tip must be kept away from the canal wall.
(5) Debris in ear canal. The ear canal should be inspected before testing to ensure that it is clear.

GENERAL CONSIDERATIONS FOR BOTH HEARING AND IMMITTANCE SCREENING

Equipment

The specifications for the equipment that should be used in the screening program are described in Chapter 1. One additional criterion in selecting equipment for use in the screening program is the quality and availability of maintenance service. All audiometric equipment must be serviced on a regular basis, and the location and efficiency of the service center should be considered before making a purchase. It would not be advisable to purchase an instrument from a dispenser 1000 miles away, when a local dealer who provides direct service is available.

Whenever possible, each school system should purchase its own equipment, so that a procedure can be implemented for proper maintenance and calibration, and records maintained. However, if circumstances do not permit the school system to buy its own audiometer, the following are major sources for borrowing or renting equipment:

(1) State education departments.
(2) State and/or county health departments.
(3) Other schools.
(4) County health associations.
(5) Local speech and hearing clinics.

The audiometer used for diagnostic purposes should have the capability of performing air and bone conduction tests, masking, speech audiometry, and special diagnostic tests. Most schools will not have this equipment available in the system. However, assurances should be made that these services are available at the referral facility performing the diagnostic procedures.

Teacher's Contribution

There are many behaviors which have been associated with auditory impairment in children, and it is important that school personnel become familiar with signs of classroom behavior or physical symptoms of hearing loss which might give them clues as to children in need of audiologic examination. Behaviors and physical symptoms that may indicate auditory impairment in a child are listed in Table 3-11. While these signs may also be associated with other types of school problems, any child exhibiting one or more of them should be referred for audiometric screening, and diagnostic evaluation when indicated.

Several studies have been conducted on the efficacy of teacher identification of school children with hearing loss. Early studies reported that teachers were able to correctly identify only one of four to six children with significant

Table 3-11 Behaviors and Physical Symptoms in Children That May Indicate Hearing Loss

Behaviors
a. Frequently asks to have things repeated
b. Turns one side of head toward speaker
c. Talks too loudly or too slowly
d. Shows strain in trying to hear
e. Watches and concentrates on teacher's lips
f. Is inattentive in classroom discussion
g. Makes frequent mistakes in following directions
h. Makes unusual mistakes in taking directions
i. Tends to isolate self
j. Tends to be passive
k. Is tense
l. Tires easily
m. Has a speech problem
n. Is not working up to apparent capacity
o. Has academic failure following severe illness

Physical Symptoms
a. Mouth breathing
b. Draining ears
c. Earaches
d. Dizziness
e. Reports of ringing, buzzing, or roaring in ears (tinnitus)

hearing loss.[68,69] In a more recent study, Nodar[70] compared teachers' identifications with audiometric and immittance screening data. Results from this study indicated that teachers were able to identify almost 50% of the children in the hearing loss group. This study shows that while not always accurate, classroom teachers can play a valuable role in detecting children with hearing problems, and their observations should definitely be considered as an adjunct to the screening process. However, in no way should these data be interpreted to imply that teachers are an adequate substitute for auditory screening procedures.

Periodicity of Testing

Few would argue that the ideal program would test every child every year. However, screening all children annually is not practical most of the time and many compromises have been suggested. Virtually all published guidelines support two general principles with regard to periodicity of testing[29,36]:

(1) There is a greater need for screening children in the lower grades than children in higher grades.
(2) There are populations of children with a higher incidence of hearing loss and ear disorders who warrant testing outside of the routine schedule.

The need to concentrate screening on the lower grades is based on two observations. First, during the early school years there is a higher prevalence of transient hearing loss due to middle ear pathology; and second, mild, and frequency-selective hearing losses are many times undetected in the early school years.[12] Based on these principles, annual screening of all children in grades K, 1, 2, and 3 is highly recommended.[36]

Controversy exists on the cost benefit of screening after grade 3. After analyzing the data from 14,800 10th graders, Downs and Doster[1] concluded that audiometric screening programs should be relaxed in the upper grades. This conclusion is based on the low yield of previously undetected hearing impairment in the upper grades.

Although there is a general reduction in the incidence of hearing loss in the upper grades, results from two studies have shown that the incidence of high frequency loss significantly increases in the 4000 to 6000 Hz region beyond grade 8, especially in males. Weber, McGovern, and Zink[26] reviewed the audiometric configurations from 1000 students failing the screening procedures performed by the Colorado Department of Health. Thirty percent of the losses identified were in the 4000 Hz region, with 24.9% in males and 5.1% in females. As age increased to 16+ years, there was a significant increase in the losses at 4000 Hz.

Hull et al[27] report data from 38,568 children in grades 1 through 12. In comparing all grade levels across frequencies, the highest incidence of hearing loss exceeding 25 dB HL (ISO, 1964) was at 4000 Hz in the male population in the 11th and 12th grades. Since the losses are typically greater in males who engage in noisy activities, implementing a hearing conservation program for the students in the industrial arts program should detect most of the hearing losses, because these students most likely are those who will engage in hobbies with high noise levels. The benefits of implementing such hearing conservation programs in the schools extend beyond identifying existing hearing loss. Through education, students become aware of the effects of noise on their hearing, which may prevent occupational hearing loss from noise exposure in later years.[71]

With respect to special populations, the following guidelines should be applied. Testing should be performed on:

(1) Children who are new to the school or to the school district.
(2) Children with delayed or defective speech and language before they are enrolled in therapy.
(3) Pupils returning to school after a serious illness.
(4) Pupils who appear to be retarded.
(5) Pupils having emotional or behavior problems.
(6) Pupils referred by the classroom teacher for hearing testing for any reason.

Regardless of grade level, annual testing should also be performed on pupils discovered by previous tests to have hearing impairment, and on pupils enrolled in adjustment or remedial classes.

The exact procedures used for follow-up will vary considerably from district to district, but provisions for three areas of concern must be made: audiologic, medical and educational.

Audiologic Follow-Up. In many traditional school hearing conservation programs, all children who fail the screening are immediately referred for medical follow-up. Such referral is important to identify significant medical problems, but might be considered premature in the sequence for some categories. As indicated in Table 3-9, there are categories of failures that should be referred for audiological follow-up before a medical referral is made. The screening tests administered in the schools must be considered only as a preliminary indication of the presence of hearing loss and/or a middle ear disorder. Before the exact nature and extent of the loss can be determined, additional audiologic testing should be performed on those indicated in Table 3-9 by an audiologist, if at all possible, under acceptable testing conditions.

It would be ideal for all failures to be referred to a clinic where both medical and audiologic facilities are available. In that way the physician and audiologist could work together in assessing the nature and extent of the problem and in providing appropriate follow-up. Many of the larger metropolitan areas have such facilities. However, where such facilities are not available, follow-up audiologic threshold testing should be performed and the results evaluated by a senior member of the school's testing staff. In this way the physicians will have necessary audiological data available.

The current guidelines of the American Speech-Language-Hearing Association[36] (1975) support the need for audiological follow-up before medical referral. In addition, the guidelines give the following priority for audiologic evaluation for those children failing the hearing screening and rescreening procedures:

(1) Binaural loss in both ears at all frequencies tested.
(2) Binaural loss at 1000 *and* 2000 Hz only.
(3) Binaural loss at 1000 *or* 2000 Hz only.
(4) Monaural loss at all frequencies.
(5) Monaural loss at 1000 and 2000 Hz only.
(6) Binaural or monaural loss at 4000 Hz only.

Medical Follow-Up. One of the dilemmas regarding medical follow-up for children failing the screening is the choice of the physician to whom to send the child. Traditional medical ethics dictate that the child must be referred to the family physician. Typically, the family physician is a general practitioner or pediatrician. The general medical practitioner plays a very important role in the overall management of the family's medical needs, but often does not have the expertise required in the diagnosis and management of otologic problems. For this reason, those children failing the screening program may be best served if referred directly to an ear specialist (otologist). For the overall well-being of the child, the referral to the otologist, with proper notification and approval from the managing physician, is most appropriate when auditory disorders are found.

Whenever referral is made for medical follow-up, the parents must be contacted. Initially contact can be made by phone, but written recommendations also should be made. In addition, feedback from the physician should be requested and records kept on all medical referrals. Anderson[2] provides examples of forms that can be used for follow-up purposes.

A very useful way to establish a liaison with the medical community is through a School Medical Advisory Board. Many school systems have need for an avenue by which to communicate with the medical community. Having the expertise of several of the community physicians available to the school allows for direct and frequent interaction with them, resulting in a better understanding of the procedures that are used in the schools. Many physicians will also welcome such an opportunity to serve the school.

Educational Follow-Up. In all cases when auditory disorders are found, teachers must be notified so that special provisions can be made in the classroom. In many cases, the hearing loss will be transient and the extent and duration of the impairment will depend on the nature of the abnormal condition. However, even for these children, the teacher must take into account the effect of the loss and make special provisions in the classroom. Part II of this book deals with remedial aspects of hearing loss in school children.

REFERENCES

1. Downs MP, Doster MF, Weaver M: Dilemmas in identification audiometry. *J Speech Hear Disord*, 30 (1965), 360–364
2. Anderson CV: Conservation of hearing, in Katz J, ed: *Handbook of Clinical Audiology*, ed 2 (Baltimore: Williams & Wilkins, 1978).
3. Melnick W, Eagles EL, Levine HS: Evaluation of a recommended program of identification audi-ometry with school-age children. *J Speech Hear Disord*, 29 (1964), 3–13.
4. Brooks DN: A new approach to identification audiometry. *Audiology*, 10 (1971), 334–339.
5. Eagles EL: Hearing levels in children and audiometer performance. *J Speech Hear Disord*, suppl 9 (1961), 1–274.
6. Cooper JC, Gates GA, Owen JH, et al: An abbreviated impedance bridge technique for school screening. *J Speech Hear Disord*, 40 (1975), 260–269.
7. American Speech-Language-Hearing Association (ASHA) Committee on Audiometric Evaluation Guidelines for acoustic immittance screening of middle ear function. *ASHA*, 21 (1979), 283–288.
8. Frankenberg WK: Selection of diseases and tests in pediatric screening. *Pediatrics*, 54 (1971).
9. Wilson WR, Walton WK: Identification audiometry accuracy: Evaluation of a recommended program for school-age children. *Lang Speech Hear Serv Schls*, 5 (1974), 132–142.
10. Frasier GR: The genetics of congenital deafness. *Otolaryngol Clin North Amer*, 4 (1971), 227–247.
11. Stewart J: *HRS screening*. Paper presented at the annual meeting of the Western Society for Pediatric Research, Carmel, CA, 1974.
12. Northern JL, Downs MP: *Hearing In Children*, ed 2 (Baltimore: Williams and Wilkins Co, 1978).
13. Berg F: Definition and incidence, in Berg F, Fletcher SG: *The Hard of Hearing Child* (New York: Grune and Stratton, 1970).
14. Klein JO: Epidemiology of otitis media, in Harford ER, Bess TH, Bluestone D, et al, eds: *Impedance Screening for Middle Ear Disease in Children* (New York: Grune and Stratton, 1978).
15. Jerger J: Dissenting report: Mass impedance screening. *Annals Otol Rhinol Laryngol*, 89 suppl 69 (1980), 21–22.
16. Brooks DN: Impedance in screening, in Jerger J, Northern J, eds: *Clinical Impedance Audiometry* (Acton, Mass: American Electronics Corp, 1980).
17. Silverman RS, David H, eds: *Hearing and Deafness* (New York: Holt, Rinehart, Winston, 1978).
18. Eagles EL, Wishik SM, Doerfler LG: Hearing sensitivity and ear disease in children: A prospective study. *Laryngoscope* (Monograph), 1967, 1–274.
19. Connor LE: Determining the prevalence of hearing impaired children. *Except Child*, 27 (1961), 337–344.
20. Fay TH, Hochberg I, Smith CR, et al: Audiologic and otologic screening of disadvantaged children, in Glorig A, Gerwin K, eds: *Otitis Media* (Springfield: Charles C. Thomas, 1972).
21. Robinson GC, Anderson DO, Mogohodam HK, et al: A survey of hearing loss in Vancouver school children: In Methodology and preva-

lence. *Canad Med Assoc J*, 97 (1967), 119–1207.

22. Newman MH: Hearing Loss, in Strom M, ed: *Differential Diagnosis in Pediatric Otolaryngology* (Boston: Little, Brown & Co., 1975).

23. Weit P: Patterns of ear disease in the southwestern American Indian. *Arch Otolaryngol*, 105 (1979), 381–385.

24. Kaplan GY, Fleshman JK, Bender TR, et al: Long-term effects of otitis media: A ten year cohort study of Alaskan Eskimo children. *Pediatrics*, 52 (1973), 577–585.

25. McEldowney D, Kessner PM: Review of the literature: epidemiology of otitis media, in Glorig A, Gerwin KS, eds: *Otitis Media* (Springfield: Charles C. Thomas, 1972).

26. Weber HJ, McGovern FJ, Fink D: An evaluation of 1000 children with hearing loss. *J Speech Hear Disord*, 32 (1967), 343–354.

27. Hull FM, Mielke PW Jr, Timmons RJ, et al: The national speech and hearing survey: Preliminary results. *ASHA*, 13 (1971), 501–509.

28. Northern JL: Impedance screening in special populations: State-of-the-art, in Harford E, Bess F, Bluestone CD, et al, eds: *Impedance Screening for Middle Ear Disease in Children* (New York: Grune and Stratton, 1978).

29. Darley FL: Identification audiometry for school-age children: basic procedures. *J Speech Hear Disord* (Monograph), suppl 9, 1961, 26–34.

30. Fisher LI: Efficiency and effectiveness of using a portable audiometric booth in school hearing conservation programs. *Lang Speech Hear Serv Schls*, 7 (1976), 242–249.

31. Roeser RJ, Glorig A: Pure tone audiometry in noise with auraldomes. *Audiology*, 14 (1975), 144–151.

32. Roeser RJ, Seidel J, Glorig A: Performance of earphone enclosures for threshold audiometry. *Sound and Vibration*, 10, No. 9 (1975), 22–25.

33. Roeser RJ, Musket CH: Noise attenuating earphone systems. *Maico Aud Library*, Series 15, Report 4, 1976.

34. Stark EW, Borton TE: Noise excluding earphone enclosures for audiometry. *Audiology*, 14 (1975), 232–237.

35. Musket CH, Roeser RJ: Using circumaural enclosures with children. *J Speech Hear Res* 20 (1977), 325–333.

36. American Speech and Hearing Association (ASHA) Committee on Audiometric Evaluation Guidelines for Identification Audiometry. *ASHA*, 17 (1975), 94–99.

37. Griffing TS, Simonton KM, Hedgecock LD: Verbal auditory screening for pre-school children. *Trans Am Acad Ophthalmol Otolaryngol*, 71 (1967), 105–111.

38. Ritchie BC: Review of the literature: Verbal auditory screening for children, in Gerwin KS, Glorig A, eds: *Detection of Hearing Loss and Ear Disease in Children* (Springfield: Charles C. Thomas, 1974).

39. Ciocco A, Palmer CE: The hearing of school children. *Society for Research in Child Development* (Monograph 4), Nat Res Council, 1941.

40. Johnson KO, Newby H: Experimental study of the efficiency of two group hearing tests. *Arch Otolaryngol*, 60 (1954), 702–710.

41. Mencher GT, McCullock BF: Auditory screening of kindergarten children using the VASC. *J Speech Hear Disord*, 35 (1970), 241–247.

42. Fowler EP, Fletcher H: Three million deafened school children. *JAMA*, 87 (1926), 1877–1882.

43. Reger SN, Newby HA: A group pure-tone hearing test. *J Speech Hear Disord*, 12 (1947), 61–66.

44. Johnston PW: The Massachusetts hearing test. *J Acoust Soc Am*, 20 (1948), 697–703.

45. Bennet SM: A group test of hearing for six-year-old children. *Br J Educ Psychol*, (1951), 45–52.

46. Johnston PW: An efficient group screening test. *J Speech Hear Disord* 17:8–12, 1952.

47. DiCarlo LM, Gardner EF: The efficiency of the Massachusetts pure-tone screening test as adapted for a university testing program. *J Speech Hear Disord*, 18 (1953), 175–182.

48–49. Newhart HA: A pure tone audiometer for school use. *Arch Otolaryngol*, 28 (1938), 777–779.

50. Hood B, Lamb LE: Identification audiometry, in Gerwin KS, Glorig A, eds: *Detection of Hearing Loss and Ear Disease in Children* (Springfield: Charles C. Thomas, 1974).

51. Villchur E: Audiometer—earphone mounting to improve intersubject and cushion-fit reliability. *J Acoust Soc Amer*, 48 (1970), 1387–1396.

52. House HP, Glorig A: A new concept in auditory screening. *Laryngoscope*, 67 (1957), 661–668.

53. Norton MC, Lux E: Double frequency auditory screening in public schools. *J Speech Hear Disord*, 26 (1961), 293–299.

54. Siegenthaler BM, Sommers RK: Abbreviated sweep check procedures for school hearing testing. *J Speech Hear Disord*, 24 (1959), 249–257.

55. Maxwell WR, Davidson GD: Limited frequency screening and ear pathology. *J Speech Hear Disord*, 26 (1961), 122–125.

56. Ventry I, Newby H: Validity of the one-frequency screening principle for public school children. *J Speech Hear Res*, 2 (1959), 147–151.

57. Stevens DA, Davidson GD: Screening tests of hearing. *J Speech Hear Disord*, 24 (1959), 258–261.

58. Illinois Dept. of Public Health: *A Manual for Audiometrists* (Springfield, Illinois, 1974).

59. Downs MP: Auditory Screening. *Otolaryngol Clin North Amer*, 11 (1968), 611–629.

60. Matkin ND: Assessment of hearing sensitivity during the preschool years, in Bess F, ed: Child-

hood Deafness: Causation, Assessment and Management (New York: Grune and Stratton, 1977).

61. Bricker DD, Bricker WA: A programmed approach to operant audiometry for low-functioning children. *J Speech Hear Disord*, 34 (1969), 312–320.

62. Northern JL: Impedance screening: An integral part of hearing screening. *Annals Otol Rhinol Laryngol* 89, suppl 68, (1980), 233–235.

63. Holm VA, Kunze LH: Effect of chronic otitis media on language and speech development. *Pediatrics*, 43 (1969), 833–839.

64. Tos M: Spontaneous improvement of secretory otitis and impedance screening. *Arch Otolaryngol*, 106 (1980), 345–349.

65. Bess FH: Impedance screening for children: A need for more research. *Annals Otol Rhinol Laryngol*, 89, suppl 68, (1980), 228–232.

66. Musket CH, Dowraczyk RD: Using an otoscope with preschoolers in acoustic immittance screening programs. *Lang Speech Hear Serv Schls*, 11 (1980), 109–111.

67. Roeser RJ, Dunckel DC, Soh J, et al: Comparison of tympanometry and otoscope in establishing pass/fail referral criteria. *J Acous Soc Am*, 3 (1977), 20–25.

68. Curry ET: The efficiency of teacher referrals in a school hearing testing program. *J Speech Hear Disord*, 15 (1950), 211–214.

69. Kodman F: Identification of hearing loss by the classroom teacher. *Laryngoscope*, 66 (1956), 1346–1349.

70. Nodar RH: Teacher identification of elementary school children with hearing loss. *Lang Speech and Hear Serv Schls*, 9 (1978), 24–28.

71. Roeser RJ: Industrial hearing conservation programs in the high schools. *Ear and Hearing*, 1 (1980), 119–120.

TESTS OF CENTRAL AUDITORY FUNCTION

4

Robert W. Keith

DEFINITION OF CENTRAL AUDITORY FUNCTION

In this chapter, approaches to the identification of children with problems of central auditory function will be discussed. Only children with normal hearing sensitivity will be considered, since very little is known about the relationship of conductive or sensorineural hearing loss to central auditory dysfunction. Currently, the term *central auditory function* is used interchangeably with other terminology that includes, for example, central auditory ability, central auditory perception, and central auditory processing. A deficiency in this area might be called a central auditory dysfunction, an auditory perceptual disorder, a nonsensory auditory deficit, or an auditory processing problem. In fact, the lack of agreement on terminology is an indication of the general lack of agreement and understanding about central auditory problems.

To better understand auditory language-learning disorders, it is helpful to review recent progress in technology, and the resultant educational expectations for our children. During the 20th century, an exponential growth in knowledge and technology occurred. This growth created a demand for formally educated persons who can work in a complex society. Without the benefit of an education or training in a skilled trade, one's social status, income, and opportunity are severely limited.

The educational demands of increased technology have placed significant stress on each child's sensory and learning abilities. To progress through school, one must be able to use the senses of sight and hearing. To learn auditorily, a child should have normal hearing sensitivity, and should be able to listen for significant time periods during a long school day. The child must learn in somewhat noisy, large classrooms (or even worse, in open classrooms), where the teacher's voice competes with background noise. The child must remember more complex information at an earlier age, and memorization is required not only for short durations (until the next test), but for long durations (when the ACT or SAT college entrance exams are given). This information must be categorized adequately for memory storage and sequenced properly upon retrieval to be useful.

Children with problems in these and other areas may have academic difficulty even though they may have normal or above-average intelligence. In the past, these children may not have had problems because the educational requirements were so different. At present, failing to achieve at the rate expected for a given chronologic age during elementary school, or even failing to surpass the achievements of peers, is considered a significant problem—a disability—a learning disability.

What is an auditory processing problem and how does it contribute to an overall learning disability? The Association of Children and Adults with Learning Disabilities (ACLD)[1] quotes the Education of the Handicapped Act of 1975, which defines specific learning disabilities as "a disorder in one or more of the basic psychological processes involved in *understanding* or in using language . . . which may manifest itself in an imperfect ability to *listen* . . . ." The ACLD further describes specific learning disabilities as "a chronic condition of presumed neurologic origin which selectively interferes with the development, integration, and/or demonstration of verbal and/or non-verbal abilities." This author has defined an auditory processing disorder as "the inability or impaired ability to attend to, discriminate, recognize, or comprehend information presented auditorily even though the person has normal intelligence and hearing sensitivity. These difficulties are more pronounced when listening to low-redundancy (distorted) speech, when there are competing sounds, or in poor acoustic environments. In the normal child, auditory processing abilities develop in a parallel or reciprocal relationship with language abilities. Children with auditory processing disorders are a subset of children with receptive and/or expressive language disorders."[2] What is implied in these definitions is the construct that auditory processing disorders contribute to developmental language disorders and interfere with academic achievement in the classroom.

A simplified definition of an auditory processing disorder could be any breakdown in the child's auditory abilities that results in diminished learning through hearing, even though peripheral auditory sensitivity is normal. In an effort to be systematic, various authors have attempted to identify and define those auditory processing abilities that may be important to the child's learning through hearing. These abilities are listed in Table 4-1. Although many other auditory processing abilities can be identified and labeled, Table 4-1 shows that auditory ability can be approached systematically and categorically. However, a direct cause-and-effect relationship between the abilities listed in Table 4-1 and achievement in language acquisition, reading, or academics has not been established. It is true that many children who fail to achieve in language, reading, and academics have auditory processing problems. However, many children who achieve normally also have poor auditory processing skills, and some poor readers and students with low achievement have normal auditory processing abilities. This apparent dilemma will be discussed later in this chapter.

As with learning disabilities, significant auditory perceptual problems exist in combination with other disorders and may, in fact, be due to many factors. For example, auditory perceptual problems may stem from neurologic problems such as seizure disorders, mental retardation, or cerebral palsy. Other factors may include: (1) the social and environmental conditions of poverty and malnourishment; (2) other medical problems, including peripheral hearing loss whether conductive (even a "mild" loss) or sensorineural; (3) brain damage from head trauma, meningitis, or other viral infections; and (4) childhood schizophrenia or other emotional disturbances. Drug abuse also may result in auditory perceptual disorders. Finally, there are undoubtedly genetic factors involved, since many family members have similar educational histories of learning problems. While some of these factors complicate the assessment of auditory perceptual abilities, they should not be used as "excuses" to exclude a child from an auditory-language remediation program.

PREVALENCE OF AUDITORY LANGUAGE-LEARNING DEFICITS

According to the Association for Children with Learning Disabilities, between 8,000,000 and 12,000,000 children in the United States are learning-disabled. Many of these children have auditory processing problems. One difficulty in establishing the number of children with auditory processing problems is that no standard definition of terminology is used in

Table 4-1 Auditory Processing Abilities Important to the Learning Process

Descriptive Term	Ability
Discrimination	To differentiate among sound of different frequency, duration, or intensity
Localization	To localize the source of sound.
Auditory attention	To pay attention to auditory signals, especially speech, for an extended time.
Auditory figure ground	To identify a primary speaker from a background of noise.
Auditory discrimination	To discriminate among words and sounds that are acoustically similar.
Auditory closure	To understand the whole word or message when part is missing.
Auditory blending	To synthesize isolated phonemes into words.
Auditory analysis	To identify phonemes or morphemes embedded in words.
Auditory association	To identify a sound with its source.
Auditory memory; sequential memory	To store and recall auditory stimuli of different length or number in exact order.

discussing them. Thus, estimates of prevalence will vary, depending on definitions used in different localities.

Another problem with prevalence studies is that mild cases of auditory processing problems are inconspicuous or easily compensated for when educational demands are at a minimum. With increased pressure for academic achievement, however, mild problems can become educationally significant. Matějček[3] points out that if one assumes that the incidence of severe learning disabilities is more or less constant, the presence of mild learning disabilities will vary, depending on a number of health, social, and educational factors and on the level of diagnosis and treatment. Matějček states further that the greater the general knowledge of learning disabilities and the higher the level of diagnosis, the greater the likelihood that even mild cases will be discovered.

In addition, as Benson pointed out in writing about dyslexia,[4] factors other than definition must be considered when determining frequency data. One consideration is age. A great deal of variability in auditory performance in children up to 12 or 13 years of age makes it even more difficult to specify precise expectations of performance in the young. This normal variability in performance leads to different interpretations by different clinicians. A given performance on one task may be viewed by one examiner as being within the normal range, while another examiner might view the same performance as indicating auditory processing problems. Also, while auditory processing problems seem to be common in children, they have only recently been mentioned in the literature that deals with adults, implying either a smaller prevalence in that population or ignorance of the problem on the part of clinicians. It may be that adults with auditory language-learning problems are absorbed into the stream of society. As with dyslexia, the frequency of occurrence of auditory processing problems is impossible to ascertain.

BEHAVIORS OF CHILDREN WITH AUDITORY PROCESSING PROBLEMS

When asked what behaviors were typical of children with auditory processing problems, a teacher noted that such children often seem to be "in a fog" and to say "Huh?" all the time. The teacher explained that such children often do not do their schoolwork, do not follow directions, and do not respond to auditory stimuli. She remarked, "When I talk to children with that kind of problem, they just look at me."

The following observations appear to be characteristic of children with auditory processing problems:

(1) Most are male.

(2) They have normal pure-tone hearing thresholds.

(3) They generally respond inconsistently to auditory stimuli. They often respond appropriately, but at other times they seem unable to follow auditory instructions.

(4) They have short attention spans and fatigue easily when confronted with long or complex activities.

(5) They are easily distracted by both auditory and visual stimulation. Brutten et al[5] describe these children as being at the mercy of their environment. Unable to block out irrelevant stimuli, they must respond immediately and totally to everything they see, feel, or hear, no matter how trivial. According to Rampp and Plummer,[6] in a survey of 164 children with auditory processing disturbances, 90% were hyperactive.

(6) They may have difficulty with auditory localization skills. This may include an inability to tell how close or far away the source of the sound is, and an inability to differentiate soft and loud sounds. There have been frequent reports that these children become frightened and upset when they are exposed to loud noise, and often hold their hands over their ears to stop the sound.

(7) They may listen attentively, but have difficulty following long or complicated verbal commands or instructions.

(8) They often request that information be repeated.

(9) They are often unable to remember information presented verbally for both short-term and long-term memory. They may have difficulty in counting or in the alphabet, or in remembering the days of the week and months of the year or addresses and phone numbers.

(10) They are often allergic to various things in the environment.

(11) They often have a significant history of chronic otitis media.

Other behavioral characteristics of children with auditory processing problems include poor listening skills, taking a lot of time to answer questions, having difficulty relating what they have heard to the words they see on paper, and being unable to appreciate jokes, puns, or other humorous twists of the language.

Cohen[7] points out that in addition to specific auditory behaviors, many of these children have significant reading problems, are poor spellers, and have poor handwriting. They may have speech, articulation, or language problems. They may also act out frustrations that result from their perceptual deficits in the classroom, or they may be shy and withdrawn because of the poor self-concept that results from multiple failures.

These examples are only a few of the behaviors that are associated with auditory processing problems. It should be noted that not every child with an auditory processing problem will exhibit all of the behaviors mentioned. The number of problems experienced by a given child will be an expression of the severity of the auditory learning disability. A child with problems in only one or two auditory areas would have only a mild auditory learning problem. If the difficulty is profound, affects language comprehension severely, and persists for years, it is called receptive aphasia, or central deafness,[5,8] or auditory agnosia.

One should note that these behaviors are not unique to children with disorders of auditory processing. They are common to children with peripheral hearing loss, attention deficit disorders, allergies, and other problems. It should not bother clinicians to find similar behaviors among children with various language learning problems. Children (and adults) are capable of a limited repertoire of responses to the problems of life. While children have similar behaviors, they do not represent a homogeneous group. In fact, it is the task of the clinician to determine whether children with similar behaviors have different underlying problems that require different remediation approaches.

One possible way of determining the severity of the auditory processing disorder is to cite the circumstances under which the problem is identified. A preschool child with a mild auditory processing problem will not experience a great deal of difficulty in learning through the auditory system, since the intense one-to-one interaction between parent and child is sufficient compensation and will allow the child relatively normal speech and language devel-

opment. A moderate auditory processing problem is likely to be more confusing to the parents. The child who is inconsistent in his/her responses may be considered simply to be "slow." A test might be done to rule out a hearing loss; but when that is eliminated, the presence of a central auditory problem might not be considered.

Both mild and moderate auditory processing deficits will emerge as problems when the child enters school and is required to learn auditorily under less favorable listening conditions. When the auditory processing problem is finally diagnosed, the parents may understand retrospectively some of the problems and behaviors that confused them earlier. When a severe auditory processing problem is present, a child may fail to develop speech and language normally; then the problem may be discovered before the child enters school.

IDENTIFICATION AND ASSESSMENT OF AUDITORY PROCESSING PROBLEMS

Peripheral Hearing Loss

When thinking about behaviors of children with central auditory processing problems, one should recognize that many of these same behaviors are found in children with a peripheral hearing loss, whether it is conductive or sensorineural. A conductive hearing loss results from damage or disorders in the sound-conducting mechanism, including the external ear canal, eardrum, middle ear space, or the bones of the middle ear (see Chapters 1 and 2). Examples of a conductive loss include wax that occludes the ear canal, a hole in the eardrum, or fluid in the middle ear from a cold or allergy. A hearing loss in the cochlea (inner ear) is called a sensorineural hearing loss (see Chapter 1). When these losses are severe, they are relatively easy to identify because the child will not respond to sound or develop speech and language.

Mild peripheral hearing loss at all frequencies, or normal hearing at some frequencies and abnormal hearing at others, is likely to produce an inconsistent auditory response, difficulty in localizing the source of sound, poor auditory attention, and other behaviors that indicate auditory difficulty in learning.

Therefore, one must first determine by hearing testing whether a child who exhibits these behaviors has a peripheral hearing loss. It is vitally important to recognize that the pure-tone hearing screening tests usually done in the schools are not sensitive to the presence of small amounts of fluid in the middle ear or to other ear disorders, and that these tests fail to identify mild hearing loss with both conductive and sensorineural origins. It is necessary to do both air and bone conductive threshold measurements in a quiet environment to adequately measure hearing sensitivity. The addition of immittance measures will give additional information about middle ear function, and is a necessary component of school hearing screening programs.

It is also important to keep in mind that a single hearing test performed on a child may not be adequate. Fluctuating hearing loss associated with allergies or colds, or the possibility that a sensorineural hearing loss is progressive, makes it unwise to plan a child's long-term educational experience on the basis of a single hearing test.

A final word about conductive hearing loss. Until recently, little information was available on the long-term effects on central auditory abilities of early and prolonged otitis media with static or fluctuating hearing loss. Presently, however, there is growing evidence that otitis media can cause pronounced auditory learning problems, and it is not the innocuous disease that it was once considered to be.[9-15] The residual effects can be severe central auditory processing problems that may cause language and learning delays long after the middle ear problem itself has been resolved. Therefore, children with histories of frequent colds or chronic middle ear disease should be watched carefully for signs of auditory language-learning problems. This subject is covered in detail in Chapter 9.

ASSESSMENT PROCEDURES

When a peripheral hearing loss has been ruled out in a child with speech and language problems or when behaviors indicate that an auditory processing problem is present, a thorough evaluation of central auditory abilities should be performed. The assessment of central auditory abilities is more difficult than the assessment of peripheral hearing because of the complexities involved.

History

The assessment should begin with careful observation of the child, with particular attention to the auditory behavior patterns described previously in this chapter. Care should be taken to identify strengths as well as weaknesses, and to note performance in other modalities including sight, motor coordination, tactile response, and speech.

When possible, an in-depth history from the child's parents or guardian should be taken. Rosenberg[16] called the case history "the first test" because of the value of the information obtained. He pointed out that a carefully taken history can be extremely useful in differentiating among various problems, can supplement results from auditory tests, and can help in making decisions about the child's educational management.

The case history should be taken systematically to avoid missing important information. The person taking the history should provide an opportunity for the parents to state their concerns about their child, to describe the child's behaviors, and to express any other related concerns. Specific information that should be requested includes: (1) information about the family; (2) the mother's pregnancy; (3) conditions at birth, the child's growth and development, health, and illnesses; (4) general behavior and socioemotional development; (5) speech and language development; (6) hearing and auditory behavior; (7) nonauditory behavior; and (8) educational progress. The specific questions asked of parents will depend on the setting in which the testing is being done, and the purpose of the examination. History-taking forms are published by Katz and Strickmann[17] and Myklebust.[8] Areas to be investigated in the history when an auditory processing problem is suspected are given in Table 4-2.

Tests of Central Auditory Abilities

There are at least two very different approaches to tests of central auditory abilities that depend in part on the examiner's understanding of auditory processing disorders. But-

Table 4-2 Information Model for Taking a Case History

Area	Information Needed
Family history	History of the family's difficulty in school achievement. The language spoken in the home.
Pregnancy & birth	Unusual problems during pregnancy or delivery. Abnormalities present at the birth of the child.
Health & illness	Childhood illnesses, neurologic problems, psychological trauma, head trauma or injury, middle ear disease, allergies. Drugs or medications prescribed by a physician.
General behavior & social-emotional development	Age-appropriate play behavior, social isolation, impulsiveness, withdrawal, aggression, tact, sensitivity to others, self-discipline.
Speech & language development	Evidence of articulation, voice, or fluency problems. Ability to verbally communicate ideas. Ability to formulate sentences correctly. Appropriateness of verbal expression to subject or situation.
Hearing & auditory behavior	Ability to localize sounds auditorily. Ability to identify sound sources. Ability to listen selectively in presence of noise. Reaction to sudden, unexpected sound. Ability to ignore environmental sounds. Tolerance to loud sounds. Consistency of response to sound. Need to have spoken information repeated. Ability to follow verbal instructions. Ability to listen for appropriate length of time. Ability to remember things heard. Ability to pay attention to what is said. Ability to comprehend words and their meaning. Ability to understand multiple meanings of words. Ability to understand abstract ideas. Discrepancies between auditory and visual behavior.
Nonauditory behavior	Motor coordination: gross, fine, and eye-hand. Hand dominance. Visual perception. Spatial orientation. Any unusual reaction to touch.
Educational progress	Reading ability, math ability, and art ability.

ler (personal communication, 1986) pointed out that there is a traditional audiologic perspective, a speech language pathologist's perspective, and a teacher's perspective. Fundamentally, the audiologist's past "anatomic" perspective has led to development of an assessment approach based on the processing of auditory signals along the auditory pathway leading to the language centers of the brain. This approach has differed from the speech language pathologist's cognitive perspective, which stresses information processing strategies. Teachers often view the problem in terms of the child's ability to follow oral directions, comprehend academic instructions, etc.

The assessment can be approached using the model of the speech language pathologist's nonstandardized expressive language sample. That is, substantial information can be obtained from a "nonstandardized auditory receptive language sample." For example, Lasky and Cox[18] describe a systematic approach to observation of the child's auditory behavior in

their SPERS remediation model. They recommend observational evaluation of the child under different conditions of Signal, Presentation, and Environment, while evaluating the child's Responses, and Strategies.

Some of the auditory abilities that are assessed include:

Auditory Attention. The ability to sustain attention over time can be assessed by observing the child in comparison with his/her peers. The child should have the ability to direct attention toward a relevant acoustic signal, whether speech or music, and to sustain that attention for an appropriate length of time. When a child is not tuned in to listen, the child cannot learn auditorily. Some preliminary research in our laboratories indicates that tests of auditory vigilance may be useful in describing the child's auditory attention.[19] This Auditory Continuous Performance Test may eventually help separate children with disorders of attention from those with auditory figure-ground problems.

Auditory Figure Ground. Auditory figure ground is the ability to understand speech in the presence of a competing background noise. The ability to understand speech in noise varies widely among individuals. However, some children experience extreme problems with background environmental noise that have adverse affects on academic achievement. Observation of the child can help determine how behavior changes when it is quiet and in the presence of competing talkers and other environmental noise. When observing these changes, it is necessary to determine whether a child's decreased ability to perform in noise is due to diminished auditory abilities or to a more generalized attention-deficit disorder. Formal testing under standardized conditions can help differentiate between these problems. Because of the wide range of individual abilities to resist background noise, the examiner should have adequate normative data with adequate numbers of subjects to define ranges of performance in a normal population for the test conditions used. Only a few commercial tests have adequate normative data available. Informal observations of figure-ground performance must be made very carefully since the situation is subjective.

Tests of auditory figure ground are usually administered using tape-recorded speech in the presence of competing background speech or environmental noise. The test must be recorded with the speech at a favorable signal-to-noise (S/N) ratio or the test becomes a masking study that measures auditory closure. Tests that use competing speech, ranging from a single talker to a speech babble background, are preferable to those that use white or "speech" noise.

Auditory Discrimination. Auditory discrimination can be assessed at many levels. For example, when a child has repeated a monosyllable word correctly, the child has demonstrated an ability to discriminate speech sounds at the imitative level. When syllables or word pairs are presented orally (e.g., the Wepman Auditory Discrimination Test[20]) and the child is asked to report whether they were exactly the same or different, another level of discrimination is introduced. In that example, the child must understand the concept of same and different, and a cognitive aspect to auditory discrimination is introduced. When children can repeat words correctly but cannot tell whether the sounds are the same or different,

there is a cognitive problem and not a problem of auditory discrimination. Another test difficulty is that there is no assurance that the child is listening to all parts of the word pairs and not simply to the initial, middle, or final part.

Some tests of auditory discrimination require the child to point to a picture in response to stimulus words. In some cases, the pictures represent words that are phonetically similar. The difficulty with any picture-pointing test is that it is cross-modality, requiring visual recognition of all of the pictures and an auditory-visual association between word and picture. Because these tests rely on visual perception and auditory-visual integration, it is difficult to attribute any breakdown to auditory discrimination in the narrow sense. Nevertheless, because they are common behaviors asked of a child, an inability to respond appropriately to a picture-pointing task indicates a possible delay in the child's development.

Another level of "auditory discrimination" testing is demonstrated by the Lindamood Auditory Conceptualization test.[21] In this test, the child is asked to associate sounds with colored blocks, and to manipulate them to demonstrate their ability to discriminate one speech sound from another; and their ability to perceive the number, order, and sameness or difference of speech sounds in different sequences. This highly cognitive task is on the opposite end of the continuum of auditory discrimination abilities that range from imitation to cognition. In the assessment of auditory discrimination abilities, the examiner should determine the level at which the child's auditory processing abilities break down.

Auditory Closure. Auditory closure is the ability to understand the whole word or message when part is missing or missed. Being a linguistically based cognitive ability, auditory closure can be assessed using tasks that require the child to fill in missing parts of a word. One example is the auditory closure subtest of the Illinois Test of Psycholinguist Abilities (ITPA).[22] In this test the child fills in missing parts of a word. For example, the examiner will say "airpla   ," or "ea_ter _unny"; the correct responses are airplane and Easter bunny.

A different approach to testing auditory closure is to eliminate certain frequency components of spoken words by electronic low-pass filtering. Eliminating the high frequencies of speech results in a signal that sounds muffled. Research has shown that low-pass filtered speech effectively separates children with learning problems from those who are normally achieving.[23] According to Costello,[24] depressed scores on the Central Auditory Abilities Test, which contains a filtered speech subtest, are often found in children with language and/or learning problems.

Auditory Blending. Sometimes called auditory synthesis or phonemic synthesis, this auditory ability is considered by many to be a fundamental requisite to learning to read by a phonic method.[25,26] According to Bannatyne,[27] a child may sound out the phonemic units of a word successfully, but may be unable to approximate a normally spoken word. Bannatyne states that auditory blending and closure abilities are significantly correlated. Several standardized tests assess auditory blending abilities by presenting isolated sounds that make up a word.[22,28,29] The child must combine those sounds to tell what the word is. Examples of stimuli are: f-oot (foot), t-oa-st (toast), and k-e-tch-u-p (ketchup).

Auditory Analysis. The ability to identify phonemes, syllables, or morphemes embedded in words requires both auditory processing and linguistic processing abilities.[30] Some diagnostic reading tests contain subtests of auditory analysis abilities.[31,32] The Auditory Analysis Test[33] requires the subject to form a new word when a phoneme or syllable is removed from a larger word. For example, gate without "g" is ate, trail without "t" is rail, glow without "l" is go.

Auditory Memory. Like auditory discrimination, memory exists at many levels including perceptual or echoic memory, short-term memory, long-term memory, and episodic memory. Many parents do not recognize these several levels, and it is difficult for them to reconcile the fact that a child can remember an incident from the distant past, but cannot remember a spelling lesson from the previous evening's practice to the next day's test. Therefore, innumerable tests have been designed to assess auditory memory using all kinds of speech stimuli from phonemes to sentences, paragraphs, and short stories. Two aspects of memory that are typically assessed are memory span[34,35] and sequential memory.[22,36] The Memory for Content subtest of the GFW Auditory Memory Test[37] uses a different test approach. A picture-pointing task is used in which the child is asked to indicate the two pictures that were *not* named.

Comment. In these paragraphs, different auditory abilities have been discussed as if they each occurred in isolation. It should be clear to the reader that while it may be necessary to describe the components of auditory perception, it is virtually impossible to actually test auditory abilities independent of each other. A number of specialists have noted that each of these skills overlap, and that they are inseparable.[38–40] Since the first edition of this volume, investigators of language and learning disabilities have shifted their attention from *auditory perceptual skills* to *higher-order cognitive strategies*. In so doing, the listing of auditory processing abilities as described here has fallen into research disrepute. Nevertheless, investigation and description of auditory processing abilities in a child who is having problems with language and learning continue to be important parts of the process necessary for developing an effective remediation program. This approach will continue to be important as clinicians adopt the point of view that some combination of bottom-up and top-down strategies, discussed in the next section, are necessary for development of language and for learning.

Dilemmas of the Auditory Processing Test Battery

There is presently a great deal of controversy about whether the specific auditory skills, as they have been defined, form the basis of learning language, or whether these skills are acquired as a result of having learned the language. Some experts state that auditory perception is fundamental to learning language, and that auditory processing deficits cause disorders in areas of language, reading, and learning.[41] These experts further state that auditory perception can be readily broken into specific deficits that are amenable to training,[30,42] that a hierarchy of auditory perceptual skills exists with processes moving from simple to complex, and that remediation should follow the same order.[21,30,43–45] Others[46–49] feel that poor performance on auditory skills may result from a language disorder, since these children do not have sufficient linguistic, semantic, and cognitive skills to enable them to develop strategies for dealing with the auditory tasks.

It is important to discuss these different positions, because the selection of remedial techniques will depend directly upon which philosophy is adopted. If one holds that specific auditory deficits, such as auditory closure, auditory blending, and so forth, are responsible for the language deficit, then remediation would proceed via training of those specific skills on a hierarchical basis. If, on the other hand, one takes the position that central auditory problems result from a language disorder, then remediation would proceed strictly on a language basis, in which the therapist would use intervention strategies such as those described in Chapter 16.

A point about measurement of specific auditory skills is that many of the tests are language-based. That is, in order to perform on these tests, the child must have basic language skills; the more advanced the child's language, the better the child will perform. In the discussion of auditory discrimination, it was observed that the child needs to understand same-different concepts in order to perform the task. Similarly, all of the following are language-based: (1) the Flowers-Costello CAA Sentence Completion task, which is a cognitive-based language task ("On Halloween we carved a _____."); (2) the *auditory closure* tasks (tele_____one as telephone); and (3) the *auditory analysis* task (gate without g is ate). Certainly, the GFW auditory memory test requires more than basic auditory abilities when a child is asked to point to the two pictures that were not named. And in the GFW Auditory Discrimination Test,[50] when the word stimulus is "big," the correct response is to point to the picture of the elephant and mouse, which is a cognitive response.

To assess auditory abilities, therefore, it is critical to evaluate each test for prelinguistic and linguistic or precognitive and cognitive language content. The brief analysis of auditory perceptual tests just presented identified a number of language factors that would affect results. A prelinguistic task is one in which a stimulus sound is simply imitated, without the need to understand it, define it, or associate a visual object with it. For example, to repeat the nonsense syllables "ba" and "da" is the simplest form of imitation and is a prelinguistic skill, but to know whether these two sounds are the same or different requires higher linguistic competence. Repetition of syllables or words heard in the presence of a background noise at a favorable S/N ratio is a low-level

cognitive imitative speech task. When the intensity of the noise is equal to or exceeds the intensity of the speech, direct masking occurs, and the task becomes a higher-level cognitive task of auditory closure. Repeating nonsense syllables or simple words presented simultaneously to opposite ears is a low-level language task. Repeating a string of unrelated syllables, digits, or words is a simple linguistic memory task; but remembering groups of related words becomes a complex cognitive task, since the person is required to see relationships among words, develop categories, and through a cognitive process increase recall abilities.

This discussion is not intended to deny categorically that there may be children who fail to learn because of fundamental auditory processing disorders. Its purposes are to raise issues of cause and effect and to avoid classifying language disorders as deficits in basic auditory perceptual processes when the task used in assessing auditory processes is actually a language task.

In fact, while in the past, there was a lack of well-documented examples of children with auditory perceptual rather than primary linguistic-cognitive problems, that situation is beginning to be remedied. There is "mounting evidence of auditory perceptual impairments in children with language disabilities."[51] In the 1970s, research on fundamental auditory processing abilities in children was conducted by Tallal. Her research findings indicated that basic temporal processing deficits could play a critical role in the speech and language disorders of children, and that an auditory rate processing deficit is the primary deficit in specifically language-impaired children.[52,53] These results are similar to the findings of prolonged auditory fusion times for children with language and reading disorders compared to normals.[54] Other behavioral research from the 1970s indicated problems in dynamic auditory localization in children with language learning disorders,[55] difficulty in processing time-compressed speech,[56,57] difficulty in processing speech in the presence of competing background noise,[58] difficulty in processing filtered speech,[23] difficulty in processing competing speech materials,[59] and problems in perceptual memory for information presented through the auditory system.[60] There continues to be a great need for basic research in using psychophysical techniques to learn more about auditory perceptual deficits in children and adults.

The Audiologic Evaluation

A second and very different approach to assess auditory processing abilities is used by audiologists. This approach evaluates the child's ability to respond under different conditions of signal distortion or competition. The principle of this approach assumes that a normal listener can tolerate mild distortions of speech and still understand it. A listener with an auditory processing deficit will encounter difficulty with the distorted speech due to added internal "distortion."[61] Results of these tests can be used to infer the developmental status of the child's central auditory nervous system, and to help determine whether auditory perceptual problems may form a basis for language and/or reading problems. Although the cause-and-effect relationship between auditory perception and language has not been established, there is reason to believe that growth of language function relates to progressive maturation of the cerebral cortex.[62] When it is shown that prelinguistic auditory processing abilities are poorly developed, the child may not have the neurologic potential necessary to organize and develop a linguistic system, or development may be slower than normal. The more severe the auditory abnormalities, the greater the effect on acquisition of language. When auditory abnormalities occur in combination with abnormalities among other sensory systems, or when associations among visual, tactile, or other sensory systems are not established, the effect is more devastating, and the child will have difficulty in overall learning.

Diagnostic auditory tests used in assessing developmental integrity or maturation of the auditory nervous system include *masking level differences* (MLD), binaural fusion of filtered speech, competing sentence tests, the Staggered Spondaic Word (SSW) test, competing word tests, dichotic consonant vowel (CV) identification tests, auditory figure ground testing, testing for auditory fusion time, and time-compressed speech tests. The Pediatric Speech Intelligibility Test[63] is a well-designed and normed diagnostic test that can be administered to children as young as three and four years of age. An in-depth description of each of these tests, including the stimulus, response, and interpretation of results, is beyond the scope of this chapter, but is available elsewhere.[64,65]

There are a few screening tests available to identify children with auditory processing disorders. These tests were designed to be administered in the schools, and do not require two-channel diagnostic audiometers. Tests introduced in the 1970s include the Goldman-Fristoe-Woodcock Test of Auditory Discrimination[50] and the Flowers-Costello Test of Central Auditory Abilities.[66] More recently McCroskey[57] introduced the Witchita Auditory Processing Test that presents several conditions of time-compressed/time-expanded speech. The SCAN Screening Test for Auditory Processing Disorders[2] has three subtests, including filtered words, auditory figure ground, and competing words. SCAN was normed on 1034 children between 3 and 11 years of age. In addition to mean and standard deviation of subtest and composite test results, the SCAN normative data includes standard scores, percentile ranks, age equivalents, and standard score confidence levels. Many of the available central auditory tests have a poor normative data base. The author of SCAN hopes that it will serve as an example for others who endeavor to develop auditory test batteries in the future.

As a group, these tests all share certain characteristics. For example, they are applicable only after the emergence of language, since they require either verbal repetition of syllables, words, or sentences or pointing to pictures that represent the stimulus words. Most of the tests show substantial maturational effects. No age-related data are reported for the MLD and binaural fusion tests. Generally, if given to children at early ages, the results of these tests are highly variable, with average performance improving remarkably up to 12 years of age. By about 12 years of age, the auditory system of normal children has matured to the point where their responses approximate those of adult listeners. Children with speech, language reading, and learning problems have been reported to perform poorly on these tests, although some children with language or reading problems yield normal scores.

The use of these tests is increasing, although there is a great deal to learn about interpretation of obtained results. In an attempt to place central auditory tests into perspective, the following factors should be considered:

(*1*) The test results describe the maturation level of the central auditory pathways; and through longitudinal studies on a given child, they demonstrate development of central auditory abilities.
(*2*) The test results provide data to document the neurologic origin presumed to exist in children with specific learning disabilities.
(*3*) The test results help to identify progressive neurologic disease.
(*4*) The test results can be used to assess the effect of medication on auditory abilities.
(*5*) The test results can aid in ruling out abnormalities of the central auditory pathways as contributing to a language-learning problem.
(*6*) The test results help to describe whether cerebral dominance for language has occurred.
(*7*) The test results describe whether the auditory channel is "weak" or "strong," and whether classroom, tutoring, or remedial material should be modified to account for auditory processing abilities.
(*8*) The tests are useful in research on auditory processing abilities.

Tests of central auditory function cannot be expected to indicate specific language, learning, or reading deficits. To describe these specific problems, the examiner needs to administer tests that are appropriate for that purpose. The central auditory test battery does provide information that can be used to develop remedial strategies for language-learning disordered children. These strategies include both classroom management suggestions to teachers and parents and direct intervention techniques that are generally administered by speech-language pathologists.

Case Histories 1, 2, and 3 presented in this chapter detail both the central test results obtained on three different children and their implications.

IMPLICATIONS FOR THE FUTURE

It is impossible to consider the subject of auditory processing and language disorders without feeling that there continues to be a need for information on many basic questions. We still do not "know" whether auditory perceptual abilities are fundamental to language disorders, or whether auditory processing disorders exist as symptoms of a language disorder. The interest in bottom-up or top-down theories of information processing (to the exclusion of the other) has diminished somewhat over time, possibly because many have come to understand the process as some combination of the two.

Those who are attempting to understand auditory perception and language appear to be faced with the same set of problems as those who are attempting to understand reading problems. In a textbook on dyslexia,[67] there is lengthy discussion of problems in defining terminology. The authors also present

---

Case history #1. Julian was referred for central auditory testing at the age of 9 years, 2 months. His educational history revealed that his "verbal abilities indicated average intelligence, but he had severe problems in reading and writing." He was also below grade level in math skills. He was reported to have problems concentrating on tasks that required independent work. He was also delayed in developing a hand preference. Julian was referred for testing to determine whether he had auditory perceptual deficits that were contributing to his learning problems.

Results of auditory testing indicated normal findings on the Wepman and Morency Auditory Memory Span and Auditory Sequential Memory tests, and the Wepman Auditory Discrimination tests. He had normal results for speech-in-noise testing and filtered speech testing. The Competing Sentence subtest of the Willeford battery was 100% in both ears, and the Staggered Spondaic Word test indicated normal right ear effects, with raw score results in the normal range.

These results indicated that Julian's auditory development and abilities were completely normal, and that any academic problems were unrelated to auditory factors.

Case history #2.   Charlotte was referred for central auditory testing at 13 years, 6 months of age. She had a long history of speech and language problems, academic failure, and repeated chronic middle ear infections. Routine hearing tests revealed a 25 to 30 dB conductive loss in both ears, which was consistent with her medical history. At the time of the test, it was realized that the conductive loss could affect the results of the central auditory battery, but the tests were given because the parents had travelled a great distance for the tests.

The outcome of the central test battery indicated normal speech-in-noise test results at +6 dB S/N ratio. The Auditory Memory, Sequential Memory, and Auditory Discrimination tests all yielded low raw scores that fell below the adequacy threshold for 8 year olds. The staggered Spondaic Word test results were similar to norms obtained on a normal 6 year old. Finally, the Competing Sentence subtest of the Willeford battery achieved a 100% score in the right ear and 0% score in the left ear—a result that would not be expected beyond 7 years of age.

The central auditory test results obtained on this particular child are difficult to interpret because of the interacting factors that are present. In the first place, Charlotte's conductive hearing loss was of sufficient magnitude to have caused a language-learning problem. In addition, the abnormal central test findings could have resulted from the simple presence of the conductive hearing loss at the time of the test or could have been caused by chronic sensory deprivation from middle ear disease that caused a lack of maturation of central auditory pathways. The poor memory and discrimination test results reflect her language-learning problems. The net result of audiologic test findings indicates that Charlotte has significant peripheral hearing problems that require medical attention and probable central perceptual deficits that are undoubtedly related to her language-learning status.

Case history #3.   Martin was 7 years, 11 months old when he was referred for central auditory testing because of language-learning problems. Martin had mild-to-severe asthma attacks three to four times per year, several allergies, and occasional ear infections when he was younger. Martin was cooperative, and had a WISC full scale IQ of 103 and similar verbal and performance scores. He was delayed in speech and language acquisition and spoke no recognizable words until the age of 3. The speech pathologist reported that Martin had problems in sequential production, arrhythmic rate, word-finding and word-ordering, and in omitting language markers. Test results were normal on the Carrow test of auditory compre-hension of language, but below the average for 6 year olds on the Carrow elicited language inventory. His lowest score on the ITPA was in auditory memory (scaled score of 28), but other scaled scores were normal.

Results of the hearing test indicated normal peripheral hearing levels. Central auditory test findings indicated that his performance was at the level expected of a 6 year old. Repeated testing was done over the next two years with a battery of tests, including speech-in-noise, Dichotic CV identification, the SSW, the competing sentence subtest of the Willeford battery, and Auditory Memory Span and Sequential Memory tasks. The results of repeated tests showed that his central auditory test scores improved, indicating continued maturation of his central auditory pathways. At the age of 10, Martin's auditory test scores were approximately two years below his age norms. Meanwhile, his spontaneous speech showed an increase in the types and complexity of sentence structure, sentence use incorporating more word units, a better sense of time sequence when describing events, and self-correction of noun-verb agreement. His school achievement also progressed.

These test results indicate that Martin has had apparent delayed auditory pathway matura-tion with concurrent language problems. No evidence here suggests that one caused the other. There is evidence to suggest that with continued speech and language therapy and special attention in school, Martin can be expected to continue to develop and his language-learning problems can be expected to be resolved.

theories of both reading deficits in relation to perceptual deficits and deficits in language and verbal skills that are similar to those discussed here in relation to audition. In addition, material is presented on psychological factors, genetic aspects, and prediction and remediation of dyslexia—concerns that are relevant to auditory processing problems but were not developed here.

One would expect to find parallels between auditory and visual perceptual problems, since both sensory systems feed information to the same brain. It is highly probable that similar answers will be found for problems in both areas.

In the end, those questions may be of interest only to those involved in research to understand and explain how these systems interact. They are probably of little immediate concern to the clinician who is faced with a case load of children with auditory and language disorders. Teachers and clinicians who work with children who are not performing at their potential level must learn as much as they can about concepts such as those presented in this chapter. They need to select information that is relevant and helpful for them in working with their children. They must be critical when using test instruments offered on the commercial market. They need to analyze the tasks involved in the tests, and to interpret the results carefully. Normative data should be accepted only when its applicability is established for the specific population of children with which educators are involved.

Most of all, the teacher and clinician must be careful about accepting simplistic explanations about complex and poorly understood behaviors. A great deal of progress has been made in our understanding of these problems, but the search continues.

REFERENCES

1. ACLD Newsbriefs: *ACLD Description: Specific Learning Disabilities*, No. 166 (Sept-Oct 1986).
2. Keith RW: SCAN: A Screening Test for Auditory Processing Disorders (San Antonio, Psychology Corp., 1986).
3. Matejcek Z: Specific learning disabilities. *Bull of the Orton Society*, 27 (1977), 7–25.
4. Benson DF: Is dyslexia a neurologic disorder? In Brockhurst R, Boruchoff S, Hutchinson B, et al, eds: *Controversy in Ophthalmology* (Phila-

delphia: W.B. Saunders Co., 1977), pp 796–797.
5. Brutten M, Richardson SO, Mangel C: *Something's Wrong With My Child* (New York: Harcourt Brace Jovanovich, 1973), p 29.
6. Rampp DL, Plummer BA: A child in jeopardy: Medical and educational profiles of children with auditory processing learning disabilities. Read before the Sixth Annual Meeting of the Society for Ear, Nose and Throat Advances in Children, Santa Barbara, CA, December 6–9, 1978.
7. Cohen RL: Auditory skills and the communicative process, in Keith RW, ed: *Seminars in Speech, Language and Hearing* (New York: Thieme-Stratton, Inc., 1980), chap 2.
8. Myklebust H: *Auditory Disorders in School Children: A Manual for Differential Diagnosis* (New York: Grune and Stratton, 1954), p 14.
9. Holm VA, Kunze LH: Effect of chronic otitis media on language and speech development. *Pediatrics*, 43 (1969), 833–839.
10. Schlieper A, Kisilevsky H, Mattingly S, Yorke L: Mild conductive hearing loss and language development: A one year followup study. *Develop and Behavior Leds*, 6 (1985), 65–68.
11. Brandes P, Ehinger D: The effects of early middle ear pathology on auditory perception and academic achievement. *JSHD*, 46 (1981), 250–257.
12. Welsh L, Welsh J, Healy M: Effect of sound deprivation on central hearing. *Laryngoscope*, 93 (1983), 1569–1575.
13. Sak R, Ruben R: Recurrent middle ear effusion in childhood: Implications of temporary deprivation for language and learning. *Ann Otol* 90 (1981), 546–551.
14. Hanson DG, Ulvested RF: Otitis media and child development of speech, language and education. *Ann Otol Rhinol Laryngol*, suppl 60, 88, pt 2 (1979).
15. Lehmann MD, Charron K, Kummer A, et al: The effects of chronic middle ear effusion on speech and language development: A descriptive study. *Pediatr J Otorhingolaryngol*, 1, pt 2 (1979), 137–144.
16. Rosenberg PE: Case history: The first test, in Katz J: *Handbook of Clinical Audiology*, ed 2 (Baltimore: Williams and Wilkins Co., 1978), chap 7.
17. Katz J, Struckmann S: A case history for children, in Katz J: *Handbook of Clinical Audiology*, ed 1 (Baltimore: Williams and Wilkins Co., 1972), chap 25.
18. Lasky E, Cox C: Auditory processing and language interaction, in Lasky E, Katz J, eds: *Central Auditory Processing Disorders* (Baltimore: University Park Press, 1983), chap 13.
19. Keith RW, Krafft K: The auditory continuous performance test: Research in progress.
20. Wepman JM: *Auditory Discrimination Test* (Los

Angeles: Western Psychological Services, 1973).

21. Lindamood CH, Lindamood PC: *Lindamood Auditory Conceptualization Test (Revised)* (Hingham MA: Teaching Resources Corp., 1975).

22. Kirk S, McCarthy J, Kirk W: *Illinois Test of Psycholinguistic Abilities* (Urbana: University of Illinois Press, 1968).

23. Keith RW, Farrer S: Filtered word testing in the assessment of children with central auditory disorders. *Ear and Hearing*, 12 (1981), 267–269.

24. Costello MR: Evaluation of auditory behavior of children using the Flowers-Costello test of central auditory abilities, in Keith RW, ed: *Central Auditory Dysfunction* (New York: Grune and Stratton, 1977), chap 8.

25. Katz J: Phonemic Synthesis, in Lasky E, Katz J, eds: *Central Auditory Processing Disorders* (Baltimore: University Park Press, 1983).

26. Katz J, Harmon C: Phonemic synthesis: Testing and training, in Keith RW: *Central Auditory and Language Disorders in Children* (San Diego: College Hill Press, 1981).

27. Bannatyne A: *Language, Reading and Learning Disabilities* (Springfield: Charles C. Thomas, 1971).

28. Roswell FG, Chall JS: *Roswell-Chall Auditory Blending Test* (New York: Essay Press, 1963).

29. Goldman R, Fristoe M, Woodcock R: *GFW Sound Symbol Tests: Blending* (Circle Pines, MN: American Guidance Service Inc., 1974).

30. Wiig E, Semel EM: *Language Disabilities in Children and Adolescents* (Columbus: Charles E. Merritt, 1976).

31. Karlsen B, Madden R, Gardner F: *Stanford Diagnostic Reading Test* (New York: Harcourt Brace Jovanovich, 1966).

32. Gates AI, McKillop AS: *Gates-McKillop Reading Diagnostic Tests* (New York: Columbia University Teacher's College Press, 1962).

33. Rosner J, Simon D: The auditory analysis test. *J Learn Disabil*, 4 (1971), 384–392.

34. Wepman JM, Morency A: *Auditory Memory Span Test* (Los Angeles: Western Psychological Services, 1973).

35. Wechsler D: *Wechsler Intelligence Scale for Children* (New York: Psychological Corp., 1949).

36. Wepman JM, Morency A: *The Auditory Sequential Memory Test* (Los Angeles: Western Psychological Services, 1975).

37. Goldman R, Fristoe M, Woodcock R: *GFW Auditory Memory Tests* (Circle Pines, MN: American Guidance Service Inc., 1974).

38. Williamson DG, Alexander R: *Central Auditory Abilities*. (Minneapolis: Maico Audiological Library Series 13, 1970).

39. Sanders DA: *Auditory Perception of Speech* (Englewood Cliffs, NJ: Prentice-Hall, 1977).

40. Witkin, BR: Auditory perception. Implications for language development. *Language, Speech and Hearing Science*, 4 (1971), 31–52.

41. Rampp D: *Proceedings of the Memphis State University First Annual Symposium on Auditory Processing and Learning Disabilities* (Las Vegas, 1972).

42. Butler KG: Auditory perceptual processing and dysfunction, in *Sixteenth International Congress of Logopedics and Phoniatrics*. Interlaken, 1974 (Basel: Karger, 1976), pp 65–69.

43. Kirk S, Kirk W: Psycholinguistic learning disabilities, in *Diagnosis and Remediation* (Urbana: University of Illinois Press, 1971).

44. Butler KG: Auditory perceptual training. *Acta Symbolica*, 3 (1972), 123–125.

45. Lasky E: An approach to auditory processing. *Acta Symbolica*, 4 (1973), 51–62.

46. Sanders DA: *Auditory Perception of Speech* (Englewood Cliffs, NJ: Prentice-Hall, 1977), p 187.

47. Rees N: Auditory processing factors in learning disorders: A View from Procrustes' bed. *J Speech Dis*, 38 (1973), 304–315.

48. Rees N: The speech pathologist and the reading process. *Asha*, 16 (1974), 155–158.

49. Marquardt T, Saxman J: Language comprehension and auditory discrimination in articulation deficient kindergarten children. *J Speech Hear Res*, 15 (1972), 382–389.

50. Goldman R, Fristoe M, Woodcock RW: *Test of Auditory Discrimination* (Circle Pines, MN: American Guidance Service Inc., 1970).

51. Tallal P: Neuropsychological research approaches to the study of central auditory processing. *Human Comm Canada*, 9 (1985), 17–22.

52. Tallal P: Auditory perceptual factors in language and learning disabilities, in Knights R, Bakker D, eds: *The Neuropsychology of Learning Disabilities* (Baltimore: University Park Press, 1976), p 320.

53. Stark R, Tallal P, Mellits E: Expressive language and perceptual and motor abilities in language impaired children. *Human Comm Canada*, 9 (1985), 23–48.

54. McCroskey R, Kidder H: Auditory fusion in learning disabled, reading disabled and normal children. *J Learning Dis*, 13 (1980), 69–76.

55. Devens J, Hoyer E, McCroskey R: Dynamic auditory localization by normal and learning disability children. *J Amer Auditory Soc*, 3 (1978), 172–178.

56. Beasley D, Freeman B: Time altered speech as a measure of central auditory processing, in Keith RW, ed: *Central Auditory Dysfunction* (New York: Grune and Stratton, 1977).

57. McCroskey R: *Wichita Auditory Processing Test* (Tulsa: Modern Education Corp., 1984).

58. Cherry R, Kroger B: Selective auditory attention abilities of learning disabled and normal achieving children. *J Learning Dis*, 3 No. 4 (1983), 202–205.

59. Keith RW: Special issue: Dichotic listening tests. *Ear and Hearing*, 4, No. 6 (1983).

60. Butler K: Language processing, "selective attention and mnemonic strategies," in Lasky E, Katz J, ed: *Central Auditory Processing Disorders* (Baltimore: University Park Press, 1983).

61. Teatini GP: Speech audiometry, in Rojskjaer C, ed: *Second Danavox Symposium* (Odense, Denmark, 1970).

62. Chase RA: Neurological aspects of language disorders in children, in Irwin J, Marge M, eds: *Principles of Childhood Language Disabilities* (Englewood Cliffs, NJ: Prentice-Hall, 1972).

63. Jerger S: Evaluation of central auditory function in children, in Keith RW, ed: *Central Auditory and Language Disorders in Children* (San Diego: College Hill Press, 1981).

64. Keith RW: *Central Auditory Dysfunction* (New York: Grune and Stratton, 1977).

65. Keith RW: Speech, language, and hearing, in Lass NJ, McReynolds LV, Northern JL, et al (Philadelphia: W.B. Saunders Co., 1980), chap 27.

66. Flowers A, Costello R: *Flowers-Costello Test of Central Auditory Abilities* (Dearborn, MI: Perceptual Learning Systems, 1970).

67. Benton AL, Pearl D: *Dyslexia: An Appraisal of Current Knowledge* (New York: Oxford University Press, 1978).

5 | THE PSYCHO-EDUCATIONAL ASSESSMENT OF HEARING IMPAIRED CHILDREN

Robert E. Kretschmer and Stephen P. Quigley

At the heart of most direct services provided by the school psychologist are the psycho-educational evaluation and the *diagnostic-prescriptive* process. The goals of this chapter are to provide relevant definitions of terms connected with the notions of *evaluation* and *the diagnostic process*, and to discuss topics related to the assumptions and prerequisites of conducting any evaluation, especially that of a hearing impaired student. Issues related to the identification-placement process and the application of various evaluation materials and results to the programming of individual children will also be addressed.

THE DIAGNOSTIC PROCESS

The term *diagnostic process* as used by practicing psychologists appears to have taken on two meanings or connotations. The first of these relates to the entire sequence of events associated with a handicapped child moving through the educational system from the point when a handicapping condition is suspected to the actual placement and programming for a child. A second, more limited meaning of this term refers to the sequence of events that any given individual professional within this larger framework goes through to arrive at his or her own conclusions about the functional status of the child suspected of having a handicapping condition.

When the diagnostic process is thought of as a movement through the educational placement and programming system, the sequence of events generally involves: (*1*) the screening of individual children to identify those who possibly need special educational consideration; (*2*) the actual certification by one or more specific professionals of the disabling conditions; (*3*) the verification by a team of individuals, including the parents and/or their representatives, of one or more handicapping conditions; (*4*) the making and delineating of various placement and programmatic decisions, if any are required; and finally, (*5*) the actual implementation of the prescribed program and the subsequent follow-through monitoring evaluations, as required by law.[1]

Although many severely and profoundly hearing impaired children will have been certified and verified as handicapped before they enter school, they typically will still go through the diagnostic process in order to be placed within the educational system. Many mildly and moderately hearing impaired children, children with high-frequency hearing losses, or children with unilateral hearing losses, may initially be identified through auditory screening procedures. Other forms of screening commonly used to identify handicapped children are visual screening through the use of such instruments as the Snellen Chart, developmental screening during kindergarten or first grade *round-up*, and schoolwide achievement testing programs. Thus, one definition of *screening* is the use of any systematic behavioral observation, checklist, rating scale, or objective test to initially establish the possibility of a disability (see Chapter 3).

Once a child has been screened and a potential handicapping condition is suspected, a sequence of events is set into motion. Usually, a referral is made to those individuals within the school system who are responsible for making sure that all the necessary information pertinent to the resolution of the particular child's educational problems is gathered. This would include collecting a social and family history, obtaining informed consent for further diagnostic testing, and scheduling the necessary evaluations with one or more professionals.

The ultimate goal of the diagnostic process is to obtain the necessary information to make appropriate decisions regarding placement and subsequent programming of individual children. Ideally and legally, this process should be performed by a team, which would include the participation of the parents. Deciding whether a child is handicapped and in need of special educational consideration is a group process; a handicapping condition is verified by the documented diagnosis of the disabilities or handicaps made by a *multidisciplinary team* (M-team) after reviewing and synthesizing all the pertinent background, observations, and test materials collected on a child. Although the team of individuals, including the classroom teacher and the parents, verifies the salient handicapping conditions, individual members of the team may certify specific disabilities or handicapping conditions appropriate to their professional specialties. Each professional, at the conclusion of his or her evaluation, generally presents a series of recommendations. The *individual educational program* (IEP) is the composite of the recommendations of all the M-team members with regard to educational placement and programming. These recommendations should be written in behavioral terms, and should address all major aspects of development and the child's specific strengths and weaknesses. In addition to specific recommendations, time frames and performance criteria should be specified, as well as the person who is to implement each recommendation.

ASSUMPTIONS UNDERLYING TESTING

A number of assumptions underlie any evaluation process. Newland,[2] in considering the case of psychological testing, cites six such assumptions. The first is that the person administering the test is properly trained to do so. Any violation of this assumption could yield results of questionable validity.

Recently, several national and regional surveys of psychological services for hearing impaired individuals have been conducted.[3–5] Each of these studies have indicated that the majority of the providers of these services do not have formal or special preparation to work with deaf persons. For example, in 1974, Levine[3] in a national survey found that only 10% of her respondents were employed on a full-time basis to work with deaf persons, and only

17% of the sample had specialized training to do so. By 1981, there had been a slight increase in the percent of full-time service providers (21%) but little change in the fact that relatively few providers of psychological services to deaf persons had specialized preparation in the area of hearing impairment (15%).[4] In addition, in the Levine[3] study, 90% of the sample was unfamiliar with or poorly skilled in manual communications, even though approximately 65% of the clients relied on or used manual forms of communication in combination with other forms. According to Spragins et al,[4] however, the situation had improved somewhat in that seven years later, 30% of these service providers indicated that they had average to above-average manual communication skill. As might be expected, it was also found that a greater percentage of full-time service providers (83%), particularly those with special training in the area of hearing impairment, rated themselves as having average to above-average skills as opposed to part-time service providers (16%). Based upon the data provided by McQuaid and Alovisetti,[5] regional differences may exist—since these researchers found a greater percentage of full-time service providers (54%) in the Northeast, and a far greater percentage (34%) of individuals who had specialized training and used total communication (71%).

The issue of communication difficulty, and the possible test bias resulting from failure to understand the directions of a test, are at the heart of a number of Furth's studies[6] and a study by Ray.[7] They, as well as Vernon and Brown,[8] note that failure to perform on a task may simply be a function of not understanding the directions, rather than an inherent disability. It is therefore essential that the examiner have experience with deaf clients and be proficient in all forms of communication used by deaf people.

Those tests that have been standardized on hearing impaired persons have usually taken into account the problem of communication and have provided for standardized instructions and procedures. For example, the Hiskey-Nebraska Test of Learning Aptitude has two sets of instructions, one verbal and one pantomime, and the Stanford Achievement Test-Hearing-Impaired edition[9] has a series of special instructions and practice items for each battery level. Unfortunately, most of the tests that have not been standardized on hearing impaired people have verbal directions. Some notable exceptions are the Leiter International Performance Scale and the Chicago Nonverbal Examination, which have essentially panto- mime directions. (The references for all the tests can be found in either Salvia and Yssel- dyke[10] or Buros.[11])

Investigations into the influence of various forms of test administration and modification for the Wechsler Intelligence Scale for Children- Revised (WISC-R) Performance Scale have been conducted by Sullivan[12] and Courtney et al[13]; and Ray[7] investigated the influence of a standardized method of administration on how hearing impaired children performed on this same test. Courtney et al found that when subjects were administered the WISC-R Perfor- mance Scale exclusively by means of panto- mime gestures, the resulting effect was a 5 intelligence quotient (IQ) point decrement (resulting IQ = 90) when compared to the Anderson and Sissco[14] norms for hearing im- paired children and youths. Likewise, Sulli- van,[12] in comparing pantomime, visual aids, and total communication test administration modifications (using a residential school sam- ple of children with genetic, questionable, and multiply handicapped etiologies), found an even greater decrement when using panto- mime gestures (IQ = 88). Although the use of visual aids resulted in slightly better perfor- mance, they—with the use of pantomime di- rections—still resulted in as much as a 15 point poorer performance than when total communication was used.

Ray attempted to investigate the possibility that the Performance Scale scatter profile, of- ten associated with the Wechsler Scales for hearing impaired children, was a function of misunderstanding the task, due to certain com- munication variables. Although he was not able to demonstrate this, he did provide the field with a standardized method of adminis- tration for the WISC-R, which can be used with any hearing impaired child, whether the child relies on oral communication, simultaneous communication, or gestures/pantomime; and he was able to eliminate the typical overall decrement associated with most forms of test modification. These studies and tests may help in meeting the spirit of the law, which requires that the child be evaluated in his native lan- guage or mode of communication unless it is clearly not feasible to do so.[1]

The second assumption noted by Newland is that any test only samples behavior to some statistically satisfactory degree of adequacy. By this, it is meant that the test should be both reliable and valid. These two terms are dis- cussed in detail in Chapter 3. Briefly, a reliable test is one that yields similar scores for individ- uals after repeated administrations over time. Validity, on the other hand, is the degree to which a test actually measures what it purports to measure. A valid test by definition must be a reliable test, but the reverse is not true. These notions of reliability and validity refer to both norm-referenced as well as criterion-refer- enced tests. Thus, even teacher-made tests should demonstrate reliability and validity.

The third assumption underlying psycho- logical testing is that the individuals on whom a particular test is to be used have been ex- posed to learning experiences or accultura- tion comparable to the original norming group. This particular point addresses itself directly to the issue of test bias. That is, a test can only be considered valid in relationship to particu- lar individuals or groups of individuals. What may be valid for one group of individuals may not be valid for another group. This notion of test bias has been the point of much discussion and the source of much litigation, which has finally resulted in certain statements being made within the federal mandate governing the rights of all handicapped children.[1] This mandate has stated that information concern- ing cultural and social background, among a number of other variables, must be taken into account when making placement decisions and when planning for any handicapped child. Newland[2] has suggested that validity with re- spect to acculturation is probably not an all-or- nothing matter, but that there are degrees of validity. The mere fact that a test is normed on a population or that certain subcultures were included in the norming process does not guarantee a nonbiased valid test. Similarly, the fact that other subgroups were excluded from the norming process does not automatically invalidate a test's use with these subgroups. If the test can be found to perform the same function with a special group as it does with the normed population, then it should be con- sidered valid. In fact, this has been the focus of much of the psychological literature on the hearing impaired population that will be dis- cussed later in this chapter.

This notion of test bias is complicated not only by the issue of hearing impairment, but also by the fact that a large percentage of the hearing impaired population is comprised of individuals from backgrounds other than Caucasian, whereby the culture may be different and English may not be the language spoken in the home.

The fourth assumption noted by Newland is that error is associated with all measurement. This means that the instruments used, the conditions under which the individual is examined, and the examinee are not perfect. This is true even under what are seemingly ideal testing conditions. Because of this implicit error, an individual's performance on any particular test is usually reported as a spread of scores, rather than a single score, which increases the chances of being accurate. The more that the testing situation departs from the ideal, the less accurate the obtained scores on a test become.

Finally, the fifth and sixth assumptions noted by Newland are that only present behavior is observed and all future behavior, abilities, and disabilities are inferred. For example, when a youngster fails a test, all that is observed is that the student did not complete the task. Any statements concerning inability to complete the task or future behavior, although *educated* in nature and based upon known relationships (predictive validity), are considered inferences rather than fact.

In discussing the nature of psycho-educational evaluations and the diagnostic-prescriptive process, Ysseldyke and Salvia[15]—advance four additional assumptions that are fairly self-explanatory. These four assumptions are:

(1) Children enter into a teaching situation with identifiable strengths and weaknesses.
(2) The strengths and weaknesses are causally related to academic success.
(3) Strengths and weaknesses can be reliably and validly assessed.
(4) Pupil performance on diagnostic devices interacts with intervention strategies to produce differential instructional gains.

These assumptions are thought to be in operation whether one is concerned with normally hearing children or hearing impaired children, and are central to the notion of individualized educational programming.

IDENTIFICATION AND PLACEMENT

Assessment data are collected for a number of purposes.[10] One of these purposes is for the classification and placement of handicapped individuals in the most appropriate instructional setting possible. Two types of decisions are involved in this process. The first is whether a child should be placed in a special class or left in regular classes. The second has to do with choosing specific methodologies, teaching strategies, or communication modes that should be used with a child. The former decision is, in part, determined by the general philosophy of the school system. That is, if the system's organization is highly predicated upon ability or homogeneous grouping, the criteria for entrance into or staying within a particular classroom are apt to be very stringent. If, on the other hand, a more heterogeneous grouping philosophy is adopted, less stringent criteria will be used. Typically, though, most school systems have adopted a philosophy of homogeneous grouping; and as a result, have developed local plans that include a variety of placement options. If the placement decision is to situate the child in a self-contained classroom, another decision must be made as to which classroom, implying further homogeneous grouping and often decisions as to what communication mode will be used. For the most part, these decisions will be based upon the use of some form of norm-referenced test. That is, the child will be *grouped* with other children who perform similarly on a norm-referenced test. In fact, this is one of the primary values of such tests. These tests assist in making various classification, selection, and placement decisions; and when used in this manner, they can serve a legitimate function.

There are some unfortunate side effects of norm-referenced placement: first, once the child is classified, he or she is labeled, and this label then becomes the explanation for all subsequent learning difficulties or behavioral styles; second, an attempt might be made to use the norm-referenced test to develop diagnostic-prescriptive programs; and third, there is not unanimity in the criteria used by various professionals in placing hearing impaired children within the continuum of possible educational options.[16] The former situation is referred to as *nominalism*, and the second assumes that certain children, given a particular aptitude or ability, will learn better under one condition than under another. This situation refers to the second type of placement decision mentioned previously. Although it would be highly desirable to use these tests to develop individual programs, the research into "ability by treatment interactions" has not yet provided support for this notion.[17]

DOMAINS ASSESSED

Myklebust et al[18] have suggested a comprehensive evaluation scheme for hearing impaired individuals in which information is collected in each of the following areas: (1) general background information and developmental history; (2) sensory functioning; (3) cognition or intelligence; (4) language and academic achievement; (5) psycho-motor functioning; (6) social maturity and adaptive behavior; and (7) emotional adjustment. Tables 5-1 and 5-2 summarize the information needed in each of these areas. A discussion of each area and its concerns follows.

History and Background Information

The first area to be considered in the evaluation of any hearing impaired youngster is the collection of thorough birth, genetic, developmental, educational, familial, social/emotional, work (if applicable), and previous evaluation (including any previous speech and hearing, educational, medical, and/or psychological evaluations) histories. In addition to these areas of concern, parental expectations, attitudes, observations, judgments and concerns should be obtained as well. When the referral source is not the parent but another professional, such as the teacher, the professional's expectations, attitudes, observations, judgments, and concerns should be elicited and recorded as well, since the referring agents should feel that their concerns are recognized and considered when the evaluation process has been completed. Table 5-1 provides a brief overview of some of the major areas to be covered in a life history interview.

While it is important to obtain as complete a history as possible on an individual, certain research studies have indicated that not all of these data are equally predictive of academic success or language development, which are

often two of the major criteria used in placement decisions for hearing impaired children. There have been conflicting reports about the significance of the age at which a hearing loss is identified, the age at which initial training and/or admission to school begins, or the age at which amplification is initiated on predictions of academic success. However, Laughton[19] and Pressnell[20] found these variables to have an effect on the achievement of certain oral and written language structures and written language productivity. In terms of family characteristics, family size has been found to be related to academic success for integrated oral children, with children from smaller families achieving more than children from larger families.[21] However, surprisingly, socio-economic status (SES) has not been found to significantly affect academic success.

Although certain parental attitudes, expectations, and child-rearing practices have been found to have low-to-moderate correlations with academic success, as defined by scores on tests of academic achievement, for orally integrated hearing impaired children, they have not generally been found to predict success but with a few exceptions.[21] With young children, parental expectations for achievement potential were found to be highly predictive, but as the child became older, the predictive power of parental expectation decreased. Interestingly, the parental assessment of the child's athletic or artistic abilities became increasingly more important as a predictor when the child entered adolescence. Neuhaus[24] also found a definite relationship between the positive and negative attitudes of parents toward their hearing-handicapped children, and their children's subsequent emotional adjustment, which in turn should relate to academic success. Some researchers have noted that parents tend to overestimate the potentials and abilities of their hearing-handicapped children. Also, parents tend to have unrealistic future expectations that reflect more their own ambitions than the capacities and abilities of their children.[21]

It has been found that teacher ratings of intellectual ability correlate very well with children's performance on the Leiter International Performance Scale,[25] and a teacher's initial assessment of the academic potential of children has been cited as a significant predictor of future academic success.[21] However, in considering this, one must entertain the possi-

Table 5-1   Life History Outline

Medical, Genetic and Developmental	Clinical Evaluation	Family	Educational	Emotional and Social	Vocational	Familial Observations, Expectations, Judgments, and Attitudes	Teacher Observations, Expectations, Judgments, and Attitudes
Pre-, peri-, post-natal conditions of mother and child	When first noticed hearing loss	Genetic basis for hearing loss	When entered school	Method and style of communication and interaction with family members	Vocational and prevocational training	Statement of suspected problem	Statement of suspected problem
Medical history of illnesses	When began to wear a hearing aid	Other handicapping conditions	Type of school	Relationships with peers and neighbors	Work history	Cognitive abilities	Cognitive abilities
Genetic milestones	Type of hearing aid used	General family structure	How long in school	Relationship with community	Occupational preferences and goals	Language abilities	Language abilities
Sensory development	Auditory evaluations	Family milieu	Schools attended	Preference for friends (deaf or hearing)		Academic abilities	Academic abilities
Language development	Medical evaluations		Academic achievement, adjustment, progress	Leisure time (play) activities and preferences		Sensory abilities	Sensory abilities
Cognitive development	Psychological evaluations			Participation in deaf clubs		Motor abilities	Motor abilities
	Educational evaluations			Social interests		Social abilities	Social abilities
	Other evaluations			Marital preference and status		Emotional abilities and stability	Emotional abilities
				Social independence		Vocational abilities	Vocational abilities
				Self-evaluation and attitude toward self and deaf and hearing peers			

Table 5-2   Psycho-educational Assessment: Sensory Functioning

Audition	Vision	Touch

1. *Hearing sensitivity*
  a) Pure tone audiogram (a/c +
     b/c)
  b) Speech detection/reception
  c) Word discrimination
  d) Tests of middle ear function
  e) Results from hearing aid
     evaluation
  f) Special tests
2. *Auditory perception*
  Test of Auditory Comprehension
	1. *Visual acuity**
	  a) Snellen Chart
	  b) Keystone Telebinocular
	  c) Bausch and Lomb Othorater
	  d) Timus Vision Screener
	2. *Visual-motor perception**
	  a) Bender Gestalt Test for Young Children
	  b) Frostig
	  c) Graham and Kendall Memory for
	     Designs Test
	  d) Developmental Test of Visual-Motor
	     Integration
		No tests available

*NOTE: Provide valuable, but incomplete data (see text).

bility that a self-fulfilling prophecy may be in operation as much as a legitimate predictive relationship.

Finally, in terms of integrating hearing impaired children into a regular classroom, the regular teacher's attitude toward handicapped children in general and hearing impaired children specifically should be considered. Alexander and Strain[27] have found that regular teachers often have negative attitudes about and may be less accepting of special education children introduced into their classrooms. The regular teacher's attitude toward the number of hearing impaired children that should be enrolled in a single classroom has been found to be predictive of academic success for oral-integrated students.[21] The sensitivity of administrators to various individual differences and needs of these children is also predictive of academic success for these children.[21] Haring et al[28] have developed two instruments which may be helpful in determining the attitudes and knowledge of regular education teachers or administrators about various handicapping conditions, including hearing impairment. Unfortunately, no studies investigating the predictive variables associated with integrating children who use the simultaneous or total form of communication have been found.

Sensory Functioning

Although the child possesses five basic senses, only two and possibly three are of concern here. These are audition, vision, and possibly the tactile sense (see Table 5-2). Obviously, any child who has been identified and certified as hearing impaired will have had an audiometric evaluation. Generally speaking, one would minimally expect an air conduction and (if possible) bone conduction pure tone audiogram, speech threshold, and (if possible) discrimination test results, and some statement and/or objective test results concerning the youngster's candidacy for amplification. In addition, there may be reports of middle ear functioning, as determined by immittance measures, and the results of any special testing that may be warranted by the child's particular case (see Chapter 1).

Although the hearing impaired child should have undergone a thorough audiologic evaluation, the child's functional use of residual hearing may still be unknown. In order to fulfill a need in this area, the Test of Auditory Comprehension (TAC) has been developed.[29] This test was designed to evaluate the functional auditory status of moderately to profoundly hearing-impaired children along a continuum of auditory skill development. More specifically, the test was designed to assess the auditory discrimination of suprasegmentals and segmentals, memory sequencing, story comprehension, and figure-ground discrimination of hearing-impaired children ages 4 to 12 years, 11 months. The test was designed to be used as both a criterion-referenced, curriculum-based test in conjunction with its companion auditory training curriculum, as well as a norm-referenced test. Although there were some technical problems in the selection of a standardization sample, the reliability and validity data presented in the manual suggest that this test and its associated auditory training curriculum may be quite useful. Additionally, according to the manual, since substantial and positive correlations were obtained between scores on this test and functioning within different types of educational settings, this test may be useful in making placement decisions.

An individual with an auditory sensory impairment is typically required to rely more heavily upon the senses of vision and touch. Of these two, more attention has been given to the screening and evaluation of vision. In all the identified studies designed to investigate the incidence and types of visual problems in hearing impaired individuals, all but one have found a greater incidence of visual difficulties than that existing in the hearing population.[30] The reported incidence of visual problems has ranged from 38%[31] to slightly over 50%[32] and many of these problems do not appear to be acuity problems. Greene,[33] for example, using a sophisticated in-depth optometric clinical screening program, noted that the combined categories of binocularity problems and pathology were greater than all of the categories of refractive errors. Greene also commented on the inefficiency of the typical screening programs that consist of only the Snellen Chart. The Snellen Chart could account for the identification of only 23% of his sample of visually impaired, hearing impaired children. He further noted that other typical vision screening instruments, such as the Keystone Telebinocular, the Bausch and Lomb Orthorator, and the Titmus Vision Screener, although improvements over the simple Snellen Chart, are still incomplete. Thus, he recommended the establishment of a complete optometric clinical screening program, as do Walters et al.[34]

As noted previously, some children failing vision tests might do so not because of acuity problems, but rather because of some form of "perceptual" problem. Essentially, a perceptual problem is one in which the person is unable to be aware of (as opposed to sense), organize, and/or understand particular stimuli. Thus, although the sense receptor is intact, the "sensor" is unable to understand or has difficulty in processing the visual stimulus. This difficulty apparently can be a function of the individual, the stimulus structure, or the interaction of the two. Occasionally, the term *visual perceptual problem*, as used by some psychologists and other special service providers, refers to difficulty in visual-motor integration. That is, this "perceptual problem" manifests itself in the inability to copy specified designs or figures. Actually, the inability to complete such a task may be due to either difficulties in visually analyzing and organizing stimuli, or to the execution of the motor act in making a visual-motor match. In terms of the former, Locher and Worms[35] have suggested that visual perceptual difficulties may actually be due to difficulties in focusing or regulating attention, rather than an actual visual disability. Such inappropriate scanning of the visual stimulus would not permit the youngster to extract effectively all the necessary information to respond adequately to the task.

Among the most common visual-motor tasks used by psychologists in their assessments of children are the Bender Gestalt Test for Young Children (Bender-Gestalt), the Developmental Test of Visual Perception (Frostig), the Graham and Kendall Memory for Designs Test, and the Developmental Test of Visual-Motor Integration (VMI). Salvia and Ysseldyke[10] have indicated that most tests of visual motor perception lack the technical adequacy to be used in making important instructional decisions. Despite this, these tests are often used in the evaluation of most children, including hearing impaired children, and they have been used in various research projects. Generally speaking, when a child is found to have a deficit in this area, it is usually interpreted to mean that either the child has a legitimate visual-motor or visual-perception problem, possibly symptomatic of "minimal brain damage," or emotional difficulties and anxieties. Unfortunately, there is little empiric evidence to support these claims for most of these tests.

A few of these instruments have been used in research projects with hearing impaired individuals with inconsistent results. Although many hearing impaired individuals are found to perform poorly on the Bender-Gestalt Test, Keogh et al[36] have found the interjudge reliability scoring of these drawings to be very poor. Interestingly, in contrast to the findings of poor visual motor integration, Blair[37] among others, has found hearing impaired subjects to do well on a memory-for-designs test, which involves a design drawing component in addition to a memory component. Conflicting results have also been reported for other such "perceptual" tests, which may be due to the unreliability of the tests themselves. As a result, these tests should probably only be used as a rough screening instrument and only grossly deviant reproductions should be considered abnormal.

The fact that visual perceptual functioning is difficult to assess does not detract from its possible importance. Sharp[38] attempted to isolate the visual perceptual correlates of speech-reading in children by comparing the performance of good and poor speechreaders on various measures of visual perceptual and visual perceptual speed tasks. She found that performances on the Porteus Mazes, the Visual Sequential Memory subtest of the Illinois Test of Psycholinguistic Abilities (which is a memory task involving geometric designs), and three tests specially designed by the researcher (i.e., Rhythm Patterns: A Test of Movement, the Hidden Figures Test, and the Hidden Objects Test) were all related to good speechreading ability. The latter two tests essentially were figure-ground tests. These results, then, suggest that visual memory for movement, rhythm perception, speed of visual perception, and figure-ground ability are associated with speech-reading ability.

To date, there has only been one study investigating the visual-perceptual correlates of sign language acquisition. Siple et al[39] in a longitudinal study, investigated the visual perceptual correlates of sign language acquisition by deaf and hearing students at the National Technical Institute for the Deaf. Two different sets of predictors were isolated. For the *hearing impaired students* whose initial sign language scores were poor, improvement in sign language ability was significantly associated with initial scores on a rapid visual perceptual discrimination test (Perceptual Speed Identical Form Test), and the Embedded Figures Test. The predictors of the *hearing individuals'* progress in sign language were initial performances on the Flags Test, involving spatial manipulation, and the Visual Closure Speed Test, which assesses the speed at which an individual can recognize or infer a whole from minimal cues. These results suggested to the investigator that the deaf individuals acquired facility in sign language by attending to details and analyzing the whole, whereas hearing individuals used a process of synthesizing whole patterns and gestalts.

Cognition (Intelligence)

The intent of testing in this domain is to obtain general and specific measures of intelligence, creativity, and the mode of internalized mediation. The intelligence tests most widely used with hearing impaired individuals are shown in Table 5-3. Only the Hiskey-Nebraska Test of Learning Aptitude was specifically designed for and standardized on the hearing impaired population. While a few other scales standardized on hearing impaired individuals are available, the Hiskey-Nebraska and several tests not standardized on hearing impaired persons are in much greater use in this country. Although not standardized on the hearing impaired population, the Leiter Scales do not require verbal instructions and the Chicago Nonverbal Examination has two sets of directions and norms—one for pantomime directions and one for verbal directions.

The Wechsler Scales probably have been the most researched instrument used with the hearing impaired population. Presumably because of the popularity of the WISC-R, norms

Table 5-3 Psychoeducational Assessment: Cognition (Intelligence)

Tests Available	1. Weschler Scales
	   Adult Intelligence Scale (WAIS)
	   Adult Intelligence Scale-Revised (WAIS-R)
	   Intelligence Scale for Children (WISC)
	   Intelligence Scale for Children-Revised (WISC-R)

	2. Hiskey-Nebraska Test of Learning Aptitude*
	3. Harris-Goodenough Draw-A-Man
	4. Leiter International Performance Scale
	5. Leiter International Performance Scale—Arthur Adaptation
	6. Ravens Colored Progressive Matrices
	7. Kaufman Assessment Battery for Children
	8. Learning Potential Assessment Devise[40]
	9. Torrance Tests of Creative Thinking
	10. Test for Internal Speech

*NOTE: This is the only intelligence test specifically designed for and standardized on hearing impaired individuals.

for the hearing impaired population have been developed.[14]

The Wechsler tests are comprised of two scales, each containing a series of subtests. The two scales are a verbal scale, in which sets of verbal questions are posed to the examinee, and a performance scale involving various manipulation tasks. More precisely, the verbal scale is comprised of six subtests:

(1) *Information*, which requires the subject to answer factual type questions.
(2) *Comprehension*, which requires answering open-ended questions involving social awareness and practical knowledge and judgment.
(3) *Arithmetic*, requiring the solution of orally presented story problems.
(4) *Similarities*, which ask the subject to induce a superordinate term (*e.g.*, dishes, when given two subordinate terms such as cup and saucer).
(5) *Vocabulary*, which asks the subject to define words.
(6) *Digit Span*, in which the subject has to recall a series of digits presented orally.

The performance scale is also comprised of six subtests:

(1) *Picture Completion*, requiring the subject to identify missing parts of familiar objects.
(2) *Picture Arrangement*, requiring the subject to sequence a series of pictures.
(3) *Block Designs*, which requires the subject to copy mosaic designs utilizing a series of multi-colored block cubes.
(4) *Object Assembly*, which is a type of jigsaw puzzle task.
(5) *Coding*, which is a symbol association task whereby the subject is to draw simple designs underneath a series of numbers based upon a key that is provided.
(6) *Mazes*, which requires the subject to trace through a series of mazes.

Since there are two scales and 12 subtests each yielding their own scores, it is possible to have interscale and subtest comparisons on an individual, and to engage in profile analyses to determine relative strengths and weakness. However, extreme care must be taken when performing such analyses, since serious placement and intervention system decisions may be based upon unreliable or chance/error factors. Taking this point into account, the Wechsler tests still permit one to observe an individual's performance under several conditions,

and it is the only test mentioned in this chapter that permits the comparison of both verbal and nonverbal performances. However, it has become almost axiomatic that the verbal sections of these tests are considered invalid as measures of intellectual abilities for hearing impaired individuals, since they are assumed to be testing language and language functioning as opposed to inherent *intellectual* or *cognitive* abilities.[8] (Henceforth, any reference to any of the Wechsler Scales will refer to the Performance section only unless otherwise stated.) While it may be true that failure to perform on the verbal scale might be caused by a failure to understand specific questions or other related language factors, rather than a lack of more basic cognitive skills required to acquire the necessary information, the ability to score well on this test is still highly correlated with academic achievement. As a result, it would be very helpful to obtain verbal scale scores, whenever and however possible, to assess the hearing impaired person's ability to compete verbally with hearing peers. Such scores should properly be treated as verbal achievement scores and be reported in the language section of any psycho-educational report.

It has been demonstrated that there can be as large as a 16 to 44 IQ point difference between the overall performance scores and verbal scores on these scales for middle childhood to adolescent hard-of-hearing children[41] and congenitally deaf adults.[42,43] The discrepancy between verbal and performance scores is greater for congenitally deaf students than for hard-of-hearing or post-lingually deafened children,[44] and is related to the degree and type of high-frequency hearing loss in white children only.[45] It should be pointed out that Hine[41] found the Picture Arrangement subtest correlated best with the results of the verbal scale. This correlation, although low, was positive and statistically significant.

A number of studies have attempted to determine whether hearing impaired youngsters and adults did as well on the Wechsler Performance tests as normally hearing individuals, and whether a characteristic profile of subtest performance could be identified. The majority of these studies have found little or no difference between the overall performance of the two populations. The composite of the results of these studies suggests that a characteristic profile of subtest performance for the hearing impaired population may exist. This composite profile has these characteristics:

(1) performance on the Picture Completion subtest varies from slightly less than the hearing mean to slightly above it;
(2) performance on the Picture Arrangement subtest varies from no difference to slightly less than the hearing mean;
(3) performance on the Block Designs subtest ranges from no difference to slightly above the hearing mean;
(4) performance on the Object Assembly subtest ranges from the hearing mean to slightly above it; and
(5) performance on the Coding subtest ranges from no difference to slightly below the hearing mean.

This profile appears to be more evident with the younger deaf children and is statistically controlled for in the norms provided by Anderson and Sisco.[14] Ray[7] has challenged the utility of these norms, though, since they were compiled post hoc and no attempt was made to control for standardization of the administration procedures, and Sullivan[12] argues that the above-mentioned profile is an artifact of test administration modifications. Thus, norms are available, but they might not be standardized.

Some investigators have attempted to determine the reliability, validity, and utility of the Wechsler Scales with hearing impaired individuals. In general, the WISC and the WISC-R have been found to correlate moderately well to well with such other measures of intelligence as the Hiskey-Nebraska,[46,47] and the WISC-R has been found to be a reliable instrument when used with deaf persons.[48] The overall performance IQ has been found to be predictive of academic success,[26,49] and performance on all of the subtests (with the exception of Mazes) has been found to discriminate between high and low academic achievers. The Picture Arrangement, Block Design, and Coding subtests in particular, discriminate well between high and low achievers,[50] and it has been noted that these same three subtests correlate significantly with speechreading ability.[51] Finally, it has been noted that comparable results are obtained when youngsters at the upper-age limits of the WISC-R are subsequently evaluated using the WAIS-R.[52]

The Hiskey-Nebraska Test of Learning Aptitude is the only commonly used test of intelligence designed specifically for the hearing impaired population in this country. Because of this, some individuals have used it as the standard against which other tests are measured. The test has 12 subtests, many of which involve visual memory, and two sets of directions and hearing norms (i.e., verbal directions and hearing norms, and pantomime directions and hearing impaired norms). Salvia and Ysseldyke,[10] in reviewing the technical adequacy of the test, note several limitations and suggest that the results should be interpreted with caution. Recently, Watson[53] established moderate test-retest reliability even after a five-year interval span (r = .65). Watson and Goldgar[54] found high concurrent validity when the Hiskey was compared to the WISC-R, except that the Hiskey yielded a greater number of subjects with extreme upper and lower limits scores. It has also been reported that the Hiskey-Nebraska scores correlate highly with such various measures of academic success as the Stanford Achievement Test, the Gates Reading Test, the Metropolitan Achievement Test, and teacher ratings of academic achievement in the early elementary years but not during the middle school and adolescent years (e.g., grades 5 to 9[55]). Also, the Hiskey Learning Quotient (LQ) score and those subtests stressing visual memory have been found to be moderately predictive of performance on the Test of Language Development and the Reynell Developmental Language Scales administered via total communication.[56] Finally, it has been noted that the Block Patterns, Paper Folding, Picture Association, and the Visual Attention Span subtests, in particular, are predictive of academic achievement with 6- to 12-year-old orally trained deaf children.[57]

The Leiter International Performance Scale and its Arthur adaptation have also been used to assess the hearing impaired individual, and have been found to be highly predictive of academic achievement, as defined by teacher ratings and performance on tests of reading, despite their technical inadequacy.[10] This relationship has even held up longitudinally over an 11- to 13-year period.[49,58] Bonham[59] found the Leiter, in combination with the WISC, to be an exceptionally good predictor of success in the reading comprehension subtests of the Metropolitan Achievement Test. The Leiter was designed to be used with individuals with speech and language difficulties, aged 2 to 18 years, and was standardized on a hearing sample. The Arthur adaption is identical to the original Leiter but is only appropriate for children aged 2 to 12. There are no subtests to these tests; instead, they are comprised of a series of graduated but essentially unrelated tasks. In order to facilitate test interpretation, Levine et al have suggested an item classification scheme.[60]

In a series of concurrent validity studies, the Leiter has been found to correlate well with numerous other tests, including the Hiskey-Nebraska,[61] the Ravens Colored Progressive Matrices,[62] the WISC,[62] and the ITPA.[63] Although the Leiter has been found to be predictive of academic achievement, and appears to be sensitive to learning problems, Ratcliffe and Ratcliffe[64] warn that caution should be exercised when using this instrument in decisions of placement, since a few studies using both hearing and hearing impaired youngsters have found as much as an 11- to 20-or-more point discrepancy between scores on this and other tests. Also, Mira[61] found that the test-retest reliability for young deaf children was very low (with a reliability coefficient of .36).

The Ravens Progressive Matrices and its revision, the Ravens Colored Progressive Matrices, have been used in a few research projects with hearing impaired individuals. In essence, the test involves the pattern completion of a number of items. The Ravens Colored Progressive Matrices have been described as tapping a special aspect of intelligence, and some believe that it measures pure g (pure global or general intelligence). Carlson,[65] however, provides data on hearing children which suggest that on the Colored Progressive Matrices, sets A and Ab test perceptual pattern completion, whereas set B actually evaluates the ability to solve analogies by operations or rules.

The composite picture from studies using the Ravens Colored Progressive Matrices with hearing impaired individuals suggests that younger children have difficulty with the test, but that by the time they become young adults, performance improves.[66] Goetzinger and Houchins[67] and Ritter[62] found essentially normal performance with younger deaf and hard of hearing children. Ritter also found the Colored Progressive Matrices to correlate well with the Leiter and moderately well with the WISC, and James[68] found a high correlation with the WISC-R.

The last two tests of intelligence that have received some attention from researchers in hearing impairment are the Harris-Gooden-ough Draw-A-Man test and, more recently, the Kaufman Assessment Battery for Children (K-ABC). Although early studies using the Draw-A-Man test found hearing impaired children to do poorly on this test, more recent studies have found hearing impaired children to perform within average limits up to 13 years of age.[42] After this age, decrement of performance to below average was found. As for the K-ABC, Porter and Kirby[69] established that deaf children 7 to 12 years of age did not differ in their performance from the normative sample, nor was performance affected by the use of pantomime directions or directions communicated via American Sign Language. High correlations were obtained between the K-ABC and performance on the WISC-R, and moderate correlations were obtained between K-ABC scores and scores on the Metropolitan Achievement Test.

The Learning Potential Assessment Device, while employing standard instruments or "tools," is not a standard test in the traditional sense. Rather, it is a collection of commercially available tests and some specially designed instruments for which no norms are reported or available. It is one of the newer instruments out of the growing trend away from "static" norm-referenced tests toward dynamic measures of learning ability or potential. The 16 (five verbal and 11 largely performative) instruments are to be used in a Test-Teach-Test paradigm, wherein the "teaching phase" is to follow the tenants of the author's theory of mediated learning. Mediated learning in this context emphasizes that the role of the examiner is one of assisting the child to regulate metacognitively in a clear and accurate manner the input, elaboration, and output phases of the child's information processing, and to guide and provoke the use of appropriate learning strategies that will hopefully generalize or *transcend* to other stimuli and events. The extent to which this can be done is a measure of the child's modifiability and potential for learning. Keane and Kretschmer[70] reported on the application of this technique and noted its superiority in assessing the learning potential of deaf children over that of traditional psychometric approaches and even dynamic approaches that provide feedback.

The Torrance Test of Creative Thinking is a test of cognitive functioning. More precisely, it purports to measure an individual's flexibility, fluency, originality, and elaborative skills of thinking. Both verbal and performative tasks are available. Laughton[71] recommended that the Torrance Thinking Creatively with Pictures, Form *A* be included with the routine battery used to evaluate hearing impaired children, since in her study of hearing impaired children, several scores derived from this measure were found to predict the development of morphologic, phrase structure, and transformational rule usage. The originality score in particular predicted usage of all the linguistic structures studied, and the elaboration score aided in the prediction of morphologic rule development. Kaltsounis[72] has demonstrated in a number of studies that hearing impaired children did as well on this test as did hearing children. Average-to-superior performance on the "nonverbal" form has been supported by several other studies.[73,74]

One of the implicit purposes in formal testing of intelligence and cognition is to gain some insight into the thinking and problem-solving abilities of the examinee. Of particular interest are insights into the examinee's ability to handle symbolic material, since they may reveal information about the examinee's mediational processes and capacity to handle symbols in general. Occasionally, the results of some of the more symbolically oriented nonverbal subtests on intelligence tests (e.g., the Picture Arrangement and Coding subtests on the Wechsler tests and the Picture Analogies or Picture Association subtests on the Hiskey-Nebraska Test) are used for this purpose, and we already discussed the LPAD. But while these tests give us insight into the child's ability to deal with symbolically oriented materials, they do not directly assess the mode of internal symbolic representation. Modes of internalized representation must be inferred from behavioral observations and tests.

Recently, however, attempts have been made by some researchers to determine empirically the nature of the mediating process. Odom et al[75] and Bellugi et al[76] have suggested that with deaf children, the mediating process involves the use of signs. Locke and Locke[77] made the alternative suggestion that hearing children and many deaf children with intelligible speech tend to recode internally certain visually presented symbolic material phonetically. Deaf children without intelligible speech were found to prefer a dactylic (finger-spelling) and/or visual recoding system. Conrad,[78] reporting on a series of studies he had conducted, argued that the use of a phonetic internal coding system probably is not an all-or-nothing matter, but exists in degrees. The use of a phonetic code by hearing impaired individuals, according to Conrad, is strongly associated with their use of external intelligible speech, although he noted that many profoundly deaf youngsters, whose speech would be considered unintelligible, use this code form. He concludes this from observing that their speech, although unintelligible to a listener, is consistent and probably *intelligible* to the speaker.

Conrad, as a result of his work, has developed a testing procedure that he believes can discriminate between children who use a phonetic coding system and those who use a visual coding system. However, his test does not discriminate among individuals who might use other possible coding strategies (i.e., those who might prefer finger-spelling, signs, or a combination of all possible internal codes). There is a need for such tests and for further research into what determines mediation preferences. Such knowledge should help in the decision-making process regarding placement and programming for hearing impaired children.

Language and Academic Achievement

Although this is probably one of the most important areas to be assessed, few studies have been conducted using formal assessment techniques with the hearing impaired (Table 5-4). As noted in the Cognition (Intelligence) section of this chapter, the verbal scale of the Wechsler test has been used with hearing impaired children and adults under limited circumstances. The results on this test, although very helpful in providing an index of the hearing impaired child's verbal understanding of the world, do not specify more precisely the particular linguistic structures or lexical items (with a few exceptions) that the child knows.

Ideally, in a full-language evaluation, all aspects of language functioning should be considered. This would include: (*1*) communication modality preference; (*2*) articulation skills in terms of speech, sign language, and signs; (*3*) knowledge and use of morphologic rules of English and American Sign Language, if appropriate; (*4*) knowledge and use of the syntactic rules of English and American Sign Language, if appropriate; (*5*) vocabulary/semantic

Table 5-4 Psycho-educational Assessment: Language and Academic Achievement

Ability Tested	Test
Articulation	Ling Speech Articulation Assessment[79]

Syntax	Berko Test of Morphology[81]
	Grammatical Closure Subtest of the ITPA
	Berry Talbot Exploratory Test of Grammar
	Northwestern Syntax Screening Test
	Carrow Elicited Language Inventory
	Boehm Test of Basic Concepts
	Grammatic Analysis of Elicited Language Presentence Level[84]
	    (specifically for hearing impaired population)
	Grammatic Analysis of Elicited Language: Simple Sentence[85]
	    (specifically for hearing impaired population)
	Grammatic Analysis of Elicited Language: Complex Sentence Level[86]
	    (specifically for hearing impaired population)
	Rhode Island Test of Language Structure
	Test of Syntactic Abilities[88]
	    (specifically for hearing impaired population)
	Analysis of Spontaneous Language Samples Procedure[90,91]

Lexical development	Peabody Picture Vocabulary Test
	    (limited use for manually oriented students)
	Word Recognition Subtests of Achievement Tests
	    (tests knowledge of printed work)
	Vocabulary Subtest of the Wechsler Scales

General verbal ability and knowledge	Verbal Scale of the Wechsler Scales
Interactive language	*Informal*	*Formal*

	Parent interviews
	Naturalistic observations
	Standardized observations
	Contained observations
		Bales Interactive Process Scale[95]
		Flanders Interactive Scale
		Craig & Collins Analysis of
		    Communicative Interaction[96]
		Cognitive Verbal/Nonverbal
		    Observation Scale

Academic achievement	Stanford Achievement Test Battery Hearing-Impaired edition Metropolitan Achievement Battery Brill Educational Achievement Test for Secondary Age Deaf Students[99]

aspects of the language used; (6) pragmatic uses of language; and (7) ability to engage in metalinguistic behaviors such as making judgments of grammaticality and being able to paraphrase; and (8) in the case of bilingual/bicultural youngsters, other preferences for, dominance, and abilities in a language other than English or signs.

To review all the possible issues and procedures associated with these topics is beyond the scope of this chapter. As a result, the reader will be referred to other resources when appropriate. Ling,[79] for example, describes in detail a procedure for assessing speech articulation. In terms of certain aspects of speech,

Pflaster[21] has emphasized the importance of suprasegmental control (e.g., speech rhythm) over actual articulation ability, in that this factor significantly entered into a prediction equation of success for orally integrated children up to age 10. After that age, apparently the oral receptive skills of the children were more important.

Although there undoubtedly exists an entire range of articulation ability in terms of fingerspelling and signing, no formal testing procedure for school age is known to exist. Taking a lead from assessment procedures for oral speech, though, various rating systems and articulation tests might be devised by utilizing the information reported by Wilbur[80] and others concerning the "phonology" of finger-spelling and signs.

A number of evaluation instruments and techniques currently are available for the assessment of syntactic and morphologic rule knowledge of English. Cooper[81] successfully administered the Berko test of morphology to a group of hearing impaired children. The Berko test attempts to assess the child's ability to generalize the use of certain inflectional endings and markers, such as the plural [s] or the regular past tense marker [-ed]. The grammatic closure subtest of the Illinois Test of Psycholinguistic Abilities and the Berry Talbot Exploratory Test of Grammar are adaptations of this test and are commercially available. Three other tests that have been used with hearing impaired individuals are the Northwestern Syntax Screening Test (NSST), the Carrow Elicited Language Inventory, and the Boehm Test of Basic Concepts.

The NSST, as the name suggests, is a screening test of receptive and expressive language abilities. Only 40 syntactic structures are used in the test. The Carrow Elicited Language Inventory is meant to evaluate a slightly wider scope of linguistic constructions. The Boehm Test of Basic Concepts was developed to be a criterion-referenced test of certain beginning, academically related concepts; and it involves concept identification, statement repetition and comprehension, and pattern awareness. No attempt was made by the author of the test to specify the specific linguistic constructions that are being evaluated, but a visual inspection of the items by the user can easily reveal their nature. As might be expected, studies employing these instruments have shown that hearing impaired individuals perform more poorly than their hearing counterparts.[20,82,83] These tests may be used as a type of criterion measure to identify specific language structures with which the individual may be having difficulty. It should be pointed out, however, that these instruments test only a very limited number of possible constructions, and thus give only a very narrow picture of the child's linguistic understanding and capacity.

These tests have been standardized on and for a hearing population. Recently, several formal instruments have been developed for the hearing impaired population. These are: (1) the Grammatical Analysis of Elicited Language—Presentence,[84] Simple Sentence,[85] and Complex Sentence Levels[86]; (2) the Rhode Island Test of Language Structure[87]; and (3) the Test of Syntactic Abilities.[88] The first three tests use a format similar to that of the Carrow Elicited Language Inventory, with the exception that the various activities or tasks are structured so that they are a natural consequence of the context. The tests were standardized on orally taught hearing impaired children, ages 3 to 5 years, 11 months, 5 to 8 years, 11 months, and 8 to 11 years, 11 months, respectively, although norms are now available for the Simple Sentence Level when the items are communicated via total communication. Norms for normally hearing children are also available. The Rhode Island Test of Language Structure is a test of receptive understanding of various grammatic constructions designed to be administered via total communication. The format involves discriminating a correct picture from a series of foils that depict a sentence with a given syntactic structure. The test is designed for hearing impaired youngsters from ages 3 to 20 years and normally hearing youngsters from ages 3 to 6 years.

The third test devised for use with a hearing impaired population is the Test of Syntactic Abilities (TSA). It consists of a screening test and 20 individual paper-and-pencil tests covering nine of the major syntactic structures of English. It was designed to be both a criterion-referenced and a norm-referenced in-depth diagnostic battery, appropriate for 10- to 19-year-old hearing impaired youngsters. The constructions that are evaluated are negation, conjunction, determiners, question formation, verb processes, pronominalization, relativization, complementation, and nominalization. One virtue of this particular test is that it is criterion-referenced, and that it systematically explores in-depth the hearing impaired child's knowledge of a number of syntactic constructions. From a technical standpoint, extreme care was taken to make the norming population as representative as possible. The reliability of this test in terms of internal consistency and test-retest is high, and the individual subtests have been found to correlate well with results obtained on the Stanford Achievement Test and with written language, thereby giving evidence of validity. The TSA has a related curriculum, the *TSA Syntax Program*,[89] which was designed and field tested for teaching the major structures of English evaluated by the TSA.

Another procedure that has growing acceptance is the use of analysis of spontaneous language samples. In this procedure, a corpus, or sample, of spontaneous language is elicited from the child and a grammatic, semantic, and/or pragmatic analysis of the production is made using some *a priori* classification scheme. A number of these schemes are available.[90,91]

Unlike syntax, which is thought to be comprised of a finite number of rules that can be evaluated exhaustively, lexical development is theoretically infinite. As a result, it is impossible to obtain a complete inventory of the child's vocabulary. A number of receptive vocabulary tests that have been standardized on the normally hearing population are available. One such test is the Peabody Picture Vocabulary Test (PPVT). All of these tests generally follow the same format. A word is spoken and the examinee is expected to select the appropriate corresponding picture. When administered to hearing impaired individuals in the prescribed fashion, the test becomes as much a test of speechreading and auditory processing as a test of vocabulary. If a simultaneous form of communication is used, inflated scores may result, since the iconic nature of the signs may induce a correct response without actual lexical knowledge. Similarly, problems arise if the items are administered via finger-spelling or presented in a written format, since the tests were not intended to be used this way. As a result, tests like the PPVT have limited value with many hearing impaired individuals. Another index of vocabulary development, however, which would not involve any task modification, is the use of word recognition subtests of various achievement tests. Such tests, however, tap only one aspect of lexical knowledge—knowledge of the printed word.

Language learning, for both normally hearing and hearing impaired children, at least in part, involves an interactive process; and as a result, the child's participation in these interactions needs to be assessed. The interactive patterns of the primary caretaker and the child or the interaction between a classroom teacher and the students are examples of interactions that could be used for assessment. Or, one could also assess the interaction patterns of a group of hearing impaired children among themselves or in an integrated situation.

The methods used to investigate these interactive patterns are of several types—verbal statements gathered from interviews with parents, naturalistic observation, standardized observation, and containing observation, which is the limiting of one's observation to a specifically prescribed behavior.[92] In terms of mother-child, as well as teacher-child interactions, the behaviors of most interest are those that would most promote intellectual development, psychosocial attachment and development, academic achievement, and language development. An excellent review of the current studies and strategies in observing normal mother-infant interaction is provided by Ramey et al[92] and Feuerstein.[40] The need for considering these interactions is amply demonstrated by Collins and Rose[93] and Goss,[94] who has shown that hearing mothers of deaf children respond differently and less effectively as teachers of language than hearing mothers of hearing children.

Similarly, a number of interaction scales are available to investigate classroom and teacher-child interactions. Among these are the Bales Interaction Process Analysis,[95] the Flanders Interactive Scale, Craig and Collins Analysis of Communicative Interaction,[96] and the Cognitive Verbal/Nonverbal Observation Scale.[97] Recent studies using these scales have shown that, at least in some classes for hearing impaired students, the conversations tend to be teacher-dominated (with few student-initiated communications),[96] the activities center around memory work as opposed to inference building,[97] and the children lack the ability to ask for information, make suggestions, provide orientations, or clarify other's opinions in group problem-solving situations.[98]

A number of academic achievement tests that can be used with hearing impaired students are available. Three of these have norms for the hearing impaired population, as well as norms for the normally hearing population. These are the Stanford Achievement Test Battery-Hearing Impaired Edition, the Metropolitan Achievement Battery, and the Brill Educational Achievement Test for Secondary Age Deaf Students.[99] Of these, the Stanford Achievement Tests are the most popular and technically adequate. One advantage that the Stanford tests have is that they are both norm-referenced and criterion-referenced, and thus theoretically are amenable to direct translations into an educational program. Given that most diagnostic reading tests are phonically based, their utility with the hearing impaired population is limited. Obviously, these tests would be limited to use with hard-of-hearing children or phonically oriented deaf children. However, Ewoldt[100] has recently discussed the application of the Goodman-Burke Reading Miscues Inventory, which is a test of oral reading fluency, to a group of hearing impaired children who used simultaneous communications. Her findings suggested that the hearing impaired children made the same kinds of reading errors that hearing children made, and that the reading processes of the two groups were in many ways very similar.

Psycho-Motor Functioning

Although the psycho-motor integrity of the individual may provide the examiner with one more piece of information concerning the total development of the hearing impaired child, few studies have been performed in this area and few tests of psycho-motor ability are available. The studies that have been conducted have suggested that some hearing impaired individuals have difficulties in terms of static balance (standing on one foot), and psycho-motor speed (doing a manual task with speed), with lesser but still significant difficulties in maintaining balance while in motion (dynamic balance). These identified motor difficulties are the result of a study using the Oseretsky Test of Motor Proficiency.[42]

Social Maturity and Adaptive Behavior

Social maturity essentially is the ability to take care of oneself and to assist in the care of others. The related concept of adaptive behavior is defined by the American Association of Mental Deficiency (AAMD) as the "effectiveness with which the individual copes with the natural and social demands of the environment." The AAMD further explains that "This definition has two major facets: (1) the degree to which the individual is able to function independently, and (2) the degree to which s/he meets satisfactorily the culturally imposed demands of personal and social responsibility."[10] The importance of including measures of this kind in a total assessment is emphasized by the official position of both the AAMD and the Office of Civil Rights.[101] Both organizations have stated that an individual can be classified as mentally retarded only if the individual is

found to be subnormal in both intelligence and in adaptive behavior.

Although a number of adaptive scales are available, only one has been used with hearing impaired individuals in research studies—the Vineland Social Maturity Scale. This instrument is administered in a structured interview situation with someone who is very familiar with the child being rated. The scale is comprised of eight clusters of items: self-help general, self-help eating, self-help dressing, locomotion, socialization, occupation, communication, and self-direction. The test was intended to assess the social competency of individuals from birth to adulthood.

Myklebust[42] and others have used the Vineland Social Maturity Scale with residential school students and have found that in the early years, very little difference existed between normally hearing and hearing impaired youngsters, except in items directly evaluating communication skills. However, as the children matured, the pervasiveness of the language problem was found to have serious effects in other areas, so that by age 15, the mean social quotient was in the low 80s. (A social quotient is similar to an intelligence quotient in that 100 is considered the average.) A recent investigation by Quarrington and Solomon[102] studied the social maturity of three groups of hearing impaired children ages 5 to 16. The groups studied were a group of day students in a public school setting, a group of students attending a residential school but who had numerous trips home, and a group of residential students who rarely went home. The first two groups had social quotients in the mid-80s, as might be expected, whereas the latter group had a mean social quotient in the mid-70s, which is distinctly below average.

Emotional Adjustment

In terms of the child's emotional development, the psycho-educational assessment team needs to be concerned with (a) the child's overall mental health and behavioral functioning, and (b) the child's motivation to learn. The need to consider the former is emphasized by the fact that several surveys have suggested that the incidence of emotional disturbance and behavioral disorders in the hearing impaired population is greater than in the normally hearing population.[103] In terms of the latter, the psycho-educational evaluator should also be interested in those behaviors that, although not pathological, do affect learning and functioning within the classroom.

A number of studies have been conducted to examine the personality characteristics of the hearing impaired. Many of these investigations have been based on the use of projective techniques (Table 5-5).[104] Unfortunately, a few of the instruments require extensive verbalization on the part of the examinee, which limits their use to a portion of the hearing impaired population and calls into question the conclusions derived from the use of such instruments. These criticisms are in addition to those generally leveled against all projective and most personality tests—that they generally lack the necessary technical adequacy to be considered highly valid or reliable. Despite these limitations, the same findings have been obtained repeatedly when using different tests.[104]

The general pattern obtained from these studies is emotional immaturity, adaptive rigidity, sociocultural impoverishment, narrowed intellectual functioning, short attention span, and poor impulse control. Hogan[107] has likened these characteristics to an authoritarian personality, whereas Levine and Wagner[104] have suggested that these characteristics are similar to those of culturally deprived individuals. Although the personality profiles obtained from projective tests give the impression of severe maladaptive behavior, in all probability, they actually reflect relatively good

coping skills, considering the impact of the physical disability and the psycho-social reactions to it.

Recently, several investigators have begun to study various aspects of these personality *traits* as they relate to the academic setting. More specifically, interest is being expressed in the interrelated notions of impulsivity, external versus internal locus of control, learned helplessness, and the need for achievement. Impulsivity refers to the tendency to make fast decisions with many errors, whereas its opposite, reflection, refers to the tendency to react slowly with relatively few errors. According to Harris,[108] reflectivity is associated with age, reading ability, adjustment, social class, high motivation to achieve, persistence, and long attention spans. Similarly, the bipolar dimensions of external versus internal locus of control have also been associated with several of these variables, as has field dependency.[109] For example, locus of control has been associated with greater or lesser information learning, information seeking, academic achievement, and motivation to achieve.[110]

Some of these ideas have been investigated with hearing impaired individuals. Both Altshuler et al[111] and Harris[100] have found hearing impaired persons to be less reflective and thus more impulsive than their hearing counterparts. Harris also found deaf children of deaf parents to be more reflective than deaf children born to hearing parents. Apparently, the nature of the home environment in terms of parent-child interactions and communication patterns has a bearing on the extent of the child's reflectivity or impulsivity. Similarly, Stinson[112] found that the hearing impaired child's motivation to achieve, his persistence and his actual achievement were a function of the mother's interaction with her child in a learning/teaching situation. Thus, the quality of the mother-child interaction and the extent of the actual external (locus of) control placed upon the child has an effect on immediate achievement and probably on the child's eventual perception of locus of control. To the extent that hearing impaired children are actually overprotected and controlled, they may not learn to take responsibility for their behavior, and thus develop what McCrone[113] has identified as learned helplessness. Learned helplessness is characterized by: (*1*) an external locus of control; (*2*) underachievement; and (*3*) reduced performance when faced with

Table 5-5 Psycho-educational Assessment: Emotional Adjustment*

Tests Available

1. Rorschach
2. Make-A-Picture-Story-Test
3. Draw-A-Person Test
4. Mosaic Test
5. Id-Ego-Superego Test
6. Missouri Children's Picture Series
7. Rotter Incomplete Sentences
8. Meadow/Kendall Social-Emotional Assessment Inventory for Deaf Children[105]
9. Meadow's Assessment of Social-Emotional Adjustment in Hearing-Impaired Preschoolers[106]

*NOTE: Limited use—results questionable.

failure. These are characteristics that are very common in many hearing impaired children.

Since these behaviors appear able to be modified,[40,70,114] it would seem important to include various measures of impulsivity and locus of control within a standard battery, if possible. Some instruments that could be used are shown in Table 5-6.[115,116]

Table 5-6 Psycho-educational Assessment: Measures of Impulsivity and Locus Control

Materials Available
1.   Matching Familiar Figures Test[114]
2.   Timed Draw-A-Man Test
3.   Porteus Mazes
4.   Wechsler Mazes
5.   Id-Ego-Superego Test
6.   Rotter Test of Internal/External Control

SPECIFIC CRITERIA FOR INTEGRATION

In this chapter, instruments and procedures have been described that have been used in identifying and programming for the academic and language needs of the hearing impaired child. No attempt was made to discuss minimal competencies needed to integrate hearing impaired children into a regular classroom either on a full- or part-time basis. There are very few studies of this problem. Reich et al,[117] on the basis of a study of 195 integrated hearing impaired children, suggested several sets of minimal criteria that depend upon the type of program and the age of the child. Criteria were derived for *elementary-age children* who were candidates for either *full integration* (EFI) or *integration with itinerant help* (EIH), and *secondary-age children* who were candidates for *full integration* (SFI), *integration with itinerant help* (SIH), or *partial integration* (SPI). The minimum requirements for full integration at the elementary level were:

(*1*) No greater than a moderate (70 dB HL) pure tone average hearing loss.
(*2*) No greater than a severe (90 dB HL) high frequency average (HFA, the average of the thresholds at 4000 and 8000 Hz).

(*3*) Aural functioning of 62% or better correct response to a specially designed test of sentence and paragraph understanding.
(*4*) Oral functioning of 78% or better on a test similar to that used to assess aural functioning.
(*5*) An English language background.
(*6*) Parents who had no less than a high school education.
(*7*) Parents who had aspirations for their child of high school graduation or college.
(*8*) Some degree of help at home, and good parental contact with the school.
(*9*) An IQ of no less than 90.
(*10*) Diagnosis of hearing impairment no later than age 7, with a hearing aid being fitted no later than age 8.

Almost identical criteria for the other four groups were reported, with the exception of permitting:

(*1*) Severe hearing losses in the case of pure tone averages for the EIH and the SPI children.
(*2*) Profound HFA losses for all four groups.
(*3*) Slightly lower aural functioning (58%) for the EIH children.
(*4*) Slightly higher oral functioning (86%) for all the secondary groups.
(*5*) Slightly lower intelligence for the EIH children, but slightly higher intelligence for the SIH and SPI children (IQs of 97 and 95, respectively).
(*6*) Slightly later age of diagnosis (9 years) for the SIH and SPI children.
(*7*) Slightly younger age (5.5 years) for a hearing aid fitting for the EIH children, but slightly older for all the secondary children (age 9 years).

Rudy and Nace[118] also have developed criteria whereby an individual's candidacy for integration can be estimated. The procedure is based upon ratings in the areas of intelligence, academic achievement, social adjustment, and degree of loss. These ratings yield a composite score that can be compared with a decision-making cut-off point provided by the researchers to determine eligibility for integration.

While these minimal criteria can be very useful, it should be remembered that they have not been tested beyond the initial populations studied. Thus, they should only be used as guidelines.

CONCLUSION

An attempt has been made in this chapter to briefly cover issues related to the appropriate psycho-educational assessment of hearing impaired children. It has been indicated that a number of domains of behavior and social functioning must be considered in making educational decisions regarding hearing impaired children. More specifically, it was recommended that information be collected in each of the following areas: life history, sensory functioning, cognition, language and academic achievement, motor functioning, social maturity, and emotional behavior. In collecting this information, it was recommended that the individual involved (in this case, the psychologist) should have some experience with hearing impaired individuals, and that technically sound and appropriate evaluation instruments be used. In terms of the former, very few training programs exist that prepare psychologists with a specialty in hearing impairment, and fewer yet provide an adequate background in this disability to the general school or clinical psychologist. This is unfortunate, since the psychologist in the local school system is being required more and more often to evaluate hearing impaired as well as other low-incidence disabled children. In terms of the latter point, a few tests have been developed that are specifically designed for hearing impaired individuals, and a number of other tests have been found to have varying degrees of utility. In general, however, efforts in developing adequate evaluation procedures have been rather piecemeal.

These facts point to several obvious needs and conclusions. Among these are: (*1*) that the training of psychologists should be supplemented at the pre- and in-service level through specific coursework and intensive workshops possibly offered during the summer months; and (*2*) that large-scale projects should be implemented to develop appropriate evaluation procedures and instruments that take into account the pluralistic and heterogeneous nature of the hearing impaired population. Although some initial work has been done in the area of establishing criteria for integration, further research is needed in utilizing different integration plans—for example, having the primary teacher be dually certified or sending an interpreter-tutor with a child who uses simultaneous communication—and in the determinants of successful academic and language achievement.

Although the emphasis of this chapter has been on formal and norm-referenced evaluation procedures for purposes of placement, this is but the initial step in programming for a child. As noted elsewhere in this chapter, most norm-referenced tests do not lend themselves to specific programming for children, since they were initially designed to provide comparative information so that classification of placement decisions could be made. On the other hand, criterion-referenced tests, curriculum-based testing, and the progress of task analysis lend themselves directly to teaching programs. In fact, it is through the use of appropriate curriculum-based, criterion-referenced testing and task analysis that the most effective remedial programs can be devised. Unfortunately, many teachers and evaluators both at the pre- and in-service level have not developed a sound theoretic understanding of the organization of knowledge itself, which should be the basis for a curriculum, or of how to analyze and identify accurately the hierarchy of subskills of a task. As a result, every effort should be made to incorporate this information within the pre- and in-service training of these professionals.

REFERENCES

1. Rules and Regulations for Implementation of the Education for All Handicapped Children Act of 1975. U.S. Dept. of Health, Education, and Welfare. *Fed Reg*, 42 (1977), 42474–42518.
2. Newland TE: Assumptions underlying psychological testing. *J Sch Psych*, 11 (1973), 316–322.
3. Levine ES: Psychological tests and practices with the deaf: A survey of the state of the art. *The Volta Review*, 76 (1974), 298–319.
4. Spragins AB, Karchmer MA, Schildroth AN: Profile of psychological service providers to hearing-impaired students. *Am Ann of Deaf*, 126 (1981), 94–105.
5. McQuaid MF, Alovisetti M: School psychological services for hearing-impaired children in the New York and New England area. *Am Ann of Deaf*, 126 (1981), 37–42.
6. Furth HG: A review and perspective on the thinking of deaf people, in Hellmuth J, ed: *Cognitive Studies* (New York: Brunner/Mazel, 1970).
7. Ray S: An Adaptation of the *Wechsler Intelligence Scales (Performance) For Children Revised*, dissertation (Knoxville, TN: University of Tennessee, 1979).
8. Vernon M, Brown DW: A guide to psychological tests and testing in the procedures evaluation of deaf and hard of hearing children. *J*

Speech Hearing Dis, 29 (1964), 414–423.

9. *Academic Achievement Test Results of a National Testing Program*. Office of Demographic Studies, Series D, No. 9. (Washington, DC: Gallaudet College, 1972).

10. Salvia JA, Ysseldyke JE: *Assessment in Special and Remedial Education* (Boston: Houghton-Mifflin, 1978).

11. Buros OK: *The Eighth Mental Measurement Yearbook* (Highland Park: The Gryphon Press, 1978).

12. Sullivan PM: Administration modification on the WISC-R performance scale with different categories of deaf children. *Am Ann of Deaf*, 127 (1982), 780–788.

13. Courtney AS, Hayes FB, Couch KW, Frick M: Administration of the WISC-R performance scale to hearing-impaired children using pantomimed instructions. *J Psychoeduc Assess*, 2 (1984), 1–7.

14. Anderson RJ, Sissco FH: *Standardization of the WISC-R Scale for Deaf Children*. Office of Demographic Studies, Series T, No. 1 (Washington, DC: Gallaudet College, 1977).

15. Ysseldyke JE, Salvia JA: Diagnostic-prescriptive teaching: Two models. *Exceptional Children*, 41 (1974), 181–185.

16. Spear B, Kretschmer RE: The use of criteria in decision making regarding the placement of hearing impaired students. *Special Services in the Schools* (in press, 1987).

17. Ysseldyke JE: Diagnostic-prescriptive teaching: The search for aptitude-treatment interactions, in Mann L, Sabatino DA, eds: *The First Review of Special Education*, Vol. 1 (Philadelphia: JSE Press, 1973).

18. Myklebust HR, Neyhus A, Mulholland AM: Guidance and counseling for the deaf. *Am Ann Deaf*, 107 (1962), 370–415.

19. Laughton J: *Nonverbal Creative Thinking Abilities as Predictors of Linguistic Abilities of Hearing-Impaired Children*, dissertation (Kent, OH: Kent State University, 1976).

20. Pressnell L: Hearing impaired children's comprehension and production of syntax in oral language. *J Speech Hearing Res*, 16 (1973), 12–21.

21. Pflaster G: *A Factor Analytic Study of Hearing Impaired Children Integrated Into Regular Schools*, dissertation (New York: Teachers College, Columbia University, 1976).

22. Serwatka TS: *Nonverbal Predictors of Reading Achievement in Hearing Impaired Children*, dissertation (Kent, OH: Kent State University, 1976).

23. Anderson MW: *Psycholinguistic Abilities and Academic Achievement of Hard of Hearing Students*, dissertation (Gainesville, FL: University of Florida, 1974).

24. Neuhaus M: Parental attitudes and the emotional adjustment of deaf children. *Exceptional Children*, 35 (1969), 721–727.

25. Birch JR, Birch JW: Predicting school achievement in young deaf children. *Am Ann of Deaf*, 101 (1956), 348–352.

26. *Hard of Hearing Child in the Regular Classroom*. Pontiac, Michigan. Oakland County School, final report, Eric number ED 145646, 1975.

27. Alexander C, Strain PS: A review of educators' attitude toward handicapped children and the concept of mainstreaming. *Psych School*, 15 (1978), 390–396.

28. Haring N, Stern G, Cruickshank WM: *Attitudes of Educators Toward Exceptional Children* (Syracuse, NY: Syracuse University Press, 1958).

29. *Test of Auditory Comprehension*. Office of Los Angeles County Superintendent of Schools, (North Hollywood: Foreworks, 1976).

30. Levin S, Erber NP: A vision screening program for deaf children. *The Volta Review*, 78 (1976), 90–99.

31. Braly EW: A study of defective vision among deaf children. *Am Ann of Deaf*, 83 (1938), 192–193.

32. Lawson LJ, Myklebust HR: Ophthalmological deficiencies in deaf children. *Exceptional Children*, 37 (1970), 17–20.

33. Greene HA: Implications of a comprehensive vision-screening program for hearing-impaired children. *The Volta Review*, 80 (1978), 467–475.

34. Walters JW, Quintero S, Perrigin DM: Vision: Its assessment in school-age deaf children. *Am Ann of Deaf*, 127 (1982), 418–432.

35. Locher PJ, Worms PF: Visual scanning strategies of neurologically impaired, perceptually impaired, and normal children viewing the Bender-Gestalt designs. *Psych School*, 14 (1977), 147–157.

36. Keogh BK, Vernon M, Smith CE: Deafness and visuo-motor function. *J Spec Educ*, 4 (1970), 41–47.

37. Blair F: A study of the visual memory of deaf and hearing children. *Am Ann of Deaf*, 102 (1957), 254–263.

38. Sharp EY: The relationship of visual closure to speech reading. *Exceptional Children*, 38 (1972), 729–734.

39. Siple P, Hatfield N, Caccamise FF: The role of visual perceptual abilities in the acquisition and comprehension of sign language. *Am Ann of Deaf*, 123 (1978), 852–856.

40. Feuerstein R: *The Dynamic Assessment of Retarded Performers* (Baltimore, MD: University Park Press, 1979).

41. Hine WD: The abilities of partially hearing children. *Brit J Educ Psych*, 39 (1969), 171–178.

42. Myklebust HR: *Psychology of Deafness* (New York: Grune and Stratton, 1960).

43. Ross DR: A technique of verbal ability assessment of deaf adults. *J Rehab Deaf*, 3 (1970), 7–15.

44. Smith CS: The assessment of mental ability in partially deaf children. *Teacher Deaf*, 60 (1962), 216–224.

45. Roach RE, Rosencrans CJ: Intelligence test performance of black children with high frequency hearing loss. *J of Aud Res*, 11 (1971), 136–139.

46. Hiskey M: Hiskey-Nebraska Test of Learning Aptitude (Lincoln: Union College Press, 1966).

47. Hirshoren A, Hurley OL, Hunt JT: The reliability of the WISC-R and the Hiskey-Nebraska test with deaf children. *Am Ann of Deaf*, 122 (1977), 392–394.

48. Hirshoren A, Kavale K, Hurley OL, Hunt JT: The reliability of the WISC-R performance scale with deaf children. *Psych School*, 14 (1977), 412–415.

49. Fiedler M: *Developmental Studies of Deaf Children* (Washington, DC: ASHA, 1969).

50. Lavos G: WISC psychometric patterns among deaf children. *The Volta Review*, 64 (1962), 547–552.

51. Jeffers J: The process of speechreading viewed with respect to a theoretical construct, in *Proceedings of International Conference on Oral Education of the Deaf, Vol. II*. (Washington, DC: Alexander Graham Bell Association, 1965), pp 1530–1561.

52. Braden JP, Paquin MM: A comparison of the WISC-R and WAIS-R Performance Scales in deaf adolescents. *J Psychoeduc Assess*, 3 (1985), 285–290.

53. Watson BU: Test-retest stability of the Hiskey-Nebraska Test of Learning Aptitude in a sample of hearing-impaired children and adolescents. *J Speech and Hearing Disorders*, 48 (1983), 145–149.

54. Watson BU, Goldgar DE: A note on the use of the Hiskey-Nebraska Test of Learning Aptitude with deaf children. *Language, Speech and Hearing Serv Schools*, 16 (1985), 53–57.

55. Giancreco C: The Hiskey-Nebraska Test of Learning Aptitude (Revised) compared to several achievement tests. *Am Ann of Deaf*, 111 (1966), 556–577.

56. Humphrey JM: *Performance of Deaf Children on Tests of Cognitive, Linguistic, and Academic Achievement*, dissertation (Houston: University of Houston, 1976).

57. Birch JR, Stuckless ER, Birch JW: An eleven year study of predicting school achievement in young deaf children. *Am Ann of Deaf*, 108 (1963), 236–240.

58. Bonham SJ: Predicting achievement for deaf children, *Psych Serv Ctr J*, 14 (1974), 34–44.

59. Levine MN, Allen RM, Alker LN, et al: Clinical Profile for the Leiter International Performance Scale. *Psych Serv Ctr J*, 14 (1974), 45–51.

60. Mira MP: The use of the Arthur Adaptation of the Leiter International Performance Scale and the Nebraska Test of Learning Aptitude with preschool deaf children. *Am Ann of Deaf*, 107 (1962), 224–228.

61. Ritter DR: Intellectual estimates of hearing-impaired children: A comparison of three measures. *Psych School*, 13 (1976), 397–399.

62. Taddonio RO: Correlations of Leiter and visual subtests of the Illinois Test of Psycholinguistic Abilities with deaf elementary school children. *J Sch Psych*, 11 (1973), 30–35.

63. Ratcliffe KJ, Ratcliffe MW: The Leiter Scales: A review of validity findings. *Am Ann of Deaf*, 124 (1979), 38–45.

64. Carlson JS: A note on the relationship between Raven's Colored Progressive Matrices Test and operational thought. *Psych Schools*, 10 (1973), 211–214.

65. Goetzinger CP, Wills RC, Dekker LC: Non-language IQ tests used with deaf pupils. *The Volta Review*, 69 (1967), 500–506.

66. Goetzinger MR, Houchins RR: The 1947 Raven's Colored Progressive Matrices with deaf and hearing subjects. *Am Ann of Deaf*, 114 (1969), 95–101.

67. James RP: A correlation analysis between the Raven's Matrices and WISC-R Performance Scale. *The Volta Review*, 86 (1984), 336–341.

68. Porter LJ, Kirby EA: Effects of two instructional sets on validity of the Kaufman Assessment Battery for Children-Nonverbal Scale with a group of severely hearing impaired children. *Psych School* 23 (1986), 37–43.

69. Keane J, Kretschmer RE: The effect of mediated learning intervention on task performance with a deaf population. *J Educ Psychol*, 79 (1987), 49–53.

70. Laughton J: Nonlinguistic creative abilities and expressive syntactic abilities of hearing-impaired children. *The Volta Review*, 81 (1979), 409–420.

71. Kaltsounis B: Differences in verbal creative thinking abilities between deaf and hearing children. *Psych Reports*, 26 (1970), 727–733.

72. Pang H, Horrocks C: An exploratory study of creativity in deaf children. *Percep Mot Skills*, 27 (1968), 844–846.

73. Silver RA: The question of imagination, originality, and abstract thinking by deaf children. *Am Ann of Deaf*, 122 (1977), 349–354.

74. Odom PB, Blanton RL, McIntyre CK: Coding, medium and word recall by deaf and hearing subjects. *J Speech Hearing Res*, 13 (1970), 54–58.

75. Bellugi U, Klima E, Siple P: Remembering in signs. *Cognition*, 3 (1975), 93–125.

76. Locke SL, Locke VL: Deaf children's phonetic, visual and dactylic coding in a grapheme recall

task. *J Exper Psych*, 89 (1971), 142–146.

77. Conrad R: *The Deaf School Child* (London: Harper & Row, 1979).

78. Ling D: *Speech and the Hearing Impaired Child Theory and Practice* (Washington, DC: AG Bell Association, 1976).

79. Wilbur RB: *American Sign Language and Sign Systems* (Baltimore: University Park Press, 1979).

80. Cooper R: The ability of deaf and hearing children to apply morphological rules. *J Speech Hearing Res*, 10 (1967), 77–86.

81. Geers AE, Moog JS: Syntactic maturity of spontaneous speech and elicited imitations of hearing impaired children. *J Speech Hearing Dis*, 43 (1978), 380–391.

82. Davis J: Performance of young hearing impaired children on a test of basic concepts. *J Speech Hearing Res*, 17 (1974), 342–351.

83. Moog JS, Kozak VJ, Geers AE: *Grammatical Analysis of Elicited Language: Pre-Sentence Level* (St. Louis: Central Institute for the Deaf, 1983).

84. Moog JS, Geers AE: *Grammatical Analysis of Elicited Language: Simple Sentence Level (GAEL-S)* (St. Louis: Central Institute for the Deaf, 1979).

85. Moog JS, Geers AE: *Grammatical Analysis of Elicited Language: Complex Sentence Level* (St. Louis: Central Institute for the Deaf, 1980).

86. Engen E, Engen T: *Rhode Island Test of Language Structure* (Baltimore: University Park Press, 1983).

87. Quigley SP, Steinkamp MW, Power DJ, et al: *Test of Syntactic Abilities* (Beaverton: Dormac, Inc., 1978).

88. Quigley SP, Power DJ: *The TSA Syntax Program* (Beaverton: Dormac, Inc., 1980).

89. Bloom L, Lahey M: *Language Development and Language Disorders* (New York: John Wiley & Sons, 1978).

90. Kretschmer RR, Kretschmer LW: *Language Development and Interaction with the Hearing Impaired* (Baltimore: University Park Press, 1978).

91. Ramey CT, Farran DC, Campbell FA, et al: Observations of mother-infant interactions: Implications for Development, in Minifie FD, Lloyd LL, eds: *Communicative and Cognitive Abilities—Early Behavioral Assessment* (Baltimore: University Park Press, 1978).

92. Collins JL, Rose S: Communicative interaction patterns in an open environment for deaf high school students. *Am Ann of Deaf*, 121 (1976), 497–501.

93. Goss RN: Language used by mothers of deaf children and mothers of hearing children. *Am Ann of Deaf*, 115 (1970), 79–85.

94. Bales RE: *Interaction Process Analysis* (Reading: Addison-Wesley Press, 1950).

95. Craig WN, Collins JL: Analysis of communication interaction in classes for deaf children. *Am Ann of Deaf*, 115 (1970), 79–85.

96. Wolff S: Cognitive and communication patterns in classrooms for deaf students. *Am Ann of Deaf*, 122 (1977), 319–327.

97. Pendergrass RA, Hodges M: Deaf students in group problem solving situations: A study of the interactive process. *Am Ann of Deaf*, 121 (1976), 327–330.

98. Brill RG: *Brill Educational Achievement Test for Secondary Age of Deaf Students* (Northridge: Joyce Media, 1977).

99. Ewoldt C: Reading for the hearing or hearing impaired. A single process. *Am Ann of Deaf*, 123 (1978), 945–948.

100. Oakland T: *Psychological and Educational Assessment of Minority Children* (New York: Brunner Mazel, 1977), p 149.

101. Quarrington B, Solomon B: A current study of the social maturity of deaf students. *Canad J Behav Sci Rev Canad Sci Comp*, 7 (1975), 70–77.

102. Schlesinger HS, Meadow KP: *Sound and Sign Childhood Deafness and Mental Health* (Berkeley: University of California Press, 1972).

103. Levine ES, Wagner EE: Personality patterns of deaf persons: An interpretation based on research with the Hand Test. *Percept Mot Skills*, 31 (1974), 1167–1236.

104. Meadow KP, Karchmer MA, Petersen LM, Rudner L: *Meadow/Kendall Social-Emotional Assessment Inventory for Deaf Students* (Washington DC: Gallaudet College, Pre-College Programs, 1980).

105. Meadow KP: An instrument for assessment of social emotional adjustment in hearing-impaired preschoolers. *Am Ann of Deaf*, 128 (1983), 826–834.

106. Hogan HW: Authoritarianism among white and black deaf adolescents: Two measures compared. *Percept Mot Skills*, 31 (1970), 195–200.

107. Harris RI: The relationship of impulse control to parent hearing status, manual communication and academic achievement in deaf children. *Am Ann of Deaf* 123 (1978), 52–67.

108. Davey B, LaSasso C: Relations of cognitive style to assessment components of reading comprehension for hearing-impaired adolescents. *The Volta Review*, 87 (1985), 17–27.

109. Chan KS: Locus of control and achievement motivation—critical factors in educational psychology. *Psych Schools*, 15 (1979), 104–110.

110. Altshuler KZ, Deming WE, Vollenweider J, et al: Impulsivity and profound early deafness: A cross-cultural inquiry. *Am Ann of Deaf*, 121 (1976), 331–345.

111. Stinson M: Deafness and motivation for achieve-

ment: Research with implications for parent counseling. *The Volta Review*, 80 (1978), 140–148.

112. McCrone WP: Learned helplessness and level of underachievement among deaf adolescents. *Psych Schools*, 16 (1979), 430–434.

113. Chandler TA: Locus of control. A proposal for change. *Psych Schools*, 12 (1975), 335–339.

114. Kagan J: Impulsive and reflective children. Significance of conceptual tempo, in Krumbolid JD, ed: *Learning and the Educational Process* (Chicago: Rand McNally, 1965).

115. Rotter JB: Generalized expectancies for internal versus external control of reinforcement. *Psychol Monographs*, 80 (1966), 1–28.

116. Reich C, Hambleton D, Houldin BK: The integration of hearing impaired children in regular classrooms. *Am Ann of Deaf*, 122 (1977), 534–544.

117. Rudy JP, Nance JG: A transitional instrument, in Northcott WH, ed: *The Hearing Impaired Child in a Regular Classroom* (Washington DC: The Alexander Graham Bell Assoc., 1973).

6 | PSYCHO-EDUCATIONAL ASSESSMENT OF CHILDREN WITH AUDITORY LANGUAGE LEARNING PROBLEMS

R. Ray Battin

The learning and behaviorally disturbed child has been described by more than 40 labels over the years. In many instances, these labels were a reflection of the practitioner's bias. The term in vogue at this time, *specific learning disability*, was preceded by the term *minimal brain dysfunction*. Both terms are used to describe children with average or above-average general abilities, but with specific learning or behavioral disabilities ranging from mild to severe, which were assumed to be associated with deviations of the central nervous system.

In 1971, Battin and Kraft described learning-disabled children as being dysynchronous.[1] The concept of dysynchrony is shown in Figure 6-1. In this figure, the solid lines represent synchronous behavior—that behavior which occurs at regularly scheduled and expected intervals. As shown by the dotted lines, the learning impaired, dysynchronous child does not follow expected developmental patterns because he/she is out of phase with all or part of his/her environment, including siblings, parents, neighborhood, and school. The severity of disruption can be related to the degree of perceptual deficit present, as well as to the health status and potential of the child's family. In contrast, the child who develops without perceptual deficits can generally accommodate to his/her environment if dysynchrony appears, unless pertinent elements of psychopathology interfere.

This dysynchrony can be from one or a combination of causes: physical (allergies, hypothyroidism, hypoglycemia), organic (neurologic impairment), educational, environmental, and/or familial. Furthermore, dysynchrony may be evidenced very early, and in some, it is thought to be apparent in utero. The child with a central auditory processing disturbance qualifies for the dysynchronous label.

Auditory verbal language disturbances can range from the severely involved, as seen in children with aphasia, auditory agnosia, or autism, to the more mildly involved children with auditory imperceptions and/or learning disabilities.

For the child with severe auditory-verbal-language problems, psycho-educational assessment will, by necessity, consist of a modified test battery tailored to the perceptual and the communicative skills of the child. Test instruments typically used for evaluating the severely hearing impaired are also applicable to this population (see Chapter 5).

Children with auditory language-learning problems are more difficult to identify than those with peripheral hearing loss and/or impaired vision. Their behaviors may be misunderstood. As a result, these children are frequently labeled immature or inattentive. Their performance in school worsens each year, and by grades 3 or 4 they are either making failing grades or significantly underachieving for their abilities level. At this point, the teacher or parent may seek further evaluation of these children.

The child is referred to the educational diagnostician, counselor, or school psychologist because of school or behavioral difficulties. It is the responsibility of the examiner to assess the child's general abilities, how he/she learns, and how he/she perceives and deals with new situations. The examiner must also present an extensive analysis of independent responses and test scatter. Specific test data, if properly analyzed, may delineate the child with an auditory perceptual problem.

This chapter will deal with the selection and interpretation of psycho-educational tests and their use in evaluating the child with an auditory-verbal processing or perceptual disturbance. It will attempt to demonstrate how the

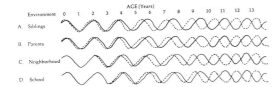

Figure 6-1. Illustration of dysynchrony in children (from Battin and Kraft[1]).

child's test profile can be used in educational planning and in establishing a remedial program directed to specific deficits.

VALIDITY AND RELIABILITY

Care must be taken when choosing an assessment instrument. With the proliferation of tests (they sprout like leaves on a tree), the examiner must know how to choose appropriately.

Standards, as recommended by the Committee on Standards of the American Psychological Association, apply to any published test used in evaluation, diagnosis, or prognosis. Each test should have data available on validity and reliability, directions for administration and scoring, and qualifications required to administer and properly interpret the test.

A test and its manual should be revised periodically. The Standards committee recommends that a test be withdrawn from the market if the manual is 15 or more years old and no revision can be obtained.[2] It has been further stated, "If the validity of a suggested test interpretation has not been checked within 15 or 20 years, the test should be withdrawn from general sale and distributed, if at all, only to persons who will conduct their own validity studies."[2]

Test *validity* means that the test actually measures what it says it measures,[3] while *reliability* refers to the accuracy of the measurements by reflecting the degree of consistency among scores obtained by an individual (see Chapter 3).[4] The consistency or stability of a test score is usually expressed by means of a *reliability coefficient*.[5] *Standard error of measurement* expresses the consistency of performance in absolute terms and provides a statement of the size of the errors of measurement.

INFORMAL VS. FORMAL TESTING

Increasing criticism has been directed toward formal testing. Intelligence tests have come under critical review because they have been used to classify children for placement in classes for the mentally retarded. It was found that blacks tended to score lower on the Wechsler Intelligence Scale for Children (WISC) and the Stanford-Binet tests, and thus were overrepresented in these classes. As a result, a moratorium on the use of formal psychological testing for special education placement has been declared in many school districts.[6-8] To discontinue the use of generalized intelligence tests, however, is to throw out the good with the bad. The error comes when examiners use such tests as the WISC-Revised (WISC-R), the Wechsler Pre-School and Primary Scale of Intelligence (WPPSI), or the Stanford-Binet to compute a single composite score, rather than analyze the components. As will be pointed out in later sections of this chapter, both the WISC and the Stanford-Binet can provide information on auditory-verbal and visual-motor skills.

Informal assessment may provide insight into the child's problems, but with the present concern over accountability, it does not provide an adequate base on which to build a treatment or educational program. The generalized assessment utilizing well-standardized tests provides the examiner with more reliable and valid data against which treatment gains versus maturational gains may be checked. By using the child as the control, a learning and abilities profile can be plotted and used to determine if significant variations between strengths and weaknesses exist and whether therapeutic intervention is indicated. Classification can be made according to independent learning skills, as opposed to a more *global* labeling.

UNIMODAL, BIMODAL, OR MULTIMODAL ASSESSMENT

It is extremely difficult to dissect learning by modality. Jastak and Jastak theorize that the three sensory modalities—hearing, vision, and kinesthesia (touch)—are "involved in the formation of lexigraphic and other linguistic communication codes."[5]

With increasing specialization, learning disorders are divided into discipline-specific disabilities. As we test in our specialty and see what we are trained to see, we become like the proverbial blind men describing the elephant. Rarely is a learning-disabled child depressed in only a single modality. Furthermore, if we look only at a single modality when we assess a child's capabilities, we may label as deficient areas in which the child falls below what is expected according to chronologic age, when in fact the child is depressed across all modalities and is performing within abilities level. To re-emphasize, a child must be used as his/her own control if we are to understand the learning potential as well as the disabilities of that child.

HISTORY AS PART
OF THE ASSESSMENT

A detailed birth, health, family, social, educational, and behavioral history is a critical part of any comprehensive assessment. A preinterview questionnaire, which the parents can complete at home with the help of the baby book, and which is returned prior to the testing, allows the examiner some insight into the problems presented by the child.[9] A comparison of the behaviors described in the questionnaire with test behavior and performance provides the examiner with some support for the interpretation drawn from the assessment.

In addition to specific questions, the questionnaire should contain several open-ended questions that allow the parents to describe the child's behavior and personality. Methods of discipline used by the parents should also be explained in detail. The examiner will want to review the responses to questions on birth, health, and development carefully, as well as scrutinize the behavioral responses.

Behaviors that point to a disturbance in the auditory-verbal area include inattentiveness, short attention span, daydreaming, and a tendency to play with younger children. The child may also be withdrawn, unable to follow directions, and forgetful. The child may misunderstand instructions or directions, be disruptive in school and at home, fail to bring homework home, or be unable to remember assignments. For example, the child might know spelling words or other material at home, but fail a test on the material at school. Teachers may label the child as a "smart aleck" or one who "refuses to conform."

SPECIFIC TEST INSTRUMENTS

A comprehensive psycho-educational test battery for children suspected of an auditory-verbal learning disturbance should include tests which fall under five general categories. These categories are: general abilities, auditory-verbal behavior, visual-motor behavior, academic behavior, and personality. Table 6-1 summarizes the psychological tests that should be considered for assessment in these five areas.

General Abilities Assessment

The most widely used tests of general abilities are the Stanford-Binet and the Wechsler Scales.

The first scale of intelligence, the Binet, was published by Binet and Simon in 1905. It was developed to help separate the uneducable from the educable in the schools of Paris. In 1916, while at Stanford University, Terman revised the Binet test—thus, the name Stanford-Binet.[10] Since that time it has gone through several additional revisions. In 1960, the best items from the *L* and *M* forms of the 1937 scale were combined into a single scale. This revision was restandardized in 1972.[11] Thorndike et al introduced the fourth edition in 1986.[12]

The present revision covers the same age range. It requires the examiner to establish a basal age and a ceiling age, and includes many of the same types of test items. All other aspects of the test differ significantly from previous editions. Items of the same type are now grouped into 15 tests, with each test tapping different cognitive skills and different funds of information.

Four broad areas, Verbal Reasoning, Abstract/Visual Reasoning, Quantitative Reasoning, and Short-Term Memory, are assessed by the 15 tests. The tests provide a composite standard age score of general reasoning ability and standard age scores for the four areas. Standard age scores are also available for any combination of the four areas as well as for individual test scores for the 15 tests. This edition was constructed to better identify individuals who are mentally retarded, have specific

Table 6-1 Psycho-educational Test Battery

Type of Assessment	Sequence of Tests
I. General Abilities	*(appropriate instruments)* Stanford-Binet-Fourth Edition Wechsler Intelligence Scale for Children-Revised (WISC-R) Wechsler Preschool and Primary Scale of Intelligence (WPPSI) Kaufman Assessment Battery Special Abilities Tests
II. Auditory-Verbal Behavior	1. Illinois Test of Psycholinguistic Abilities (ITPA; selected subtests) 2. Detroit Test of Learning Aptitude-Revised (selected subtests) 3. Goldman-Fristoe-Woodcock Test of Selective Attention 4. Peabody Picture Vocabulary Test (PPVT) 5. Quick Test
III. Visual-Motor Behavior	1. Illinois Test of Psycholinguistic Abilities (ITPA; selected subtests) 2. Bender-Gestalt Test 3. Slosson Drawing Coordination Test for Children 4. Primary Visual Motor Test 5. Goodenough-Harris Draw-A-Person
IV. Academic Behavior	1. Wide-Range Achievement Test (WRAT) 2. Peabody Individual Achievement Test (PIAT) 3. Myklebust Picture Story Language Test
V. Personality	*(appropriate instruments)* Rorschach Test Thematic Apperception Test The Children's Apperception Test Incomplete Sentences Test House-Tree-Person Test Kinetic Family Drawing

learning disabilities, or are gifted. Once an examiner becomes familiar with the new test, he/she will find it is much more flexible than earlier editions. The new edition can be adapted more readily to the child undergoing the test, and it provides information in both the auditory-verbal and visual-motor modalities. This information can then be used in the development of a treatment program.

The complete battery consists of 8 to 13 tests and takes one hour to 90 minutes to administer. A screening battery composed of the Vocabulary, Bead Memory, Quantitative, and Pattern Analysis can be administered in 30 to 40 minutes. A six-subtest battery, which requires less testing time than the complete battery, can be assembled by adding Memory for Sentences and Comprehension to the original screening test. The authors recommend that assessment of students experiencing difficulty in school include tests that have the greatest diagnostic value and a balance of verbal and abstract/visual reasoning tests. The test manual provides recommendations for abbreviated batteries.[12]

The revised, restandardized WISC-R was published in 1974.[13] It consists of the same 12 subtests that made up the 1949 WISC, with six tests constituting the Verbal Scale and six the Performance Scale. As with the earlier WISC, 10 of the WISC-R tests are considered mandatory; the Digit Span and Mazes subtests are supplementary tests and were not included in establishing the IQ tables.

Changes were made in the administration order and in the subtest content. The verbal and performance tests are alternated, with the preferred order being: Information, Picture Completion, Similarities, Picture Arrangement, Arithmetic, Block Design, Vocabulary, Object Assembly, Comprehension, Coding, Digit Span (supplementary), and Mazes (supplementary).

I have found the new order for presenting subtests to be more interesting and less tiring, both for the child and the examiner. The subtests most relevant to auditory-verbal dysfunction are the verbal ones; however, they only reveal a disturbance within a particular child when they are compared with that child's performance areas.[14]

Analysis of a child's performance on the individual subtests of the WISC-R will indicate whether further testing in specific modalities is needed.[15] The Information subtest indicates how well the child stores information gained from education and experience and how well this information can be retrieved on command. By comparing responses on the Information, Arithmetic, and Digit Span subtests, the examiner can observe the effectiveness of the child's delayed recall as opposed to immediate recall, auditory attention and mental control. The ability to provide practical solutions to everyday problems and social adjustment may be seen through the Comprehension subtest, with the Vocabulary subtest providing an estimate of verbal fluency, word knowledge, and expressive skills. The Similarities subtest provides information on the child's logical and abstract verbal reasoning ability.

By careful observation of the child's behavior during the verbal subtests, an understanding of how the child processes auditorily emerges. Questions that indicate auditory processing function include:

(*1*) Does the child need frequent repetition or restatement of questions?
(*2*) Does the child tend to reauditorize the material, or are there long response latencies?
(*3*) How are the numbers on the Digit Span Subtest retrieved?
(*4*) Are the problems on the Arithmetic Subtest forgotten before they can be solved?
(*5*) Are there difficulties in perceiving the questions or following directions on the Information, Comprehension, and Similarities Subtests?
(*6*) Does the child appear to confuse words (e.g., pail for nail) on the Vocabulary Subtest?

Similar analysis of the subtests of the Performance Scale can pinpoint problems in visual closure, gestalt, praxis, short-term memory, scanning, and left-right tracking. Problems with delayed visual recall, visual problem solving ability, and fine motor control can also be delineated.

The WPPSI is an extension of the WISC devised for younger children.[16] It was constructed in 1963 and standardized on a sample population of 1200 children divided into six age groups clustered by half-year and ranging from 4 years of age through 6.5 years of age. The six age groups were each made up of 100 boys and 100 girls; these subjects represented the 1960 census geographically, racially, occupationally, and residentually (rural-urban) in the standardization population. In this test, the mean IQ is 100, with a standard deviation of 15. The subtests have a mean scaled score of 10 and a standard deviation of 3. The test takes approximately 50 to 75 minutes to administer, and may have to be broken into two testing sessions if the child becomes unduly fatigued. As with the WISC, the WPPSI uses 10 subtests—five verbal and five performance—to determine IQ. A review of the child's performance on individual subtests does give the examiner a pattern of strengths and weaknesses in auditory-verbal and visual-motor learning. In this author's opinion, however, it does not provide sufficient additional information over the Stanford-Binet to warrant the added time it takes to administer. The time would be more profitably used by administering a language test in conjunction with the Stanford-Binet.

The Kaufman Assessment Battery for Children was published in 1983[17] as an individually administered measure of intelligence and achievement for children 2.5 through 12.5 years of age. Administration time is approximately 45 minutes for preschool children and 75 minutes for school age children.

The test is made up of the following 16 subtests: Hand Movements, Number Recall, Word Order, Magic Window, Face Recognition, Gestalt Closure, Triangles, Matrix Analogies, Spatial Memory, Photo Series, Expressive Vocabulary, Faces and Places, Arithmetic, Riddles, Reading/Decoding, and Reading/Understanding. Seven subtests are administered to 2.5-year-old children, 9 to 3-year old children, and the maximum (13) to 7-year-old children and older. It provides standard scores (mean, 100; standard deviation, 15) in four areas: Sequential Processing, Simultaneous Processing, Mental Processing Composite (obtained from Sequencing Processing and Simultaneous Processing, which provides an IQ equivalence), and Achievement. Supplemental sociocultural norms assist in interpreting the tests of minority children. In addition, a nonverbal scale made up of selected subtests that can be administered and responded to through gestures provides assessment of the general abilities level of children with auditory processing problems, speech and language delay, or hearing impairment.

The Kaufman was developed from neuropsychological theory, but does not claim to be a neuropsychological test. However, those examiners who look at brain dysfunction, as it relates to performance and developing a therapy plan, will find the test fits well into their assessment battery.

Other intelligence tests that test special abilities are the Hiskey-Nebraska Test of Learning Aptitudes,[18] Leiter International Performance Scale,[19] Arthur Point Performance Scale,[20] Slosson Intelligence Test for Children and Adults,[21] Raven Progressive Matrices,[22,23] and the Columbia Mental Maturity Scale.

Auditory-Verbal Behavior Assessment

Although speech pathologists have laid claim to the ITPA as a language test, it was designed as a diagnostic test of psychological and linguistic function.[25] The test assesses specific ability strengths as well as weaknesses, and thus allows a plan for remediation to be developed. The experimental edition of the ITPA was published in 1961, with the present revision published in 1968. The revised ITPA extended the age range and covers children from 2.5 years through 10 years, 3 months of age. Clinically, the test is more effective for those over 4 years of age. For learning-disabled children whose age is above the test ceiling, the full test or selective subtests provide useful information on developmental lags.

The 10 main and two supplementary subtests of the ITPA are divided into two categories: auditory-verbal and visual-motor. Scaled scores, which are a linear transformation of raw scores, are used to express the child's functioning level on each subtest. There is a mean of 36 and a standard deviation of 6. While psycholinguistic age scores may provide information on the child who falls above the age ceiling of the ITPA, they do not provide the data available in the scaled scores, which take into consideration variability of performance for different ages on the various subtests. The scaled scores allow for comparison of test-retest data. An overall psycholinguistic age as well as a psycholinguistic quotient are available from the total score of the 10 main subtests. A mental age estimate and IQ equivalent are also available by using the IQ conversion tables of the Stanford-Binet.

There are five main tests and two supplementary tests under the auditory-verbal area of the ITPA. They assess the ability to gain meaning from auditorily received stimuli (auditory reception), the ability to see the relationship between stimuli received auditorily (auditory association), and the ability to convey ideas in words (verbal expression). Grammatic closure uses visual clues together with auditory clues for assessing the child's retention of syntax and grammatic form. It also assesses the child's ability to complete or *close out* an incomplete sentence. The auditory sequential memory test uses digits that are presented two per second to assess immediate sequential recall. The two supplementary tests consist of auditory closure for assessing the ability to complete or *fill in* the missing parts or part of a word, and sound blending for testing the ability to synthesize or resynthesize words or nonsense words. Both the auditory closure and the grammatic closure subtests tap long-term memory.

Although the auditory reception and association tests tap the specific skills set forth by the test, they are dependent on a child's vocabulary and are somewhat culturally biased. At times, due to the child's shyness or lack of comprehension of the task, it is difficult to obtain sufficient response on the verbal expression subtest to adequately estimate expressive skills. However, it has been observed clinically that there is a close relationship between performance on this subtest and the written expressive skills observed on the Myklebust Test of Written Expression.[26]

Each subtest of the ITPA was to measure only one discrete function via a single modality or channel without contamination by using another channel. As was seen in the discussion of the grammatic closure subtest, it is difficult to isolate a single channel or modality when developing any test. This is particularly true on the visual subtests that utilize pictures to elicit a response. Only one of the five main tests that propose to test the visual-motor skills is free of auditory-verbal contamination. The visual sequential memory test uses discrete abstract figures that restrict verbal labeling to evaluate the ability to reproduce a sequence of designs. The test provides the examiner with information on attention span, visual scanning, and directionality, as well as immediate recall of a visual sequential pattern. The ability to recognize the whole from parts or to *close out* an incomplete visual pattern is assessed through the visual closure subtest. It also provides the examiner with information on visual recall, visual scanning, left/right tracking, and how organized the youngster is in visual problem-solving. Simple line drawings of common objects (fish, shoes, bottles, hammers, and saws) are used in the four separately presented scenes. While the child is able to label the pictures, this auditory-verbal response minimally assists in the visual closure task. Both the visual reception subtest, which assesses the ability to decode visual stimuli, and the visual association subtest, which assesses the ability to see the relationship between visual stimuli, receive some contamination from the auditory channel. Children who are severely depressed in auditory verbal skills also score low on the visual association subtest of the ITPA, even though visual problem-solving tests that are not language-contaminated, such as the Raven Progressive Matrices, are well executed.

The remaining subtest of the ITPA is manual expression. This subtest deals with communicating ideas through gestures. It provides some insight into the child's inner language, particularly where there is a delay in verbal expression.

The Detroit Tests of Learning Aptitude (DTLA-2, revised in 1985)[27] is a flexible, comprehensive test. It can be used to verify areas of difficulty and to supplement the WISC-R, Stanford-Binet, and ITPA, or even in place of the ITPA for children over 10 years, 3 months of age. The DTLA-2 contains 11 subtests and nine composites. The author retained, with minor changes in administration and scoring, six of the subtests from the 1967 revision.[28] Three new tests were added, creating a total of nine subtests in the complete battery, which assess four domains: Linguistic, Cognitive, Attentional, and Motoric. The Motor Speed and Precision subtest has been dropped from the present revision. However, this subtest is useful in evaluating fine motor skills, as well as the speed at which a student can handle paper-pencil tasks.

A downward extension of the DTLA-2 was developed by Hammil and Bryant.[29] The Detroit Tests of Learning Aptitudes-Primary (DTLA-P) was designed to measure intellectual abilities of children 3 to 9 years of age. The test is organized developmentally from easiest to most difficult, and uses a Binet-type format. The examiner establishes a basal (that point where 10 items in a row are passed) and a ceiling (that point where 10 items in a row are missed). An articulation test and 8 subtests, which may be used in the identification of specific abilities, are included in the DTLA-P. A general intelligence or aptitude score is also provided.

Individual assessment places the child in an optimum testing learning situation. Children who have problems with auditory figure-ground or selective attention may do well in the one-to-one situation, but have extreme difficulty attending in the classroom. The revised Goldman-Fristoe-Woodcock (GFW) Test,[30] or discrimination tests presented both in quiet and with competing noise, should be given. Clinically, it has been found that children who have difficulty selectively attending in the classroom are depressed on the cafeteria and/or voice noise subtests of the GFW. Children who are depressed on the fan noise subtest, but who fall at or above the 50th percentile on the other two subtests (cafeteria and voice noise), show emotional rather than auditory perceptual problems.

Picture vocabulary tests are often used to assess receptive language. The results are reported by mental age and/or IQ, implying that these test results are comparable to results from more comprehensive tests of general ability. The most frequently used vocabulary tests are the Peabody Picture Vocabulary Test (PPVT)[31] and the Quick Test.[32]

The PPVT and the Quick Test are reported by Sattler[20] as measuring different facets of language skills. The Peabody appears to be less sensitive to higher-order language skills than the Quick Test. Intelligence quotients obtained from the PPVT are not interchangeable with the IQ scores obtained from either the WISC or the Stanford-Binet. The PPVT "may be useful in measuring extensiveness of vocabulary and degree of cultural assimilation of children."[33] Costello described the PPVT as a screening instrument for children who have a limited expressive vocabulary or who are verbally inhibited. PPVT scores should not be used in isolation, but rather in conjunction with other measures of general abilities.[34] The Quick Test also serves as a screening instrument and should never be used in place of the Stanford-Binet, WISC, or WPPSI. It can be used when a precise estimate of general abilities is not critical.[20]

Visual-Motor Behavior Assessment

A complete evaluation should include one or more tests of visual perception integration and execution. The Bender-Gestalt Test has been widely used since it was developed by Loretta Bender in 1938. Koppitz revised the scoring system in 1963 and again in 1975, and her scoring system has been adopted by most individuals administering the Bender-Gestalt Test.[35] She has developed an objective scoring system as well as age norms for ages 5 years through 10 years, 11 months. In addition, she has delineated indicators of brain injury for children ages 5 to 10 years.

Two other tests of visual perception and eye/hand coordination are the Slosson Drawing Coordination Test for Children[36] published in 1962, and the Primary Visual Motor Test[37] published in 1970.

The Goodenough-Harris Draw-A-Person Test[38] allows the examiner to compare the youngster's spatial, size, and shape orientation, as well as the child's sequencing ability when drawing free-hand without a pattern, as opposed to copying designs. It also provides insight into the child's body imagery and emotional state. The youngster is asked to draw a picture of a person, then a picture of the opposite sex, and then a self drawing. New norms were established for the test in 1970 for ages 6 to 11 years by the US Department of Health, Education, and Welfare.[39] The test is non-threatening and serves as a good introduction to the total test battery. It should be observed which hand the youngster uses to write and draw as well as how the pencil is held.

Academic Assessment

Some estimate of academic performance should be made during the comprehensive evaluation. This allows the examiner to observe how well the child handles academic material in a one-to-one testing situation as opposed to the group, timed achievement test administered in the classroom. The report of results should describe how the child handles different types of problem-solving, as well as areas in which there is difficulty. Difficulties should be analyzed in light of deficits observed in auditory, verbal, and visual motor areas. For example, one might report the results of testing as follows:

"The memory problems did not overly hamper her academic achievement. She worked slowly in reading; however, her performance fell in the same range as her intellectual ability. The youngster seemed to perform better when given ample time to consider her response. The memory problems did not interfere with her spelling, but did appear to hamper long-term retention of academic facts."

The Wide-Range Achievement Test (WRAT), which takes between 20 and 30 minutes to administer, evaluates arithmetic, reading (word recognition), and spelling. The test is widely used and was standardized by the Public Health Service of the US Department of Health, Education, and Welfare in 1970,[40] and revised by the authors in 1976. The test ranges from pre-kindergarten through college. The Arithmetic Subtest is timed, with a 10-minute limit. Additional information can be obtained if the examiner records what the child has completed at the 10-minute limit and then allows the youngster to continue until he/she no longer can work the problems.

The Peabody Individual Achievement Test (PIAT) takes approximately 45 minutes to administer to older or very bright children, with younger or slower children requiring about 30 minutes to complete the test.

Both the WRAT and the PIAT have limitations. Williamson[41] compared the WRAT with the Stanford Achievement Test and found that with older pupils, the WRAT tended to overestimate academic performance. The younger the student, the higher the correlation. When the WRAT and PIAT were compared by Harmer and Williams,[42] they found no significant difference between performance on the spelling and reading subtests. There was no significant difference between math scores of the PIAT and the WRAT for grades 1, 2, and 3; however, at grades 4 and above, individual cases demonstrated differences of as much as six years in grade equivalents. These findings indicate that the WRAT and PIAT math subtests are not interchangeable unless consideration is given to the differences between the two tests. When the PIAT math subtest is used for grades 4 and above, the results may overestimate achievement levels—this test should be supplemented with the subtest of the WRAT or a similar test of computation skills.

Both the WRAT and PIAT tend to overestimate when the results are compared with teacher-administered achievement tests. Williamson[41] questioned whether this was due to the diagnostician, who tests on a one-to-one basis, being in a more supportive role and thus obtaining much higher scores. It may be that group (classroom) testing underestimates the ability of the learning-disabled child.[43] It would also tend to punish the easily distracted, or children with problems in selective attention or attention span. Therefore, the individually administered achievement test may give a more accurate estimate of academic achievement of a child with auditory-verbal problems.

The Myklebust Picture Story Language Test,[26] or a similar test of written expression, allows comparison of written language with verbal expression and reading. Children who are depressed in verbal expression frequently are also depressed in the number of words and/or sentences that they use to write a story, even though the content may be age-appropriate or above. Children who are poor readers or who score low in reading comprehension often do poorly on content. Grammar and punctuation disturbance on the written test tends to reflect how well a child has acquired the rules of language.

Personality Assessment

Whether or not children are disabled, they will acquire a distinct manner of handling different situations and dealing with their environment and people. They are individuals with distinct personalities. Personality tests provide information about the *inner workings* of individuals, their perceptions of their world, how they cope, their social skills, their self-concept, and their frustration tolerance level. Such tests give the examiner some understanding of the child's attitudes toward self, family, and the outside world—how the child perceives that he "fits into the scheme of things." Personality assessment utilizes projective tests and personality inventories.[44] Many test instruments are available, and each examiner has favorites. The most popular are the Rorschach Test,[45,46] the Thematic Apperception Test, the Children's Apperception Test,[47] the Incomplete Sentences Test,[48] the House/Tree/Person Test,[49] and the Kinetic Family Drawings.[50]

One or two personality tests should be a part of the comprehensive evaluation. The examiner should be qualified to administer and interpret projective instruments. It is important that information on the perceptual disabilities

be available at the time of interpretation of the projective tests. When a child's misperceptions of the environment result from an auditory perceptual disturbance, the child's responses to the projective instrument will be affected. If a child constantly misperceives what is said by improper decoding, or if the child cannot hold information in short-term memory long enough to rescan it and interpret and act on the message, or if selective attention is disturbed, the child's environment will be constantly punishing. Frustration, poor self-worth, and a sense of failure, as well as feelings of anger, aggression, and hostility are bound to develop. These feelings are secondary to the primary disorder of disturbed auditory perception and processing. Clinically, it has been found that when specific deficits are remediated, the emotional components tend to resolve themselves. When an emotional disturbance does remain beyond specific treatment of deficits, it responds quickly to psychotherapy.

EDUCATIONAL PLANNING AND REMEDIATION

The primary purpose of a comprehensive psycho-educational evaluation is to provide the parents, school, and remediation specialists with a better understanding of the child, and the child's general abilities, disabilities, and academic strengths and weaknesses. Test results should also provide an explanation of nonconforming behavior and allow for the development of an individualized educational, behavioral, and remediation plan. The test profile may dictate such things as:

(1) Modifications in the home and school environment to allow the child to selectively attend to what is being said.
(2) Reinforcement of auditory instruction by visual and kinesthetic means.
(3) Allowing the child to record written work on a tape recorder and then transcribe from his/her own dictation.
(4) Modifying the length and sequence of orally presented material.
(5) Placement in a resource program.
(6) Individualized therapy directed to remediating specific deficits.[51]

The case evaluation in this chapter shows how information relating to intellectual, aca-

Case evaluation. Table 6-2 shows the test profile of a young man, M.B., who was seen for comprehensive neuropsychological and audiologic evaluation when he was 9 years, 3 months of age. He was the older of two boys. According to the preinterview questionnaire, both birth and developmental history were normal. Health history revealed allergies and repeated middle ear infections during the preschool years. Tubes had been inserted to relieve the fluid, and there was a history of fluctuating hearing until the adenoids were removed when M.B. was 6 years of age.

M.B. was enrolled in the third grade in a private school, and was having difficulty with reading, spelling, and math. He tried hard and made average to above-average grades; however, he had difficulty putting what he knew on paper. He tended to be a follower in play, but did get along with peers and with his brother and father. His major problem was described as a failure to follow orders.

Behavior during examination revealed a likeable youngster who was cooperative and put forth a good effort. He appeared tense, and this was sustained throughout the testing. He would often stare at the examiner as if concentrating very hard or listening intently, but would give no response. He rarely asked to have material repeated, but instead would proceed incorrectly or give the wrong answer as if he had not heard or understood what had been said. There were long response latencies, and from time to time he would say, "I don't understand what you mean."

Gross coordination fell within normal limits; fine motor coordination was somewhat disturbed. However, on the motor speed and precision subtest of the Detroit Tests of Learning Aptitude, this youngster functioned approximately two years below his chronologic age. His handwriting was difficult to read, and he had a tendency to form numbers and letters in an awkward manner. M.B. was left-handed, foot dominance was not firmly established, and he was right-eyed for near and far point vision. Visual testing revealed normal acuity, phoria, and color and depth perception.

Audiologic findings revealed a mild, bilateral conductive hearing loss with pure tone averages of 13 dB for the left ear and 18 dB for the right, speech reception thresholds of 15 dB for the left ear and 20 dB for the right, and phonetically balanced maximum responses of 100%, bilaterally. Impedance audiometry confirmed the conductive component. The boy had considerable nasal congestion and was coughing and sneezing at the time of testing. A referral was made back to his pediatrician.

The Goldman-Fristoe-Woodcock Test of Selective Attention was administered through the ear phones. Adjustments were made in output to compensate for the mild conductive hearing loss. M.B. performed 100% correct in quiet, but dropped below the baseline for his age on the three noise subtests.

Both receptive and expressive language skills were below average. M.B. was quite reticent, and spontaneous speech was very limited. He appeared to have word-finding problems when he did express himself, and he did not know the meaning of many vocabulary terms. Grammar was a bit below average, but he was able to structure his sentences in proper sequence.

Performance on the WISC-R placed this boy in the borderline-to-average range of general abilities. There was a highly statistically significant difference between his functioning in verbal and visual areas throughout the testing. His verbal abilities were uniformly below average, while all his visual skills were above average.

Testing in specific learning skill areas confirmed his extreme difficulty in discriminating and understanding the meaning of what was said. He had problems processing oral information and making appropriate word associations. If he was able to receive information accurately, he had difficulty repeating it. As a result, verbal expressive skills were well below average. While most visual perceptual skills were average to above average, he did have some difficulty with visual retention and with visual motor integration/execution. He performed better when he had to manipulate materials only minimally.

Academically, M.B. was performing at early second-grade level. He had a limited sight vocabulary and did not use phonic skills. In math, he had difficulty with terms (such as pair) and with memory problems (such as the number of pennies in a nickel and the number of days in a week). He was able to handle most single-digit addition and subtraction; however, if the problem was put in story form, he was unable to solve it. On the general information subtest of the PIAT, he worked very hard; he would occasionally work to recall the correct term by

Table 6-2 Test Profile of M.B. for Case Evaluation

THE BATTIN CLINIC
Parent-Teacher Report for: _____ M.B. _____
School: _____ C.A. _9–3_ Date: _9–25–79_

	s.s.	IQ / age	Very Poor (5)	Poor (15)	Low (30)	Average (50)	High (70)	Superior (85)	Very Superior (95)
I. PRESENT GENERAL INTELLECTUAL FUNCTIONING									
Wechsler Intelligence Scale	s.s.	IQ							
Verbal Scale Total		(77)	(X)						
Information	6		X						
Similarities	6		X						
Arithmetic	6		X						
Vocabulary	7			X					
Comprehension	6		X						
Digit Span		(5)	X						
Performance Scale Total		(102)				(X)			
Picture Completion	8				X				
Picture Arrangement	11						X		
Block Design	12							X	
Object Assembly	11						X		
Coding	10					X			
Mazes									
Full Scale Total		(87)	(X)						
Other(s) _____ Mental Age ____									
II. SPECIFIC LANGUAGE/LEARNING ABILITIES									
Illinois Test of Psycholinguistic Abilities		age							
Reception — Auditory		6–10	X						
Reception — Visual		Above Ceiling							X
Association — Auditory		5–5	X						
Association — Visual		Above Ceiling							X
Expression — Verbal		5–10	X						
Expression — Manual		Above Ceiling							X
Expression — Grammatic		6–5	X						
Closure — Auditory		7–3			X				
Closure — Visual		Above Ceiling							X
Memory — Auditory		5–8	X						
Memory — Visual		7–10				X			
Sound Blending		Above Ceiling							X
Total Language Age		(7–10)			(X)				
Ayres Figure-Ground (Visual)									
Raven (Visual Problem Solving)							X		
Bender-Gestalt (Eye-Hand Coordination)					X				
Goodenough-Harris (Draw-A-Person)							X		
Benton Test of Visual Retention						(X ——— X)			
Goldman-Fristoe-Woodcock (Selective Attention)									
Quiet									X
Fan Noise			X						
Cafeteria Noise			X						
Voice Noise			X						
Detroit Test of Learning Aptitude									
Auditory Attn: Words _6–2_ Sentences _4–6_									
Visual Attn: Objects _7–6_ Letters _7–6_									
Motor Speed: _7–3_									
Other(s) _____									

(Continued)

Table 6-2 *Continued*

	Percentile Rank						
	Very Poor / 5	Poor / 15	Low / 30	Average / 50	High / 70	Superior / 85	Very Superior / 95

III. ACADEMIC ACHIEVEMENT
Test Name: *Peabody Individual Achievement*

	grade level	Very Poor	Poor	Low	Average	High	Superior	Very Superior
Math	2.3		X					
Reading Recognition	1.8	X						
Reading Comprehension	2.7			X				
Spelling	1.7	X						
General Information	3.8				X			
Total	2.3		X					

Myklebust (Written Expression)

		Very Poor	Poor	Low	Average	High	Superior	Very Superior
Number of Words		X						
Number of Sentences		X						
Words per Sentence		X						
Syntax				X				
Content				X				
Others								

IV. SPECIAL AREAS
Test Names: *T.A.T. Projective Questions, House-Tree-Person, Motor Coordination*

V. AUDIOLOGIC FINDINGS: *Mild bilateral conductive loss*
VI. VISUAL FINDINGS: *Acuity, color, depth, phoria—normal*

---

repeating the first letter over and over until he could eventually recall the word. On the Myklebust Test, he wrote only one sentence, and the words were difficult to interpret because of misspelling.

Strong emotional components, mostly in the form of stress and its internalization, were present. He appeared well aware of his difficulties and of the extreme discrepancy between his visual problem-solving skills and his facility in language. This must have been quite frustrating to him. He wanted to be more competent and more powerful and to have more attention, particularly from his father.

To summarize, this young man was performing in the borderline-to-average range of abilities, with strong visual perceptual skills and extreme deficits in auditory-verbal areas. The history of fluctuating hearing during the formative years was believed to be a contributing factor in the language delay. M.B. was having great difficulty discriminating and understanding what was said to him, processing and retaining that information, and expressing himself verbally. There was carryover into the academic area, where he had difficulty remembering important facts and terms, understanding directions and lecture material, discriminating fine sound differences in phonics, and verbally expressing the information he did have. Academically, he was performing well below grade placement. It was recommended that he receive resource help through the schools, and that if at all possible, this be supplemented with intensive therapy directed to the specific deficits.

demic, and behavioral factors is obtained from the history and assessment and how this information may be interpreted.

SUMMARY

A comprehensive psycho-educational assessment of a child with auditory language-learning problems should use the child as his/her own control. It should evaluate general abilities as well as specific auditory, language, and learning areas. The examiner should be concerned with the child's optimum performance level at the time of testing as well as abilities when the child is under stress or fatigued, and in a variety of learning situations. Examiners should also look to specific deficits, as well as strengths, in the auditory, visual, haptic-kinesthetic, and language areas. How the child performs in a quiet, nonstimulating environment, as well as when distractions or competing messages are introduced, needs to be determined. Some understanding of family health should be a part of the assessment, as should a comprehensive history that explores birth, health, behavior, developmental milestones, academic performance, and peer and family relationships. Furthermore, the examiner must be an astute observer of behavior, noting how a child perceives questions, whether the child asks for repetition, whether restatement is necessary, how environmental noises affect him, and what type of response latency is present.

A profile of the child should be drawn to show strengths as well as deficits so that an individualized educational plan and a comprehensive remediation program can be developed. The child's strengths should be utilized for ego building, while the deficits are being remediated, thus improving the child's ability to function in the classroom, at home, and with his peers.

REFERENCES

1. Battin RR, Kraft IA: *Therapeutic Intervention for the Dysynchronous Child* (Buenos Aires: Proceedings XVth World Congress of Phoniatrics and Logopedics, 1971).
2. French JW, Michael WB: *Standards for Educational and Psychological Tests and Manuals.*

Prepared by the Committee on Standards of the American Psychological Association, a joint committee of the American Psychological Association, American Educational Research Association, and National Council on Measurement in Education (Washington: American Psychological Association, 1966), pp 8, 22–23.
3. Klein SD: *Psychological Testing of Children: A Consumer's Guide* (Boston: Psy-Ed, 1975), p 3.
4. Paraskevopoulos JN, Kirk SA: *The Development and Psychometric Characteristics of the Revised Illinois Test of Psycholinguistic Abilities* (Urbana: University of Illinois Press, 1969), p 95.
5. Jastak JF, Jastak SR: *The Wide Range Achievement Test: 1976 Revised Edition* (Wilmington: Guidance Associates of Delaware, Inc., 1976), pp 46, 65.
6. Jackson GD: On the report of the Ad Hoc Committee on Educational Uses of Tests with Disadvantaged Students: Another psychological view from the Association of Black Psychologists. *Amer Psychol*, 30 (1975), 88–92.
7. Mercer J: Sociocultural factors in labeling mental retardates. *Peabody J Educ* 48 (1971), 188–203.
8. Zimmerman IL, Woo-Sam JM: Intellectual testing today—Relevance to the school-age child, in Oettinger L, Majowski LV, eds: *The Psychologist, the School, and the Child with MBD/LD* (New York: Grune & Stratton, 1978), p 51.
9. Fox DR, Battin RR: Private practice in audiology and speech pathology, in Battin RR, Fox DR, eds: *The Clinical Aspects of Speech and Language Pathology* (New York: Grune and Stratton, 1978), chap 5.
10. Terman L, Merrill M: *Measuring Intelligence* (Boston: Houghton-Mifflin, 1937), p 461.
11. Terman L, Merrill M: *Stanford-Binet Intelligence Scale: Manual for the Third Revision Form L-M* (Boston: Houghton-Mifflin, 1962), p 362.
12. Thorndike RL, Hagen EP, Sattler JM: *The Stanford-Binet Intelligence Scale*, ed 4 (Chicago: The Riverside Publishing Company, 1986).
13. Wechsler D: *Manual for the Wechsler Intelligence Scale for Children, Revised* (New York: Psychological Corp, 1974).
14. Paul N, Westerly O, Wepfer JW: Comparability of the WISC and the WISC-R. *J Learning Disab*, 12 (1979), 348–351.
15. Vance H, Wallbrown FH, Blaha J: Determining WISC-R profiles for reading disabled children. *J Learning Disab*, 11 (1978), 657–661.
16. Wechsler D: *Manual for the Wechsler Preschool and Primary Scale of Intelligence* (New York: Psychological Corp, 1967).
17. Kaufman AS, Kaufman NL: *Kaufman Assessment Battery for Children* (Circle Pines, MN: American Guidance Service, 1983).
18. Hiskey M: *Hiskey-Nebraska Test of Learning Aptitude* (Lincoln: Union College Press, 1966).

19. Leiter RG: *General Instructions for the Leiter International Scale* (Chicago: Stoelting Company, 1969).

20. Arthur G: *Arthur Point Scale of Performance* (New York: Psychological Corp, 1947).

21. Slosson RL: *Slosson Intelligence Test for Children and Adults* (East Aurora, New York: Slosson Educational Publications, 1963).

22. Raven JC: *Guide to Using the Standard Progressive Matrices* (London: H. K. Lewis & Co., Ltd., 1960).

23. Raven JC: *Guide to Using the Coloured Progressive Matrices* (London: H. K. Lewis & Co., Ltd., 1965).

24. Burgemeister BB, Blum LH, Lorge I: *Columbia Mental Maturity Scale*, ed 3 (New York: Harcourt, Brace, Jovanovich, 1972).

25. Kirk SA, McCarthy JJ, Kirk WD: *Examiner's Manual: Illinois Test of Psycholinguistic Abilities, Revised Edition* (Urbana: University of Illinois Press, 1968).

26. Myklebust HR: *Development and Disorders of Written Language: Picture Story Language Test* (New York: Grune and Stratton, 1965).

27. Baker HJ: *Description, Interpretation and Application of the Detroit Tests of Learning Aptitude* (Indianapolis: The Bobbs-Merrill Company, 1975).

28. Hammill DD: *Detroit Tests of Learning Aptitude—2* (Austin: Pro-ed, 1985).

29. Hammill DD, Bryant BR: *Detroit Tests of Learning Aptitude-Primary* (Austin: Pro-ed, 1986).

30. Goldman R, Fristoe M, Woodcock RW: *GFW Auditory Selective Attention Test* (Circle Pines, MN: American Guidance Service, 1974).

31. Dunn LM: *Peabody Picture Vocabulary Test* (Minneapolis: American Guidance Service, 1970).

32. Ammons RB, Ammons CH: The Quick Test: Provisional manual. *Psych Rep*, 11 (1962), 111–161.

33. Cole A: A study of preschool disadvantaged Negro children's Peabody Picture Vocabulary results. *Child Study Center Bulletin*, State University College at Buffalo (1966), p 66.

34. Costello J, Ali F: Reliability and validity of Peabody Picture Test scores of disadvantaged preschool children. *Psych Rep*, 28 (1971), 755–760.

35. Koppitz EM: *The Bender Gestalt Test for Young Children* (New York: Grune and Stratton, 1963), p. 195.

36. Slosson RL: *Slosson Drawing Coordination Test for Children and Adults* (East Aurora, NY: Slosson Educational Publications, 1975).

37. Haworth MR: *The Primary Visual Motor Test* (New York: Grune and Stratton, 1970).

38. Harris D: *Children's Drawings as Measures of Intellectual Maturity: A Revision and Extension of the Goodenough Draw-A-Person Test* (New York: Harcourt, Brace & World, 1963).

39. *Intellectual Maturity of Children as Measured by the Goodenough-Harris Drawing Test*. National Center for Health Statistics Series 11, No. 105. US Dept. of Health, Education and Welfare, Public Health Service, 1970.

40. *School Achievement of Children 6-11 Years as Measured by The Reading and Arithmetic Subtests of the Wide Range Achievement Test*. National Center for Health Statistics Series 11, No. 103. US Dept. of Health, Education and Welfare, Public Health Service, 1970.

41. Williamson WE: The concurrent validity of the 1965 Wide Range Achievement Test with neurologically impaired and emotionally handicapped pupils. *J Learning Disab*, 12 (1979), 201–202.

42. Harmer WR, Williams F: The Wide Range Achievement Test and the Peabody Individual Achievement Test: A comparative study. *J Learning Disab*, 11 (1978), 667–670.

43. Miller WH: A comparison of the Wide Range Achievement Test and the Peabody Individual Achievement Test for educationally handicapped children. *J Learning Disab*, 12 (1979), 65–68.

44. Molish HB: Projective methodologies. *Ann Rev Psych*, 23 (1972), 577–614.

45. Exner JE Jr: *The Rorschach: A Comprehensive System* (New York: John Wiley & Sons, 1974).

46. Rorschach H: *Psychodiagnostics*, ed 2, Lemkan P, Krononberg B, trans. (Berne: Huber, 1942).

47. Bellak L: *The Thematic Apperception Test and the Children's Apperception Test in Clinical Use*, ed 2 (New York: Grune and Stratton, 1971).

48. Murstein BI, ed: *Handbook of Projective Techniques* (New York: Basic Books, 1965).

49. Buck JN: The H-T-P technique: A qualitative and quantitative scoring manual. *J Clin Psych*, 4 (1948), 317–396.

50. Burns RC, Kaufman SH: *Actions, Styles, and Symbols in Kinetic Family Drawings: An Interpretive Manual* (New York: Brunner/Mazel, 1972).

51. Bradley PE, Battin RR, Sutter EG: Effects of individual diagnosis and remediation for the treatment of learning disabilities. *Clin Neuropsych*, (1979), 23–35.

SUPPLEMENTARY READINGS

1. Adelman HS: Diagnostic classification of learning problems: Some data. *Am J Orthopsych*, Oct (1978), 717–726.

2. Anastasi A: *Psychological Testing*, ed 4 (New York: McMillan, 1976).

3. Barr DF: *Auditory Perceptual Disorders* (Springfield: Charles C. Thomas, 1972).

4. Blager FB: Response of emotionally disturbed children to auditory discrimination tests in quiet and in noise. *J Audit Res*, 18 (1978), 221–229.

5. Goh DS, Youngquist J: A comparison of the Mc-Carthy Scales of Children's Abilities and the WISC-R. *J Learning Disab*, 12 (1979), 344–348.

6. Guilford JP: *Psychometric Methods* (New York: McGraw-Hill, 1954).

7. Keith RW: *Central Auditory Dysfunction* (New York: Grune and Stratton, 1977).

8. Koppell S: Testing the attentional deficit notion. *J Learning Disab*, 12 (1979), 43–48.

9. Koppitz EM: *Psychological Evaluation of Children's Human Figure Drawings* (New York: Grune and Stratton, 1968).

10. McCarthy JJ, McCarthy JF: *Learning Disabilities* (Boston: Allyn and Bacon, 1971).

11. Oakland R, ed: *Psychological and Educational Assessment of Minority Children* (New York: Mazel Publishers, 1977).

12. Rampp DL, Plummer BA: A child in jeopardy: Medical and educational profiles of children with auditory process learning disabilities. Presented to the Sixth Annual Meeting of the Society for Ear, Nose Advances in Children, Santa Barbara, CA, Dec 6–9, 1978.

13. Rudel RG: Relation of forward and backward digit repetition to neurological impairment in children with learning disabilities. *Neuropsychologia*, 12 (1974), 109–118.

14. Snyder-McLean LK, McLean J: Verbal information strategies: The child's use of language to acquire language. *J Speech Hearing Dis*, 43 (1978), 306–325.

15. Tarezan C: *An Educator's Guide to Psychological Tests* (Springfield: Charles C. Thomas, 1972).

16. Wallbrown FH: Intelligence Testing. *The Directive Teacher*, 2 (1979), 20–22.

17. Wender PH: *Minimal Brain Dysfunction in Children* (New York: Wiley-Interscience, 1971).

Remediation | II

INTRODUCTION

The term "auditory disorders" represents a wide spectrum of problems within the auditory system, ranging from hearing loss due to abnormal mechanical conditions in the peripheral hearing mechanism (conductive loss), to disruption in the sensory end organ and/or auditory neural pathway (sensorineural loss), to a possible disruption of the neural system(s) responsible for the encoding of neural events (central auditory disorder). The remedial processes that have been espoused for the educational management of children with auditory disorders can vary depending on the severity of the disorder.

However, if one takes the perspective that the educational management of auditory disorders should be based on the nature of the disorder, as well as the severity, it is possible that a hierarchy of confidence levels can be put on the management strategies that should be employed. Looking at auditory disorders in this way provides a unique viewpoint that may clarify the remedial process. In order of degree of confidence, these disorders range as follows:

(1) *Congenital hearing loss*, present at birth or shortly thereafter, may be sensorineural or conductive (see Chapters 1 and 2). The language learning deficits resulting from congenital hearing loss are well documented and are directly proportional to the degree of loss, intellectual potential of the child, and environmental factors such as family inter-relationships, and the amount and quality of stimulation. There is little question that congenital hearing loss, even when it is mild, significantly affects auditory language learning skills.

(2) *Acquired hearing loss* may also be sensorineural or conductive in nature. This type of loss may also be fluctuating or permanent. As with congenital hearing loss, the language deficits resulting from acquired hearing loss are proportional to the degree and duration of the loss, intellectual potential of the child, and environmental factors. More and more, evidence is being reported suggesting that even mild fluctuating conductive hearing loss due to middle ear disorders results in language learning problems (see Chapter 8).

(3) *Inefficient auditory language learning skills due to environmental factors.* Factors which may result in inefficiency of auditory language learning skills include a lack of adequate language stimulation, sensory over-loading, and malnutrition (see Chapter 8). Even psychological trauma is suspect in this regard. Although it is documented that auditory language learning disorders may result from factors such as these, this observation is only very recent and the exact way in which these factors affect auditory language learning has yet to be established firmly.

(4) *Central auditory processing disorders* are thought to be unrelated to hearing loss caused by mechanical and sensory end organ problems in the auditory system, and in fact seem to exist in the absence of hearing loss. This type of auditory problem has been discussed and bandied about for a considerable time, but the etiological factors accounting for central auditory disorders remain elusive. There is a presumption that minimal brain damage of some sort is present in a child who is classified as having a central auditory processing disorder. However, this presumption has never been documented by histologic or neurologic evidence, or by radiologic or encephalographic techniques, except in cases of diagnosed neurological disorders where organicity is evident.

From an educational perspective, children who are classified as having central auditory disorders are indistinguishable upon examination from those children in the preceding two categories. This observation provides enough evidence to argue that children classified as having central auditory processing disorders have some form of auditory language learning problem that may be related to developmental factors, such as conductive hearing loss, or environmental factors. Because of the paucity of information on the etiology of central auditory disorders, the remedial strategies have yet to be standardized. However, it is reasonable to assume that remediation for children who are thought to manifest central auditory disorders should follow the same basis as for all categories. That is, intervention strategies should be based on normal language development and auditory training.

Part II of our book follows the above philosophy of remediation.

The pragmatic issues of state and federal guidelines and mainstreaming are presented as they influence the remedial process. Remedial aspects of peripheral hearing loss are covered in Chapters 9 through 13. What is the effect of mild hearing loss on auditory language learning? How can the teacher keep the child's hearing aid functioning in the classroom? What is the best acoustic environment, and how should amplification systems, individual and group, be managed? What new technological advances are there to assist hearing impaired students in specific listening situations? Readers will find answers to each of these specific questions and more.

Chapter 14 covers remedial strategies for the profoundly deaf child; the controversial area of cochlear implants, and presents information on tactile aids. Our assumption is that specific language intervention strategies should be based on results from psycho-educational assessment strategies described in Chapters 5 and 6. Chapters 15 and 16 apply this philosophy to auditory training and speechreading, and language remediation. The explosion of printed material makes it difficult for therapists and teachers to keep up with what is available. Chapter 17 reviews a variety of materials that are available, gives information on where to find them, and provides examples on how the materials can be used in the classroom and in individual intervention programs. Finally, once a handicapped child is identified, all aspects of the family need to be considered. This area is covered in our last chapter on family counseling.—RJR, MPD

7

REMEDIATION WITHIN AND BEYOND STATE AND FEDERAL GUIDELINES

Carol Amon

INTRODUCTION

Since Public Law 94-142[1] was enacted in 1975, there has been no option. *All children who are handicapped and in need of special education and related services must be identified, evaluated, and assured a free appropriate public education in the least restrictive environment.* In our zealous attempts to adhere to this legal mandate, we have found ourselves emerged in the golden age of special education. Knowing that regular education could not meet the needs of children with auditory disorders, specialists have assumed responsibility for designing special methodologies, curricula, and programs for these students, ranging from mainstreaming to residential placement. More recently, an emphasis has been placed on the need for a continuum of services or placement options, so that we might meet the needs of all hearing-impaired children.

If we listen to the cries of parents, therapists, educators, and administrators, however, we realize that this golden age of specialization may be a little tarnished. We are in an era of declining resources and increasing demands. Specialists in hearing are struggling to maintain their programs. Unfortunately, children with auditory disorders are often caught in the middle of these struggles. We have been concerned with the right method that will teach all things to hearing-impaired children. We have been rigid in our methods. There is currently a tendency to focus on the program, rather than on programming for each individual child.

It is, perhaps, time to move out of the golden age of special education. In special education, individual differences are the rule, not the exception. For this reason, there clearly can be no universal method and there can be no cookbooks. We must focus on programming— not on a program. Special education must become a process of individualizing.

TERMINOLOGY

A brief review of the terms and issues as they relate to auditory disorders may be helpful.

Handicapped Children. According to Public Law 94-142, this term refers to those children evaluated in accordance with the regulations as being (relating to auditory disorders) hard-of-hearing or deaf, and who (because of those impairments) need special education and related services. *Hard-of-hearing* and *deaf* mean hearing impairments that adversely affect educational performance.

Interpretation of these terms vary. Does the child with a mild hearing loss, who has an understanding teacher, and is getting average grades not qualify as handicapped? What about the child with chronic otitis media or the one with a unilateral loss? Are they not entitled to special educational and related services?

Special Education. This term refers to specially designed instruction to meet the unique needs of a handicapped child. *Related services* means such developmental, corrective, and other supportive services as are required to assist a handicapped child to benefit from special education; included are speech pathology and audiology, psychological services, physical and occupational therapy, recreation, early identification and assessment, counseling, medical services for diagnostic or evaluation purposes, school health services, social work services in schools, and parent counseling and training. The questions we must ask are: What is specially designed instruction and who does the special designing?

Identified, Located, and Evaluated. Before any action is taken with respect to the initial placement of a handicapped child in a special educational program, a full and individual evaluation of the child's educational needs must be conducted by a multidisciplinary team including at least one specialist with knowledge in the area of the child's suspected disability. The question here is who qualifies as a specialist in hearing impairment?

Free, Appropriate, Public Education. This means special education and related services provided in conformity with an individualized education program developed by a team that includes the child's teacher, parents, and evaluation personnel. What happens if there is disagreement? Are the team's decisions based on the availability of programs? Are parents truly equal partners with the educators in the decision-making process?

Least Restrictive Environment. This means that, to the maximum extent appropriate, handicapped children should be educated with children who are not handicapped. Special classes or separate schooling should occur only when the nature or severity of the handicap is such that education with the use of supplementary aids and services in a regular class cannot be achieved satisfactorily.

How does a least restrictive environment relate to productivity? Would services in a rural area be different than in a metropolitan area if we are truly basing decisions on student needs? What about value differences relating to the need to interact with hearing impaired peers?

GOOD EDUCATIONAL PRACTICE

Whether our role with children with auditory disorders is in regular education, special education, related services, administration, or parenting, we are faced with decision-making that must not only meet federal and state legislative mandates, but also constitute good educational practice. We must also consider the spirit of the law. This can only be done by considering what is best for the child. What is best for the system, the parent, the teacher, or the budget should receive only secondary consideration.

The traditional approach to educating children with auditory disorders has emphasized categorical programs, with the major responsibility for decision-making lying with specialists in hearing—specifically audiologists, teachers of hearing handicapped, and speech and hearing therapists. It seems important to examine the concept of that traditional approach. We must assume that the only reason special education emerged as a separate discipline, in

the first place, is that regular education could not individualize adequately for handicapped children. Does it make sense, then, to create special programs for all children with auditory disorders? Instead, our goal should be to develop excellent and efficient planning processes that ensure individualizing for each child, choosing from an array of both regular and special services. Should specialists in hearing be making decisions about programming for children with auditory disorders, or should they assist parents and regular educators in the process of decision-making? We must move from vertical to horizontal decision-making. *We should begin to think of special education as a collaborative process—a process of individualizing—taking the components that are available and combining them in a unique way to meet each child's needs. Indeed, if the process of individualizing took place for each child, there would be no need for special education as a categorical program. It is time we unify our educational efforts.*

THE PROCESS OF USING EVALUATION INFORMATION

The process of interpreting and sharing information about a student's current level of functioning provides the basis for individualizing. Unlike diagnosis, which is focused on confirming the existence of a particular problem or deficit, evaluation refers to the process of putting together all information in order to construct a whole picture of the student.

The intended result of the evaluation process is the most complete understanding possible of the child. This can only be done by a collaborative team effort of parents and professionals integrating the unique information that each contributes. By sharing ideas and perspectives, the team enhances the quality of planning necessary to ensure an appropriate education.

Interpreting and reporting assessment results is often seen by professionals as a logical, effortless task for which most have been trained. Parents, however, often view this process as frustrating, meaningless, and a waste of time: "Professionals spend several hours testing our children, but never share what it all means. They take our kids apart by disciplines and never put them back together as whole children. It feels like each professional must prove his or her worth by giving lengthy assessment reports that are meaningless to us and others. They usually have already discussed and made decisions about our child and are there simply to tell us parents their conclusions." Interestingly, some professionals agree with these parental perceptions: "We've got to look good to these parents. If we don't meet ahead of time, we might say something that we don't all agree on and we can't disagree in front of parents."

Parents should have had an integral part in the evaluation process from the beginning. Just as each professional assesses functioning and prepares an assessment report, so should the parents. Providing them with a worksheet that asks them to note their child's strengths and areas of difficulty at home and in the community can facilitate this.

The following letter, sent to the parents at least two weeks prior to the meeting where evaluation results are discussed, is suggested:

> Dear Parents,
> In order for us to get a better understanding of your child's strengths and areas of difficulty, it would be helpful if you and your family would provide the information listed on the attached questionnaire. Your child may function differently at home than he or she does in school; and it is important that we know and understand these differences.
> Please complete the questionnaire and bring it with you to the meeting, so that your information is used when we discuss your child's current level of functioning and needs. We look forward to working with you.

It is important that parents have the opportunity to think through and record their thoughts on their own, and not through an interview process by a professional. It then becomes even more critical that the meeting in which these thoughts and observations are shared be structured in such a way as to allow parents to contribute their own information. Parents report that there is nothing more degrading and humiliating than to have a professional report for them. Statements such as "Mrs. Jones reported. . . ," "The child's father said. . . ," "During my interview with the family, it was learned that. . . ," serve no purpose other than to confirm the parents' feelings of insecurity.

The following set of questions for parents may be useful; however, it is important to structure the questions to the language and socio-educational level of the parents.

(1) What does your family feel is the basic concern with regard to this child?
(2) How well does your child learn and remember things? How quickly does your child understand something new?
(3) How does your child communicate? Does your family understand what your child is saying? How well does your child understand?
(4) What has your child learned? How does your child learn best?
(5) How well do you think your child hears?
(6) Do you have any concerns about your child's motor abilities, such as crawling, walking, writing, cutting, etc.?
(7) How well does your child get along with others? What are your child's likes and dislikes?
(8) What's your child's view of him- or herself? What does your family see as desirable and undesirable behaviors?
(9) Does your child accept responsibility for chores at home? Does your child follow directions? How well does your child take care of his or her room and clothes?
(10) What would you like to see your child accomplish in the next year? In the next three years?

Providing parents with such a structure accomplishes several things. First, by facilitating the recording of their specific observations, this may help with the denial of reality. It is far easier and healthier for parents to recognize the child's weaknesses than for a professional to tell them. It also facilitates communication among family members, which often breaks down in families of handicapped children due to different coping styles. Third, it gives credibility to parent perceptions during the meeting in which evaluation information is discussed. Often, if a parent disagrees with a professional observation, that disagreement is viewed by the professionals as parent denial of reality or emotional reaction to information difficult to hear. When parents have noted this information previously and bring it to the meeting, it is viewed by professionals as more credible. If a professional's assessment reports are filed with the student's records, it is important to include the parents' reports.

Regular education teachers also need to be encouraged to be strong partners in the evaluation. It is important to let them know that their information is just as important as that of the specialists. Their knowledge of what and how the child learns, daily performance, learning style, group participation, and patterns of behavior is unique and critical.

THE MEETING

Public Law 94-142 mandates that a meeting should occur for the purpose of interpreting evaluation information and determining whether or not the child is handicapped and in need of special education. The structure of this meeting should be a child-centered group discussion and sharing. Too often, professionals enter into a "round robin" reporting structure in which each person gives his or her report and recommendations.

Current Level of Functioning

If we are truly going to individualize for a child, then it is important that we understand his or her current level of functioning and needs from a global point of view—not just from one tester's or observer's report. It is not just the speech and language specialist who has information about a child's communicative functioning. The child communicates at home, in the community, in school, and even when being tested by professionals in other functioning areas. All information should be heard and synthesized. The concept of wholism dictates that we look at the child comprehensively. Education is the development of a child in all functioning areas. Any attempt to separate these functioning areas is artificial and counterproductive.

The traditional "round robin" reporting does not allow this to happen for a variety of reasons. First, there is the issue of "pecking order." Many parents and professionals feel that if an expert gives an assessment report, it is not wise to offer a different opinion, since this would appear as a challenge to that expert. Second, when lengthy reports are given, it is difficult to listen to and integrate all the information. Third, it is human nature, when "in the spotlight," to perform in such a way as to impress professional peers with the breadth and length of information known. Much of the information reported is not viewed as critical to the understanding of the child.

A preferred way of structuring this meeting is to facilitate a child-centered discussion. "Let's talk about the child's communicative functioning. Mom and Dad, how does he or she communicate at home? . . . Is this what you see in the classroom? . . . What did testing reveal? . . . Why might we see that discrepancy? . . . Who else has information on this? . . . What I'm hearing as consensus, then, is . . . " It is the synthesis of information that is recorded as group consensus relating to the student's current level of functioning. It is usually helpful to provide an opportunity for the parents to share their observations first, in each functioning area discussed, before they get caught up in the jargon of others and before they may react emotionally to difficult-to-hear information. This also allows them to feel like equal partners in the discussion and decision-making process.

This child-centered discussion should occur for each area of functioning: cognitive, communicative, academic, sensory, motor, social, emotional, and vocational. After the team has a holistic picture of the child's functioning, it can then determine needs, whether or not a handicapping condition exists, and if special education is needed.

Needs

Using the collective information on the child's current level of functioning, the team now discusses and determines needs of the total child; that is, what the child needs, different from the norm, to continue to grow and learn and have "school" work for him or her. These may be internal (within the child) or external (within the environment as applied to the child). Public Law 94-142 states that a full and individual evaluation of the child's educational needs must be conducted before any action is taken with respect to providing special education. Many professionals, however, seem to skip over this function and move directly to the next step of determination of handicap. Their assumption is that if a child is hearing-handicapped, we need to place him or her in the program for hearing-handicapped, where needs and services are determined by specialists in the area of hearing. Such a procedure would not reflect special education as a process of individualizing, but rather one of categorical programming. *It is far more impor-*

tant to identify the needs of a student than it is to identify the handicapping condition. Knowledge of the handicapping condition is important only for reporting purposes—not for programming purposes.

The following may help to structure a discussion of needs from a holistic, child-centered reference.

(*1*) *Developmental, compensatory needs.* Does the student need any specific, systematic training to address deficits? (use of residual hearing, speech intelligibility, receptive or expressive language, motor skills, perceptual skills)

(*2*) *Environmental management needs.* Does the student need physical classroom modifications? (room arrangement, seating, lighting, noise level, materials, equipment) Do people in the student's environment need to understand his hearing loss, and how to communicate with him? (regular classroom, home, peers, community)

(*3*) *Academic needs.* Does the student have any specific curricular needs? Does the student need any specific modifications or adaptations? (classroom organization, classroom management, schedule modifications, methods of presentation, methods of practice, methods of testing)

(*4*) *Career-vocational-avocational needs.* Does the student have any unique needs relating to life skills? (awareness, exploration, preparation, experience)

(*5*) *Personalizing needs.* Does the student have any unique needs relating to applying and internalizing? (peer relationships, self-concept, knowledge and acceptance of handicap, coping with stress, trusting others, expressing emotion) Does the child's social or emotional environment need restructuring? (nurturing, supporting, counseling, shifting responsibility to self)

It is not appropriate to talk about specific services needed at this time or to limit the discussion of what the child needs by considering only those services that are currently available. We may state that a child needs to improve speech intelligibility or needs speech intelligibility training; however, it is not appropriate to assume that the child needs speech therapy. Speech intelligibility training can occur through many types of service, and not just by speech therapy. We may state that a child needs to learn to deal with anger appropriately; however, this is not the time to decide that he or she should see the psychologist once a week.

DEVELOPING THE INDIVIDUAL EDUCATION PLAN

If a determination is made by the team that a child is handicapped and needs special education and related services, after discussing evaluation information and needs, an individual educational plan must be developed. Public Law 94-142 mandates that the plan include:

(*1*) A statement of the child's present levels of educational performance.

(*2*) A statement of annual goals, including short-term objectives.

(*3*) A statement of the specific special education and related services to be provided.

(*4*) The extent to which the child will be able to participate in regular educational programs.

(*5*) The projected dates for initiation of services and the anticipated duration of the services.

(*6*) Appropriate objective criteria and evaluation procedures and schedules for determining whether the objectives are achieved.

The individual educational plan may be developed by the team at the same meeting in which current level of functioning, needs, and handicapping condition were determined; or it may be developed later. The requirement is that the team consists of evaluation personnel, parents, the child's teacher, the child (where appropriate), and a representative of the public agency who is qualified to provide or supervise special education. This team is clearly responsible for individualizing for this particular child.

Goals

Using information about a child's current level of functioning and needs, the team must decide what the child can reasonably be expected to accomplish in one year. Reviewing the many needs that may have been listed for a student, the team must prioritize these needs and determine the most important goals for the child. Again, it is important to use a child-centered structure for discussion and decision-making. Professionals may have a tendency to report *their* goals for a child (i.e., "My goal for him in speech is. . ."). However, this would not be a true process of individualizing; rather, it would be indicative of professional decision-making after placement in the service or program. Needs may be so great that trying to meet all of them would splinter the child's learning process so as not to meet any of them effectively. Parents should have a significant role in making this decision. Asking parents what they would like to see their child accomplish is usually an excellent initial point of discussion.

Planning and Individualizing Services

If we accept the premise that regular education curricula and methods are designed to meet the needs of the majority of students, then we must consider this also to be appropriate for students with auditory disorders, making only those modifications and adaptations needed as a result of their unique needs. Assuming that hearing-impaired students need a special program, with special curricula, methodologies, and instructional techniques, is counterproductive. It is important, however, to take into consideration their unique needs, so that these students have the same opportunity to learn as any other student. In order to individualize for these students, it is important that the team responds to the following questions, starting with the premise that regular education should be considered first.

(1) What are the subjects or activities in regular education, in which this student can participate with no modifications or adaptations, from which he or she can benefit?

(2) What are the subjects in regular education from which the student can profit, so long as specific modifications or adaptations are made? List the needed modifications or adaptations. (These should be listed with no concern, at this time, as to who makes them—the regular education teacher or a specialist.)

(3) What alternative curriculum or instruction does the student need that is not offered as a part of regular education? (This should be determined with no consideration at this time of who would be available to provide it.)

(4) What supportive training does the student need in relation to deficit areas? How often? (Again, this should be determined with no consideration of the availability of services at this time.)

(5) What behaviors need to be carried out consistently by all service providers, including the parents?

After the team reaches consensus on these questions, an individualized specific service plan can be determined for the student, selecting from the array of services offered in both regular and special education. This automatically allows the student to receive services in the least restrictive and most productive environment. Let us look at application of this individualizing process.

1. *What are the subjects or activities in regular education, in which this student can participate with no modifications or adaptations, from which he or she can benefit?* Some students may be able to benefit from many subjects or activities; others may only be able to benefit from lunch and recess activities. The real world in which the student with auditory disorders must integrate does not automatically provide modifications for his or her auditory deficits. For this reason, it is important to expose the student to that world in increased proportions throughout his or her educational experience, but only to the extent that benefit can be gained. Sometimes this would not be for entire subjects or courses, but for meaningful parts, such as hands-on experience.

2. *What are the subjects in regular education from which the student can profit, so long as specific modifications or adaptations are made? List the needed modifications or adaptations.* The team can refer back to the list of needs for much of this information. The following is an example of modification or adaptations that might be considered.

(1) Techniques:
   Direction, with instruction to be given individually or in writing.
   Key words and concepts of oral instruction reinforced in writing.
   Allow extra time for processing.
   Allow answers to be in short-phrase form.
   Require no oral assignments.
   Accompany oral information with signing.
   Advanced introduction to new vocabulary and concepts.
(2) Content, materials:
   Use high-interest, low-vocabulary materials.
   Reading level no greater than _____th grade.
   Provide scripts or notes of lecture presentations.
   Provide vocabulary lists.
(3) Environment management:
   Preferential seating.
   Direct student-to-teacher amplification.

(4) Evaluations procedures:
  Tests given orally, individually, or with reading assistance.
  Allow oral responses rather than written.
  Provide extra time to complete tests.
  Evaluate daily work and participation in lieu of tests.

After determining the regular education subjects from which the student could benefit and those relating to his or her goals, the modifications or adaptations needed by the child should also be determined by the team. After this has been done, the team states whether this will be done by the regular education teacher with no assistance, by the regular teacher with consultation from the specialist, by the regular teacher and specialist teaming together, by the specialist assisting in the regular classroom, or by the specialist pulling the student out of the regular classroom. This can easily be determined by asking the regular teacher what he or she is comfortable, able, and willing to do. There should be no judgment as to which is the best method for providing these modifications. If they can be done in the regular classroom, that is where they should happen. If not, however, it is important that they be provided in whatever manner is necessary, with pull-out services being the last alternative.

This process allows the regular classroom teacher to have ownership in the programming for the child. Too often, handicapped children are placed in the regular classroom, with specialists telling the regular classroom teachers what to do. Then when modifications or adaptations are not made, the specialists are quick to criticize. Many classroom teachers are willing to make modifications, but need assistance in doing so. It is important, then, for the specialists to provide technical assistance to these teachers through consultation or team teaching.

If specialists are needed to assist or make modifications, either in the regular classroom or in a pull-out program, the team must determine which specialists are available and appropriate to do this. Often, it is the trained teacher of hearing-handicapped children, but not always. Teachers of learning-disabled children often have the skills to make needed modifications. Who serves the child is not as important; the nature of the services is.

3. *What alternative curriculum or instruction does the student need that is not offered as a part of regular education?* Specific instruction in language or reading, functional mathematics, independent living skills, or affective education are examples of alternative instruction. Again, this should be based on the student's needs, and not on what is available. Once the nature of the instructional need is identified, along with the amount of time, the team may creatively assign any service providers capable of providing such. Students who are hearing-handicapped do not necessarily need to be served by teachers trained in the area of hearing impairment. Instruction provided by a teacher of emotionally disturbed, learning disabled, or mentally retarded students may, for some instructional areas, be appropriate.

4. *What supportive training does the student need in relation to deficit areas? How often?* This may include such things as receptive or expressive language training, speech intelligibility training, auditory training, counseling, motor skills training, or perceptual training. The team must determine the amount of individualized training needed in each area with no regard to availability of services. Once that is identified, based on student need, the team may assign any service provider or a combination of service providers. Speech intelligibility training, for example, can be facilitated by many types of service providers. Speech therapists or teachers of hearing-handicapped children may serve as leaders or consultants; but regular teachers, learning disabilities teachers, audiologists, paraprofessionals, or peer tutors may supply much of the direct service.

An example of this concept was illustrated beautifully in a junior high school where a hearing-handicapped student was having difficulty expressing anger appropriately. When angry, he would usually resort to kicking in lockers or putting his fist through classroom windows. The staffing team determined that a goal for this student would be to express anger appropriately, specifically through verbalization rather than through physical actions. A psychologist was available in that building only once a week, which of course did not usually coincide with when the student became angry. Creatively, the team decided that "one person should be available at all times to whom this student could go at will and express feelings of anger." A counselor was not available and the student did not trust his teacher or principal. It was determined that the ideal service provider would be the custodian. The custodian was approached and happily accepted this challenge, understanding that he was to listen to the student for a maximum of five minutes, and then return him to the classroom. Within three months, the student's behavior was completely reversed, and he was able to verbally express anger in all situations.

5. *What behaviors need to be carried out consistently by all service providers, including the parents?* If, for example, a goal for a child is to gain attention by vocalizing rather than gesturing, it is important that *all* service providers, including the parents, ignore gesturing and respond only to vocalization. Such consistency is also usually necessary in behavior management strategies. These types of needs should be addressed by the team and specified in the individual education plan, so that everyone has ownership in them, and will thus be working toward them. Speech therapists alone cannot "fix" speech; psychologists alone cannot "fix" behavior.

Least Restrictive Environment

Public Law 94-142 requires that handicapped children be educated with children who are not handicapped to the maximum extent appropriate. This issue has been debated greatly by specialists in hearing, and by the hearing impaired themselves. If we define special education as placement in programs for specific handicapping conditions, this indeed will continue to be debated. Individual values relating to the benefits of mainstreaming versus the benefits of association with hearing impaired peers and adults will always differ. For this reason, it seems critical that we approach programming decisions for each child individually. An excellent and efficient planning process will facilitate individualization so that each student is educated not only in the least restrictive environment for him or her, but also in the most productive one. Special education for students with auditory disorders must be a process—not a program.

PROVIDING INDIVIDUALIZED EDUCATION AND REMEDIATION

The planning and individualizing process, if applied to each student with auditory disorders, would undoubtedly provide him or her with an appropriate individual education plan. Implementation of that plan may be a different issue. For many administrators, regular education teachers, specialists, and even parents, such an integrated plan would be a drastic change from the comfortable segregated programming to which each has been accustomed. Role ambiguity, power struggles, and differences in interpersonal styles may lead to a great deal of stress, which in turn may cause people to revert back to old behavior patterns, get rigid, and protect their territory. In addition to having an efficient and effective planning process, we must also have a working structure or a framework in which methods and techniques are incorporated. We need an organizational system that permits us to draw from the vast array of special and regular education services.

Five components may be gleaned from the variety of models and practices that filter the common working of all the approaches into a few essential elements. They are: *developmental-compensatory instruction, environmental management, academic instruction, career-vocational-avocational instruction,* and *personalization instruction.* Using these essential components of the system for each student, strategies can be developed and pieced together to appropriately deliver to the hearing-impaired student an individualized plan. The use of such a structure would not limit the type of personnel able to deliver services to hearing-impaired students, but instead would offer options in using various personnel with appropriate competencies to meet student needs.

Developmental-Compensatory Instruction

Developmental-compensatory instruction is designed to provide each student with systematic training to address his or her developmental deficits. Usually, this is necessary for hearing-impaired students in the areas of audition, speech, and language. Strengthening the use of residual hearing and speech reading, improving speech intelligibility, and expanding receptive and expressive language are all factors to consider in the provision of services for hearing-impaired students (see Chapters 15 to 17). Services in these areas must be driven by the goals established by the planning committee and stated on the individual education plan, and not by the preferences of the hearing specialists. If specific services relating to developmental-compensatory instruction are indicated, they may be provided not only by audiologists, speech-language therapists, and teachers of hearing-handicapped students, but also by all other service providers through consultation and collaboration.

Environmental Management

Environmental management provides systems for structuring the student's total environment to help him or her achieve school success. Two major subsystems must be addressed: the physical environment and the interactional environment. The physical environment includes controlling things such as room arrangement, noise, lighting, materials, equipment, and amplification systems (see chapters 11 and 12). Interactional environmental management refers to helping all adults and peers in the educational system to understand and accommodate the specific hearing loss of a student in order to contribute to the success of the hearing-impaired student. Leadership for both physical and interactional environmental management usually comes from the specialist in hearing. All people with whom the hearing-impaired student interacts, should be provided with information on his or her particular hearing loss, what he or she hears and does not hear, how amplification works and sounds, and communication tips. Such in-servicing should be a continual process, and not simply a one-time explanation. As new questions arise, the hearing specialists must be available to assist with explanations. Involving the hearing-impaired child in this sharing of information is, of course, essential.

Academic Instruction

Achieving competency in curricular or academic subjects is a major goal for all students, and is obviously a goal for the student with auditory disorders. We need to provide systems that promote academic growth, using various techniques and curricula appropriate to the hearing-impaired student's individual learning needs, and as similar as possible to that of the regular student.

Flexibility in designing and teaching academic subjects is of paramount importance. Too often, there is a lack of coordination and continuity between educational goals and objectives in the regular classroom and remedial or supportive instruction in the pull-out special program.

The first step toward appropriate academic instruction is using the planning meeting to determine general curricula, techniques, modifications, and adaptations. Having an individual education plan, however, is of little value if the system is rigid and inflexible.

Openness to sharing and collaborations is the second essential step. Specialists in hearing must be willing to give up some of their old notions; specifically: (1) that only they, as trained specialists, can provide appropriate services; (2) that their role is primarily to provide direct service to the students; and (3) that their direct service has to be provided through a pull-out program. Providing direct assistance to hearing-impaired students in the regular classroom and team teaching with the regular teaching should be strongly considered. Regular educators must be willing to tailor instruction and expectations to the needs of their hearing-impaired students. Administrators must be willing to experiment with creative scheduling to facilitate this consultation and collaboration.

Career-Vocational-Avocational Instruction

One of the goals of our educational system is to prepare students for a productive and independent adult life; and this, obviously, must also be a component in the system of services for hearing impaired students. This component includes systems to develop: (1) positive attitudes toward school, work, and society; (2) social skills, life skills, and leisure time skills; (3) work ethics, values, motivation, habits, interests, behaviors, and goals; (4) occupational awareness, and (5) marketable skills for employment or continued education that will lead to employment.

Personalization Instruction

As caring individuals, we often deprive hearing-impaired students of the only experience that can really promote their growth and development—the experience of using their own strengths. In our zealous attempt to support, modify, and accept the hearing-impaired student, we may assume responsibility for his or her success. It is important to constantly remember our end product; a student who thinks for him- or herself as a self-directed, self-controlled individual. He or she needs to become personally accountable and able to act without guidance, assistance, or supervision, and to answerable for his or her behaviors. Hearing-impaired persons need to find a sense of responsibility for themselves and their actions.

An important component of the system of services for hearing-impaired students is personalization instruction. This does not happen automatically. This would include assistance in: (1) personalizing, internalizing, and applying information; (2) developing a realistic view of him- or herself; and (3) planning, implementing, and evaluating personal goals. This is accomplished by providing formal and informal "counseling" to the student, and is performed by monitoring and in-servicing professionals and parents. This must be pervasive throughout the student's program, and not a separate entity providing mostly for "here-and-now" situations. We must allow hearing-impaired students "to do," rather than being "done to." This component of servicing links together all aspects of the student's program in a personalized manner.

CONSULTATION AND COLLABORATION

Remediation and education of students with auditory disorders has been described here as a process of individualizing. Special education is the process that individualizes the system to the student's needs. As we begin to implement this collaborative process, it becomes clear that many of our traditional roles will change. The specialist now has a dual role. One is as a teacher, providing direct instruction to hearing-impaired students; the other is as a support for regular educators, helping them identify student's needs and appropriate curricular and instructional adjustments.

Much has been written on the concept of consultation, mostly from a business perspective. Dinkmeyer and Carlson[2] make a point that must be integrated into our thinking, which is that "the most effective consultation is a collaborative undertaking, rather than a relationship between an 'expert' and a 'nonexpert'." Regular education teachers and specialists must define the educational problem of the student together, and develop strategies together to deal with it. If consultation is viewed as the regular education teacher relying on the specialists to provide answers and assume responsibility, then frustration and dissatisfaction will develop when the advice does not work. Also, if the specialist assumes the role of expert, the advice may be seen as unrealistic, impossible to implement, or inappropriate by the regular education teacher, who will not follow through. The specialist may then develop antagonistic feelings toward the teacher who does not use the advice.

A team approach must be used to provide services to students with auditory disorders. This requires mutual respect and equal sharing of responsibility and concern. All members of that team share in both the successes and the failures. Team members must have clear avenues of communication and time to communicate. Together, they must decide who will do what by when and how effectiveness will be monitored. "A secondary outcome of consultation," states Brown et al,[3] "should be that both the consultant's and consultee's repertoire of knowledge and skills will be enhanced to the end that both persons will function more effectively in similar situations in the future . . ."

An example of the collaborative process may be helpful.

1. A planning meeting was held to determine the student's individual educational plan. The team had jointly determined the student's current level of functioning, goals for the year,

and a service plan that described modifications and adaptations needed along with specialized instruction and training. It also stated what service providers would be involved with this student. The regular classroom teacher may or may not have been a part of this meeting; but it was determined that the student could profit from instruction in her room if there was assistance given in making modifications.

2. The specialist, probably the teacher of the hearing-handicapped student, contacted the regular teacher to begin planning. "R.J., a hearing-impaired student, has been assigned to your class. Can we meet for an hour sometime this week to discuss her abilities and learning style along with your classroom expectations?"

3. During that meeting, the specialist described the hearing loss, amplification, and implications for the classroom. The regular teacher discussed instructional materials used, how subject matter was presented, types of responses she expects from students, how she evaluates, management of the classroom, and social interactions in the classroom. Salend and Viglianti[4] suggest the following items for classroom analysis.

  textbooks used, grade levels, reading levels
  supplementary materials used
  media frequently used
  support personnel available
  presentation style (lecture, blackboard, etc.)
  student requirements (notes, read aloud, independent work)
  how directions are given
  evaluation process (types of tests, how grades are given, homework, special projects)
  rules, consequences, reinforcement, routines
  peer interactions, interests, acceptance of differences, attitudes
  physical classroom design

4. Together they discussed where they thought the student could function independently, areas where difficulty might be expected, and assistance needed (who would do what by when). This included tailored curriculum, adapted materials, instructional strategies, modified assignments, and expectations.

5. Instruction and assistance was to be provided. The assistance could be provided in the classroom by the specialist, or the specialist could demonstrate through a team teaching concept.

6. The specialist and regular teacher were to meet often to monitor their plan and make adjustments.

7. If training or specific instruction was to be provided, that could be done within the classroom environment or through a pull-out

program. Regardless of where it would be provided, these service providers were to meet with the classroom instructors to monitor integration and carryover of training concepts.

8. At the end of the year, all service providers, including the parents, were to meet to review the individual educational plan and make plans for the next year. All had to assume responsibility for the success of that plan.

9. The regular education teacher maintained responsibility for instruction and grading for this student, consulting often with the specialists.

Such a process requires open avenues of communication and additional time for coordinating activities. The benefits are not only efficient and effective education for hearing-impaired and other students, but can also renew enthusiasm for and satisfaction with teaching and training by the regular educators and the specialists.

PREPARATION FOR TRANSITION

Transitions occur whenever roles, locations, or relationships change; and as a part of normal life they involve simple or complex changes. The transition from the role of a student to the role of an adult, has life-long consequences. The transition is complex, involving decisions about living arrangements, social life, economic goals, and career options. It is important to address the needs to be considered in this transition process for auditory-handicapped students.

Most students go through the process of transition naturally, weighing and sorting out their knowledge of themselves and their value system in relation to the world around them. This conceptual process, of which most students may not even be aware, is usually different for students with hearing impairment. They often have not heard family, peers, or members of the community discussing the multitude of issues relating to independent living as an adult. In addition, many hearing-impaired students may have been deprived of opportunities to become self-directed, self-controlled individuals, due to the overzealous support and assistance often given by teachers, parents, and specialists.

It is critically important that our service delivery system builds functional bridges that will span the gulf between the security and structure offered by the school and the opportunities and risks of adult life. Too often, hearing-impaired students leave education without meaningful occupations, skills for independent living, and knowledge of services available from other agencies. What good is an education if the student does not have a happy work and/or personal life?

Teachers, specialists in hearing, and parents must facilitate the process of transition for hearing-impaired students by using a carefully planned, outcome-oriented process that focuses on the infusion of functional career, vocational, and life skills into educational planning. Career, vocational, and life skills education must be an integral part of programming for hearing-impaired students from the elementary grades through graduation.

Elementary School Level

Students with auditory disorders at the elementary school level need to develop work values and attitudes, and to begin to perceive themselves as independent workers. Focusing on promptness, neatness, responsibility, completion of tasks, working with set time limits, acceptance of individual differences, and appropriate reactions to authority figures is important. Self-awareness goals must be incorporated into our planning for each student, relating to the student's development of feelings of self-worth and self-confidence.

The elementary school years are also used to assist students in becoming aware of different careers and life-styles. Career awareness goals should be considered to provide students with a general understanding of the nature of work (work as a part of life, how we work together for common goals, and the concept of interdependence of workers), types of work, social values, personal satisfaction from work, and material benefits of work.

Special service providers for students with auditory disorders who have traditionally focused on the development of speech, language, and audition during these early school years, must be careful to infuse the above goals into programming. When reading stories or visiting supermarkets or museums, for example, language relating to "what kind of jobs are there here?" "how many jobs can you identify?" "what do you think she has to do in that job?" "how do you think he feels?" and "do you think you would like that job?" can be used. Role playing, puppetry, values-clarification exercises, and simulated business and family activities in the classroom might be helpful. Visiting establishments where there are adult hearing-impaired persons or bringing hearing-impaired adults into the classroom is critically important, so that the hearing-impaired students have the opportunity to begin to understand family roles, life-styles, and career issues.

Through personalization instruction, we can assist students with auditory disorders in personalizing, internalizing, and applying career awareness and self-awareness information, and in developing realistic self-images.

Middle School/ Junior High Level

Middle or junior high school years are used to help students become more aware of their potential and future possibilities. This is the time when they begin to identify personal needs, interests, and aptitudes in relationship to leisure and recreational pursuits, and in relationship to work—such as pay, independence, achievement, and variety.

Career awareness information and activities continue to be infused in educational programming; however, students must also be given the opportunity to engage in a variety of hands-on experiences without pressure of making definite choices relating to independent living and career. Career exploration opportunities should be provided so that hearing impaired students can examine different occupational groupings and relate these to their aptitudes and interests. Occupational demands relating to speech, language, and auditory abilities should be openly discussed. Job shadowing is a particularly useful experience for hearing impaired students, as they are able to directly experience the job and talk individually with the involved person. In-school work experiences and summer employment should be encouraged.

Career and vocational assessment may be appropriate at this time to determine what the hearing impaired student likes to do, has motivation to do, and has the aptitude to do.

Career exploration and assessment opportunities generally available to all students within a junior high school are, at times, not provided to students with hearing impairment due to teacher unfamiliarity with hearing loss and lack of understanding of implications. It becomes important, then, for the specialist in hearing to collaborate with these individuals so that their services can be used. Specialists in hearing may have a tendency to provide the career exploration and assessment experiences to hearing impaired students, feeling that they alone understand and can communicate with these students. This may be a dangerous overprotection that prohibits the students from encountering the real world. Through collaboration, we can facilitate the real world experiences with opportunity for success. Students with auditory disorders have both the right to succeed and the right to fail, along with the right to learn from their experiences. It is our duty as educators to ensure all of these rights.

Senior High Level

It is during these last years of school that a student must develop and clarify personal, social, and occupational skills and goals to assure a productive place in society. Students with hearing impairment must decide how they want to live, what is important, and their life direction. This is the time to delineate specific interests, aptitudes, and competencies in relation to the desired life-style. Planning for independent living and career preparation becomes more formalized. Previous general goals of going to college or getting a job are not enough. "I want to be a . . . ," "I want to live . . . ," and "In my leisure time I want to . . . " are acceptable goals, and college may be a vehicle to get there.

Susan McAlonan, consultant in transition at the Colorado Department of Education, suggests that a specific high school transition plan be developed in the 10th grade and used throughout the high school years. Such a plan would be developed as part of the individual educational planning (IEP) process, with regular educators, career-vocational specialists, specialists in hearing, parents, and the student having joint responsibility for that plan. Transition goals must be considered and refined each year (see Table 7-1), and skills, interests, habits, and behaviors must be formally recorded (see Table 7-2).

Such a plan will facilitate decision-making

toward meaningful work and independent living. High school courses can be selected accordingly. Vocational education or work study programs can be used. Specific training in searching, applying for, and interviewing for a job can be provided. Specific guidance can be given on job retention skills and adjusting to competitive standards. Specific opportunities for using recreational facilities and for participating in a wide variety of leisure time activities can be provided. Specific instruction in daily living skills, such as managing personal finances, selecting and managing a household, buying, preparing, and consuming foods, and exhibiting responsible citizenship can be provided. Personal-social skills can be discussed and developed in relation to socially responsible behavior, interpersonal communication, problem-solving, independence, self-awareness, and self-confidence. Career interests can be refined to match aptitudes. A person interested in becoming a lawyer, but without the ability to do so, can be guided toward becoming a courtroom clerk or paralegal. Placement services for students upon termination from high school can be provided by a job, in a postsecondary training program, or in a college program.

Putting It All Together

Whether our role with children with auditory disorders is in regular education, special education, related service, administration, or parenting, we are faced with decision-making that will prepare hearing impaired adolescents for the transition to adult living. Giving them a diploma or a certificate of graduation and saying, "See you later; have a good life!" is not enough. Education for these individuals is a right according to Public Law 94-142. Once these individuals have left the educational system, adult services are a privilege that may or may not be available. It is our duty to see that the preparation for independent living, meaningful occupation, and quality of life includes family, health, civic, avocational, and personal development components.

Educational programming must be specifically designed to prepare hearing-impaired students to live and function in society. They must learn how to behave and function appropriately in domestic, recreational, vocational, and community life. *We may need to de-em-*

Table 7-1   High School Transition Plan

Student Name _____ District _____ School _____

Transitional Goals (Expected outcome after graduation)

1. Vocational Placement: ____ Competitive employment   Selected occupation _____
                           ____ Postsecondary education   Institution _____ Program _____
                           ____ Supported employment   Selected employment station _____
                           ____ Other   Description _____
2. Residential Placement: ____ Independent living   Location _____
                           ____ Supported living (Group home, Dorm, etc.) _____
                           ____ Living with relative _____
                           ____ Other   Description _____
3. Transportation: ____ Public transportation ____ Driver's license ____ Own car ____ Relative's car
                           ____ Other   Describe _____ Special requirements _____
4. Other: ____ Social   Description _____
                           ____ Leisure time   Description _____
                           ____ Community   Description _____
5. Community Agencies and Support Services Identified to Assist in the Transition Process (List)

_____   _____
_____   _____

From McAlonan, Colorado Department of Education, February 1986.

Table 7-2   Transition Notes and Records

9th Grade	10th Grade	11th Grade	12th Grade
Vocational assessment Skills _____	Vocational assessment _____	Vocational skill development _____	Vocational selection _____
Interest _____	_____	_____	Job-seeking skills _____
Career exploration In school _____	Career exploration _____	Job-seeking skills _____	_____
Community _____	_____	Job retention skills _____	Job retention skills _____
Work habits _____	Work habits & behavior _____	Work habits & behavior _____	Work habits & behavior _____
Social skills _____	Social skills _____	Social and leisure skills _____	Social and leisure skills _____
Independent living _____	Independent living _____	Independent living _____	Independent living _____
Related academics _____	Transportation skills _____	Transportation skills _____	Transportation skills _____
_____	Related academics _____	Related academics _____	Related academics _____

phasize our traditional remedial academic instruction and focus on the development of competencies to facilitate their living as independently and happily as possible in today's society. Seeing these students live and work in their community to the maximum extent possible, and seeing them become self-sufficient, contributing members of society, will fulfill our goals and dreams as educators.

SUMMARY

Remediation of students with auditory disorders within state and federal guidelines often appears to be a frustrating entanglement of laws, emotions, values, and traditions. We have, perhaps, been in the golden age of special education, with specialists in hearing assuming responsibility for the education and remediation of hearing-impaired students. Special education has focused on the program, rather than on programming for each individual student.

Simply assuring that a program for hearing-impaired students is available is not enough. We must begin to define special education as a process of individualizing; a process that involves collaborative decision-making and implementation of services. Only then will each student with auditory disorders not only have an individual education plan, but also a free appropriate public education in the least restrictive environment.

REFERENCES

1. *Education for All Handicapped Children Act of 1975.* Public Law 94-142. U.S. Congress, 94th Cong., 1st sess., U.S. Code, sec. 1041–1461, 1975.
2. Dinkmeyer D, Carlson J: *Consulting: Facilitating Human Potential and Change Process* (Columbus: Charles E. Merrill, 1973).
3. Brown D, Eyne M, Blackburn J, Powell W: *Consultation: Strategy for Improving Education* (Boston: Allyn and Bacon, 1979).
4. Salend SJ, Viglianti D: Preparing secondary students for the mainstream. *Teaching Exceptional Children*, 14, No. 4 (1982), 138–139.

8

MAINSTREAMING:
A PROCESS—NOT A GOAL

Gloria H. Hoversten and Diane Fomby

INTRODUCTION

The present organizational structure of the schools is an age-grade level system developed in the mid-1800s. As it became apparent that all students did not fit into the narrow range of expectancy, it was a common practice to allow some students to "skip" a grade and compel others to repeat a grade. Residential schools for the blind, deaf, and other physically handicapped students flourished. Special day classes, a major innovation of the 1920s, were "add-ons" to the *lock-step graded system*—in effect, placing the handicapped child outside the system and retaining the existing, regular graded structure.[1] The result for students in both the segregated special day classes and the residential school was, in many instances, social isolation, "minimal life exposure even to failure," the creation of stereotypes, and lowered expectancy levels.[2] Labeling of students mushroomed—partly due to the well-intentioned purpose of allowing the student to be served by special education. Labels such as "the deaf" resulted in many generalizations and perpetuated the tendency to focus on methodologies, rather than on the instructional needs of the individual child.

Personnel had to be trained to serve these students, and so there developed an entire range of specialists; for example, hearing therapist, teacher of the visually handicapped, learning disability teacher, and speech and language specialist. Teacher training institutions perpetuated the labels, and certification by category became the rule.

In the past, federal funding for education was limited to financial assistance to states through competitive application grants. State funding for special education provided the needed financial support to local school districts, and was based largely on categories of

handicapped. California, for example, funded at least 28 different special education programs. Differences in reimbursement formulas to local school districts, differences in the amount of funding by exceptionality, and differences in local tax revenues resulted in gross inequities from state to state nationwide in educational opportunities for the handicapped. When each type of exceptionality depended on a "head count" for its funding, little motivation existed for flexibility, movement across artificial boundaries, supplemental support services, and individualization.

However, some teachers and parents of hearing impaired students persisted in seeking education in the *mainstream* of the neighborhood school. The parents, by necessity, acted as academic tutors, consultants to the regular teachers, and counselors to their child. If supplementary teaching and/or services were needed, parents frequently had to either provide them personally or hire others to help. Children were placed in programs and taken out of programs often at the sole discretion of the principal or the parent; options were few. In retrospect, it was perhaps the hard-of-hearing child who suffered the most—neither fitting in the special class or the residential school, nor having the services available for support in the neighborhood school.

So neither the concept nor the practice of mainstreaming is new. What *is* new is the legal mandate and the financial assistance from the federal government. In addition, three important changes have occurred in recent years: (*1*) early identification of hearing impairment; (*2*) early education; and (*3*) early fitting of improved amplification. These changes affirm the demand for a departure from the traditional segregated system of education, and make successful education with normal children a real possibility for many hearing impaired students.

THE PHILOSOPHICAL BASIS

The case for mainstreaming, as summarized by Kaufman,[3] is based on the belief that it will remove stigma from handicapped youngsters, enhance their social status, facilitate modeling of appropriate behavior, provide a more stimulating and competitive environment, offer a more flexible, cost-effective service in the child's own neighborhood, and be more acceptable to the public, particularly minority groups. The assumption is that handicapped students have more similarities than differences in comparison to their nonhandicapped peers, and it is inherent that separate education can result in unequal education. Martin,[4] former Deputy Commissioner for Education of the Handicapped, has stated:

> Our experience with segregated societal institutions has shown them to be among our most cruel and dehumanizing activities. . . . On this basis alone, the human concern for human beings, we must attempt to have handicapped children in sight, in mind, and in settings where they will receive the fullest measure of our educational resources.

Few people question the underlying philosophical values of equality and justice; many question the practicality. However, mainstreaming is a reality. The most relevant question for us is, "How can we make it work?"

THE LEGAL MANDATE

Legislation protecting the rights of the handicapped gained major impetus from the milieu of social change brought about by civil rights laws. The commitment of the US Congress to the education of the handicapped was evidenced by the passage of three laws: (1) The Rehabilitation Act of 1973, Public Law 93-112; (2) The Education for All Handicapped Children Act of 1975, Public Law 94-142; and (3) The Education of the Handicapped Act Amendments of 1983, Public Law 98-199.

Title V of The Rehabilitation Act of 1973, Section 504, is the first major statutory civil rights enactment that protects handicapped individuals from discriminatory employment practices, and mandates equal educational opportunities for the handicapped and equal accessibility to federally supported programs and activities. The Education for All Handicapped Children Act of 1975 delineates the specific requirements for implementation of the broad civil rights provisions of Section 504, and requires that all handicapped children between 3 and 21 years of age receive an appropriate and free public education.

States may choose not to receive federal financial assistance under the formula grant funds of Public Law 94-142, but compliance with Section 504 is mandated for all 50 states and is not a matter of choice. In order to qualify for federal funds to education under Public Law 94-142, a state must establish:

> Procedures to assure that, to the maximum extent appropriate, handicapped children, including children in public or private institutions or other care facilities, are educated with children who are not handicapped and that special classes, separate schooling, or other removal of handicapped children from the regular educational environment occurs only when the nature or severity of the handicap is such that education in regular classes with the use of supplementary aids and services cannot be achieved satisfactorily.[5]

This legal mandate is referred to by a variety of terms: *mainstreaming, normalization, deinstitutionalization, integration*, and *least restrictive environment*. Regardless of terminology, the intent is to reduce or eliminate the segregation of handicapped children in special schools, and to place them with normal children as much as possible. The term least restrictive environment is currently preferred over mainstreaming, since it indicates a continuum of settings and does not imply that all handicapped children are to be taught in the regular classroom.

It is timely to reflect (with Stainback et al[1]) that: Two hundred years ago, it was the integration of the poor into the public education system that was a major issue. . . Three decades ago, with the Brown vs. Board of Education decision, it was the integration of the races. . . Twenty years later it was that landmark Supreme Court decision that separate education is not equal was applied to the handicapped population. . .[1] In all of these departures from established practice, educators have resisted the changes.

IMPLEMENTING THE LAW

A Continuum of Services

A comprehensive educational system must include a continuum of educational environments and placement options, with instructional resources and support personnel as needed. Specific options that should be included in this continuum are listed in Table 8-1.

In addition to this requirement for a continuum of program options, regulations provide that each public agency shall ensure that a handicapped child's educational placement is as close as possible to the child's home.

These requirements compound the problems for low population areas. However, it should be noted that Stanford Research Institute, reporting in 1982, found a significant expansion of program placement options by *local education agencies* (LEAs) since enactment of Public Law 94-142.[6] The National Rural

Research and Personnel Preparation Project (1980) also reported an increased use of alternative settings, personnel, and services in rural school systems.[6]

Appropriate and Nondiscriminatory Assessment

Appropriate assessment becomes crucial when the results of testing will be used to develop a child's individualized educational plan (IEP). It is the responsibility of an educational assessment team to determine a child's present level of functioning. Additionally, the law specifies that nondiscriminatory tests are to be used. For the hearing impaired, these are tests whose results will accurately reflect the child's aptitude or achievement level, rather than the child's receptive or expressive language disabilities. However, testing materials appropriate to the language level and mode of communication of hearing impaired children are only now beginning to be available. Another problem is that there are not enough appropriately trained professionals knowledgeable about deafness to perform these assessments.

In theory, the law protects a hearing impaired child from inappropriate placement based on discriminatory assessment. However, in practice, the tools and the personnel to put this unbiased assessment into effect are not widely available.

Predictive instruments to determine the most appropriate instructional setting are urgently needed. The heterogeneous nature of the hearing impaired student population, and the interaction of numerous variables related to a student's achievement, make development of such instruments extremely difficult.

An additional urgent need is for curriculum-based, criterion-referenced assessment to assist the itinerant teacher of hearing impaired students in regular classes in providing relevant instruction in speechreading skills and auditory training.

Development of the Individualized Educational Plan

The *individualized educational plan* (IEP) is a written statement that includes: (*1*) present educational performance; (*2*) annual goals, in-

---

Table 8-1   A Continuum of Services for Exceptional Children

The progression of services, from special institutional placement to regular classroom participation, should include:

Institutions, such as state hospitals.
Home or hospital instruction.
State special schools.
Nonpublic school programs (with facilities for exchange of services with public schools).
Special classes in a separate school center, with participation in the regular school environment largely on a group basis.
Special day classes at a regular school campus.
Special day classes at a regular school campus with informal and/or group level interaction to prepare for regular classroom functioning.
Integrated special day programs.
Resource specialist programs.
Regular classes with related services (i.e., speech, adapted physical education).
Regular classes with modifications as needed (i.e., special equipment, facility adaptation).
Regular classes with observation and consultation.
Regular education with no special educational support necessary.

NOTE: Adapted from *Least Restrictive Environment: Los Angeles County Operated Programs Resource Guide, 1978–1979.* Los Angeles County Office of Education.

cluding short-term instructional objectives; (3) specified support services—extent and duration; (4) degrees of participation in regular educational programs; and (5) evaluation criteria and schedules. The Office of Special Education describes the IEP as a management tool, a compliance document, and a communication vehicle. The IEP has proven valuable for several reasons: its application to every student, the completeness of its contents, its relative uniformity from school to school, and the requisite parent involvement.[7]

A survey conducted by the National Committee for Citizens in Education[7] found that 83% of responding parents attended their children's IEP meetings; over 67% felt adequately informed, and 70% agreed the IEP seemed to meet their children's needs. Only 5% refused to sign the IEP.

In reality, the development of the IEP may not be a true team effort. As Weatherly[8] points out, it is rarely acknowledged that team members are actually engaged in a political bargaining process:

> With participants of unequal rank vying with one another over issues of status, power, control, command of limited programmatic resources, and distribution of public benefits . . . the least powerful members of the team (the child, the parents and on occasion, the classroom teacher) are at a distinct disadvantage in the process and may feel their voices are not heard.[3]

Front-line administrators find themselves caught between demands from parents for services and demands from *their* supervisors to conserve resources. Regular and special class teachers can become pitted against one another in the struggle to control resources and the work environment. Solutions may be directed toward changing the child to fit into the existing structure, rather than changing the structure to fit the child.

When money is scarce, it is understandable that a school district will seek to prove that its program *is* appropriate for a specific child—rather than be faced with paying for an expensive private or residential placement. The public needs to reflect that such an outlay for one child ultimately results in fewer services for the other children in the district—and is not evidence of an uncaring staff and administration.

DEFINITION AND DELIVERY OF RELATED SERVICES

Public Law 94-142 provides for related services (transportation, developmental, corrective, and other supportive services) "as required to assist a handicapped child to benefit from special education."[9] This component has proved to be one of the most troublesome to implement effectively according to the 1985 *Seventh Annual Report to Congress on the Implementation of the Education of the Handicapped Act* (EHA).[10] Much disagreement has existed as to what services are essential. The meaning of "as required . . . to benefit from an education" is a crucial question. Schools, parents, and the courts continue to debate the extent and meaning of the law.

Of particular interest here is Board vs. Rowley, 1982, the US Supreme Court's first special education case.[11] A federal district court and the Second Circuit Court of Appeals had both held that a school district must provide a sign language interpreter as part of a deaf child's individualized education program. The lower courts found that in order to achieve comparability in education to that given nonhandicapped children, an interpreter must be provided. However, the Supreme Court reversed the Second Circuit Court of Appeals, concluding that the school had complied with the intent of Congress by providing the student access and a reasonable opportunity to learn. It concluded that Congress had not intended that the schools try to develop the handicapped child to his or her maximum potential; that is, provide the best possible program. The deaf student, in this case, had progressed from grade to grade without an interpreter, and was therefore making progress comparable to that of her nonhandicapped peers. The standard for adequacy under the law became comparability to nonhandicapped peers.

The courts have ruled that a related service is anything the handicapped child needs to benefit from an education; and, the financial burden that a broad interpretation of the related services requirement could impose on school districts is rather frightening to contemplate. However, a wide variety of interagency agreements have been negotiated to secure third-party funding, joint funding, and cooperative programming. Rural districts have joined together to use a pool of related service specialists or to purchase related services through region-wide contracts with service providers. New comprehensive programs between special education local planning agencies and community departments of mental health are being organized to provide assessment and treatment, including residential care to seriously emotionally disturbed students. These agreements negotiate such peripheral aspects as transportation and provision and maintenance of facilities. Parent rights of consent and due process are practiced as required by EHA. Occupational and/or physical therapy is being provided through similar negotiation between local children's service agencies and school districts.

The Seventh Annual Report to Congress on the Implementation of the Education of the Handicapped Act (1985) concludes that educational agencies have made progress in meeting their financial obligations to provide related services.[10] When one considers that, in the recent past, related services were usually limited to speech and language therapy, the services of a school nurse, and secondary level school counselors, it is apparent that a very large step is being taken to improve services to children. This involvement of school and community has tremendous potential for eliminating duplication of services and territorial disputes.

There continues to be a need for documentation, data, and research to support the delivery of various related services. The reality of budget limitations and the legal requirements for specification, as to extent and duration of treatment and projected outcome, are acting as a catalyst for specialties to self-examine and research the efficacy of various treatments. This, too, is an improvement over the former laissez-faire approach. Fragmentation of the child's program will decrease as specialists from various agencies share in the development and implementation of the child's IEP.

Personnel Preparation and Development

Although a comprehensive system of personnel development is required to implement Public Law 94-142, the law provides only for a state's annual program plan, which must include the in-service training of general and special education instructional and support personnel. Teachers of the hearing impaired face a new role—that of *itinerant teacher*. The teacher's role now consists of providing support and ancillary services to the mainstreamed child and the regular classroom teacher. This new role requires that special teachers expand their areas of expertise, especially their knowledge in the areas of cognition and learning theory, language acquisition, interpersonal relationships, and group dynamics. It is not to the advantage of a mainstreamed student nor to the regular classroom teacher to have an itinerant teacher who learns a new role by trial and error. Despite the legal impetus for change, very few teacher-training programs have redesigned their curriculae to prepare future teachers of the hearing impaired for roles as itinerant teachers.

Administrators who hire teachers for itinerant positions need to be aware of the "left out" feelings experienced by many itinerant teachers who are isolated from an organized teaching body. The qualifications for a successful itinerant teacher may well be different from those for a resource specialist or a special classroom teacher. Itinerant teaching demands a breadth of experience to cope with the varied needs of a mainstreamed hearing impaired child. The itinerant teacher must be able to provide diagnostic prescriptive teaching, possess strong "public relations" skills, and have the ability and the perseverance to seek out the additional specialized services needed by the child. Such an individual requires a high degree of self-motivation, as there is no one else in the field to serve as the child's advocate.

The Governance Model

The *governance model* includes the administrative structure of the program and the levels of responsibility. The model that evolves is closely tied to the method of funding the programs. Because it is far more costly for sparsely populated districts to provide a comprehensive system, many models will be inter-district or regional cooperatives. These factors bring into focus the problem of deciding who makes policy, who takes responsibility for the program operation, and who monitors and evaluates the effectiveness of the program.

There is confusion as to who is in charge. Bogdan[12] points out that the role of the director of special education was clear when classes were segregated. Now, when most school principals have autonomy over the programs in their own schools, struggles over administrative supervision occur. Both special education teachers and regular teachers are confused about who is responsible for specific children and for the program.

The temptation to place children into the categories in which the greatest reimbursement is received has existed for some time. If a special education program is fiscally neutral (i.e., with no inherent fiscal advantage or penalty to the district that administers the program), its operation can be based on quality of service.

These governance decisions will require legal clarification as well as greater flexibility than in the past on the part of school boards, administrative staff, and the community.

The Funding Gap

The cost of educating a handicapped child has been estimated at twice the cost of regular classroom instruction. The federal government, in its passage of Public Law 94-142, made a commitment to help the states and local schools pay for educating handicapped children. However, federal entitlements are based on a formula that multiplies the number of handicapped children in the state receiving special education services (not to exceed 12% of the school age population) by a percentage of the national average per-pupil expenditure ($2860 in 1986).[13] The total actual federal appropriation dropped dramatically from a fairly stable 12% of the national average-per-pupil expenditure during the late 1970s to a low of 7% in the early 1980s.

Modest yearly increases enacted by Congress would have returned the appropriations to approximately 10% in 1986. However, a 4.3% across-the-board cut in the approved education budget for 1986 resulted from the passage of the Gramm-Rudman-Hollings bill. This bill necessitates cuts in future budget proposals submitted by the President to Congress. Despite Congress's efforts to maintain current appropriation levels (i.e., not reduce the actual dollars allocated), the percentage of the national average-per-pupil expenditure allocated declines. State funds and local revenues continue to provide the major portion of special education expenditures. Local school district budgets are being stretched to pay for huge increases in special education costs brought about by significant increases in numbers of students identified and served, the mandated provision of full-service programs, and additional rising peripheral costs (e.g., lawyers' fees, transportation costs). Political considerations have forced a shift in funding for schools from the local property tax base to state funds. State legislators, in turn, are balking at increased expenditures for schools. Congress has, however, re-authorized the EHA for five years and increased total funding dollars for special education from 1.35 billion in 1986 to 1.74 billion in fiscal year 1987.

At present, expenditure data within and across states is not readily available for comparative analysis due to both the disparity in data maintained by the states and the variations in funding formulas used to finance special education programs. However, it is the intent of Congress to look beyond implementation and toward impact; studies of effectiveness and costs of services are in process.

The National Association of State Directors of Special Education[13] provides the following examples of the impact of fiscal restraints:

> Class sizes are growing; newly identified children are remaining longer on waiting lists; little growth is occurring in the needed expansion of program options; related services are being curtailed; vital initiatives toward provision of comprehensive early intervention services to handicapped children birth through five are being reduced; age eligibility is being narrowed to reduce responsibilities for older handicapped youth; and eligibility criteria for special education generally are being narrowed to constrain the number of children to be served.

In the absence of any explicit federal or state guidelines for establishing priorities for referral, assessment and services, priorities are established by local administrators in line with the funding available to them. The potential for conflict grows between the parents of students with mild handicaps and parents of students with severe handicaps as to who has the better "right" to services.

In addition, there is no incentive for schools to develop high-quality services—a rather moot point in the current fiscal crises.

Weatherly[8] reminds us that our tradition of reform legislation is one in which "lofty objectives are espoused but minimal resources committed. . . . The war on poverty was fought with resources and tactics sufficient only for a brief skirmish preceding what has become a major retreat." It is hoped that a similar fate does not befall the education of the handicapped.

PROGRESS REPORT

The Seventh Annual Report to Congress on the Implementation of The Education of All Handicapped Children Act examines the progress made in implementing the requirements mandated by the public law as amended by Public Law 98-199. This report of 1983–1984 activities continues to portray a shift in emphasis from procedures to quality that was first evident in the report of 1982–1983 activities. Congress is being told that the states have successfully implemented the procedural features of the EHA, and that the states continue to strive for quality in all aspects of programming for handicapped children and their parents. Problems still remain.

> There are continuing needs to stimulate preschool services, to provide for more effective transition from school to meaningful work, to more effectively serve deinstitutionalized children and youth and to develop effective models of interagency collaboration to make more efficient use of available resources. In particular, as better data on the costs of special education and related services are obtained, it becomes increasingly apparent that more effective interagency relationships have the potential to simultaneously increase services and decrease costs.[10]

In the report, the Office of Special Education and Rehabilitation Services presents these priorities relative to the Act:

(*1*) Commitment to early intervention.
(*2*) Extension of community living experiences.
(*3*) Expansion of educational services in the least restrictive environment.
(*4*) Improvement of services available to handicapped adolescents moving from education to the world of work.

The report further notes that, nationwide, the number of special education teachers in all fields is increasing, but data do not necessarily indicate a concomitant increase in skills. Preservice and in-service personnel development remains a priority, as are parent education and the training of specialists in infant and vocational education.

THE MAINSTREAMING PROCESS

Determining the Least Restrictive Environment

Turnbull and Schulz have defined mainstreaming as the instructional and social integration of the handicapped into the regular class structure.[14] It is not just the physical presence of the handicapped child.

Instructional integration is involvement in the curriculum of a classroom. These authors, as well as others, point out that not all students necessarily need to be working on the same skills and concepts. Through such strategies as individualized programming, cooperative activities, and flexible grouping, individual needs can be met.

Social integration has, as its basis, a respect for the strengths and weaknesses of all students, and provides the opportunity to gain status and acceptance and to feel comfortable as a full member of the classroom group. Implicit in this concept is that mainstreaming is a planned process of progressive inclusion, not a "dump and hope" goal.

In considering placement for any hearing impaired child, it is critical to consider the particular needs of that individual child. Although a child with a mild-to-moderate hearing loss may be referred for evaluation to a hearing impaired program, in no way can that child's needs be met in the same way as those of a child who exhibits a severe or profound loss.

In discussing an environment that is *least restrictive* for a child whose aided sound field audiologic results show responses near to normal, it is imperative to consider accommodation within the general education program, with support as necessary. The public law seeks, in particular, to deinstitutionalize moderately impaired students. It is neither necessary nor appropriate to remove students who, with improved teacher skills and support, can be accommodated within the general education program. On the other hand, in seeking a *least restrictive environment* for a profoundly deaf child with unintelligible speech and weak auditory/speechreading skills, it is equally imperative to consider the relative restrictiveness of the same setting in educating the whole child.

Not all hearing impaired children will be successful in fully integrated regular classrooms. Some will benefit from a partially integrated program, while others will always need a special day class in a regular school or a special school. The principle of *progressive inclusion* may result in a student being appropriately placed in a special day class (or residential school) for his or her early elementary education and moving up the continuum as his or her development warrants.

The rate at which progressive inclusion occurs will differ and be based on the large number of variables that affect educational progress in the hearing impaired: such as amount and configuration of residual hearing, additional handicaps, and response to amplification.

Residual hearing, although important, is not a variable upon which all placement decisions must rest. For years, audiologists have been calling attention to the fact that individuals with the same degree of hearing loss (i.e., similar audiograms) may perceive speech quite differently. Audiologists working in the schools have recognized the interpretation of aided auditory functioning levels as a top priority in assisting with the development of the IEP. Recently published materials provide assistance in determining use of residual hearing and auditory skills.[15]

It is the function of the IEP team to determine for a child an appropriate placement in the least restrictive environment. If a child is in the least restrictive environment, the placement cannot be inappropriate. Least restrictive environment is a concept complementary to the most appropriate placement, and is always relative to the needs of the child.

Unfortunately, in practice, in mediation, and in fair hearing processes, least restrictive environment has been misunderstood to be synonymous with mainstreaming. A trend is developing which places the hearing impaired child in a mainstream situation, with the social interaction of regular students on a regular education campus as a single-minded goal.[14] Nationwide, we discover some hearing impaired students as islands in the mainstream;

that is, physically present, but both socially and intellectually absent.[16]

The *islands in the mainstream* phenomenon results from several causes. Primarily, the intent of the public law has been misinterpreted to suggest that interaction with regular students on a regular campus is the immediate mandate. This is not true.

Problems also arise when schools are expected to furnish a continuum of services that they have not been designed to handle and are hard-pressed to provide. The result is that a hearing impaired child is likely to be placed in an existing setting. The variety of educational settings and comprehensive related services to meet the individual needs of each child in a heterogeneous hearing impaired population is often insufficient. Settings may well be *appropriate* without being *most appropriate*. Additionally, *most appropriate* does not have to mean most expensive, although it may require a considerable expenditure of flexibility, ingenuity, and creativity.

Consider this successful two-year experiment developed outside of San Francisco.

Mariam Allen, a teacher of the hearing impaired in northern California, proved that innovative mainstreaming strategies that greatly benefit hearing impaired children do not need to be stopped by budgetary constraints.[17] Mrs. Allen felt particularly sensitive to the developing self-image of a mainstreamed child who found him- or herself to be the only hearing impaired individual in a class or a school. It seemed to Mrs. Allen that none of the existing mainstreaming options for hearing impaired children in her district were appropriate. She proposed that all six of the children she taught needed to be placed in a full-time class that would be co-taught by a special education teacher who used sign language and by a regular classroom teacher. Her proposal was adopted, and the demonstration program that she taught with a regular classroom teacher received an award as exemplary education after being implemented for two years.

Mrs. Allen described the first year as being somewhat difficult for the hearing impaired children. They complained about the noise level in the room, wanted continual contact with adults, and were misunderstood by their hearing peers. During the second year, the group as a whole was quieter, the schedule was less complex, and the hearing impaired students interacted far more in the class. Sociograms showed that the hearing impaired children were seldom the isolates. Academic scores for the entire group improved at an expected rate during both years. Some of the hearing impaired children showed unusual academic and social growth.

Mrs. Allen concluded that "conventional mainstreaming [sending a student out alone or with an interpreter who is not a teacher] does not always address all of the needs of hearing impaired children nor does it deal with the problems of the regular classroom teacher who is asked to meet those needs as well as those of the regular students." Her inventiveness holds promise for solving both of those problems.

In comparison, the *conventional* practice of isolating each of these six children in his or her neighborhood school seems archaic. Yet, daily, IEP teams, goal-oriented toward mainstreaming, intellectually shackled by existing programs, and with the very best intentions, are creating islands in the mainstream.

During the 1983–1984 school year, 4,300,000 handicapped children 3 to 21 years old were served by the EHA. Learning disabled, speech-impaired, mentally retarded, and emotionally disturbed children made up 93% of that total. Hearing impaired children accounted for less than 2%.

To fairly interpret the least restrictive environment section of the public law, one must consider the "nature or severity of the handicap" that deafness imposes. For the majority of the children served by the public law, oral communication will develop, although delayed, distorted, or disordered. For the severely to profoundly deaf, communication *must be taught*. We must commit ourselves to providing the most appropriate educational setting for these hearing impaired youngsters to acquire the linguistic, cognitive, experiential, and social skills they will need to reach their full potential. If being "educated with children who are not handicapped" can meet these varied needs, then it should be implemented. If not, then the least restrictive setting outside "the regular educational environment" that will get the job done must be provided.

Social Interaction

The relative restrictiveness of a placement lies not in the setting itself, but in the closeness of the match between programming and student needs.[16] The IEP team cannot afford to let the current enthusiasm for mainstream placements blind them to the needs of the individual child. In particular, social needs may be overlooked. Research has not substantiated arguments that the increased contact between deaf and hearing peers as a result of mainstreaming will lead to increased *social interaction*.[18] Apparently, placement in the mainstream alone is not enough. The child must first have the prerequisite skills to benefit from the opportunity the mainstream placement provides. Mainstreaming will not create the skills. In fact, inappropriate or premature mainstreaming seems likely to have long-term detrimental effects both academically and socially.[19]

Many studies over the last 40 years have found deaf children to be less socially mature than hearing children. Delayed language acquisition experienced by most deaf children leads to more limited and constrained opportunities for social interaction.[19] A growing body of literature describes the language competencies required of normal-hearing children to compete in the classroom environment successfully.[20] Hearing impaired children frequently enter the classroom with less than competent conversational skills.[18] One of the theoretic bases for mainstreaming is that it gives hearing impaired children the benefit of socialization input from their normal-hearing classmates. However, the social isolation that many mainstreamed hearing impaired students experience suggests that communication skills closely approximating the norms of hearing children are a prerequisite for functioning well in the classroom environment. The two groups of children most likely to be successfully mainstreamed are those with mild-to-moderate losses and those with severe hearing impairments who have benefited from early intervention and maximum use of amplification.[21]

Achievement

Deaf children usually score within the normal range on nonverbal intelligence tests, although their mean scores are somewhat lower than those of hearing children. However, the general academic achievement in deaf children is much below what could be expected from performance on tests of cognitive development.[19]

The Office of Demographic Studies has provided surveys of Stanford Achievement Test results for more than 17,000 hearing impaired students.[22] These surveys show a growth rate of approximately 0.2 grade levels per year, culminating in an average reading level of less than grade 4 by 19 years of age. The delay in reading appears to increase with age, with different studies showing a leveling off at grade 2 to 4.

Language (English) is another area characterized by significant deficits and early plateaus. Language tests administered to a group of 5- to 20-year-old hearing impaired students showed that the students achieved language ages of 6 to 7 years in syntax and 8 to 10 years in content, with little growth or change after 12 years of age. Even by 18 years of age, most hearing impaired students have not mastered the major syntactic structures of English. Many hearing impaired children 5 to 9 years of age cannot produce structures that are well established by normal-hearing 4 year olds.[22]

Evidence of some individual hearing impaired children achieving at levels significantly above the national average has been associated with consistent and high-quality educational programs. Deaf children of deaf parents consistently perform at a higher level than deaf children of hearing parents, regardless of the educational setting. Ironically, the children of deaf parents are more likely to be in special classes or special schools than in the mainstream.[19]

Students who are mainstreamed constitute a population with different characteristics from those shown by students who receive instruction in special education settings only. Integrated students tend to have less severe hearing loss than students who are not integrated, are more likely to have been postlingually deafened, and are rated by teachers as having intelligible speech.[21]

Allen and Osborn[21] concluded that analysis of current data does not reveal the effects of mainstreaming on achievement. Hearing impaired students are not mainstreamed randomly. Those placed in the mainstream are thought by teachers or parents to be capable of doing well in an integrated setting. In fact, they do out-perform their nonintegrated hearing impaired peers on achievement tests.

However, comparisons of the achievement levels of students who are integrated with those who are not integrated show differences not attributable to integration. Given the differences between the group that is integrated and the group that is not, it can be expected that integrated students will perform at higher levels because they possess demographic and handicapping characteristics that have been shown to be related to higher achievement.

Research is needed that examines placement decisions in a systematic way before an adequate examination of the causal effects of mainstreaming on academic achievement can be undertaken.

Deinstitutionalization

There may exist among special educators, hearing impaired individuals, and their parents a difference in values that is reflected in their opinions of what is restrictive and what is not. Some argue that the regular classroom is restrictive because it cannot guarantee a communicating milieu for all hearing impaired children, and that the lack of comprehensive services offered in a mainstreamed setting restricts a child from reaching full potential.

The current view of mainstreaming as a goal relegates both special schools and substantially separate programs to positions at the *more restrictive* end of the cascade of services. But, for some students, the special school or substantially separate program may indeed provide the least restrictive alternative. The decision will always need to be made in terms of the individual child.

US Department of Education guidelines for compliance with the least restrictive environment provision of the EHA are contained in *Manual 10*, published by the US Department of Education.[23] In the spring of 1986, educators at a public briefing on *Manual 10* complained to Assistant Secretary of Education Madeleine Will that the manual gives the impression that regular school placement must be the least restrictive environment for all handicapped children. Will agreed that is just one of several misconceptions that professionals and parents hold regarding the new directive. She denied that the Department of Education considers any educational placement outside the neighborhood school a violation of the spirit of Public Law 94-142. She conceded that some disabled children will still need special schools, stating that "any placement on the continuum could be least restrictive for a particular child."

In making educational programming decisions under Public Law 94-142, the courts and impartial hearing examiners have defined education to include not only the teaching of academic and vocational skills, but also non-academic skills such as self-help, social, interpersonal, independent living, play, and recreation.

Based on a survey of legal precedents, Silverstein[24] deduced that three legal and policy conclusions are evident when residential programming is required:

(1) More than six hours per day is necessary to meet the students' educational needs.
(2) The severity of the child's language deficit precludes meaningful benefit from peer group learning and interaction in the mainstream setting.
(3) Social and emotional adjustments are poor in the mainstream setting.

The public law has considerably changed the role of residential schools. *Manual 10* does require that students in more restrictive environments be provided with opportunity for interaction with nondisabled peers as much as possible. Residential programs nationwide are working hard to find the right opportunities for their deaf students to interact with hearing peers.

The expanding population of multihandicapped deaf youngsters and of severely emotionally disturbed deaf students may find their needs best met by residential school placement. Residential schools can serve as a short term *living skills* environment for older deaf students who have not learned these skills in a day school setting. State schools will continue to serve children from sparsely populated areas, although changing demographics are reducing this number as more families migrate to urban centers. Additionally, these schools will carry on the demonstration site, curriculum center, and diagnostic functions that have been established. Special schools serving large populations reduce their seeming restrictiveness by offering varied coursework designed to serve a diverse group, and by staffing with specialists trained to communicate with the deaf.

Hearing impaired children and their parents should be granted public support for the educational setting determined to be appropriate. If it is deemed most appropriate for a hearing impaired child to be placed in a residential facility, the child and parents should receive attitudinal and fiscal support.

The Mainstream Classroom

It is the regular education teacher who is at the receiving end of responsibility as mainstreaming becomes more widespread. The National Education Association (NEA) has addressed regular classroom teacher concerns in their 1986 legislative program.[25] The NEA supports the spirit of the law and looks to the federal government for 100% funding of federally mandated services. For the mainstream teacher, the organization favors: (1) reduction in class size commensurate with the added responsibility of providing educational services to handicapped students; (2) teacher involvement in the determination of placement of handicapped children; (3) a procedure for speedy teacher appeal of placement decisions when necessary; (4) access to resource personnel; and (5) preservice and in-service training.

Turnbull and Schulz[14] report that:

> In pinpointing the particular concerns of regular teachers in inservice training sessions, we have consistently found that regular teachers generally ask for more information on assessing a student's level of achievement, strategies for individualizing instruction, appropriate instructional materials for various student characteristics, and ways to manage behavior problems.

Colleges and universities are challenged to prepare all education majors for successful mainstreaming practices. Educators are challenged *to mainstream the system* before mainstreaming students.

The majority of hearing impaired students who are mainstreamed typically have sufficient residual hearing and oral skills to understand speech and to speak intelligibly. Even some profoundly deaf students have remarkably developed receptive and expressive skills that enable them to communicate effectively in the regular classroom. However, the majority of children with profound hearing losses lack the requisite auditory skills to communicate orally in the mainstreamed classroom, especially when acoustic information must be relied upon for understanding. The regular classroom teacher cannot be expected to communicate effectively with most profoundly deaf children. When children are unable to communicate in the classroom, support systems must be provided. Interpreters and tutors can be useful. The use of oral interpreters in the classroom has recently been advocated. The oral interpreter is a trained and certified person who provides simultaneous lip-reading cues as the teacher is instructing. Oral interpreters may provide valuable information to the hearing impaired child, but this is a new service and its overall effectiveness has yet to be proven. Assistive devices might also be useful (see Chapter 13).

With proper planning, the integration of a hearing impaired child in a regular classroom can be made nondisruptive. All those concerned—the child's teacher, administrator, parents, the child when possible, and other specialists when needed—should participate in developing the IEP before placing a hearing impaired student into a regular classroom. At this time, it should be decided whether the child can be successfully integrated into the classroom without becoming a drag on the other students and failing to learn at his individual rate. This is the essence of appropriate class placement.

Appropriate class placement assumes particular importance for a child whose academic and social skills may be widely disparate. Hearing impaired students frequently function higher in math than in language areas. Social immaturity is also a problem common to hearing impaired children. Appropriate placement in which both curricular and social areas are considered will help to alleviate the problem of the special child disrupting the regular class.

Even after well-planned placement, it is possible for a mainstreamed child to disrupt the normal function of the classroom. If it becomes obvious that the placement is not appropriate, the planning team should convene as soon as possible, so that the child can be transferred to a more appropriate setting.

Possible compensations could be made to teachers who receive mainstreamed children into their regular classrooms. Class size could be reduced to enable the regular teacher to spend needed time with mainstreamed students. Any one teacher should not be overloaded with mainstreamed students. Teachers should be allowed options in the placement of mainstreamed students. Time should be allowed to the teacher for extra work created by placement, and opportunities for reverse mainstreaming should be provided.

The practice of *reverse mainstreaming*, in which hearing children are brought into the special class for the hearing impaired for various learning activities, is frequently welcomed by regular teachers. Hearing children from bilingual homes or lower-functioning hearing children may profit from the language instruction to a small group that the teacher of the hearing impaired provides. Larger groups of hearing children may be invited to participate with the hearing impaired children in art or cooking activities, or in viewing a captioned film.

Blackwell draws some important conclusions in his guide, *Teaching Hearing Impaired Children in Regular Classrooms.*[26]

> Whatever the reason for placing a hearing impaired student in a regular classroom, the task of helping that child move through the very difficult task of mastering the English language is a great responsibility.
>
> In reality, perhaps, that responsibility can never be carried by one person alone. The audiologist must make sure the student's hearing aids are of good quality and work properly. The teacher of the hearing impaired, the speech therapist or the resource teacher will need to provide sufficient tutoring, skill building, auditory training, speech training, and counseling. The responsibility must surely be seen as a shared task.

Too frequently, classroom teachers accept the hearing impaired student's presence in the class, believing that because they are unfamiliar with the implications of a hearing loss, the real work will be done by the itinerant support staff.

While this is partly true, regular classroom teachers must see themselves as a much more critical influence in the language development process. More language issues will be observed and dealt with in daily class activities than in any tutoring session.

Furthermore, while classroom teachers may not know much about deafness, they probably know a great deal about the nature of language or the structure of content matter and how they must be learned. That kind of information is invaluable in the educational process.

Attitudes

Having a regular teacher view a mainstreamed child's disability as a manageable difference rather than a classroom problem will take more than a public law. It will require an attitude change. Lauber,[27] a regular class teacher who has cerebral palsy and uses a wheelchair, states:

> It's the telethon mentality that gets in the way. We've seen too much of charming disabled children, usually referred to as 'helpless cripples,' and most often paraded across a stage while a weeping star begs the audience for money. As a result, the general public thinks of disabled people in very dependent, unrealistic terms.

Studies on attitudes indicate that society regards the handicapped with prejudice. This is the attitude that the public law seeks to address. A hearing impaired child eating lunch alone in a sea of hearing peers can hardly be considered part of the mainstream.

Much can be done to educate hearing children in regular classes to ensure their cooperation in making mainstreaming a success. Many classes in which hearing-impaired children are mainstreamed could profit from an understandable presentation for children about hearing loss and its effects on speech, language, and behavior. Other activities, such as the learning of sign language, listening to a hearing aid, and learning about the ear and hearing are examples of planned experiences that can have a positive effect. Acceptance needs to be understood as a process rather than a set of procedures; as such, it takes time. Simple exposure, as well as planned experiences, and the example of adult routine acceptance will facilitate the process of social acceptance of the hearing impaired child by hearing classmates.

It is important to remember that the similarities between children who hear and hearing-impaired children are greater than their differences. A hearing impaired child's social and emotional needs can be met in a regular class if special attention is given to providing a climate of support and understanding for all the students in the class.

Johnson and Johnson[28] describe ways in which teachers can structure the interactions between handicapped and nonhandicapped students to promote positive attitudes. They report on cooperative learning situations in which students coordinate their actions to achieve a mutual goal. Compared to individual or competitive learning situations, cooperative learning tasks promoted positive interdependence.

The REACH Project in San Francisco noted successful acceptance of handicapped children by their nonhandicapped peers, who served as peer tutors or special friends.[29] These two roles provided structured interaction between disabled and able-bodied students. Peer tutors had curricular focus; special friends interacted on a regularly scheduled basis at recess. The motivation for playground involvement was provided by new, age-appropriate equipment (e.g., frisbee, ring toss, card games such as fish or Uno) otherwise unavailable.

In our society, attitudinal changes seem to follow institutional changes rather than the other way around. The courts have demonstrated that they can make substantial changes in education regarding segregation, teacher rights, student rights, and allocation of financial resources. None of these changes are accomplished swiftly or easily. There is no reason to think that Public Law 94-142 will achieve a perfect educational milieu for every handicapped child in a short period of time.

Acceptance of the handicapped child in the regular classroom will materialize when educators and related professionals feel informed and reasonably well supported in their efforts to deal with the special needs of mainstreamed children. People tend to resent what they do not understand. An informed public is more willing to change. The presence of the different child in the educational mainstream will help to dispel the ignorance and concomitant fear experienced by those of us who consider ourselves to be normal.

Environmental Strategies

The mainstream environment can be modified to accommodate hearing-impaired students. Various strategies will make incidental school information and extracurricular activities available to mainstreamed pupils.

Notetakers, peer tutors, special friends, and buddy system support not only fill the communication gap experienced by hearing-impaired students, but also provide student interactions and social contact. Teacher reinforcement of oral information, with its written counterpart on the board or overhead projector, will profit all visual learners in the class. Notification of assignments in written form should be a policy, rather than a special strategy, for handicapped students.

It may take years to impress upon regular school educators the need to provide visual reinforcement for the hearing impaired child. The hearing impaired student must have an opportunity to read as well as hear the daily bulletin, codes of conduct and policy statements, and procedural information (library rules, schedules, etc.). Someone needs to interpret announcements made on the public address system. Scripts can be provided for films or videotapes that are not captioned, and for audiotapes. Hearing impaired students may need interpreters or other special support in order to participate fully in after school activities. These activities, in addition to regular schoolwork, are vital to a student's ability to function successfully in the social mainstream.

Counselors and other student placement personnel need to be aware that English as a Second Language (ESL) classes offer an appropriate learning environment for some hearing impaired students. The English vocabulary and syntax used by the teacher in talking to students may be far less complicated than the language structures used in regular classes. An abundance of high-interest/low-language level instructional materials used in ESL classes is also suitable for hearing handicapped students.

Counselors are frequently reluctant to place handicapped students in ESL classes, since the classes may be overcrowded or funded differently. The strategy should be one of meeting needs rather than affixing labels or categorizing according to origins of the deficit.

Special classes, which often overprotect students in attempting to assist them, prevent the acquisition of skills in daily living, decision-making, and social interaction. To be successful, students must learn these survival skills. Fending for oneself in a regular public school, and learning campus survival skills—especially the person or persons to go to for which kinds of help, and when—may benefit a child who can be appropriately placed in such an environment.

Reverse mainstreaming can be a successful strategy in building social skills among chil-dren in a hearing impaired classroom. Reverse mainstreaming allows the special education teacher to retain some control, while increasing the social interaction of hearing impaired children in structured activities with normal-hearing peers. The activity should be planned so that cooperation between hearing and hearing handicapped youngsters is necessary. One method to increase interaction between members of a hearing impaired class and grade 1 students on the regular school campus where the special education class was situated was successful. The first-grade teacher agreed to integrate her 28 children into the authors' physical education lesson one afternoon per week. Teams were formed with mixed hearing/hearing impaired groups; large group activities involved interdependent play (e.g., parachute games) and mixed pairs supported one another in cooperative play. Additionally, art lessons weekly involved half-class integration. Half of the hearing impaired children went to the first grade while half the first-grade class came to the special day class. Each teacher taught a different art lesson, which required the sharing of materials. The following week, the other half of each class made the switch, and each teacher taught the same art lesson to the second half of the students. These strategies not only provided student models and peer interaction, but allowed each teacher to plan an art activity every other week instead of weekly.

Although hearing impaired students at first tended to over-react to events in the reverse mainstream situation, they soon modified their behaviors to more socially acceptable levels. There was far less pushing and shoving, more sportsmanship demonstrated, more patience in turn-taking, and generally fewer exhibitions of egocentric behaviors. These newly learned social skills combined with specific skills developed in physical education class, related to ball handling and game rules, greatly improved the hearing impaired children's abilities to spontaneously participate in recess activities with hearing children.

Social integration of hearing impaired children involves not only physical proximity of hearing peers, but their interactive behavior and acceptance as well. Physical proximity by itself will not promote interaction. The special education teacher's role in preparing a student to integrate socially is important. The parents' role is even more crucial. The lack of conversational skills on the part of a hearing impaired student will greatly reduce both the child's initiating communication with hearing peers and his or her likelihood of responding to initiations.[18] Furthermore, many studies support the finding that hearing impaired children may depend socially on teachers rather than on peers. Special educators must insure that they do not perpetuate this dependence. Some special educators may perceive themselves as having gained status by their ability to teach children who are so communicatively different and dependent that only the enlightened professional can deal with them.[29]

Acoustic Environment of the Regular Classroom

A major drawback to the successful mainstreaming of hearing impaired children may be the background noise and competing messages that commonly occur in a regular classroom of 25 or 30 children (see Chapter 11). Research has provided a great deal of information on this subject, and has shown that the relative effect of noise on hearing impaired listeners is significantly greater than the effect on normal listeners.[30] Awareness of the interacting effects of noise, reverberation, and hearing aid usage is essential for management of the hearing impaired child's listening environment.

At present, not even the majority of self-contained special classes have acoustically treated environments (e.g., carpeting and limited reflective surfaces). Thus, the hearing impaired child in the regular class has little hope of encountering anything beyond a quiet, controlled classroom, a good place to sit, and a teacher with a good voice. The use of a teacher FM transmitter in conjunction with the pupil's own personal ear-level aid is a new technologic development that could be of great help, but has been slow to catch on. When it is recognized that the signal-to-noise (S/N) ratio in the regular classroom may frequently be as poor as 0 dB (i.e., the competing noise is at the same intensity as the desired message), it is clear that something must be done. As demonstrated in Chapter 11, future research may prove that a controlled sound environment is desirable for all learners.

Adequate Population in Receiving Schools

The low incidence of deafness creates special problems for local districts trying to offer a continuum of services to a small and heterogeneous hearing impaired population. A concurrent problem for many suburban districts is a declining enrollment among their regular students. If special day classes are to be situated on a regular campus to avoid a segregated setting, how many special classes can a regular school receive without overwhelming the site with exceptional children?

The Southwest School for the Hearing Impaired operates special day classes in one area of Los Angeles County. Some 11 classrooms, located on six regular school campuses, make up the program; there is no single site housing the school. The experience of operating these classes confirms that a regular elementary school campus should not house more than one or two special day classes. More than two classes increases the tendency for the special teachers and the hearing impaired pupils to cling together, although as many as three classes can be tolerated. The number of receiving classes available for hearing impaired children needs to be considered, since this variable will affect the number of hearing impaired children partially integrated into any one teacher's class; more than three pupils in a class probably represents an overload. If all the hearing impaired pupils on a school campus are close to the same age, there is a high probability of overloading in receiving classes. Regular campuses generally house many grade levels; two or three special day classes located on these campuses should cover the same number of grades.

Paradoxically, the same scheme does not necessarily benefit hearing impaired high school students. Regular high school populations are generally much larger than elementary school populations. Frequently, high schools accept students from a number of feeder schools. The instructional program, staffing, and extracurricular activities differ vastly from their elementary school counterparts. High schools need a large population to offer a sufficient variety of coursework, from college preparatory to vocational training, for a diverse population. Adolescent hearing im-

Case history #1.   David, 23 years old, has had a severe-to-profound hearing impairment since birth (see Fig. 8-1). He is a junior at a large state university with a strong disabled student program for the hearing impaired, which includes counseling, interpreters, tutors, notetakers, and social services. David goes to school part-time and has a part-time job with an aerospace contractor. His major is computer science, and his job involves the development of software. David already knows that when he obtains his degree he will seek employment with a smaller organization, one with more flexibility and opportunity for creative development than he can experience now in a job with a government-specified outcome. David is taking advantage of the large and effective network of support provided for hearing impaired students at his university. He chose his job, his classes, his church, even his girlfriend, and many of his social activities with information derived from, and counseling supplied by, the Disabled Students' Center.

Things have not always gone this smoothly for David despite above-average intelligence and highly supportive parents. He was in special day classes for the hearing impaired with partial mainstreaming at the junior high level before he entered high school. When David began high school as a fully mainstreamed student, he had the services of a speech therapist one hour per week and an itinerant teacher of the deaf three hours per week. With these support services, David found his first year in high school fairly easy.

With this false sense of security, he scheduled algebra, chemistry, German, and English along with physical education and driver's education for his sophomore year. He continued to have itinerant help three hours weekly, but dropped speech therapy because he was missing too many classes. Chemistry lectures were hard to follow because of the laboratory working arrangements. Even though notetakers were available, David did not request one, and the school did not have oral interpreters. Both of these services would have helped, especially in chemistry.

Instead, David found that he was studying six to eight hours after school in order to earn a B or C. He had given up his job delivering newspapers to have more time to study. The pace was too much. He was losing weight, developing skin problems, and had virtually no social life.

David's itinerant teacher attempted to counsel him about study habits, and encouraged him to add some extracurricular activities and ease up on the academics. The teacher conferred with the counselor, the classroom teachers, David's father, and the administrator of the hearing impaired program.

A meeting was called to consider alternative educational services for David. The meeting presented ideas for change in the curricular areas and educational settings. David was present at the meeting; as a result, he was enrolled in an experimental program at his local high school, which permitted selected students to learn at their own pace. Classes were smaller, more individual attention was available to each student, and there were fewer lectures to attend. David accepted the responsibility of earning credit in the areas that posed particular problems for him.

David responded well to the challenge, adjusted his expectations to a more comfortable level, and completed the year in the experimental program as a happier, better-adjusted student.

By March of his senior year, he asked to have itinerant instruction dropped. He wanted to see if he could complete his studies unassisted. He feels pleased that he was able to complete the final months of high school on his own.

College proved to be something else. David's intelligible speech and listening and lip-reading skills had permitted him to function fairly well in small groups. However, despite all the time he had put into language work in high school, David found it almost impossible to keep up on his own with the vocabulary and concepts as well as the large-sized classes of his college coursework. He required the assistance of notetakers and interpreters in order to succeed. David also learned sign language and felt a great sense of relief that he would not miss important information. He is now a quite comfortable total communicator with real options in a true mainstream environment. He feels he is making satisfying choices about how he wants to live his life and is looking forward to meeting life's challenges.

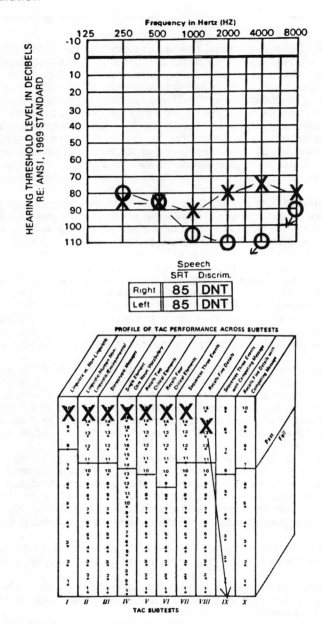

Figure 8-1. Audiometric and TAC data for David (Case history #1).

paired youngsters can benefit if the same arrangements occur in the hearing-impaired high school program. The key is to gather a substantial hearing-impaired high school population. Local school districts in Orange County, California have banded together to provide an extensive high school program to all of the hearing-impaired students in the county. The receiving school has a huge and expanding population. The program is able to offer a multitude of options because it has the numbers to meet the needs of a varied population. High school programs for the deaf that serve a small population could considerably close the gaps in the continuum by consolidating themselves into a larger district. Politicians and pro-

Case history #2.   Six-year-old Jack's slight size does not deter him from joining any of the ball games on the playground at his elementary school. Third and fourth graders accept his presence on the courts because of his skills, his almost intuitive knowledge of game rules, and his good sportsmanship. The fact that Jack was born with a severe-to-profound hearing loss makes his ready acceptance and seemingly easy socialization all the more remarkable (see Fig. 8-2).

Jack suffered multiple difficulties at birth when his parents were told first, that he would not live; and later, that he would never walk. He does exhibit some fine motor difficulties, although his gross motor skills are far above average. Jack has worn binaural ear-level aids since his loss was confirmed at 22 months of age, and he began in an infant total communication program for the hearing impaired. Jack's hearing continues to fluctuate because of recurring middle ear problems.

Jack's mother explained that Jack was a spectator at sports long before he became a participant. His grandparents are soccer coaches, and various members of his large family are ball players. Jack adopted these family values, and even as a toddler was a patient observer of team play. Now, at 6 years of age, Jack is beginning his third year on a soccer team.

Academics do not come easily to Jack. He is mainstreamed for 30 minutes each day in a regular kindergarten, and he spends about 45 minutes several days per week with a resource teacher. The rest of the time, Jack is placed in a total communication special day class for the hearing impaired. Although students in the special day class use an FM system, Jack's mother insists that he wear his own ear-level aids at all times. He is an eager, highly motivated, attentive learner. Although his parents were reluctant to do so, they now have Jack on medication to reduce hyperactivity. Preschool teachers had found him highly distractible and inattentive. He is tolerating the medication well and showing good work and study habits.

Jack's etiology seldom results in an individual with his positive prognosis. His parents have provided him with an accepting and varied environment. He has the good fortune of experiencing new and different events regularly. He has learned intuitively how to observe others at play, deduce their rules, and then join them when he understands their game. His parents and the experiences, motivation, and values they have provided have helped Jack achieve this elusive (for many hearing impaired children) goal. A classroom teacher for the hearing impaired would be hard-put to duplicate that learning process.

These important social skills will carry Jack throughout his schooling to whatever degree he is academically mainstreamed. He is bringing to the mainstream process skills that will guarantee his social integration, rather than expecting mainstreaming to bring the skills to him.

---

fessionals alike may oppose such a structure, since it minimizes local control; but hearing handicapped young people stand to benefit.

A brilliant, profoundly deaf college freshman, who won a college scholarship from her local district, complained that English classes she had taken as a mainstreamed student at her local high school had been a waste of time. "My high school English teachers understood that because of my handicap I could not compete with the class. They tried to be fair. But to tell you the truth, I learned nothing well." She recognized this immediately when she began taking a freshman English class designed for hearing impaired students and taught by a deaf woman in a special disabled students program at a huge university in southern California.

It is the students at both ends of the spectrum who suffer most from conventional programming. Even very bright deaf students cannot be expected to compete linguistically with hearing peers at a high school level. At the opposite end, severely involved or multiply handicapped deaf students cannot be expected to extract equal benefits from a conventional program.

In mainstreaming, it is not only existing ed-

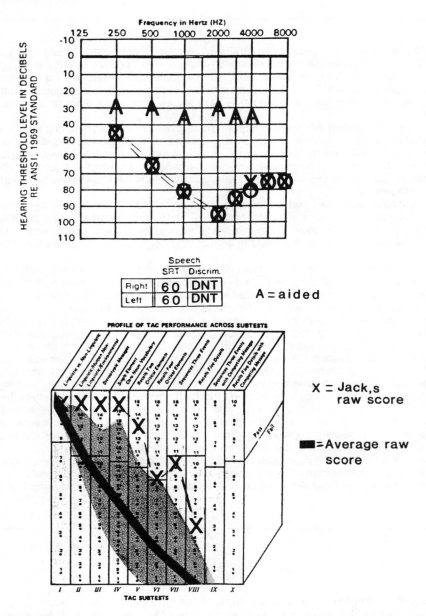

Figure 8-2. Audiometric and TAC data for Jack (Case history #2). On the TAC the X's represent Jack's raw score and the solid line the average raw score. The shaded area on the TAC represents ± 1 standard deviation.

ucational programming that needs to be modified, but the service delivery model, which includes the administrative structure and the levels of responsibility. As stated elsewhere in this chapter, it is necessary to mainstream the system serving the students before the students can be mainstreamed.

The Pull-Out Program

The current delivery of speech and language services to handicapped students within a school program is based on a medical model originally developed in what were designated *speech and hearing clinics*, which were often

Case history #3.   Molly, 15 years old, has a severe hearing impairment (see Fig. 8-3). A gifted student, she is enrolled in a hearing impaired program, but is fully mainstreamed into the regular classes of the high school in which the program is housed. Molly's standardized test scores are at or above grade level on every subtest. She is an avid reader, writes well, and expresses herself well enough orally to be understood by her hearing peers. She uses a sign language interpreter in her classes and has been popular with both hearing and hearing-impaired students since she became a freshman last year.

Despite these many positive attributes, Molly has problems. Her grades are good enough only to get by; she has been removed from a physical education class for refusing to wear required clothes; she has been suspended from the school twice for actions that foolishly endangered other students; she seldom does homework, refuses to work in class, lacks respect for authority, and generally does what she pleases.

Molly's hearing loss was detected early, and she was enrolled in a special day class using total communication when she was 18 months old. With this early support and above-average intelligence, Molly's academic progress has been extraordinary. However, attempts to mainstream Molly at the third- and fourth-grade levels were unsuccessful. She was socially immature, and did not take responsibility for paying attention or receiving information.

Molly's special day class teacher developed a reverse mainstream program to give Molly opportunities for increased interaction and development of social maturity with hearing peers. Her teacher invited a small group of hearing students to learn an academic subject with Molly. In this small group, Molly's teacher could closely monitor specific learning behaviors and could structure the environment so that Molly would be able to take increasing responsibility for herself. It was hoped that Molly would learn these skills in a supportive environment, and then would apply them in a mainstream setting.

Molly was fully mainstreamed in her neighborhood school for fifth grade. At the end of that year, she requested to be returned to the hearing impaired program. Molly felt isolated socially. Professionals who had worked with Molly found her attitude toward learning poor, and her lack of attention in class a severe problem. She was returned to the junior high school program for the hearing-impaired, but was fully mainstreamed with interpreter assistance. It was felt that the special program would meet her educational and social needs and improve her academic performance.

Molly's story has not changed since junior high school. Her mother finds it difficult to modify Molly's behavior at home with consistent rewards and consequences, although counseling has been offered through the high school.

Apparently, Molly's least restrictive environment has not been devised yet. The fact that her standardized test scores reflect grade or above-grade level ability indicates that Molly is learning despite the system. If the system cannot meet this student's needs, it would seem she is destined to drop out.

Most districts have devised alternative high school programs for students who have social problems. Generally, classes are smaller, students work under contracts, consequences are certain, and counseling is an important part of the curriculum. Perhaps something similar needs to be investigated for Molly. She does not know what she wants because existing programs do not fill her needs. A least restrictive environment for Molly is a challenge and a necessity.

contained within hospital and university settings. This model when applied to the public school setting results in the *pull-out approach*. Most special services within schools use this approach, and a variety of negative effects are frequently seen. Students miss out on the important preparations for a test or (more likely) some pleasurable activity thought by the specialist to be less important. This lessens the opportunity for social integration, and can lead to feelings of resentment. It highlights the students' differences, contributes to problems in self-acceptance and assimilation, and lowers achievement expectations. Often, the regular teacher resents what is seen as an intrusion; it becomes very easy to abdicate responsibility

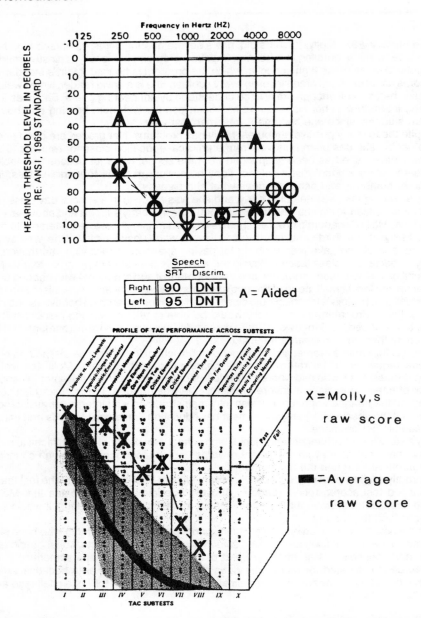

Figure 8-3. Audiometric and TAC data for Molly (Case history #3). On the TAC the X's represent Molly's raw score and the solid line the average raw score. The shaded area on the TAC represents ± 1 standard deviation.

to the specialist. (How often our itinerant teachers of the hearing impaired have been welcomed at the classroom door as the *savior* of the problem child; it is difficult, if not impossible, to be a savior with two to three times per

has not been tested to any satisfactory degree. Experience indicates that students seem to continue their support service programs, graduating only when age demands an end.

Some speech-language programs are incor-

Case history #4. Andy's severe hearing loss went undetected until he was 3 years old (see Fig. 8-4). Although his adoptive parents felt he had suddenly lost his hearing, personnel experienced in working with hearing-impaired youngsters saw no evidence that Andy's hearing had ever been normal. He demonstrated the language delays and speech difficulties expected of a child his age with a congenital loss of this degree.

Andy was enrolled in an oral preschool program for the hearing impaired soon after his hearing loss was documented. His affluent family continued to provide him with varied experiences, and Andy made excellent progress. By the time Andy was 5 years old, his parents expected the hearing impaired program to start the child on a first-grade reader. Only extensive assessment and conferencing convinced the parents that an academic program in a reading series was premature. Andy continued to work on building the linguistic and cognitive skills he would need to become a successful reader.

When Andy was 6 years old, the location of his special day class on the campus of a regular elementary school made partial mainstreaming possible. Andy's entire class was reverse mainstreamed for physical education and art taught by the special education teacher and aide. Andy and a hearing impaired classmate were mainstreamed in the same first-grade math class. Andy showed remarkable strength in math computation.

The following year, Andy's mainstream experience was expanded to include reading as well as math in second grade. Andy, one of 28 children in the class, joined a group of 10 children in the lowest reading group. Reading was more of a challenge, and Andy struggled to keep up with the group. His special day class teacher provided considerable tutoring.

The special day class teacher and the regular teacher agreed that Andy's fine behavior, good work, and study habits and remarkable listening skills made him a candidate for a fully mainstreamed placement in his neighborhood school, with the assistance of an itinerant teacher of the hearing-impaired and a speech teacher.

When almost 8 years old, standardized test results indicated that Andy read at about a 2.3 grade level, spelled at 2.5, and computed arithmetic at 3.2. His listening comprehension (Stanford Achievement Test—H.I.) was at an amazing 2.3 grade level. However, math concepts, math application, science, social science, and vocabulary were at a first-grade level. The special day class teacher further observed that Andy had problems with abstract concepts, written expressive language, and decoding new vocabulary.

Andy's neighborhood school in an upper-class area had a very accelerated program. The professionals working with Andy all agreed that his full integration into an accelerated second grade would be most appropriate. Andy's parents refused that recommendation; and over the objections of the professionals involved, they insisted on Andy's placement in a third-grade class. The parents had been told by a clinical audiologist, when Andy's hearing loss was discovered, that their child would be mainstreamed by third grade. The district met the parent's wishes.

After two years as a fully mainstreamed student, Andy's itinerant teacher notes that Andy continues to work hard and struggles to maintain the pace of the fifth-grade class. The itinerant teacher reflects that had Andy's placement been initiated at second grade instead of third, he may have closed some gaps and may have found himself under less pressure today. The teacher further suggests that as Andy's education progresses, the gaps may widen and become significant. As a beginning fifth grader, Andy is frequently frustrated and sometimes distressed as he tries to meet the demands of his mainstream class. An FM system is being used this year; acceptance by Andy and the regular teacher is good; it is hoped that Andy will realize the benefits and be willing to use the system when he enters junior high school and encounters many different teachers.

Socially, Andy has problems, too. He tends to be withdrawn. When he does interact with other children, he chooses playmates from a special day class for educationally handicapped children on the campus.

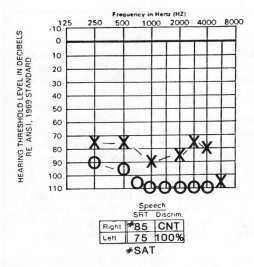

Figure 8-4. Audiometric data for Andy (Case history #4). The left ear discrimination score was obtained using the NU 6 test.

research data are increasing. These are hopeful trends.

Another related problem that needs resolution is the confusion of roles. The language, speech, and hearing specialist and the itinerant teacher of the hearing impaired are both concerned with communication skills. Who provides the academic support needed to maintain the hearing impaired student in the regular classroom? Is this the role of the itinerant teacher of the hearing impaired, or is it the role of the resource specialist? And what is the role of the classroom teacher in all of this?

The teaching of reading is a skill that touches many communication avenues thought to be the prerogative of a particular specialist. The *fragmentation of learning* referred to by Will[31] is abundantly clear.

The authors believe that the solution does indeed lie in the integration of special education with regular education and the eventual elimination of the lock-step graded structure based largely on chronologic age. Small steps are no doubt needed to point the way toward such sweeping changes. A place to begin might be the granting of greater flexibility to the specialists and the regular classroom teacher to seek solutions outside the traditional approaches. There will be innovative teachers who may very well devise solutions.

The role of the sign language interpreter in the regular classroom is worthy of attention. We need to ask such questions as: "Is this the best way to enable the deaf child to understand the subject matter?" Perhaps, the interpreter should be a trained teacher, fluently expressive in sign language, who could interact with the regular teacher and jointly carry some of the class responsibilities. If this were possible, social and academic interaction would be given a powerful stimulant.

CONCLUSION

The case histories in this chapter were selected to illustrate the complexities involved in responding to the mandate in Public Law 94-142 to serve individual needs. Public Law 94-142 is a challenge—not an answer. The practicality of the law has been questioned, but the underlying premise of the right of handicapped children to an appropriate education with full participation in society as much as possible has not.

The reality is, however, that the spirit and intent of Public Law 94-142 are sometimes overlooked in zealous attempts to adhere to the letter of the law. The best-intentioned educators, legislators, and advocates for handicapped children have not been able to remedy educational inadequacies with the passage of a law. It will take time to refine and develop policy that clarifies the interpretation of Public Law 94-142. Major national issues have surfaced. Some issues may require amendments to the statute. The Office of Special Education hopes that problems with the law can be resolved primarily through interpretation or clarification of policy.

Bogdan[12] comments on changes brought about by the mainstreaming movement as follows:

> Change is difficult to accomplish and in our travels we have observed remarkable movement. There is active participation of parents in demanding quality education for their disabled children; parents who at an earlier time took what they could beg. Children who were once sentenced to the back wards of huge institutions are side by side with high achieving youngsters in prestigious schools. All over, people are talking a different language, being sensitive to the derogatory connotation of

Case history #5.   Candy, 9 years old, is a multiply handicapped, profoundly deaf girl (see Fig. 8-5). Her hearing loss was suspected and confirmed at 9 months of age; she was binaurally aided at 1 year of age. Candy entered an experimental infant program when she was 17 months old and continued in a total communication preschool and primary special day class placement for hearing-impaired children through 8 years of age. Throughout this period, she received speech therapy and adaptive physical education for motor skill delays in addition to her special day class placement.

Candy's parents and other family members had learned sign language and were extremely supportive. They diligently provided her with a multitude of experiences and an environment designed to stimulate language and learning. Yet Candy's language improvement and living skills were not commensurate with the extensive schooling and family support she received.

Candy was a very cooperative student who followed class routine well and demonstrated good visual memory. However, she had an extremely short attention span, appeared to have receptive and expressive skills for only a very basic noun vocabulary, could not sequence, and had difficulty communicating information outside the immediate environment.

At the IEP, the teacher and parents agreed that further diagnostic testing was necessary for appropriate program planning. Candy's progress did not reflect the effort made by educators and her parents.

The state provided an extensive three-day evaluation at the state residential school for the deaf. Following the testing, an IEP was held for Candy, and these results and observations were discussed: severe attention deficit, significant motor skill delays, inability to visually track moving objects, and sensory-integration deficits in addition to the language delays noted previously by the classroom teacher. The diagnostic team recommended a complete neurologic work-up to pinpoint anomalies not identified by broad assessment, medication to reduce distractibility, further sensory integration testing, and placement in the deaf multihandicapped unit at the state residential school. The IEP set these recommendations in motion.

A part of neurologic testing, a computed tomographic (CAT) scan, could not be administered because Candy could not be sedated into stillness. Sensory-integration testing disclosed that Candy was unaware which of her two arms was touched if she could not see the contact. Medication to reduce distractibility proved to be very helpful, and Candy has been receiving it for 18 months with good results.

Candy's program in the deaf multihandicapped unit includes occupational therapy twice weekly, remedial physical education daily, computer activities designed to help her focus attention two hours weekly, participation in a team village life skills program twice weekly, and such extracurricular activities as a Brownie Troop and experiential field trips. Candy has won a Super Citizen Award for her residential dorm, where she lives during the week with 19 girls, ages 5 to 12 years, all of whom are multihandicapped and deaf. Candy's parents report that she is happy to see them on the weekends, but very eager to return to school each Sunday night. Candy was removed from speech therapy at her most recent IEP. The team saw no progress, and recognized that neuromuscular difficulties made intelligible speech highly unlikely.

Even though Candy still cannot communicate effectively, sequence, or read easily, her parents feel that she has improved in self-help skills, self-confidence, and language. They attribute Candy's progress to the tailor-made program designed for her special needs—a program beyond the scope of a day school setting. These parents—highly educated activists—have become members of the advisory council to the educational program. Although extensive assessment has not discovered the cause of Candy's profound hearing loss and other handicapping conditions, the parents are confident that her current placement meets her needs better than any place she has been.

This residential placement, although removed from the home with fewer chances for interaction with hearing peers, provides a setting that is less restrictive than any other, because all of Candy's multiple needs are being met.

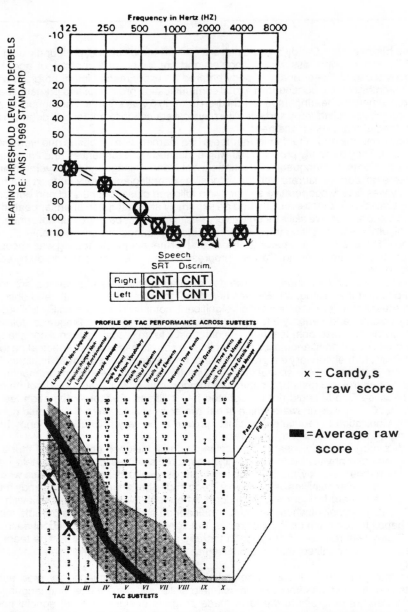

Figure 8-5. Audiometric and TAC data for Candy (Case history #5). On the TAC the X's represent Candy's raw score and the solid line the average raw score. The shaded area on the TAC represents ± 1 standard deviation.

words such as "cripple" and "handicapped," and understanding disabled students as people who have rights. We have seen examples of teachers who have flourished under the challenge of doing something different for someone who is different. A core of change agents, administrators, teachers, and others are pres-

ent in the schools, and they are becoming a force which will be felt.

Will,[31] Assistant Secretary of Education for the National Office of Special Education and Rehabilitation Services, finds that

Case history #6.   Denise, 16 years old, has a severe hearing loss in her right ear and a profound loss in her left ear (see Fig. 8-6). The loss (probably present at birth) was not suspected until she was 2.5 years old. She received her first hearing aid (for the right ear only) before 3 years of age, and was enrolled in an oral program at 3 years of age. She remained in a special day class until grade 6, at which time she was thought to be ready for mainstreaming.

At this time, she began to use an FM system coupled with her personal ear-level hearing aid, and has continued to use the system for all of her remaining school years.

At present, Denise is a senior in a large high school of 2000 students. She carries the teacher transmitter with her to each of her six classes; all teachers have cooperated in wearing the transmitter. Denise has always accepted the FM system in a very matter-of-fact way. She hears well enough with the system to take her own notes in class. The parents described the difference made by the FM system as the difference "between night and day." (Her fellow students have even profited from the system, asking Denise to tell them when she hears the teacher [who is wearing the transmitter] returning to his class.)

Most of Denise's classes are remedial classes designed for slower students. She has passed the proficiency test needed for graduation in written language and math, but has failed the reading proficiency test each time. It is expected that she will pass it and graduate this year. Denise is seen twice weekly for 50 minutes by an itinerant teacher of the deaf to work on vocabulary building, and to provide assistance in academic subjects.

Denise's itinerant teacher describes her as self-contained, well adjusted, and very secure. Many individuals with whom Denise comes in contact think of her as shy and do not identify her as hearing impaired. Her speech is readily intelligible. She is able to converse on the telephone with family and some friends. Denise has a close normal-hearing girlfriend whom she met while taking up cross-country running.

She played basketball, but dropped out because the coaches had "a tendency not to play her," and most did not talk to her (i.e., tell her when she did well and explain what she was doing wrong).

Denise has an intact family (both parents and one younger brother); both parents have been very supportive of Denise and of her schools and teachers. Both have served as PTO President, and both have served on the Parent Board. They express some concern about her social life, recognize that she is quiet and studious rather than a "social butterfly," and are very proud of her achievements.

Her father described the sixth grade as a "bear," and one which was emotionally draining on everyone. Denise was new to the school and the only hearing impaired student; the teachers were lenient and permitted Denise to get away with things for which others were reprimanded. At one point, the students "ganged up" on Denise and were about to beat her up. Her father convinced Denise to ask the teachers to be more strict with her, and the uproar gradually dissipated.

Denise's itinerant teacher feels she functions well in the hearing environments. She has maintained friendships with deaf classmates and asked a deaf young man to a school dance. She has recently started taking sign classes.

Denise has an interest and talent in art, and hopes to become a cartoonist. Her itinerant teacher is helping the parents and Denise to select and apply to appropriate colleges or trade schools. The future is bright for Denise.

Special Education in the 10th year since the passage of PL 94-142 has 1) refined the concept and practice of individualized instruction, 2) redefined the role of parents in the education of the child, 3) made education possible for ½ million previously unserved handicapped children, 4) improved services for several million others.

Will concludes that programs within the separate special education system have achieved mixed results for some children. In an address (1985) on educating children with learning problems, she makes the point that the pull-out approach

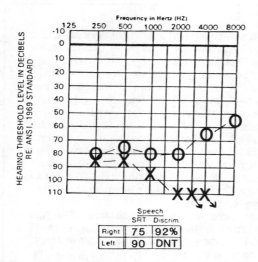

Figure 8-6. Audiometric data for Denise (Case history #6).

Considerable research evidence exists showing that all children of the same age are not ready to be taught the same objective; that all children do not learn a given objective at the same rate, nor do they master given objectives in all curricular areas during the same year. Despite this evidence, Stainback et al[1] find that traditional instructional practices have been slow to change. Attention needs to be focused on the underlying educational structure, rather than continuing to place responsibility on overworked teachers. Special education consulting and resource personnel need to go into regular classrooms and "help teachers implement individualized, cooperative and adaptive learning environments." Little real chance of ever achieving integration for all students is seen unless *special* and *regular* resources, personnel, and program merge into one unified system.[1]

These recommendations are reinforced when one considers the dramatic increase, approximately 20 to 30% estimated by Will, in students unable to learn adequately in the present regular education system.[31] The reasons for this are probably inherent in our changing social and economic climate of working parents, single-parent homes, *latch-key* children, non-English speaking immigrants, and the survival of many infants designated as high risk at birth.

The worst of the initial Public Law 94-142 adjustment period is over. The great fear that hoards of handicapped children would overwhelm each classroom has not been realized. Now educators can begin to think about ways to improve their programs. A panel of experts assembled by the Ford Foundation wrote:

> What may emerge from the new emphasis on special education is not just a rearrangement of programs for the handicapped, but possibly a pervasive change in the processes of schooling for all children.

. . . has failed in many instances to meet the educational needs of these students and has created, however unwillingly, barriers to their successful education. . . the language and terminology we use in describing our education system is full of the language of separation, of fragmentation, of removal. . .philosophers say that ideas have consequences and that one must know the consequences of one's ideas.

She summarizes four consequences of the present system: (*1*) rigid eligibility requirements and screening procedures exclude many from needed support; (*2*) poor performance is equated with a handicap leading to stigmatization and lowered expectations; (*3*) special programs are made available only *after* serious deficiencies are identified (i.e., after failure); and (*4*) incipient problems are not ameliorated in the early developmental stages.

Reform at the building level, suggested by Will,[31] would empower the building administrator to assemble and mold all the resources in his or her program to produce effective programs. Skills to carry out the individual educational plans would be collectively contributed by special education teachers and regular education teachers.

Bogdan[12] sees the supposed failures of mainstreaming as problems of organizational arrangements, internal politics, and a lack of will and skill in school personnel.

Society has made a national commitment to educating every child successfully, regardless of his or her social background, native language, or handicap. Public Law 94-142 may "show the way to a new educational structure that will benefit every child and hence the nation as a whole for generations to come."[7]

Case history #7.   Barbara, a 16 year old, has a profound bilateral hearing impairment due to meningitis at 2 years of age (see Fig. 8-7). She began attending special day classes in an oral program at 3 years of age. She was fully mainstreamed in her neighborhood school by fourth grade, and received four hours weekly of service from an itinerant teacher of the deaf.

When Barbara entered sixth grade, she transferred to a private religious school. The services of an itinerant teacher were provided once weekly for 50 minutes.

At present, she attends a private religious high school known for its high academic standards and strict discipline. Classes, averaging 40 students in each, are mainly in a lecture format. Barbara has six different teachers. A state law prohibits Barbara from being served by the itinerant teacher, a public school employee, on the grounds of the private school. So the itinerant teacher meets Barbara at a nearby public high school. She works on written language, vocabulary development, and grammatic structure using a program developed specifically to assist students in passing the proficiency examinations for a high school diploma.

Barbara has become increasingly unhappy during the past year. Her grades, always A and B level, dropped last semester; she received several D's. Her grandparents (with whom Barbara lives) have been concerned because Barbara comes home from school, goes directly to her room, and spends many hours there including the majority of her time on the weekends. She has only one girlfriend at school (also an outsider) who is always in difficulty and on probation. Barbara, herself, was tardy to class and frequently disregarded campus rules.

The school year ended with Barbara being expelled due to cheating—giving her friend the answers during an examination. Barbara's mother was given the option to appeal the suspension. A hearing with the Board of Education was held, and the itinerant teacher and Barbara spoke to the Board. After the itinerant teacher explained the severity and ramifications of Barbara's hearing loss, she learned that (unknown to her) Barbara always sat in the back of the room and that several of her teachers did not know the extent of the hearing loss. The school board approved readmittance, and recommended that the school counselor meet weekly with Barbara, meet weekly with each of Barbara's teachers, and confer weekly with the itinerant teacher.

An excellent student was *assigned* to take notes for Barbara in each of her classes. (This had been suggested to Barbara earlier by the itinerant teacher, but Barbara was adamant, insisting that she did not need or want a notetaker.)

The counselor is initiating a program to involve Barbara in extracurricular activities. Barbara had tried out for the school softball team, but was not accepted. Even though she had played during junior high school, this school's strong athletic competitive tradition probably worked against her acceptance. This was a crushing blow to Barbara.

At the moment, Barbara seems happier. She still objects strenuously if it is suggested that she might ask a speaker to repeat, and she continues to expend great effort to hide her hearing loss. She does not want to learn signs, does not want her itinerant teacher to use any signs, rejects the idea of a home teletypewriter, and refuses to contact former deaf classmates.

Barbara has the intellectual gifts to succeed in college; whether she can surmount her present difficulties in social adjustment and self-acceptance remains to be seen. She is a lonely girl. Her itinerant teacher as well as the school counselor continue to look for ways to broaden Barbara's social contacts.

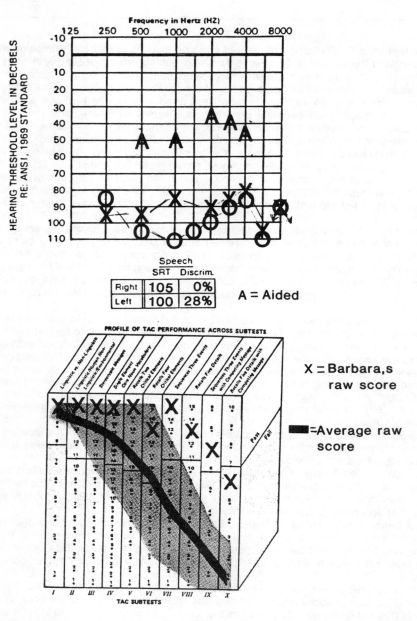

Figure 8-7. Audiometric and TAC data for Barbara (Case history #7). On the TAC the X's represent Barbara's raw score and the solid line the average raw score. The shaded area on the TAC represents ± 1 standard deviation. The discrimination scores were obtained using the NU 6 test.

REFERENCES

1. Stainback W, Stainback S, Courtnage L, Jaben T: Facilitating mainstreaming by modifying mainstream. *Exceptional Children*, 52 (1985), 144–152.

2. Northcott WH: *Implications of Mainstreaming for the Education of Hearing Impaired Children in the 1980's*, pamphlet (Washington, DC: A.G. Bell Publications, 1979).

3. Kaufman M, et al: Mainstreaming: Toward an explication of the concept. *Focus on Exceptional Children*, 7 (1975), 1–12.

4. Martin EW: Some thoughts on mainstreaming.

Exceptional Children, 41 (1974), 150–153.

5. *Education for All Handicapped Children Act of 1975.* Public Law 94-142. 20 U.S. Code 1412, sec. 612(5).

6. Weintraub F, Ramirez B: Progress in the education of the handicapped and analysis of PL 97-199. The Education of the Handicapped Act Amendments of 1983, in *Special Education in America: Its Legal and Governmental Foundations Series* (Reston, VA: Council for Exceptional Children, ERIC Clearinghouse on Handicapped and Gifted Children, 1985), ED 255011.

7. Lazarus M: *Educating the Handicapped: Where We've Been, Where We're Going* (Arlington, VA: National School Public Relations Association, 1980), pp 27–94.

8. Weatherly R: *Reforming Special Education: Policy Implementation from State Level to Street Level* (Cambridge: MIT Press, 1979).

9. *Education for All Handicapped Children Act of 1975.* Public Law 94-142. 20 U.S. Code 1401, sec. 4(17).

10. *Seventh Annual Report to Congress on the Implementation of the Education of the Handicapped Act* (Washington, DC: U.S. Department of Education, 1985).

11. Turnbull H: Appropriate education and Rowley. *Exceptional Children,* 52 (1986), 347–352.

12. Bogdan R: A closer look at mainstreaming. *Educational Forum,* 47 (1983), 425–434.

13. National Association of State Directors of Special Education: Personal communication (Washington, D.C., 1986).

14. Turnbull A, Schulz J: *Mainstreaming Handicapped Students: A Guide for the Classroom Teacher* (Boston: Allyn and Bacon, 1979).

15. *Auditory Skills Curriculum: Test of Auditory Comprehension.* Los Angeles County, Office of Education (North Hollywood: Foreworks, 1976). *Auditory Skills Curriculum Preschool Supplement.* Lexington School for the Deaf (North Hollywood: Foreworks, 1986).

16. Mullen Y: *A Psychologist Looks at Mainstreaming.* Paper presented at the International Convention of The Alexander Graham Bell Association, Portland, OR, June 26–30, 1984.

17. Allen M: *A Cooperative Integration (Mainstreaming) Program between Millbrae Elementary School District and San Mateo County Office of Education's Classes for the Deaf and Severely Hard of Hearing Program. Results of a Two Year Study. 1979–1981.* (Redwood City, CA: San Mateo Office of Education, 1981).

18. Antia S: Social integration of hearing impaired children: Fact or fiction? *Volta Review,* 87 (1985), 279–289.

19. Meadow K: *Deafness and Child Development.* (Berkeley, CA: University of California Press, 1980).

20. Weiss A: Classroom discourse and the hearing-impaired child, in Butler KG, ed: *Hearing Impairment: Implications From Normal Child Language* (Gaithersburg, MD, Aspen Publishers, 1986).

21. Allen TE, Osborn TL: Academic integration of hearing impaired students: Demographic, handicapping and achievement factors. *Am Annl Deaf* 2, No. 2 (1984), 100–113.

22. Moog J, Geers A: EPIC: A Program to Accelerate Academic Progress in Profoundly Hearing-Impaired Children. *Volta Review,* 87 (1985), 259–277.

23. Pre-College Programs: *The Progress Report.* (Washington, DC: Gallaudet College, April 1986).

24. Silverstein R: The legal necessity for residential schools serving deaf, blind and multi-handicapped sensory-impaired children. *American Annl Deaf* 131 (1986), 78–84.

25. National Education Association: *Legislative Program for the 100th Congress, Resolution, No. B-21. Education for All Handicapped Students.* Resolutions of the 1986 National Education Association Representative Assembly.

26. Blackwell PM: *Teaching Hearing-Impaired Children in Regular Classrooms. Language in Education: Theory and Practice* (Washington, DC: No. 54 Center for Applied Linguistics, July 1983).

27. Aiello B: *The Hearing Impaired Child in the Regular Class.* Teachers' Network for Education of the Handicapped (Washington, DC: American Federation of Teachers, 1981).

28. Johnson DW, Johnson RT: Classroom learning structure and attitudes toward handicapped students in mainstream settings: A theoretical model and research evidence, in Jones RL, ed: *Attitudes and Attitude Change in Special Education: Theory and Practice* (Reston, VA: ERIC Clearinghouse on Handicapped and Gifted Children, 1984).

29. Murray C, Beckstead SP: *Awareness and Inservice Manual* (San Francisco, San Francisco State University, 1980).

30. Tillman TW, Carhart R, Olsen WO: Hearing aid efficiency in a competing noise situation. *J Speech Hear Res,* 13 (1970), 789–811.

31. Will MC: Educating children with learning problems: A shared responsibility. *Exceptional Children,* 52 (1986), 411–415.

9

CONTRIBUTION OF MILD HEARING LOSS TO AUDITORY LANGUAGE LEARNING PROBLEMS

Marion P. Downs

INTRODUCTION

The concept of an *educationally handicapping hearing loss* has recently undergone dramatic changes. Traditionally, it has been thought that if a child passed a school hearing screening test at the usual 25 dB HL screening level, his/her hearing was adequate for educational purposes. But, in 1964, a large school study[1] found that pure tone screening at 25 dB HL missed ear disorders in 52% of the children tested. Later studies[2] are finding that almost all middle ear disorders result in conductive losses that can be educationally handicapping to some degree. This changing concept of a handicapping loss is of immediate concern to educators, school nurses, health service personnel, physicians, and school administrators.

Conductive hearing loss from active ear disease is the most frequently occurring type of loss in school children. Although sensorineural losses are more distressing because of the severity of the handicap, conductive losses should be of more widespread concern because these losses may be responsible for many of the language disorders that are seen in the *normal-hearing* school population. Often termed *central processing disorders*, the language problems may be due to developmental language dysfunction caused by recurrent ear disease. Recognition of this fact will make a difference in the therapeutic techniques used with such children.

What kind of a hearing loss caused by ear disease would result in educational handicap? What decibel level is educationally handicapping? Why should mild losses from common ear disease become learning handicaps? What evidence suggests that ear disease in early life results in language learning disorders? These questions will be thoroughly covered in this chapter because they represent a revolutionary change in our way of looking at hearing

loss in school children. In addition, some other environmental deprivations that affect the auditory language learning process will be explored—for almost all of our language is learned through audition.

THE HANDICAP OF CONDUCTIVE HEARING LOSS

Just for a moment, perform a little experiment on yourself. With your index fingers extended, press the tabs in front of your ears into the ear canals, occluding the ear canals completely. Press tightly. You have just given yourself a 25 dB HL average hearing loss, as shown in Figure 9-1. Try carrying on a normal conversation with this hearing loss, or try listening to someone talk in a crowd. You will find that you have to strain a great deal in order to catch what people are saying. Yet this kind of hearing loss would have passed the traditional school screening tests, where only 1000, 2000, and 4000 Hz were screened at 25 dB HL. This kind of loss results from the ear disorder called otitis media, extremely common in children. Table 9-1 shows the approximate prevalence of ear disease in children as delineated in a Washington, D.C. survey by the National Academy of Sciences.

But for the benefit of physicians and nurses, we must reiterate which kind of otitis media is the culprit in such hearing losses. As detailed in Chapter 2 there are three types of otitis media:

(1) *Acute suppurative otitis media*, characterized by fever, pain, redness of the drum, and a significant conductive hearing loss (see Fig. 9-2). There is no missing these symptomatic episodes of acute otitis media. Because this disease is caused by bacteria, it may yield readily to antibiotics, so it is easily medically treated.

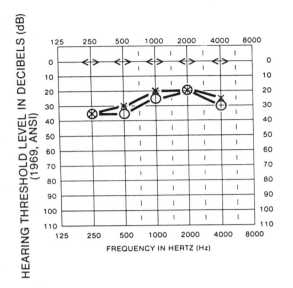

Figure 9-1. Simulation of conductive-type hearing loss obtained when occluding ears with fingers.

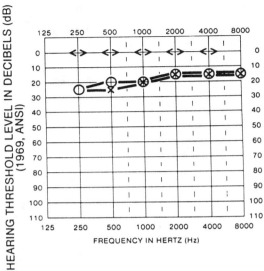

Figure 9-2. Mild conductive hearing loss characteristic of acute suppurative otitis media.

(2) *Chronic otitis media*, usually characterized by a perforated eardrum accompanied by purulent (pussy) drainage. There may be some pain, and the hearing loss can be quite severe.

(3) *Serous otitis media* (sometimes called secretory otitis media), an almost completely asymptomatic disease, unless one is able to identify the mild conductive hearing loss that usually results.

Figure 9-3 shows the mean conductive hearing loss of serous otitis described by Bluestone.[3] There is no pain, no fever, no drainage, no bulging drum, and only a thin fluid behind the

eardrum that may be difficult to see in a cursory examination. This is the ear disease that we are particularly concerned with, both in the infant and in the school child, because the mild hearing loss that results may be a great deal more educationally handicapping than has been thought. Estimates of its prevalence range from 4% in 7- and 8-year-olds[4] to 14% or more in the entire child population.[5]

When present, serous otitis media usually affects both ears (see Chapter 2). It may be continuous, causing a constant reduced level of hearing, or it may be recurrent, causing a

Table 9-1 Distribution of Otologic Examination Results in Children Age 6 Months to 11 Years: Community Sample, Selected Areas in Washington, D.C., 1971

Otologic Examination Result*	6 mo–3 yr (%)	4–5 yr (%)	6–7 yr (%)	8–9 yr (%)	10–11 yr (%)	Total All Ages (%)
Bilaterally normal	68.8	74.3	72.2	81.2	78.8	74.6
Small fibrotic scarring only	3.6	4.6	8.0	5.6	6.7	5.7
Ear pathology	27.6	21.1	19.8	13.2	14.4	19.7
TOTAL	100.0	100.0	100.0	100.0	99.9	100.0
Total number	499	411	451	407	390	2,158†

*Total chi square (4 d.f.) = 34.132, $p < 0.001$; regression within chi square (1 d.f.) = 30.401, $p < 0.001$.
†Excludes 22 who could not be examined.
Reprinted with permission from Kessner DM, Snow CK, Singer J: *Assessment of Medical Care for Children*, Vol. 3 (Washington DC: National Academy of Sciences).

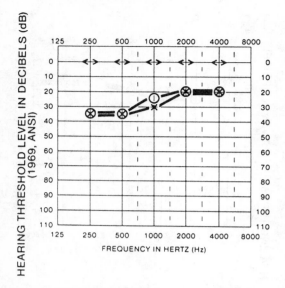

Figure 9-3. Mean conductive hearing loss characteristic of serous otitis media described by Bluestone.[3]

fluctuating hearing loss. Even when fluctuating, serous otitis media handicaps the overall language learning situation of the child, for acoustic information will be heard sporadically and differently from time to time and cause confusion in the child's learning strategies. Figure 9-4 shows where various speech sounds are heard in relation to the mild conductive hearing loss of otitis media. It can be seen that although the voiced vowel and consonant sounds may be heard at around 40 dB HL on the audiogram, a great many of the unvoiced consonant sounds may be heard faintly or not at all with even a mild conductive hearing loss. It is important to understand what this means in terms of the learning strategies of the child.

When you occluded your ears in the exercise above, you found that you could still hear ordinary conversation, even though it was considerably muffled. However, what you may not have realized is that there were some speech sounds that you could not hear at all or could not hear distinctly. You never missed them, for you have been so familiar with the strategies for understanding speech through contextual clues that you were not aware of not hearing some of the sounds. What if you had been a first grader who was learning a variety of words for the first time? It is exceedingly more important for a first grader to hear all of the speech

sounds in a new word than it is for you as an experienced listener to hear them. Figure 9-5 illustrates why some of the sounds may be missed. It shows that the voiceless stop consonants and the voiceless fricative consonants are in some cases 30 dB less intense than the vowels and other consonants. Voiceless stop consonants include the /p/ as in *pay*, /t/ as in *to*, and /k/ as in *key*; and the unvoiced fricatives include the /f/ as in *for*, /s/ as in *see*, /th/ as in *thin*, and /sh/ as in *she*. This is illustrated by the word *teak* in Figure 9-5 where the /e/ sound is almost 29 dB more intense than the /k/.

For the child who is still learning language, a mild conductive hearing loss may place an unbearable strain on coping abilities. Only the rare child—one with unusually high intellectual abilities—can surmount this learning hazard without being affected in some way. Thus, when speech sounds are missed entirely or not heard distinctly, or are heard differently from one time to another, the usual learning strategies of the child become disorganized and ineffective.

However, the normal background noise level of our present-day environment can be a most destructive liability when added to a conductive hearing loss. Stop for a moment and do another experiment in hearing. Wherever you are, sit back and listen to the ambient noise in your environment. You will hear noise from air conditioning, fluorescent lights, heating blowers, people talking, etc. According to Skinner,[6] this background noise is usually 10 to 15 dB below the level of speech, giving a +10 to +15 dB signal-to-noise (S/N) ratio (see Chapter 11). Skinner states that this S/N ratio is not difficult for the normal-hearing adult, because an adult is able to fill in with contextual clues for the missed acoustic signals. But, Skinner says, if children are to hear all of the acoustic clues clearly, the noise should be 30 dB below the level of speech. Unfortunately, our classrooms do not get a clean bill of health so far as S/N ratio is concerned. Chapter 11 describes the studies that have shown that there are unfavorable S/N ratios in most school classrooms.

The environmental noise problem in the schools has been exacerbated by open-plan or open area classrooms, air conditioning, and heating systems, and by the lack of good acoustic treatment of most classrooms. Even the normal-hearing child may be affected by this rising ambient noise level. A study by Cohen[7] demonstrated that groups of children who

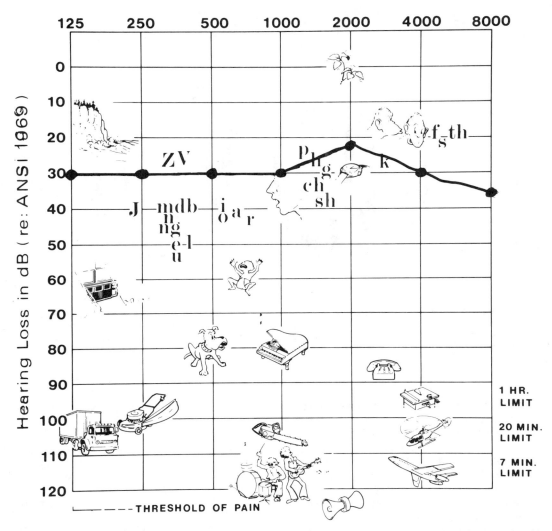

Figure 9-4. Comparison of the frequency and intensity of various environmental and speech sounds in relationship to the mild conductive hearing loss of otitis media. (Reprinted with permission from Northern and Downs: *Hearing in Children*, ed 2. [Baltimore: Williams and Wilkins, 1978], p 12.)

lived in high environmental noise backgrounds tended to have more reading difficulties than did children who lived in lower background noise levels. An ingenious proposal to remedy the background noise situation in the classroom has been described. The procedures appear to be beneficial both for the child with conductive hearing loss and the normal hearing child.

Results from an investigation by Dobie and Berlin[8] provide dramatic support confirming the acoustic liabilities of mild conductive hearing loss. Knowing that a child with a 20 dB HL loss would pass a screening test that used 20 dB HL as the criterion intensity level, Dobie and Berlin undertook to find out what kind of speech perception problems such a child would have in language learning situations. They treated recorded speech sample utterances, first by recording them through *correct-*

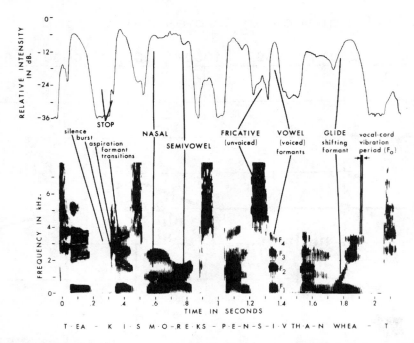

Figure 9-5. Spectrographic analysis and relative intensity of a speech sample showing why some acoustic cues may not be perceived when mild hearing loss is present. (Reprinted with permission from Skinner MW: The hearing of speech during language acquisition. *Otolaryngol Clin North Amer* 11, No. 3 [October 1978], p 634.)

ing filters, which shaped the signal as if it were processed through an ear at about the 40 phon level. They then displayed these utterances oscillographically and attenuated them by 20 dB (to simulate how a 20 dB conductive hearing loss would receive the material). These oscillographic samples were then displayed underneath the unattenuated samples, and spectral analyses of each 600 msec of the speech samples were prepared. A number of readers then read the oscillographs to segment and mark the onsets of the various phonetic utterances.

The readings of these treated utterances revealed the following two observations: (1) there was a potential loss of transitional information, especially plural endings and related final-position fricatives; and (2) very brief utterances or high-frequency information could conceivably either be distorted or degraded if S/N conditions were less than satisfactory (remember that the S/N ratios in almost all schools are inadequate).

Dobie and Berlin reasoned that on the basis of their findings, a child with a 20 dB hearing loss from otitis media might be handicapped acoustically in the following ways:

(1) Morphologic markers might be lost or sporadically misunderstood; for example, "Where are Jack's gloves to be placed?" might be perceived as "Where Jack glove be place?"
(2) Very short words that are elided often in connected speech (see "are" and "to" above) will lose considerable loudness because of the critical relationship between intensity, duration, and loudness.
(3) Inflections, or markers, carrying subtle nuances such as questioning and related intonation contouring can at the very best be expected to come through inconsistently.

In addition, the authors found that there was a great deal of variability in the acoustic input. As a result, markers for the beginnings and endings of words and ideas could be inconsistently noted.

This study by Dobie and Berlin completely corroborated the acoustic liabilities that Skinner had predicted would result from mild conductive loss. She was concerned about the S/N ratios, about the variability of the acoustic input, and about the loss of morphologic markers. The study brought scientific evidence supporting her theories.

Central Nervous System Studies

Several animal studies and one human study provide initial evidence to explain what happens in the central nervous system when there has been a sensory deprivation of hearing due to mild conductive hearing loss. The first was by Webster and Webster,[9] who were able to give a group of mice conductive hearing losses shortly after birth. At 45 days, these experimental mice and a control group of normal-hearing mice were sacrificed, and the neurons of their central auditory nervous system were analyzed. It was found that in the experimental mice, there were significantly fewer neurons in specific brain stem pathways of the auditory system, and also significantly smaller neurons in these pathways. Therefore, in animals, it could be shown that the central nervous system was indeed affected by deprivation.

To discover whether these effects were permanent, Webster and Webster undertook an additional similar study[10]; only this time, they restored the hearing of the mice with conductive loss after 45 days. This group and the normal-hearing controls were all sacrificed and analyses made. Again it was found that there were significantly fewer and smaller neurons in the auditory pathways of the experimental mice with conductive hearing loss. The authors reasoned that there must be critical periods for the development of central auditory processing, and that if there is interference during these periods, permanent central auditory deficits will exist.

Other reports by Clopton and Silverman[11] have confirmed that there are indeed central effects in animals who have had early auditory deprivation. And other animal investigations have shown that even experiential deprivation results in neurologic deficits. Greenough,[12] for example, completely isolated a group of rats, giving them no contact with other rats or with objects or other sensory inputs. When the rats were sacrificed, analyses showed that the neurons of these rats had fewer dendritic branches in their central nervous system and fewer dendritic synapses than did rats reared in stimulating environments.

The only human study corroborating these animal findings has been reported by Dobie and Berlin.[8] They anticipated that there might be physiologic changes following conductive losses from recurrent otitis media, and looked for the effects to show up in the central binaural interaction phenomenon. They reasoned that the absence of auditory binaural interaction in the brainstem could be predicted by *auditory brainstem response* (ABR) audiometry (see Chapter 1), by subtracting the sum of the right and left ear monaural responses from the binaurally evoked ABR. The result of the subtraction would be a straight line in the absence of interaction. However, in normal humans, Dobie and Berlin found a marked and consistent nonlinearity, showing the presence of binaural interaction. In a child with a long history of conductive loss, but normal hearing at the time of the test, there were great differences and inconsistencies when the summed monaural ABR responses were subtracted from the true binaural interaction ABR. The authors feel that this result may represent a measurable central physiologic correlate of the effects of long-standing, but resolved, conductive loss.

From the above studies, one would venture predictions that: (1) conductive loss is more devastating to the educational activity of the school child than had previously been suspected; and (2) children who have a history of recurrent otitis media with mild conductive hearing loss might be expected to have central-like symptoms that would masquerade as central processing disorders and language learning problems. There is a great deal of evidence indicating that such is the case. The following will attempt to summarize some of the studies that have demonstrated these conditions.

SEQUELAE OF CONDUCTIVE HEARING LOSSES

A large number of retrospective studies have appeared in the literature describing the effect of otitis media on the language functioning of children. The retrospective nature of the studies has been severely criticized by Ventry,[13] who feels that only prospective studies will reveal the pathophysiologic effects of otitis media on language development in children. However, the sheer number of studies that have appeared indicates that they cannot be overlooked when considering this problem. A brief review of some of the pertinent studies follows.

Zinkus et al[14] investigated 213 school children grouped into two major categories. Group A consisted of educationally handicapped children with significant central or auditory processing deficits. Group B was composed of learning-disabled children with no evidence of auditory perceptual disturbances. Careful histories were taken to classify children into a group with recurrent otitis media and those with the absence of middle ear disease. Physical, neurologic, developmental, and intellectual tests were given to both groups. The latter included the Wechsler Intelligence Scale for Children-Revised (WISC-R), the Wide Range Achievement Test (WRAT), and the Illinois Test of Psycho-linguistic Abilities (ITPA). Their findings included the following:

(1) Among the educationally handicapped subjects with auditory perceptual disturbances, the rate of reported severe recurrent otitis media was 46.3%; whereas the incidence of middle ear disease in learning-disabled children with no evidence of central auditory processing deficits was 22%. The association between chronic ear disease and auditory processing deficits was found to be statistically significant. The authors felt that these results point to middle ear disorders as a possible cause for certain types of auditory processing deficits.
(2) The incidence of language delays among the two groups did not appear to be a significant factor. However, the authors state that one of the first indications for auditory processing deficits may well be a delay in the ability to develop sequential language skills. The mean verbal IQ of 96.4 for group A was significantly lower than the verbal IQ of 111 for group B, although the two groups did not differ significantly in performance scores. Therefore, the authors conclude that the auditory processing deficits in group A exerted considerable influence on verbally oriented tests.
(3) The behavioral characteristics of group A activity level, attention span, distractability, and aggressive and disruptive behaviors were found to be significantly worse (59.3%) than group B (27.7%).

Zinkus et al conclude that recurrent ear disease during the first three years of life may be an important associated factor in the development of certain types of auditory processing deficits.

Kessler and Randolph[15] evaluated children with histories of middle ear problems in a different way. From the total third-grade population of a school system, they selected 29 children with functionally normal hearing who presented with histories of middle ear disease before the age of three years. A carefully matched control group of 19 third-grade children with no histories of otitis media was also identified. Nine measures of auditory abilities were obtained from these groups. Table 9-2 lists the measures used and the results obtained.

In addition to these findings, information was obtained on the academic achievement of the children as assessed by the Word Study Skills and Reading Comprehension subtest of the Stanford Achievement Tests. The experimental group was found to score significantly lower than the total third-grade population on both subtests. Also, 55% of the experimental group were receiving supportive services from the schools in one of the areas of speech and language, remedial reading, and/or learning disabilities; whereas only 31% of the control group was receiving such services. The authors conclude that early middle ear disease can result in auditory inefficiencies and that children who cannot effectively compensate for these inefficiencies for whatever reason may have difficulty acquiring adequate language and academic skills.

Needleman[16] identified 20 children ages 3 to 8 years who had recurrent serous otitis media with the first episode between birth and 18 months, and who also had a history of episodes of otitis media continuing for at least two years. She also selected a matched group of otitis-free children. She chose to study a facet of language: the comprehension and production aspects of the phonologic system as measured by various tests.

Needleman's results showed that, on total performance, there were significant differences between the two groups, with the otitis media group scoring lower than the nonotitis group, particularly in production of phonemes in words, production of phonemes in connected speech, the use of combinations of phonemes in word endings, and in varying morphologic contexts. One encouraging aspect of this study was the finding that as their age increased, the experimental subjects came relatively closer to the performance of the normal subjects, indicating the possibility that such children may eventually be able to catch up in

Table 9-2 Measures of Auditory Ability Used and Results Found in Kessler and Randolph's[15] Study of Children with an Early History of Otitis Media

Test Administered	Scores of Experimental Group and Control Compared*
1. Digit-span subtest of Wechsler Preschool and Primary Scale of Intelligence.	Experimental group scored significantly lower.
2. Goldman-Fristoe-Woodcock Auditory Skills Test Battery, Memory of Sequence subtest.	Results not significantly different.
3. Detroit Tests of Learning Aptitude, Auditory Span for Related Syllables.	Experimental group scored significantly lower.
4. Detroit Tests, Oral Direction subtest.	Results not significantly different.
5. Goldman-Fristoe-Woodcock Battery, Selective. Auditory Attention in Fan-like Noise subtest.	Experimental group scored significantly lower.
6. Goldman-Fristoe-Woodcock Battery, Auditory Attention in Cafeteria Noise subtest.	Results not significantly different.
7. GFW Battery, Selective Auditory Attention in Linguistic Noise subtest.	Results not significantly different.
8. Illinois Test of Psycholinguistic Ability, Auditory Closure subtest.	Results not significantly different.
9. Illinois Test of Psycholinguistic Ability, Sound-Blending subtest.	Experimental group scored significantly lower.

*The Experimental Group consisted of 29 third-grade students with functionally normal hearing and a history of otitis media symptoms before 3 years of age. The Control Group consisted of 19 third-grade students with normal hearing and no history of otitis media.

their phonologic development. Needleman pointed out that the phonologic skills that were poorer in the otitis media group were those that are requisite for learning to read, and that these phonologic difficulties may account in part for the educational retardation that has been observed in children with recurrent otitis media.

An Australian study by Lewis[17] identified a group of 14 Aboriginal children between 6 and 9 years of age who had documented ear infections before age 2. Another group of 18 children was found to have been disease-free over the same period. The average hearing level of the otitis media group was only 10 dB poorer than the normal group. All the children were given a variety of auditory skills tests; and in every instance, the control group performed better than the experimental group. Statistical differences were found in: (1) the Wepman Auditory Discrimination Test; (2) the Phonemic Synthesis Test of the ITPA; and (3) the Enticknap Picture Vocabulary Test. Lewis felt that the magnitude of the pure tone sensitivity differences was not responsible for the demonstrated effects, but the important consideration seemed to be the existence of the middle

ear disorder at an early age. He felt that this early ear disease tended to encourage inefficient listening strategies that persisted well beyond the episodes of active ear disease. This statement was the first recognition that mere presence of otitis media may be considered as presumptive evidence that a hearing disability may exist. If this proposition is true it lends weight to the urgency of establishing effective programs to identify middle ear disorders in school screening programs (see Chapter 3).

The studies discussed represent retrospective investigations that have been reported in the literature. Other reports similar to these include those by Eisen,[18] Kaplan,[19] Holm and Kunze,[20] Howie,[5,21] Hersher,[22] Masters and March,[23] Freeman and Parkins,[24] Quigley,[2] Kodman,[25] Palfrey,[26] and Hook.[27] What is particularly significant about all of these reports is that the children studied may be classified as having "central auditory processing deficits, auditory perceptual problems, language learning problems, auditory language deficits, etc." Yet all of their deficits appear to be developmental in origin, caused by early deprivation in a sensory avenue. This calls for a reconsideration of the entire question of labeling children as having central auditory deficits or auditory perceptual problems.

The identification of one group of children whose problems are developmental in origin due to early deprivation casts a doubt on the whole concept of *central* problems originating from some congenital brain dysfunction. If auditory deprivation causes central-like disorders, what happens when there is environmental deprivation in language due to reduced or low-quality language stimulation in the home? This too is auditory deprivation, whether it is reduced quantity of auditory input or whether the input is of poor quality. An analogy might be drawn to the studies of Dobie and Berlin previously described, where they showed the auditory deprivation as representing *degraded auditory input*. Reduced, low-quality language input can certainly be considered degraded.

Studies have indeed demonstrated that exposure to low quality language or reduced opportunities for listening have the same effect on language skills as does auditory sensory deprivation. Wachs et al,[28] Uzgiris,[29] Uzgiris and Hunt,[30] and Wachs[31] found that infants raised in slum environments will show significantly slower development at a much earlier age than previously suspected. These differences appear as early as 11 months and increase from 18 months on. Messer and Lewis[32] also found that lower-class 13-month-old children vocalize less than their middle-class peers, and are also less mobile in the playroom. They state that understimulation produces apathy and reduced language skills. These are the children who end up in language learning classes.

Not only lack of language stimulation may victimize children; Wachs et al[28] found that high intensity stimulation and exposure to an excessive variety of circumstances can also be responsible for lower levels of cognitive development. They used the Uzgiris and Hunt infant psychological development scale, and found that stimulus bombardment actually resulted in developmental problems.

Other studies have shown that children raised in noisy environments do not respond as well in a distractive situation, as do their peers from quiet homes.[33-35] Thus, these environmental conditions, in effect, may constitute sensory deprivation just as devastating as hearing loss.

A PROPOSED BASIS FOR REMEDIATION

A matrix of possible conditions that can affect a child's development in language learning skills and cognition has been presented. In view of the multiple factors involved, the question must be asked, "How adequate is the concept of auditory perceptual deficit for education?"—a question also posed by Zach and Kaufman.[36] These authors questioned how perceptual deficiency in any given child is assessed, how relevant the remedial programs for these children are, and how perceptual deficit is conceptualized ideologically. They undertook a study in which they administered the Bender Visual Motor Gestalt Test to 70 children who were then required to perform a discrimination task using the same forms. Half of the children were given the Bender test first, and then the discrimination test; and the other half, the discrimination task first, and then the Bender test. The results showed that performance on one task was not related to performance on the other—that it was possible for a child to discriminate forms adequately and still obtain a score on the Bender that indicated perceptual difficulties existed and vice versa. Thus, to subject a child labeled as having perceptual problems to remedial tasks requiring visual discrimination if, in fact, the child can perform visual discrimination quite well would be highly questionable. This question regarding adequate understanding of *perceptual deficit* can also be asked of the remedial programs that are presently recommended for auditory *perceptual* disorders.

A large number of tests has been devised for children who seem to have language disorders, as described in Chapters 5 and 6. These tests measure specific, discrete auditory skills that are presumed to be responsible for language learning. Where deficiencies occur in these specific skills, therapies have been built around the particular disabilities identified in an effort to remediate the language disorder. For example, if the child scores low in sound blending, auditory closure, or auditory discrimination, therapy may be directed at recognition of certain combinations of sounds either in nonsense syllables or words, or the blending of the sounds. Although these therapies are used routinely, it is felt that such therapies are built on a faulty premise. Rather than the language deficit having been caused by these discrete disabilities, it is believed that the basic language disability is the cause of the specific, discrete problems that are measured in the tests described. Hence, under this assumption to build a therapy around these specifics would be a disservice to the child and to the therapist. Hamill and Larson,[37] in 1978, questioned the effectiveness of training that used the ITPA as a criterion for improvement, or that was based on the model represented by this test. They reviewed a series of 38 studies that reported attempts to train psycholinguistic skills using the ITPA as a criterion and model, and found that such training has not proved valid by a preponderance of studies.

Rees and Shulman[38] have pointed out the deficiencies in current clinical approaches to the assessment of language comprehension in children. They state that most tests that measure comprehension of spoken language examine only the subjects' ability to comprehend lexical items and relational or grammatic meanings and do not go beyond the literal meanings of words and sentences. These tests do not tap the ability of children to determine the speaker's intended meaning when it is different from literal meaning, or to relate a sentence to its linguistic and nonlinguistic context. Yet these are quite ordinary abilities that are used in regular discourse. These authors further point out that language comprehension is a much more complex function than just retrieving the literal meaning of spoken sentences. A discussion of these complexities is found in Chapter 16 by Miller.

Leonard et al[39] in 1978 questioned whether standardized language tests should be used to plan goals and procedures for intervention. These authors state that the present standardized language tests serve only one purpose: to separate the impaired language user from the normal language user. Such tests simply document clinical observations of the child's difficulties in acquiring language. The authors furthermore feel that these tests do not form a basis for devising effective intervention strategies. They quote Siegel and Broen[40] as pointing out that "the question clinicians most often have to face is not whether the child has a problem but rather what the nature of the problem is. Norms are not especially useful when the content of performance needs to be

described,[41] and it is the content that should serve as the basis for developing a therapy program." Leonard et al suggest the use of nonstandardized, clinician-constructed measures to help in devising intervention procedures.

Thus, the problem is not whether the available tests identify those children with a language learning problem, but whether the tests are able to give direction for remediation procedures. Rees, in 1973,[42] reviewed the tests presumed to show that auditory processing disorders, such as auditory memory, auditory sequencing, auditory blending, etc., are responsible for language disorders, and she concluded that the children who were studied had a basic language dysfunction rather than *auditory processing deficiencies*. She pointed out that the search for the fundamental psychologic unit of auditory processing of sentences has led from the phoneme to the underlying sentence itself. She shows that individual speech sounds follow one another too rapidly in ordinary speech to allow them to be analyzed separately and therefore even the discrimination of simple paired words like "feed" and "seed" rests on a linguistic rather than an auditory ability. She feels that it is the entire sentence, with all its semantic and syntactic implications, that is the basic unit of language, and that none of the subskills that are tested in the *auditory reception tests* have any relationship to language acquisition.

From the above, two premises can be made: (1) the problem designated, as *perceptual*, or *auditory processing*, disorders in the child with a language learning disability are due to a fundamental language problem, rather than to specific auditory function disorders; and (2) such fundamental language deficiencies may be due, in many cases, to early environmental deprivation of auditory input, whether it is early conductive hearing loss, lack of sufficient or adequate language input, or sensory overload, as has been suggested. If one accepts these premises, then the formulation of remedial measures becomes very simple, as it follows the line of pure language remediation, such as is found in Chapter 16. The clinician who is working with any child with an auditory disorder, whether it be a hearing loss or an auditory language learning problem, will do well to follow the simple language remediation directives that are found in Chapter 16.

DEMOGRAPHIC IMPLICATIONS OF OTITIS MEDIA

The need for remediation may become more and more widespread if the present trends in the demography of otitis media continue. In the general population, Teele et al[43] showed that 71% of children have had at least one episode of acute otitis media by 3 years of age, and 33% have had three or more such episodes. However, this percentage escalates in *day care centers*, where 80% of the children have three or more episodes of acute otitis media by age 3.[44] With the proliferation of such centers caring for the children of working mothers, the incidence of recurrent serous otitis will continue to increase alarmingly.

The peak occurrence of otitis media in day care centers is now at 6 months of age, and studies show that such early occurrence places a child at risk for recurrence of the disease.[45] Teele et al[43] reported that the longer the disease process for serous otitis in infants 6 to 12 months of age, the worse the language levels of the children later on. Thus, school systems can expect an escalation of language-learning problems with this increase in early otitis.

Unless otitis media is treated vigorously, it can recur repeatedly into the school years, resulting in a growing problem for school health departments. No current figures on the numbers of school children with ear disease are available in the United States, but an in-depth study was reported from New Zealand.[46] One hundred children 7 to 8 years old were given audiometry and tympanometry tests every two to three weeks throughout a school year. An average prevalence of 62% of some ear abnormality was found, with a mean duration of six weeks for an episode. A correlation between educational tests and threshold audiometric results was reported, showing that the children with poorer hearing had poorer scores on language and achievement tests. The authors concluded that one audiometric test per school year was not adequate to identify hearing loss and ear disease. They suggested that tympanometry tests three times per year will be the most cost-effective program to detect ear disease, with threshold audiometry once per year. That recommendation was subsequently adopted by the New Zealand Public Health Department for all its schools.

The effects of escalation of otitis media may be felt in the schools within a short time. Feagans[47] followed a group of school age children with histories of recurrent otitis media beginning by 6 months of age. They were found to have lowered narrative and discrimination skills that were mediated by problems in attentional processes. These children had difficulty in attending to a stimulus, probably due to poor hearing during early critical years.

Another significant finding in the school age child has been that gifted children who have had early recurrent otitis may be misperceived as lower functioning[48,49] because of poor school performance. Yet, when given in-depth testing, they are found to be highly gifted. Again, deficits in attending seem to be responsible, along with marked weaknesses in sequential processing. Downs[50] has related these problems to auditory processing deficits.

The schools may also find an increase in behavioral problems as a result of early hearing deficits. Silva[51,52] followed a group of children with early recurrent otitis media through the age of 11 years. In addition to persistent reading and articulation problems, the behavior ratings by teachers also were lower in the otitis group than in the normal controls. All the effects were at significant levels at 3, 5, 7, 9, and 11 years of age.

In managing children with otitis media, school health departments may be guided by a Policy Statement of the American Academy of Pediatrics:[53]

Middle Ear Disease and Language Development. There is growing evidence demonstrating a correlation between middle ear disease with hearing impairment and delays in the development of speech, language and cognitive skills. A parent or other caretaker may be the first person to detect such early symptoms as irritability, decreased responsiveness and disturbed sleep. Middle ear disease may be so subtle that a full evaluation for this condition should combine pneumatic otoscopy, and possibly tympanometry, with a direct view of the tympanic membrane. This statement is not meant to be a recommendation for specific treatment methods. When a child has frequently recurring acute otitis media and/or middle ear effusion persisting for longer than three months, hearing should be assessed and the development of communicative skills must be monitored.

The Committee feels it is important that the physician inform the parent that a child with middle ear disease may not hear normally. Although the child may withdraw socially and diminish experimentation with verbal communication, the parent should be encouraged to continue communicating by touching and seeking eye contact with the child when loudly and clearly speaking. Such measures, along with prompt restoration of hearing whenever possible, may help to diminish the likelihood that a child with middle ear disease will develop a communicative disorder. Middle ear disease can occur in the presence of sensory neural hearing loss. Any children whose parent expresses concern about whether the child hears should be considered for referral for behavioral audiometry without delay.

It seems clear that the schools may see a growing number of children with the kinds of deficits that have been described,[52] attributable to early mild hearing losses or present hearing losses from otitis media. Remediating these problems as basic language delays and as problems in attending is the road to follow.

UNILATERAL HEARING LOSS

Hearing loss in only one ear was formerly considered to involve no handicap as long as preferential seating was given in the classroom, with the child sitting near the teacher, and with his or her good ear toward the teacher. However, a new study reported by Bess et al[54] seriously challenges that philosophy and cautions schools not to be sanguine about children with unilateral hearing losses.

Bess et al studied 60 children 6 to 13 years old who had normal hearing in one ear, but sensorineural hearing losses of over 45 dB in the other ear. Although all of them had been given preferential seating in the classroom, 35% of them had failed one or more grades in school, and another 13% were in need of special resource assistance—a total of almost 50% with educational problems. Further testing and analysis showed that:

(1) Children with unilateral hearing loss exhibited greater difficulty than children with normal hearing in understanding speech in the presence of a competing noise background, even when the good ear was on the side of the speech and the bad ear on the side of the competing noise. Thus, preferential seating in the classroom is not an adequate solution to the problem.

(2) Those children who had severe-to-profound unilateral hearing loss (greater than 61 dB) exhibited significantly lower full scale IQs than those children with milder losses (45 dB to 60 dB). Thus, the degree of loss made a difference in the severity of the effect on the IQ.

(3) Teachers consistently rated unilaterally hearing-impaired children as having greater difficulty in peer relationships, less social confidence, greater likelihood of *acting out* behavior or withdrawal from social situations, greater frustration, increased need for dependence on the teacher, and more frequent distractability.

(4) Factors in common among those unilaterally impaired children who had greater educational problems included: (a) Early age of onset of the hearing loss; (b) Perinatal (e.g., prematurity) and/or postnatal (e.g., meningitis) complications; (c) Severe-to-profound sensorineural impairment (over 61 dB); and (d) Right ear impairment. Of the children who failed one or more grades, 63% had right ear hearing losses; and a large mean difference was found between verbal IQ scores of children with left ear hearing impairments and those with right ear impairment: left, 108; right, 99).

Bess concludes that it is no longer appropriate to assume that preferential seating will solve the problems of the child with unilateral hearing loss. Innovative solutions must be devised for these children. Bess offers possible interventions that schools can employ, including applying FM wireless systems to the good ear, using infrared systems, or simply amplifying the entire classroom to improve the S/N ratio. Special resource assistance is another alternative, but is an after-the-fact remedy. Whatever is done for the child with unilateral hearing loss, it must go beyond the traditional recommendations.

SUMMARY

Mild hearing losses of any type or cause (among school children) result in language deficits, lowered academic performance, reduced cognitive skills, and/or behavioral problems. Many of the problems are due to otitis media, whether incurred in infancy or at school age. Such hearing losses must be zealously identified and remediated, both medically and educationally. The language problems that are found can best be remediated by the comprehensive therapy described in Chapter 16.

REFERENCES

1. Jordon RE, Eagles EL: The relation of air conduction audiometry to otologic abnormalities. *Ann Otol Rhinol Laryngol*, 70 (1961), 819–927.
2. Quigley, SP: Some effects of hearing impairment upon school performance. Prepared for the Division of Special Education Services, Office of the Supt. of Public Instruction, State of Illinois, 1970.
3. Bluestone CD, Beery QC, Paradise JL: Audiometry and tympanometry in relation to middle ear effusion in children. *Laryngoscope*, 83 (1975), 594–604.
4. Virolainen E, Pukahha H, Aantaa E, et al: The prevalence of secretory otitis media in 7- to 8-year-old school children, in *Recent Advances in Otitis Media* (Athens, OH: Dept. of Otolaryngology, Ohio State Univ., 1979). In press as a supplement to *Laryngoscope*.
5. Howie VM, Ploussard JH, Sloyer J: The "otitis-prone" condition. *Am J Dis Child*, 129 (1975), 676–678.
6. Skinner MW: The hearing of speech during language acquisition. *Otolaryng Clinics of North Amer*, 11 (1978), 631–650.
7. Cohen, SA: Cause vs. treatment in reading achievement. *J Learning Disabil*, 33 (1970), 163–166.
8. Dobie RA, Berlin CI: Influence of otitis media on hearing and development. *Ann Otol Rhinol Laryngol*, 88, suppl 60 (1979), 48–53.
9. Webster DB, Webster M: Neonatal sound deprivation affects brain stem auditory nuclei. *Arch Otolaryngol*, 103 (1977), 392–396.
10. Webster DB, Webster M: Effects of neonatal conductive hearing loss on brain stem auditory nuclei. *Arch Otol Rhinol Laryngol*, 88 (1979), 684–688.
11. Clopton BM, Silverman MS: Plasticity of binaural interaction: II. Critical period and changes in midline response. *J Neurophysiol*, 40 (Nov 1977), 6.
12. Greenough WT: Experiential modification of the developing brain. *Am Sci*, 63 (1975), 37–46.
13. Ventry IM: Effects of conductive hearing loss: Fact or fiction. *J Speech Hear Disord*, 45 (1980), 143–156.
14. Zinkus PW, Gottlieb ML, Schapiro M: Developmental and psychoeducational sequelae of chronic otitis media. *Am J Dis Child*, 132 (1978), 1100–1104.
15. Kessler ME, Randolph K: The effects of early middle ear disease on the auditory abilities of third grade children. *J Acad Rehab Aud*, 12 (1979), 6–20.
16. Needleman H: Effects of hearing loss from early recurrent otitis media on speech and language development, in Jaffe B, ed: *Hearing Loss in Children* (Baltimore: University Park Press, 1977), chap 44.
17. Lewis N: Otitis media and linguistic incompetence. *Arch Otolaryngol*, 102 (1976), 387–390.
18. Eisen NH: Some effects of early sensory deprivation on later behavior: The quondam hard-of-hearing child. *J Abnorm Soc Psychol*, 65 (1962), 338.
19. Kaplan GK, Fleshman JK, Bender TR, et al: Long-term effects of otitis media: A 10-year cohort study of Alaska Eskimo children. *Pediatrics*, 52 (1973), 577–585.
20. Holm VA, Kunze LH: Effect of chronic otitis media on language and speech development. *Pediatrics*, 43 (1969), 833–838.
21. Howie VM: Developmental sequelae of chronic otitis media: A review. *Develop Behav Pediatr*, 1 (March 1980), 34–38.
22. Hersher L: Minimal brain dysfunction and otitis media. *Perceptual & Motor Skills*, 47 (1978), 723–726.
23. Masters L, March GE: Middle ear pathology as a factor in learning disabilities. *J Learn Disabil*, 2 (1978), 54–57.
24. Freeman BA, Parkins C: The prevalence of middle ear disease among learning disabled children. *Clin Pediatrics*, 18 (1979), 205–212.
25. Kodman F: Educational status of the hard-of-hearing children in the classroom. *J Speech Hear Res*, 28 (1963), 297–299.
26. Palfrey JS, Hanson MA, Pleszczynska C, et al: Selective hearing screening for young children. *Clin Pediatrics* 19 (July 1980), 473–477.
27. Hook PE: Learning disabilities in the hearing-impaired. *Ear, Nose & Throat J*, 58 (1979), 40–52.
28. Wachs TD, Uzgiris IC, Hunt J McV: Cognitive development in infants of different age levels and from different environmental backgrounds: An exploratory investigation. *Merrill-Palmer Quarterly of Behavior & Development*, 17 (1971), 283–317.
29. Uzgiris IC: Socio-cultural factors in cognitive development, in Haywood HC, ed: *Social-Cultural Aspects of Mental Retardation* (New York: Appleton-Century, 1970).
30. Uzgiris IC, Hunt J McV: An instrument for assessing infant psychological development. Prepared for the Psychological Development Laboratory, University of Illinois, 1966.
31. Wachs U, Hunt J McV: Cognitive development in infants of different ages and from different environmental backgrounds. *Merrill-Palmer Quarterly of Behavior & Development*, 17 (1971), 288–317.
32. Messer SB, Lewis M: Social class and sex differences in the attachment and play behavior of the year-old infant. Presented at the Annual Meeting of the Eastern Psychological Association, Atlantic City, 1970.
33. Deutsch CP: Auditory discrimination and learn-

ing: Social factors. *Merrill-Palmer J Behav Dev*, 10 (1964), 277–296.

34. Clark AD, Richards CJ: Auditory discrimination among economically disadvantaged and non-disadvantaged preschool children. *Exceptional Children*, 33 (1966), 259–262.

35. Nober LW: *A Study of Classroom Noise as a Factor which Affects the Auditory Discrimination Performance of Primary Grade Children*, dissertation, University of Massachusetts, Amherst, 1973.

36. Zach L, Kaufman J: How adequate is the concept of perceptual deficit for education? *J Learn Disabil*, 5 (1972), 351–356.

37. Hammill D, Larson S: The effectiveness of psycholinguistic training: A reaffirmation of position. *Exceptional Children*, 44 (1978), 402–417.

38. Rees NS, Shulman A: I don't understand what you mean by comprehension. *J Speech Hear Disord*, 43 (1978), 208–219.

39. Leonard L: What is deviant language? *J Speech Hear Dis*, 37 (1972), 427–466.

40. Siegel G, Broen PL: Language assessment, in Lloyd L, ed: *Communication Assessment and Intervention Strategies* (Baltimore: University Park Press, 1976).

41. Muma J: Language assessment: Some underlying assumptions. *ASHA*, 15 (1973), 331–338.

42. Rees NS: Auditory processing factors in language disorders: The view from Procrustes' bed. *J Speech Hear Disord*, 38 (1973), 304–315.

43. Teele DW, Klein JO, Rosner BA, and the Greater Boston Otitis Media Study Group: Otitis media with effusion during the first three years of life and development of speech and language. *Pediatrics*, 74 (1984), 282–287.

44. Denny FW: Article on otitis media. *Pediatric News*, 18 (1984), 1, 38.

45. Howie VM, Ploussard JG, Sloyer J: The "otitis-prone" condition. *Amer J Dis Child*, 129 (1975), 676–679.

46. West SR: Audiometry and tympanometry in children throughout one school year. *New Zealand Med J*, 737 (1983), 603–605.

47. Feagans L: Otitis media: A model for long term effects with implications for intervention, in Kavanaugh J, ed: *Otitis Media and Child Development* (York Press, 1986), in press.

48. Silverman LK, Chitwood DG, Waters JL: Young gifted children: Can parents identify giftedness? *Topics in Early Childhood Spec Ed* 6 (1986), 23–38.

49. Silverman LK: Hunting the hidden culprit in underachievement: Is it ear infections? *Gifted Child Testing Service* (Denver, 1986), in preparation.

50. Downs MP: Effects of mild hearing loss on auditory processing. *Otolaryngol Clin North Amer* 18 (1985), 337–344.

51. Silva PA: Some long-term psychological, educational and behavioral characteristics of children with bilateral otitis media with effusion, in Sade J, ed: *Proceedings of the International Symposium on Acute and Secretory Otitis Media* (Jerusalem, 1985).

52. Davis JM, Elfenbein J, Schum R, Bentler RA: Effects of mild and moderate hearing impairments on language, educational and psychosocial behavior of children. *J Speech Hear Dis*, (1986), 53–61.

53. American Academy of Pediatrics Policy Statement: Middle ear disease and language development. *News and Comment* (September 1984).

54. Bess FN: Special issue: Unilateral sensorineural hearing loss in children. *Ear and Hearing*, 7 (1986), 3–54.

10 | MAINTENANCE OF PERSONAL HEARING AIDS

Carolyn H. Musket

BACKGROUND

Hearing aids are the most important resource available for the habilitation of hearing impaired children. However, the instruments are prone to physical and electroacoustic breakdowns. Common defects include clogged earmolds, weak batteries, intermittent controls, frayed cords, cracked tubing, poor frequency response, and excessive distortion. The need for vigilance in hearing aid maintenance is illustrated by the case of Ted P in Case History 1.

Investigators first were alerted to these problems when they evaluated hearing aids worn by children in regular school programs. In 1966, after examining the physical condition of hearing aids used by 134 hearing impaired children seen in a university clinic, Gaeth and Lounsbury[1] reported that 69% of the aids were inadequate. Zink[2] published results in 1972 from a two-year electroacoustic study of hearing aids worn by school children. The first year he found that 58% of the aids in use were unacceptable; during the second year, 45% failed his criteria. In 1976, Schell[3] presented findings from a three-year longitudinal evaluation of hearing aids used by school children in Cincinnati. She conducted both a physical inspection and an electroacoustic analysis of the aids and concluded that 57% of them were deficient. Findings of still another investigation, in which Bess randomly selected 121 hearing aids from those worn by hearing impaired children in the Los Angeles schools, appeared in 1977.[4] Bess inspected the physical condition of each aid and performed electroacoustic measurements as well. A minimum of 25 to 30% of the hearing aids were found unsatisfactory in the various areas analyzed.

Another group of studies describes the functioning of hearing aids worn by children in educational facilities for the severely hearing impaired. Coleman[5] monitored hearing aids worn by 25 preschool hearing impaired children during a school year, and released data in 1972 that indicated 40 to 50% of the aids were unsatisfactory. This same year, Northern et al[6] reported physically examining 138 aids used by residents in a school for the deaf; 69% of the aids were not in acceptable condition. Similarly, Porter[7] inspected and conducted an electroacoustic analysis of 82 aids worn by the younger children at the Kansas School for the Deaf. In a 1973 article, he stated that 51% of the aids performed inadequately. Roeser et al[8] wrote in 1977 that annual surveys of aids worn by children in a program for the severely hearing impaired revealed that 30 to 40% of the instruments had significant malfunctions. Finally, Mynders[9] physically checked 165 hearing aids at a day school for the deaf and, in 1979, revealed that 59% of them did not function properly.

Unfortunately, these studies conducted over a 13-year period unanimously agree. After reviewing the data available in 1975, Coleman observed, "The overwhelming conclusion . . . is that in programs designed to take advantage of the acoustic capabilities of a handicapped youngster, 30 to 50% of the aids in the classroom are not performing satisfactorily on any given day."[10(p103)] The implications of these studies cannot help but cause dismay for those educational approaches that assume the child's own hearing aid is an integral part of rehabilitation, either in the classroom or in the home.

One important reason for this repeated finding in connection with children's hearing aids is the lack of knowledge about all aspects of amplification. Zink noted this when he commented, "Teachers were found to have limited background information regarding care and operation of hearing aids. As long as the child wore the aid, teachers did not question the adequacy of the aid."[2(p46)] And the teachers are

Case history #1. Ted P., a 5-year-old, was recently seen at a university center for communication disorders. Ted, who had been wearing a hearing aid since the age of 2, had a severe, flat bilateral sensorineural hearing loss. Figure 10-1 shows his unaided responses to warble tones presented through a loudspeaker in the test suite. His average minimal response level was 77 dB HL. However, when wearing a hearing aid his aided responses to these same warble tones occurred at an average hearing level of 45 dB HL. His aided speech threshold was 40 dB HL. These numbers indicated that this child, who has a hearing loss so severe that he cannot hear conversational speech at all, functions with a hearing aid as a child who can detect conversational speech if he is close to the talker. This is an important difference for Ted as he strives to acquire speech and language.

One week later, Ted returned for further exploration of his performance with amplification. At the start of the session, the aided results from the week before were rechecked. This time, however, Ted's aided speech threshold was 90 dB HL—not 40 dB HL—and his aided responses to warble tones agreed with this new finding. Ted was not receiving any help whatsoever from the hearing aid! Figure 10-2 displays these second test results. The audiologist soon determined that these discrepancies occurred because Ted's earmold was completely occluded by cerumen (earwax). Even though the hearing aid was working, the amplified sound could not pass through the earmold into Ted's ear because the earmold was blocked by the presence of cerumen. Once the earmold was cleaned, Ted's aided scores agreed with those of the previous week.

Why did this happen? It happened because Ted's parents, who invested in a hearing aid and faithfully had him wear it to school each day, did not have one minute in the evening to listen to the aid to ensure that it was functioning. It happened because Ted's teacher, intent upon preparations for the day's lessons, did not have time to inspect his hearing aid to make sure he would profit to the maximum from her instruction. In this teacher's priorities, presenting information and structuring learning activities ranked higher than checking the hearing aid. Sometime between February 20th and February 27th, Ted ceased to hear sound and reverted into a world of silence. Just how long this situation would have continued if he had not returned for testing is cause for considerable professional concern. Ted's story is not unusual; unfortunately, his is not an isolated case.

not alone. Gaeth and Lounsbury found in interviews with the parents of 120 children that parents too "know very little about a hearing aid and its care."[1(p287)] These statements present a challenge that must not go unanswered if a solution to the dilemma of malfunctioning hearing aids is to be found. This chapter is an attempt to meet the crucial need for practical, applicable information about hearing aids for those persons in direct daily contact with them—teachers and parents.

THE HEARING AID

No one hears perfectly all of the time. In everyday life, even persons with normal hearing experience difficulty in certain listening situations, such as a large meeting where the speaker addresses a group from some distance away. It would not be possible for those in the audience to hear well without the help of amplification. Some device must be used to intensify the speaker's voice to make it audible to the listener out of normal conversational range. Fortunately, amplification by public address systems is available. The speaker talks into a microphone; this signal is then carried to an amplifier, where it is intensified greatly and directed to loudspeakers strategically placed around the meeting room. From these loudspeakers the magnified voice is delivered to the audience. In addition, this system uses some source of electrical power. The amplification arrangement described above is an accepted feature of auditoriums, stadiums, and theaters.

It is helpful to know that a wearable electronic hearing aid really is a miniature public address system. As shown in Figure 10-3, it has the same components that were just described:

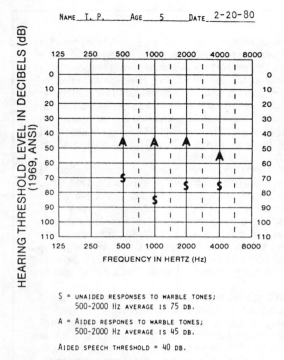

NAME T. P. AGE 5 DATE 2-20-80

S = UNAIDED RESPONSES TO WARBLE TONES;
   500-2000 Hz AVERAGE IS 75 DB.

A = AIDED RESPONES TO WARBLE TONES;
   500-2000 Hz AVERAGE IS 45 DB.

AIDED SPEECH THRESHOLD = 40 DB.

Figure 10-1. Unaided (S) and aided (A) responses to sound field warble tones for Ted P (see Case History 1 in this chapter).

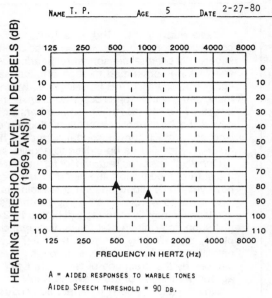

NAME T. P. AGE 5 DATE 2-27-80

A = AIDED RESPONSES TO WARBLE TONES
AIDED SPEECH THRESHOLD = 90 DB.

Figure 10-2. Aided sound field responses for Ted P, one week after the results shown in Figure 10-1 were obtained (see Case History 1 in this chapter).

microphone, amplifier, loudspeaker (receiver), and power source. Basically, it is designed to accomplish the same goal. The purpose of a hearing aid is to make sound stronger so that it may be heard more easily by an impaired ear. This increased intensity is needed not because a great distance exists between speaker and listener, but because the impaired ear has a loss in hearing sensitivity. In hearing aids, the recognizable parts of a public address system are not easily discernible because they are extremely small and packaged together in the unfamiliar form of a hearing aid case. Therefore, instead of being in front of the speaker, the microphone is worn on the body of the hearing impaired person (the listener) as a built-in part of the hearing aid. This explains

why hearing aids work most effectively in quiet, structured surroundings, where the speaker is 3 to 4 feet away. When greater distances are involved, the speaker is not within the range of the microphone. When noise is present, it reaches the microphone too, and is amplified making it difficult for the listener to separate the desired speech sound from this interference.

Hearing Aid Components

Microphone. Sound travels through the air by movement of the molecules of air. This acoustic transmission is cumbersome and difficult to magnify, although it can be done.

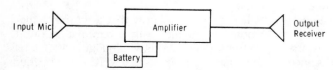

Figure 10-3. A simple block diagram of a hearing aid.

When one cups a hand behind the ear, more sound waves are collected and directed into the ear, thus enlarging the original signal. An old-fashioned ear trumpet took advantage of this fact. However, increase in intensity that may be obtained in this way is minimal. If the acoustic transmission of sound is converted into electric energy, a much greater increase is possible. This desired energy conversion— acoustic energy into electric energy—is the function of the hearing aid microphone. As the sound waves strike the diaphragm of the microphone, their acoustic energy causes it to mechanically move back and forth. The vibrating motion of the diaphragm in turn initiates a change in electric voltage according to principles that vary with the type of microphone used. Variations in the sound waves impinging upon the microphone create corresponding variations in an electric signal flowing from it. Most hearing aids manufactured at present achieve this transformation by using an electret condenser microphone.

The microphone itself is housed inside the hearing aid case. The location of the microphone may be detected by looking for a small opening or grid in the case. It is important to identify this sound inlet, because it should not be obstructed when the instrument is worn.

Some hearing aids have microphones that are *directional*. A directional microphone receives signals from two locations—it has both a front-facing and a rear-facing opening. In such a microphone, sounds occurring from the rear are attenuated, thereby giving emphasis to sounds happening in front of the hearing aid user.

Amplifier. As the electric current from the microphone passes through the amplifier, its magnitude is increased. This is accomplished through various stages of complex circuitry, which rely mainly upon the transistor for amplification. In all hearing aids, the amplifier is contained within the case of the hearing aid. It is an extremely small component.

Receiver (Earphone). The part of a hearing aid that corresponds to a loudspeaker usually is referred to as a receiver. Less often, the term *earphone* identifies this component. The function of the receiver is to convert the amplified electric energy back into acoustic energy. Through magnetic action, the electric current from the amplifier causes physical movement of the diaphragm of the receiver. This movement disturbs the adjacent air mole-

cules, thereby creating sound waves again. Now, however, the converted sound waves are of much greater magnitude than those that originated at the diaphragm of the microphone.

An air conduction receiver may be built internally into the hearing aid, or it may be a separate part connected to the aid by a cord. For both types, the amplified sound eventually will be directed into the child's ear canal. For a small number of hearing aid users, such a fitting is not advisable due to draining ears or a malformed or absent ear canal. These children use a *bone conduction oscillator* for a hearing aid receiver. An oscillator is a small, box-like device attached to the hearing aid by a cord; it fits onto a headband that holds it against the prominent bone behind the external ear. Mechanical vibrations from the side of the oscillator's case transmit sound to the inner ear through the skull.

Battery. Also housed with the hearing aid case is a small battery, which provides the electric power for the instrument. The battery is a reservoir of stored chemical energy that is converted into electric energy when used in the hearing aid. Several different types of batteries, more accurately termed *cells*, are available for use in hearing aids. These include mercury, silver oxide, zinc air, and nickel cadmium. The most common hearing aid batteries come in four sizes, as seen in Figure 10-4. Specifications from the manufacturer indicate the size and type of battery recommended for use in a particular aid, as well as the voltage it should supply. Generally, hearing aids require 1.3 to 1.5 volts.

Figure 10-4. Common hearing aid batteries. The two on the left are used in body-worn aids; the two on the right are for the ear-level instruments.

Hearing Aid Arrangements

Wearable hearing aids are available in four different styles, which are named according to their location on the user. They are pictured in Figure 10-5.

Body-Worn. The term *body-worn* refers to a small, rectangular instrument usually worn on the chest. Either it may be clipped to an article of clothing, such as a shirt pocket; or, with young children, it may be inserted into a cloth carrier or harness, which is strapped around the chest. The microphone, amplifier, and battery on a body-worn aid all are within the case of the hearing aid. A flexible cord, which is composed of wires encased in plastic, leads from the body-worn aid to an external, button-sized receiver. In recent years, there has been a definite decline in the use of body-worn hearing aids. With children, they primarily are reserved for the very young (below 3 years of age), or for those whose profound losses or other physical disabilities necessitate the use of a more powerful or more durable body aid. In most other instances, children now may be fit appropriately with behind-the-ear instruments.

Behind-the-Ear. Another term for behind-the-ear is *postauricular*. In this hearing aid model, all components of the system—microphone, amplifier, receiver, and battery—are contained within a small, slightly curved case, which is designed to fit behind the ear of the wearer.

Eyeglass. Eyeglass hearing aid models, although seen infrequently on children, also are available. In this style of hearing aid, all components are built within the temple bar of an eyeglass frame. This fitting is not recommended often for young children because of its bulk and the problems associated with maintaining two sensory aids concurrently.

In-the-Ear. In this style, all parts of the hearing aid, including the battery, are contained within a plastic shell that fits entirely into the outer ear itself. An *in-the-canal* aid is an even smaller version of this style. Because of tiny controls, lack of flexibility of electroacoustic parameters, and the fact that it is not modified easily as the size of the ear canal changes, in-the-ear aids have not been used widely with children.

As a group, behind-the-ear, eyeglass, and in-the-ear instruments are referred to as *ear-level* hearing aids.

Monaural, Binaural. In a *monaural* hearing aid arrangement, the output from a single hearing aid system is directed into only one ear of the wearer. A *binaural* fitting refers to the use of a complete hearing aid for each ear. A *pseudobinaural* fitting means that the output of one hearing aid is channeled to both ears. This is accomplished through the use of a Y-cord or V-cord that is connected to a body-

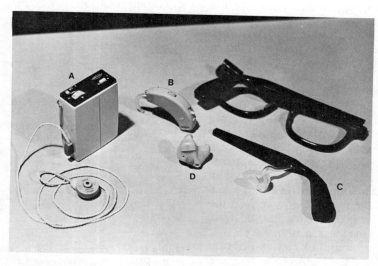

Figure 10-5.   Styles of hearing aids. A. Body-worn; B. Behind-the-ear; C. Eyeglass; D. In-the-ear.

worn aid with one plug; then, it divides into two branches so that a cord goes to a receiver in each ear.

CROS. CROS is an acronym for the *contralateral routing of signals.* Various forms of this term describe innovative ways in which the components of a hearing aid are arranged on the head and coupled to the ear.[11] For example, in a typical CROS fitting, the microphone is housed remotely in a separate unit worn behind one ear, while the amplifier, receiver, and battery are contained in a case that fits behind the opposite ear. A cord joins these two parts, as pictured in Figure 10-6.

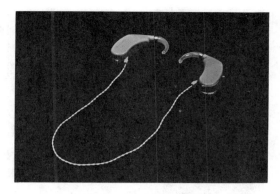

Figure 10-6. A CROS hearing aid. The unit containing only the microphone is on the left; the amplifier, receiver, and battery are in the case on the right.

Hearing Aid Controls

The hearing aid is controlled through dials, switches, and screw adjustments. Figure 10-7 shows a body-worn hearing aid and Figure 10-8 depicts a behind-the-ear instrument. These figures should help to clarify the descriptions of hearing aid controls in this section.

On-Off Switch. The switch that turns on the aid may be found in various locations, depending upon the design of the aid. It may be incorporated into the swing-out battery compartment, especially in ear-level instruments. Snapping the plastic battery tray completely shut turns on the aid. This switch also may be combined with the rotary volume control, so that the first click when this dial is advanced signals that the aid has been turned on. Or the aid may have a separate on-off switch with a plus (+) sign indicating when it is working. Finally, in some aids this switch may be combined with the input control where *O* indicates the aid is off and not operating.

Input Control. The input control determines what signal is being transmitted to the amplifier. The choices available for input on a specific hearing aid include: *M*, which means that the microphone is picking up airborne signals; *T*, which shows that the aid will interact

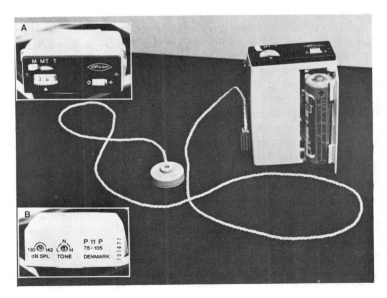

Figure 10-7. A body-worn hearing aid with insets showing a closer view of (A), the top of the aid, and (B), the bottom of the instrument.

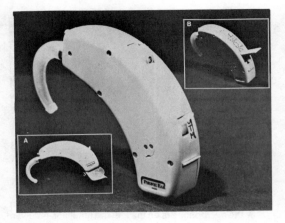

Figure 10-8. A behind-the-ear hearing aid with insets showing (A), the sound inlet of the microphone above the earhook and the battery compartment, and (B), the adjustment screws.

with the telephone; *MT* or *B*, which indicates that both the microphone and telephone inputs are functional; and ⊕, which denotes that the aid may be coupled to an external audio source. Although this latter symbol is advocated by the International Electrotechnical Commission to indicate audio-input entry, some manufacturers use other markings.

When the control is on *T*, the microphone of the aid is not operational. Instead, a telecoil placed within the case of the hearing aid receives a magnetic signal that comes directly from the handheld telephone receiver, provided that it is in close proximity to the hearing aid. This signal continues through the circuitry of the hearing aid amplifier. When the telephone switch is in use, the only signal amplified comes from the message emitted over the telephone. And it is not the actual acoustic sound of the voice itself that enters the hearing aid, but rather a magnetic signal that exists simultaneously with it. Other sounds such as room noise and the user's own voice are not intensified since the microphone of the aid is not functioning. Some telephone sets come with a receiver that does not have a usable magnetic signal; consequently, a hearing aid telecoil is not compatible with such telephones unless a separate adapter unit is used with the hearing aid.

Also of interest is the fact that in the *T* position, the hearing aid will pick up magnetic signals emanating from an *induction loop*. An induction loop is created by connecting a loop of wire, which encircles a given area, with a microphone and amplifier. Sound from the microphone is carried through this wire and may be received by the hearing aid in the *T* position. Such an amplification system can be used in classroom settings (see Chapter 12). The advantage of *MT* or *B* is that with input from both the microphone and the telecoil, the user may monitor his/her own voice and respond to the voices of others while receiving the signal from the telecoil.

An audio-input option is available on some instruments. When set for this mode of operation, the hearing aid may be connected directly to an external audio source via an auxiliary cord. In this way, it is possible for a child's personal hearing aid to receive input from FM auditory training equipment (see Chapter 12) and such devices as a television set, a radio, or a tape recorder. An alternative setting exists that allows for use of both the microphone and the external audio input at the same time.

Gain (Volume) Control. This rotary dial allows the user to adjust the sound of the hearing aid from minimum to maximum amplification. It operates much like the volume control on a radio. Most often it is continuously adjustable, but on some aids it may move in discrete steps. The dial also may be numbered or color-coded to assist the user in finding the desired setting.

Directional-Omnidirectional Switch. On some hearing aids the use of a directional microphone is optional. A standard omnidirectional microphone may be changed to one with directional capabilities when a selector switch is placed in a certain position.

Tone Control. With the tone control, the relative strength of the high frequency and low frequency sounds that are amplified may be changed. A tone control appears either as a selector switch available to the user or as a screw adjustment that is preset when the aid is dispensed. When the tone control is set at *L*, the low frequency range is emphasized by suppressing amplification of high frequencies. On *H*, the opposite occurs: the high frequency sounds are emphasized because low frequency sounds are suppressed. The position *N* denotes the standard or normal frequency response for that particular instrument.

Output Control. This screw adjustment imposes a limit to the maximum amount of sound the hearing aid will transmit. It sets a ceiling—the hearing aid will not produce a more intense sound than this limiting level no matter how great the input to the microphone. This output limiting may be achieved in the aid through either *peak clipping* or *compression*; the latter also is referred to as *automatic gain control* (AGC).

Earmolds

In almost all hearing aid arrangements, it is necessary to couple the hearing aid to the user's ear with an individually made earmold. An earmold is a piece of plastic with a channel called the *sound bore* running through the center; the earmold is attached to the hearing aid and inserted into the wearer's ear. Its purpose, of course, is to deliver the amplified sound directly from the receiver into the ear canal.

There are many different types of earmolds. The National Association of Earmold Laboratories (NAEL) uses standard nomenclature to classify them.[12] Only a few are mentioned here. On body-worn hearing aids, the external receiver button snaps onto a solid mold, which fills the ear; it is termed a *receiver mold*. For behind-the-ear instruments, sound from the internal receiver is directed through a rigid plastic hook or elbow; then a piece of flexible plastic tubing carries sound from this hook to the mold, which usually is either a *shell mold* or a *skeleton mold*. Eyeglass aids use only plastic tubing between the outlet for the internal receiver and the often used *canal-lock mold*. With in-the-ear aids, the earmold itself forms the enclosure for the hearing aid components. Sample earmold styles may be seen in Figure 10-9.

Each earmold is custom-made. An impression is taken of the user's ear to reproduce exactly the contours of the canal and bowl-like portion of the ear flap; this is done by packing these areas with a soft impression material. After this substance has set, it is carefully removed, packaged, and mailed to an earmold laboratory with an order describing the type of earmold desired. Following these specifications, the earmold laboratory fabricates the actual mold. Materials from which earmolds are made include acrylic, silicone, vinyl, and polyethylene. The result may be either a hard mold or a soft one. The more pliable molds often are used with children since these are

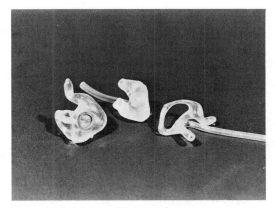

Figure 10-9. Sample styles of earmolds. From *left* to *right*: a receiver mold, a shell mold, and a free-field mold.

less likely to cause injury as a result of any boisterous activity. In fact, Ling and Ling[13] report following two groups of ten children throughout a school year; one group had hard earmolds and the other used a soft type. They found that the children with hard earmolds were without aids from one to five weeks during the year due to ear damage, whereas the problem was negligible among those using soft earmolds.

An earmold must fit comfortably and securely in the ear in order to retain the hearing aid there. In addition, a snug fit ensures that amplified sound from the hearing aid receiver actually will arrive at the eardrum. A properly fitting earmold, which prevents sound from leaking out at the sides of the canal, often is a concern when powerful hearing aids are used on children with severe losses. Special care may be needed to obtain a mold with a tight enough seal. Conversely, however, for some children with certain audiometric configurations, special earmolds or earmolds with certain modifications are recommended to provide a pathway for amplified sound to escape. This usually is done in order to alter the output of the hearing aid in some way. The special earmolds are described as *free-field* (open, nonoccluding); the modification frequently made to other molds is termed a *vent*.

Since the outer ear grows as the child matures, it is expected that new earmolds will be needed periodically to maintain a proper fit. Children under 4 years of age may require a new earmold as often as every three to six months; older youngsters may need to exchange their molds yearly until the age of 8 or 9 years.[14]

Electroacoustic Characteristics

A hearing aid is described and compared with other hearing aids according to the way it amplifies sound. Such information about a hearing aid indicates how sound coming from the receiver (output) differs from what entered the microphone (input). These measures of various input-output functions of a hearing aid are referred to as electroacoustic characteristics. The way in which these performance measurements are made and expressed is mandated in the *American National Standard Specification of Hearing Aid Characteristics*.[15] This standard was approved by both the American National Standards Institute (ANSI) and the Acoustical Society of America in 1976; it was revised in 1982, and is referred to as ANSI S3.22-1982 (ASA 7-1982). The intent of such a standard is to enable measurements of hearing aid performance obtained at different facilities to be compared with one another. It is noteworthy that this standard became law in this country in August 1977. This is when the Food and Drug Administration's (FDA) Rules and Regulations Regarding Hearing Aid Devices: Professional and Patient Labeling Conditions for Sale went into effect.[16] As a part of this FDA document, it was specified that the performance characteristics of hearing aids be determined in accordance with the existing American national standard. The FDA regulation was later updated to require adherence to the 1982 revision of ANSI S3.22. Thus, this standard for hearing aid characteristics became the first ever to be enforceable.

Another noteworthy feature of ANSI S3.22-1982 is that it stipulates tolerance limits for each characteristic measured. The reason for having a tolerance limit, or range of acceptable deviation, is to improve quality control. Because of these requirements, each hearing aid of a particular model manufactured after August 1977, should perform within the tolerance limits allowed by the standard, when measured accurately. Some of the more common measurements from ANSI S3.22-1982 will now be discussed.

Gain. Gain refers to the amount in decibels by which the hearing aid amplifies or intensifies sound. If a sound of 70 dB enters the hearing aid microphone and a sound of 115 dB is measured coming from the receiver, then the gain of this hearing aid, or the additional intensity supplied by the amplifying circuit, is 45 dB. The amount of gain a hearing aid offers varies with the frequency of the entering signal; that is, a hearing aid does not amplify all incoming sounds by the same amount. ANSI S3.22-1982 specifies that the gain present at 1000, 1600, and 2500 Hz, with an input of 60 dB SPL, be averaged. This figure is reported for two conditions. When this average is obtained with the gain (volume) control rotated to the full-on position, the resulting gain is referred to as the *high-frequency-average full-on gain*. When it is measured with the gain control rotated to a specific setting more nearly simulating use conditions (less than full-on), it is called *reference test gain*.

SSPL 90. This term is used to describe the maximum sound pressure level output that a hearing aid is able to produce at its receiver. Previously, it has been referred to as the maximum power output. Procedures of ANSI S3.22-1982 call for the saturation sound pressure level of a hearing aid to be measured with the gain control full-on, and with an input signal of 90 dB SPL applied to the hearing aid microphone. The output for frequencies from 200 to 5000 Hz is recorded. Again, the values at 1000, 1600, and 2500 Hz are averaged, and the resulting figure is reported as the *high-frequency-average SSPL 90* for the hearing aid. In addition, the maximum decibel output present for a single frequency is noted and reported, along with the frequency at which it occurred, as the *maximum SSPL 90*. SSPL 90 and, to a lesser extent, gain values are used in determining the relative power of a given hearing aid.

Frequency Response. The frequency response refers to descriptive information about the way in which a hearing aid amplifies various frequencies, since it does not increase all frequencies equally. According to ANSI S3.22-1982, a frequency response curve is a graph that illustrates how the output of the aid changes as frequencies progress from 200 to 5000 Hz. It is measured with an input of 60 dB SPL at the microphone and the aid's gain control in reference test position. It is possible, then, to use this graph to determine the *frequency range*, or that band of frequencies from low to high for which the aid provides enough amplification to be potentially useful.

Harmonic Distortion. Distortion is present in an amplifying system when the acoustic parameters of the input sound at the microphone are not reproduced exactly in the output at the receiver. One form of such distortion is harmonic distortion. This occurs when new frequencies that are whole-number multiples of the input frequency appear. ANSI S3.22-1982 states that this should be reported in terms of *percentage of total harmonic distortion* (%THD). Total harmonic distortion is measured at 500 and 800 Hz with an input of 70 dB SPL, and at 1600 Hz with an input of 65 dB SPL. The gain control of the aid is in reference test position.

Equivalent Input Noise Level. This measurement pertains to the internal noise present in the hearing aid or the *on* noise found in many electroacoustic devices. It is calculated according to a formula given in ANSI S3.22-1982.

HEARING AID MAINTENANCE

A maintenance program to ensure continued maximum performance of a hearing aid should be composed of: (*1*) a daily visual inspection and listening check; and (*2*) periodic electroacoustic measurement. Through a daily monitoring program, obvious causes of hearing aid malfunction may be identified quickly and sometimes resolved. A few supplies should be assembled to simplify this inspection. The electroacoustic measurements, which require more elaborate equipment, provide information of a different type about the way the hearing aid amplifies sound.

Hearing Aid Maintenance Kit

To implement the first step of this program, it is recommended that several items be obtained and kept, ideally, both in the classroom and in the home of each hearing aid user.[17,18] These articles will fit into a small utility box; having access to it facilitates the task of caring for a hearing aid. The suggested contents are listed below and appear in Figure 10-10.

A. *Battery Tester (Voltmeter).* A battery tester of the moving coil type, which will read up to 3 volts, is adequate. The tester is used to ascertain whether a battery has the voltage necessary for a particular hearing aid. It may be obtained from a hearing aid dispenser or a supplier of hearing aid accessories.

B. *Hearing Aid Stethoscope and Adapter.* Use of a hearing aid stethoscope enables one to listen only to sounds amplified by the aid, since both ears of the listener are occluded. It may be used with any style of hearing aid, and is available from a hearing aid dispenser or a supplier of hearing aid accessories.

C. *Forced-air Earmold Cleaner.* This device is used to remove moisture from ear-

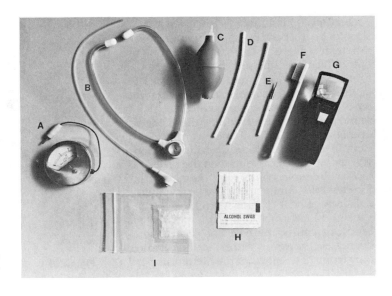

Figure 10-10. Hearing aid maintenance kit. See text for description of contents.

molds and tubing after they have been cleaned. It is helpful, too, in determining if there is an obstacle to the passage of sound through an earmold. Those with a small extension (as opposed to a snap) on the end may be used with any type of earmold. Those air blowers are sold by hearing aid dispensers and suppliers of hearing aid accessories.

D. *Pipe Cleaners.* These are used in removing earwax from an earmold. Pipe cleaners also may be used to dry out the sound bore after an earmold has been washed.

E. *Small, Soft Brush.* This brush helps in clearing dust or lint from hearing aid switches and the grill over the microphone.

F. *Child-sized Toothbrush.* This brush is useful when washing an earmold.

G. *Small, Lighted Magnifying Glass.*

H. *Individual Packets of Alcohol-Saturated Swabs.* If corrosion is noted on battery contacts, they may be cleaned by wiping with these swabs. Restricted locations may be accessible with a cotton-tipped applicator.

I. *Packet of Silica Gel and a Lock-Top Plastic Bag.* This chemical will remove moisture from the air; thus, it keeps dry or dries out the contents of the bag. Spare batteries may be kept in such a bag, as well as the hearing aid itself, when it is not in use, especially during humid periods. Kits to dry out hearing aids may be obtained from hearing aid dispensers or suppliers of hearing aid accessories.

Visual Inspection

Battery. First on any maintenance list should be inspection of the battery. When Coleman surveyed hearing aids worn by preschool hearing impaired children, he initially found that 40% of them had batteries that lacked sufficient voltage; in the second semester of the study, this figure was 29%.[5] That he found the battery reversed, and therefore nonoperational, in 20% of the hearing aids he examined was even more appalling. Other investigators also have identified the battery as a most vulnerable component. Kemker et al,[19] for example, conducted a five-year longitudinal study of hearing aids worn by children in special education. During this period, malfunctions caused by weak or dead batteries decreased; however, since the incidence fell only from 72 to 44%, the problem remained a

significant one. Fortunately, battery faults are among the easiest to rectify.

Initially, one should determine that the correct battery is used. Both the desired battery size and the nominal voltage are specified in information supplied with the aid by the manufacturer. Also, the maximum voltage available in each cell may be labeled on the battery. This battery voltage should be checked with a battery tester as shown in Figure 10-11. Actually, it is preferable to test battery voltage in the evening when the battery is taken out of the hearing aid. To do this, of course, means that parents should be involved in routine hearing aid care. It is possible for batteries temporarily to recover voltage during the night when they are not used; if checked in the morning, misleading information could result because a satisfactory voltage reading might not result in optimal performance. Decreased battery voltage is a significant factor in the unsatisfactory electroacoustic function of hearing aids.[5,20] A battery should be considered weak and be replaced if the voltage reading obtained is 0.2 to 0.3 volts below the amount specified by the manufacturer.[17–19]

One should observe whether the battery and the battery contacts in the aid yield evidence of corrosion. Corrosion on battery contacts may cause a hissing sound in the aid. If minimal corrosion is present, the white powdery substance that forms on the battery contacts may be wiped away with a soft cloth or an alcohol swab. However, care must be taken not to get alcohol on the plastic case of the aid or

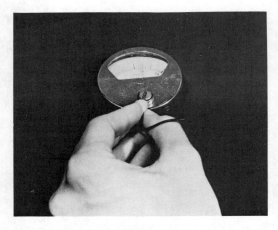

Figure 10-11. Testing battery voltage.

on the earmold. In some cases it may be necessary to rub battery contacts with a pointed eraser to remove all traces of corrosion. Only gentle pressure should be applied, so that any coating covering the battery contacts will not be damaged. A battery that is extensively corroded should be discarded. To minimize the possibility of corrosion, the battery should be removed from the aid overnight.

Finally, one should observe if the battery is installed properly in the aid. The plus (+) side of the battery should be aligned with the plus (+) marking usually stamped or engraved in the battery compartment. Instead of this marking, some aids have battery compartments which will only accept placement of a battery in the correct position. If the battery compartment will not close, it is likely that the battery has not been inserted correctly.

Earmold.   The earmold should be examined both alone and coupled to the ear of the child. Note whether the earmold is cracked or chipped, because any rough edge will cause discomfort to the wearer. It is vital that the sound bore of the earmold not be occluded with earwax. Such an accumulation in this opening may be removed with a toothpick and then the channel cleaned out with a pipe cleaner. Care must be taken not to push earwax back into the mold, where it is more difficult to remove. When the earmold is inserted into the child's ear, it should fit comfortably; a whistling sound, known as acoustic feedback, should not occur when the aid is in use.

An earmold may be separated from an external receiver simply by unsnapping it. To remove a mold from a behind-the-ear aid, gently slip the tubing from the earhook. The tubing must not be pulled from the earmold itself because it is permanently secured there. With the earmold separated from the aid, it is possible to use the forced-air earmold cleaner to demonstrate that there is, indeed, a clear passageway through the earmold (and tubing) for amplified sound. Position the bulb at one end of the mold (or tubing), squeeze it, and feel the flow of air at the other end, as shown in Figure 10-12. The earmold may be washed in warm water and mild soap *provided it is detached from the hearing aid*; dry it and use a pipe cleaner and the forced-air earmold cleaner to remove moisture from the sound bore. Make sure the earmold is completely dry before joining it again to the hearing aid. Moisture will

Figure 10-12.   Using a forced-air earmold cleaner.

damage the hearing aid. The earmold should be cleaned periodically, but unless the child accumulates an unusual amount of earwax, it should not be necessary to wash the earmold daily. Removing the earmold from an external receiver of a body-worn aid does not present a maintenance problem. However, detaching an earmold from a behind-the-ear aid by slipping the tubing off the earhook eventually will stretch the tubing somewhat. When this connection becomes loose, the amplified sound passing through it can escape and cause acoustic feedback.

Tubing.   Any tubing that forms a loose connection, has yellowed, or is hardened and brittle needs to be replaced by an audiologist or a hearing aid specialist. Check to see that moisture has not collected inside the tubing to block the passage of sound. If moisture problems persist, consider the use of special tubing designed to absorb and exhaust moisture as it accumulates. When the aid is in place on the child, the tubing should not be twisted, thereby obstructing sound.

Receiver.   If the hearing aid has an external receiver, look to see if it is cracked or damaged in any way. Often a washer of thin plastic film is placed around the nubbin of the receiver to ensure a tight seal when it is snapped onto the earmold. A receiver-saver also may be used; this is a strip of plastic that forms an additional connection between the receiver and the cord to prevent an accidental separation.

Cord.   Determine if any sections of the cord appear to be frayed. Connections at the plug receptacles of the receiver and the hearing aid case should be firmly attached.

Settings and Controls.   The input switch, if included, should be on *M* unless the telecoil (*T*) is being used for a personal or group amplification system. The tone and gain control settings should be those recommended for the child.

Hearing Aid Case.   If necessary, the case itself should be cleaned with only a soft cloth. A brush from the maintenance kit may be used to clean crevices and around controls.

Listening Check

It is important to listen to the hearing aid to obtain information about the function of the switches and controls and to monitor, as much as possible, the quality of sound reproduction. If parents begin this practice when their child's instrument is new, they will establish a reference for future listening checks.

Standard Listening Check.   The listener may attach the hearing aid either to a personal earmold, if available, or to a hearing aid stethoscope. As seen in Figure 10-13A, the external receiver of an aid may be snapped onto the stethoscope. Figure 10-13B shows an adapter in use for aids with internal receivers; a connecting tube is slipped over the aid's sound outlet, and the other end of the tube is attached to the stethoscope. Still another alternative is to use a tubing extension that terminates in a nozzle that may be placed over the canal portion of an earmold; this adapter appears in Figure 10-13C. In this way, one may listen to the combined system of any hearing aid and earmold together, or to an in-the-ear aid. This latter adapter, especially, offers some practical advantages in daily listening checks of behind-the-ear aids by teachers and parents. Because it may be fastened directly over the end of the earmold, it does not necessitate routinely separating the tubing from the earhook; thus, fewer problems would be likely to develop at this point. In a school program, where several aids are to be checked, the outside of each earmold should be sanitized by wiping it with Cetylcide, or a similar product, before it is inserted into the end of the adapter. Cetylcide is an antibacterial instant earmold cleaner available from a supplier of hearing

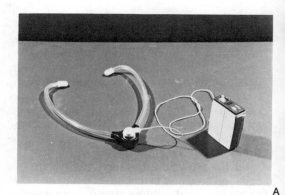

A

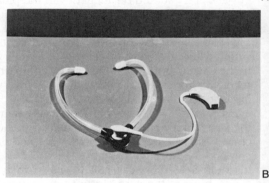

B

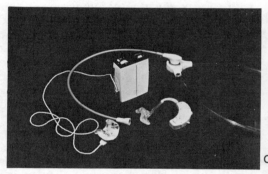

C

Figure 10-13.   A, Attachment of a hearing aid stethoscope directly to the external receiver of a hearing aid. B, Attachment of a hearing aid stethoscope adapter to a behind-the-ear hearing aid. C, A hearing aid stethoscope adapter, which may be connected directly to an earmold.

aid products. It will not harm plastic as alcohol will.

The input switch of the aid, when it is present, should be set on *M*, the aid should be off, and the gain control should be turned down. Because it may be difficult to talk and listen simultaneously, one may want to listen to speech on a tape recorder or radio during this check. While the tester is listening, the aid should be turned on and the gain control rotated slowly back and forth and it should be noted if there is a smooth change in intensity, if there is a constant signal, and if the control operates quietly. The various switches should be moved to determine if they are functional. The cord, if the aid has one, should be rolled gently between the fingers in several places; a "break" in the incoming sound would identify a defective cord that should be replaced. Finally, the case should be rotated slightly to ascertain whether this causes interruption of the sound.

Such a listening check will identify faulty controls. Noting a decrease in the quality of sound reproduction is more difficult, especially for an examiner with an untrained ear. Deterioration in the quality of sound may occur gradually over a period of time, and not be readily apparent on a day-to-day listening basis. Another consideration is the intensity of the speech input. When the gain control is set in the position used by the child, the microphone normally responds to speech input from about 3 feet away; this is an average conversational distance. Should the person making the listening check use his/her own voice, as so often happens, input to the aid would be of much greater intensity than normal because of its proximity to the microphone. Such an increase in intensity might also cause distortion to occur at this gain control position when it would not be present under ordinary listening conditions. Finally, it must be recognized that those with normal hearing may find it uncomfortable to listen to the high output levels of the more powerful hearing aids at gain control settings used by the child. This discomfort precludes careful listening at such a setting. While distortion of sound may be present for the child, it may not be detected at the lower gain control setting preferred by the adult performing the listening check. Use of a tape recorder that may be coupled to a hearing aid may be helpful in performing listening checks. For more information, consult the Appendix at the end of this chapter.

Five-Sound Test. Ling and Ling suggest an approach that uses sounds representing the range of speech frequencies, from low to high, to monitor the frequency response of a hearing aid.[13] They advocate listening to five speech sounds—*oo, ah, ee, sh,* and *s*—as they are transmitted by the aid. If parents do this daily, they will become familiar with how these sounds are reproduced by their child's hearing

aid and be able to identify a change with confidence. In the classroom, this test may be given while the child wears the aid to observe any deviation from his usual response. The teacher presents the five sounds, one at a time, without visual clues. The child claps after hearing each sound, and if capable, repeats the sound.

In discussions at a 1975 conference on amplification held at the Lexington School for the Deaf, Rubin offered an example of the effectiveness of this technique.[21(p133)] A child's failure to reply to the *ee* sound as usual made the school aware that he was turning the aid's gain control down because the earmold fit poorly.

Bone Conduction Hearing Aids. There is not a satisfactory way to perform an adequate listening check on a bone conduction instrument. When the instrument is in actual use, the tension with which the oscillator is held against the head is very important. If the headband does not have sufficient tensile strength, it eventually might be stretched by being placed repeatedly on an adult's head for a listening check. Also, the listener would have to occlude both ears with earplugs or by pressing them shut to hear only through the bone conduction oscillator. It is possible for an audiologist or hearing aid specialist to check the integrity of the aid's controls and switches after substituting an appropriate air conduction receiver. Such persons should provide frequent routine maintenance for these aids. The parents and teacher can be responsible for testing the battery voltage and inspecting the aid visually.

Acoustic Feedback

Acoustic feedback is the term for the high-pitched whistling sound so annoying to those in the company of hearing aid users. Many times the hearing aid user does not hear this sound because of hearing loss. Acoustic feedback occurs whenever there is a clear pathway between the high output from a hearing aid receiver and the microphone of the same hearing aid. In a body-worn hearing aid, one may "make it whistle" or induce feedback if the aid is turned on and the receiver held near the microphone opening; feedback will cease if the receiver is moved some distance away from the microphone. Ordinarily, this whistling interaction is avoided because the output of the receiver is directed through the earmold and away from the hearing aid microphone. However, if the earmold does not fit snugly in the ear canal, the amplified sound waves may escape around the sides of the mold and be reproduced as feedback when they reach the aid's microphone. This happens more often in an ear-level instrument because the receiver and microphone openings are so close together. The amplified sound also might leak through a crack or pinhole in the tubing or earhook of a behind-the-ear aid, or through the wall of tubing if it is too thin.

Preventing acoustic feedback, then, becomes a matter of determining where the sound leakage is occurring by the process of elimination. Once the trouble spot is identified, the cause may be corrected. These four procedures show how to check for the source of the leak when whistling is heard:

(1) Remove the hearing aid, with the earmold attached, from the child.
(2) Place your thumb over the earmold opening, turn the aid on, and rotate the gain control to its maximum. If squealing is heard, quickly turn the aid down and detach the earmold.
(3) With a body-worn aid, place your thumb tightly over the nubbin of the external receiver and increase the gain control to its maximum. If the feedback does not occur this time, it must have occurred before from a leak in the earmold itself or in its attachment to the receiver. If the feedback remains, it must be internal in the aid and should be taken for repair. When following this procedure, occlude the receiver nubbin only for a brief period.
(4) With a behind-the-ear aid, place your thumb over the end of the earhook after slipping off the earmold and tubing. Increase the gain control to maximum for only a short time. If the feedback is gone, it must have been present due to damage to the earmold or tubing. If the whistling continues, it must be caused by a leak in the earhook or a problem internal to the aid. Consult an audiologist or hearing aid specialist for replacement of the earhook or repair of the aid.

It may be that feedback occurs when the hearing aid is on the child, but not during this check. In such cases there are two considerations: (1) this may be an indication of a middle ear problem, and immittance measurements should be obtained to investigate this; or (2) a new earmold may be needed.[22] The latter cause is a frequent one with growing children.[23] Once the other causes of feedback have been eliminated, a new earmold should be obtained.

Caring for a Hearing Aid

Batteries.   Batteries should be stored in a cool, dry place in an airtight container not accessible to children. Prevent the batteries from touching metal. Do not carry them loosely in a pocket with change and keys, or in a purse. Segregate used batteries immediately away from children; batteries may be returned for recyling. Wipe the contact surfaces of the battery before inserting the battery into the aid. Remove batteries from the hearing aid at night. This will prolong their life and decrease the possibility of corrosion. Extra batteries should be kept at school so that they may be replaced there.

Battery Ingestion.   *Button* batteries, which power ear-level hearing aids as well as other devices, such as calculators and watches, present a potential health hazard because they may be swallowed easily.[32–34] Their growing popularity and availability has resulted in increasing instances of battery ingestion, especially for children who are attracted to loose or discarded batteries within their reach, or they may remove batteries from hearing aids or other products. The National Poison Center Network has estimated that 510 to 850 button battery ingestion cases occur annually in the United States.[33] In 1983, Litovitz reviewed 56 cases of battery ingestion;[33] age could be determined for 50 cases; and of these ingestions, 78% occurred in children under 5 years of age. This incidence is typical, in general, of poisonings. Hearing aids were the most common intended use of these batteries. In the majority of cases summarized, Litovitz found the ingested battery was passed spontaneously without complications; but serious and even fatal injuries may result. Consequently, it is of paramount importance that parents and teachers be counseled regarding the inherent dangers of button batteries to children. These small batteries may also cause injury if placed in the nose or ears.

Prevention of battery ingestion and other misuses must be stressed at all times. Some hearing aid manufacturers now offer the option of a tamper-resistant closure on the battery compartment of a hearing aid; and battery manufacturers are printing warning statements on product packages. Clinicians and educators should give the following precautions in verbal and written form to all hearing aid users and those working with aided children:

(1) Keep unused batteries and hearing aids not in use out of children's reach.
(2) Dispose of batteries properly away from children.
(3) Never change batteries in front of children.
(4) Never put batteries in the mouth for any reason, as they are slippery and are easily swallowed accidentally. A child may mimic you.
(5) Whenever possible, secure the battery drawer from casual access by children (may use tape, a tamper-resistant compartment, or a hearing aid retainer).
(6) Always check medications; batteries have been mistaken for tablets.
(7) *If a battery is swallowed:*
    a. Find another battery exactly like the one swallowed, or the package from which the battery came, to obtain the identification number.
    b. Telephone, collect, the National Button Battery Ingestion Hotline—(202) 625-3333 (voice) or (202) 625-6070 (TDD)—for battery contents and recommended treatment.

Cords. Cords can be obtained in several lengths. One of an appropriate size should be used with a child so that it will not have to be wrapped or twisted around the aid to be kept out of the way. A spare cord should be available so that immediate replacement will be possible.

Hearing Aid. Keep the hearing aid away from excessive heat and humidity. Food guards may be purchased for body-worn aids with top-mounted microphones. A food guard is a cover designed to protect the microphone opening from food spills. During especially humid times of the year, place the aid overnight in a plastic lock-top bag with a drying agent (silica gel). Avoid dropping the receiver as well as the hearing aid itself. Keep the aid turned off when it is not in use, and *never* open the case of the hearing aid in an attempt to repair it yourself.

Consult an audiologist or hearing aid specialist promptly if you have any questions or concerns about the function of the hearing aid.

Hearing Aid Retainers. It is often difficult to secure a behind-the-ear aid on a small child, and some dispensers have advocated the use of toupee tape in such situations. Recently, a retainer for behind-the-ear hearing aids has

been developed. It consists of a plastic loop that encircles the external ear flap; this loop contains two plastic clips that fit tightly around the aid. These clips have the possible added advantage of preventing tampering with the aid's gain control and battery compartment, depending upon their positions. Other styles of retainers are available for the external air conduction receivers of body-worn aids and auditory trainers, for bone conduction receivers, and for holding aids to the heads of difficult-to-fit children who have absent or deformed ears or mis-shapened heads. For more information, consult the Appendix at the end of this chapter under suppliers of accessory items.

Electroacoustic Analysis

An effective hearing aid maintenance program must include monitoring the electroacoustic performance of a hearing aid. While a visual inspection and listening check will contribute to an aid's optimal operation, with the possible exception of the Five-Sound Test, they will not reveal problems in electroacoustic performance unless the aid is grossly malfunctioning.[2,3,7,35] Electroacoustic measurements in educational settings may be made with a portable hearing aid test set.

Hearing Aid Test Set. A commercially available hearing aid test set is pictured in Figure 10-14. The function of a test set may be understood through a description of its components.

Test Chamber. Measurements must be performed with the aid in a sound-free environment. This is accomplished by placing the aid in an insulated chamber. Spaces all around the sides and the lid of the chamber are filled with sound-absorbent materials, such as sand and glass wool, so as to prevent outside noises from reaching the microphone of the hearing aid. A test point is indicated in the chamber where the hearing aid microphone should be placed.

Loudspeaker. A loudspeaker is situated in the test chamber oriented towards the test point. Usually, it is located in the bottom of the chamber facing upward; however, one current model houses the loudspeaker within the lid of the chamber. A pure tone of a known frequency and intensity is directed from the loudspeaker to the microphone of the hearing aid.

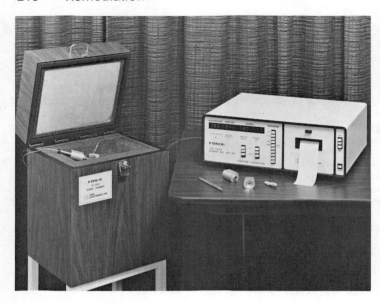

Figure 10-14. A hearing aid test set. The test chamber is on the left; the analyzer and recorder is on the right, with 2cc couplers on the table in front of it. A behind-the-ear aid attached to a 2cc coupler is shown in the test chamber; the measuring microphone is inserted into the other end of the coupler (courtesy of Frye Electronics, Inc).

Regulatory System. Some system is used to ensure that input from the loudspeaker does not vary from the desired intensity as it enters the hearing aid microphone. A regulating microphone may be positioned inside the chamber at the test point only one-quarter inch from the microphone of the hearing aid. It cooperates with a measuring amplifier to regulate the output of the loudspeaker in order to keep the input to the aid at a constant level across frequencies. Another way in which this uniformity may be achieved is by the use of a predetermined and stored correction curve that compensates for the effects of the test chamber. A dummy microphone having the same physical dimensions as the measuring microphone should be used with this latter system.

2cc Coupler. Output from the receiver of the hearing aid is sent into a 2cc coupler. The hearing aid snaps onto the 2cc coupler, which is a stainless steel cylinder containing a cavity with a volume of 2 cc. This size was selected as the standard because it was thought to approximate the space between the tip of an earmold and the eardrum in an adult ear.

Measuring Microphone. Another microphone is inserted into the opposite end of the 2cc coupler to receive the amplified signal from the hearing aid receiver. The diaphragm of this microphone forms the bottom boundary of the 2cc space. Thus, sound leaves the hearing aid receiver, passes through the 2cc hard-walled cavity, and activates this measuring microphone.

Analyzer and Recorder. The signal from the measuring microphone is fed into components that analyze this output, and its intensity is determined. In addition, some type of filter is employed so that harmonic distortion measurements may be made—the signal entering the hearing aid must be filtered from the output, so that only sound energy present in its harmonic frequencies may be measured. Data resulting from these various measurements appear visually in a graphic or numeric display, which may be recorded permanently in printed form.

Hearing Aid Measurement. Educational programs should take advantage of the availability and ease of operation of these portable hearing aid test sets. Measurement procedures with them were developed explicitly for the purpose of maintaining quality control and product uniformity. It is in just this way that the test set may help to meet the needs of rehabilitative programs. Routine electroacoustic monitoring should be used to verify that the amplification characteristics of the hearing aid are consistent over time and in agreement with those that the aid had when it originally was selected for the child.

How often a child's aid should be evaluated depends realistically upon the accessibility of the test set and the number of children it must serve. A recommendation resulting from investigations of hearing aids worn by school children is that aids receive at least an annual electroacoustic evaluation.[4,7] Certainly, any program would be strengthened if it were possible to include such monitoring as often as two to three times per year.[24-26] Moreover, Ross and Tomassetti[22] recognize that the need for this monitoring varies with the age of the child. Small children lead more active lives; consequently, it has been found beneficial to check the performance of younger children's aids monthly. In addition, such measurements should be made whenever there is a change in a child's aided abilities without apparent reason, or whenever a problem in the aid's electroacoustic performance is suspected on the basis of the daily listening check.

The manufacturer's written performance specifications for the various instruments worn by children in the school must be on file. Only then may measurements made with the test set be used to determine if an aid is functioning as originally designed. As additional information, it would be ideal to include in each child's records an electroacoustic analysis obtained with the aid adjusted to the use settings recommended when the aid was fit. This is not unrealistic in terms of the printout capabilities of some test sets. The aid could be monitored periodically with this information as a reference. The difficulty lies in coordinating this exchange of information between those who fit and dispense the aid and those who monitor its functioning.

Generally, electroacoustic monitoring should consist of determining the major characteristics previously described in this chapter— gain, *saturation sound pressure level* (SSPL), frequency response, and harmonic distortion. A measurement of the internal noise level also may be included. Instruments whose performance deviates significantly from the reference data would be identified as malfunctioning. Limits of acceptable variation, however, must be somewhat arbitrary until the relationship these electroacoustic characteristics have to speech intelligibility and hearing impairment in children is more clearly defined.

Testing Repaired Hearing Aids. Schell[3] noted that most of the problems detected with electroacoustic analysis of children's hearing aids were repairable ones. Therefore, a hearing aid test set is an asset to a maintenance program in yet another way. Measurements may be made when aids are returned from repair to ascertain if indeed they received adequate service.[2,27,36] Investigations in this area report discouraging findings. Zink[2] repeated electroacoustic measurements on 52 hearing aids returned following repair, and concluded that 35% of the aids still were unacceptable. Most of the continuing problems were in the areas of frequency response and harmonic distortion. Warren and Kasten,[27] although not confined to reporting only on children's hearing aids, assessed the electroacoustical performance of 41 hearing aids after repair; 63% did not approximate manufacturer's specifications. In fact, 15% malfunctioned to such an extent that they had to be returned for further repair Marston[36] found only 3 of 25 repaired aids passed all of the 10 ANSI standard tests he included in his investigation. In view of these findings, it would seem prudent to require that all repaired aids be evaluated electroacoustically before they are used.

Testing Loaner Hearing Aids. A hearing aid test set may be used with loaner hearing aids. Unless the hearing impaired child with residual hearing is using a functioning hearing aid, the child will not profit to the fullest from an educational program. Accordingly, some schools supply loaner aids to students whose personal aids are being repaired. With a hearing aid test set, the performance characteristics of a loaner aid may be verified before the aid is issued to the child. If loaner aids do not perform adequately, there is little sense in using them; their condition will only cause children to reject amplification.[28] Zink analyzed 35 aids that had been donated for children's use, and found 92% unacceptable.[2] Without a doubt, loaner instruments will be needed; resources, however, should be found to ensure that they are kept ready and in good condition.

IMPLEMENTATION OF A HEARING AID MAINTENANCE PROGRAM

School administrators should be aware that the Education of All Handicapped Children Act (Public Law 94-142) states in Section 121(a)303:

> *Proper Functioning of Hearing Aids:* Each public agency shall insure that the hearing aids worn by deaf and hard of hearing children in school are functioning properly.[29]

As a result of this mandate, Public Law 94-142 funding may be a source of revenue for hearing aid maintenance programs.

Audiologists should be used as resource

personnel in the schools since their specialized training includes the study of amplification systems. In 1976, the American Speech-Language-Hearing Association (ASHA) and the Conference of Executives of American Schools for the Deaf jointly approved *Guidelines for Audiology Programs in Educational Settings for Hearing-Impaired.*[30] These guidelines delineate the role of audiology in comprehensive programs for hearing impaired children who are receiving special educational and habilitative services. They particularly address the special problems associated with the high incidence of malfunctioning hearing aids. In connection with this, the guidelines suggest that audiologists conduct in-service training for teachers and other staff members in the daily monitoring and trouble-shooting of hearing aids as well as consult individually with the teachers. Providing such instruction and counseling for parents also is mentioned. In 1983, ASHA adopted another position statement, *Audiology Services in the Schools*, which offers recommendations for feasible delivery systems to provide comprehensive audiologic services to school children with hearing impairment.[31] Again, programs to monitor hearing aid performance are endorsed. Suggestions for resource materials are given in the Appendix at the end of this chapter. In addition, it should be noted that the FDA's *Rules and Regulations Regarding Hearing Aid Devices* also require that an instructional brochure for the user accompany each hearing aid purchased.[16] This pamphlet from the manufacturer must contain, among other things, information on the care and maintenance of the hearing aid.

Several experts suggest that the daily visual inspection and listening check might be performed by teacher aides who have been trained to do this activity.[4,5,19,37] Another possibility would be using parent volunteers who would rotate in taking this assignment.[17] Certainly such participation would heighten parents' awareness of common maintenance needs, and the time commitment is reasonable. Hanners and Sitton[17] reported that a daily monitoring program with preschoolers took 90 seconds per child. Problems other than those of simple, ordinary care would require consultation with an audiologist or hearing aid specialist. Kemker et al[19] and Mynders[9] both found weekly visits to the school to be an effective supplement to daily monitoring by the teachers

or teacher aides. Moreover, large metropolitan school districts may find it advantageous either to employ a hearing aid repair technician or to contract for this service.[4]

There can be no doubt that the need to establish an intensive, routine hearing aid maintenance program for children is of the utmost importance. Teachers, parents, and the children themselves, when they are old enough, must share this responsibility. The immediate result will be more consistent, functional amplification for the child; the additional benefits may be even more far-reaching as children actually experience this improved auditory input in their rehabilitative program.

ACKNOWLEDGMENT

The author wishes to express appreciation to Jonathan P. Miller who provided all photographs appearing in this chapter, with the exception of Figure 10-14.

REFERENCES

1. Gaeth JH, Lounsbury E: Hearing aids and children in elementary schools. *J Speech Hear Dis*, 31 (1966), 283–289.
2. Zink GD: Hearing aids children wear: A longitudinal study of performance. *Volta Review*, 74 (1972), 41–51.
3. Schell YS: Electro-acoustic evaluation of hearing aids worn by public school children. *Aud Hear Educ*, 2 (1976), 7, 9, 12, 15.
4. Bess FH: Condition of hearing aids worn by children in a public school setting, in Withrow FB: *The Condition of Hearing Aids Worn by Children in a Public School Program*, Report No. (OE)77-05002. US Dept. of Health, Education and Welfare, Public Health Service 1977, chap 2.
5. Coleman RF: *Stability of Children's Hearing Aids in an Acoustic Preschool*. Final Report, Project No. 522466, Grant No. OEG-4-71-0060, US Dept. of Health, Education and Welfare, Office of Education, 1972.
6. Northern JL, McChord W, Fischer E, et al: *Hearing Services in Residential Schools for the Deaf. Maico Audiological Library Series*, 11 (1972), Report 4.
7. Porter TA: Hearing aids in a residential school. *Am Ann Deaf*, 118 (1973), 31–33.
8. Roeser RJ, Gloria A, Gerken GM, et al: A hearing aid malfunction detection unit. *J Speech Hear Dis*, (1977), 351–357.

9. Mynders JM: A beginning hearing aid maintenance program. *Hear Aid J*, 32 (1979), 9, 40, 41.
10. Coleman RF: Is anyone listening? *Lang Speech Hear Serv in Schools*, 6 (1975), 102–105.
11. Harford E, Dodds E: Versions of the CROS hearing aid. *Arch Otolaryngol*, 100 (1974), 50–57.
12. Pollack MC, Morgan R: Earmold technology and acoustics, in Pollack MC, ed: *Amplification for the Hearing-Impaired*, ed 2 (New York: Grune and Stratton, 1980), chap 3.
13. Ling D, Ling AH: *Aural Habilitation: The Foundations of Verbal Learning for Hearing-Impaired Children*. (Washington DC: AG Bell Assoc, 1978).
14. Northern JL, Downs MP: *Hearing in Children*. ed 2 (Baltimore: Williams and Wilkins, 1979).
15. *American National Standard Specification of Hearing Aid Characteristics*. ANSI S3.22-1982 (Revision of S3.22-1976) (ASA 7-1982) (New York: Acoustical Society of America, 1982).
16. Rules and Regulations Regarding Hearing Aid Devices: Professional and Patient Labeling and Conditions for Sale, Part IV. Food and Drug Administration, *Federal Register*, (February 15, 1977), 9294–9296.
17. Hanners BA, Sitton AB: Ears to hear: a daily hearing aid monitor program. *Volta Review*, 76 (1974), 530–536.
18. Rubin M: *All About Hearing Aids* (Washington, DC: AG Bell Assoc, 1975).
19. Kemker FJ, McConnell F, Logan SA, et al: A field study of children's hearing aids in a school environment. *Lang Speech Hear Serv in Schools*, 10 (1979), 47–53.
20. Lotterman SH, Kasten RN, Majerus DM: Battery life and nonlinear distortion in hearing aids. *J Speech Hear Dis*, 32 (1967), 274–278.
21. Rubin M: *Hearing Aids: Current Developments and Concepts* (Baltimore: University Park Press, 1976).
22. Ross M, Tomassetti C: Hearing aid selection for preverbal hearing-impaired children, in Pollack MC, ed: *Amplification for the Hearing-Impaired*, ed 2 (New York: Grune and Stratton, 1980), chap 6.
23. Walker C: The incidence of earmold replacement in an urban school for the deaf. *Hear Aid J*, 33 (1980), 6, 50.
24. Downs MP: *Maintaining Children's Hearing Aids: The Role of the Parents. Maico Audiological Library Series*, 10 (1971), Report 1.
25. Sortini AJ: A new method of evaluating hearing aid performance. Paper presented before Oticongress 3, Copenhagen, Denmark, February 26, 1973.
26. Ross M, Giolas TG: Issues and exposition, in Ross M, Giolas TG, eds: *Auditory Management of Hearing-Impaired Children* (Baltimore: University Park Press, 1978), chap 9.
27. Warren MP, Kasten RN: Efficacy of hearing aid repairs by manufacturers and by alternative repair facilities. *J Acad Rehab Aud*, 9 (1976), 38–47.
28. Zink GD, Alpiner JG: Hearing aids: One aspect of a state public school hearing conservation program. *J Speech Hear Dis*, 33 (1968), 329–344.
29. Education of All Handicapped Children Act (PL 94-142): Implementation of Part B. Office of Education, Dept. of Health, Education and Welfare. *Federal Register*, 42 (August 23, 1977), 42474–42514.
30. Joint Committee on Audiology and Education of the Deaf: Guidelines for audiology programs in educational settings for hearing-impaired children. *ASHA*, 18 (1976), 291–294
31. ASHA Ad Hoc Committee on Extension of Audiological Services in the Schools and the ASHA Ad Hoc Committee on the Provision of Audiologic Services to Persons in the Schools: Audiology services in the schools. *ASHA*, 25 (1983), 53–60.
32. Bebout JM: Hearing aid battery ingestion: Incidence, treatment, and prevention. *Hearing J*, 37 (1984), 12–16.
33. Litovitz TL: Button battery ingestions. *JAMA* 249 (1983), 2495–2500.
34. Rumack BH, Rumack CM: Disk battery ingestion. *JAMA*, 249 (1983), 2509–2511.
35. Potts PL, Greenwood J: Hearing aid monitoring: Are looking and listening enough? *Lang, Speech, Hearing Serv Schools*, 14 (1983), 157–163.
36. Marston LE: Performance of reconditioned hearing aids. *J Acad Rehabil Audiol*, 18 (1985), 123–127.
37. Benedet RM: A public school hearing aid maintenance program. *Volta Review*, 82 (1980), 149–155.

APPENDIX

Source for Materials and Equipment Helpful in a Hearing Aid Maintenance Program for Children

Booklets for children and older students:

Ear Gear by C. B. Simko, 136 pp, 1986. Available from Gallaudet University Press, Box 87, 800 Florida Avenue NE, Washington, DC 20002. This workbook uses the rebus approach to teach elementary-age, hearing-impaired students about hearing loss and hearing aids. Second-grade reading level ($4.50).

Wired for Sound by C. B. Simko, 156 pp, 1986. Available from Gallaudet University Press, this workbook is the secondary school edition of *Ear Gear* (see above). It is designed to teach the older student about hearing loss and hearing aids. Fifth-grade reading level ($4.95).

Getting the Most Out of Your Hearing Aid by J. M. Armbruster and M. H. Miller, 40 pp, 1981. Available from Publications Sales Dept., AG Bell Association for the Deaf, 3417 Volta Place, NW, Washington, DC 20007-2778. This booklet includes information on hearing aid components, becoming accustomed to wearing an aid, and caring for a hearing aid ($3.00, quantity prices offered).

Hearing Aids for You and the Zoo by R. Stoker and J. Gaydos, 32 pp, 1984. Available from the AG Bell Association for the Deaf (see above). Zoo animals are used in this booklet to help young hearing-impaired children learn to accept and care for their hearing aids ($4.95).

Orientation to Hearing Aids by J. S. Gauger, 1978. Available from the AG Bell Association for the Deaf (see above). Programmed instruction to help students understand, use, and care for a hearing aid; written at eighth-grade vocabulary level. Consists of a series of six workbooks ($9.45).

Audiovisual programs:

Changing Sounds produced by the Bill Wilkerson Hearing and Speech Center, Nashville, TN, 1974. Available for purchase ($16.00) as a slide/tape program from HOPE, Inc, 1780 North Research Park Way, Suite 110, Logan, UT 84321. Familiarizes the viewer with the parts of a hearing aid and procedures to detect and correct malfunctioning instruments. A daily check of the aid is emphasized.

Hearing Aids produced by Oakland Schools, Pontiac, MI, 1971. Available on loan free as a sound filmstrip from Project TALK, Oakland Schools, 2100 Pontiac Lake Rd, Pontiac, MI 48054. Shows what a hearing aid wearer experiences and discusses the types, parts, and care of hearing aids.

Hearing Aids: A Daily Check produced by Design Media, San Francisco, CA, 1980. Available as a sound filmstrip ($45.00) or as a slide/tape program ($75.00) from Design Media, 2235 Harrison St., San Francisco, CA 94110. Add $2.00 shipping and handling fee. Shows parts of a hearing aid and steps of a daily check. The sounds of common hearing aid malfunctions are duplicated and practical solutions are given.

Suppliers of accessory items for hearing aid maintenance:

Hal-Hen Company, 36-14 Eleventh St, Long Island City, NY 11106 (catalog available). This firm will fill orders from educational institutions, but not from individuals.

HARC Mercantile, Ltd, 3130 Portage Road, PO Box 3055, Kalamazoo, MI 49003-3055 (catalog available). Orders from individuals accepted by mail; credit card holders may order by phone.

Hearing aid retainers are available from Huggie Aids™, 837 NW 10th St, Oklahoma City, OK 73106.

Checksette, a tape recorder that may be coupled to a hearing aid, is available from Oval Window Audio, 306 Congress Street, Portland, ME 04101.

Manufacturers of portable hearing aid test sets:

B & K Instruments, Inc, 5111 W. 164th St, Cleveland, OH 44142.

Frye Electronics, Inc, PO Box 23391, 9826 SW Tigard St, Tigard, OR 97223.

Phonic Ear, Inc, 250 Camino Alto, Mill Valley, CA 94941.

CLASSROOM ACOUSTICS

Terese Finitzo

For a normal-hearing adult observer, the effects of a noisy, reverberant classroom may not be immediately apparent. But for a teacher who is transmitting information all day long, the experience may be fatiguing. Moreover, a young child who is trying to learn unfamiliar concepts may find this room stressful, while a hearing impaired youngster may understand almost none of the information presented. Although considerable theoretic research is being done concerning the detrimental effects of poor classroom acoustics, acoustics are often not considered in school planning sessions. The following letter from a school principal shows what occurs when the special needs of hearing-impaired students are not considered in decisions about the acoustic qualities of a classroom.

> We are faced with a problem that was not anticipated in planning our new school. While the physical space is excellent, our hearing impaired students are refusing to use the auditory training units in the open-plan classrooms—presumably because of the high noise levels. We recognize that those students with considerable residual hearing are being forced to rely primarily on visual channels for learning. What can we do to improve the situation?

The inappropriate acoustic design in this school is a needless barrier to achievement for both hearing impaired students and their teachers. Unfortunately, such a design reflects a familiar attitude taken in planning classrooms for hearing impaired children. An unknown author in a booklet on sound control states, "If people were deaf, architects and builders wouldn't have to worry about acoustics."[4] Yet, most hearing impaired children have residual hearing, and room acoustics do matter if an aural or total approach to education is emphasized. Whether the child is educated in a self-contained class or mainstreamed with normal-hearing children, the effects of room acoustics

can no longer be forgotten. Architects and engineers must work with school personnel and audiologists to create educational environments that are conducive to learning.

This chapter reviews the *acoustic* factors critical to speech intelligibility in the classroom. These factors include noise and reverberation, and their effect on the understanding of speech. Guidelines are suggested for modifying or minimizing the effects of noise and reverberation in the classroom, particularly for hearing impaired students who use group amplification systems.

NOISE

Noise is any unwanted disturbance that interferes with what we want to hear. At a symphony, a nearby couple whispering would be considered "noise." Later, at a restaurant, "noise" might be the nearby band that prevents a friend's conversation from being heard. In this chapter, noise will be classified according to its location or source, its description, and its effect on listening.

Location: External or Adjacent Noise Sources

Noise sources can be external or adjacent to the classroom, or inside the classroom itself. External or adjacent noise problems can be solved by careful planning of the location of the school building in the community. A quiet, residential street away from traffic noise, railroads, and airports is ideal. When the location of an existing school is not optimal, certain steps can be taken to decrease the outdoor noise. A wall or a large mound of earth in front of the school building will serve as a partial barrier and absorb sound that is en route to the class, assuming that the school is within the *shadow* provided by the barrier. Planting noise-abating trees and shrubs will also deflect unwanted external sounds. For this step to be effective in summer and winter, both deciduous and evergreen trees should be used. An occasional tree or hedge will not deflect unwanted sound.

In addition to the location of the school building in the community, the wall construction and the window treatment will determine how much outdoor noise will be reduced as it travels indoors. Certainly, a portion of the outdoor sound will be transmitted inside the building, while another portion will be absorbed by the wall, and a third portion will be reflected back from the wall. Figure 11-1 illustrates how sound is transmitted through walls. As shown in this figure, if a sound of a given frequency is reduced from 70 dB on one side of a partition to 40 dB on the other side, the partition has a transmission loss of 30 dB at this frequency. The better the noise reduction or transmission loss that a wall has, the more efficient the construction. Architects and builders should strive for a noise reduction of at least 50 dB between critical learning spaces, and 40 dB between less critical spaces in schools for hearing impaired children.

A solid concrete wall is superior in reducing noise to lighter partitions, temporary building construction, or to large expanses of glass. However, double-wall structures with air spaces between them can be used, particularly in reducing the transmission of high-frequency noises. The two separate walls should be structurally independent. For maximum efficiency,

an absorbent material can fill the space between the two structures. When windows are needed, double-pane glass windows will lessen outdoor noise better than single-pane windows. Of course, the windows must be kept closed to be effective.

Location: Internal Noise Sources

Both the location of the classroom in the school building, and the activities taking place in the classroom are potential sources of noise. Before calling in acoustics consultants, the teacher and principal can often evaluate a classroom at no extra cost and with no additional equipment. Looking and listening in the classroom when it is unoccupied, and then returning to the same classroom when it is occupied will identify many simple noise problems. Solutions to the problems may be apparent and further assistance unnecessary. If consultation and additional measures are needed, the teacher's description of the classroom will be valuable.

When programs for hearing impaired children are being developed, three considerations should be made when evaluating classroom location:[5]

(1) A classroom located near concentrated student activity, such as a major hallway junction or restroom, will tend to have greater sound levels throughout the day than one located off the beaten path.
(2) A classroom near a high noise area, such as the band or orchestra room, gymnasium, computer terminal, maintenance or mechanical room, cafeteria, or playground, is not acceptable.
(3) Classes for hearing impaired children should not be near or in teaching centers or open-plan areas with minimal sound isolation from suspended ceilings, temporary partitions, or sliding walls or doors.

It may be more feasible simply to relocate those rooms that are unacceptable, rather than to structurally alter an existing building. Advanced planning is ideal, but whether a new school is built or an existing one is modified, the following suggestions may be helpful for any critical listening areas:

(1) Locate the noisy activities previously mentioned in one area of the school, and front these classes toward the playground or any other outdoor

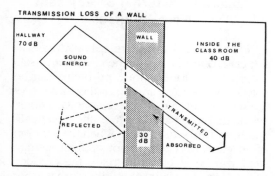

Figure 11-1. The transmission loss of a wall. The amount of sound that is transmitted through a wall depends both on how much sound is reflected back from the wall and how much is absorbed by the wall.

noise source. Space near these areas is best suited for storage.[6]

(2) Locate (or relocate) special classrooms with hearing-impaired children away from high-noise activities, preferably in a single-level building or on the first floor of the school building, away from the mechanical equipment room or other noise sources.

(3) Carpet corridors to decrease the sound of footsteps outside the classroom.

(4) Make certain that solid-core, well-constructed doors lead into the classroom. However, the best door will not decrease the traffic noise from the corridor if it is left open.[7] An open door, a door with a ventilation duct, or even just a door that fits poorly will be a weak link in an otherwise good wall. If funds are limited, felt (or rubber) can be used around the door frame for a tight seal.[8]

(5) Room partitions that end in suspended ceilings or have a continuous air space above the ceiling, either between the rooms or between a room and a hallway, are obvious sources of unwanted noise. Along with temporary partitions or folding walls, they should not be considered a solution to decreasing noise levels in large, multipurpose rooms. A temporary partition is little better than none at all![9] Partitions between classrooms or between classrooms and corridors must be fully contiguous between the floor and the solid ceiling above.[6]

Three classroom activities that can generate noise are: (1) the movement of children, teachers, or desks on hard surface floors; (2) noisy or malfunctioning equipment; and (3) multiple teaching activities that occur simultaneously in the same classroom.

Wall-to-wall carpeting in all rooms (and corridors if possible) will reduce the noise associated with the movement of children and teachers. A durable, wall-to-wall, indoor/outdoor carpet is usually sufficient, since the primary purpose of the carpet is to reduce the extraneous *kid noise* that occurs when children slide in and out of their desks. Carpeting is particularly important if the desks are not bolted to the floor. For this reason, area rugs would not be adequate. Matkin[10] suggests that in uncarpeted schools, the Parents-Teachers Association (PTA) might try to obtain carpeting as a project for the year, focusing first on the most critical classrooms.

An acoustic ceiling tile is one of the most effective solutions for absorbing extraneous sound within the classroom. At first, money can best be spent on a good acoustic ceiling.

This and other measures will be discussed further under the section dealing with reverberation.

Solving noise problems due to malfunctioning equipment may require outside assistance, although the source of noise may be readily apparent. In one classroom, the air-conditioning fan was malfunctioning, and communication near it was impossible. In another room, a noisy clock was a distraction, although it was not particularly restrictive to communication. No assistance was needed to identify these noise sources.

The noise problems involving multifunctional or open-plan classrooms usually generate two complaints. Either the teacher cannot be heard, or students attend to adjacent instructional activities rather than their own. In many well-designed open classrooms, the key ingredient in achieving privacy is the insertion of a broadband masking noise throughout the space. That is, noise from ventilating systems or other mechanical equipment may be purposefully designed into the classroom by the architect to ensure privacy between adjacent activities. In other open classrooms, the *masking noise* is composed of other children's voices. Several researchers[11,12] have stated that listening in a background of other voices may be the most troubling type of competition encountered, because the frequency content of the message and the competition are alike.

The reason that masking noise is often purposely injected into an open classroom is that such noise is felt to be essential for instruction without interference from nearby students. On the other hand, this method of achieving privacy seriously violates a primary design criterion for classrooms with hearing-impaired children—that of maintaining a minimum background noise level. Consequently, placing hearing-impaired children in open classrooms with high noise levels cannot be recommended. Unfortunately, many hearing impaired children are placed in open-plan classrooms.[7] Additional information about this type of classroom will be presented later in this chapter.

The Measurement of Noise

When specific questions are raised about the amount of noise present in or around the classroom, the educational audiologist or acoustic consultant can measure the noise levels with a *sound level meter*. Sound level meters may take many forms—from compact, battery-operated instruments to more complicated, stationary meters that can automatically record the data. For most applications in the schools, a small, portable instrument is sufficient. Figure 11-2 is a photograph of two portable sound level meters that can be used in the schools.

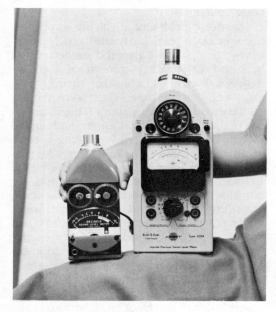

Figure 11-2. Examples of portable battery-operated sound level meters. On the left is a general, less expensive meter, and on the right is a precision sound level meter that can be used with an octave filter network (see Fig. 11-4).

The audiologist taking the measurement has the option to choose from three weighting networks or filters available on sound level meters for general use. These networks are referred to as dB(A), dB(B), and dB(C), and provide some general indication of the frequency distribution of the noise. As shown in Figure 11-3, the dB(C) weighting curve has the flattest frequency response, and thus gives an indication of the overall sound pressure level of the noise. While both dB(A) and dB(B) filter out more low-frequency energy, the dB(A) weighting curve is the most widely used, because it closely corresponds to the frequency response of the human ear. In instances where the dB(A) and dB(C) scale measurements are essentially the same, the sound probably predominates in frequencies above 600 Hz.

Table 11-1 lists the ranges of noise levels, using the dB(A) and dB(C) weighting networks of the sound level meter, recorded from various locations in six representative school buildings. While room size and number of students in the various classrooms differed, measurements were made during similar activities and during the same time of the day. The noisiest locations measured were the gymnasiums, with cafeterias a close second. Carpeted classes tended to have lower noise levels than uncarpeted classes, and the open-plan environments had the highest noise levels of all types of classrooms. Not surprisingly, the best classroom was a self-contained class for hearing impaired children. This class had a small number of students and only one teacher. The noise levels in Table 11-1 are in general agreement with those found by other investigators. Ross and Giolas[8] found the ambient room

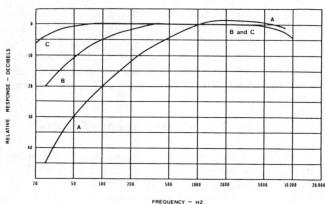

FREQUENCY – HZ

Figure 11-3. Standardized weighting curves required for general use on sound level meters.

Table 11-1 Noise Measurements in Decibels for Activities Occurring in Representative Classrooms in the Dallas and Chicago Areas

Type of Environment	Range of Measurements (dB Scale)	
	A	C
Traditional classrooms		
Unoccupied (morning, with traffic noise)	42–44	55–58
With 25 students, 1 teacher	58–60	62–65
Open-plan classrooms		
Unoccupied (morning)	42–47	63–64
With 100 students, 10 teachers	66–73	69–74
Classes for hearing impaired children in mainstream environment		
1. *Carpeted classroom*		
Unoccupied (morning)	36–39	52–55
With 15 students, 2 teachers	55–62	63–65
2. *Uncarpeted classroom*		
Unoccupied	42–44	56–58
With 5 students, 1 teacher	60–67	68–72
Self-contained school for hearing impaired children (carpeted)		
1. Unoccupied (morning)	35–38	50–55
2. With 5 students, 1 teacher	40–45	53–56
Gymnasiums		
Occupied	82–86	85–88
Cafeterias		
Occupied	75–80	79–81
Computer terminal	73–79	80–87

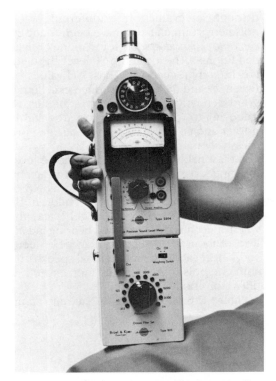

Figure 11-4. A precision sound-level meter with a filter network attached to the bottom.

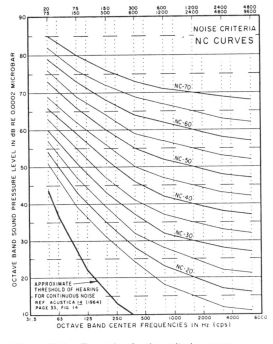

Figure 11-5. Example of noise criteria curves.

noise to be 60 dB(C) in a classroom selected to be average in size, location, and acoustics, while Watson[13] recorded 59 dB(C) and 56 dB(A) in a number of primary schools.

In addition to measuring the intensity of sound for dB(A), dB(B), and dB(C), it is also possible to measure octave band noise levels by using a separate filter network available on some sound level meters (Fig. 11-4). Octaves from 31.5 Hz through 8000 Hz are commonly measured. When an octave band analysis is performed, the data can then be plotted on a *noise criteria* (NC) curve, shown in Figure 11-5. This family of noise curves has evolved through an evaluation of different indoor noise environments that have been found *acceptable* or *unacceptable* for working or living conditions.[14] The lower the NC level, the better the listening situations. Thus, NC values between 20 and 35 would produce excellent to good acoustic environments. A higher NC value (45 to 65) means that the area will be noisier and communication will become progressively more restricted.

A reasonable goal for ambient noise levels in empty classrooms for normal-hearing children is 35 dB on the A scale, or about NC 30. However, for hearing-impaired children, the criteria are more stringent. Gengel[15] states that when speech is delivered to a hearing aid at a level of about 60 dB SPL at a distance between 3 and 15 feet (about conversational speech), the ambient noise level should not exceed 30 dB(A), or about NC 20 to 25.

Figure 11-6 presents the NC curve in an un-

occupied, acoustically well-designed classroom for hearing impaired preschoolers. The NC value obtained in this classroom was 25. The NC value was determined by noting the highest curve that intercepted the octave band measurements. This occurred at 500 Hz, where a 31 dB octave band SPL reading was obtained. This value falls on the NC 25 curve.

In comparison, the data from another classroom for hearing-impaired elementary school children is shown in Figure 11-7. This class was on the second floor of an old school building that became the *home* for the district's hearing impaired students. The classroom was across the hall from a noisy computer terminal. The unoccupied NC value of 55 means that communication was difficult in this room. Notice that the NC value was 27 when the computer was not operating and the door to the classroom was closed.

Figure 11-8 is an example of NC curves for an

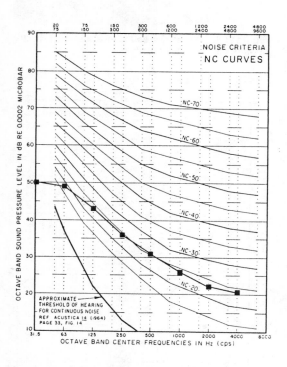

■   UNOCCUPIED CLASSROOM FOR
     HEARING IMPAIRED CHILDREN

Figure 11-6. Noise criteria curve on an acoustically well-planned unoccupied classroom for hearing impaired children.

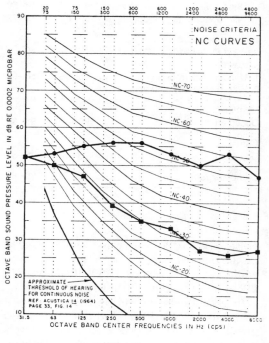

■   UNOCCUPIED (EARLY A.M.)

●   UNOCCUPIED
     (COMPUTER IN USE ACROSS HALLWAY)

Figure 11-7. Unoccupied and occupied noise criteria curves in a classroom with a noisy computer terminal across the hallway.

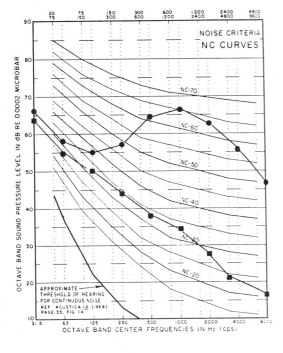

NOISE CRITERIA
NC CURVES

■ UNOCCUPIED OPEN CLASSROOM
● OCCUPIED OPEN CLASSROOM

Figure 11-8. Unoccupied and occupied (100 students) noise criteria curves for model open classroom.

unoccupied and occupied 8000 square foot, open-design classroom. The school building and classrooms were the district's showcase facilities. The unoccupied space does meet an open-plan design criteria of NC 35 to 40. Remember that many well-designed, open-plan rooms have a steady background sound to ensure privacy between activities. Although this room fails to meet the hearing impaired child's need for low background noise, NC 35 is considered acceptable for normal listeners in a room of this type. However, introducing students into the classroom definitely alters the picture. The space was planned for 200 students, 10 teachers, and 10 teacher's aides. On the day the classroom was evaluated, there were approximately 100 students present, and the occupied NC value was 65. The fear that students in this open class would attend to adjacent activities was needless. It was surprising that they could hear their own teachers, since an NC value this high is acceptable only in kitchens, shops, and laundries.[14]

In this classroom, the *noise* (as seen from its spectrum in Fig. 11-8) was composed primarily of children's voices. As stated earlier, listening in a background of other voices may be the most troubling type of competition, because the frequency content of the message and the competition are alike. To reiterate, placement of hearing impaired children in open-plan classrooms on a full-time basis cannot be recommended.

If there are indisputable pedagogic advantages to open classrooms, or if a school system is already trapped into open classes, completely closed rooms must also be provided for critical listening and instruction. The open areas can be maintained for selected instructional activities (perhaps art?). Minimal teacher-to-student distances (6 feet or less) in these spaces are essential. In addition, hearing impaired students should use FM auditory trainers rather than individual hearing aids. With the FM system, the teacher can use a lavalier microphone that will ensure minimal mouth-to-microphone transmission. In fact, the appropriate use of classroom amplification systems as discussed in Chapter 12 can be a powerful acoustic tool in all educational environments.[16,17]

Signal-to-Noise (S/N) Ratio

The purpose of reducing the noise level in the classroom is so that the teacher's speech level (signal) will be sufficiently high to maximize the information that the students receive in the presence of background noise. The *signal-to-noise* (S/N) ratio is the difference in decibels between the speech signal and the extraneous background noise in the environment. An S/N ratio of 0 dB would mean that the speech and noise were the same decibel level. An S/N ratio of +6 means that the speech is 6 dB greater than the noise, while an S/N ratio of −6 dB means that the speech is 6 dB less than the noise. The amount of information that is understood in a classroom will decrease as the S/N ratio decreases. Ross[18] states that a favorable S/N ratio will allow an individual to understand as clearly as the individual's auditory problems permit. Gengel[15] found that the S/N ratio had to be at least +10 dB and preferably +20 dB for hearing impaired children to function effectively in the classroom. Finitzo-Hieber and Tillman[3] are in agreement with Gengel.

They state that the S/N ratio should be no less than +12 dB for hearing impaired listeners. Unfortunately, few existing classrooms meet this criteria.

Sanders[19] reported that S/N ratios in certain kindergarten and elementary school classrooms varied from +1 to +5 dB, respectively. In addition, the noise levels were found to vary considerably more in kindergarten than in elementary classes. The poorer S/N ratios and more varied noise levels in the kindergarten class were due to the diversified classroom activities and teaching methods used at this level, ranging from free play to relatively quiet story times. The S/N ratio in open-plan classrooms will be similar to that found in kindergarten classes because of their multipurpose nature. As an example, the open-plan classroom described above in Figure 11-8 had S/N ratios that varied between +1 to −6 dB at certain times during the day.

Because little data has been reported on S/N ratios in total communication classes for hearing impaired children, which use both the auditory and visual modes simultaneously, a pilot study was undertaken by this author in which S/N measurements were made in several local total communication classes. Results of this informal study revealed that the S/N ratios that were measured were only +2 to +4 dB. A most interesting finding was that the teachers in these rooms were using unusually low speaking voices while simultaneously signing what they were saying. These findings mean that a child listening with a hearing aid could realistically hear little of what the teacher was saying. The information was being transmitted manually, rather than in a total communication approach. When the teachers became aware of their reduced voice levels, S/N ratios did improve, but not to levels considered acceptable for hearing impaired listeners.

REVERBERATION

When sound is introduced in a room, a continual process of reflection takes place from the floor, the walls, and the ceiling. This reflection results in a prolongation of the sound, which is known as reverberation.[20] In very large, reverberant halls, or in a canyon, reflected sound may be referred to as an echo because of the distinct delay in the arrival of the sound back to the listener. In rooms, these reflections generally are shorter and blend together. The reverberation time (T) in a room is most directly responsible for the quality of the listening environment.[18]

Reverberation time (T) is defined as the time it takes from the moment a sound source has stopped until it is reduced 60 dB from its original intensity. For example, if a 100 dB SPL signal takes one second to decay to 40 dB, the T in that room would be one second. Since speech is a broadband signal, reverberation time in a room is generally taken at 500, 1000, and 2000 Hz, and the average of reverberation times at these three frequencies is calculated. The specifics of how to measure reverberation time have been adequately covered elsewhere; the reader who needs this information can find detailed descriptions in these sources.[16,21]

Reverberation time is influenced by the distribution and absorption of sound in a room and by the size of the room. Sound distribution in a classroom (e.g., from the teacher's voice) is composed of both direct and reflected (reverberant) energy. The distribution of sound from the direct signal will decrease in intensity with distance according to the inverse square law (see Chapter 12). That is, sound will drop 6 dB in intensity with every doubling of the distance from the sound source. The reverberant energy reflected from the room's surfaces will not decrease inversely with the distance, but may build up and even exceed the intensity of the direct sound. Figure 11-9 illustrates the direct path and some of the reverberant paths of a sound source present in a classroom. The reverberant energy in the classroom may be detrimental to understanding the teacher's message, as the teacher's voice may be buried in the background of reverberant sound. In summation, the delayed, reflected energy in a classroom changes some of the important aspects of a speech signal and interferes with speech intelligibility by masking and distorting the message.

The amount of reverberant energy in a room depends on the type of material on the surface on the walls, floor, and ceiling. Reverberant sound will last longer if the room's finish is concrete or hard plaster than if acoustic tile and carpet are present.

Table 11-2 lists average sound absorption coefficients of common materials and room surfaces. The absorption coefficient is the ratio of the sound energy absorbed to the total en-

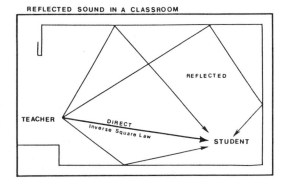

Figure 11-9. Direct and reverberant transmission of sound in a classroom from teacher to student.

ergy present. Thus, a 0% absorption coefficient would mean that no sound is absorbed, while a 100% coefficient would mean that all of the sound is absorbed. As shown in Table 11-2, absorption coefficients are frequency-dependent. That is, the material varies in its effectiveness in absorbing sound as a function of the frequency, and it is more difficult to absorb sound at lower frequencies than at higher frequencies. Moreover, by comparing the differ-

ence between ¾-inch acoustic tile placed on a solid wall with the same material suspended, it can be seen that absorption can be increased at low frequencies by extending the distance between the room's surface and the material used to absorb sound.

Since highly absorptive surfaces will decrease the number of reflections and hence, the reverberation in the room, sound treatment should be provided for as many vertical surfaces as possible in all classrooms for hearing impaired children. Opposite parallel surfaces should be treated so that sound will not be continually reflected between walls. Tilting blackboards at a 6° angle may be useful if they are opposite a hard, untreatable area like the locker area. As can be seen in Table 11-2, a good acoustic ceiling is one of the most effective ways to minimize reverberation, since treatment of wall and window areas is more difficult. Corkboard on walls and heavy drapes on windows will help to a degree. Certain companies, such as Armstrong, Johns-Manville, and Modern-Fold Industry, make effective sound-soak panels designed specifically for walls, file cabinets, or other reflective surfaces.

Not all reflections due to reverberant energy are necessarily detrimental to under-

Table 11-2 Average Sound Absorption Coefficients of Common Materials and Room Surfaces

Room Surface	Frequency in Hz					
	125	250	500	1000	2000	4000
Floor finishes						
Concrete, stone, etc.	.01	.01	.02	.02	.02	.03
Resilient tile on concrete	.03	.03	.04	.05	.05	.05
Carpet without pad	.07	.12	.20	.35	.50	.65
Carpet (unbacked) on pad	.10	.25	.55	.70	.70	.75
Wall finishes						
Brick (painted)	.02	.02	.02	.03	.03	.03
Plaster on lath	.05	.05	.05	.05	.05	.05
Thin wood paneling (½")	.28	.24	.17	.09	.09	.10
Normal window glass	.25	.15	.10	.07	.05	.03
Ceiling finishes						
Plaster on solid	.02	.02	.03	.04	.04	.05
¾" acoustic tile on solid	.10	.25	.80	.95	.80	.65
¾" acoustic tile suspended	.60	.60	.70	.95	.85	.65
Sound-absorbing treatments						
1" glass fiber on solid	.15	.30	.60	.80	.80	.80
3" glass fiber on solid	.30	.75	.85	.90	.90	.90
4" glass fiber on solid	.40	.85	.90	.95	.95	.95

Source: Crum.[2]
Note: See text for definition of *absorption coefficient*.

standing speech. However, in a classroom with a T of just one second, the number of reflections that are present will at least partially disrupt speech.[18] Obviously, how the room is used will be important in determining the optimal reverberation. In general, reverberation time should be shorter in smaller rooms.

A survey by John and Thomas[22] of the then recently constructed classrooms for deaf children in England revealed that the reverberation time for different frequencies varied from 1.3 to 3.4 seconds. McCroskey and Devens[23] measured reverberation times in nine elementary schools constructed between 1890 and 1960, and found T greater than one second in the older buildings and 0.6 seconds in some of the newer buildings. Our experience has been similar. Older buildings that have high, hard plaster ceilings and wooden floors have longer Ts than newer buildings with carpet, acoustic tile ceilings, and perhaps drapes.

THE EFFECT OF REVERBERATION, NOISE, AND ITS INTERACTION ON MONOSYLLABIC WORD DISCRIMINATION IN NORMAL AND HEARING IMPAIRED CHILDREN

A few studies have actually measured the effects of reverberation and noise on the discrimination of speech, using normal-hearing and hearing impaired children as subjects. In general, results from these studies have revealed that the interaction of these two variables in a classroom does distort the speaker's message and make understanding difficult. As an example, Finitzo-Hieber and Tillman[3] evaluated 12 normal-hearing children and 12 hard-of-hearing children with mean pure tone thresholds (500, 1000, and 2000 Hz) of 45 dB HL. The test conditions included three reverberation times (0.0 or anechoic, 0.4, and 1.2 seconds), and four S/N ratios (quiet, +12 dB, +6 dB, and 0 dB). The task was to repeat monosyllabic test words introduced into the room from a loudspeaker 12 feet in front of the youngsters, who listened through a mild-gain monaural hearing aid. The background noise was a babble of eight talkers.

Table 11-3 shows mean scores obtained from both groups of subjects at each of the three reverberation times in the quiet condition. The contribution of reverberation time is illustrated by viewing the scores from left to right for both groups. The discrimination ability of the normal-hearing listeners were excellent in the quiet (anechoic) condition, with a mean score of 95%. The 0.4 second increment in reverberation did not significantly alter the performance of the normal-hearing children. However, the distortion produced by a 1.2 second reverberation time in quiet substantially degraded discrimination even for the normal-hearing children.

Performance of the hearing impaired children who used monaural hearing aids is recorded in the second line of the table, and demonstrates a significant reduction when compared to the performance of the normal-hearing children. Note that while there is a relatively good mean score (83%) at the 0.0 second reverberation time, the 0.4 second increment caused speech to be degraded to 74%. At the 1.2 second reverberation time in

Table 11-3 Mean Monosyllabic Word Discrimination Scores in Percent Correct Under Three Conditions of Reverberation Without Any Extraneous Background Noise

Subjects*	Reverberation Time (sec)		
	0.0 (no reverberation)	0.4 (good classroom)	1.2 (older classroom)
Normal-hearing children (n = 12)	95%	93%	77%
Hard-of-hearing children with a hearing aid (n = 12)	83%	74%	45%

NOTE: This study included 24 participants, 12 normal-hearing students, and 12 hearing impaired students.

quiet, performance was only 45%. Moreover, in the nonreverberant environment, the difference in the scores of the two groups was 12%; at the 0.4 second reverberation time, the difference was 19%; and at the 1.2 second reverberation time, the difference between the two groups was 32% without the introduction of background noise.

Table 11-4 gives data for the combinations of reverberation times and S/N ratios. In general, results showed that the introduction of noise along with an increase in reverberation time compounded the complexity of the listening situation for both groups. At the 0.4 second reverberation time and the +12 dB S/N ratio, discrimination for the normal hearing children was 83%, which is considered good. In contrast, the performance of the hearing impaired subjects was only 60%. Yet, few existing classrooms are sound treated to achieve either a 0.4 second reverberation time or an S/N ratio of +12 dB. For the T of 1.2 seconds at the favorable +12 dB S/N ratio, the normal listener's score was below 70%, while the hearing impaired peer was capable of identifying only about 40% of all monosyllabic words presented.

The intermediate S/N ratio used in this study (+6 dB) is more likely to be obtained in traditional classrooms. With a reverberation time of 0.4 seconds, the mean score was 52% for the hearing impaired children. With a T of 1.2 seconds, the mean score of 27% for the hearing impaired subjects was half that of the normal-hearing children.

An S/N ratio of 0 dB is similar to the noise level found in the open-plan classroom discussed earlier in this chapter. For this noise condition, the message and the background noise are at equal intensity levels. This level of competition created a very difficult listening environment for both groups. The 1.2 second environment at the 0 dB S/N ratio was the most difficult listening condition in this study. Intelligibility for the normal-hearing listener was 30%, compared to 11% for the hearing impaired. In this acoustic environment, many hearing impaired children were able to correctly discriminate only two or three words out of the 50 stimuli presented. Finitzo-Hieber and Tillman[3] state:

> We have taken a group of hard-of-hearing children who were capable of efficiently processing speech through audition alone and now find that they are processing little if any information auditorily, in a situation which characterizes a reverberant classroom with a high noise level.

Blair, Ross and Giolas, and Borrild support these findings.[7,8,16]

Crum and Matkin[5] report that the child most often considered for integration into a regular class is a successful hearing aid user who has developed good auditory learning skills with the visual modality supplementing the auditory modality. However, in certain classrooms, the hard-of-hearing child with good auditory potential is being forced to rely upon visual processing as the primary channel for learning. Integration may, in fact, be isolation if the room acoustics are not stringently controlled.[10]

Classrooms where hearing impaired children are to be integrated should be designed to meet these acoustic goals:

Table 11-4   Mean Monosyllabic Word Discrimination Scores in Percent for Combinations of Reverberation Times and S/N Ratios*

Reverberation Time (T) (sec)	S/N ratio (dB)	Scores of Normal-Hearing Children (%)	Scores of Hard-of-Hearing Children with Hearing Aids (%)
0.4	+12	83	60
	+6	71	52
	0	48	28
1.2	+12	70	41
	+6	54	27
	0	30	11

*S/N = Signal-to-noise.

(1) Have S/N ratios no less than +20 dB, with very low continuous background noise levels.[7,24]

(2) Provide high isolation against outside intrusion and superior absorption within the class for a reverberation time of 0.4 to 0.6 seconds.[4,21]

(3) Maintain teacher-student distances of 6 feet or less to minimize the detrimental effects of reverberation and maximize visual cues for the child.

(4) Provide the student with both auditory and visual cues to maximize information from the spoken message.[6,7]

SUMMARY

The integration of hearing impaired children into normal classrooms is presently being emphasized by many educators. Their goal is to ensure normal social and emotional growth, rather than to make the child appear different through isolation in self-contained classrooms. Such a goal is a valuable one, if the hearing impaired child is capable of acquiring information at a rate similar to that of the normal-hearing youngster. The potential problems for hearing impaired youngsters in understanding speech in the classroom when compared to their normal-hearing peers have been identified in this chapter.

While the delayed educational achievement of hearing impaired children has more complex causes than poor acoustics alone, poor environmental acoustics represent one more barrier for the hearing impaired child otherwise capable of competing with normal-hearing children. In addition, poor acoustics make it difficult to distinguish the child's real deficiencies from learning problems specifically caused by unacceptable classroom acoustics.

Reverberation and noise in a classroom may not entirely prohibit understanding, but these two factors may make learning a more difficult task. Educators must understand the importance of optimal acoustics, and the acoustics of the classroom must be considered before hearing impaired children are integrated with normal-hearing children or placed in any classroom environment.

ACKNOWLEDGMENT

The author wishes to thank Trudy Coleman, M.S. for her assistance in both the classroom measurements and the artwork for this chapter.

REFERENCES

1. Nabelek A, Pickett J: Monaural and binaural speech perception through hearing aids under noise and reverberation with normal and hearing impaired listeners. *J Speech Hearing Res*, 17 (1974), 724–739.

2. Crum M: *Effects of Speaker to Listener Distance Upon Speech Intelligibility in Reverberation and Noise*, dissertation (Evanston, IL, Northwestern University, 1976).

3. Finitzo-Hieber T, Tillman T: Room acoustics effects on monosyllabic word discrimination ability for normal and hearing impaired children. *J Speech Hearing Res*, 21 (1978), 440–458.

4. The use of architectural acoustical materials. Acoustical Materials Association. AIA No. 39-A, 1963.

5. Crum M, Matkin N: Room acoustics: The forgotten variable? *Lang Speech Hearing Serv Schools*, 7 (1976) 106–110.

6. Olsen W: Acoustics and amplification in classrooms, in Bess F, ed: *Childhood Deafness* (New York: Grune and Stratton, 1977).

7. Blair JC: *The Contributing Influences of Amplification, Speechreading, and Classroom Environments on the Ability of Hard of Hearing Children to Discriminate Sentences*, dissertation (Evanston, IL, Northwestern University, 1976).

8. Ross M, Giolas T: Three classroom listening conditions on speech intelligibility. *Amer Annals of the Deaf*, 116 (1971), 580–584.

9. Roller S: Personal communication (1974).

10. Matkin N: Personal communication (1977).

11. Miller G: Effects of noise on people. *J Acoust Soc Amer*, 56 (1974), 724–764.

12. Carhart R, Tillman T, Greetis B: Perceptual masking in multiple sound backgrounds. *J Acoust Soc Amer*, 46 (1969), 694–703.

13. Watson T: The use of hearing aids by hearing impaired pupils in ordinary schools. *The Volta Review*, 66 (1964), 741–744.

14. Beranek L: *Acoustics* (New York: McGraw-Hill, 1954).

15. Gengel R: Acceptable speech-to-noise ratios for aided speech discrimination by the hearing impaired. *J Audit Res*, 11 (1971), 219–222.

16. Borrild K: Classroom acoustics, in Ross M, Giolas T, eds: *Auditory Management of Hearing Impaired Children* (Baltimore: University Park Press, 1978).

17. Hirsh I: Use of amplification in educating deaf children. *Amer Annals of the Deaf*, 113 (1968), 1046–1055.

18. Ross M: Classroom acoustics and speech intelligibility, in Katz J, ed: *Handbook of Clinical Audiology* (Baltimore: Williams and Wilkins, 1972), pp 756–771.

19. Sanders J: Noise conditions in normal school classrooms. *Except Child*, 31 (1965), 344–353.

20. Sabine W: *Collected Papers on Acoustics* (New York: Dover Publications, 1964).

21. Finitzo-Hieber T: *The Influence of Reverberation and Noise on the Speech Intelligibility of Normal and Hard of Hearing Children in Classroom-size Listening Environments*, dissertation (Evanston, IL, Northwestern University, 1975).

22. John J, Thomas H: Design and construction of schools for the deaf, in Ewing AWG, ed: *Educational Guidance and the Deaf Child* (Washington, DC: The Volta Review, 1957).

23. McCroskey R, Devens J: Acoustic characteristics of public school classrooms constructed between 1890 and 1960. Presented at the American Speech and Hearing Association, Las Vegas, Nevada, November 1974.

24. Peterson A, Gross E: *Handbook on Noise Measurement* (Concord, MA: General Radio, 1972).

12 CLASSROOM AMPLIFICATION SYSTEMS FOR THE PARTIALLY HEARING STUDENT

Richard G. Pimentel

INTRODUCTION

For the hearing impaired student, proper selection of amplification is extremely important to language and speech development. Unlike adults who have acquired their hearing loss later in life (after developing language and speech), hearing impaired children must develop language and speech through impaired ears. Because of the adverse effects of the hearing impairment, the amplification system selected must provide the highest quality signal possible, so that the child is provided with the best possible acoustic signal.

Properly selected amplification will have an impact on language and speech acquisition because the development of language and speech relies heavily on the auditory modality. Properly selected amplification will also enhance speech intelligibility for the students, which may be a primary factor in their educational progress.

In the classroom setting, three options for amplification are available: personally owned hearing aids, school-owned auditory training systems, and school-owned systems that may be used in conjunction with personally owned hearing aids. The use and maintenance of personally owned hearing aids is covered in Chapter 10. This chapter reviews auditory training systems that are available for classroom use, with specific emphasis on FM free-field systems. In addition, the chapter outlines the factors that should be considered when school personnel select systems to be used in their programs.

THE IMPORTANCE OF THE AMPLIFICATION SYSTEM AND OF A CONTROLLED SOUND PRESSURE OF THE ACOUSTIC SIGNAL

The proper selection of an amplification system is of prime importance due to its effect on the student's educational development, and because it may improve the quality of the auditory signal the student receives. Other factors that will affect the auditory stimulus include the acoustics of the room, the distance of the teacher from the student when speaking, the background noise in the environment, and the clarity of the speaker's voice.

The concept of a controlled sound pressure level of the acoustic signal, usually the speaker's (teacher's) voice, will be presented throughout this chapter, and is an important consideration when discussing amplification systems for hearing impaired students. This concept implies that acoustic information delivered to the ear(s) of a student with hearing loss should be regulated as closely as possible. The reasons for such regulation are:

(1) Most hearing impaired students depend entirely on their amplification systems for the auditory signals that they receive.
(2) Hearing impaired students may have a narrow range of hearing. Even though hearing impaired children require additional intensity before the signal is perceived, many will not be able to tolerate the signal at high intensities. Technically this is known as a reduction in the *dynamic range*. Because some children have

reduced dynamic ranges, the signal delivered by the amplification system must be controlled for its maximum amount of amplification, or maximum saturation sound pressure level.

(3) A controlled sound pressure level will enhance the student's ability to receive the teacher's speech with greater intelligibility.[1]

THE EFFECTS OF DISTANCE AND ENVIRONMENTAL NOISE ON SIGNAL RECEPTION

One of the major reasons why auditory training systems were developed was to overcome the problems of distance and poor room acoustics (see Chapter 11). Virtually all auditory training systems use microphones that are designed to be worn or held by the teacher in a fixed position. Because the microphone is in a fixed position, a relatively constant distance is maintained between the speaker's mouth and the microphone, which provides a controlled sound pressure level to the student's ear(s). In this way, the speech signal delivered to the student's ear(s) can be maintained at a fixed range of sound pressure levels, and the acoustic signal is less affected by distance, environmental noise, and other interfering factors.

DEVELOPMENT OF AUDITORY TRAINING SYSTEMS IN THE SCHOOLS

Auditory training systems were introduced into the schools over 40 years ago to enhance the language and speech acquisition, and through high-fidelity amplification—speech intelligibility; and to provide the hearing impaired student with acoustic information at a controlled sound pressure level. The systems that are and have been used in the classroom will now be briefly reviewed in chronologic order of their development.

Hardwire. The first auditory training system introduced into the classroom consisted of an amplifier, microphone, and listening stations at each student's desk. The system is called a *hardwire* system because wires actually ran from the amplifier to each student's desk; and at each desk, the student had an individual volume control and a headset. The

teacher spoke through a microphone connected to the amplifier. This system provided a controlled sound pressure level of the teacher's voice and relatively high-fidelity amplification for the technology available for that era. The system did not provide mobility for the teacher or student, so that, for example, when the student went to the blackboard, amplification had to be left at the student's desk. (Later systems incorporated hardwire microphones at the students' desk to help them self-monitor.)

Portable Desk Auditory Trainer. Portable desk auditory trainers were designed to provide students with high-fidelity amplification and mobility—so that they could be used at the desk or carried by the student. These systems are still available in monaural, pseudobinaural (Y-cord), or binaural (true stereo) configurations (explained below). These systems use environmental microphones, which are attached to the units and move about the classroom with the student. Therefore, with these instruments, a controlled sound pressure level of the teacher's voice is not maintained. The desktop auditory trainer amplifies all sounds equally, so background noise, as well as the speech signal, is delivered to the hearing impaired child's ear(s). The effective use of portable desk trainers is limited to quiet, controlled listening environments, similar to those used in individual speech therapy sessions.

Loop (Induction). The loop induction system was introduced in an attempt to meet the requirements to control the sound pressure level of the teacher's voice, to maintain consistency in auditory cues between home and school, to provide a favorable environmental *signal-to-noise* (S/N) ratio, and to provide maximum mobility within a classroom.[2] The induction loop system is constructed by placing a wire *loop* around the room, usually in the ceiling or on the floor under the carpet. The wire loop is then connected to an amplifier. Also connected to the loop amplifier is a microphone worn by the teacher. As the microphone picks up acoustic signals, an inductive field is created in the room and each student's hearing aid picks up the inductive signal. The students wear their personal hearing aids in either the telephone (T) or microphone/telephone (MT) position (hearing aids must have a telecoil) to receive the teacher's voice through magnetic induction while within the looped area.

Loop induction systems have been found inadequate in meeting the needs of hearing-impaired students because of their poor acoustic performance. These systems do not provide a controlled sound pressure level of the teacher's voice in the classroom. In fact, there are many variables that may adversely affect a hearing aid's performance when used in a classroom with a loop induction system.[3] Loop induction systems also added a new detrimental dimension to auditory training systems, called *spillover*. Spillover is cross-talk between rooms, which means that the students may receive the voices of the teachers in the rooms next to them, or above or below them, if the systems are not adequately balanced.

Loop Radio Frequency (RF).   RF loop systems were designed to provide a controlled sound pressure level of the teacher's voice, high-fidelity amplification, mobility within the classroom, and to eliminate spillover. RF loop systems were constructed by placing a hard-wire loop around the room, which was called the *learning antenna*. Depending on the type of system used, the teacher's voice was transmitted either by AM or FM radio frequency. The students wore specially designed radio receivers, which were referred to as student units or auditory trainers. The students had to be within the looped area to receive the teacher's voice. The teacher's microphone could be either hardwired, or wireless and operated through the loop amplifier.

RF loop systems were an improvement over the induction loop systems, and they provided for a controlled sound pressure level of the teacher's voice. However, with RF loop systems, high-fidelity amplification can be infringed upon by outside interference from commercial radio bands. Furthermore, spillover is a problem with these systems.

Free-field FM.   The free-field FM system is currently the most widely used auditory training system in the education of the hearing impaired. It has been designed to provide a controlled sound pressure level of the teacher's voice, high-fidelity amplification, mobility inside or outside of the classroom, and to eliminate spillover and the need for costly classroom installation. Free-field FM systems operate like a miniature radio transmitter and receiver. The teacher's unit picks up the teacher's voice and transmits it to the student's receiver, where the sound is amplified and then transferred to the student's ears either through small earphones or the student's personal hearing aid.

The free-field (wireless) FM system requires no special installation and is completely portable. It is available in several configurations, designed to meet specific acoustic and educational needs that will be discussed in greater detail later. The systems consist of two basic components: the teacher's transmitter/microphone and the student's receiver; these units may be powered by rechargeable or disposable batteries. If rechargeable batteries are used, a third component, the charging unit, is added to the system.

The FM frequency band between 72 and 76 MHz has been allocated by the Federal Communications Commission (FCC) especially for the education of hearing impaired students. All teacher transmitters must have FCC certification, which means that they must be type-approved by the FCC and have the type-approval number clearly marked on them. The special frequency allocation and the regulation by the FCC is helpful in preventing interference from other RF sources and spillover or cross-talk in a school where classrooms next to each other are using FM systems on different frequencies. Thirty-two frequencies are available in the allocated band, so that a school may use 32 different teacher microphones simultaneously without having to worry about spillover and cross-talk.

Infrared.   Infrared is the newest type of technology applied to auditory training systems. This type of system provides a controlled sound pressure level of the teacher's voice, high-fidelity amplification, and mobility within the classroom. However, this system does require special installation and is not readily movable to another classroom or educational setting. The system consists of two main components: the infrared light emitter and the students' receiving units. Infrared is invisible light used to transmit the teacher's voice to the students. A hardwire microphone or wireless transmitter transmits the teacher's voice to the infrared emitters that are mounted in the classroom, and the students wearing the infrared receiver units receive the teacher's voice. Infrared systems can transmit stereophonically, and the signal quality is very good. However, daylight can interfere with signal quality, since the infrared signal can be canceled out by light. At present, this type of system has not been widely accepted for use in the education of hearing impaired students primarily because the FM system provides more versatility.

Table 12-1 summarizes the characteristics of the systems reviewed above, and provides the reader with a convenient comparison of the features of auditory training systems that are currently available.

Direct-Signal Input Hearing Aids

Direct-signal input hearing aids represent a new type of technology that has been applied to enhance listening conditions for the hearing impaired. Although they are not technically considered auditory training systems, direct-signal input hearing aids are discussed in this chapter because they have features that will be beneficial in the educational setting. This type of system consists of a standard *behind-the-ear* hearing aid that has been modified so that audio sources can be connected directly to the hearing aid preamplifier via an audio patch cord, allowing a student to receive the auditory signal through his/her prescribed amplification system. Figure 12-1 shows two direct-signal input hearing aids, one connected to a patch cord, which attaches to the audio source. How direct-signal input hearing aids are used in the classroom setting is shown in Figure 12-2.

Through the years, hearing aids have improved greatly. The concept of direct-signal input expands the ability of the hearing aid to be adapted to more listening situations that the hearing impaired individual may have to deal with. For the hearing impaired student, direct-signal input is a good way to provide acoustic information from an audio source. It works well with FM systems and may also be used

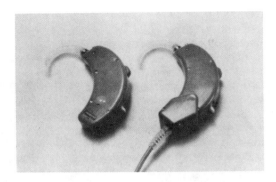

Figure 12-1. Hearing aids with direct-signal input connections. The patch cord attached to the hearing aid at right connects to an audio receiver worn by the student.

effectively with other audio sources such as card readers, tape recorders, televisions, etc.

The advantages of direct-signal input are not limited to educational environments. Direct-signal input provides a means of adjusting to the individual listening conditions at home, at work, or at play. For example, the hearing impaired business professionals who rely on the telephone may be able to more effectively use it through direct-signal input; and at home, the television may be enjoyed more thoroughly.

Advantages of the Free-field FM System

Auditory training systems were not designed specifically to replace the student's personal hearing aid, but to improve listening conditions in the educational environment. All systems discussed meet that goal, but most sys-

Table 12-1   Comparison of Auditory Training System Features

System	Good Fidelity	Complete Mobility	Constant Sound Level	Prevents Spillover	Easy Installation
Hardwire	Yes	No	Yes	Yes	No
Loop (Induction)	No	No	No	No	No
Loop (RF)	Yes	No	Yes	No	No
Infrared	Yes	No	Yes	Yes	No
Free-field FM	Yes	Yes	Yes	Yes	Yes

Figure 12-2. Personal FM system used with hearing aids having direct-signal input connections or telecoil.

tems have certain restrictions, making one system more applicable to the individual program where it is to be used.

Of the systems mentioned in Table 12-1, the free-field FM system is most commonly used in the classroom today. The reason that the free-field FM system is most commonly used is that it offers the most versatility in meeting program needs. Table 12-2 describes the features of the free-field FM system and what function these features fulfill in a classroom environment with hearing-impaired students. In addition to the features listed in Table 12-2, FM systems require no special installation and are completely portable for use in the classroom, auditorium, home, museum, zoo, or any setting that the educational process may occur.

FM systems, as well as other types of amplification systems, can be either *monaural, pseudobinaural,* or *binaural (stereo)*. This feature is determined by the student's receiver; the teacher's transmitter is always monaural. In addition to these options, the system can be duplex.

Monaural.   A monaural auditory training system has an FM receiver built into a monaural hearing aid. Monaural means that there is one environmental microphone, one amplifier, one tone control, and one output control.

Pseudobinaural.   In the monaural system only one ear is stimulated. Pseudobinaural systems provide binaural (two-ear) stimulation through a Y-cord; however, they do not provide true binaural amplification or fitting flexibility. A balance control, if present, does

give the audiologist some degree of adjustment of the output for each ear independently.

Binaural or Stereo.   The binaural or stereo auditory training system has an FM receiver with a built-in stereo hearing aid. Stereo means there are two environmental microphones, two amplifiers, two tone controls, two output controls. These systems provide true binaural or stereo amplification, and allow more fitting flexibility for the audiologist. FM systems usually divide the transmitted FM signal between the two amplifiers, allowing independent adjustment of the FM signal as well as the signal from the two environmental microphones to each ear.

Duplex.   Duplex auditory training systems can be either monaural or binaural as described above. In the duplex system concept, the student not only receives the transmitted voice of the teacher, but also receives the transmitted voices of the other students. Each student receiver contains a built-in transmitter. This feature enhances the interaction between students, and prevents the student's voice from being lost due to distance or room noise. This type of system would be most applicable in special or contained classroom for hearing-impaired students.

The teacher's microphone of the FM system is worn around the neck or on the lapel, maintaining a constant distance of the microphone from the teacher's mouth. The teacher's voice is then transmitted by radio waves to an FM receiver worn by the student. This arrangement effectively simulates a distance of the

Table 12-2   Advantageous Features of the Free-field FM System for Use in the Classroom

Feature	Purpose
High-fidelity amplification with low-harmonic distortion and a high signal-to-noise (S/N) ratio.	To enhance speech intelligibility.
A controlled sound pressure level of the teacher's voice, particularly in the presence of background and room noise.	To help improve speech discrimination.
Mobility for the student and teacher.	To enable the auditory training system to be used in all educational experiences—within the classroom, throughout the school, on field trips, and in other school activities.
Elimination of spillover or cross-talk between classrooms.	To allow students to receive only their own teacher's voice and not the voice of the teacher in the room next to, above, or below them.
Electroacoustic fitting flexibility.	To provide the audiologist with the range of adjustments needed to best meet the needs of the hearing impaired student.

teacher's voice from the student's ear of 6 to 8 inches, thus presenting a controlled sound pressure level of the teacher's voice. An example of a free-field FM system in use is given in Figure 12-3.

Ross and Giolas[1] reported results from a classic study in which the effects of three classroom listening conditions on speech intelligibility were measured. These investigators obtained speech discrimination scores from 13 hearing impaired students in three different educational environments: (1) under usual student listening conditions (seven of the children routinely wore hearing aids and six did not wear hearing aids); (2) in a binaural listening situation, with all students wearing a binaural auditory trainer/FM receiver with the wireless transmitter turned off; and (3) a binaural listening situation with both the environment microphones and the teacher's FM transmitter turned on. In this study, the speech discrimination scores improved 27% between listening condition 1 and listening condition 3. What appears to be a reasonably quiet classroom for the normal-hearing student may be far from ideal for the hearing impaired student.

Today approximately one-third of the deaf and hard-of-hearing students are being served in the contained classroom. The other two-thirds are being served in classrooms with hearing children, referred to as *mainstreamed* or *integrated* classes. Many of the hearing impaired students in these classrooms may benefit greatly from the proper use of amplification and improved listening conditions.

Public Law 94-142 requires that more handicapped students be educated in the *least restrictive environment* (LRE), which will have an impact on the education of hearing impaired students. Public Law 94-142 has not been mentioned to discuss who should or should not be educated in the LRE, but to emphasize a new movement that will affect listening conditions for the student even though it may be detrimental to that student's educational development. It may not be feasible to acoustically treat all classrooms for hearing impaired students with carpet, acoustic tile, drapery, etc. The school administrators will have budgetary constraints, and they will have to assess how best to serve all their students with the funds available.

The FM system is one form of investment the school can make in improving the listening conditions for each hearing impaired student to be served in the hearing classroom. The controlled sound pressure level of the teacher's voice, the mobility for teacher and student, and the system's portability and lack of installation requirements provide a cost-effective means of meeting the student's auditory needs, while at the same time allowing the program to meet the requirements of Public Law 94-142.

Figure 12-3. FM in the main-streamed classroom.

FACTORS IN CONSIDERING AMPLIFICATION SYSTEM SELECTION

The factors to be considered when selecting an amplification system for the schools are shown in Table 12-3. A discussion of each factor follows.

Location Where System Is to Be Used

The location in which the equipment is going to be used should be a consideration when selecting the most appropriate system. The physical facility and the movement of the students within that facility will influence the decision about which system is to be purchased. If the program uses the *open class-*

Table 12-3   Factors to Be Considered When Purchasing an Amplification System for the Schools

Location where the system is to be used
Age of students
Educational program control over amplification
Fitting flexibility
System operation
Service
Other considerations
　Consult with other programs
　In-service to staff

room, an FM wireless system may be most appropriate because of its ability to eliminate spillover and its ease of installation. If the students will be changing classes each period, a system with readily interchangeable FM frequency selecting modules should be considered (see Figs. 12-4 and 12-5). Auditorium use and field trips should also be considered during the selection process.

If the hearing impaired student is going to be *mainstreamed* or *integrated* in the hearing classroom, there are social as well as acoustic factors to be considered. The traditional larger-sized auditory trainer may be rejected or resented because of peer pressure. A less conspicuous FM system in conjunction with the student's own personal hearing aid may be more appropriate. One appealing factor about FM free-field systems is that they are flexible and may be used in all educational settings without special installation. If the hearing impaired students change schools or classrooms from year to year, the school system does not incur any additional cost.

Age of Students

The age of students being served will influence the amplification being selected, since attitudes concerning auditory trainers may change as the student becomes older. Whereas the traditional body-worn type auditory trainer is more acceptable and easy to manage with

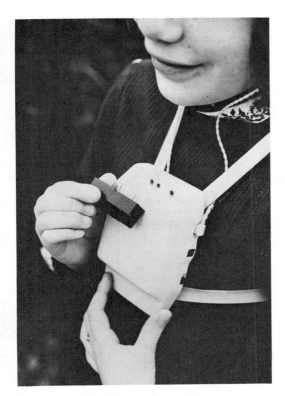

Figure 12-4. Readily interchangeable frequency selecting modules allow children to change their auditory trainers from class to class with relative ease.

Figure 12-5. The features of the free-field FM system make it readily usable on field trips.

preschool and elementary school students, secondary school, mainstreamed, and college students may prefer a system with more cosmetic appeal, which can be used with their personal hearing aids.

For preschoolers and elementary students, the audiologist, teacher, and parent may want to consider an auditory trainer with a broad degree of fitting flexibility. As the student develops more language and speech, the audiologist may want to change the frequency response, gain, and output characteristics of the amplification. The audiologist would also have an opportunity to try different acoustic fitting parameters in more normal listening conditions than in a test suite with two good observers: the teacher and parent. Thus, with the younger student, an auditory training system having variable electroacoustic parameters should be considered.

Older students, especially those in junior high and high school, tend to reject the larger auditory trainers worn when they were younger. If these students are using their hearing abilities well and have good hearing aids, a personal-type FM system may be most appropriate. In many cases, this system meets both the acoustic and social needs of the student. Direct-input FM systems may be less noticeable when worn, so that the students may feel more comfortable with their peer group.

Hearing-impaired college students are now starting to use FM systems to improve their listening environment. Even with special seating arrangements, the large lecture halls with room noise and reverberation make the unaided speech of professors difficult to understand. Direct FM transmission of the professor's voice may make these adverse listening conditions much less objectionable for the student.

The Educational Program's Control Over Amplification

Control over personal hearing aids by the educational program is important. If a system is selected that uses the student's personal amplification, it must be in good working order or the system will not help the student (see Chapter 10). In public schools, it is sometimes very hard to have any control over personal amplification because it is owned by the student. Schools that want FM systems that use hearing aids will sometimes purchase both the FM units and the hearing aids to ensure their control over the system.

An approach to ensure continued amplification for students who use their own personal hearing aids is to purchase back-up hearing aids with multivariable fitting flexibility or auditory training units to be used when the student's aid is malfunctioning. It should be realized that in some cases, the only amplification from which a student may benefit will be in school, because personal aids may not function properly or the student may not own one. It is unfortunate that in some cases, a more direct effort is not made to ensure proper amplification at home. However, through a properly used and maintained amplification system, the school can at least provide good auditory input for the student while at school.

Fitting Flexibility

Fitting flexibility will have a great effect upon the student's use of amplification. Just because a student has a hearing impairment that is apparently unchanging, it does not mean that a system with a *fixed gain, frequency response, or maximum output* (SSPL) will always be appropriate. An audiologist should fit the auditory trainer to meet the student's acoustic needs. The amplification system purchased should have wide-range fitting capabilities to allow the audiologist the fitting flexibility necessary to meet the acoustic needs of the student. Systems are available today with a wide range of frequency response, output, and gain adjustments (see Figures 12-6 and 12-7).

Today, many programs serving hearing-impaired students have educational audiologists on staff responsible for the audiometric and acoustic management of their systems. Programs that do not have audiologists on staff may bring in consultants, or they can send the student to a personal audiologist for complete testing and fitting.

To properly fit the auditory trainer or hearing aid to the needs of the student, the complete capabilities and specifications of the system must be known. As stated earlier, hearing aids and auditory trainers are class II medical devices regulated by the Food and Drug Administration (FDA), and all manufacturers are required to provide complete operating instructions and specifications as outlined in the

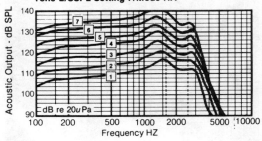

Figure 12-6. Example of the variable output (SSPL) control available on some auditory training units to limit acoustic output to help protect children from overamplification.

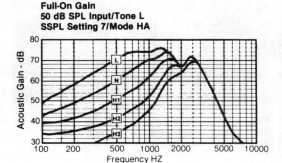

Figure 12-7. Example of frequency response adjustability in some auditory trainers to provide wide-range fitting capability.

guidelines published by the American National Standards Institute (ANSI).[4] This information should be made available to and read by the audiologist who is making the proper selection and fitting of the auditory training system, and by the teachers who use the equipment.

System Operation

Operational details of a system are important if it is to be used effectively. The teacher wants a system that is easy to use, so that he or she can spend time teaching students, rather than manipulating the units. Experienced teachers of hearing-impaired students are accustomed to working with auditory trainers and hearing aids. On the other hand, general education teachers of mainstreamed students will require systems that are easy to operate because of their responsibilities to all the students in the class.

Service

Service of the equipment purchased is as important as the equipment itself. Auditory training equipment will require service on an ongoing basis, and a service program should be planned in the operating budget. Objectively, when selecting a service program, one should look for quality service by competent technical people who have the equipment necessary to repair equipment electromechanically and acoustically. Reliable, expedient service is a very important consideration when investing in amplification equipment, and it should be thoroughly discussed with the company interested in selling equipment to the program. Fast turn-around of serviced equipment is required to minimize the time that a student may have to go without amplification. Some programs will purchase back-up equipment or will purchase a service contract that provides it to ensure that their students will not be without amplification during repair time.

Some manufacturers have service contracts available that offer different options and may include, in addition to service of the equipment, on-site inspections, back-up equipment, and an in-service training program for the staff. Service contracts allow school systems to budget in advance for service, and the contract can sometimes be considered an insurance policy covering equipment maintenance for the school year.

One way a school program may reduce the cost of service is to have the teachers and/or teachers' aides and other staff members regularly monitor the equipment and send it to the repair center, rather than to have this done by a company representative. Such a procedure can be effective, but the school must be sure that those monitoring the equipment are properly trained and capable of detecting those problems that can cause the equipment to malfunction. Chapter 10 provides excellent information on this subject and should be read by school personnel considering this option.

Other Considerations

Consultation with Other Programs.
Most of the auditory training systems available today cost about the same per student. To be sure that a program receives the greatest value for each dollar spent, all features and options should be considered before purchase of the system. One consideration is the reputation of the manufacturer of the equipment. Administrators should always consult with other schools where successful programs have been instituted. Ask about reliability, ease of operation, service, cost, and the responsiveness of the manufacturer to questions and problems. If possible, it would be best to visit these programs to assess first-hand how they operate and to see and touch the equipment.

In-Service to Staff.
In-service training includes orientation for the school staff on how the auditory training systems function, and a review of the procedures that should be followed to assure optimum use of the system. A representative of the company selected should be prepared to offer a complete in-service training program to the staff. Ongoing, in-service training programs should be set up to optimize the use of amplification systems. This may be done monthly by the educational audiologist and perhaps two to three times per year by the manufacturer's representative. Such an ongoing in-service training program will provide reinforcement for the staff and also bring new staff members up to date on the equipment operation. The more support the teaching staff receives in using an amplification system, the more confidence they will develop in its use.

An area of in-service that is becoming more in demand is instruction directed to the general classroom teacher, who may be unfamiliar with auditory training systems and amplification. It is critical that the teacher understands the rationale for using auditory training systems, and the impact that the type of system used in their teaching program will have on the hearing impaired student's ability to discriminate in the presence of background noise. Audio demonstration material that provides clear examples of how a teacher's voice is received by a hearing impaired student under several different listening conditions is available.[5,6] Taking the time to thoroughly orient the regular classroom teacher on the amplification needs of the hearing impaired student enhances successful integration of the hearing impaired student into the hearing classroom.

ONGOING AMPLIFICATION MONITORING PROGRAM

Although this subject is covered in detail in Chapter 10, this chapter would be incomplete without stating that the educational audiologist or program coordinator has a responsibility to set up an ongoing program for checking the amplification worn by each student. There are many ways to administer and implement a program that assures properly working amplification. Some programs have each student check their own amplification each morning. A simple listening check each morning by the teacher or teacher's aide or by the students themselves, if reliable, should be implemented as a standard operating procedure. This listening check also includes the checking of cords and of the reception of the teacher's transmitter for FM systems. Units that are questionable should be thoroughly checked as specified by the manufacturer.

An electroacoustic testing program that measures frequency response, SSPL (output), acoustic gain, and total harmonic distortion should be implemented on a weekly or monthly basis. A weekly testing program would be ideal and could be developed, depending on the program size. There are several good, easily operated acoustic test systems available that are appropriate for most educational programs for the hearing impaired. Even though a number of parameters can malfunction with classroom amplification systems, many simple problems can be readily corrected in the school, without having to send the unit off for repair. Some of the problems most frequently encountered are broken cords, dead batteries, batteries that were not completely charged, defective earphones, and incorrect amplifier adjustments.

FM SYSTEMS YESTERDAY, TODAY, TOMORROW

FM auditory trainers—1986. The radio FM band 88 to 108 MHz was allocated by the Federal Communications Commission (FCC) for wireless microphones that limit their radiated power (effective transmitting range), and the FCC established the rules for use without interference to other services.

In 1972, through the efforts of equipment manufacturers, the FCC approved new rules to allocate 32 special frequencies in the 72 to 76 MHz band for exclusive use by hearing impaired children in educational settings. Even though these new systems were still required to have low-power transmitters, the effectiveness of the system was increased and little interference was experienced because of the exclusive operating frequencies. However, over the following decade, changes in the FCC regulatory environment allowed new radio services—such as paging systems, construction communication, model radio controls, and others—to use frequencies close or adjacent to those set up for auditory training systems. In almost every case, these new systems were allowed to use many times the radiated power allowed for auditory trainers, thus creating the potential for interference to the school setting.

In 1980, the FCC was petitioned to allow the original frequencies assigned for educational purposes to be used also for assistive listening devices to benefit the hearing impaired in places such as theaters, churches, concert halls, and meeting rooms. This rule change use was granted by the FCC in 1982.

As more auditory training systems and FM systems for the hearing impaired are installed nationwide (especially in large metropolitan areas), and as additional radio services are permitted to operate, the number of cases of interference has grown. Unfortunately, this increased use of FM systems by the hearing impaired, combined with the additional radio services being allowed by the FCC, continues to increase the numbers of interference. Under the FCC rules, it is the auditory training and assistive listening systems that must accept this interference. Thus, these systems are forced to change if they wish to continue to operate. So far, those systems forced to change have been able to select a new operating frequency from the 32 now allowed. How much longer this will be possible is uncertain at present.

In the next decade, interference problems will be more frequent with educational FM systems. Eventually, alternatives will have to be implemented that will include the use of other frequency bands that will eliminate or reduce interference problems, but will result in incompatibility of present and future systems.

Infrared technology may be improved to a point where dead spots or shadow effects will not interrupt single emission. Ultrasonic transmission technology will also be explored for application to wireless auditory training systems, and new systems will evolve through applied research as the need arises.

SUMMARY

Hearing impaired students must deal with many different listening conditions in the educational environment. Their reduced sensitivity to sound, reduced ability to discriminate speech, and narrow dynamic range can cause them great difficulty in receiving the teacher's voice intelligibly. Furthermore, speech intelligibility deteriorates as distance and background noise increase. Although several types of amplification systems have been designed to help hearing impaired students in the school, FM systems are most commonly used because of their versatility in meeting different educational objectives. FM systems are available in different configurations for the school system, and school administrators must choose those characteristics that best meet the acoustic and social needs of the students served in their program.

For college students, secondary students, and mainstreamed students, the new direct-signal input concept of using the student's own hearing aid with an FM receiver is an option that provides clean listening and is a more aesthetically appealing system to wear. The development of the direct-signal input hearing aid is making the personal-type FM systems more desirable and is also improving listening conditions in many listening situations for the hearing impaired individual.

Administrators have the responsibility to select the most appropriate amplification system for the students they serve. Factors included in choosing the most appropriate amplification system include location where the system is to be used, age of students, control over the system, fitting flexibility, system operation, service, etc. These factors have been discussed in this chapter.

REFERENCES

1. Ross M, Giolas TG: Three classroom listening conditions on speech intelligibility. *Amer Ann of Deaf*, 116 (1971), 580–584.
2. Holden RJ: *Acoustics for Amplifications*. (San Francisco, HC Electronics, Inc, 1971).
3. Matkin ND, Olsen WO: Induction loop amplification systems: Classroom performance. *ASHA*, 12 (1970), 239–244.
4. American National Standards Institute Specification of Hearing Aid Characteristics. *ASA STD* 7 (1976), *ANSI* 53:22.
5. Glorig A: *Getting Through* (Chicago: Zenith [Zenetron] Radio Corp, 1971).
6. Harford E: *How They Hear* (Northbrook, IL: Gordon Stowe, Assoc, 1964).

SUGGESTED READINGS

Hawkins DB: Comparisons of speech recognition in noise by mildly-to-moderately hearing impaired children using hearing aids and FM systems. *J Speech Hear Dis*, 49 (1984), 409–418.
Hawkins DB, Schum DJ: Some effects of FM system coupling on hearing aid characteristics. *J Speech Hear Dis*, 50 (1985), 132–141.

13

ASSISTIVE LISTENING DEVICES AND SYSTEMS (ALDS) FOR THE HEARING IMPAIRED STUDENT

Carolyn H. Musket

INTRODUCTION

In the field of hearing impairment, the term *assistive listening devices and systems* (ALDS) has come to refer to a wide variety of equipment designed to improve communication for those with hearing loss.[1] As currently used, this term does not include wearable hearing aids. ALDS either may be used alone or may supplement hearing aid use in special situations. For example, some ALDS arrangements will transmit amplified sound more effectively from the source to the listener, which may be especially helpful in noise and in large rooms. Other devices may improve use of the telephone or TV. Still additional assistive devices will alert a person to environmental events by transforming an auditory signal into a visual or vibrotactile stimulus. ALDS usually are electronic or electromechanical devices and systems; many are available. In 1982, the Gallaudet Research Institute reported finding almost 200 devices and simple systems for the hearing impaired other than a hearing aid.[1] The purpose of this chapter is twofold: (*1*) to provide an overview of the help available to the hearing impaired student through the use of ALDS; and (*2*) to consider the role of the school with regard to ALDS.

OVERVIEW OF ASSISTIVE LISTENING DEVICES AND SYSTEMS

Telephone Communication Assistive Devices and Systems

Telephone and Hearing Aid Compatibility. Some hearing aids include a telecoil, also known as an induction coil, to help the wearer use the telephone. Telecoils usually are found in behind-the-ear or body-worn hearing aids; it is more difficult to use them effectively in small in-the-ear aids because of space restrictions. When the input switch of the hearing aid is on T (telecoil), the hearing aid will amplify only the telephone signal (see Chapter 10). However, for this to occur, the telephone receiver must generate a magnetic field sufficient to induce current flow in the hearing aid telecoil.

Problems arise because not all telephone handsets are capable of producing a suitable magnetic field and, therefore, are not compatible or usable with hearing aids having a T switch. This situation was somewhat improved in 1983 with the enactment of Public Law 97-410—the Telecommunications for the Disabled Act of 1982—and the adoption of implementing regulations by the Federal Communications Commission (FCC).[2] These measures stipulate that all essential telephones must be compatible with hearing aids. The term *essential telephones* includes all coin-operated telephones, which have been required to be hearing aid compatible since January 1985. In addition, these federal regulations specify hearing aid compatibility for the following essential telephones: (*1*) new telephones in isolated areas or used for emergency calls, such as police and fire department call boxes; (*2*) new telephones in businesses and public buildings provided for use by the public, such as hotel house phones and airport paging phones; (*3*) new telephones installed in hotels and motels until 10% of the rooms meet this requirement; and (*4*) new telephones installed in hospital and other care facilities since January 1985. It is important for consumers to know that federal law requires that packages containing telephones must be labeled to provide information about compatibility with hearing aids. Moreover, the FCC has adopted and made mandatory technical standards setting the strength of a magnetic field that must be gener-

Case history. Amy T., age 9, had a moderately severe, bilateral sensorineural hearing loss above 500 Hz and wore binaural behind-the-ear hearing aids most of the time. She was mainstreamed and attended third grade with normal-hearing youngsters. Like all children, Amy enjoyed watching TV, but sat very close to the set at home and did not use her hearing aids. Mrs. T. brought Amy to our Assistive Listening Devices Center to investigate help when viewing TV. We showed this mother and daughter a closed-captioned version of the previous day's *Sesame Street* program, which we had recorded in anticipation of this appointment. In addition, we outfitted Amy with an infrared receiver coupled to the aid (on T setting) in her right ear via a silhouette induction loop placed between the aid and her head (see Fig. 13-6). We thought this wireless system was desirable because of other small children in the family. Amy watched and listened from across the room. "Gee, Mom," she volunteered, "I never knew that fellow's name before!"

Amy's parents purchased a telecaption decoder and an infrared TV listening system. Later, the grandparents presented this family with a videocassette recorder so Amy could enjoy closed-captioned movies. Moreover, Mrs. T. moved the infrared system to another room in the evenings to use as a personal communicator when she tutored Amy in her lessons. Speaking into a microphone held 6 inches from the mother's mouth provided an improved instructional mode. Next, Amy started taking the infrared system to school whenever use of TV or a tape recorder was scheduled for the class. Her teacher used the system when announcing the weekly spelling test words.

In fact, Amy's use of an infrared listening system with her personal hearing aid demonstrated to both family and teachers that improved performance was possible in certain situations. At the last meeting of her school district Admission, Review, and Dismissal Committee, the decision was made to provide and individual auditory trainer for Amy to use daily in the classroom. Surely, Amy is one of our success stories!

---

ated by telephones labeled hearing aid compatible.

Handset Amplifiers. Telephone handset amplifiers, which are hearing aid compatible, provide extra loudness to the telephone acoustic and magnetic signals (Fig. 13-1). These receivers have built-in amplifiers with a volume control wheel in the handset handle that may be rotated to increase the intensity of the signal. One model has a touch bar in the middle of the handle that is lightly depressed to increase or decrease loudness; the volume on this handset returns to normal when the receiver is replaced on the base which is an advantage if the telephone will also be used by those with normal hearing. These handsets are available in several colors, and are easily installed on modular telephones by inserting the existing cord into a plug receptacle in the end of the handset. For older style, nonmodular telephones, handset amplifiers may be obtained with an attached cord to connect inside the base of the telephone.

Modular Amplifiers. Modular amplifiers may be plugged into the base of the telephone; the existing telephone handset cord is then plugged into the amplifier (Fig. 13-2). Either a rotary dial or a sliding switch on the amplifier is used to increase the intensity of the telephone signal.

Portable Amplifiers and Adapters. A portable amplifier or adapter may be carried with the user and put over the receiver end of a telephone handset when the need arises; the unit is held tightly in place by an elastic band (Fig. 13-3). A rotary dial controls the intensity, and power is supplied by a battery.

Various models of these portable devices perform different functions. One model amplifies only the acoustic signal from the telephone. Another model must be used with hearing aids having a telecoil; it transforms an acoustic signal into the strong magnetic field necessary for the telecoil to operate. Such an adapter is useful because it allows noncompatible telephones to be used with hearing aids. Finally, there are portable assistive devices available for the telephone that will both amplify the sound and generate a magnetic signal.

Telecommunication Device for the Deaf (TDD). A telecommunication device for the deaf (TDD) resembles a small type-

Figure 13-1. Telephone handset amplifiers with a volume control wheel (*bottom*) and a touch bar (*top*) to regulate intensity.

Figure 13-2. Two telephone modular amplifiers shown alone (*left*) and connected for use with the telephone (*right*).

writer because of its keyboard; it also has a screen to display the message visually. Some TDDs have a paper printout to record a permanent copy of the conversation. When using this device, a telephone handset is placed in the rubber cups of an acoustic coupler on the TDD (Fig. 13-4). The user types a message that is converted into tones and conveyed over the phone line to another TDD, which transforms the message back into printed form. In this system, both the sender and receiver of the message must have a TDD. However, TDDs are unique, because they allow communication in printed form using the telephone.

TDDs are available in several sizes: portable, semiportable, and nonportable; they are powered by household current or batteries. The more elaborate models offer the user an array of options, which may include automatic answering and memory for storing messages.

TDDs transmit information to each other through the Baudot code, which has been used by teletype machines since the early 1900s. However, most data communication systems, which include personal computers, use the ASCII code (American Standard Code for Information Interchange).[3] Consequently, special provisions must be made if one wishes to use a TDD to communicate with a personal computer. It is possible to obtain a TDD that has the added capability of using the ASCII code. In addition, modems are available that allow personal computers using ASCII to communicate with TDDs using Baudot.

Another telecommunication device for the hearing-impaired also uses tonal signals from

Figure 13-3. Telephone portable amplifiers and/or adapters.

Figure 13-4. A telecommunication device for the deaf (TDD) coupled for use with the telephone.

the telephone. A portable communicator may be placed over the receiver end of the telephone and secured with a rubber strap (Fig. 13-5). When a connection is made with a push-button telephone, tones that result from depressing the buttons of this phone cause letters, numbers, and symbols to appear on the screen of the communicator. This arrangement allows a severely hearing impaired person with speech to talk over the telephone and receive a visual reply; only one device is needed. Some TDDs also possess the optional feature of receiving such messages from push-button telephones used alone without another TDD.

Television (TV) Assistive Devices and Systems

Many assistive devices and systems are available for improved television (TV) viewing; some are also suitable for the radio. Those devices involving an auditory signal are based upon the concept of presenting the TV sound much closer to the ear of the hearing impaired listener, and thus overcoming the problems associated with distance, room reverberation, and noise. The systems described for classroom amplification in Chapter 12 may also be used in connection with TV; they appear as the first four options in the following section.

Hardwire. In these arrangements, an actual wire will connect the device worn by the user to the TV. For example, earphones may be plugged into an output jack on the TV set. If necessary, such a jack may be added to a TV set.

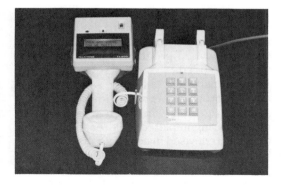

Figure 13-5. A portable telecommunication device for the deaf coupled for use with the telephone.

Dual jacks offer the option of having the TV sound heard only through the earphones, or through both the earphones and the regular TV speaker. In the latter case, others may watch TV along with the hearing impaired viewer.

Audio Loop. A wire induction loop that receives sound from the TV may extend around the room, may encircle only the chair of the hearing impaired viewer, or may be worn as a silhouette or neckloop by the person with a hearing loss. In the case of the latter, a wire would lead from the neckloop to the TV set. An audio loop allows a hearing impaired viewer to listen to the TV sound through the telecoil on a hearing aid; it must be used in connection with a hearing aid input switch in the T position.

FM Systems. The transmitters of most FM systems may be coupled to the TV through a cable. The sound from the TV is then sent via this transmitter to a receiver worn by the user and connected to a button earphone or hearing aid in the ear. This arrangement is wireless between the TV and the viewer.

Infrared. An infrared system also is wireless from the TV set to the viewer. A small microphone, held in place by an adhesive tab, is positioned in front of the TV speaker; a cord connects this microphone to a transmitter the size of a small pencil box, which sits atop the TV set. This infrared transmitter is powered by household current and contains several *light-emitting diodes* (LED). The LEDs transmit the TV sound by means of invisible infrared light beams to a battery-powered receiver worn by the viewer. One model of receiver may be worn by those with mild-to-moderate hearing losses. Another style of receiver, which interfaces with a hearing aid having a telecoil or direct auditory input, is available for those with more severe impairments (Fig. 13-6).

TV Band Radio. A simple, yet effective, way to amplify TV sound for some hearing impaired viewers is with a portable radio that receives the audio portion of television programs. Radios are manufactured that receive VHF and UHF TV audio in addition to regular AM and FM radio frequencies. The radio may be located beside the viewer, tuned to the station also on the TV, and adjusted to a comfortable volume. If desired, an earphone or headset may be jacked into the radio and worn.

Closed-Captioned TV. Closed captioning is a process in which the audio portion of a

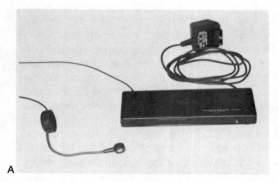

A

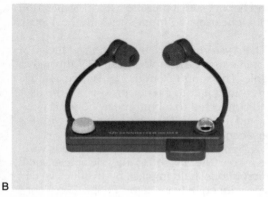

B

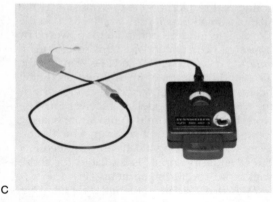

C

Figure 13-6.   A TV infrared listening system having a transmitter and microphone (*top*), a receiver for use without a hearing aid (*middle*), and a receiver with a silhouette induction loop for use with a hearing aid having a telecoil (*bottom*).

television program is translated into captions which appear on the screen, much like subtitles in a foreign film. Thus, a hearing impaired viewer can read dialogue and narration to supplement whatever may be heard. These captions appear as white letters against a black background and are broadcast on line 21 of the commercial television signals, which has been reserved by the Federal Communications Commission for hearing-impaired services.[4] However, closed captions may be seen *only* when a telecaption decoder or adapter is connected to a television set (Fig. 13-7). When the decoder is turned on, closed captions appear. When the decoder is turned off, only the picture is seen.

The National Captioning Institute (NCI) was established by the US Congress in 1979 for the purpose of conveying the aural information of TV broadcasts to the hearing-impaired.[4] NCI captions all types of TV programs. Prerecorded shows are captioned in advance of the broadcast. News programs and live events, such as sports, are captioned as they happen with real-time captions created on a modified stenotype machine linked to a computer. All networks— ABC, CBS, NBC, and PBS—broadcast closed-captioned programs. Some cable programming is also closed-captioned. Program listings in the newspapers and magazine guides identify a closed-captioned program through use of the initials *CC*, the words *closed-captioned*, or NCI's registered service mark, ⌼ .

Telecaption decoders also may be used with videocassette recorders. A large number of home videocassette movies are closed-captioned, and are identified as such on the packages. Instructional materials for classroom use are also available on videocassettes with closed-captions.

Studies have shown that hearing-impaired students who read at the third-grade level and above significantly increase their comprehension of televised programs when closed-captions are added.[5,6] Captioned television has the potential to not only increase comprehension of a program, but also to improve reading and language skills when used over a period of time. Hearing-impaired children, like all children, find televised material highly interesting. Certainly, closed-captioned television gives the hearing-impaired student access to spoken language and a means of enriching vocabulary never before available. Such educational applications of closed-captioned television are still in the developmental stages.[7]

Figure 13-7. Telecaption decoder and remote control (courtesy of the National Captioning Institute).

Figure 13-7. Telecaption decoder and remote control (courtesy of the National Captioning Institute).

Alerting and Warning Assistive Devices and Systems

As a part of daily activities, one must respond appropriately to a variety of nonspeech auditory signals. The ring of the telephone, the chime of a doorbell, and the buzz of an alarm clock are essential cues for independent living. Moreover, one's actual safety depends upon being able to hear the sound of a fire alarm or smoke detector. These signals may not be heard by those with impaired hearing. Consequently, there is a wide array of devices and systems on the market to offer assistance in this area. There are devices that monitor and receive alerting signals via a microphone, an inductive pick-up when magnetic leakage is available, or a direct electric connection. They transmit the occurrence of this signal via a wireless FM radio frequency or through a wire to a receiver. This receiver, in turn, may either emit a much louder sound or transform the signal into a visual indicator, such as a flashing light or a vibrotactile stimulus. There are single-purpose devices as well as systems designed for total home monitoring. The number of options and combinations makes this a complex topic. However, the following list of possible solutions for certain situations should help acquaint the reader with the type of help available to improve the detection of alerting and warning sounds.

Ring of the Telephone. Portable telephone ring amplifiers may be plugged into any modular telephone outlet and placed in a convenient location through use of an extension cord (Fig. 13-8). Some of these amplifiers change the ring itself into a horn, warble tone, or low-pitched sound more likely to be heard by those with hearing losses. Units are available that feature a strobe light; the device is plugged into an electric outlet, and a modular cord from the telephone is connected to it. Then, a brilliant, flashing strobe, which often may be seen in adjacent rooms, occurs to signal a telephone call. With another arrangement, it is possible to use a flashing household lamp as the signal. In a more elaborate version of the latter, a remote receiver may be plugged into a wall outlet in another room and a lamp plugged into this receiver. Then, the existing household wiring will carry the signal from a transmitting unit plugged into an electric out-

Figure 13-8. Telephone portable ring amplifier.

let by the telephone to this remote receiver, thus causing a lamp in another room to flash when the phone rings. Another type of telephone ring indicator operates on leakage from a magnetic ringer bell; however, this leakage will not be available on all styles of telephones. Such a device is plugged in a wall outlet and attached to the telephone via a small suction cup; it will then flash any lamp plugged into it when the telephone rings.

Doorbells. Doorbell chimes may be replaced with extra volume bells or buzzers that are more likely to be audible to the hard-of-hearing. One system connects a transmitter plugged into a wall outlet to the present chime with a wire; then, a second unit, which is a buzzer, may be plugged into an electric outlet in any room of the house. This arrangement uses the home's present electric wiring to transmit a signal from the transmitter and activate the remote buzzer; buzzers may be placed in several locations. As with the telephone, it is also possible for a microphone in a transmitter to be activated by the sound of the doorbell, and to relay this information to a receiver that will activate a flashing light. In another variation, the sensor-transmitter may be wired directly into an existing doorbell.

Wake-up Alarms. Alarm clocks are manufactured that have built-in flashing lights to awaken a sleeper. Other bedside clock timers have an outlet at the back into which a lamp, strobe light, or vibrotactile device may be plugged to serve as the alerting signal. The vibrotactile device may be either a bed shaker permanently attached to the frame of the bed or a portable vibrator to be placed under the pillow or mattress. Still, another electric device is sensitive to the sound of any alarm clock placed on it, and will cause a lamp or bed shaker plugged into it to respond whenever the alarm sounds.

Smoke Detectors. Several devices are available that will activate a strobe light or bed shaker plugged into them when they sense the occurrence of the sustained, intense sound of a smoke alarm. In another system, the smoke detector itself is both mounted on the ceiling and plugged into an electric outlet; remote receivers with visual, vibrotactile, or loud auditory signals may be plugged into a wall outlet in each bedroom. Again, transmission occurs through existing household wiring.

Multipurpose Systems. The monitoring of several auditory signals in an environment may be accomplished in different ways. One system uses a master control unit that regulates input from sensor-transmitters placed in strategic locations. The control unit flashes differing light codes in remote receivers to identify the source. These various components are plugged into the building's electric outlets. Another system uses sensor-transmitters mounted near each sound to be monitored (doorbell, telephone), which send a radio signal when activated to a receiver worn on the wrist (Fig. 13-9). The user feels a vibrotactile signal on the wrist and determines where the sound occurred by looking at the series of lights on the wrist receiver. This wireless, battery-powered paging system operates within a range of 100 feet.

Personal Assistive Listening Systems

Personal assistive listening systems refer to amplification arrangements designed to improve interpersonal communication in difficult listening situations. In most instances, they offer the user a way to overcome problems occurring in noise. Personal communication systems may be used alone or in connection with hearing aids. Personal communicators for stationary, one-to-one use are less elaborate and inexpensive when compared to current classroom auditory trainers described in Chapter 12. Usually, personal communicators are hardwire devices; the various components of an amplification system—microphone, amplifier, and receiver or earphone—are separated

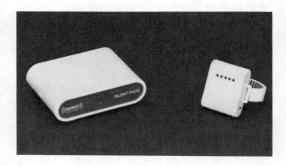

Figure 13-9. A vibrotactile alerting system having a transmitter (*left*) and a wrist-worn receiver (*right*).

and connected to each other by wires. Thus, it is possible for the person talking to hold the microphone near the mouth, or clip it to a lapel, making the message spoken much louder than any surrounding noise. The listener, a comfortable conversational distance away, is connected to the talker with cords but profits from the enhanced signal-to-noise (S/N) ratio this system allows. An unaided user may wear the system's earphone. An aided listener may combine the system and a hearing aid through direct auditory input if the aid has this option, or an induction neckloop or silhouette if the aid has a telecoil. Such a listening arrangement has been found to be helpful in restaurants and in automobiles. Personal communication systems are flexible. The microphone, for example, may be placed near the speaker of a television set, radio, or stereo as well.

Several manufacturers produce personal assistive listening systems (Fig. 13-10). It is also possible to assemble a simple personal communicator from components readily available at most radio or electronics stores.[8,9] One needs a tie clip or hand-held microphone, a miniamplifier-speaker, and a monaural or binaural headset (Fig. 13-11).

Sudler and Flexer reported on the success they encountered when using an inexpensive personal communicator as an auditory trainer during speech-language therapy.[9] They noted improved articulation and self-monitoring skills

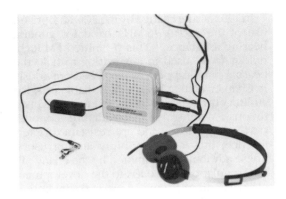

Figure 13-11. A personal assistive listening system assembled from components available at an electronics store.

in high school hearing impaired students. Children with normal hearing also had better self-monitoring of speech with the system, and were more motivated when using it.

Still another application of personal assistive listening systems occurs during conferences. Having a personal communicator available at the school makes it possible for a counselor, nurse, or teacher to talk more easily with a hearing impaired parent or other family member who is not aided.

Large Area Assistive Listening Systems

Assistive listening systems for the benefit of the hearing impaired may be found in large assembly areas, such as auditoriums, theaters, and houses of worship. A survey being conducted by a consumer organization, Self-Help for Hard of Hearing People (SHHH), has identified that over 12,000 large area assistive listening systems are in operation nationwide.[10] The National Association for Hearing and Speech Action has published a *Directory of Assistive Listening Devices*, which lists more than 4000 public places equipped with large area listening systems (see Appendix B). Recent growth in the availability of such assistance is due to several factors, which include government regulations, new technology, and consumer advocacy.

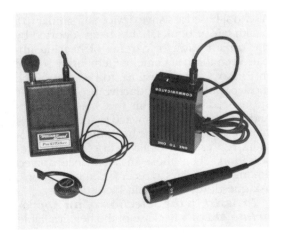

Figure 13-10. Two personal assistive listening systems available from manufacturers.

In 1982, a rule change by the FCC authorized use of the 72- to 76-MHz band for general hearing assistance.[11] This permitted FM technology to be used in any setting to help the hearing-handicapped. As discussed previously in Chapter 12, that band was available only for auditory trainers confined to educational institutions. FM transmission systems are economical for large areas, and are resistant to interference; they allow mobility among users. These advantages, prompted by the change in FCC regulations, have led to the development of FM listening systems for use in settings other than schools.

Infrared is the newest technology for large area assistive listening systems (see Chapter 12). In recent years, infrared listening systems have been installed in theaters across the United States, as well as in other assembly areas. Infrared light waves cannot penetrate walls, which makes this arrangement most suitable in theaters where security of the program material presented is of prime importance. An infrared transmission system prevents the possibility that someone nearby having the proper equipment could record and subsequently market the sound track of a theatrical production. The hearing impaired who use infrared receivers at home when viewing TV may now take these same receivers with them to enjoy the theater. Of course, infrared receivers for others may be obtained at the theater.

Another important influence originated with the Rehabilitation Act of 1973, Public Law 93-112. Section 502 of this act created an independent federal agency, the Architectural and Transportation Barriers Compliance Board (ATBCB) to enforce the Architectural Barriers Act of 1968.[12] This 1968 law prohibits architectural barriers in federally funded buildings to ensure accessibility to disabled people. The elimination of communication barriers in assembly areas is included in the "Minimum Guidelines and Requirements for Accessible Design" adopted by the ATBCB in 1982.[13] These regulations define an assembly area as a room or space accommodating 50 or more persons. Such areas with audio amplification systems are required to have a listening system to assist a reasonable number of people, but no fewer than two, with severe hearing loss. Audio loops and radio frequency systems, which include light wave systems, are listed as acceptable. For assembly areas without amplification systems, a permanently installed or portable listening system is mandated. Many states also have similar architectural barrier laws.

Finally, consumer groups, most notably SHHH, have been active in educating their members about the technology and laws available to help them. In fact, in 1986, SHHH initiated an ALDS advocacy program among its chapters specifically aimed at finding places in each community that should have a large area assistive listening system in order to be in compliance with federal regulations.[14] SHHH chapters will then work towards achieving such installations.

ROLE OF THE SCHOOL WITH REGARD TO ASSISTIVE LISTENING DEVICES AND SYSTEMS (ALDS)

To Disseminate Information. It is important that those who are in daily contact with hearing impaired students and their families be knowledgeable about all of the resources that are available to help those with hearing loss function more effectively. Teachers, administrators, counselors, and nurses may contribute by providing information and referrals regarding ALDS to students and families. A school library might add a videotape that demonstrates ALDS to its collection, and make it available to those interested (see Appendix B). A program concerning assistive listening devices and systems may be scheduled for meetings of parent groups affiliated with the school. A school-based assistive device fair, similar to a health fair or book fair, has been reported by the organization of parents of hearing impaired children at Camelot Elementary School in Fairfax County, Virginia, to be "one of the most popular and productive programs ever sponsored."[1,p 36] At this fair, manufacturers and distributors were invited to set up displays of their products. At the beginning of the program, representatives gave a brief product presentation. Then, those in attendance rotated among the displays to receive demonstrations, ask questions, and obtain literature.

To Assist in the Selection of an Appropriate ALDS. Because of the help available in everyday life with various ALDS, it seems logical that recommendations concerning their use will become a part of a student's comprehensive aural rehabilitation program. However, the large number of devices and systems on the market, as well as their varying technologies, makes the actual selection process difficult. At this time, objective information about the comparable performance of most ALDS is lacking, except in the area of classroom auditory trainers. The following criteria have been identified as important factors to consider when selecting an ALDS[15]:

(1) Degree of hearing loss.
(2) Compatibility of existing personal hearing aid and/or large area system with proposed ALDS.
(3) Listening situations in which the ALDS will be used.
(4) Availability of ALDS, durability and service, length of warranty, Underwriter Laboratories approved, if applicable.
(5) Acceptance by the user with regard to cosmetic consideration and comfort.
(6) Affordability with regard to both initial cost and cost of operation and maintenance.
(7) Feasibility with regard to ease of operation and portability.
(8) Flexibility.

In addition, provisions for a trial period with the selected ALDS would be helpful.

To Provide Training in the Use of ALDS. While some ALDS are relatively uncomplicated, others require a period of training to be used most effectively. Consequently, in addition to providing information about the availability of ALDS, educators should offer help in showing hearing-impaired students how and when to use them.[16] This training with some ALDS is necessary if they are actually to be used in everyday life. Such efforts have been made in the area of telephone communication. Both Castle[17] and Erber[18] have developed and written about instructional programs to facilitate telephone communication with the hearing-impaired. The materials these authors make available may be modified for various ages of childhood.

Since assistive devices are to be used in the home, sessions may be organized to provide parents with training in use of ALDS. Once parents become familiar with these devices, they will encourage and require their children to take advantage of this help.

Finally, school systems should schedule periodic in-service sessions to keep teachers and other staff members up-to-date in the area of assistive listening devices and systems.

REFERENCES

1. Fellendorf GW: *Current Developments in Assistive Devices for Hearing Impaired Persons in the United States* (Washington, DC: Gallaudet Research Institute, 1982).
2. *Telecommunications for Disabled Act of 1982 (Act)*. Public Law 97-410. 47 USC *Fed Reg*, 49 (January 11, 1984), 1352.
3. Hocker C: TDDs and computers. *The Voice* 2, (1986), 14.
4. Crane D: Writing for closed-captioned television for the hearing-impaired. *IEEE Trans Profess Comm*, 28 (1985), 15–18.
5. Braverman B: Television captioning strategies: A systematic research and development approach. *Amer Annals of the Deaf* 126 (1981), 1031–1036.
6. National Captioning Institute: Hearing impaired children's comprehension of closed captioned television programs, research report 83-5 (Falls Church, VA: National Captioning Institute, 1983).
7. National Captioning Institute: Using closed-captioned television in the teaching of reading to deaf students, research report 85-2 (Falls Church, VA: National Captioning Institute, 1985).
8. Vaughn GR, Lightfoot RK, Gibbs SD: Assistive listening devices . . . Part III: Space. *ASHA*, 25 (1983), 33–46.
9. Sudler WH, Flexer C: Low cost assistive listening device. *Lang, Speech, Hearing Serv Schools*, 17 (1986), 342–344.
10. Centa JM: Assistive listening systems are taking off! *Hearing Instr*, 37 (1986), 6.
11. Williams GI: The five technologies of large space hearing assistance systems, *Assistive Listening Devices and Systems* (Rockville, MD: ASHA, 1985), chap 4.
12. National Center for Law and the Deaf: *Legal Rights of Hearing-Impaired People* (Washington, DC: Gallaudet College Press, 1984).
13. Architectural and Transportation Barriers Compliance Board (ATBCB): Minimum guidelines and requirements for accessible design. *Fed Reg*, 47 (August 4, 1982), 33862.
14. Stone H: A triangle of hope: Industry, hearing health professionals and the consumer. *Hearing Instr*, 37 (1986), 34.
15. Vaughn G, Lightfoot RK: How to select assistive listening devices and systems, paper presented at a workshop on Assistive Listening Devices and Systems for the Hearing Impaired sponsored by the American Speech-Language-Hearing Association in Rockville, MD, 1984.
16. Fellendorf GW, Castle DS, Ravich R, Gammel C: Institutional panel on trends and issues, in Fellendorf GW, ed: *Develop and Deliver II: The Proceedings of the Second International Forum on Assistive Listening Devices and Systems*

for Hearing Impaired Persons (Washington, DC: Fellendorf Associates, Inc, 1985).

17. Castle D: *Telephone Training for Hearing-Impaired Persons: Amplified Telephones, TDD's, Codes* ed 2 (Rochester, NY: NIID/RIT Press, 1984).

18. Erber NP: *Telephone Communication and Hearing Impairment* (San Diego, CA: College Hill Press, 1985).

APPENDIX A

Assistive Devices and Listening Systems Demonstration Centers November 1, 1986*

ARIZONA

Heidico, Inc.
444 S. Montezuma Street
Prescott, AZ 86301
Tel: (602) 445-9554 (V) (TDD)

Tucson Hearing Society
University of Arizona
Department of Speech & Hearing
Tucson, AZ 85721
Tel: (602) 621-7070

Sunburst Tele-Com, Inc.
1016 N. 32nd Street, Suite 6A
Phoenix, AZ 85008
Tel: (602) 274-0203

CALIFORNIA

Hearing Society for the Bay Area
1428 Bush Street
San Francisco, CA 94109
Tel: (415) 775-5700

H.E.A.R. Center
Providence Speech and Hearing
1301 Providence Avenue
Orange, CA 92668
Tel: (714) 639-4990

House Ear Institute
256 South Lake Street
Los Angeles, CA 90057
Tel: (213) 483-4431 (V)
    (213) 484-2642 (TDD)

_____

*(Compiled by Fellendorf Associates, Inc., 1300 Ruppert Road, Silver Spring, MD 20903)

COLORADO

The Hearing Store
2308 S. Colorado Boulevard
Denver, CO 80222
Tel: (303) 757-4327

DISTRICT OF COLUMBIA

Gallaudet University
Assistive Devices Center
800 Florida Avenue, N.E.
Washington, DC 20002
Tel: (202) 651-5328

ILLINOIS

Charles Silberman Assistive Devices Center
Chicago Hearing Society
10 West Jackson Boulevard
Chicago, IL 60604
Tel: (312) 939-6888

Sound Resources, Inc.
201 East Ogden
Hinsdale, IL 60521
Tel: (312) 325-6133

KANSAS

Institute of Logopedics
2400 Jardine Drive
Wichita, KS 67219
Tel: (316) 262-8271

MARYLAND

Assistive Devices Center
The National Association of the Deaf
814 Thayer Avenue
Silver Spring, MD 20910
Tel: (301) 587-1788
    (V) (TTY)

Hearing and Speech Agency of Metro Baltimore, Inc.
2220 St. Paul Street
Baltimore, MD 21218
Tel: (301) 243-3800 (V)
    (301) 243-1274 (TDD)

Self-Help for Hard of Hearing People
7800 Wisconsin Avenue
Bethesda, MD 20814
Tel: (301) 657-2248 (V)
    (301) 657-2249 (TTY)

Potomac Telecom, Inc.
1010 Rockville Pike

Rockville, MD 20852
Tel: (301) 762-4005 (V)
       (301) 762-0851 (TDD)

MASSACHUSETTS

The Clarke School for the Deaf
Round Hill Road
Northampton, MA 01060-2199
Tel: (413) 584-3450

NEW YORK

Hearing Rehabilitation Center
Albany Medical Center Hospital
New Scotland Avenue
Albany, NY 12208
Tel: (518) 445-3125

Mill Neck Foundation
P.O. Box 100
Mill Neck, NY 11765
Tel: (516) 922-3880

National Technical Institute for the Deaf
One Lomb Memorial Drive
Rochester, NY 14623
Tel: (716) 475-6473
       (716) 475-6476

New York League for the Hard of Hearing
71 West 23rd Street
New York, NY 10010
Tel: (212) 741-7650 (V)
       (212) 255-1932 (TTY)

OKLAHOMA

HearCare
5077 South Yale
Tulsa, OK 74135
Tel: (918) 622-2721
       (800) 722-6220

OREGON

Eugene Hearing and Speech Center
1201 Almaden Street
P.O. Box 2087
Eugene, OR 97402
Tel: (503) 485-8521

PENNSYLVANIA

Johnson ENT Associates
321 Main Street
Johnstown, PA 15901
Tel: (814) 536-5161

Hearing Resource Center
Chestnut Hill Hospital
Medical Office Building, Suite 16
8815 Germantown Avenue
Philadelphia, PA 19118
Tel: (215) 247-4400

TENNESSEE

Bill Wilkerson Hearing and Speech Center
1114 19th Avenue S.
Nashville, TN 37212
Tel: (615) 320-5353

TEXAS

Callier Center for Communication Disorders
The University of Texas at Dallas
1966 Inwood Road
Dallas, TX 75235
Tel: (214) 783-3037

CANADA

The Canadian Hearing Society
271 Spadina Road
Toronto, M5R 2V3
Canada
Tel: (416) 964-9595

APPENDIX B

Sources of Information and Materials about Assistive Listening Devices and Systems (ALDS)

A.G. Bell Association for the Deaf
Publication Sales Dept.
3417 Volta Place, N.W.
Washington, DC 20007-2778
(202) 337-5220 (Voice) (TDD)

Offers a six-page pamphlet: Castle DL: *Signaling and Assistive Listening Devices for Hearing Impaired People*. Single copies free; quantity prices available.

Fellendorf Associates, Inc.
1300 Ruppert Road
Silver Spring, MD 20903
(301) 593-1636 (Voice) (TDD)

Offers publications in the area of ALDS; a list of ALDS Demonstration Centers (see Appendix A); and an audiotape: Fellendorf GW, ed:

Conversation IV: Assistive Listening Devices and Systems. $4.95.

National Association for Hearing and Speech Action
10801 Rockville Pike
Rockville, MD 20852
(800) 638-8255 (Voice) (TDD)

Publishes *Directory of Assistive Listening Devices*, which lists more than 4000 public places equipped with large area amplification devices; cost is $12.95. Listings for a single state are available at no fee. Also offers a free packet of information about assistive listening devices and instructions on how to use a TDD.

National Captioning Institute, Inc. (NCI)
5203 Leesburg Pike
Falls Church, VA 22041
(703) 998-2400 (Voice) (TDD)
(800) 528-6600 (Voice) for information on telecaptioning

Provides a newsletter and lists of closed-captioned videocassettes/discs currently available.

National Information Center on Deafness
Gallaudet University
800 Florida Avenue, N.E.
Washington, DC 20002
(202) 651-5109 (Voice)
(202) 651-5976 (TDD)

Offers an eight-page pamphlet: DiPietro L, Williams P, Kaplan H: *Alerting and Communication Devices for Hearing Impaired People: What's Available Now.*

National Technical Institute for the Deaf
One Lomb Memorial Drive
P.O. Box 9887
Rochester, NY 14623
(716) 475-6824

Offers a pamphlet: Castle DL: *What You Should Know About TDDs.* Free (limit 25 copies).

New York League for the Hard of Hearing
71 West 23rd Street
New York, NY 10010-4162
(212) 741-7650 (Voice)
(212) 255-1932 (TDD)

Offers a videotape: *Assistive Devices for Hearing Impaired Persons,* in either ½" VHS or ¾" U-matic tapes. Cost of tape is $75; handling charge, $5.

Organization for Use of the Telephone, Inc. (OUT)
P.O. Box 175
Owings Mills, MD 21117
(301) 655-1827

A consumer organization dedicated to promoting the effective use of telephones by the hearing-impaired. Offers a pamphlet: *All Telephones Must Work with All Hearing Aids—Everywhere.* Cost, $.30.

Self Help for Hard of Hearing People, Inc. (SHHH)
7800 Wisconsin Avenue
Bethesda, MD 20814
(301) 657-2248 (Voice)
(301) 657-2249 (TDD)

A consumer group that has been active in promoting the use of ALDS. Offers a series of six pamphlets titled, *ALDS (Assistive Listening Devices) and YOU,* for $2.50 and a poster, *Communication Access Systems for Groups and Large Rooms,* for $3.50 (postage included).

Telecommunications for the Deaf, Inc. (TDI)
814 Thayer Avenue
Silver Spring, MD 20910
Voice and TDD: (301) 589-3006

This organization will answer inquiries about TDD. They publish newsletters and a directory of TDD numbers.

Catalogs are available from the following:

AT&T National Special Needs Center
2001 Route 46
Parsippany, NJ 07054-1315
(800) 233-1222
(800) 833-3232 (TDD)

Hal-Hen Company, Inc.
P.O. Box 6077
Long Island City, NY 11106-4416
(800) 242-5436 (Outside New York state)

Request pamphlet on ALDS. This firm will fill orders from educational institutions, but not individuals.

Heidico, Inc.
(see Arizona, Appendix A)

HARC Mercantile, Ltd.
P.O. Box 3055
Kalamazoo, MI 49003-3055
(800) 445-9968 (Voice)
(800) 962-6634 (in Michigan)

Nationwide Flashing Signal Systems, Inc.
8120 Fenton Street
Silver Spring, MD 20910
(301) 589-6671 (Voice)
(301) 589-6670 (TDD)

Radio Shack, Dept. 87-A-250
300 One Tandy Center
Fort Worth, TX 76102

Request catalog titled: *Selected Products for People with Special Needs*.

Sound Resources, Inc.
(see Illinois, Appendix A)

14 | COCHLEAR IMPLANTS AND TACTILE AIDS FOR THE PROFOUNDLY DEAF STUDENT

Ross J. Roeser

INTRODUCTION

Conventional amplification through personal hearing aids provides significant benefit to the majority of hearing impaired children and adults. With conventional hearing aids, acoustic signals are amplified to an intensity great enough to make them audible to the impaired ear. In the preschool and school-aged child, the added acoustic stimulation should help to improve the reception of speech and, as a consequence, foster the development of speech and language skills. A basic tenet of audiologic management for hearing-impaired children is to provide amplification as soon as possible to promote communication skills (see Chapters 10, 12, and 13). Although the vast majority of hearing impaired children and adults benefit significantly from conventional amplification, it is quite clear that there are those who do not. Specifically, those with severe-to-profound deafness typically receive so little additional information from the amplified signal that they will not wear a hearing aid(s) when given the choice.

When children or adults with severe-to-profound deafness who cannot benefit from conventional amplification are found, alternative methods must be considered. Two techniques that are available for such individuals are cochlear implants and tactile aids. The cochlear implant is a relatively new device that involves electric stimulation of the auditory nerve through the use of an electrode, having one or more channels, surgically implanted in the cochlea. Since surgery is needed, the technique requires the expertise of a specially trained otolaryngologist for implanting the electrode, and it is expensive. Initial costs, including the hardware, hospitalization, surgery, and other services, can vary from $16,000 to $25,000.[1]

The costs of cochlear implants severely limit their availability to most profoundly deaf persons, but some insurance carriers are now covering the procedure, and Medicare now covers the costs in some states. Wallace[2] indicates that the Medicaid payment will vary from approximately $7500 to $13,500, depending on the geographic location of the hospital, length of stay, and the hospital's cost history. Cochlear implants were first available only for adults; but in 1985, the Food and Drug Administration (FDA) approved their use for children. As a result, school personnel in selected areas nationwide now have children using cochlear implants in the classroom.

With tactile stimulation, acoustic signals are changed into vibratory or electric patterns, which are delivered to the skin. The goal of a tactile communication system is to extract relevant information from the acoustic signal, and to present it to the individual in a tactile mode as a means of supplementing the auditory reception of the acoustic signal—with the successful reception of speech as the ultimate challenge. Surgery is not required for tactile stimulation, and the typical cost of a tactile aid ranges from about $500 to $1500.

Several types of cochlear implants and a number of tactile aids are now available commercially, and are being used in the educational setting. Who are candidates for cochlear implants or tactile aids? What is the need for these instruments? How do they work? What devices are available? Are they safe? Are they effective? What differences are there between the two devices, and is one more efficient than the other? What intervention therapy techniques should be used with those receiving the devices? These, as well as other issues, are addressed in this chapter.

WHO ARE THE CANDIDATES?

Case history #1 presents data from a child who would be considered a potential candidate for a cochlear implant or a tactile aid. As indicated in this case history, despite the fact this child was shown to be receiving some benefit by formal hearing aid evaluation, she was demonstrating little or no advantage with the use of conventional amplification in her everyday listening environment. This is one primary reason accepted by clinicians for considering any profoundly deaf, hearing impaired patient for either a cochlear implant or a tactile aid. Besides the lack of benefit from traditional amplification, what other criteria make K.S. a potential candidate?

Windmill et al[3] provide guidelines for (adult) patient selection that are typical for cochlear implant teams. These guidelines include:

(1) Must be an adult 18 years or older.
(2) Postlingual profound hearing loss.

(3) No benefit from traditional amplification devices.
(4) Otologically normal (no active pathologic condition).
(5) Psychologically acceptable (normal IQ and stable).
(6) No bone growth in cochlea (by computed tomographic [CT] scan).
(7) Absence of response on *auditory evoked response audiometry*.
(8) Positive response to electric stimulation of promontory.
(9) No general medical or surgical contraindications.

Although these criteria are commonly accepted by most implant teams, and procedures are used to assess each area, some controversy exists regarding the value of psychological testing, radiologic studies, and the electric promontory tests. For example, Windmill et al[3] report that while all of the other test procedures eliminated at least one of their adult

---

Case history #1. K.S. had no significant clinical history, except that a series of ear infections beginning at about 1 year of age had required pediatric consultation. At 1 year, 7 months of age, K.S. contracted meningitis. Following hospital discharge, her parents noted a lack of awareness to sound and, on recommendation by their pediatrician, had K.S. evaluated by an audiologist. Despite her attentiveness, behavioral testing over two sessions revealed a lack of response to auditory stimuli, except for low frequencies presented at the limits of the audiometer. Auditory-evoked response testing indicated no response at audiometric limits. The clinical diagnosis was significant hearing loss, most likely in the severe-to-profound range.

K.S. was fit with binaural amplification, and she and her family were placed in a parent education program for the hearing impaired. Formal hearing aid evaluations showed that she was demonstrating benefit from her hearing aids; low-frequency unaided thresholds improved from 95 to 100 dB to the 55 to 65 dB range with her instruments. Initially, both parents reported more awareness to environmental sounds and speech when K.S. was wearing her hearing aids, and felt that she was benefitting from them. At 3 years of age, K.S. was placed in a preschool program for the hearing impaired, which she attended daily. Her teachers felt that she had excellent learning potential, but her limited speech was unintelligible, and she was significantly delayed in her language skills on formal tests. None of her teachers felt that she was benefitting from hearing aid use, as evidenced by her performance on tasks requiring use of listening skills. She consistently was unable to perform auditory tasks whether aided or unaided. On occasion, routine daily checks of her hearing aids would reveal that one or both were not always functioning, and she would not indicate knowing a difference.

At 14 years of age, K.S. finished grade school and entered into a high school program for the hearing impaired with 27 other deaf students. She no longer wore her hearing aids voluntarily, and reacted when attempts were made by her parents to encourage their use. At 18 years of age, after graduating from high school, she discontinued the use of her hearing aids altogether.

patients, not one of their potential or actual patients was determined unsuitable for a cochlear implant by the psychological evaluation. They also point out that the results from the psychological evaluation have limited prognostic value, since one of their most successful patients was judged to have an adequate psychological profile on preimplant testing, but was determined to be manic-depressive following the surgery; the use of lithium was recommended as a controlling agent.

While all of the above procedures have some value in determining candidacy, results from the audiologic evaluation, and past experience with hearing aids—more than any of the other single presurgical considerations—are the primary considerations used to determine candidacy. Patients who receive cochlear implants must unquestionably be shown to have profound deafness and not be able to benefit from conventional amplification. Results from Owens and Telleen[4] reinforce the need for conclusive documentation of hearing aid performance prior to cochlear implant surgery. They studied the performance of two profoundly deaf patients with hearing aids compared to three patients with single-channel cochlear implants on audiometric and speechreading procedures. Those using the cochlear implants showed wide variations in their responses, but results from the two patients using conventional amplification were consistently superior to those of the subjects with implants. From their results, it is clear that experience with a suitable hearing aid is mandatory before an implant procedure is considered. Tests of auditory speech perception and speechreading with a suitable hearing aid are necessary as part of the preimplant testing.

A past history of unsuccessful hearing aid use should not be used as an indication for cochlear implant candidacy. Improved engineering and hearing aid fitting strategies, as well as innovative supplemental audiologic test procedures for assessing patients with severe-to-profound deafness, have made hearing aids a viable option for many patients who have attempted to wear hearing aids in the past. The limited gains that are available through cochlear implants in their present form may not provide as much benefit as those available through conventional hearing aids.

The criteria for cochlear implants in children are essentially the same as for adults, with minor differences. One established criterion

for children is that they must be at least 2 years of age. This requirement is needed not as the result of technical surgical considerations, but to establish firmly the presence of deafness and the lack of benefit from traditional amplification. Such a time period is required when deafness is established at birth.

Even though the age of 2 years has been set as a minimum criterion for cochlear implant candidacy, there are those who feel that this is by far too young. They argue that audiometric testing on children age 2 years and below is much too variable to ensure that profound bilateral deafness is present with 100% accuracy. Although auditory brainstem evoked response (ABR) audiometry is available, the maximum stimulation levels are limited and low frequency hearing can be present when ABR responses are absent. Behavioral audiometry using observation techniques can be used, but responses are influenced by the maturational level of the child and the observers' experience and response criteria. In addition, especially for the child with acquired deafness, at 2 years of age the benefits of hearing aid use can not be firmly established. Sufficient time is needed with appropriately fit amplification before the decision is made to implant a young child. Based on these concerns many feel that specifying a minimum age for a cochlear implant is not appropriate. Unfortunately, this minimum age becomes the accepted standard for all children to receive an implant. Instead, each child must be considered individually and candidacy be determined only when profound deafness and the inability to benefit from appropriately fit amplification are firmly established.

Intelligence testing for children who meet the hearing loss criteria is critical. Due to the questions that still surround cochlear implants in children, candidates must present with no other complicating factors, such as low intelligence; it would not be clear whether any lack of progress in an implanted child with below-normal intelligence was a result of the cochlear implant or the child's intellectual level. Due to the inherent difficulties in establishing intellectual function in deaf children, each child's age, motor performance, and communication level and skills must be considered in selecting the most appropriate measures. Children with autism and significant learning disabilities should be categorically eliminated from candidacy.[5]

A unique criterion, *evidence of strong family support*, was unanimously accepted at a recent conference on cochlear implants in children as a key ingredient for successful use in this population.[5] The obligations and responsibilities surrounding cochlear implant surgery are considerable and critical to the overall success of the procedure. The family must be aware of the requirements through preimplant counseling, and then be able and agreeable to meet the increasing needs following surgery. Table 14-1 provides examples of how family support can be documented overtly.

THE NEED FOR COCHLEAR IMPLANTS AND/OR TACTILE AIDS

The need for cochlear implants and/or tactile aids depends entirely on the incidence of severe-to-profound deafness, and an estimate of those among this population who might benefit from their use. Following approval of the 3/M House Urban Cochlear Implant by the FDA in 1984, sensationalism by the news media resulted in claims that the device represented the solution for deafness for millions of people.[6] This claim, quite obviously, is an overstatement of the application. An early attempt to delimit the eligible population for cochlear implants was undertaken by Carhart.[7] He estimated that, in 1974, there were between 70,000 to 80,000 children and adults in the United States who were potential candidates for cochlear implants. A more recent estimate was provided by The American Speech-Language-Hearing Association (ASHA) Ad Hoc Committee on Cochlear Implants.[6] This committee used data reported by The National Center for Health Statistics,[8] and indicated that there were between 131,000 to 294,000 individuals 3 years of age and above nationwide who would be candidates for cochlear implants.

The above estimates represent the population of all profoundly deaf individuals 3 years of age and above in the United States. Clearly then, the number of eligible school age children is less than the figure above. Karchmer[62] reviewed data from the 1982 Annual Survey of Hearing Impaired Children and Youth, and reports that 51,962 hearing impaired school children were identified in 6000 schools. Among this population, there were 35,735 children with no additional handicapping conditions that potentially could eliminate the child from cochlear implant candidacy; and of the 35,735, there were 16,607 with hearing loss in the profound (91 dB ISO or above) range. To account for error, Karchmer recommended increasing the estimates by one-third, giving a range from 16,607 to 22,087. If one eliminates the 20 to 55% of this population who would not stimulate due to insufficient nerve fibers,[6] the result would be from 9170 to 17,670 school age children nationwide who are eligible for cochlear implants.

With regard to tactile aids, except for rare sensory disorders of the skin, there are no clear physiologic contraindications. Also, a favorable aspect of tactile aid use is that a trial period can be carried out with little difficulty, because the instrument is not permanently implanted in the body through surgery. Thus, tactile aids have a potentially wider application and can be used with less trauma than cochlear implants. As many as 367,000 profoundly deaf individuals 3 years of age and above, 22,087 school age children, and an even greater number of children (if those under 3 years of age are included) can attempt using and ultimately may benefit from tactile aids.

Table 14-1 Evidence of Strong Family Support*

Accept child's hearing loss
Keep appointments
Are knowledgeable about child's hearing aids
Communicate well with child
Have appropriate expectations
Display high interest and motivation levels
Spend ample time with child
Use same language at home and school
Have concern for child's educational and physical development

*From Northern et al.[5]

SAFETY AND EFFECTIVENESS— THE ROLE OF THE FOOD AND DRUG ADMINISTRATION

The Food and Drug Administration's (FDA) Medical Device amendments of 1976 initiated regulations to guide the medical devices industry. In essence, these amendments set up guidelines to be followed by medical device manufacturers before the devices are offered to the public for use and sale. In 1982, the Center for Devices and Radiological Health (CDRH) was established to protect public health in the fields of medical devices and radiologic health. One purpose of the CDRH program is to assure the *safety*, *effectiveness*, and *proper labeling* of medical devices. Medical devices that are not "substantially equivalent" to devices that were on the market prior to May 28, 1976, must now be approved by the FDA before they can be sold in the United States. The term *substantially equivalent* implies that the device has the same function and/or composition.

The procedures that are required to gain FDA approval of a medical device are quite complex and need not be detailed here. However, two requirements apply to the cochlear implant. (Tactile aids are exempt from FDA approval because of their substantial equivalence; i.e., there were tactile aids on the market prior to May 28, 1976.) As part of the process, manufacturers must first submit an *investigational device exemption* (IDE), which outlines procedures to collect data on safety and effectiveness. Once the IDE is approved, a limited number of investigators are selected to use the device under controlled conditions. After completion of the IDE stage, a *premarket approval application* (PMA) is filed, describing the device in detail and outlining procedures that have been conducted to assure its safety and effectiveness. The PMA also contains information on labeling. IDEs and PMAs are reviewed by a panel of experts who act as consultants to the FDA to determine whether the claims made by the manufacturer are supported by the data collected.

The FDA approved the first PMA for cochlear implants for adults in 1984, and later approved the device for children 2 years of age and above in 1985. The initial device approved was the 3M/House single-channel cochlear implant. At present, a number of other devices have been approved and/or are under consideration by the FDA. It is quite clear that in the future, clinicians and educators will be faced with providing for the habilitative/rehabilitative and educational needs of an expanding population of profoundly deaf children and adults.

COCHLEAR IMPLANTS

Figure 14-1 is a schematic showing one type of cochlear implant system; most systems use the basic techniques shown here. During surgery, an active electrode is placed through the round window of the cochlea into the scala tympani, and an internal receiver/stimulator is secured in the temporal bone above and behind the ear. As sound is picked up by the microphone (#1), it is converted into an electric signal and delivered to a speech processor (#3), where selected acoustic characteristics are coded. The electric code from the speech processor is then delivered to a transmitter coil (#5), and is electromagnetically induced across the skin to an internal receiver/stimulator (#6). The internal receiver/stimulator converts the code to electric signals, and they are delivered to the electrode(s) placed in the cochlea (#7). As the electric signals stimulate the cochlea the signals are recognized as sounds, and a sensation of hearing occurs (#8).

Most systems work essentially in this way, although some have direct input, meaning that they are *hardwired* using a percutaneous plug; some have multiple channels, with one system having up to 22 channels, 21 of which are available for stimulation. And some use an extracochlear electrode, meaning that the electrode is placed on the round window rather than being inserted into the cochlea. Not all channels are typically used with the systems having multiple channels. Instead, only the channels that are found to be functional through testing are activated. Extracochlear electrodes are desirable because they do not invade the cochlea and cause damage to the inner ear structures, making revision surgery more easy if needed. While this is a desirable feature, preliminary indications suggest that open-set speech understanding using an extracochlear implant system is inferior to intracochlear implants.[10]

Table 14-2 lists 11 cochlear implant systems that are currently available in the United States and Europe, and provides information on their operating characteristics. As indicated in this table, four systems (the first four listed) use an extracochlear electrode. It is also clear, from Table 14-2, that the majority of the systems use a transcutaneous induction coil rather than direct coupling. Also indicated in this table is that

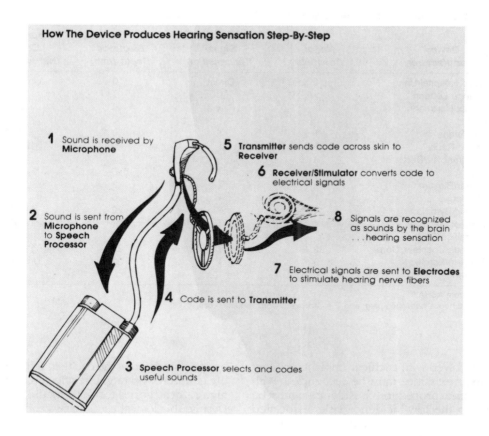

How The Device Produces Hearing Sensation Step-By-Step

1 Sound is received by **Microphone**

2 Sound is sent from **Microphone** to **Speech Processor**

3 **Speech Processor** selects and codes useful sounds

4 Code is sent to **Transmitter**

5 **Transmitter** sends code across skin to **Receiver**

6 **Receiver/Stimulator** converts code to electrical signals

7 Electrical signals are sent to **Electrodes** to stimulate hearing nerve fibers

8 Signals are recognized as sounds by the brain . . . hearing sensation

Figure 14-1.   Illustration of how cochlear implants produce sound sensations (see text for detailed explanation). (Courtesy of Cochlear Corporation.)

electrode depth for the intracochlear systems ranges from 3 to 25 mm, and hardware costs range from $4500 to $12,000. As indicated earlier, only the 3M/House and Nucleus systems have received PMA approval from the FDA for adults. For children 2 years of age and older, both the 3M and Nucleus systems have IDE approval, meaning that they are only available as an investigational device in designated locations in the United States.

In 1985, there were more than 1000 cochlear implants in adults worldwide and several investigator groups were implanting children.[6] By now, this number most certainly has doubled. As a result of this significant activity, numerous reports can be found in the literature on all aspects of cochlear implants, providing basic information on their construction and design, and giving detailed information on

their clinical use and the educational benefits. The information presented in these reports is too detailed to summarize here. For a more thorough review of the literature, the interested reader is directed to reports by Berliner et al,[11] ASHA,[6] Mecklenburg,[12] and Tyler et al.[13] A review of the major issues surrounding cochlear implant use will be presented in this chapter, including potential risks, single versus multiple channels, and implants in children.

Potential Risks

Proponents of the cochlear implant believe that the benefits provided by the implant far outweigh the potential risks involved, even though it is recognized that most users will not be able to discriminate ongoing speech. The

Table 14-2   Cochlear Implants Available in the United States or Europe*

Device/ Manufacturer	No. of Channels	Signal Transmission	Electrode Depth (mm)	Approximate Cost ($) (Hardware only)
1. Guys Hospital/Univ. College London	1	Direct	0	Unknown
2. Implex/Hortmann, GmbH	1	P or T	0	6000
3. 3M/Vienna	1	T	0	9500
4. Prelco/Racia	1	T	0	12,000
5. Chorimac 12/Bertin et Cie	12	T	0–3	9000
6. Boiear/Biostim	1	T	3	4500
7. 3M/House	1	T	6	6500
8. Ineraid/Symbion	4	P	22	11,000
9. Univ. of CA, San Francisco Storz	4	T	24	12,000
10. Nucleus/Cochlear Corp.	22	T	25	11,000
11. Antwerp/Forelec/Ku-Leuven	16	T	22	Unknown

*Modified from ASHA.[6]
P = Percutaneous *hardwired* plug; and T = Transcutaneous induction coil.

risks involved with cochlear implants are low, but their existence must be recognized. With any surgical procedure, consideration must be given to the low-incidence risks associated with general anesthesia and with possible infection. Besides these general considerations, there are several others that are specific to the cochlear implant. Initially, concern was raised about the possibility of bone growth in the cochlea, because animal studies have shown that electric stimulation of the cochlea will cause this condition to occur, which results in disruption of hair cell function.[14] However, clinical experience has demonstrated that many patients have used cochlear implants for five to seven years and even longer—up to 12 years—without significant changes in electric threshold sensitivity.[13] This finding would suggest that there are no obvious adverse affects of cochlear implant use for these time periods, but does not address the important question of lifetime use for periods of 70 to 80 years for the infant wearing a cochlear implant. The question also remains as to what effects there might be on discrimination ability or recognition of more complex sounds over extended use.

Downs[9] expressed concern for children being considered for cochlear implants who were at risk for recurring otitis media; during the infection stage, there is the potential for

bacterial invasion of the cochlea. To help identify children who might be affected, she gives high-risk categories for otitis media pronicity. Despite this logical cautionary stance, studies have failed to document a higher incidence of otitis media and/or secondary complications in patients receiving cochlear implants.[15] As a result, otitis media does not appear to be a major complicating factor at present.

A particular concern with children is head growth. At birth, the cochlea has reached adult size. However, the temporal bone that houses the components of the cochlear implant continues to grow and enlarge as the infant develops. As a result, allowances need to be made with infants, so that the intracochlear electrode will not be distracted from the cochlea. O'Donoghue et al[16] found that maximum head growth occurs in the first two years of life, and recommended prolonging surgery until after this age. In addition, these investigators recommended that a stretching allowance of 1 to 3 cm be made for the intracochlear electrode in young children to account for head growth.

Device malfunctions have occurred in some patients. In fact, one manufacturer voluntarily called a moratorium on implanting a device due to a failure of the internal coil in several patients. When device malfunctions occur, reimplantation is necessary, and reports have indicated auditory sensations are possible from the reimplanted electrode.[17] However, there are no data to indicate what effect reimplantation has on the ability to discriminate sound. Also, there are patients who do not stimulate on reimplantation. At The Callier Center, we have provided postimplant basic guidance to five implant patients. After more than one year of using their implants, two of these patients had device failures due to internal coil malfunctions. Neither patient restimulated when reimplanted. No data have been published to document the incidence of this unfortunate situation, but through reports such as ours, failure to stimulate on reimplantation is known to exist.

Other possible complications include tinnitus, dizziness, and facial muscle twitching; facial muscle twitching is most likely with extracochlear devices. Although these potential complications exist, their occurrence is reportedly rare since they have been found in only a few patients.[13]

Single Versus Multichannel Implants

One of the major design considerations to be made by the cochlear implant candidate is single or multiple channels. It is logical to conclude that a multiple-channel system will provide superior performance because of the additional information that can be coded for processing in the cochlea. However, surprising as it may seem, there have currently been only limited attempts to compare performance between single- and multiple-channel systems. Some of the limited data available have failed to show a significant performance difference between single- and multiple-channel implants.[18]

There are several reasons why comparative studies are not readily available. First, since each device is permanently fixed in each subject, within-subject comparisons using different electrode designs is impossible. This limitation leaves only the possibility of between-subject comparisons, and there is a wide range of variability in performance when different subjects are compared. In addition to this factor, many of the available devices have been implanted in only a few patients, making data obtained from between-subject comparisons on these small numbers difficult or impossible to interpret. Moreover, there are no standardized testing protocols. Many of the investigation centers use tests that were devised by their own team. Finally, there is only a small handful of independent research centers specifically evaluating cochlear implant patients. The majority of the data currently available on the cochlear implant are from enthusiastic development centers.[13]

One recently published report indicates that patients using a multiple-channel implant perform better than those with a single-channel system. Gantz and Tyler[19] evaluated the performance of 10 adults who were implanted with three different devices: seven with a single-channel system and three with up to 20 channels. All three of the implant systems enhanced speechreading ability and improved performance on tests using speech and nonspeech stimuli. However, superior performance was found on open-set speech tests for the three patients who were fit with the multichannel devices. These results are among the first to provide objective evidence that multiple-channel cochlear implants are superior to single-channel implants. More data are needed before firm conclusions can be made regarding this vitally important area.

Cochlear Implants in Children

The most controversial issue surrounding cochlear implants is their use with children. On the one hand, there are major consequences of severe-to-profound deafness, especially for children with congenital losses. Language learning and speaking will be significantly impaired when profound deafness exists and the child is made to rely on speechreading alone. For most profoundly deaf children, total communication is the only means of providing language. Vocabulary development and reading skills will be affected—compared to a vocabulary of 5000 to 26,000 words for the normal 5-year-old child, a deaf child will have a speaking vocabulary of about 200 words. One study reported that 50% of children having hearing loss greater than 85 dB HL had no reading comprehension at all.[21] Severe-to-profound deafness impacts all aspects of educational and psychosocial development, and will greatly influence socioeconomic status.

On the other hand, there are uncertainties about the potential benefits from cochlear implants, there is the possibility of irreversible damage to the cochlea, and the costs (monetary, psychological, time, effort, etc.) are high. These factors must receive serious consideration in the decision to implant children.

Those who favor implanting for children argue that the device provides valuable timing and intensity cues for contact with the sound environment, and it assists in speechreading. It is their contention that the information processed by the cochlear implant will provide significant benefit in speech and language development. They argue that even if irreversible damage occurs in the implanted ear, the other ear is available for implantation if improved technology leads to a better system. Failing to implant will deprive the child of the potential benefits during the critical years for speech and language development. Few would argue with these principles, but the fact remains that the exact benefits a child will derive from a cochlear implant remain uncertain.

The House Ear Institute (HEI) is responsible for the greatest number of cochlear implants in children; results from the HEI program represent the primary source of information available to assess the benefits of this technique. Results from 164 children, 2 to 18 years of age, who had received a single-channel cochlear implant through the HEI investigator program were recently published in a comprehensive monograph.[11] Significant gains in sound discrimination/recognition[22] and speech production[23] were reported for 143 regular implant users, and the investigators have attributed these gains to the use of the cochlear implant. While these results are encouraging, the methods used to collect the data are open to question due to the lack of appropriate controls and other methodologic problems. In addition, the investigators failed to compare performance with cochlear implants to performance with tactile aids, which raises a question about the need for cochlear implants when a noninvasive and less expensive alternative is available.

Data questioning the benefits derived from cochlear implants in children have also been reported. Miyamoto et al[24] studied speech production and language changes in 15 children who had received single-channel cochlear implants. Contrary to the significant gains reported by the HEI referred to above, Miyamoto et al[24] failed to document significant gains in either speech production (vocal duration, intensity, and pitch) or language skills that could be attributed to the cochlear implant. While

growth was seen in language skills following implantation, the growth did not exceed that expected in profoundly deaf children reported in the literature.

Until conclusive data are made available documenting the advantages that can be gained from cochlear implants in children, this will continue to be a hotly debated issue. Well-designed studies comparing performance with cochlear implants and alternative devices (hearing aids and tactile aids) are needed before this issue will be resolved.

ASHA Recommendations

In 1984, The American Speech-Language-Hearing Association (ASHA) formed an ad hoc committee on cochlear implants, and the committee published its report in 1985.[6] This report presents a comprehensive review of cochlear implants, covering major issues dealing with their development and use, and presents a series of recommendations developed as a result of the data presented. Because of the insightful nature of these recommendations, they are presented in their entirety in Table 14-3. As indicated by these recommendations, the committee clearly favored adults as the primary recipients of cochlear implants, and strongly endorsed the use of hearing aids and tactile aids for at least several months prior to implanting children. The committee recommended that controlled studies be performed with small groups of children before large-scale implantation begins.

TACTILE AIDS

Acoustic signals that are presented at a sufficiently high-enough intensity can be perceived by the skin (through the tactile mode), rather than the ear (through the auditory mode), by profoundly deaf individuals. Nober[25,26] was among the first to caution clinicians that, at high intensities, acoustic signals presented by air and bone conduction can be felt rather than heard by the profoundly deaf individual. For air conduction stimuli, he demonstrated that low-frequency pure tone thresholds obtained from the ears and hands of 94 profoundly deaf subjects were almost identical once the intensity reached levels of 75 to 105 dB HL at 125 to 1000 Hz, respectively.[25] For bone conduction,

Table 14-3   Recommendations of the ASHA Ad Hoc Committee on Cochlear Implants*

1. Adults with minimal or no residual hearing are the primary candidates for a cochlear implant after it is clearly demonstrated that a hearing aid or tactile device will not be used successfully. This recommendation must include long-term training with hearing aids and tactile devices.

2. For the profoundly deaf child, the early fitting of hearing aids and/or tactile aids is essential. Early intervention with these devices represents less risk than the cochlear implant.

3. To assure adequate hearing testing, especially in children (to determine extent of residual hearing), audiometers should be used that enable testing up to 120 dB HL.

4. There is a need to develop standardized testing materials for profoundly hearing impaired persons to determine candidacy for the cochlear implant versus alternative devices.

5. It is important for children to have an adequate trial (several months) and training with available noninvasive devices prior to consideration of a cochlear implant.

6. In order to improve selection of cochlear implant patients, there should be continued investigation of tests, such as evoked potentials with electrical stimulation, as a means to assess the status of auditory nerve fibers and pathways.

7. At present, the risks of neural damage and degeneration associated with the intracochlear device (long-term effects) are not clearly known for the growing child. However, a sufficient number of children have now been implanted with the 3M/House device to allow appropriate evaluation of that implant. The committee recommends that further implants in children should be limited to extracochlear and multichannel intracochlear devices in controlled studies involving small groups of children before large-scale implantation begins again.

8. Pre- and postimplant counseling are essential to assure the selection of appropriate candidates and the effective use of the cochlear implant devices.

9. Research is necessary regarding the development of psychophysical measures that will improve the selection of patients and evaluation of device effectiveness.

10. There should be continued research regarding the development of speech processors.

11. Habilitation/rehabilitation training procedures need to be refined to make them valid, quantifiable, and cost effective.

12. Audiologists must be able to assure that a cochlear implant candidate cannot benefit more effectively from a hearing aid, even if worn in only one ear, than from a specific cochlear implant device.

*Used with permission from ASHA.[6]

the levels were between 25 and 55 dB HL. This finding helps to explain why the profoundly deaf individual obtains minimal benefit from conventional amplification; the high-intensity acoustic stimuli delivered through the hearing aid provide tactile, rather than acoustic, stimulation.

Providing tactile stimulation through hearing aids has adverse consequences. Whereas the individual with some residual hearing should be able to obtain spectral and temporal cues through the amplification provided by a hearing aid, the profoundly deaf individual who relies on tactile sensations will receive only rudimentary awareness and possibly temporal cues from the low frequencies delivered to the ear canal by the hearing aid.[27] Additional detail regarding this concept is provided in Figure 14-2. In this figure a comparison is made between the frequency sensitivity of the ear (see Chapter 1, Fig. 1-2) and the skin measured at the forearm and fingertips. Two impor-

tant points are made in this figure. The first is that the frequency response of the skin and tactile sensitivity vary with the body location. In this figure, the fingertip is shown to be more sensitive and has a greater frequency range than the forearm. It is known that the fingers and lips are among the most sensitive locations for tactile stimulation,[28] but (as will be discussed in a later section of this chapter) neither location is ideally suitable for tactile stimulation using a communication aid.

Figure 14-2 also points out that compared to the broadband frequency response of the ear, the skin is limited to only low frequencies. The frequency response of the ear is between 20 and 20,000 Hz, with the optimal frequency response between 300 and 3000 Hz. However, the skin is limited to frequencies of 10 to 500 Hz, with the optimal frequency response at 220 to 240 Hz. The reduced frequency response of the skin only to low-frequency stimulation is a major limiting factor when hearing

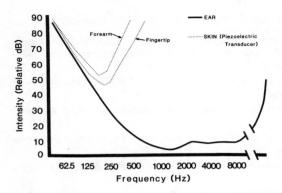

Figure 14-2. Frequency response of the skin measured at the forearm and fingertip compared to the normal frequency response of the human ear.

aid amplification is used, because hearing aids typically do not amplify frequencies below 400 to 500 Hz. This most likely is the primary reason why the majority of individuals with profound deafness obtain little benefit from hearing aid use, and as many as 23% of the profoundly deaf school-aged population choose not to wear hearing aids.[29] The goal of a tactile aid is to improve communication by changing acoustic signals into vibratory or electric signals and delivering them to the skin in the most efficient way possible, maximizing the physiologic capabilities of the skin.

Educators of profoundly hearing impaired students have for years been using tactile stimulation informally. For example, having a student touch the therapist's larynx during phonation is one approach used to teach voicing. A unique approach to teach musical rhythm is to have students hold large balloons between their hands in the presence of music presented through a phonograph or tape recorder at a

high intensity, allowing them to feel the low frequencies. Or, placing a loudspeaker on the chest of the student and playing music or speech will provide a form of tactile stimulation. Although these techniques have been used for quite some time they provide a limited, but still effective, form of tactile stimulation.

Unlike the recent formal efforts to develop cochlear implants, systematic work on tactile aids dates back more than 60 years.[30,31] Over this span of years, a number of devices with varying characteristics have been developed and evaluated. Kirman[32,33] and Sherrick[28] both provide excellent historic reviews of this early work and major issues that are in this area.

At present, there are five major tactile aids commercially available in the United States. Table 14-4 lists each of the devices, provides information on their operating characteristics, and gives their approximate costs. This table shows that there are a number of simple and complex instruments now commercially available. Issues concerning tactile aids have centered around the type of stimulation, location of stimulation, and single versus multiple channels.

Type of Stimulation

As shown in Table 14-4, tactile aids can use two types of stimulation: (1) *vibrotactile*, in which acoustic signals are presented as vibrations to the skin using mechanical transducers; and (2) *electrotactile* (or electrocutaneous), in which acoustic signals are presented to the skin as electric currents. The use of the vibrotactile approach has been preferred over the electrotactile approach due to the availability of vibrators for experimental use, and also the inherent difficulties experienced with apply-

Table 14-4   Commercially Available Wearable Tactile Aids*

Name	Company	Type of Stimulation	Channels	Approximate List Price ($)
Tactaid I	Audiological Engineering	Vibrotactile	1	435
Tactaid II	Audiological Engineering	Vibrotactile	2	825
KS 3/2	Telex	Vibrotactile	2 or 3	1600
Mini-Fonator	Siemens	Vibrotactile	1	895
Tacticon	Tacticon Corp.	Electrotactile	16	3300

*United States manufacturers only.

ing an electric current to the skin. Many early investigators used standard audiometric bone conduction vibrators, causing serious drawbacks due to their poor frequency response characteristics and their high power requirements. Recently, specially constructed vibrators have been developed to match the impedance characteristics of the skin.[34] This development is the most significant factor that has allowed efficient, wearable vibrotactile aids to be introduced within the past two to three years.

The majority of the work on electrotactile stimulation has been done by Saunders et al.[35–38] The original version of his instrument was a two-channel device providing stimulation to the forehead. Later versions of the instrument contained 20, and then 32 electrodes applied to the abdomen using a linear display; the 32-electrode device was the prototype of the Tacticon (see Table 14-4). A concern when using electrical stimulation is the adverse effect of using electric currents on the skin over an extended period. After using electrotactile stimulation over extended periods, Saunders et al[37] report that the electric sensations produced by the aid can be tolerated with no side effects, and that the intensity level was unaffected by perspiration and other changes in skin resistance.

In addition to the work of Saunders et al,[37] other investigators have experimented with electrotactile stimulation. Sparks et al[39] developed the Multipoint Electrotactile Speech Aid (MESA)—a highly complex experimental electrotactile device with 288 electrodes in a 36 × 8 array presented to the abdomen. In one study with MESA, it was found that electrotactile stimulation enabled receivers to achieve excellent recognition of vowels in consonant vowel consonant (CVC) context and the consonantal features of voicing and nasality.[40] Findings obtained from another study with three subjects revealed that after initial training, performance with MESA improved lip-reading performance of connected discourse significantly. In addition, Sparks et al[39] reported no problems with painful stimuli or untoward side effects.

Most recently, Grant et al[41] used an electrotactile aid with 10 electrodes arranged in a linear array along the forearm with one profoundly deaf subject and one normal-hearing subject whose hearing was masked during testing. Speechreading performance was examined for both sentence and connected discourse materials in aided condition, and was compared to an unaided condition. For both types of materials, there was significant improvement for both subjects with the aid compared to performance without the aid. Patterns of intonation, stress, and phrase structure, which are not easily speechread, were readily available with the aid. Overall, studies using electrotactile stimulation support its use as a means to supply tactile stimulation.

Comparison of vibrotactile and electrotactile devices suggest that vibrotactile devices may be more efficient for the lower frequencies and electrotactile devices for higher frequencies.[42] Although each type of stimulation has advantages and disadvantages, comparative longitudinal clinical research is needed to determine which will be the most efficient form of stimulation. A combined approach might also be tried. DeFilippo[43] compared the performance of a single-channel vibrotactile aid with that of a combined vibrotactile and electrotactile aid on the hand, and found that the combined system produced superior scores. This isolated report should encourage further comparative investigations.

Location of Stimulation

Unlike cochlear implants, which are designed to stimulate only structures within the cochlea, a decision has to be made with tactile stimulation as to where on the body to provide stimulation. The majority of studies have used parts of the hands, arms, abdomen, jaw, thorax, forehead, or thighs as locations of stimulation. As a sensor for vibrations, the fingers of the hand have structural and functional characteristics indicating they are among the more sensitive body parts.

Only a limited number of comparative studies with tactile aids using different body parts in clinical trials are available. Early studies failed to show an apparent advantage of one body location over the other. For example, Englemann and Rosov[44] trained their subjects using the forearms and fingertips. When the transducers were relocated to the thighs of their subjects, transfer was reported to be immediate. Also, Yeni-Komshian and Goldstein[45] transferred tactile patterns from the right hand to the left, and from the fingers to the palm of the same hand and found no performance differences. Findings from these studies support the interpretation that tactile performance is a function of pattern recognition, more than increased sensitivity of a particular body part or neurologic adaptation.

Geldard and Sherrick[46] reported data indicating that the fingertips of the hand are superior for recognizing vibratory patterns compared to the arm, thigh, and thorax. Additional data supporting the superiority of the fingertips for tactile recognition comes from Spens.[47] He used a variety of different tactile arrays on seven different body locations of one subject (himself); the task was number identification. Results from this study are shown in Figure 14-3. As displayed in this figure, performance ranged from a low of 46% for a single vibrator placed on the wrist, to a high of 77% for a 6 × 16 vibrator array placed on the index finger. From these results, as well as those of Geldard and Sherrick,[46] it is clear that for maximum discrimination, consideration should be given to including the fingertips in tactile stimulation. One problem with using the fingertips is their accessibility; using them for tactile stimulation would affect manual dexterity and, perhaps, be a serious drawback.

Sherrick[28] suggests an intriguing clinical approach in which due to their increased sensitivity, the fingers and hands are used initially to learn tactile patterns. Once learned, these vibratory patterns are transferred to a less conspicuous part of the body, such as the abdomen. This *double-barreled* approach would use the hands for fine discrimination by grasping a tactile display, and a second body part (the abdomen or thigh) for constant monitoring and alerting. This type of system would take advantage of the important characteristics of the tactile signal—the superiority of the fingers and hands in sensing finer discriminations while providing for constant monitoring of the sound environment, as well as allowing the hands to be free for manipulations. Research is needed to explore this type of tactile system.

Another intriguing clinical approach would be to stimulate the skin close to the ear; perhaps the pinna or outer ear canal itself. This may have the psychological advantage of associating tactile stimulation with hearing sensation. After all, sound reception is not associated with the hands, abdomen, or other body parts, especially by the adult with acquired deafness. In fact, one of the clinical observations made by those fitting tactile aids is the comment that even though there may be clear

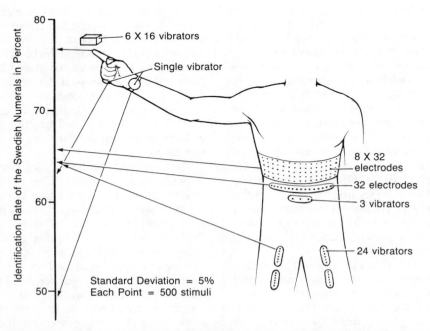

Figure 14-3.   Identification rate of Swedish numbers as a function of the stimulating place, the stimulating method, and the number of stimulators. (From data presented by Spens.[47])

sound awareness, it is not associated with *hearing*. No direct data are available on the tactile sensitivity of the skin on the ear,[28] but indirect evidence from Nober[26] suggest that the vibrotactile thresholds of the pinna and ear canal are within 5 dB of those for the hand. These data would indicate that the ear may be an excellent location for stimulation.

While the data are beginning to favor the fingertips as the ideal location for tactile stimulation, commercial devices are not yet available to use the apparent superiority of this location. The clinician choosing to use tactile stimulation must explore various body locations (abdomen, sternum, forearm, thighs) in choosing which location is best for a given patient. One clinical method to select location of stimulation is to obtain sound field awareness thresholds for warbled pure tones and speech in making the initial placement decision. The location on which the best thresholds are obtained is used for the initial stimulation site. After using this location for several days, alternate sites are selected for comparison until a preferred site is found. In some cases, there does not appear to be a clear superiority of one body location over another.

Single Versus Multichannel Tactile Aids

Simple one-channel to extremely complex multichannel devices with up to 288 different points of stimulation have been developed and tested under different conditions.[33] With single-channel devices, the available information is limited to simple awareness of environmental sounds and temporal cues (stress patterns and prosody). For speech, the single-channel device is severely limited, and is capable of displaying only rudimentary fundamental frequency (Fo) information. However, single-channel devices, as limited as they are, have proven to be beneficial in supplementing speechreading.[48]

Multichannel aids can present tactile information using a one-dimensional (linear) or two-dimensional display. A one-dimensional display is like a piano keyboard with low frequencies at one end and high frequencies at the other. In this type of display, spectral cues are presented in a manner similar to that in the cochlea. Frequency is coded by place of stimulation, as on the piano keyboard, and intensity is coded by vibratory amplitude. For example,

if the abdomen is being used as the location of stimulation, low frequencies might be presented on the right, midfrequencies in the center, and high frequencies on the left.

Two-dimensional arrays code frequency along one spatial axis and intensity along another. An analogy of a two-dimensional array is a pure tone audiogram, where frequency is on the horizontal axis and intensity on the vertical axis. If this analogy was applied to a tactile array on the abdomen, then frequency would be coded along the belt line and intensity from the waist to the sternum. It is theorized that the two-dimensional array would make it possible for the skin to extract both frequency and intensity cues from the complex speech signal in a more efficient manner than a one-dimensional array.

Although both one- and two-dimensional arrays have been developed and evaluated, optimum values for basic considerations are yet to be established. Before conclusive clinical decisions can be made regarding the efficacy of each system, optimum values of critical variables—including display size, number of channels, and coding strategies—must be made. Currently, there are no direct comparisons available using one- and two-dimensional displays, so it is not known which of these is actually superior.[28] With the advent of wearable tactile aids, it is now possible to field test performance with single-channel and multichannel tactile aids, and it is expected that data on this type of comparison will be forthcoming in the near future.

COMPARISON OF COCHLEAR IMPLANTS AND TACTILE AIDS

The goals of cochlear implants and tactile aids are essentially the same: (*1*) to provide wearers with increased auditory contact with their environment, including awareness of their own voice; (*2*) improve their ability to speechread; and (*3*) ultimately to provide the ability to discriminate connected discourse. Based on these common goals, one would assume that there are numerous studies comparing performance between the two systems. Unfortunately, this is not the case. It is quite apparent that those working with cochlear implants do not feel obligated to undertake comparative studies, and those working with tactile aids do not have populations of implant subjects available for study. In this section, a comparison of cochlear implants and tactile aids is made. Included is a review of a small number of comparative studies that have been reported.

Functional Differences

One way to evaluate functional differences between the available systems is to look at their primary differences compared with those of conventional hearing aids. This comparison is made in Table 14-5. In this table, hearing aids, cochlear implants, and tactile aids are compared by seven performance factors. The information in this table should be quite clear, but some elaboration may be helpful. Hearing aids are recommended for daily use. Audiologists encourage parents of hearing impaired children and classroom teachers to monitor hearing aid use to ensure maximum wearing time. Daily usage of cochlear implants is also encouraged, although no hard data are available to support this philosophy. However, with tactile aids, the question of daily usage pattern remains. There is no question that tactile aids (as well as the other systems) provide maximal benefit in face-to-face conversation, where the signal-to-noise (S/N) ratio (see Chapter 11) is favorable and the use of visual cues is maximized. Tactile aids can also provide alerting signals to inform the wearer of the presence of warning or functional acoustic signals. However, whether the wearable tactile systems available provide tactile information in a sophisticated enough manner to be useful in a

normal, everyday environment has not been demonstrated.

Some preliminary evidence exists to indicate that tactile aids are of limited use in situations other than face-to-face interactions. Friel-Patti and Roeser[49] documented highly significant improvements in the communication skills of four profoundly deaf children who were fit with a three-channel vibrotactile aid and placed in individual, triweekly language intervention sessions. As part of the study, the four children were also monitored in the classroom, and careful monitoring of their behavior in this environment failed to show significant carryover into general classroom activities.[50] Most likely, the lack of carryover was a result of hardware limitations, because the noise rejection system in the aid used in the study was highly limited. Many of the currently available aids have refined noise rejection systems, which might expand their use to a variety of listening situations.

Information on trial period, initial costs, risks, safety, and long-term sequela has been presented elsewhere in this chapter and needs no further expansion. The issue of effectiveness is of major importance. With conventional amplification, effectiveness depends on the type of loss and the amount of residual hearing. Patients with conductive loss receive maximum benefit from hearing aid usage. In fact, for most patients with conductive loss, their threshold sensitivity can be brought within the range of normal limits, and they will have normal discrimination ability. With sensorineural hearing loss, the major factors determining effectiveness are the degree and configuration of the loss. Those with mild or mild-to-mode-

Table 14-5   Primary Differences Between Hearing Aids, Cochlear Implants, and Tactile Aids

Factor	Hearing Aid(s)	Cochlear Implants	Tactile Aids
Daily usage	Yes	Probably	?
Trial period	Yes	No	Yes
Initial cost	$550–1200	$10,000–20,000	$450–3000
Risk	None	Yes	None
Safety	Safe	?	Safe
Long-term sequela	Minimal	?	None
Effectiveness	Depends on type of loss and amount of residual hearing	Depends on residual neural population and coding/processing technique	Depends on skin's ability to process sound and processing technique

rate losses generally obtain more benefit than those in the severe range.

It is only speculative that both the number of residual neural populations in the cochlea and VIII nerve and the coding techniques used by the implant system to process the electric signal are the primary factors determining effectiveness of cochlear implants. Exactly why some patients are able to function at extremely high levels of accuracy, even to the point of communicating over the telephone, remains a mystery. Could this behavior be accounted for by their ability to synthesize the limited information delivered through the system? Or is the system delivering a superior signal for these patients? This question cannot be readily resolved, because there are currently no noninvasive techniques to determine the number or integrity of neural populations in the cochlea.

With tactile aids, as discussed previously, the skin's limited ability to process sound is a major limiting factor. Whereas the ear has: (1) a dynamic range of 130 dB, the tactile system has a range of only 30 to 35 dB; and (2) a frequency response between 20 and 20,000 Hz, with an optimal frequency range from 300 to 3000 Hz. The tactile system has a frequency range of only 10 to 400 or 500 Hz, with an optimal range at 220 to 240 Hz.[51] These limitations inflict serious restrictions on the ability of the skin to process sound, and dictate the maximum benefits and use that can be expected. An ideal tactile aid would best stand alone as a substitute for the ear. However, with the limitations of the skin as a receptor of sound, it is quite probable that the tactile mode may not, in fact, be able to substitute for the ear. Sherrick[28] recently addressed this issue. He argues that since speech is a special code that only the auditory system can process, and since the skin is limited in its ability to process sound, it is probable that tactile aids will not function as a substitute for hearing, but rather as a supplement to communication by facilitating speechreading. Support for this philosophy is available, since only modest gains have been realized by even the most complex tactile systems available.

Despite the limitations of the tactile system outlined above, there are those who maintain that it will be possible to communicate successfully with a tactile aid if the system is designed to maximize the processing features of the skin, thus representing speech in a well-organized manner. Those holding this philoso-phy contend that only minimal gains have been made with tactile aids up to this point due to factors including limited training time, inappropriate training strategies, and inadequate hardware. They feel that if proper instruments were developed and used appropriately, it will be possible to replace the auditory system with the tactile system. Both longitudinal studies with instrumentation having flexible coding strategies and the ability to handle complex sound processing will resolve this question.

Sound Awareness/Detection

Sound awareness is the ability to detect the presence of auditory stimuli in the environment. Detection of sound is important in providing alerting signals, and must be present if discriminations are to be made. However, simple detection of sound does not imply that the acoustic signals detected can be discriminated. Regardless, sound awareness is an important behavioral measure, and it is based on highly objective information in a cooperative patient. How do sound awareness thresholds compare for cochlear implants and tactile aids?

Table 14-6 shows published data comparing awareness thresholds for the two systems when the instruments were set at their typical volume settings. The data for cochlear implants were taken from a summary of findings from a large number of children,[22] and the data for tactile aids were from four children fit with a three-channel vibrotactile aid.[49] As indicated by this comparison, awareness thresholds from the two devices are similar, being within 0 to 4 dB for the frequencies 500 to 4000 Hz. Speech awareness thresholds were slightly better for the tactile aid than the cochlear implant: 47 dB compared to 55 dB, respectively. Overall, these data indicate essentially the same performance is possible when using tactile aids compared to cochlear implants when sound awareness is measured.

Comparable findings for sound awareness with cochlear implants and tactile aids are not surprising, since the amplitude of the stimulating signal—whether it is an electric signal delivered to the cochlea or tactile signal delivered to the skin—is determined by the volume setting of the amplifier. The higher the volume setting, the greater the gain of the amplifier, the more sensitive the system, and the lower the

Table 14-6   Comparison of Mean Aided Awareness Thresholds for Cochlear Implants and Tactile Aids (dB SPL)*

	Warbled Pure Tones(Hz)						Speech Awareness Thresholds
	250	500	1000	2000	3000	4000	
Cochlear implants at 24 mo[†]	59	56	57	57	59	64	55
Tactile aid[‡]	68	58	60	61	59	63	47

*Data were obtained at user-level volume settings.
[†]From Thielemeir et al.[22]
[‡]Thresholds converted from HL to SPL. From Friel-Patti and Roeser.[49]

intensity at which the wearer will respond. In fact, it would be quite possible to increase the volume setting of either a cochlear implant or a tactile aid, and to significantly reduce the levels at which the patient will be aware of sound. However, the negative effect of increasing the sensitivity of an amplifier is that there will be increasing difficulty with background noise as the sensitivity is increased; that is, the background sounds will increasingly disrupt the processing of the primary signal as the sensitivity is increased. The application of microprocessing techniques, such as automatic noise suppression circuits, should significantly improve sound detection thresholds for both cochlear implants and tactile aids without the effects of background noise.

Research Studies

Pickett and McFarland[52] present a thorough review of the literature and address several issues on cochlear implants and tactile aids. In this paper, a cross-comparative analysis of data from numerous studies is made. Data from studies using speech tracking, consonant identification, phonetically balanced (PB) monosyllabic word recognition, and recognition of CID Everyday Sounds were compared on performance with cochlear implants and tactile aids. A conclusion made by this comparison was that, conservatively, the data showed that performance with the cochlear implant is not much better than tactile aids. This comparison also revealed that a relatively small amount of coded information available through tactile stimulation may provide as much benefit as a complex multichannel implant system. Pickett and McFarland[52] warn that their cross-comparative technique has inherent problems. However, the fact that this comparison did not

overwhelmingly support the superiority of cochlear implant use gives significant support for the use of tactile aids as a viable alternative.

Additional data are also presented by Geers and Moog[53] and Miyamoto et al.[54] Geers and Moog[53] observed performance in two large samples of profoundly deaf children with hearing aids, 10 children with single-channel vibrotactile aids, and two children with single-channel cochlear implants. Included in their analysis was a comparison of their findings to results reported by the HEI for 54 implanted children. Performance was compared on a number of audiologic tests, and measures of speech production and language development were obtained. Children were placed in one of four categories based on their test performance: category 1, *no pattern perception*; category 2, *pattern perception*; category 3, *some word recognition*; and category 4, *consistent word recognition*. Their results indicated that single-channel devices provide only pattern information (category 2) not spectral information. For children in category 2 who had learned to categorize words according to stress pattern, and had learned to monitor their vocalizations through hearing aids, the single-channel devices appeared to provide little advantage. Based on their findings, Geers and Moog[53] concluded that, in most cases, single-channel vibrotactile aids and single-channel cochlear implants provide similar information with no apparent advantage to either device. These authors encourage the development of multichannel tactile aids and cochlear implants.

Miyamoto et al[54] have incorporated vibrotactile aids into their cochlear implant program, allowing their patients to experience tactile stimulation prior to receiving the implant. They report this experience to be highly favorable. Through this approach, basic stress differentiation and temporal concepts can be taught, and the ability of the subject to incorporate these cues into speech identification can be assessed. Since the procedure can be incorporated into the initial phases of cochlear implant rehabilitation, they can be demonstrated prior to surgery and greatly enhance the probability of success. As part of their report, Miyamoto et al[54] presented vibrotactile data from one adult and one child and compared them to scores using cochlear implants. From these limited data, it was concluded that the tactile aid provided notable benefit on most of the suprasegmental tasks and some of the segmental tasks, with little difference in performance observed between the two types of stimulation.

One additional factor is patient acceptance. Is there a preference of one type of device over the other? No formal efforts have been made to address this question, although anecdotal reports are available. In the studies we have conducted, we allowed two patients who had been fit with cochlear implants to use wearable tactile aids.[55] When given the option of using either of the instruments, both subjects indicated preference for the cochlear implant, mainly because they associated stimulation from the instrument with *hearing*, whereas the tactile aid was not. It is difficult to factor out patient preference in subjects who already have received cochlear implants due to the *aura* and expectations surrounding the procedure. However, the concept of hearing restoration appears to be favored over replacement of hearing with tactile sensations.

It is possible to predict expected performance from cochlear implants and tactile aids on a number of different tasks by retrospective analysis of available research studies. Table 14-7 compares expected performance between the two devices on seven different auditory functions. As shown by this comparison, for six of the auditory functions there does not appear to be a difference between the two devices in expected performance. One factor that does appear to be different between the two systems is the ability to discriminate between environmental sounds. For environmental sounds, it appears that cochlear implant stimulation provides superior input than for a tactile aid, at least as they are presently configured. However, through this type of comparison it is again surprising that only minor expected differences exist in performance when comparing the two devices.

Table 14-7   Comparison of Cochlear Implant and Tactile Aid Expected Performance*

Task	Cochlear Implant	Tactile Aid
Discriminate loud and soft sounds	Yes	Yes
Discriminate continuous and interrupted sounds	Yes	Yes
Discriminate long and short sounds	Yes	Yes
Differentiate no. of sounds	Yes	Yes
Differentiate no. of syllables in words	Yes	Yes
Differentiate no. of syllables in sentences	Yes	Yes
Differentiate different types of sounds in the environment; e.g., door knock vs. speech	Yes	No

Sources: Thielemeir et al[22]; Geers et al[60]; Proctor and Goldstein[61]; Goldstein and Proctor[20]; and Geers and Moog.[53]
*Courtesy of A. Proctor.

The data available fail to show major performance differences between cochlear implants and tactile aids. Clearly, the need for comprehensive intrasubject comparisons of performance with cochlear implants and tactile aids is shown by this review. An important overriding conclusion from the data available is that tactile aids appear to provide as much benefit as cochlear implants in their present configuration. Or, when the costs/risks/benefits are considered, there appears to be questionable justification for cochlear implants when wearable tactile aids are available.

THERAPY

Comprehensive training is required for implant team members who are responsible for providing rehabilitation (*basic guidance*) of the cochlear implant patient. However, for audiologists, speech-language pathologists, or teachers who are not part of the implant team and are faced with a patient having an implant, there may be some questions about the ways in which therapy techniques may be useful. Or, for those working with tactile aids, a similar question may be raised. Basically, since the two instruments provide similar results, the therapeutic strategies can be interchanged.

Eisenberg[56,57] has developed a comprehensive therapy program (*basic guidance*) for use with patients receiving cochlear implants at The House Ear Institute (256 Lake Street, Los Angeles, CA 90057). Clinicians could apply these techniques to any of the other available implants or to therapy with tactile aids. Generally, as with most auditory training programs (see Chapter 15), the training progresses in a hierarchy from simple to complex as follows:

(*1*) Presence or absence of sound.
(*2*) Onset or cessation of sound.
(*3*) One versus two sounds.
(*4*) Long versus short sounds.
(*5*) Fast versus slow sounds.
(*6*) Continuous versus interrupted sounds.
(*7*) Gross word discrimination.
(*8*) Voiced versus voiceless phonemes.
(*9*) Telephone training.
(*10*) Recognition of environmental sounds.
(*11*) Speech-tracking.

Clinicians can use a number of techniques from auditory training manuals, or devise their own to work on each of these areas.

Telephone training is unique to implants and tactile aids, and involves teaching wearers to use coded signals to make emergency and simple informational communications over the telephone with the assistance of their implants or tactile aids. Training begins by having the patient practice listening (or feeling with a tactile aid) for a dial tone. After its presence is established, the phone number is dialed and the patient listens/feels for the ring or, if the phone is in use, the busy signal. Practice is given with the three signals (dial tone, ring, and busy signal) until the patient can differentiate them. A code can be set up with family and close friends using one through four syllable phrases. For example:

No .... One syllable
Yes, Yes .... Two syllable
Please, repeat .... Three syllables
I don't know that .... Four syllables

In this way, the hearing impaired implant/aid user could ask a series of questions and have them answered using this code. This type of communication is limited to family members

and close friends for prelingually deaf implant/aid users, since their speech is often difficult or impossible to understand by others. For the postlingually deafened adult with good speech, telephone code could be used in a variety of situations by beginning the conversation with instructions to the listener that the caller is deaf, by using an implant/aid, and by giving instructions on how to use the code. In emergency situations the ability to use telephone code may be vitally important.

Speech tracking is a procedure that was first described by DeFilippo and Scott[58] as an objective measure of speechreading. Subsequent to their introduction, the technique has been used to train and measure speechreading performance by a number of clinicians and investigators. In the procedure, a talker—reading from a text, a novel, or short story—presents short segments to a receiver who then attempts to repeat the text back verbatim. Performance is measured by the number of correct words per minute that the hearing impaired speechreader is able to repeat back; that is, tracking is performed over 10-minute intervals, and the measure of performance is the mean number of words correctly repeated by the subject per minute. As a guide, normal-hearing subjects average about 100 to 120 words per minute when this type of sender receiver/exchange is used.

Robbins et al[59] point out a number of limitations with speech-tracking. Included are: (*1*) possible bias of the sender; (*2*) lack of standardization; (*3*) the receiver must have a basic knowledge of the English language (which limits its application to postlingually deafened subjects); and (*4*) learning. Despite these limitations, Robbins et al conclude that speech-tracking is an excellent strategy for teaching speechreading. Its use is especially applicable for patients with implants and tactile aids. The clinician must realize that tracking is a time-consuming technique, requiring about 40 minutes to complete three 10-minute sessions, which is about all that the average patient will be capable of completing because of the concentration required. A good therapy strategy is to have implant/aid users track with their spouses or others who they regularly communicate with, and keep a record of their performance. This way, the patient can work on speechreading skills outside of the therapy sessions, and others can become involved in the therapy process.

SUMMARY

This chapter reviews the techniques that are available for the profoundly deaf individual. Hearing aids, tactile aids, and cochlear implants can be provided so that even the most severely hearing impaired students can be aided and can achieve their maximum educational potential. Since cochlear implants pose risks that are not presented with hearing aids or tactile aids, and their potential benefits in children do not appear to be firmly documented in the literature, their use should continue to be experimental.

ACKNOWLEDGMENTS

Portions of this work were supported by NIH Grant No. 1, R01 NS 15982-01A1.

REFERENCES

1. Sonnenschein MA: Cochlear Implant Update. *SHHH J*, 7 (1986), 16–19.
2. Wallace MA: Clarification of the relationship between medicare and the cochlear implant. *SHHH J*, 8 (1987), 7.
3. Windmill IM, Martinez SA, Nolph MB, Eisenbenger BA: The downside of cochlear implants. *Hearing J*, 40 (1987), 18–21.
4. Owens E, Telleen DD: Speech perception with hearing aids and cochlear implants. *Arch Otolaryngol*, 107 (1981), 160–163.
5. Northern J, Black FO, Brimacombe JA, et al: Selection of children for cochlear implantation. *Semin Hearing*, 7 (1986), 341–446.
6. ASHA Ad Hoc Committee on Cochlear Implants. *ASHA*, 28 (1985), 29–52.
7. Carhart R: Sensorineural hearing loss: An overview, in Merzenich MM, Schindler RA, Sooy FA, eds: *Proceedings of the First International Conference on Electrical Stimulation of the Acoustical Nerve as a Treatment for Profound Sensorineural Deafness in Man* (San Francisco: University of California, 1974).
8. Ries PW: *Hearing Abilities of Persons by Sociodemographic and Health Characteristics: United States* Series 10. No. 140 (Washington, DC: National Center for Statistics, 1982).
9. Downs MP: Implanting electrodes? *ASHA*, 23 (1981), 567–568.
10. Burian K, Eisenwort B, Brauneis K: Comparative investigations of auditory perception on selected patients stimulated with extra- or endoco-

11. Berliner KI, Eisenberg LS, House WF: Preface: Cochlear implant an auditory prosthesis for the profoundly deaf child. *Ear and Hearing*, 6 (1985), 4S–5S.
12. Mecklenburg DJ, ed: Cochlear implants in children. *Semin Hearing*, 7 (1986), 341–440.
13. Tyler RS, Davis JM, Lansing CR: Cochlear implants in young children. *ASHA*, 29 (1987), 41–49.
14. Sutton D: Cochlear pathology: Hazards of long-term implants. *Arch Otolaryngol*, 110 (1984), 164–166.
15. House WF, Luxford WF, Courtney B: Otitis media in children following the cochlear implant. *Ear and Hearing*, 6 (1985), 24S–27S.
16. O'Donoghue GM, Jackler RA, Jenkins WM, Schlinder RA: The problem of head growth. *Otolaryngol—Head and Neck Sur*, 94 (1986), 78–81.
17. Luxford WM, House WF: Cochlear implants in children: Medical and surgical considerations. *Ear and Hearing*, 6 (1985), 20S–24S.
18. Hochmair-Desoyer IJ, Hochmair ES, Burian K, Stiglbruner HK: Percepts from the Vienna cochlear prothesis. *Ann NY Acad Sci*, 403 (1983), 295–306.
19. Gantz BJ, Tyler RS: Cochlear implant comparisons. *Amer J Otolaryngol* (1985), 92–98.
20. Goldstein MH, Proctor A: Tactile aids for profoundly deaf children. *J Acoustic Soc Amer*, 77 (1985), 258–265.
21. Berliner KS, Eisenberg LS: Methods and issues in the cochlear implantation of children: An overview. *Ear and Hearing*, 6 (1985), 6S–13S.
22. Thielemeir MA, Tonokawa LL, Peterson B, Eisenberg LS: Audiological results in children with a cochlear implant. *Ear and Hearing*, 6 (1985), 27S–35S.
23. Kirk IK, Hill-Brown C: Speech and language results in children with cochlear implant. *Ear and Hearing*, 6 (1985), 36S–47S.
24. Miyamoto RT, Myres WA, Pope ML, Carotta CC: Cochlear implants for deaf children. *Laryngoscope*, 96 (1986), 990–996.
25. Nober EH: Pseudoauditory bone conduction thresholds. *J Speech Hear Res*, 29 (1964), 469–476.
26. Nober EH: Vibrotactile sensitivity of deaf children to high intensity sound. *Laryngoscope*, (1967), 2128–2146.
27. Sweetow RW: Amplification and the development of listening skills in deaf children. *Audiol, An Audio J Cont Educ*, 4 (1979).
28. Sherrick CE: Basic and applied research on tactile aids for deaf people: Progress and prospects. *J Acoust Soc Amer*, 75 (1984), 1325–1342.
29. Karchmer MA, Kirwin L: *The Use of Hearing Aids by Hearing Impaired Students in the United States*. Series No. 2, (Washington, DC: Office of Demographic Studies, 1977).

30. Gault RH: Progress in experiments on tactual interpretation of oral speech. *Social Psychology*, 14 (1924), 155–159.

31. Gault RH: Touch as a substitute for hearing in the interpretation and control of speech. *Arch Otolaryngol*, 3 (1926), 121–135.

32. Kirman JH: Tactile communication of speech. A review and analysis. *Psychol Bull*, 80 (1973), 54–74.

33. Kirman JH: Current developments in tactile communication of speech, in Schiff E, Foulke E, eds: *Tactual Perception: A Sourcebook* (Cambridge, UK: Cambridge University Press, 1982), pp 234–262.

34. Franklin D: Tactile Aids: New help for the profoundly deaf. *Hearing J*, 37 (1984), 20–24.

35. Saunders FA, Collins CC: Electrotactile stimulation of the sense of touch. *J Biomedic Syst*, 2 (1971), 27–37.

36. Saunders FA: An electrotactile sound detector for the deaf. *IEEE Trans Audio Elect*, 21 (1973), 285–387.

37. Saunders FA, Hill WA, Easley TA: Development of a PLATO-based curriculum for tactile speech recognition. *J Educ Technol Syst*, (1978–1979), 19–28.

38. Saunders FA, Hill WA, Franklin B: A wearable tactile sensory aid for profoundly deaf children. *J Medial Syst*, 5 (1981), 265–270.

39. Sparks DW, Kuhl P, Edmonds AE, Gray GP: Investigating the MESA (Multipoint Electrotactile Speech Aid): The transmission of segmental features of speech. *J Acoust Soc Amer*, 63 (1978), 246–257.

40. Sparks DW, Ardell LA, Bourgeois M, et al: Investigating the MESA (Multipoint Electrotactile Speech Aid): The transmission of connected discourse. *J Acoust Soc Amer*, 65 (1979), 810–815.

41. Grant KW, Ardell LH, Kuhl PK, Sparks DW: The transmission of prosodic information via an electrotactile speechreading aid. *Ear and Hearing*, 7 (1986), 328–335.

42. Sachs RM, Miller JD, Grant KW: Perceived magnitude of multiple electrocutaneous pulses. *Percept Psychophysics*, 28 (1980), 255–262.

43. DeFilippo CL: Laboratory projects in tactile aids to lipreading. *Ear and Hearing*, 5 (1984), 211–227.

44. Englemann S, Rosov R: Tactual hearing experiments with deaf and hearing subjects. *Exceptional Children*, 41 (1975), 243–253.

45. Yeni-Komshian GH, Goldstein MH: Identification of speech sounds displayed on a vibrotactile vocoder. *J Acoust Soc Amer*, 62 (1977), 194–198.

46. Geldard FH, Sherrick CE: The cutaneous saltatory area and its presumed neural basis. *Percept Psychophysics* 33 (1983), 299–304.

47. Spens KE: *Experiences of a Tactile "Hearing" Aid*. Paper presented at the International Congress on the Education of the Deaf (Tokyo, Japan, 1985).

48. Reed CM, Durlach NI, Braida LD: Research on tactile communication of speech: A review. *ASHA*, 20 (1982).

49. Friel-Patti S, Roeser RJ: Evaluating changes in the communication skills of deaf children using vibrotactile stimulation. *Ear and Hearing*, 4 (1984), 31–40.

50. Roeser RJ, Friel-Patti S, Scott B, et al: *Evaluating a Vibrotactile Aid With Profoundly Deaf Subjects*. A miniseminar presented at the Annual Meeting of The American Speech-Language Hearing Association (Cincinnati, OH, 1983).

51. Roeser RJ: Tactile aids for the profoundly deaf. *Semin Hearing*, 6 (1985), 279–298.

52. Pickett JM, McFarland W: Auditory implants and tactile aids for the profoundly deaf. *J Speech Hear Res*, 28 (1985), 134–150.

53. Geers AE, Moog JS: *Long-term Benefits From Single-Channel Cochlear Implants*. A paper presented at the Annual Meeting of The American Speech-Language-Hearing Association (Detroit, MI, 1986).

54. Miyamoto RT, Myres WA, Punch JL: Tactile aids in the evaluation procedure for cochlear implant candidacy. *Hear Inst*, 38 (1987), 33–37.

55. Cummins CC, Roeser RJ: *Tactile aids: A case report*. A paper presented at the annual meeting of the Texas Speech-Language-Hearing Association (Ft. Worth, TX, 1987).

56. Eisenberg LS: *Basic Guidance for Children with the Cochlear Implant*, rev. ed (Los Angeles: House Ear Institute, 1983).

57. Eisenberg LS: *Introduction to Sound: A Therapy Program Developed for the Prelingually Deaf Adult Using a Cochlear Implant*. (Los Angeles: House Ear Institute, 1980).

58. DeFilippo CL, Scott BL: A method for training and evaluating the reception of ongoing speech. *J Acoust Soc Amer*, 63 (1978), 1186–1192.

59. Robbins AM, Osberger MJ, Miyamoto RT, et al: Speech-tracking performance in single-channel cochlear implant subjects. *J Speech Hear Res*, 28 (1985), 565–578.

60. Geers A, Miller J, Gustus C: *Vibrotactile Stimulation—Case Study with a Profoundly Deaf Child*. Paper presented at The Annual Meeting of The American Speech-Language-Hearing Association (Cincinnati, OH, 1983).

61. Proctor A, Goldstein MH: Development of lexical comprehension in a profoundly deaf child using a wearable, vibrotactile communication aid. *Lang, Speech, Hear Serv Schools*, 14 (1983), 138–149.

62. Karchmer MA: A demographic perspective, in Cherow E, ed: *Hearing Impaired Children and Youth with Developmental Disabilities*. (Washington, DC: Gallaudet College Press, 1985).

TECHNIQUES AND CONCEPTS IN AUDITORY TRAINING AND SPEECHREADING

15

Ethel F. Mussen

DEFINITION OF TERMS

The terms *auditory training, aural habilitation*, and *aural rehabilitation* are often used synonymously. This chapter is addressed to auditory training and speechreading as part of the habilitation/rehabilitation process.

Aural Rehabilitation. This encompasses all instruction required to *restore* skills in communicating effectively for either a child or adult who once had normal hearing during the period of language development; that is, a *postlingual* hearing loss.

Aural Habilitation. This is applied to the same procedures used with the child who has not known completely normal hearing. The hearing loss may be congenital or acquired early in life; that is, *prelingual*, and it is sufficient to interfere with the normal acquisition of language.

Auditory Training. This is specific instruction in listening awareness and perception of the characteristics of speech and environmental sounds. As the oldest term, it is often used generically instead of the other two.

Speechreading. This is generally used to describe instruction in using the visible and audible aspects of speech to compensate for hearing loss that has impaired understanding. *Speech-* is preferred to *lip*reading; it includes not only the interpretation of lip and mouth movements, but also facial expression and gestures, prosodic and melodic aspects of speech, and the structural characteristics of language.

Contemporary methods of aural rehabilitation and speechreading have been linked with the history of clinical audiology since World War II, but schools of lipreading preceded audiology by one century.[1] While lipreading classes were developed for adults, sign language remained the more frequently taught communication method for the severely hearing impaired individuals, usually in residential schools. The language systems were sufficiently different that deaf children usually grew up as part of a deaf, non-oral community. This development of a different social and educational group has been a continuing source of heated argument between the proponents of signed and oral language systems. The general belief now is that the system in which the individual child succeeds most is better.

The acceleration of technologic changes in amplification since 1950 has made it possible to fit thousands more with hearing aids and assistive listening devices. More accurate assessment of the hearing of children and infants has permitted early amplification and some degree of aural/oral communication. This has facilitated the mainstreaming of many children in regular classes with their peers, but requires the classroom teacher or resource person to use materials and techniques that once were confined to hearing societies and hospital clinics. This chapter will attempt to summarize some of those techniques and their rationale.

Social and family patterns have also changed dramatically within the last decade. The increasing number of working mothers and single-parent families have placed a greater burden upon school personnel to provide the largest part of remediation. Even the most willing parent can only supplement a plan if both parent and child are outside the home five days per week. In addition, many parents have unresolved emotional barriers to dealing with the hearing handicap in their child, and even less can be delegated to them. Nevertheless, the parent, the resource person, and the teacher must constitute one team in evaluating the needs of the child, devising and revising a socio-educational plan, and carrying it out.

THE DEVELOPMENT OF LISTENING

The identification and assessment of hearing loss is discussed in Chapters 1 to 6. Recent investigations have revealed unusual patterns of residual hearing, and resulted in special designs of aids and rehabilitation protocols; Chapters 13 and 14 have dealt with some of these. Beyond the hair cells, as we have seen, the auditory pathways distribute impulses through the midbrain to the cortical levels, where the neural traces translate into the sensation of hearing. Once transmitted to and stored in the association areas, the repeated experience develops into the intellectual process of listening, matching, and perceiving. Figure 15-1 is a simplified version of the *feedback loop*, which is a useful diagram for visualizing the transformation of sensory intake into cognition, and then into communicative or expressive skills. (*The Brain*, a 1979 issue of *Scientific American*, has the most lucid description of the structure and functions of that organ.[2]) At this point, only the simplest aspects of reception and awareness will be discussed.

Awareness of Gross Sound. This is the most primitive level of hearing, and is basic to all animals with auditory systems for their survival. The more vulnerable the creature, the earlier in its life it must learn how to cope with imminent danger beyond the instinctive flight-or-fight reaction. *Detection* and *localization* of marked danger occur at the lowest levels of the visual-acoustic reflex mechanisms (see Fig. 15-1). This alarm system produces the rapid rush of adrenaline and muscular preparedness to fend off attack or step out of the path of an oncoming threat, such as a speeding automobile. (Good illustrations and graphic explanations of this may be found in *Sound and Hearing*, from Life Science Library.[3])

The marked startle response of the infant persists to some extent throughout life, but stimulation and experience teach us to identify strange noises as friend or foe, danger or comfort, or food or other pleasure. With maturation, the diffuse, exaggerated startle becomes precise, controlled, and more appropriate to the nature of the sound detected. *Detection* thus evolves through *discrimination* and *identification* to *inference* and *comprehension* of an ever-increasing body of knowledge of our physical world.

Carhart[4] listed these steps when he first set up an orderly system of auditory training for children and adults. Hirsh,[5] Ling,[6] and Erber and Hirsh[7] have redefined the terms as *levels of audition* that lead to *conventional skills*, and

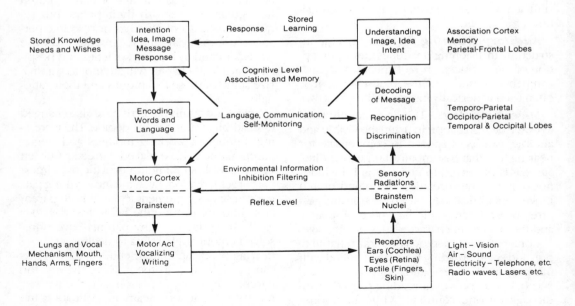

Figure 15-1. Simplified version of a feedback loop used in the sensory intake and development of cognitive and communicative or expressive skills.

they have outlined programs that develop these skills systematically. Ling[6] distinguished the processing of environmental sounds from those discrimination skills necessary for learning language. However, the sensations of the world *beyond* speech contribute to the understanding and semantic properties of words in the fullest sense of language enrichment and quality of life.

Experiences for a hearing-impaired child may vary from learning the attributes of "hot, cold, wet" for water, pots, and pans or for him- or herself to a "warm and soft" blanket or kitten. "Soft," however, may also mean the kitten's mew as well as its fur or the sound of a small bell. With hearing loss, the bell may not be heard at all by one child, or may be heard only as a metallic clink by another, even with amplification. A different hearing aid may more accurately transmit the sound, creating a completely new experience for the individual, with new meaning for the words "bell" and "tinkle." Not identifying the warning sound of a backing truck or the ring of a distant phone can mean real danger in one case or restricted communication in the other. Unfamiliarity with sounds in different regions can lead to confusion or danger when a child moves from rural to urban settings, from home to school, or from neighborhood to inner city.

Selective Listening

A corollary to attending to important signals is the ability to tune out the background appropriately; that is, to develop significant figure-ground discriminations. The child described in Case History 1 had become excellent at tuning out whatever was unclear or difficult to cope with. The effort of listening to half-heard signals is always great. The shy or phlegmatic child with partial hearing may not expend the energy required to attend selectively. One with recurrent otitis media and enlarged adenoids and tonsils may frequently have difficulty breathing, and may be drowsy from medications in addition to suffering fluctuations in hearing.[8]

When this child becomes involved in a task, a minor change in background noise or the voice of an approaching parent or teacher may not capture his attention. Normal-hearing children respond to changes in a teacher's tone of voice, and are easily alerted to a new task or change of activity. These nuances may be unclear to the child with an impairment; the absence of sound may also lack significance. In these ways, hearing impairment deprives one of many changes in the environment.[9]

Learning how to tune in and out occurs in the first few years, and it seems to be estab-

---

Case history #1. W.F., a 6-year-old boy with a moderate, bilateral, high-frequency hearing loss (see Fig. 15-2) showed early reading difficulties in school and some language and articulatory errors. He was fitted in our clinic with a CROS mold and high-frequency hearing aid to implement articulation, language, and reading therapy. His mother reported that during his first days with an aid, he was transfixed with the sounds of traffic, birds, and neighborhood pets. Over the next weeks, he repeatedly discussed background sounds that needed new dimensions of identification. Auditory training to environmental sounds was included in therapy as well as at home. It was surprising that it was required, since his thresholds of hearing for frequencies below 1000 Hz were normal.

Speech therapy and training in phonics was provided concurrently in the clinic with his first and second grades at school, and revealed greater deficits in understanding than would have been anticipated on the basis of audiogram alone. Shy and reluctant to ask for repetition or clarification, he had developed better patterns of tuning out confusing stimuli than of making fine discriminations and filling in. Although his articulation improved rapidly and he developed richer language, he did not attain the level of his schoolmates until the fourth grade. (Some months later, the family moved to a different area and the pediatrician suggested that the child no longer required the aid since there was no apparent handicap.)

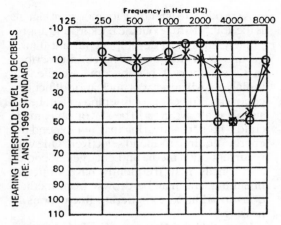

Name: W.F. Age:6 years

Figure 15-2. Case history #1. Six-year-old boy with congenital bilateral high-frequency hearing loss.

lished by the second grade in most children. This period seems to be the most critical for personal safety and for the rapid acquisition of the *figure-ground* skills that are so vital to other educational processes.[10–12] (The *hyperactive* child also has difficulty by being overly responsive to stimuli that cannot be tuned out.) Both types of children require continued training to meet their very different needs.[13]

A part of selective hearing and listening depends on the ability to hold an auditory event in time and space. The first part of a sentence is often not clear until the end has been uttered, and since speech is fleeting, all the words must be remembered until the last. Children interrupt partly from the need to clarify concepts, and partly because they do not yet retain long sequences nor recall everything that has been said or implied. Also what often seems like poor short-term memory is the child's inexperience with predicting what might come next.[14,15]

Physiologically, selective hearing is believed to develop with the maturing use of the reticular formation—cell structures in the brainstem and auditory pathways to the temporal cortex (represented in the second and third boxes in Fig. 15-1). Understanding speech is more complicated than perceiving and recognizing a particular voice. Yet the *familiarity* of a voice implies a host of learned experiences: how that person behaves, speaks, uses language, whether he or she holds promise of

pleasure or chastisement. The maturing listener develops countless sets of anticipatory responses. The teacher at the beginning of the school year usually speaks a little slower for a new class than at midsemester. The child with impairment may require this special thoughtfulness even longer.

Clearly, developing rich language requires a higher order of learning than discriminating most gross environmental sounds. Yet for training a very young or very impaired child, one may begin by focusing on obvious differences and foreground/background distinctions. Class activities may be geared to the age level of the group with short periods of *sensory awareness*.[16–18] An example of this approach is given in Therapy Strategy #1.

Several sets of materials are available, such as the Utley or Goldman-Fristoe-Woodcock (GFW) tests, which use a variety of environmental sounds both as tests and for training. One may also record many of these sounds with a cassette recorder and high-quality tape. (Use a separate microphone for greater fidelity.)

The child with hearing loss and no other neurologic impairment is capable of developing the same skills and processes as his or her normal-hearing peers. Yet fluctuating hearing renders the world sometimes normal and sometimes muffled. With fluid or scarring of the middle ears, the child may react only if sounds are very near or very loud. A flat hearing loss of 30 to 40 dB dampens the clarity of all sharp noises, yet the child may accept the change and not mention that his or her world has "gone soft." The child with a consistent sensorineural loss assumes everyone hears as he or she does, and self-esteem suffers because the child does not react as rapidly or with the same accuracy as his or her friends.[19,20]

Teachers should note changes in behavior that signal periods of infection: physical lethargy, inattention, straining to understand, asking for repetitions, speechreading in normal conversation, and watching classmates to clarify teacher's instructions.[21]

Some assume that a person wearing an aid hears normally. A child may wear a powerful aid, yet his or her hearing loss may be so severe that only portions of complex sounds are heard accurately and other parts may be missed entirely, making them difficult to identify. A new hearing aid with different amplification characteristics or a change in the child's

Therapy strategy #1. Increasing sensory awareness. An introductory game might be a 30-second period of listening to outside sounds—how many airplanes, how many sirens, dogs barking, etc.—depending upon the sounds typical of the neighborhood. The first game could be the actual count; the next might attend to the kind of sound: sharp, high, low, short, or any description that will progress from discrimination of these gross sounds to cognition of their implications and the incidental enrichment of language.

A secondary approach is primarily cognitive and language-building, and is good for all older children, with or without hearing loss. Sound discrimination may be embedded within an activity centered on *how* sounds are made and some physical characteristics of the noise source.

An example of sound source variation might be a comparison of crickets or other insects and birds, including the brevity or length of song, rubbing of wings or legs versus vocalization, etc. Compare insects and animal voices. Expand this to include differences in the medium carrying the sound, or the size, shape, and nature of vibratory source. Go on to the nature of communication and how it varies among species.

hearing may require a period of reorientation to those same sounds and others that were not heard at all. An aid may be set properly for the perception of speech, and yet not be adjusted to avoid distortion of music, shouting, and rough-housing that are common school experiences. Evidences of discomfort should be noticed and the child questioned about any unpleasant experiences. Often, the audiologist or dispenser can reduce this stress by simple adjustments of an aid and/or earmold.[22–24]

Special Needs in Amplification

Screening tests often reveal a mild hearing loss in children without middle ear disease who do not seem to be candidates for amplification. They may learn many strategies for hearing efficiently within a school or family setting without ever experiencing *normal* hearing. When they move into their first work setting or large school experience (as with T.F, in Case History 2), distance and noise create unfavorable signal-to-noise (S/N) ratios, and some amplification is sought. This author's clinical experience has been that such young adults seldom experience initial success, but require almost two years to adapt to amplification. This seems to occur partly because of the pathologic inner ear's physiologic sensitivity to changes in intensity, and partly because these adults are intellectually unfamiliar with the full dimension of normal sounds and are unable to evaluate whether they are hearing accurately or not.[25]

Room Acoustics. These may often cause distortion, feedback, and blurring of speech in the presence of other sounds. Many auditoriums and classrooms use assistive systems where the sound source is transmitted directly to the telephone circuit of the hearing aid. This avoids loss of energy of those sounds most difficult to distinguish at a distance, and also eliminates interference in the space between the speaker and listener. All means of creating a more favorable S/N ratio (see Chapter 11) should be explored, so that important speech is 20 to 30 dB higher than the background noise level.[16] When the background interference cannot be lessened, communication should be as unimpeded as possible. *Adequate light on the speaker's face, better ear toward the speaker, slower, better phrasing, are all strategies for improving communication in noise* (see Fig. 15-4).[26–32]

Everyone has experienced reverberation or echoing of speech, or the muffled qualities of certain rooms and auditoriums for both music and speech. Hard surfaces, irregular walls, and high ceilings may bounce sounds about a room in varying time and phase relationships that are often unfavorable. It is difficult to hear one voice in a cafeteria or gymnasium. The masking effects of multiple voices and echoes on running speech is so common a complaint among people with even mild hearing losses that it must be assumed to be a constant prob-

Case history #2.   T.F., an 8-year old boy, was referred for amplification because he was having difficulties in school. He had a congenital conductive hearing loss on the right ear and a mixed loss on the left ear with excellent speech discrimination on the left (see Fig. 15-3). The teacher reported that he often missed instructions and required special prompting to do assignments or tasks. He was a "loner," and often described as sullen and disagreeable. He was fitted with a high-frequency, moderate-gain aid on the left ear, and was seen in the clinic for a two-month program of aural rehabilitation, including auditory training, speechreading, and management skills.

During this follow-up period, his teacher reported that he asked to be excused from certain activities that she thought he should enjoy. T.F. reluctantly admitted that the music was painful to him because so many of the instruments were shrill and distorted with his hearing aid. He was hearing better in class and winning more approval from the teacher in academic respects, but still found many of the group activities a strain. The aid was adjusted and the earmold vented. Both teacher and parents felt that T.F. became a much happier and more successful student.

Ten years later, T.F. returned with his parents for re-evaluation of his needs. His thresholds had not changed, although he now seemed like a better-adjusted young man. His school record had been excellent and he was planning to enter a university in the fall. He also was obtaining summer employment where his hearing status had to be known for optimum placement. He presented the same aid and earmold that had been fitted initially, and then admitted that he had not worn the aid since he was 14, since the other boys made fun of it. His parents had not insisted as long as he did well in school, but they now were concerned for the larger school setting, and questioned whether his right ear should be aided also. A matched pair of moderate-gain directional aids was fit with appropriately vented earmolds to be used in the outdoor summer job, where he needed localization and maximum information about oncoming traffic. It was further felt that this might be optimal in larger classrooms in college. The second aid contributed measurably to localization and discrimination in open spaces, but in close, noisy settings the single aid on the better ear served more effectively. Having two identical behind-the-ear aids gave him one good aid at all times with a spare always available. As an adult, he may choose to have in-the-ear aids, but the clinician felt that he needed the binaural aided experience before he could make this choice or use such noninterchangeable amplification effectively.

---

lem for hearing impaired children in the normal school setting. Carpeted classrooms and acoustic tile ceilings and wall surfaces are all ways of treating the noise architecturally. Busy, open classrooms with steady movement and a background hum of voices have exaggerated effects on the hearing impaired child (and are similarly disturbing to the hyperactive child). The awareness of noise as an irritant and distraction cannot be overemphasized.

Localization.   This is achieved in the few milliseconds required for a sound to evoke the reflexive turn toward its direction. The localizing function of the auditory system is among the most basic, and it takes place in the brainstem at the reflex or most primitive neural level. Accuracy, however, requires similar sensitivity in both ears to perceive relative differences in speed, intensity, and phase relation-

ships of the sound. Precision is easier if the sound is continuous rather than brief. When it is in the midline, directly behind the listener, exact location is difficult.

Adults who lose hearing on one side complain of not locating speakers if they are in another room or speaking against a noisy background. Children with a severe unilateral loss, either congenital or acquired early, have initial difficulty in localizing, but learn to use other auditory and visual cues as they mature. Even partial hearing on both sides seems to establish the use of binaural auditory pathways for this purpose. Without some experience, however, amplification on the severely impaired side is often rejected, because it confuses rather than helps the wearer.[33-36]

Distortion.   This often occurs with hair cell damage in the inner ear (sensory losses),

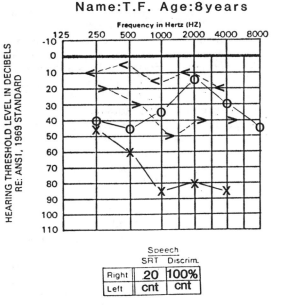

Name:T.F. Age:8years

	Speech SRT	Discrim.
Right	.20	100%
Left	cnt	cnt

MASKING USED WHEN NEEDED

Figure 15-3. Case history #2. Eight-year-old boy with congenital conductive hearing loss, right, mixed loss, left.

and is as often accompanied by *recruitment*, which makes sound increase in loudness more rapidly than in the normal ear. This loudness growth phenomenon can add to the shock of sudden sounds nearby, such as sudden laughter or slammed doors. Hearing aids may amplify the peaks of these sounds, yet may not seem to be distorting to the normal ear when the aid is checked. If an aid needs repair or adjustment, it can exaggerate the discomfort felt by the ear. An adult will remove such an aid, as may the child. However, many well-meaning adults will replace the child's aid "for his own good" unless the child can explain the problem.[37,38]

The introduction of probe microphone measurements is a technique that rather successfully measures what a hearing aid is transmitting to the canal of even small ears. This has aided many dispensers in fitting aids and earmolds more accurately (see Chapter 10). The behavior or complaint of the wearer, however, should be the primary criterion for adjustment of the instrument, since no one can duplicate the stimuli affecting the inner ear. Teachers and family members should be sensitive to these

Figure 15-4. Typical handout material on better communication techniques for instructing family and friends.

signs of discomfort, and be able to check the sound of the hearing aid or evaluate those situations that cause distress. If further adjustments cannot be made to the amplifying system, the situation may require intervention.

In general, alertness to those environmental conditions that affect a child's hearing loss, and his or her amplification should be built into the teacher's educational plan for that child. The family, medical, and resource personnel should be in frequent contact to keep informed about changes in states of health or attention to assure that the child can maximize educational opportunities.[39-43]

ASPECTS OF SPEECHREADING

Language as Communication

The highest form of social development that separates humans from all other vertebrates is language, both spoken and written. Like many other species, we incorporate body language into our signals and emotional display; we alter melody, pitch, and intensity of utterance. More easily than other animals, we can change our plumage with occasion as well as season. We can express many needs and feelings with or without sound, and with or without words. The use of sign language is evidence that speech is not intrinsic to communication. The comprehension of abstract and time-related, historic language is uniquely human and common to all members of the species, whether they live in isolated desert tribes or high-tech urban centers.

Speechreading. This is one means of facilitating communication that is used with varying degrees of skill by most people at some time. How much one can improve this skill and depend on it as a major means of comprehension has been studied by many investigators in an effort to find those aspects that can be taught to the hearing impaired. No studies have discovered magic formulae that work universally. Most investigators recognize that effective communication is a two-way process that depends on the speaker and the environment, as well as on the viewer-listener. Fortunately, the increased sensitivity to all kinds of handicap and *difference* has encouraged the open statement of needs by the hearing impaired. Suggestions for *speaking to* the hear-

ing impaired are available in many forms, as are suggestions for *more effective speechreading and situation management*. Table 15-1 (see the end of this chapter) is specifically designed for classroom teachers and, as with other such "hints," places responsibility on the speaker or adult, rather than the child. The maturing child and the adult, however, should be taught as soon as possible their own best needs for optimal understanding and how to meet these most effectively. Whether they become skilled speechreaders depends upon a number of factors, but they may become more effective as social *listeners* and students.

There is no consensus in recent studies on what constitutes the good speechreader. No studies have found that intelligence or motivation per se made significant differences between good and poor speechreaders. Clinical experience has shown that the ablest speechreaders exhibited the following characteristics (language experience is understood):

(1) *Empathy* with the speaker and what he or she is trying to convey.
(2) *Willingness to anticipate* the next phrase or thought.
(3) *Flexibility to shift* possible words or topics.
(4) *Adequate language or vocabulary* for the level of the speaker and for substituting words or phrases.
(5) *Adequate information* for the topic being discussed, or at least to ask the pertinent questions to obtain more information.
(6) *Awareness of phonemic confusions* and familiarity with speech sound placement.
(7) *Awareness of prosodic elements* of language.
(8) *Speed* of response (an age-related variable also dependent on good health and lack of fatigue).[1,44-46]

Content and Information

Since meaning, association, and information are complex aspects of cognitive development, they are dependent upon maturation and unimpeded avenues of experience. Conversely, they are sensitive to sensory handicap. The earlier and more extensive the deprivation, the greater may be the delay or distortion in learning. Thus, the child with a major hearing loss who is mainstreamed in the integrated school or classroom has the exposure to normal language experiences of his or her peers, but must have average or superior intelligence, motivation and energy to compensate for that loss and to acquire the same information as his or her classmates. The child with a milder loss but less drive or resourcefulness may miss a great deal of incidental information, and may overlook both opportunities for compensating and the cues that would fill in the gaps. When hearing loss is extreme and inner resource is impoverished, especially if it has been present since early childhood, the gap between information and use of language in deaf and normal-hearing age peers widens steadily.[47,48] Even with average or better intelligence, the child whose first language is a sign system may find it difficult to speechread non-signing speakers, because the syntax of sign language varies from spoken and the child seldom stores a large unaccustomed vocabulary for only occasional recognition.

The bank of linguistic possibilities is acquired over time and is generally used in communication; but it becomes more crucial for a speechreader. Older adults often complain of difficulty in understanding people with accents or their "mumbling" adolescent grandchildren. Both cases present a mixture of different rhythms of speech and syllabic stress, some differences in articulating specific words and sounds, and unfamiliar idioms. The young child can often understand friends whom adults consider unintelligible precisely because he or she is more attuned to the topic of play or conversation, and because the child is anticipating the next words, phrases, or questions that the other child might ask.

Most children's discourse uses concrete references that relate to immediate activities or needs. Thus, children of similar levels can converse with each other acceptably without expanding sentences into elaborate abstract ideas or using a varied rich vocabulary. The use of adult language forms is the basis for many a "precocious" child story, precisely because of its novelty. However, maturity is expected to bring acquisition of subtle, related, or different meanings. Lack of vocabulary may restrict information-gathering, social pleasure, and especially the understanding of humor and jokes, which depend on word-play.[49,50]

The teacher or resource person should try to provide ample stimulation for the hearing-impaired child, which includes *multiple meanings* of words and *multiple experiences* of relating the same stories or events using *different* words.[17] This has the virtue of:

(1) Enlarging the child's semantic vocabulary.
(2) Increasing the awareness of different means of saying the same thing.
(3) Noting the difference in patterns of relative visibility and audibility.
(4) Alerting the child to asking for and/or anticipating various options.
(5) Providing practice for the teacher and class in rewording phrases or sentences.
(6) Becoming aware of how some key words cannot be substituted, but the sentence form or inflection can be changed for improved visibility or understanding.

Note that this expansion of the shorter sentences asks for more concrete information as well as informing the child/class about implications of wet weather. With older children or if the teacher is sure she is understood, the simplest form is adequate and customary. The last form is not only more explicit with its use of larger vocabulary, but it has greater emotional content, will probably be said with more breaks between the phrases, and with more gestures and facial expression. It will command more attention from the class, yet center on the specific child's problems within the teacher's concern for the whole group. *This type of expansion or elaboration of simple sentences and questions is recommended in early life to develop the child's vocabulary and language; but it remains necessary throughout the lifetime of the hearing impaired person when a brief comment or question is not comprehended.*[51–54]

Formal lessons for language expansion can follow this same form by beginning with the shortest sentences, and by having the child or group contribute the alternatives, think about the implications, list adjectives, nouns, or phrases that convey the desired meaning, and review which are easier to see or to hear.

Example:	
rain	
wet weather	
pouring rain	light rain
downpour	mist
heavy storm	fine rain

Many available books on speechreading include such lessons, yet much of the vocabulary and idioms are obsolete soon after the book is published. It is more useful to understand the techniques of such expansions, and to devise

---

Therapy strategy #2. Varying Words and Sentence Form for Greater Visibility and Clarity.
Form 1.   It's supposed to rain later. Are you prepared? Is someone picking you up?
Form 2.   Did you bring your raincoat to school? It may rain this afternoon. How will you be going home? Will your mother come for you or are you going on the school bus?
Form 3.   It's pouring rain now! I don't want anyone to get wet and catch a cold. Does everyone have a raincoat? Do you all have rides home? Johnny, is your mother coming for you? Will she pick you up in the station wagon (car)?

---

the specific lesson from the interests, environment, or grade level of the class than to look for ready-made "cookbook" lesson plans. An imagined excursion to McDonald's or any local favorite is more pertinent than some of the published exercises on "going to a restaurant."

The young child may be asked to repeat a direction or plan, such as, "Now, what time are we leaving?" or "Where will we be going?" to make sure that he or she heard correctly. This *validation* technique has been frowned upon by some,[55] but is used by many others in the field as a means of training the hearing impaired child or adult to tell others when important information has been unclear.

The Act of Speaking

The child learns to speak his or her *mother tongue* by practicing what he or she sees and hears of speech and modeling his or her own production after others. Earliest words usually have the greatest relative importance to the infant. Sounds that are mastered first are among those most audible, most visible, requiring the least muscle control, or having an idiosyncratic attractiveness to the individual. All sounds and languages worldwide are possible for the young child, but once a phonemic system is fixed, some *foreign* sounds may seem forever impossible to produce.[56]

The familiar substitutions and omissions of *baby talk* are examples of sounds that are confused because of similar qualities and unclear placement in the mouth. [w/r] as in "wed/red," [w/l/y] as in "wady/lady," "lellow/yellow," or "yiddow/little" are all common in youngsters because of the similar acoustic properties of these *glides* and the maturational delay in mastering subtle tongue-tip movements.

Coping strategy #1. How to Ask for Repetition. The listener's reaction should inform the speaker what was *understood* or *not understood*. An appropriate answer indicates adequate, if not complete, understanding, and a conversation or class activity can proceed. If only part of the instruction or question was understood, it is more effective for the listener to ask: "What did you say about the weather?" (my mother?, my lunch?) than to say "Huh," "What?," or "Could you repeat that?" The former response elicits a repetition of the missing or wrong information that is usually shorter and pronounced with greater clarity and emphasis. If the word cannot be understood or is unfamiliar, then the specific area of misunderstanding is indicated, and substitution or elaboration can be made. *This is one of the most important strategies used by the hearing impaired, and should be encouraged in earliest childhood until it is incorporated into his or her communication behavior.*

> The [w] is often the sound used for all the others since it is formed on and by the lips and is completely visible. [f/th] "baf/bath," [t/k] "titty- tat" are examples of other phonemes that are frequently substituted because of similar acoustic characteristics and less visible means and place of production.

During the process of learning to discriminate among sounds of one's language, the child with normal hearing makes a series of increasingly fine modifications of production until the acoustic and visible characteristics of his or her speech duplicate those of family or region; the child will also use their characteristic idioms. While vocabulary and meanings can be a life-long learning process, accent is fixed early in childhood; and for most people, it can be modified only for a few years (or with heroic effort). The child will be able to identify most words by listening, and may need to watch the speaker for clarification only when words are very similar, when there is a great deal of noise, or if the vocabulary or accent is very different from his or her own.[57,58]

Visibility

Methods of describing the sounds of speech vary from the diacritical markings used in many dictionaries to indicate pronunciation, to Northampton Charts for teaching American speech to the deaf, and to the International Phonetic Alphabet used by linguists for recording a variety of accents and languages. Regardless of their original purposes, systems useful for speechreading must include degree of visibility on the lips or within the mouth. Most charts indicate that the sound is made at the front, middle, or back of the mouth, with the lower jaw relatively high (closed) or low (open). Lips, tongue, and jaws interact in *place* and *manner of articulation* to distinguish groups of sounds from each other. However, so few different movements are available to the human speaker that *acoustic differences, including presence or absence of voice*, are necessary to furnish phonemic and morphemic variety. (The Chinese languages add as many as 4 to 10 different tones or inflections to the same syllable to convey as many different meanings.[59,60])

The person with hearing impairment either learns or is taught that there are many confusions of phonemic place or sound that are sorted only by careful listening, reviewing context, or watching the speaker for visible, emotional, or gestural cues. In the 1920s and 1930s, one popular teacher of lipreading, Nitchie,[61] used words that looked alike (homophenes) or sounded alike (homophones) as the basis for drills to establish speed of recog-

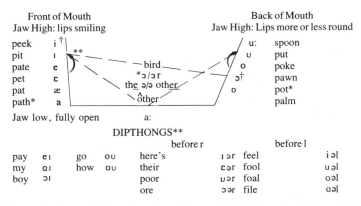

Figure 15-5. Phonetic chart of General American Vowels. *Variable vowels: Eastern seaboard accents. **Indicates direction of movement from strong to weaker vowel. †Indicates variable duration of vowel; may be held longer before voiced sound than voiceless (as in fawn—fɔin vs. fought—fɔt).

nition in different sentence contexts. Sentences and lists of *homophenous* words have been used widely ever since, but it would be an endless task to train for all the combinations of words in use. Knowing many words look alike and learning which *sounds* can be mistaken for each other is more useful. Because the number of different words is vast and clarity of articulation varies, a large vocabulary and the knowledge of context or *redundancy of language* is paramount.[62–64]

The phonetic charts of consonants and general American vowels shown in Figure 15-5 is one adaptation of the International Phonetic Alphabet. It displays the *manner* of articulation horizontally and the *place* where the sound is produced in the oral cavity vertically. If the *phonemes* or *families of sounds* are studied from left to right on the chart together with the introduction of homophenous words, this introduces the most visible sounds first and the sources of visible versus audible confusion. Pairs of voiceless and voiced sounds are presented at the same time. The technical designation of how the phoneme is produced can be used for some groups, or the description can be made in layman's terms. The difficulty with phonetic alphabets for populations old enough to be established readers is that the one symbol-one sound rule is confusing when that symbol varies from the visual association of written English. For young readers who are just learning phonics, the stricter system can assist the reading process, especially in noting the irregularities of English spelling.

Example of early lesson:

Bi-labials: Consonants made by the two lips coming together

	Voiceless	Voiced (vocal cords vibrating)
Stop/plosives (air stopped, then exploded)	/p/ as in pay, happy, step	/b/ as in boy, harbor, cab
Nasals (air continues through nose)		/m/ as in more, among, from
Glides (lips come together, then move during sound)	/hw/ as in where	/w/ as in wear

---

The sounds /p/ or /b/ are not the words "pea" or "be," but are the process of the lips closing, holding the position long enough to build up air pressure, then exploding the air in a little puff. The strength of the puff depends upon what follows—another consonant, a vowel, or a pause. The distinctive aspect of the /p/ is its visibility and its lack of vocal cord vibration or voicelessness. The exploded air and its relationship to the next phoneme creates a weak high-frequency sound that may be inaudible to many people with hearing loss. The /b/ is less explosive, but has voice to identify it, while the voiced /m/ should have a continuous, resonant nasal quality without explosion.

A silent lipreading drill would demonstrate that the words "pay," "may," and "bay" look exactly the same (are homophenous) and will be differentiated from each other only by sound and/or context. Thus, silent delivery of the sentences

"Pay the bill."
"Let's cross the Bay Bridge."
"April showers bring May flowers."

demonstrates the importance of context. Using even a low voice adds the distinction of type of sound production.

Sentences such as

"She fell in the bus." and
"She fell in the mud."

demonstrate the difficulty of distinguishing homophenes when context is the same, and the need for re-wording if precise information is necessary.

It is clear from these examples that an infinite array of sentences could be devised and practiced to demonstrate either difference or similarity. The essential point to be mastered is that certain sounds will be perceived as the same, and either increased loudness, exaggerated articulation, spelling, or rewording will be necessary to distinguish among them if the sentence structure is the same. Many examples can be made from /p/ /b/ /m/ alone as in peat-beet-beat-meet, or meet-mean, heap-keep, arbor-harbor-armor, step-stem.[65]

This chapter does not attempt to include a thorough speechreading course. It introduces the matrices of confusion and the reasons why certain sets of sounds are so easily mistaken. Calvert's[59] excellent book on phonetics illustrates and explains the field clearly and wittily with unusual historic detail. All sounds are illustrated in the International Phonetic Alphabet, Northampton, and diacritical systems. Additional references are available that are more directly related to aural rehabilitation and speechreading, including materials and lessons by Davis and Hardick,[1] Alpiner,[45] Kaplan et al,[46] and Schow and Nerbonne.[54]

Visible confusion sets or *visemes* are made in the same or nearby place in the mouth. They have been divided into five to nine different groups by Binnie et al[66] and Woodward and Barber,[67] and are the basis of different identification studies:

(*1*) *p, b, m* as in *pea, be, me*. Lips closed; stops or nasal continuant.

(*2*) *w, r, u* as in *woo, rue, who*. Lips rounded; note glide movements in w and r.

(*3*) *f, v* as in *fine, vine; half, have*. Upper teeth against lower lip; continuant, fricative sound.

(*4*) *th, th* as in *thin, this*. Tongue tip between teeth; continuant, fricative.

(*5*) *t, d, n, l* as in *tot, dot; not, lot*. Alveolar; tongue tip against gum ridge; stops or continuants—nasal or lateral.

(*6*) *s, z* as in *seal, zeal, gas, has*. Tongue tip pointing at but not touching gum ridge; fricative continuant.

(*7*) *sh, zh, ch, dg (j)* as in *sure, measure, shoe, chew, jewel*. Lips rounded while tongue tip humps toward hard palate; fricative continuant or affricate (t + sh, d + zh).

(*8*) *k, g, ng* as in *cold, goal, talk, dog, dong*. Velar (soft palate); stop or nasal continuant.

(*9*) *h* as in *how*. Glottal, open throat; fricative continuant.

Clearly, groups 5, 6, 8, and 9 are difficult to see since they are made in the middle or back of the mouth; but the lips, tongue, and jaw do move differently for the different groups, and if any sound is perceived, the combination of visibility and audibility helps to reduce ambiguity.[68–71]

Audible dimensions of *phonemes* vary from *voicing* or *voicelessness* to *nasality* versus *orality*, to *continuants* versus *stop-plosives*, and to qualities of *hiss* or *friction*. Although the voiceless consonants have some sound, the frequency spectrum is high and the intensity or power is weak in rapid conversation. In repetition, excitement, or stress, both the intensity and duration may be increased to a level of audibility. Thus, a word such as "signed," if held and stressed sufficiently, can be distinguished from "pined," "find," or "kind" by eliminating the /p/ and /f/ from the visible cues and the /k/ from the continuant hiss, rather than the voiceless stop. Visibility might separate "path" from "pass," but it would be very hard to distinguish "pats/past/pass and paths" with the rapid blending of similar sounds. The stops, /p/t/k/ are frequently substituted for each other as in "pear/tear/care," as are the /b/ d/g/ of "bun/done/gun." Visibility helps only to eliminate the /p-b/ phoneme from the others. The /m/ and /n/ sounds are so close acoustically that "m as in Mary, n as in Nancy" is almost standard telephone courtesy.[72–77]

Vowels. The word *vowel* is derived from voice, and there is no voiceless distinction between one vowel and another. The *vowels* of American English fall mainly into three categories, characterized by the triangle or rectangle representing the oral cavity. The jaw is high for the top sounds /i/ and /u/ and lower to wide open for the /a/. The major visible difference between the *front* vowels (with the tongue tip low and the blade of the tongue high in the mouth) and the *back* vowels (with the back of the tongue humped) is the lip rounding that characterizes the /u/U/o/aw or back sounds. The front vowels may be made in succession after fixing the lips in a high smile, and only dropping the jaw so that the smile drops lower in order from /i/I/e/E/ae/a/.

Diphthongs. These are indicated as moving from a stronger vowel to an unstressed or weak half—the two vowels together making a different sound than either one alone. It is the movement that distinguishes them from pure vowels and their relatively greater duration. Some of the vowels are long and can be held without changing character—(/ju/ as in you, /aw/ as in law)—others must be short—(/I/ as in pin, /U/ as in book or put)—or they move toward the central unstressed schwa or weak /ə/, becoming diphthongized as "pill, full"/ pIəl, fUəl/.

Although all of the vowels are voiced, they differ enough acoustically to be distinguished. This harmonic difference occurs in the resonance of the oral cavity. In general, vowels produced at the same jaw height share the same fundamental pitch; it is the overtones of the sound that give the clue to /i/ or /u/: "three" or "two." Because the shape differs markedly, the impaired listener who can see the speaker clearly can sort out such errors; but over a telephone, in dim light, or across the classroom, the hearing impairment leads to confusion. Vowel confusion is difficult for others to understand, since the orthographic distinction seems so clear. Diphthongs also are error prone since the second half is sufficiently weak to be missed or substituted.[78]

Prosody

The prosodic elements of speech are among the most important cues to communication, since they transcend *content* to reflect *intent*. Prosody includes *rhythm, melody, pitch, inflection, stress, intensity, and duration*—in fact all aspects of delivery of speech other than the phonemes. When this is accompanied by *expression and gesture*, language may be irrelevant. Anger, distress, threat, nurturance, and delight, for example, can be understood even when the words are strange. (The Russian actress, Alla Nazimova, used to bring tears to her audiences with fervent recitations of the Russian alphabet.) A teacher can alert her busy or dreaming students to a change in activity simply by uttering a firm or colorful *"Now, class! . . . ."*[82]

The Mueller-Walle method of lipreading was based on recognition of single syllables, and on how strings of different syllables changed appearance and rhythm in context.[1] This was well suited to speakers of German, and was not sufficient alone for American use. However, the bouncing or clapping out of a rhythmic pattern can be an aid for recognizing stress or emphasis within a word, phrase, or sentence.

Example: NA-tion   IN-ter-NA-tion-al

TWENty NAtions are atTENDing an interNAtional MEETing.

Again, demonstrations of *timing and stress* in question or statement forms is a means of emphasizing what every child has been responding to all of his or her listening life. The reprimand, *"What did you say!"* is more similar to "You said *what?*" than to the request for repetition, *"What did you say?"*—although the grammatic form is identical. "That's *some* present!" can express irony, disgust, delight, or disbelief. This sort of exercise can be a good class project at many grade levels to review the semantic variability of common words and phrases. (It is especially valuable for those learning English as a second language, although the expression in emphatic comments is fairly clear.)

For the hearing impaired, one of the more difficult aspects of American prosody is the pattern of *downward inflection* at the ends of phrases and sentences, which often makes key words inaudible. Thus, a long, rapid sentence such as,

"I saw you the other day, but you were too far away for me to talk to you."

may be heard only partially, evoking the response,

"Why didn't you speak to me?"

Coping strategy #2.   *Mouthing* or *shadowing* the speech of the person one is listening to is an effective *learning* tool in speechreading. The Jena method of lipreading relied on kinesthesis and was not sufficient on its own.[79] However, intellectual familiarity with how the sounds are made in isolation is only half the battle; feeling how they change in context permits rapid shifts in probability. As one practices the phonemes and stimulus words, kinesthetic awareness facilitates the matching of audible and visible aspects to the pattern of movement and use of breath. The words-in-sentences drill material is of value primarily if the stimuli are "rolled, . . . trippingly on the tongue" of the listener, rather than presented by a leader for recognition only. A good speechreader can silently repeat what was observed in order to clarify a sentence or phrase that was not understood. *This is not recommended as a regular habit, since it does interfere with normal communication*, but it can be used in class to heighten this skill.[80,81]

The reply, "You were too far away," illustrates a short, well-stressed response. The good speechreader, however, would have caught the visible portion, "too far away for me," and filled in the last part, thereby responding appropriately,

"Oh, too bad! I would have liked being with you."[83,84]

Table 15-1 lists some helpful hints for teachers with hearing impaired children in their classes. These procedures should ensure adequate communication within the classroom, and help to provide the hearing impaired child with additional cues for better educational achievement.

SUMMARY

The effects on school performance and social/intellectual development are the same whether a child has an intermittent hearing loss from disease with its fatigue, pain, and physical interference with sound transmission, or has a mild-to-severe congenital defect. If the disorder is one of inattention, confusion, or poor auditory memory, the effects are similar. Learning to read may suffer, acquisition of in-

Table 15-1   Hints to the Teacher with a Hearing Impaired Child in the Classroom

1. Write assignments or important instructions on the blackboard, or have the child confirm assignments at the end of the school day.
2. When using the blackboard for instruction, keep the head up and face the class directly.
3. Always explain multiple meanings of words and idioms.
4. When instructing, stand still and maintain good light on your face.
5. Never have light behind you when giving instructions.
6. Preferential seating includes placing a child with the better ear toward the teacher, as well as seating the child within 6 feet of the teacher.
7. Lipstick helps in lipreading, but beards and (walrus) mustaches do not.
8. Rephrase a sentence that is not initially understood (never repeat it exactly the same way).
9. When addressing a hearing impaired student, call the student's name, wait until he or she is attending, and then speak.
10. For children wearing hearing aids, if an adverse reaction to loud sounds is noted, such as in the band session, report it to the audiologist.
11. Consider using a buddy system, which involves having a nearby normal-hearing child in the class clarify misunderstandings and/or help in classwork.

Coping strategy #3. Key Words and Specific Repetition.   The usefulness of *key words* for both speaker and listener is tied to the prosodic element of *stress*, which is made of *intensity, duration, pitch, and inflection*. "*Where* are you going?" and "*When* are you going?" require two very different answers. The key words may be so embedded in the question that the listener may need to ask "Where?" or "When?" The repetition will most often isolate the first word.

In the same way, a teacher giving an assignment of homework should stress each significant part of the assignment when facing the class, and then write it on the board for later reference.

"I'd like you to read *Chapter Three* (pause), *Pages 40 to 45 (pause)*, and answer *Questions 10 to 25* at the *end* of the chapter."

The student asking for clarification should first repeat what he heard, as in "Chapter Three, pages forty to forty-nine?" or "Which pages?" (which should not be necessary if the assignment is on the board).[85]

Ongoing conversation cannot be stopped at every phrase or sentence to clarify all bits of information; casual, social discussions do not always require complete comprehension. However, it is possible to follow a give-and-take conversation with occasional interpolated questions to keep up, such as,

"*Where* did you say Mary was going?"

"*When* did this happen?"

"Was this on the *bus*?"

formation may be below age-grade level, articulatory skills may be poor, understanding of syntax and semantic richness may be impoverished, and the recognition and identification of environmental sounds may be limited or distorted. Self-esteem may suffer because of uncounted reactions of impatience or annoyance experienced in peer, school, or family situations.

Compensatory skills should be taught as early as possible to alert the hearing impaired person *and those around him or her* to the visible, audible, syntactic, and semantic aspects of speech and language. Techniques of recognition and identification of sounds, words, expressions, and language idiosyncrasies should be continued as long as necessary to permit useful exchange of information for education or socialization. It is important for the school, health personnel, and family to act as a cohesive team, but this is not always possible. Thus, the child who is affected most should have all the tools and confidence necessary for either understanding what is said or requesting additional information in the most expedient and least emotional way.[86]

REFERENCES

1. Davis JM, Hardick EJ: *Rehabilitative Audiology for Children and Adults* (New York: John Wiley & Sons, 1981), chap 3.
2. N. Geschwind: Specializations of the human brain, in *The Brain* (San Francisco: WH Freeman & Co, 1979; or chap 9 in *Scientific American*, 1979).
3. Stevens SS: *Sound and Hearing* (New York: Life Science Library, Time Inc, 1965).
4. Carhart R: Auditory training, in Davis H, Silverman RD, eds: *Hearing and Deafness* (New York: Holt, Rinehart, Winston, 1960).
5. Hirsh I: Audition in relation to the perception of speech, in Carterette E, ed: *Brain Function III: Speech, Language and Comprehension* (Los Angeles: UCLA Press, 1966).
6. Ling D: *Speech and the Hearing Impaired Child* (Washington, DC: AG Bell Association, 1976).
7. Erber N, Hirsch I: Auditory training, in Davis H, Silverman S, eds: *Hearing and Deafness* (New York: Holt, Rinehart, Winston, 1978).
8. Kessler M: Effects of middle ear disease on the development of audition and language skills in children. *J Acad Rehab Audiol*, 12, Pt. 2 (1979), 6–19.
9. Rupp RR: A review of the auditory processing skills of 50 children and recommendations for educational management. *J Acad Rehab Audiol* 12 (1979), 62–85.
10. Maccoby E, Konrad K: Age trends in selective listening. *J Exp Psychol*, 3 (1966), 113–122.
11. Willeford J, Bilger R: Auditory perception in children with learning disabilities, in Katz J, ed: *Handbook of Clinical Audiology* (Baltimore: Williams and Wilkins Co, 1978).
12. Katz J, Illmer R: Auditory perception in children with learning disabilities, in Katz J, ed: *Handbook of Clinical Audiology* (Baltimore: Williams and Wilkins Co, 1972).
13. Keith RW: *Central Auditory Dysfunction* (New York: Grune and Stratton, 1977).
14. Kirchner DW, Klatzky RL: Verbal rehearsal and memory in language-disordered children. *J Speech Hear Res*, 28 (1985), 556–565.
15. Glass MR, Franks JR, Potter RE: A comparison of two tests of auditory selective attention. *Lang Speech Hearing Serv in Schools*, 17 (1986), 300–306.
16. Grammatico L: Cognition in the development of listening skills, in Rubin M, ed: *Hearing Aids* (Baltimore: University Park Press, 1976).
17. Moeller MP, Eccarius MP: Evaluation and intervention with hearing-impaired children: A multidisciplinary approach. *J Acad Rehab Audiol*, 3 (1980), 13–31.
18. Moores D, Weiss K, Goodwin M: Early education programs for hearing impaired children: Major findings. *Amer Ann Deaf*, 123 (1978), 925–936.
19. Northern J, Downs M: *Hearing in Children* (Baltimore: Williams & Wilkins Co, 1987).
20. Ross M, Brackett D, Maxon AB: *Hard of Hearing Children in Regular Schools* (Englewood Cliffs, NJ: Prentice-Hall, 1982).
21. Quigley S, Thomure R: *Some Effects of a Hearing Impairment on School Performance* (Urbana, IL: Institute of Research on Exceptional Children, University of Illinois, 1968).
22. Matkin N: Hearing aids for children, in Hodgson W, Skinner P, eds: *Hearing Aid Assessment and Use in Audiologic Habilitation* (Baltimore: Williams and Wilkins Co, 1977).
23. Garwood V: Audiological management of the hearing-impaired child in the public schools, in Martin F, ed: *Pediatric Audiology* (Englewood Cliffs, NJ: Prentice-Hall, 1978), pp 446–487.
24. Ross M, Calvert D: Guidelines for audiology programs in educational settings for hearing-impaired children. *Volta Review*, 79 (1977), 153–162.
25. Beattie RC, Boyd RL: Relationship between pure-tone and speech loudness discomfort levels among hearing-impaired subjects. *J Speech Hear Disord*, 51 (1986), 120–125.
26. Ross M: Classroom amplification, in Hodgson W, Skinner P, eds: *Hearing Aid Assessment and Audiological Habilitation* (Baltimore: Williams and Wilkins Co, 1977).

27. Ross M, Giolas T: Three classroom listening conditions on speech intelligibility. *Am Ann Deaf*, 116 (1971), 580–584.

28. Ross M, Giolas T: *Auditory Management of Hearing-Impaired Children* (Baltimore: University Park Press, 1978).

29. Sanders D: Noise conditions in normal school classrooms. *Exceptional Children*, 31 (1965), 344–353.

30. Nabelek A: Effects of room acoustics on speech perception through hearing aids, in Libby ER, ed: *Binaural Hearing and Amplification*, Vol. 1 (Chicago: Zenetron, 1980).

31. Webster JC, Snell KB: Noise levels and the speech intelligibility of teachers in classrooms. *J Acad Rehab Audiol*, 16 (1983), 234–255.

32. Bricault M, Stinson M, Gauger JS: Young-adult students' ratings of the relative performance of hearing aids, FM, and loop amplification systems. *J Acad Rehab Audiol*, 18 (1985), 55–72.

33. Bess F: Children with unilateral hearing loss. *J Acad Rehab Audiol*, 15 (1982), 131–144.

34. Stein DM: Psychosocial characteristics of school-age children with unilateral hearing loss. *J Acad Rehab Audiol*, 16 (1983), 12–22.

35. Giolas T, Wark D: Communication problems associated with unilateral hearing loss. *J Speech Hear Dis*, 41 (1967), 336–343.

36. Ross M: Binaural vs. monaural hearing aid amplification for hearing impaired individuals, in Bess F, ed: *Childhood Deafness: Causation, Assessment, and Management* (New York: Grune and Stratton, 1977).

37. Madell JR: Hearing aid evaluation procedures with children, in Rubin M: *Hearing Aids* (Baltimore: University Park Press, 1976), pp 103–108.

38. Rubin M: Hearing aids for infants and toddlers, in Rubin M, ed: *Hearing Aids: Current Concepts and Developments* (Baltimore: University Park Press, 1976).

39. Davis J: *Our Forgotten Children: Hard of Hearing Pupils in the Schools* (Minneapolis: Audio-Visual Library Service, University of Minnesota, 1977).

40. Davis JM, Elfenbein J, Schum R, Bentler RA: Effects of mild and moderate hearing impairments on language, educational and psychosocial behavior of children. *J Speech Hear Disord*, 51 (1986), 53–62.

41. Moores D: *Educating the Deaf: Psychology, Principles and Practices* (Boston: Houghton-Mifflin, 1978).

42. Gilston P: The hearing impaired child in the classroom: A guide for the classroom teacher, in Northcott WH, ed: *The Hearing Impaired Child in the Regular Classroom* (Washington DC: AG Bell, 1973).

43. Berg F: *Facilitating Classroom Listening.* (Boston: Little, Brown & Co, College Hill Press, 1986).

44. O'Neill J, Oyer H: *Visual Communication for the Hard of Hearing* (Englewood Cliffs, NJ: Prentice-Hall, 1961).

45. Alpiner J: *Handbook of Adult Rehabilitative Audiology*, ed 2 (Baltimore: Williams and Wilkins Co, 1982).

46. Kaplan H, Bally S, Garretson C: *Speechreading: A Way to Improve Understanding* (Washington, DC: Gallaudet College Press, 1985).

47. Osberger MJ, et al: *Language and Learning Skills of Hearing-Impaired Students*, ASHA monograph No. 23 (Rockville, MD: American Speech-Language Hearing Assn, 1986).

48. Hutchinson J, Smith LL: Language and speech of the hearing impaired, in Schow RL, Nerbonne MA, eds: *Introduction to Aural Rehabilitation* (Baltimore, MD: University Park Press, 1980).

49. Kretschmer R, Kretschmer L: *Language Development and Intervention with the Hearing Impaired* (Baltimore: University Park Press, 1978).

50. Mussen EF: *A Study of the Relationship Between Measures of Speech Reception and Proficiency in Language*, dissertation (Columbus, OH: Ohio State University, 1954).

51. Jeffers J, Barley M: *Speechreading* (Springfield, IL: Charles C. Thomas, 1971).

52. Kelly JF, Whitehead RL: Integrated spoken and written English instruction for the hearing-impaired student. *J Speech Hear Dis*, 48 (1983), 415–422.

53. Sanders D: *Aural Rehabilitation* (Englewood Cliffs, NJ: Prentice-Hall, 1982).

54. Schow RL, Nerbonne MA: *Introduction to Aural Rehabilitation.* (Baltimore, MD: University Park Press, 1980).

55. Sanders D: Auditory perception of speech, in *Aural Rehabilitation* (Englewood Cliffs, NJ: Prentice-Hall, 1977).

56. Slobin D: Cognitive prerequisites for grammar, in Ferguson C, Slobin D, eds: *Studies in Child Language Development* (New York: Holt, Rinehart, Winston, 1973), pp 175–208.

57. Stoel-Gammon C, Otomo K: Babbling development of hearing-impaired and normally hearing subjects. *J Speech Hear Disord*, 51 (1986), 33–41.

58. Stoel-Gammon C: Phonetic inventories, 15–24 months: A longitudinal study. *J Speech Hear Res*, 28 (1985), 505–512.

59. Calvert D: *Descriptive Phonetics* (New York: Thieme-Stratton, Inc, 1980).

60. Van Tassell DJ: Auditory perception of speech, in Davis JM and Hardick EJ: *Rehabilitative Audiology for Children and Adults* (New York: John Wiley & Sons, 1981), pp 13–58.

61. Nitchie E: *New Lessons in Lip Reading* (Philadelphia: New York: JB Lippincott Co, 1950).

62. Seewald RC, Ross M, Giolas TG, Yonovitz A: Primary modality for speech perception in children with normal and impaired hearing. *J*

Speech Hear Res, 28 (1985), 36–46.

63. Liberman A, Cooper F, Shankweiler D, Studdert-Kennedy MD: Perception of the speech code. *Psychol Rev*, 74 (1967), 431–461.

64. Lloyd L: Sentence familiarity as a factor in speech perception. *J Speech Hear Dis*, 29 (1967), 409–413.

65. Boothroyd A: Speech perception and sensorineural hearing loss, in Ross M, Giolas T, eds: *Auditory Management of Hearing-Impaired Children* (Baltimore: University Park Press, 1978).

66. Binnie CA, Montgomery AA, Jackson PL: Auditory and visual contributions to the perception of consonants. *J Speech Hear Res*, 17 (1974), 619–630.

67. Woodward MF, Barber CG: Phoneme perception in lipreading. *J Speech Hear Res*, 3 (1960), 212–222.

68. Owens E, Blazek B: Visemes observed by hearing impaired and normal hearing adult viewers. *J Speech Hear Res*, 28 (1985), 381–393.

69. Sher A, Owens E: Consonant confusions associated with hearing loss above 2000 Hz. *J Speech Hear Res*, 17 (1974), 669–681.

70. Erber NP: Auditory, visual and auditory-visual recognition of consonants by children with normal and impaired hearing. *J Speech Hear Res* 15 (1972), 413–422.

71. Erber NP: Effects of angle, distance, and illumination on visual reception of speech by profoundly deaf children. *J Speech Hear Res*, 17 (1974), 99–112.

72. Owens E, Benedict M, Schubert E: Consonant phoneme errors associated with pure tone configurations and certain types of hearing impairment. *J Speech Hear Res*, 15 (1972), 308–322.

73. Owens E: Consonant errors and remediation in sensorineural hearing loss. *J Speech Hear Dis*, 43 (1978), 331–347.

74. Nabelek AK, Mason D: Effect of noise and reverberation on binaural and monaural word identification by subjects with various audiograms. *J Speech Hear Res*, 24 (1981), 375–383.

75. Nabelek AK, Pickett JM: Reception of consonants in a classroom as affected by monaural and binaural listening, noise, reverberation, and hearing aids. *J Acoustic Soc Amer*, 56 (1974), 628–639.

76. Dorman MF, Lindholm JM, Hannley MT: Influence of the first formant on the recognition of voiced stop consonants by hearing-impaired listeners. *J Speech Hear Res*, 28 (1985), 377–380.

77. Bilger R, Wang M: Consonant confusions in patients with sensorineural hearing loss. *J Speech Hear Res*, 19 (1976), 18–748.

78. Garstecki D: Auditory, visual, and combined auditory-visual speech perception. *J Acad Rehab Audiol*, 16 (1983), 221–233.

79. Bunger A: *Speechreading—Jena Method*. (Danville, IL: Interstate Press, 1932).

80. Fletcher SG: Visual feedback and lip-positioning skills of children with and without impaired hearing. *J Speech Hear Res*, 29 (1986), 231–239.

81. Erber NP, McMahan DA: Effects of sentence context on recognitions of words through lipreading by deaf children. *J Speech Hear Res*, 19 (1976), 112–119.

82. Weiss AL, Carney AE, Leonard LB: Perceived contrastive stress production in hearing-impaired and normal-hearing children. *J Speech Hear Res*, 28 (1985), 26–35.

83. Keith RW: *SCAN: A Screening Test for Auditory Disorders* (San Antonio, TX: Harcourt Brace Jovanovich, Psychol Corp, 1986), pp 36–39.

84. Picheny MA, Durlach NI, Braida LD: Speaking clearly for the hard of hearing I: Intelligibility differences between clear and conversational speech. *J Speech Hear Res*, 28 (1985), 96–103.

85. Brackett D, Maxon AB: Service delivery alternatives for the mainstreamed hearing-impaired child. *Lang, Speech Hearing Serv in Schools*, 17 (1986), 115–125.

86. Picheny MA, Durlach NI, Braida LD: Speaking clearly for the hard of hearing II: Acoustic characteristics of clear and conversational speech. *J Speech Hear Res*, 29 (1986), 434–446.

APPENDIX

Language Arts Series, 1980. Incentives for Learning. 600 West Van Buren Street, Chicago, IL 60607.

PEP: Auditory Perceptual Enhancement Program, 1978. 4 Volumes. Modern Education Corp., Tulsa, OK. Each volume has cassettes with a manual.

Subtelny J, Lieberth AK: *Speech and Auditory Training: A Program for Adolescents with Hearing Impairments and Language Disorders.* Communication Skill Builders, PO Box 42050, Tucson, AZ 85733. Manual and three easel/flip books.

Utley J: *What's Its Name?* Maico Hearing Instrument Co., 7375 Bush Lake Road, Minneapolis, MN 55435.

Whitehurst MW: *Auditory Training for Children* (Washington, DC: AG Bell, 1986).

16

REMEDIATION OF CHILDREN WITH AUDITORY LANGUAGE LEARNING DISORDERS

Lynda Miller

INTRODUCTION

This chapter is not a how-to-do-it guide. Rather, it represents my attempt to share with the reader my ideas about language and language intervention as they relate to the child with an auditory language disorder. Because I believe strongly that you cannot *know* something intimately (an idea, a manner of interacting, a technique, for example) until you have actively shaped it to fit your own perceptions, I have set two major objectives for the chapter. The first is to acquaint (or reacquaint) the reader with topics related to language and some of the roles language plays in human development and communication. The second goal is to provide an exploratory framework for the reader to create meaningful strategies, according to individual situations, for use in attempting to facilitate the acquisition of language in children who are experiencing difficulties with the process.

There are no hard, definitive answers in this chapter. Among the ideas presented here, some are tentative and not as well tested as others. All have been derived from an attempt to meld theory with its sometimes limited practical applicability, and clinical findings with their inherent constraints that become manifest in any endeavor to teach language to a child with a language disorder.

The study of language acquisition and language disorders has undergone a variety of rapid and occasionally revolutionary developments in the last two decades. The ideas in this chapter reflect that growth and many of its associated growing pains. Much of the information included here is based on theoretic work that has not previously been thoroughly reviewed in the applied arena. Thus, the intent of the chapter is to cause the reader to begin thinking about what these ideas mean; and in so doing, to test theory against application.

A few remarks need to be made at this point about the term *language disorders*. The use of the term throughout this chapter reflects Bloom and Lahey's[1] practice of using the term not as a diagnostic entity or as an explanation of behavior, but rather as a descriptive label. Thus, using Bloom and Lahey's definition, a language disorder is "any disruption in the learning of a native language—that is, in the learning or use of the conventional system of arbitrary signals used by persons in the environment as a code for representing ideas about the world for communication" (p 298). Thus, the term *language disorder* as it is used here should be interpreted in a general and broad descriptive sense. Because a language disorder is regarded as any disruption in the learning of one's native language, a portion of the chapter will be devoted to discussion of the *normal* process of communication and the use of language as a means of achieving communicative ends.

Communication, Language, and Speech

When asked if communication, language, and speech are identical, most of us would agree that they are not. Yet, when pressed to specify what the differences among the three processes are, many would be unable to provide more than a vague description. The intent of this section is to remove some of that vagueness by characterizing each of the three and relating it to the others. Let us begin by focusing on communication, the process which encompasses the broadest, most general set of characteristics of the three.

Communication can be viewed as the transfer of information or knowledge. More specifically, human communication involves some sort of sharing or joint participation. Colin

Cherry[2] has defined communication as a "*sharing* of elements of behavior, or modes of life, by the existence of sets of rules, " (emphasis in the original) and as the "sharing of common sets of rules." Communication processes contain an organization reflected in the rules people adhere to in their communicative interactions. People follow the various rules of communication to share with each other ideas, feelings, news of importance, impressions, and judgments. Some of the rule systems governing human communication will be discussed in greater depth in later sections of this chapter. For now, it is important to realize that human communication is not chaotic or haphazard but organized and predictable in how it proceeds.

Also, it is necessary to realize that human communication can be carried out in a variety of modes. That is, an idea can be conveyed through the use of a picture, such as a smiling face or a traffic sign. It can be conveyed through one's body posture, movement, and facial expression, as in a shrug of shoulders, raised eyebrows, or tentative posture to indicate puzzlement; or an idea can be indicated through the use of linguistic signs, as in the word *beautiful*. The point is, communication between people can be realized in a variety of ways, including pictorial, nonlinguistic, and linguistic. It is to the linguistic mode that we turn now.

The term *linguistic* refers specifically to language, which in its most general sense means an organized system of signs* used to stand for, or represent, the people, objects, events, and processes of the world in which we live. A language is a code or set of rules agreed upon by the members of a given community, used to refer to the world as that community perceives it. That is not to say that a group of elders in any given language community ever actually sat down together to formally agree that the word *mastodon*, for example, should be used in reference to the great hairy beast that is the forerunner of the modern elephant. The so-called *rules of language* have most likely evolved, much as humanity has, into distinct and unique groups, each of which can be called a language in its own right. Each modern language community makes use of its particular set of rules for organizing human ideas into forms suitable for transmission via speech, print, and manual sign language, among others, from one person to another. The term *language* does not usually nor appropriately include the use of the body and its various roles in communication; for example, the raised eyebrow and shoulder shrug to indicate puzzlement. In its most precise sense, language indicates the relationship between speech sounds, manually produced signs, or the written word and the meanings underlying these overt signals. As such, language is only one of several devices used in communication. In fact, Langacker calls language an "instrument of communication,"[3] implying that communication is a general and broad process, while language as a relatively restricted process provides one specific means by which to engage in communication. To continue with the example of the raised eyebrow, one can easily and efficiently communicate an idea (e.g., *I don't know*) by using the raised eyebrow, shrug of the shoulders, and outspread hands, all without the use of what we refer to as language; that is, without a word being spoken or signed.

Where does speech fit into this scheme? As language can be viewed as one of many possible devices used to communicate, speech can be viewed as one of several possible devices used to translate language structures into a form suitable for transmitting information between speaker and listener. That is, language structures can be transformed into many different yet related formats, such as the spoken word, *justice*, the printed word, *justice*, or the signed form could be used as well. Similarly, a native speaker of English may choose for reasons of style or emphasis to say, "The ant was eaten by the aardvark" rather than "The aardvark ate the ant." These sequences of speech sounds are both possible and are governed by the rules of English regarding the relationship between active and passive sentences. A native user of *American sign language* (ASL) would sign the two forms differently. Again, each sequence of manual signs is possible within the constraints of the language rules of ASL. Both of these examples serve to clarify the relationship between speech (or manually produced signs or the written word) and language; that is, speech is merely one way in which the forms of language may be realized. Speech may be regarded as a tool for rendering one's

---

*A *sign* is defined by Cherry as "any physical event used in communicating" (p 7).[2]

intentions into a form that will be recognizable and interpretable by another speaker (or signer or reader) of the same language. Speech is obviously not the same as language, but rather, can be considered a subsystem of language, just as language may be considered a subsystem of communication. Context and its influence on communication and language will be discussed in the section on language function.

Communication Function: Its Influence on Language Structure

Until recently, the emphasis in language intervention had rested squarely and solely on language structure, particularly syntax, or the grammatic forms of language. For example, most people involved in language intervention focused attention on word order in sentences; proper verb markers, as in "The lady is eating," where the *is* and the *-ing* were stressed; on prepositions such as *on, in, ahead*; on the articles *the, a,* and *an*, and so on. Over the past several years, however, students of language acquisition and language disorders have begun emphasizing the uses to which language structures are put, or the functions that language structures serve. The shift in emphasis reflects a growing awareness that language is merely one tool by which humans communicate, and that communication is the basic process; language structures vary as a direct result of communicative need. Hence, any plan to design intervention procedures must of necessity include designs for language structures that are matched with the communicative functions those structures are to serve. As we will see in the later discussion, language structures vary according to one's intention in communicating, and the circumstances under which those intentions are shared. For instance, the language structures one chooses to address a close friend are quite different from those chosen for an elderly aunt. One would most likely not say to the elderly aunt, "Hey, turkey, how's tricks?" although such a greeting is not unlikely between affectionate male friends. To clarify the relationship between communicative function and language structure, it is helpful at this point to describe briefly the communicative functions that have been receiving the most attention in recent work.

Communicative Intentions

The purpose of communication is to share something; for example, an idea, a feeling, new information, a desire. Humans intend to do something when they communicate with each other. They intend for something to happen, for the listener to be affected in some way by the communicative acts that have taken place. Exactly what are people's intentions in communicating? It may be argued that people basically wish or intend to be acknowledged, and they engage in communicative acts to share attention with others of the same species. However, more to the present point is that people wish to convey relatively specific intentions by their communicative acts. For instance, people frequently want someone to perform some act, such as taking out the trash or walking the dog. People also often wish to obtain new information. One may ask, for example, "What is the name of that ant-eating animal with the long nose?" Although there are as many communicative intentions as there are human desires, it is possible to provide a partial listing of common human communicative intentions. Such a listing is presented in Table 16-1. Following each intention are examples of language structures that might be used to signal that intention to another.

It is readily apparent from Table 16-1 that a wide variety of language structures may be used to signal one's communicative intentions. Some of the examples directly illustrate the intent underlying the communicative act, while others only indirectly reflect intent.

Degree of Directness in Communicating Intent

Consider this Halloween conversation between a teacher and a kindergartner:

Teacher:	"We're almost finished with these pumpkins. All we need are the eyes."
Child:	"I'm making big, *giant* eyes!"
Teacher:	"Good idea. I like those eyes . . . That's fine. Want to help me clean up now?"
Child:	"No."

Table 16-1 A Partial Listing of Communicative Intentions

Intention	Spoken Variants Used to Signal Intention
Share knowledge	"This is a carburetor and here's how it works." "Did you know the geese are back on the lake?"
Request information	"What's that called?" "Where's the can opener?" "Who is that woman on the bus?"
Negation	"I'm not going." "It isn't in the drawer." "I didn't see it."
Demand	"Close the door quietly." "Hit the ball." "Would you mind passing the salt?" (implied) "I'd certainly like a warmer room."
Greeting	"Hi, George." "Good evening, Senator Jones."
Ritualizing	"How are you?" "Hope the weather changes soon."

It is apparent from the final exchange that the teacher has used a language form that adults recognize as a politely stated command to clean up, but the child has interpreted it on the basis of its overt form as a question that ostensibly allows for a choice on the child's part. The example shows that adults use a wide variety of language forms that state only indirectly the underlying communicative intent, while children in the process of acquiring language rely on more basic means of interpreting intent. That is, children respond to the literal meanings of language structures, such as "You're pulling my leg," long before they begin discovering that many language forms carry multiple meanings. Several types of language structures carry multiple meanings, some of which evolved as meaning in general; for example, idiomatic expressions, others of which seem related more closely to social patterns such as polite forms used to indirectly express demands (e.g., "Would you mind emptying the trash?"), or socially appropriate forms of address (e.g., "Hi, sweetie" vs. "How do you do, Mr. President?"). Other indirect forms for con-

veying communicative intent are related to humor, as in riddles and sarcasm. For instance, if two friends have agreed to attend a fund-raising dinner together, and one friend arrives dressed in her best attire, the other might indirectly compliment her by saying, "I don't know if I can be seen with anyone in such rags."

There appears to be a continuum of degrees of directness in communicating intent ranging from extremely direct to extremely indirect. The direct forms are straightforward and immediately apparent, while the most indirect forms are covert, often extending over lengthy periods of time. Table 16-2 shows possible degrees of directness for certain language structures in order of decreasing directness.

Choosing which form to use in any circumstance depends not only on one's knowledge about multiple levels of meaning in language, but also on one's knowledge of how social contexts affect the choice of language structure; that is, what is appropriate in a given context. Language choices are constrained by the communicative function of the language. By using the appropriate degree of directness in communicating, one can match structure with function in order to communicate effectively and efficiently.

Related to the communication of intentions is the process whereby speakers, singers, and writers (hereafter referred to generically by the term *speakers*) decide exactly what infor-

Table 16-2 Degrees of Directness in Communicating Intent

Language Form	Intent
"Close the door."	Demand (close the door)
"Can you put your coat on?"	Demand (put your coat on)
"Can you tell me the time?"	Demand (tell me the time)
"Would you mind closing the door?"	Demand (close the door)
"Did you know Bill quit?"	Sharing information (Bill quit)
"It's certainly warm in here."	Demand (open the window)
"Mom, you make the best cookies!"	Demand (give me a cookie)
"Dear, isn't that new Schooner a cute little car?"	Demand (give me a new car)

mation must be provided to their listeners so as to convey the underlying intent of the message; or how much background must one provide the listener with before revealing the actual intent of the communication? In other words, what is the relationship between old and new information in any given conversation?

Relationship Between New and Old Information

A 4-year-old girl walked into our preschool one day and said to me, "She did it again." With only the information provided in the child's sentence, I could not ascertain the exact nature of her intent. Obviously, more information was needed. The 4-year-old had given me too much new information and not enough old to relate to the new. Specifically, I needed to know who "she" was and what "it" entailed. I could only deduce that whatever had happened must have occurred previously. Because I did not have enough clues to discern her intent, her utterance failed as a successful conveyor of intent.

Speakers must decide how much and what information their listeners already have in order to provide just the right type and the correct amount of new information to effectively carry communicative intent. The speaker must not provide too much nor too little, and what is provided must be couched in a form that matches the circumstances in which the conversation is taking place. How do speakers judge what their listeners already know? They do so on the basis of a wide variety of clues, only some of which have been identified. Some characteristics of listeners that provide primary clues upon which most speakers decide how to structure their language are age, sex, skin color, dialect, dress, hair style, beliefs (e.g., religious, political), personality characteristics (e.g., warm, outgoing, cool, distant), and power relationship (e.g., employer-employee). Other variables include geographic location of the conversation, weather, season, physical surroundings, what is happening at the present, what just happened, and one's general knowledge about the world, especially knowledge about human behavior. To get an idea of the effects these variables have on the speaker's choice of what and how much information to provide for a listener, compare Examples 1A, 1B, 2A, 2B.

In these two examples, the speaker altered the amount and type of information provided to his listeners according to assumptions he had made about their prior knowledge from clues provided by the listeners themselves, and from the social contexts surrounding each conversation. In the first example, the rancher made assumptions on the basis of external cues, such as the license plate, car, dress, and mispronunciation of a word. In the second, the assumptions centered on the ages and the degree of intimacy shared by speaker and listener.

Adults routinely and unconsciously make assumptions about their listeners like those exemplified above. Children, however, assume that everyone knows everything about them and their world; and as a consequence, many of their utterances fail to convey intent accurately or effectively, as with the 4-year-old previously mentioned. The task children face is learning what *not* to assume about their listeners in order to judge exactly what and how much information is needed. The child gradually becomes able to recognize the signs about a listener that signal which assumptions may be made safely. As a child develops facility in recognizing such clues, the child's speech begins to reflect that facility, so that a 5-year-old child might have been able to give me, a naive listener, enough background to know that "She did it again" refers to her older sister who had yet another automobile accident. The 5-year-old child would establish enough old information for the new to make sense.

How Conversations Work

When asked to produce a set of rules that explain what people do when they converse with each other, most of us would be unable to do so. Yet most people are vaguely aware that some conversations are easier to participate in than others, and that it is easier to grasp the meanings contained in some conversations than in others. What are we aware of about conversations? People seem to engage in conversations by adhering to and systematically violating a set of tacit rules for ensuring cooperation in communicating. More will be said later about violations. This set of rules has been described by Bates as a boy scout code of

Example 1A

A slightly battered pick-up truck with a local license plate drives up to a Montana ranch. The occupants, dressed in hiking attire, get out of the truck to talk to a man in the corral.

"Nice looking horse. He registered?"

"Nope. Just a grade horse I use to work cattle."

"How do you get to the road to Yanqui Lake?"

"Well, you have to go back down to Peterson's upper ranch road. Follow it to the first fork and then take a right. It's on up there. How long you going for?"

"About a week, if the fishing's any good. Otherwise 'til our food gets low."

"Fishing should be good right now. The lake's settled and nobody's been up there all week."

Example 1B

A foreign compact car with an out-of-state license drives up to the same ranch. These occupants, too, are dressed in hiking clothing, but it is obviously new and expensive.

"How do you get to the road to Jackie Lake [Yanqui Lake]?"

"Have you ever been up here before?"

"No."

"Well, you have to go back down this road to the country section road you crossed on the way up. It's marked with a sign that says '8.' Turn right and go about 9 miles until you come to a big sign that says 'Peterson Ranch' on it. Go up to the house and ask for Emma. She'll tell you how to go from there."

Example 2A

Conversation between teenaged boy and his father's friend:

"Hi, Mr. Longgren."

"Hello, Terry."

"Come on in. Dad's out back. Would you like to sit down while I go get him?"

"That would be fine."

"Can I get you a glass of iced tea or some water while you wait?"

"Why, yes. That'd be real nice. It's sure a hot one out there."

Example 2B

Conversation between 2 teenaged boys:

"Hi, Terry."

"Hi, James. Hey, come on in. Let's go up and listen to my new album. It's primo, man. Those guys are outrageous."

"OK. But I'm really thirsty."

"OK, man, grab a Coke. Grab one for me too while you're in the fridge."

ethics governing conversations.[4] In general, these rules of conversation as stated by Bates are "that speakers will tell each other the truth, that they will only offer information assumed to be new and relevant to the listener, that they will request information that they sincerely want to have, and so forth" (p 27). More specifically, Grice[5] has identified four conventions that people should adhere to in their conversations: (1) contribute just the right amount of information, neither too much nor too little; (2) tell the truth by not stating what you believe to be untrue and do not state something without possessing supporting evidence; (3) be relevant given the circumstances surrounding the conversation at hand; and (4) be brief, orderly, clear, and unambiguous in what you say. Unless both listener and speaker share the knowledge that one of these conventions has been violated, as when a speaker asks, "Can you tell me the time?" and both speaker and listener know that the speaker does not wish to know whether the listener has the ability to tell time but the time itself, the listener grasps the speaker's meaning and intent by using these rules of cooperation as guides to determine the most likely meaning. If the listener is unable to determine what rules are being used, the speaker's intent is either not understood, and/or the conversation breaks down. Another sort of conventionalized violation includes idiomatic expressions and forms of humor such as irony and sarcasm. Expressions of this type use the indirect forms for communicating intentions described previously in this chapter. This second violation can be illustrated by returning to the example of finding out the time. The sentence, "Can you tell me the time?" clearly violates the principle of asking only for what one sincerely wants to know. Obviously, the speaker is not asking a question about the listener's ability to tell time; because it is such a clear violation, both speaker and listener treat it as a polite variant on the demand, "Tell me the time."

How conversations work depends also on a different sort of agreement among speakers alternating speaking turns and how the turns are determined. Rees[6] cites work by Sacks in which stretches of conversations were analyzed. Their analysis revealed that although no rules were formally specified prior to the conversation, speakers took turns, they usually did not talk at the same time (or knew how to resolve the overlap when it did occur), they showed signs that designated who the next speaker would be, and so forth. How children are thought to acquire knowledge about engaging in conversations will be treated in more detail in another section.

Summary

Language can be thought of as a component within the larger context of communication, which in its broadest sense refers to the transfer of information. More specifically, human communication involves a sharing of ideas, thoughts, feelings, and news, among others. In communicating, humans use a variety of language forms, or structures, to convey any of several basic intentions. Each of several degrees of directness used to communicate intention results in a separate language form. Thus, language form varies according to intention and the degree of directness with which that intention is communicated.

Language structure also varies as a function of the amount of old or prior information a speaker judges the listener needs or has in order to effectively and appropriately understand the speaker's intent. A speaker makes assumptions about how much information the listener already knows, and modifies language structures as a result of those assumptions.

Conversations between two or more speakers are governed by a tacitly agreed upon set of conventions for cooperating in communicating. People make reference to these basic conventions in their attempts to capture the underlying intents of others, and they use conventionalized violations of these cooperative principles to add information and variety to the form of their utterances.

LANGUAGE INTERVENTION: GOALS

Before attempting to plan and implement any language intervention with a child exhibiting a language disorder, it is very useful to recognize the highly social nature of language use. It has been suggested that language structures are determined in large part by the communicative function to which they are to be put. Communication has been described as a highly social process involving sharing attention with another person, and language was viewed as one means by which people share or communicate. The most convincing argument that this is so comes from Jerome Bruner,[8] who has stated very cogently that language develops to ensure the communicative cooperation constructed between an infant and its primary caretaker (usually the mother) in their earliest social interchanges. Bruner suggests that the mother and child mutually develop a set of routines that allow them to attend to the same object (or *referent*) or activity. These early routines serve as the basis for communication development in that they establish procedures for cooperation in attending. The procedures that mother and child develop include taking turns, following the other's gaze to the object of attention, providing visible and audible (in hearing children) feedback for the other, and (in the mother's case) linguistically marking the entire process with sounds or signs, words, or short phrases or sentences.

Bruner further suggests that these social procedures provide the infant with experience in participating in what he calls the *communication game*. As the child grows and matures, the child acquires more facility with the communication game, and in fact constructs variants on the basic communication game in the form of alternate language forms. As the child develops greater facility with various language structures, he becomes more adept at appropriately matching language structures to the social circumstances in which the conversation occurs. Once again, language function can be seen to determine the choice of language structure used to communicate.

The implications for those engaged in language intervention are twofold: (*1*) the more experience the child has in constructing language structures to match actual social or contextual constraints, the easier for the child to develop facility as an effective and appropriate communicator; and (*2*) with one exception, focus on language structure in isolation, or as an abstract exercise devoid of context, is *not* likely to result in any change in the child's striving to communicate well in a variety of circumstances. The exception is a child who is linguistically (and cognitively) advanced enough to be able to understand that one can actually talk *about* language. That is, for direct teaching of specific language structures to produce desired change, the child must be able to understand that such a thing as language exists, that

there are entities we call sounds, signs, words, sentences, and so on, and that one can consciously manipulate these entities to produce a desired effect on a listener. This knowledge is termed *metalinguistic awareness*. An excellent discussion of this and other higher level language functions can be found in Wallach and Butler.[9] Most children who demonstrate a language disorder seem unable to reflect on language in this manner.

It was argued in the preceding paragraphs that language structures can be thought of as tools for use in the social process of communicating with others. To put it another way, the use of language structures can be viewed as a game—a variation of the basic communication game to which Bruner refers.[8] Specific suggestions for both indirect and direct means for facilitating the acquisition and use of particular language structures are included later in this chapter.

To build language-based objectives suitable for a particular child, the interventionist must have made a decision that the patterns of language currently used by the child do signify a disorder that is, or has, a high probability for becoming, handicapping. Making such a decision requires that the interventionist gather and analyze carefully several types of evidence regarding the child. Specifically, evidence must be obtained about the child's history and patterns of physical growth, including the motor production of speech and/or sign, emotional development, cognitive growth, and communication. While the first three areas of development are closely interrelated with communication, emphasis will be placed on obtaining and analyzing information regarding the child's development of and current patterns of functioning in communication.

Goals for Language Intervention: Ongoing Assessment

To construct goals for language intervention, the clinician must focus on the *content* and the *process* as separate aspects of intervention. The process component of language intervention is defined as the methods and procedures by which the intervention plan is carried out (to be discussed later); the content component can be described as the particular communicative and language structures, contents, and functions to be included in the intervention plan. To state intervention objectives for a given child, then, the clinician must describe the specific structures, contents, and functions judged to be appropriate for that child, considering the child's unique patterns of development and functioning in all areas of growth. The clinician carefully structures objectives so that they reflect the child's ongoing development. In other words, the clinician must constantly be aware of the child's communication needs and design goals to match those needs. How does the clinician judge which structures, contents, and functions are appropriate? The clinician continually assesses the effectiveness and appropriateness with which the child matches language structures and contents to communicative intent and to the surrounding social context. This ongoing assessment yields critical information about the child's communicative and language growth, from which the clinician can derive intervention objectives.

To begin designing these objectives, it is useful to organize the assessed content areas of communication and language into a manageable format. The next section consists of a detailed outline of content areas for assessment. One should note that the outline presented is far from complete. This lack is largely because most of the descriptive evidence about the development of language in nonhandicapped children has been gathered on very young children. Relatively little research has centered on the developing language of older children. Also, the vast majority of descriptions deal only with the acquisition and development of oral language. Almost no evidence documents the acquisition and development of sign as a natural language. For these reasons, the bulk of the examples cited in the next section reflects the development of communicative facility with oral language. With three exceptions that will be noted, the information to be presented can be obtained by observing the child communicate in a variety of settings. If the clinician and the child are communicating, a tape recording can be made from which the information can later be transferred. For a thorough analysis, it is most helpful to record a spontaneous conversation between the child and a peer or a young child's primary caretaker. The purpose of the recording is to obtain a sample of the communication and language patterns most representative of that child. For this reason, the conversation recorded should

be spontaneous and free-flowing, and free of the didactic questioning adults often use to get children to talk. For a more complete discussion of obtaining a spontaneous sample of conversation, see Hubbell.[10] The tape should include approximately 100 utterances from the child. The clinician can transfer into written form what each person says, being careful not to accidentally include a form the child did not actually produce (e.g., "The dog is eating," when the child said "Doggie eating.") Any ongoing contextual information that will aid in the analysis should also be included. For instance:

Clinician:	"Here's a big horse." (Indicates a toy horse near the toy barn.)
Child:	"Horsie drinking." (Pretends to make horse drink imaginary water.)

Organizing the Evidence: A Narrative Outline

What follows is a detailed outline, in narrative form, for use in comparing the communication and language patterns of the normal and the language-disordered child. Although the information in each category is in a roughly developmental sequence, it should not be construed as being ordered in any kind of interval fashion. The reader should also note that for any given child, one need not attempt to apply each and every descriptive category. Once the clinician has obtained a conversation sample, it can be analyzed according to the categories of the outline which best fit the child's level of development.

I. Communicative Interactions: An Analysis of the Functions of Communication and Language[11]

A. Joint Attention and Joint Activity.
Bruner[8] has cogently argued that children develop facility in communicating through the process of interacting with an adult as they mutually attend to some object, person, process, or event. In addition to mutually sharing attention, child and adult also share some activity; that is, they share joint attention around an activity of mutual interest. The shared activ-

ity typically includes ritualized components, such as "peek-a-boo," which develop into the basic rules or routines characteristic of play. Thus, engaging in communication involves playing the communication game described previously. To play the communication game, the participants share attention with each other as they engage in some activity of mutual interest. Bruner[8] has contended that learning to play the communication game is a necessary prerequisite for the emergence of language. In other words, language emerges as an efficient means of playing the communication game, although the use of language is only one tool of the game.

The following behavioral components are typical of children as they engage in joint attention and activity with an adult:

(1) The child shows (or points out) to another person an object, person, event, process, etc.
(2) The child watches another when the other points out, shows, or verbally directs the child's attention to an object.
(3) The child engages in ritualized routines such as peek-a-boo, bye-bye, pushing a ball back and forth, etc.
(4) The child engages in cooperative play.

B. Joint Referencing. The notion of joint referencing is closely related to the concepts of joint attention and joint activity, and is again drawn from the work of Bruner.[8] To engage in joint referencing means that the child is able to indicate to another (and to understand another's indication) what the child is attending to and communicating about. In other words, the child must be able to indicate to others specific persons, objects, events, processes, and so on; he or she must also be able to ascertain which specific persons or objects, the other is discussing.

Children engage in joint referencing by exhibiting the following:

(1) The child engages in eye-to-face contact with an adult.
(2) The child follows an adult's line of regard to an object, person process, etc.
(3) The child follows the physical movement of an adult's hand or body.
(4) The child follows the adult's verbal pointing to an object, etc.
(5) The child uses physical movement, gaze, or verbal indicator to point to an object, etc.

C. Conversational Participation. A large part of being able to play the communication game is the ability to engage in conversations, verbal and nonverbal, with others. The developing child, by joint attending, acting, and referring with an important adult, develops strategies for taking turns in the communication game. At first a child's strategies are quite undifferentiated and general, such as nonspeech vocalizing and gesturing broadly with arms, legs, head, and trunk. Later the child becomes more specific in conversational turns by including intonation contours in vocalizing, and by using gestures more suited to specific reference. The critical aspect in this category is not the exact *form* of conversational turn, but the fact of taking turns.

Two aspects of conversational turn-taking are of interest:

(1) The child takes conversational turns non-verbally through the use of intonation, body posture and gesture, voice quality, and gestural reference to context.
(2) The child takes conversational turns verbally.

D. Intentions in Communicating. The description of one's intentions in communicating has received a great deal of attention within the framework of pragmatics theory. Pragmatics involves the study of communication intentions, or performative intentions as Bates[4] terms them, and allows for the analysis of one aspect of pragmatic development in the child. To describe communication intentions, two components should be analyzed: types of intentions used by the child, and degree of directness in communicating intention.

(1) Types of Intentions. Adults typically hold a variety of intentions in communicating. They use a plethora of structures to communicate; for example, the intentions to persuade, to convince, to cajole, to promise, or to anger. Children, on the other hand, seem to use a more restricted set of intentions in communicating, among them the following:

(a) To share attention with another. This intention perhaps best describes the communication of very young children before they become able to incorporate differentiated intonation into their conversations.

(b) To declare, to demand, to question, and to negate. These four intentions are characteristic of children before they can use referential speech to convey intention, and after they

become able to use differentiated intonation. Each of the four intentions listed here is characterized by a unique intonation contour, accompanied by a unique vocal quality, set of facial expressions, general and specific body postures and movements, and set of contextual conditions.

(c) Dore's nine primitive speech act types.[12] Dore's model was derived from the study of communicative intentions used by children at the one-word utterance level of development. Examples of each of the nine types are: *Labeling:* the child says "Doggie" while pointing to the dog. *Repeating:* the child repeats a word used by an adult (e.g., "doll"). *Answering:* the child responds when the mother asks, "What's this?" *Requesting action:* the child indicates a desire for an adult to do something. *Requesting answer:* the child uses a questioning intonation. *Calling:* the child says someone's name clearly to gain that person's attention. *Greeting:* the child says, "Hi." *Protesting:* the child says, "No." *Practicing:* the child uses a word out of context and with no response from the other.

(d) Halliday's adult intentions.[13] Halliday proposed that as the child makes the transition from the one-word utterance level to more sophisticated language forms, the intentions the child becomes able to communicate undergo a corresponding shift. The child becomes able to use the same surface form (word or phrase) to exemplify different intents and in different structural contexts. Halliday classifies communication intentions as falling into two major categories:

> *Pragmatic:* the child uses language to effect a desired change. For example, the child says, "I want milk," or "Throw me the ball."
> *Mathetic:* the child uses language in a learning fashion, or to facilitate cognition. For example, the child says, "Why is candy hard?" or "This is a green car."

(2) Degree of Directness in Communicating Intention. The reader will recall that there are both direct and indirect means by which one can communicate intent. Children appear to begin playing the communication game by very directly communicating their intentions so that their conversational partner can quite easily discern their intended meaning. As children develop facility with communication and with language, they become able to communi-

cate the same intention using different forms, and eventually engage in the use of very indirect language forms to signal underlying intent. There appear to be three major stages in the development of the means to communicate intention:

(a) Direct communication of intent occurs preverbally, or before the emergence of referential speech. The *prelinguistic imperative* is when the child uses the adult to get what is wanted; for example, by pointing and whimpering, looking back and forth from adult to object, or taking the adult to or near the desired object. The *prelinguistic declarative* is when the child uses an object, process, event, state, or self to obtain and share the adult's attention; for example, by bringing a toy to the adult, vocalizing, and indicating the toy. The *prelinguistic negative* occurs when the child uses body and voice to express negation; for example, by shaking the head, whining, and using facial grimaces. The *prelinguistic interrogative* is used when the child uses body and voice to indicate a question; for example, by rising intonation, tentative posture, and quizzical facial expression.

(b) Direct verbal communication of intent accompanies the emergence of referential speech. During this period, the child operates as if there is a direct correspondence between what one says and what one means. In other words, the child may have several different forms of indicating needs and intention, but does not realize that language form can be totally separated from underlying intent. To illustrate, a child may be able to indicate the intention of *Give me a cookie* by saying, "I want a cookie," or "I need a cookie." However, the child most likely would not be able to indicate this intention by saying, "Your cookies are delicious."

Characteristics of children at this stage include adherence to the cooperative rules for conversation described earlier, and one-to-one mapping of language structure to underlying intent; that is, the child says exactly what he means.

(c) Indirect verbal communication of intent occurs only after the child develops the cognitive awareness that language structures can be separated from the things for which they stand. In other words, when the child understands that language is arbitrarily related to the objects and ideas that it represents, the child can begin camouflaging intentions with a variety of

surface forms that are likely to result in obtaining the desire. Aspects of indirect communication of intent are seen in the child's ability to use a many-to-one correspondence between form and meaning. Such forms include: (1) idiomatic expressions (e.g., "You're pulling my leg"); (2) softened forms (*Child:* Please? *Adult:* No. *Child:* Pretty please? *Adult:* No. *Child:* Pretty please with ice cream on top? *Adult:* No. *Child:* Pretty please with ice cream and a cherry on top? *Adult:* Oh, alright); (3) polite forms ("How do you do, Mr. Smith?"); and (4) sarcasm ("Gee, you look terrific.").

E. Providing Old and New Information, or Keeping the Meaning Going. The relationship between new and old information, or keeping the meaning flowing in conversations has already been discussed. It was pointed out that conversational partners must make assumptions about what each already knows or brings to the conversation so as to supply just the right amount of information to make one's point, or to get across one's communicative intent. The ability to provide one's partner with new information is closely related to being able to engage in joint referencing. Out of a background of available information, one indicates to the conversational partner exactly what it is he is referring to. In other words, within context and around a theme or topic, one chooses aspects of personal interest and makes a comment (or comments) about them. How children indicate topic and comment or what they want to talk about is not precisely known. However, the following characteristics appear in the conversations children have with adults.

(1) The child indicates he is establishing comment, or providing new information through gaze or line of regard, through nonverbal pointing, through verbal pointing; for example, *here, it, there, this, that,* etc., or through direct linguistic markers of new information (e.g., "The point I want to make is . . ." or "You remember the guy I told you was at the bowling alley? Well, he . . . .").

(2) The child indicates establishing a topic, or providing old information in these ways: (a) through reliance on the partner's knowledge of immediate and non-immediate, relevant context; (b) through nonverbal reference to topic coupled with verbal statement of comment. For example, the child picks up an empty glass from which he has just drunk milk and says, "More!"; (c) through verbal provision of both topic *and* comment (e.g., "More [comment] milk [topic]!"); and (d) through verbal establishment of topic by name and later reference to it through use of a linguistic "shortcut." In the sentence, "You know Chuck: he's my brother, and yesterday he went skiing and said it was great." *Chuck* names the topic by name, while *he* is a linguistic shortcut by which to refer to it again once it has been established. *Yesterday he went skiing* etc. is the comment. Or, "See that *pencil sharpener* (topic named), well, *it's* (topic referred by pronoun shortcut) *broken* (comment made verbally).

II. Communicative Strategies: An Analysis of the Form or Structures of Language

While the communicative uses to which language is put are a critical part of the child's communication development, the language forms chosen in the service of those communicative functions must be examined as well. There are two major components for analysis: semantics and syntax.

A. Semantics. Semantics has to do with how the child translates what he knows about the world into language forms. A great deal of recent attention has been paid to the child's development of facility with the semantic relationships inherent in his native language. Two recent comprehensive investigations into children's semantic structures at the one-word utterance stage of development form the basis for the following descriptions.

(1) Analysis of the conversational sample by comparison with Nelson's[14] study of children's first 50 words (see McLean and Snyder-McLean[15] for a more complete description). The conversational sample can be studied and the utterances described according to the categories described by Nelson. Using such an analysis in conjunction with the one in (2) immediately following allows one to determine whether the child is limited to the use of only a few of the categories. More specifically, the analysis allows one to see which semantic structures and relationships do not appear at all or appear with very low frequency in the child's conversation, indicating that such structures or relationships are not productive for the child and are therefore candidates for intervention. The reader should keep in mind

that these categories of semantic forms did not appear with equal frequency in the children's spontaneous language. The percentage of relative frequency of appearance appears in parentheses following each class. Nelson's categories are as follows:

(*a*) *Specific nominals.* Names of specific people (e.g., "Mommy") animals, and objects (14%).

(*b*) *General nominals.* Names of objects, substances, animals, and people (e.g., "girl"), letters and numbers, abstractions, and pronouns (51%).

(*c*) *Action words.* Demand-descriptive such as "go," "bye bye," and "up" (13%).

(*d*) *Modifiers.* Attributes ("big"), conditions ("hot"), locatives ("there"), and possessives ("mine") (9%).

(*e*) *Personal-social words.* Assertions ("want") (4%).

(*f*) *Social-expressives.* ("Please") (4%).

(*g*) *Function words.* Questions ("what") (4%).

(*2*) A useful comparison can be made by using Bloom's[16] data regarding the types of semantic relationship exhibited in the child's single-word language. Bloom delineates these types: *existence*, the use of words to point out objects (e.g., "there," "uh, oh"); *recurrence*, the use of words to request an activity or object or to comment on the recurrence of activity or objective (e.g., "more"); *disappearance*, the use of words to comment on the disappearance of an object in context (e.g., "allgone"); *nonexistence*, the use of words to comment on nonexistence where existence had been expected (e.g., "no"); *cessation*, the use of words to comment on the cessation of an activity (e.g., "stop"); *rejection* or *denial*, the use of words to protest undesired action or comment on a forbidden object such as a stove (e.g., "no"); *action*, the use of words to request action (e.g., "up"); and *location*, the use of words to comment on spatial location (e.g., "there").

(*3*) To analyze the semantic relationships evidenced in the child's spontaneous multiword utterances, the reader can use the description given by McLean and Snyder-McLean,[15] shown in Table 16-3.

(*4*) For children whose utterances are at the multiword level, further useful descriptive information can be gained by analyzing the conversational sample for evidence of the child's use of word endings and prepositions according to Brown's[17] evidence regarding order of

Table 16-3   The MacLean/Snyder-Maclean Analysis of Semantic Relationships in a Child's Spontaneous Multiword Speech[15]

Semantic Classification	Example
Agent-action	"Me read."
Action-object	"Read book."
Demonstrative + nomination	"It book" or "That book."
Notice	"Hi truck."
Possessor-possession	"Daddy hat."
Recurrence	"More milk."
Nonexistence	"No doggie" or "Milk all gone."
Entity-locative	"Sweater chair."
Action-locative	"Sit chair."
Agent-object	"Bobby book."
Conjunction	"Hat coat."
Agent-action-object	"Bobby spill juice."
Agent-action-location	"Daddy sit chair."
Action-object-locative	"Throw ball here."
Agent-object-locative	"Daddy ball chair."

acquisition. Those listed in Table 16-4 are in developmental order.

(*5*) On occasion it is informative to investigate the child's understanding of the semantic components of compound words. (This information may be gained through direct questioning rather than observed or taken from the sample of conversation.) Berko[18] has suggested four stages in the child's acquisition of meaning for compound words. The first is *identity definition*. At this stage, the child defines the word by saying, "An X is called an X because it's an X," or "An airplane is called an airplane because it's an airplane." The second stage is the *salient feature* or *function definition*. This definition involves reference to a feature or function of the word but is not related to either of the two words comprising the compound. For example, "A fireplace is called a fireplace because it keeps you warm." The third stage is when the child supplies a *word-related feature* or *function definition*. At this time, the child's definition contains reference to one or another of the two words making up the compound; for example, "A blackboard is called a blackboard because of its color." The fourth stage, the *etymologic definition*, is when the child's definition takes into account both root words and their meanings. At this stage, a child could say, "A birthday is

Table 16-4   Brown's Order of Acquisition of Word Endings and Prepositions[17]*

Word Ending or Preposition	Form
Present progressive	-ing; e.g., "running"
Prepositions	up, in, on
Regular plural	-s, es; e.g., "cats," "houses"
Irregular past	came, ran, ate
Possessive	'-s; e.g., "Daddy's"
Uncontractable forms of is	is, am, are; e.g., "She is pretty."
Articles	a, the
Regular past	-d, -ed, -t; e.g., "bragged," "painted," "hoped"
Present verb tense marker for third person	-s, -z; e.g., "He hits."
Irregular third person verb tense marker	does, has; e.g., "She does it."
Uncontractable auxiliary use of forms of is	is, am, are; e.g., "He is eating."
Contractable forms of is	'-s, '-m, '-re; e.g., "They're tired."
Contractable auxiliary forms of is	'-s, '-m, '-re; e.g., "I'm singing."

*These word endings and prepositions apply only to spoken and written English and are not applicable to ASL.

called a birthday because you celebrate the day you were born."

The words Berko used were: *afternoon, airplane, birthday, breakfast, fireplace, football, handkerchief, holiday, merry-go-round, newspaper, sunshine, Thanksgiving, sunshine, Friday.* In this procedure, the child is asked "Why is a(n) ____ called a(n) ____?" and his responses are recorded for later analysis.

B. Syntax. Syntax has to do with how the child organizes what he knows into formal linguistic structures. Syntax entails analysis of the forms the child uses to match communicative intent to grammatical structures. Syntax represents a set of strategies for successfully, efficiently, and appropriately communicating one's communicative intent. Acquisition of a variety of syntactic structures allows one the freedom to choose particular structures for stylistic purposes and/or because those structures are deemed appropriate by the culture in a particular set of circumstances. Acquisition of a variety of syntactic structures allows for the use of an elaborate code for communicating intent. A child who has acquired only one set of syntactic structures is severely limited in choosing alternatives and can be said to be operating with a restricted linguistic code for communicating intent. Analysis of syntactic structure, then, gives the clinician or teacher a clear idea of the relative richness or paucity of syntactic form available to any given child. The following language patterns can be evaluated syntactically:

(1) Two-word utterances. Evaluate according to the predominant grammatic patterns listed in Table 16-5.

(2) Three-word utterances. Evaluate based on the predominant grammatic patterns, paraphrased from McLean and Snyder-McLean,[15] shown in Table 16-6.

(3) Mean Morpheme per Utterance. This syntactic analysis is based on a modification of Brown's method.[17,p 54] Because the chronologic age at which children in the earliest stages of language acquire any given grammatic form varies considerably, the *mean morpheme/utterance* (MMU) has begun to be used as a guidepost to index grammatic development. Brown has argued that virtually every new kind of grammatic knowledge increases length up to the point at which what the child says and the structures used are determined more by the nature of the communicative interaction than by what the child knows about grammar. For most children, the MMU is a valid indicator of grammatic knowledge until they are able to coordinate compound sentences using *and, or, but, because, if, then, nevertheless, although,* and so on.

Table 16-5   Syntactic Analysis of Two-Word Utterances

Syntactic Structure	Example
Noun-Verb	"Him fall," "Mommy eat."
Noun-Noun	"Daddy ball" meaning *Daddy hit the ball.*
Verb-Noun	"Drink milk."
Modifier-Noun	"Big truck," "My car," "More juice."
Noun-Modifier	"Milk allgone."
Preposition-Noun	"In sink," "On table."
Locative-Noun	"Here truck."
Demonstrative-Noun	"That doggie."

Table 16-6 Syntactic Analysis of Three-Word Utterances[15]

Syntactic Structure	Example
Noun-Verb-Noun	"Me sit chair."
Verb-Noun-Locative	"Throw ball here."
Verb-Noun-Preposition	"Put ball in."
Noun-Noun-Noun	"Me ball box."
Noun-Modifier-Noun	"It big ball."
Locative-Modifier-Noun	"Here big car."

*Rules for Calculating MMU**

(*1*) From the spontaneous conversational sample obtained and transcribed, count out 100 of the child's utterances for the calculation.

(*2*) Count the number of words in the sample according to these guidelines:

(*a*) Unless there is evidence that the child understands the individual components of compound words (explained previously), count all compound words, proper names, and ritualized words as one word (e.g., *birthday, choochoo,* and *night-night*).

(b) Do not count fillers, such as *um, oh,* but do count, *no, yeah, hi.*

(*c*) Unless there is evidence that the child uses irregular past tense markers as exceptions to the regular past tense rule, count all irregular past tense markers as one element (e.g., *ran, saw*). Otherwise count them as two (*run* + past tense marker = *ran* = two elements).

(*d*) Unless the child evidences understanding of diminutives as derived forms, count them as one element (e.g., *duckling.* Otherwise count as two (*cow* + dimunitive = *calf* = two elements).

(*e*) Count all auxiliary verbs as one element each (e.g., *is, have, will, can, must, should*). Also count as one element *gonna, wanna, hafta.*

(*f*) Count as separate elements all word endings such as the possessive *-s* forms, the plural *-s* forms, the regular past tense forms of *-ed,* the progressive verb form *-ing,* and the third person singular verb form *-s,* as in "He hits."

(*3*) Divide the total number of words and elements by the total number of utterances (100 for the MMU).

$$MMU = \frac{Total\ Number\ of\ Words\ and\ Elements}{Total\ Number\ of\ Utterances}$$

A revealing comparison can be made between the MMU and the mean number of words per utterance (M#WU).† The higher the ratio of MMU/M#WU, the more complex the child's language development. The closer to one the ratio is, the less complex the child's morphologic development. For example, if the MMU/M#WU ratio is 4:1, the child's morphologic development can be said to be more complex than if the ratio had been 1.1:1.

(4) *Question Forms.* Studying the question forms used by the child is another indicator of syntactic development. Roughly, the developmental order in the acquisition of question forms can be described as follows:

(*a*) *Yes-No* questions. First, there is the use of rising intonation alone (e.g., "The dog is eating the sandwich?"). Then, the child uses reversed word order *and* intonation: "Is the dog eating the sandwich?" Finally, the child is able to insert an extra grammatic element to indicate verb tense (e.g., "*Did* the dog eat the sandwich?").

(*b*) *Wh-* questions. First, the *wh-* element is inserted without corresponding change in word order (e.g., "What doggie eat?" "What the dog is eating?" "What the dog was eating?"). Then, the child inserts the *wh-* element plus an extra grammatic element to indicate verb tense (e.g., "What the dog *did* eat?"). Finally, the child can insert the *wh-* element, and grammatic tense marker, and also reverse word order (e.g., "What did the dog eat?").

(5) *Forms of Negation.* Negations used by the child are also manifestations of the child's syntactic development. A general developmental order is as follows: First, the child uses a head shake joined with affirmative syntactic structure (e.g., "That mine horse," with head shake). *No* or *not* is then inserted into the syntactic structure (e.g., "No mine horse," "That not mine."). This is followed by use of *can't, don't, won't* (e.g., "Me can't do it," "Him can't go"); (the use of double negatives) (e.g., "You can't have no juice," or "I'm not going to do nothing"); and finally, the use of appropriate negative form with the appropriate affirmative indefinite pronoun (e.g., "You can't have *any* juice," or "I'm not going to do *anything*").

(6) *Types of Embedding.* The use of utterances that contain one sentence included within another is called *embedding,* and reflects syntactic development (e.g., "The man

---

*Not to be used for children acquiring ASL.

†A public school clinician in northern Idaho suggested this comparison.

who came to our house is a friend"). Embedding develops according to this pattern: (*a*) Use of *think, know, hope, tell*, mean as main verb followed by an embedded sentence (e.g., "I know *what it was*," or "I hope *I can do it*"); (*b*) the use of embedded *wh-* questions (e.g., "*Whoever hit her* should apologize," "He ate *what he could*," "Do you know *where my mitt is*?"; and (*c*) the use of relative clauses (e.g., "I know *what you mean*," "The man *who left the package* is gone," and "The picture *John made* fell down").

It should be reiterated that while the clinician will wish to evaluate the major categories of communicative functions and language structures listed in the preceding outline, each of the subcategories does not apply to every child. That is, the clinician can observe the child, obtain a sample of conversation, and judge which specific areas need analysis in preparation for designing intervention goals. Once the desired information has been gathered and analyzed, specific language intervention objectives can be constructed for that particular child. Case History 1 illustrates the use of language intervention goals specifically designed for a particular child. The goals were set following information gathering and evaluation according to the model presented in the preceding discussion. The procedure for

accomplishing these goals will then be discussed.

LANGUAGE INTERVENTION: PROCEDURES

The procedural strategies for language intervention to be described next are direct outgrowths of the previous sections of the chapter. These strategies reflect the idea that human development in general, communication, and language development in particular, occur as a function of the interaction between the genetic characteristics of the organism and the environmental conditions that organism encounters. Language structures are also viewed as means by which people organize what they know about their world with their communicative intentions so as to share their intentions and their knowledge with others. In addition, the particular structures of language used in any given circumstances are seen as reflections of the unique function they must serve under those conditions, at that particular time, with just those participants. With these reminders at hand, discussion now shifts to the *process* of language intervention, or the procedures and methods whereby the clinician at-

---

Case history #1

JOHN: A SUMMARY OF CURRENT COMMUNICATIVE FUNCTIONING AND OBJECTIVES FOR LANGUAGE INTERVENTION

Summary: John, 3 years old, was observed to engage spontaneously and actively in communicative interactions with other children and with his parents. In addition, he engaged in a 30-minute communicative interaction with the clinician. Observations from that half-hour interaction indicate the following:

Communicative Interactions: John readily engaged in cooperative play with an adult. During play, John indicated ability to share joint attention and activity with the clinician, and both partners established joint reference through pointing, physical orientation, and verbal means. The communicative intentions evident during the half hour were:

Verbal labelling: "Here a cow."
Repeating adult utterance: "Drink, Mr. Cow."
Answering: "I no have hay."
Requesting action: "Bring cow here?"
Requesting answer: "Where sheep go?"
Greeting: "Hi!"

John signaled his communicative intentions through very direct verbal and nonverbal means. There was no evidence of understanding of multiple levels of meaning in language. Because the play centered on objects within the immediate, present context of a toy farm and its accompanying animals, objects, and people, there was little opportunity to determine how well John provided his listener with old and new information about topics outside the immediate surroundings. His utterances during play, however, typically included both topic (old) and comment (new); e.g., "It a *big* cow." He also made frequent use of personal pronouns to indicate referents within the context; e.g., *Clinician:* "Where's the truck?" *John:* "*It* over here."

Communicative Strategies:

Semantics: The semantic relationships evident in John's utterances were the following:

> Notice: "*Hi*, Mr. Cow."
> Agent-Action: "Horse drink."
> Agent-Action-Object: "Him eat hay."
> Agent-Action-Locative: "Him fall down."
> Agent-Object-Locative: "Man hat there."
> Possessor-Possession: "This *mine* truck."
> Recurrence: "Him want *more* water."
> Nonexistence: "Hay *allgone!*"
> Conjunction: "Here a cow *and* a horse *and* a sheep *and* a chickens."

Word Endings and *Prepositions* used by John are:

> Present progressive: "Him eat*ing*."
> Regular plural: "Truck*s* need gas."
> Possessive: "It him*s*."
> Articles: "It *a* yellow hat!"
> Regular past tense: "Him walk*ed* over there."

Syntax: The majority of John's utterances are three to five words in length and typically include two to four word ending such as *-s, -ed, -ing,* and *-'s.* The MMU for this sample was 3.5. All utterances exhibited the appropriate order of elements. Question forms were signalled through intonation alone. Few examples have been heard of insertion of *wh-* element, and none of reversal of word order; e.g., "What him eating?" and "Him eating hay?" Negatives are generally formed through the use of *no* or *not,* although an occasional *don't* or *can't* is used; e.g., "Me *don't* have it," and "Me *can't* do it." No examples of embedding were heard.

Language Intervention Objectives for John

Communicative Interactions: For John to

> (1) Increase number of instances of verbally making joining reference within a conversation.
> (2) Increase number of verbal labels for objects, events, people, and processes, within a conversation.
> (3) Increase number of verbal responses to adult utterances in conversation.
> (4) Increase number of verbal protests in conversation.
> (5) Increase number of verbal references to events outside the immediate context.

Communicative Strategies: For John to

> (1) Begin using contractible forms of *is*; e.g., "He's here."
> (2) Begin using *the* in appropriate contexts.
> (3) Begin using contractible forms of the auxiliary *is*; e.g., "I'*m* running," "He'*s* eating," "They'*re* leaving."

tempts to facilitate growth and change in the child who exhibits a handicapping language disorder.

Adults, Children, and Play

Any discussion of how to intervene in language development rests upon some sort of idea about how children learn language in the first place. Procedures for language intervention must take into account what we know about the acquisition and development of language so that we can design procedures with the greatest likelihood of facilitating the child's attaining the objectives constructed.

It can be argued that human beings develop in response both to genetic and to environmental factors. It can be further argued that the child actively constructs what that child knows about the world and how he or she knows it, given the environmental opportunities for that construction. When applied to the process of learning language, the developmental model presented here suggests that the infant comes into the world with the genetic capacity to acquire and develop some sort of language system. That is, the infant has the necessary potential (e.g., neurologic, motor, sensory) to engage in symbolization and communication through the use of an organized linguistic system. In other words, humans possess the genetic capacity for constructing a complex and efficient means for sharing ideas with other humans. That means is what we have been calling *language*. Possessing such a capacity is not sufficient to ensure the development of a language system, however. The infant must be given appropriate environmental stimulation and opportunity in order for language to develop. That stimulation and opportunity usually come in the form of the infant's primary caretakers—the parents. According to McLean and Snyder-McLean, language development occurs in the context of "mutual responsiveness between adult and child."[15,p 68] They further state that to provide appropriate environmental opportunity for language development to occur, adults must respond to the child's intents in early signaling behavior, they must demonstrate the "segmenting of dynamic events and relationship which is reflected in

the semantic component of language,"[15,p68] and they must "provide appropriate models of the lexical and syntactic structures by which this semantic component is 'mapped .'"[15,p68]

Adults initially fulfill their roles as language stimulators through play, including both routine and ritualized forms of play (peek-a-boo, rock-a-bye baby) and creative and spontaneous play (with the child's favorite bathtub toy, or with a teddy bear). Out of these play sequences, language develops as what Bruner[8] calls a means for ensuring continued cooperating in communicating, or "an instrument for regulating joint activity and joint attention." Bruner further asserts that the mutual play between mother and infant leads the child "toward elaborating rule structures in communicating." In fact, he stated that "PLAY HAS THE EFFECT OF DRAWING THE CHILD'S ATTENTION TO COMMUNICATION ITSELF, AND TO THE STRUCTURE OF THE ACTS IN WHICH COMMUNICATION IS TAKING PLACE" (emphasis in the original).[8,p 10] Mutual play provides a structural framework for the mother and child to jointly focus attention on the linguistic markers, usually words and simple phrases, used to stand for the sequences of events unfolding in the play itself. Thus, one of the primary and most important ways in which the child acquires a language system is within the context of mutual play with an adult important to that child. As the child's play develops into more complex and symbolic forms, so too does his or her need for language structures appropriately complex for communicating to others the ideas embodied in play. The process continues until the child becomes able cognitively to perceive language as a distinct entity that can be reflected upon and discussed as an object made up of parts called *words*, *sounds*, *sentences*, etc. Until the child can reflect on language with its multiple levels of meaning and its one-structure-to-many-meaning aspect, language remains a tool or instrument to be used in sharing ideas and intentions, and play remains the primary mode within which the child learns about his world and about language. For these reasons, play is the basic fabric into which the clinician can weave specific procedures for facilitating language growth in the child who does not yet use language to talk about language. Procedures for the more developed child will be discussed later.

Play and Language Intervention

The most successful language intervention contexts used with children unable to reflect on language are those which hold the promise of creativity and spontaneity on the child's part. Because they are meaningful from the child's perspective, they create the *need* for language structures to reflect what the child is doing and thinking. The child's activity can mandate the need for language. The clinician participates as an active partner, to be sure, but not to force the child to learn language structures divorced from that which holds meaning *for the child*. In Bruner's words, the process of acquiring language structures to match functional needs is "made possible by the presence of an interpreting adult who operates not so much as a corrector or reinforcer but rather as a provider, an expander and idealizer of utterances while interacting with the child."[8,pp17–18] He adds that the process of language development depends "crucially on the context in which the communication occurs. Increasingly it [the process of language development] becomes more context-free, more . . . sensitive to the rules of language . . ."[8,p18]

With this in mind, the clinician interacts with the child in differing contexts. For young children, three primary contexts can be used: the therapy room, a preschool setting (and, on a few occasions, an elementary school classroom), and the surrounding neighborhood and community. The choice of which context to use at any given time is dependent upon the judgment of the clinician, who decides on the basis of the quality of interaction afforded by each particular context, and upon the rate of change noted in the child's communication and language.

The advantage of the therapy room is that the clinician can select the materials before the child arrives. The clinician can also arrange and manage the materials; for example, bringing out one set of materials at one time and another set later, in an effort to stimulate joint attention and reference to specific items and ideas. The therapy room is typically used for one-to-one interaction, usually with the more severely handicapped child.

The preschool setting can be used for groups of children and can operate according to an early childhood nursery school model. A typical structure is the mainstream model, where half of the children are mildly to moderately language-handicapped, and half are nonhandicapped. The physical layout includes activity areas such as dress-up, housekeeping, painting, large motor equipment, music, reading, and science centers. The time is scheduled so that the children engage in free play for approximately 30 minutes in interactions with adult clinicians and other children, outdoor play if weather permits, preparation, eating, and cleaning up of snack, a directed group activity such as a song or story, followed by a group craft project in which materials and theme are suggested by the clinicians. Occasional field trips are included. The children are in the program two hours per day, three to four days per week, depending on parental scheduling constraints.

Another language intervention context used with great success is the neighborhood surrounding the clinic and preschool. An ideal setting for children is woods, a river, a creek, railroad tracks and trains, an indoor swimming pool, playing fields, and a playground. The advantage in providing language intervention in these natural settings is that they engender natural and spontaneous conversations within which to use the specific procedures that will be described. The clinician does not have to "force" conversation; and, as a result, talk is spontaneous and carries meaning and import from the child's viewpoint. The major drawback is that it is virtually imperative to carry a tape recorder or to make ongoing notes to document daily language use by the children—both formidable feats when throwing rocks into the river with 12 children. Daily written logs are kept as a matter of course, and periodic video recordings are taken of all the children for further documentation of language growth.

The use of the elementary school classroom as a context for providing language intervention has been explored in an exciting project designed and executed by Weiss.[19] In her program, called INREAL, for INclass REActive Language therapy, she trained clinicians to provide language intervention without taking children out of their preschool and kindergarten classrooms. Together, the classroom teacher and language specialist, through a variety of both observational procedures and standardized measures, identified those children with handicapping language disorders. The clinician then spent a half-day each day in the classroom participating as a colleague of the teacher in planning and executing the daily activities. The clinician's specific role in the classroom was to integrate activities into the classroom that focused on language through the use of what Weiss calls "reactive language therapy." Weiss defines reactive language therapy as multifaceted in that it includes: (1) establishing an empathic relationship with the child—that is, becoming someone important to the child; (2) using the techniques of play therapy; and (3) employing the psycholinguistic techniques of self-talk and parallel talk, verbal monitoring and reflecting, expansion, and modeling. Weiss further reports that the use of this innovative approach cost local schools significantly less than traditional speech therapy and resulted in prevention of later learning disabilities with their attendant high costs of remediation.[20] She also points out that the reactive in-class language approach she used resulted in a very important *child-saving* ensuing from early identification and intervention.

The next section of this chapter spells out in more detail specific procedures to use in providing language intervention.

Specific Language Intervention Procedures

Throughout this chapter, continued reference has been made to the nature of the relationships among language function, content, and structure. It has been reiterated that the development of knowledge about and facility with language structures evolves directly from the communicative functions to which those structures are to be put. In addition, heavy emphasis has been placed on the active role the child takes as a conversational partner in developing efforts to structure utterances that match the child's communicative intent and the special constraints of each conversational situation. The language intervention procedures described here are outgrowths of these ideas. They are based on the interaction developmental model described earlier, and they emphasize communicative success rather than structural *correctness*. These procedures rest on the premise that adults—especially those engaging in language intervention—function as facilitators for children, or, as mentioned

earlier, what Bruner calls an "expander and idealizer of utterances."[8,p17] Bruner goes on to say, "It is not imitation that is going on, but an extension of action to the (language) sphere. Grammatical rules are learned by analogy with rules of action and attention."[8,pp17–18] Thus, the language interventionist can engage in the *modeling* of appropriate language structures that match both the communicative context and the child's developmental level. To model successfully, the adult must be an active communication partner in real conversations, and have a thorough knowledge of the child's cognitive and communicative development and current level of functioning. The adult must also use in his or her own speech language structures that are developmentally appropriate to a particular child in a given circumstance. By so doing, the adult uses language structures to refer to ideas, events, things, and people in a symbolic manner, thus segmenting the ongoing communication into clusters that can be described using linguistic forms.

In one sense, all adult behavior is a model for the child. The type of modeling described here is specific to communication and language and provides the child with just that information judged by the clinician to be appropriate for the child to see and/or hear. Here are some examples of modeling for children at differing levels of development.

Clinician A:	"We need the black horse."
Child:	"Here's the cow."
Clinician A:	"Yes, but we still need the black horse."
Child:	"Where the horse go'ed?"
Clinician A:	"I don't know. I wonder where it went. Lisa, where did the black horse go?"
Clinician B:	"Here it is. It was under the table."
Child:	"I wondered where it went?"

Child:	"Me bring eggs."
Clinician:	"O.K. They're all here."
Child:	Where /ə/ milk?
Clinician:	"Here's the milk, and here's the pan, too."
Child:	"I want chicken for eat."
Clinician:	"I don't. I want fish to eat."
Child:	"Why?"
Clinician:	"I like fish because it tastes good and it's cheaper than chicken."
Child:	"Well, I'll have fish to eat, too."

A special form of modeling occurs when the clinician and child are engaged in mutual play during which the child is doing little, if any talking. The clinician can verbally describe what is happening to the child, using language structures reflective of the child's developmental level. For instance:

Child:	(Picks up toy pig and offers it to clinician.)
Clinician:	"Here's the pig. I'm putting him inside the fence."
Child:	(Moves other animals inside fence.)
Clinician:	"Now you're putting the horse and the cow in."
Child:	(Pretends to have horse drink.)
Clinician:	"He's drinking water."

Another language intervention technique that can be used very effectively is expansion. *Expansion* is a term used by Brown et al[21] to describe when the adult repeats a child's utterance, adding the parts the adult judges to have been omitted. Although several expanded utterances could conceivably fit the child's utterance, the language interventionist deliberately chooses the one which best fits the context, or the extralinguistic situation. That is, the adult infers the child's communicative intent and meaning and chooses the expanded form that best matches that inferred intent. The child may say, for example, "That Daddy shoe," which could mean, "That was Daddy's shoe you saw," "That is Daddy's shoe," or "That is on Daddy's shoe." In the context of the conversation between the clinician and child, the adult can expand the utterance into the form resembling its most likely meaning given the circumstances. Some examples help illustrate.

Child:	"Horsie drink."
Clinician:	"Yes. The horse is drinking."
Child:	"Him eat grass."
Clinician:	"Now he's eating the grass."
Child:	"Where doggie?"
Clinician:	"Where is the dog?"
Child:	"Him table."
Clinician:	"Oh. He's on the table."

Modeling in its variant forms and expansion can be intermingled throughout a conversation. Because most middle-class parents expand approximately 30% of their children's utterances,[22] in the intervention contexts described above, clinicians strive for expansion of 30% of any given child's utterances in a conversation, and modeling of another 30%. The remainder of the child's utterances can then be responded to nonverbally, or not responded to at all if that is judged to be appropriate, or responded to with what I like to call "life-saver remarks," which include such sentences as "Don't drop that glass." "No, you may *not* bang on the fish tank," "That was absolutely terrific!," "You were really scared, weren't you?," "Yes, I missed you very much, too," and so on.

It is important to make a distinction that has a direct bearing on the language intervention techniques one uses, and more importantly, on how often and under what circumstances they are used. The distinction is between communication and noncommunication. Children, like adults, do not always want or need to communicate. They enjoy silent stretches during which nothing may be communicated. Being in another's presence suffices for the moment. For this reason, I include *silence* as a language intervention technique. I urge all my highly verbal graduate student clinicians to use silence as a powerful instrument within their box of clinical tools. Similarly, all clinicians would do well to remember that not all language used by the child is for communication purposes. Children frequently engage in language for other intents, including practicing and pure playing.[11,23]

While more developmentally advanced children may be able to reflect on and discuss the structures and functions of language, they do not automatically lose their need for play as a means for learning about their world. Language intervention can fruitfully take place in the context of play with these children as well. However, because they are more developmentally advanced, the nature of their play differs from that of less well-developed children, and language intervention should make a corresponding shift. With increasing cognitive development and social experience, children construct play that is increasingly elaborate in its complexity and more highly structured in its form. Play comes to take the form of games, complete with flexible themes and rules, but language intervention can be carried out within the context of virtually any game. In fact, in the process of inventing and describing new games, the language specialist can effectively utilize the specific language techniques described previously, once again maintaining the integrity of the language structure-communicative function relationship. Because the more developed child may be able to talk about language, it is occasionally fruitful for the language specialist to make direct reference to a particular language form. For example, the clinician and child may play a game in which each takes turns describing to the other how to build a toy figure out of differently colored toothpicks and jellybeans. The object of the game, which has been mutually invented, is to make a figure that matches a photo taken earlier by the clinician of a completed *marshmallow kid*.

Clinician:	"O.K. I put the big yellow one on top of the big green one. Now what do I do?"
Child:	"You've already tooken your turn! Now you tell *me*!"
Clinician:	"Oh, yeah. I've taken my turn. *Tooken* isn't used by most people. They say *taken*."
Child:	"Oh. O.K. *Taken. Now* tell me."

Constructing games jointly requires imagination, creativity, and energy. The language specialist may need an occasional hint about games that may be used with children of the developmental level referred to above. Muma has described "gaming procedures for the communication game" that will undoubtedly stimulate the clinician's thinking and provide grist for planning.[24] In using more elaborate games and/or direct references to specific language structures, the language specialist can never lose sight of the critical importance of the communicative function, from the child's point of view, to which any particular structure is to be put.

Parents as Agents in Language Intervention

Potentially, one of the most effective means by which to provide rich and varied language models for a child is through parents. Until a child reaches school age, the majority of the child's time is spent with parents. Even once he or she enters school, the child still lives, eats, and sleeps within the family constellation. The parents continue to exert tremendous influence on the child's development. Thus, the child's parents possess the potential for effecting the greatest amount of change in language development patterns, especially in comparison to the speech-language clinician, who may be allotted anywhere from 15 minutes to one hour two to three times per week with the child. How is the clinician to heed Muma's[24,p234] warning, "The more an individual is removed from natural contexts, the more power is lost in intervention. Language intervention should occur in natural contexts in natural ways about natural things."

One approach is to teach parents to act as language intervention agents, whether their language-handicapped child is school age or younger. The role of the language clinician or teacher shifts from the provider of direct language services for the child to that of teacher/consultant to the parents of that child. Such a shift requires imaginative schedule planning, especially when including working parents. What follows is a general guide for teaching parents as language intervention agents. One should know that the guide is written for use with parents who are relatively naive about development, and communication and language development in particular. Although many parents of school-age language-disordered children will have confronted their anxieties and fears about their child before the child enters school, some parents will not have had that opportunity before the language clinician begins to teach them how to interact more effectively with their own child. Thus, the clinician will need to select and modify appropriate components of this description of the *ideal*.

The first component in teaching parents to become effective language intervention agents for their child is to skillfully lead them to describe their child's level of development, especially in communication and language. The accuracy of their description is not necessary. What is necessary is that the parents actively construct their own characterization. It is helpful if they can observe their child in play (or school activities if the child is older) with other children his or her age. The clinician should encourage the parents to make statements about the child's relatively well-developed areas as well as the less well-developed areas. For parents who are anxious and/or fearful about their child's level of development and potential for future development, the skilled language clinician, teacher (or the school psychologist) can lead the parents into discussion of their fears. Jones[25] asserts that such discussion is critical for parents of handicapped children because there is pain associated with the knowledge that their child is not normal. Jones further argues that the pain felt by these parents is dealt with in the classic stages of the grief process as defined by Kubler-Ross[26]: (1) denial; (2) anger; (3) bargaining; (4) depression; and (5) acceptance. In the parent-training program described by Jones, the parents of handicapped children meet once per week with other parents of handicapped children to talk about feelings and to begin to take responsibility for the children by moving through the *grief* process.

A second component of the parent-teaching process is the mutual construction by parents and teacher or clinician of a model of communication development. During this phase, the clinician can provide factual information, in terms easily understandable by the parents, about communication development. Emphasis should be placed on the nonverbal and preverbal aspects of communication. Care should be taken to separate speech and grammar from the functional use of language and nonlinguistic means to communicate. If the parents are observing their child in interactions with others, the clinician or teacher can point out relevant examples of effective and appropriate communication that contain no speech or that contain ungrammatic elements. The clinician or teacher can also emphasize the communicative prerequisites of speech: such developmental phenomena as joint attention and activity, joint referencing, object permanence, the emergence of communicative intentions and their prelinguistic forms, and the emergence of symbolization. Charting the child's developmental progress lends a visual aid to the discussion and gives parents less opportunity to deny their child's developmental levels. Of particular importance is that the parents and teacher or clinician establish that language, and eventually speech and/or signed forms of language, emerges out of rich and meaningful human interactions between conversational partners.

A third component of teaching parents to become language facilitators is to jointly derive a set of techniques that can be modified for parental use. One of the most effective

means for arriving at a description of techniques is to view ongoing language intervention that includes the specific techniques of modeling and expansion, both described earlier, although they need not be labeled as such. The important thing is to lead parents to see them as techniques and to see the results that accrue. One method is for the clinician and parents to watch someone else using the techniques while the clinician describes or narrates the session. Another way is for the clinician to demonstrate and to discuss the demonstration afterward with the parents. A third approach is to narrate a previously videotaped session. Once again, the important aspect is that the parents are active participants in the process of deriving descriptions of the techniques. They must be equal partners in the task of constructing the intervention model they will eventually use with their own child.

The final step in teaching parents to become language facilitators for their child is to have them begin applying the techniques they have been viewing and describing. The use of videotaping greatly facilitates this process, as the clinician or teacher and parents can later view such practice sessions together, and evaluate and criticize the interactions. It is helpful to arrange a series of parent practice sessions spaced over a few weeks, so that the parents may engage in additional practice outside of the school or clinic. The evaluation discussions that arise from the taped practice sessions are often greatly enriched by the parents' questions and comments about their experiences outside school or clinic.

To provide structure for the discussions regarding adult-child communicative interactions, whether they be clinician-child or parent-child, the clinician may wish to categorize the interactions in some way. Mash et al[27] have described a functional system for categorizing and describing adult-child interactions. Their method allows for classification of the parents' communicative behaviors as follows:

1. Command. In this category are direct commands, or statements which include *imperatives* ("Come . . .," "Let me . . .," "Put this . . .," and "I want you. . ."). A direct command may be either *specific* ("Write your name") or *general* ("Go and play").

2. Command-Question. A command-question is a suggested or "implied" command which includes an *interrogative*:

"Will you hand me . . . ?"
"Shall we . . . ?"
"Why don't you . . . ?"
"Can you . . . ?"
"Would you like to . . . ?"

3. Question.

"What . . . (color is this)?"
"What . . . (would you like to do)?"
"Where is . . . ?"
"Who . . . ?"
"How does . . . ?"
"When did . . . ?"

4. Praise. The praise category includes both verbal statements and nonverbal actions indicating encouragement, acceptance, and/or approval of the child's behavior.
Verbal.

"O.K."
"Good . . ."
"That's fine . . ."
"I like that . . ."

Nonverbal. Nonverbal actions can include a pat on the back, a hug, a kiss, a clap, a head nod, or a smile. Some judgment can be used in interpreting context and tone of voice. A general rule of thumb is that when the above statements follow a *specific* task or behavior on the part of the child, they are considered praise. For example, if on the completion of a task the mother says, "O.K.," it is praise. If, on the other hand, the child asks permission to play, and the mother says, "O.K.," it is considered an interaction for the mother.

5. Negative. The negative category includes both verbal statements and nonverbal actions indicating discouragement, nonacceptance, and/or disapproval of the child's behavior. Negative verbal statements may take two forms. They may be direct disapproval or criticism.

"No, don't . . ."
"Stop . . ."
"Quit . . ."
"Bad boy . . ."
"That's not right . . ."
"You can do better than that."
"Don't do it that way."
"You make me sick."
"I don't like that."

Or, negative verbal statements can be implied criticism or threats.

"You're acting like a two-year-old!"
"If you don't stop . . . you'll get it!"
"You'd better watch it!"
"One more time and you're in trouble!"
"Your father won't like that when he hears about it!"

Nonverbal negative statements also may be either direct (a spank or hit, a pinch, a yank, a shove back in a chair, a shake of the head "no," or a frown), or a threat (a raised hand or shaking a finger at the child). Negative behavior on the part of the mother takes precedence over commands or question-commands; that is, if the mother says, "You get over here!" in a threatening manner, this is considered negative behavior on her part, rather than a command.

6. Interaction. Interaction is an attempt to *initiate* or *maintain* some type of mutual contact. Interaction may be either verbal or nonverbal. Verbal comments may be neutral, positive, or descriptive but can contain no criticisms, commands, or questions. The mother in some way communicates attention or expresses interest.

"That's a big bridge you're building."
"You sure are running fast."
"There are some toys in the box."
"We'll be going home when we're finished."
"mmm'mmm"

Nonverbal interaction can include holding parts of the same toy, handing an object to the child, smiling at the child (in this case, eye contact with the child must occur; if the child does not look at the mother when she is smiling at the child, her response is scored as "no response"), and any physical contact that is other than negative.

Use of a categorization system such as the one described here not only provides focus and direction for the clinician or teacher-parent critiques of adult-child interactions, but also allows for the collection of evidence regarding parental change over time in communicative interaction with a child. In addition, the clinician or teacher can collect communication and language data from the child, which, when compared to parental data, will provide evidence of the relationship between parental interactive behavior and child communication and language development and change. In the author's clinic, one clinician kept such corresponding types of data for parents and child and had discovered a very clear-cut relationship. During a session in which one parent (almost always the same parent) used a high frequency of *commands* and *questions*, the child's utterances consisted primarily of one word. During sessions in which one parent (usually the other parent) used a preponderance of *interactions* and *praise*, the child's utterances, while fewer in total frequency, consisted almost exclusively of three to five words.

SUMMARY

While the focus of this chapter has been on language and strategies for language assessment and intervention, it is obvious that the major emphasis throughout has been on the larger communicative context in which language develops as one of many ways for a child to communicate needs, desires, ideas, and emotions. Each person providing language assessment and intervention for children should keep close sight of the importance of communication rather than focus only on language form. Maintaining such a global view of language within the context of communication rather than focus only on language form. Maintaining such a global view of language within the context of communication prevents us from doing a disservice to the child as the child builds a personal version of what it means to be a participating human in this society.

REFERENCES

1. Bloom L, Lahey M: *Language Development and Language Disorders* (New York: John Wiley & Sons, 1978).
2. Cherry C: *On Human Communication*, ed 2 (Cambridge: The MIT Press, 1968), pp 6, 305.
3. Langacker R: *Language and Its Structure*, ed 2 (New York: Harcourt Brace Jovanovich, 1973), p 23.
4. Bates E: *Language and Context* (New York: Academic Press, 1976).
5. Grice HP: Logic and conversation, in Cole P, Morgan JL, eds: *Syntax and Semantics: Speech Acts*, Vol. 3 (New York: Academic Press, 1975).
6. Rees NS: Pragmatics of language, in Schiefelbusch RL, ed: *Bases of Language Intervention* (Baltimore: University Park Press, 1978).
7. Sacks H, Schegloff EA, Jefferson G: A simplest systematics for the organization of turn taking for conversation. *Language*, 50 (1974), 696–735.
8. Bruner J: The ontogenesis of speech acts. *J Child Lang*, 2 (1975), 1–19.
9. Wallach GP, Butler KG, eds: *Language Learning Disabilities in School-Age Children* (Baltimore: Williams and Wilkins Co, 1984).
10. Hubbell RD: On facilitating spontaneous talking in young children. *J Speech Hear Dis*, 42 (1977), 216–231.
11. Miller L: Pragmatics of early childhood language disorders. *J Speech Hear Dis*, 43 (1978), 419–436.
12. Dore J: Holophrases, speech acts, and language universals. *J Child Lang*, 2 (1975), 21–40.
13. Halliday MAK: Learning how to mean, in Lenneberg E, ed: *Foundations of Language Development: A Multidisciplinary Approach*, vol 1 (New York: Academic Press, 1975).
14. Nelson K: *Structure and Strategy in Learning to Talk*. Monographs of the Society for Research in Child Development, 38 (149), 1973.
15. McLean JE, Snyder-McLean LK: *A Transactional Approach to Early Language Training* (Columbus: Charles Merrill, 1978).
16. Bloom L: *One Word At a Time: The Use of Single Words Before Syntax* (The Hague: Mouton, 1973).
17. Brown R: *A First Language: The Early Stages* (Cambridge: Harvard University Press, 1973).
18. Berko J: The child's learning of English morphology. *Word*, 14 (1958), 150–177.
19. Weiss RS: *INREAL Longitudinal Effects on Later Language Learning Problems of Selected Children*, thesis (Boulder, CO: University of Colorado, 1978).
20. Weiss RS: *Cost Effectiveness of the 1974–75 and 1975–76 INREAL programs*, thesis (Boulder,

CO: University of Colorado, 1978).

21. Brown R, Cazden C, Bellugi U: The child's grammar from I to III, in *The 1967 Minnesota Symposium on Child Psychology* (Minneapolis: University of Minnesota Press, 1968).

22. McNeill D: *The Acquisition of Language* (New York: Harper and Row, 1970).

23. Weir R: *Language in the Crib* (The Hague: Mouton, 1962).

24. Muma J: *Language Handbook* (Englewood Cliffs: Prentice-Hall, 1978), p 234.

25. Jones KK: *Taking a Longer Look: A Manual on the TOTS Program* (Portland, OR: Crippled Children's Division, University of Oregon Health Sciences Center, 1978).

26. Kübler-Ross E: *On Death and Dying* (New York: Harper and Row, 1969).

27. Mash EJ, Terdal L, Anderson K: *The Response-class Matrix: A Procedure for Recording Parent-child Interactions*, thesis (Portland, OR: University of Oregon Health Sciences Center, 1976).

ADDITIONAL READINGS

An excellent compendium of material related to language-learning disorders in school-age children can be found in:

Wallach, GP, Butler KG, eds: *Language Learning Disabilities in School-Age Children* (Baltimore: Williams and Wilkins Co, 1984).

Another collection of information pertinent to language-learning disorders in school children is:

Simon CS, ed: *Communicative Skills and Classroom Success: Therapy Methodologies for Language-Learning Disabled Students* (San Diego: College-Hills, 1985).

For those particularly interested in reading further about communicative functions and their impact on children's language learning, see:

Prutting CA, Kirchner DM: A clinical appraisal of the pragmatic aspects of language. *J Speech Hear Dis*, 51 (1986), 147–171.

CLASSROOM INTERVENTION STRATEGIES AND RESOURCE MATERIALS FOR THE AUDITORILY HANDICAPPED CHILD

17

Virginia S. Berry

INTRODUCTION

The hearing impaired child in the mainstream is often manipulated by the well-meaning educator falling prey to the self-fulfilling prophecy.[1] Public Law 94-142 and all other education of the handicapped laws are often double-edged swords. Certainly one of the most positive outcomes has been an increased sensitivity to identifying handicapped children, and also improving awareness of the importance of meeting their educational needs. The result has been the rapid development of services within the *local education agency* (LEA) or the home school district.

In turn, an outgrowth of these positive trends has been the surfacing of increased labeling of children. Although a necessary evil, categorizing a child is a prerequisite to providing service. However, it is this process that is the catalyst for the educator's submission to the self-fulfilling prophecy.[1]

Teachers react, although often indirectly, to labels assigned to children. When told a child is *gifted*, expectations are set. This child is often given increased attention and special privileges. If creativity is expected, a child frequently responds accordingly. After reading a previous teacher's notes on the discipline difficulties with a child labeled as learning impaired, there is often a tendency to misjudge small misbehaviors as outrageous that would normally be overlooked or excused in other children.

Similar expectations are frequently assigned by teachers who have had a hearing impaired child placed in their class, particularly if the child comes with the label of *deaf*. Well-trained and experienced educators are outstanding professionals in many areas. However, with limited exposure to hearing impaired chil-

dren (or adults), they are likely to have many common misconceptions.[1]

> "Since this child cannot hear, he won't understand when he's talked to."
> "Since this child cannot hear, he must use sign language."
> "Since this child cannot hear, he will be slow in all areas."

Thus, the self-fulfilling prophecy begins.

The intent of this chapter is to provide the tools that an educator needs to manage the hearing impaired child successfully in the classroom. This chapter hopefully will illustrate that the strategies needed for the hearing impaired child are now more overwhelming than those basic strategies that make for a good educational setting in general.

Certainly, if an educator was modifying or redirecting all teaching to serve the hearing-impaired child, then the placement staff should ask the question, "Was mainstreaming premature?" Successful mainstreaming should include only a few overt classroom changes, with most techniques being subtle differences in style. One of the most important keys to the process is a teacher with a positive attitude and confidence who is not being transformed into a deaf educator. This chapter will discuss the skill necessary to permanently eliminate the fear of deafness, thereby ending the self-fulfilling prophecy.

Who Are the Kids?

Professionals are often plagued with the attitude that the only children who have special needs are those with the most obvious, most visible, and therefore the most severe problems. It is ironic to think that the hearing impaired child who often has the least difficulty "making it" in the regular classroom is the child with the more severe hearing loss. The reason for this is likely attributed to the direct relationship between severity of handicap and level or intensity of staff involvement. The mainstreamed, severely hearing impaired child is often older than the mildly impaired child, has received years of previous direct intervention, uses in-class interpreters/tutors, has use of special assistive devices, etc. In addition, teachers selected to serve these children are chosen after careful consideration of their knowledge and experience.[2]

On the other hand, children with lesser degrees of hearing loss of varying types are often not afforded such advantages. Are their special needs any less important? In fact, these children are often more difficult to serve in the regular classroom. Children with mild hearing losses, fluctuating losses, unilateral deficits, or high-frequency disorders are often overlooked when needs are outlined or programs are planned. For many years, these children were thought to be unaffected educationally by their hearing loss.

Certain techniques specific to this population are essential to incorporate in the classroom. As professionals, we must recognize the unique differences among hearing impaired children. Therefore, throughout this chapter, an attempt will be made to address specific areas of need.

Where Are the Kids?

In addition to often overlooking certain populations of hearing impaired children, educators and other professionals often neglect the issue of what placement is chosen for the child. Mainstreaming can be a fairly generic term, sometimes simply meaning the child attends lunch or recess with regular classes. The remainder of the day, it may be that educational needs are best met in a noncategory, self-contained special education classroom. In many districts, there are not enough hearing impaired children to justify a teacher of the deaf. Hearing impaired children are often served very successfully by special education teachers holding certification in another area, and in classrooms serving a variety of disabled children with differing needs.

The intent of this chapter is not to debate the validity or appropriateness of such placement. The point to be made, rather, is that some professionals serving hearing impaired children often assume that information on hearing loss and educational intervention goals does not need to be provided to any special educator.[3] The feeling is that their efforts should be to direct the strategies of the regular classroom teacher who has no experience with *special* children. Afterall, they reason that special educators have received all the training they needed in every exceptionality, including deafness.

If professionals are operating under this philosophy, they are missing an area of great need. Experience has proven that with the exception of certified teachers of the deaf, special education classroom teachers need suggested techniques and guidance for working with hearing impaired children; and they are anxious and receptive to receiving this type of information. The environment in which the child is placed cannot be neglected. Regardless of whether hearing impaired children are in regular classrooms full-time, resource rooms for a portion of the day for isolated tutoring in selected areas, or self-contained rooms for the entire day, their special needs and the intervention plans to meet these needs do not change. Equal time and energy should be placed on informing all varieties of educators to these needs.[4]

GETTING READY

Teacher Motivation

The successful implementation of any educational program is only as strong as the professionals responsible for it. All the training and experience in the world does not guarantee the will to succeed. Success hinges on the motivation level and attitude of those involved with the program.

Hearing professionals convince themselves that simply supplying school staff with pertinent case history information on the child, a summary of previous services, and tips for teaching would ensure trouble-free entry into the classroom. What is overlooked is that all-important variable—motivation. Regardless of what role a particular school staff member plays in the hearing impaired child's program, that professional must have a receptive attitude toward serving the child. The responsibility of working with this child means extra work for everyone who is involved with the child.[3]

The first important step in establishing the necessary receptive climate is to ensure that the classroom teacher feels a part of the child's total program.[4] Too often, hearing professionals enter a school situation bringing in their "better mouse trap." They fail to remember that educators perhaps also have some critical insight to add as to what makes for good teaching practices. School hearing professionals are often guilty of forgetting to listen to suggestions or concerns from other school staff.[3] In addition, hearing professionals typically have one goal when approaching school staff—meeting the needs of the hearing impaired child. Although commendable, they often overlook the needs of the educator.

In many situations, individuals are significantly more receptive to hard work or change if they feel they are allowed input into the direction of the effort. Therefore, enthusiasm for a "better mouse trap," should be tempered, so that school staff can describe their needs and take an active part in the planning of any special training they are to provide to the child.[5] Specific teaching strategies are much more likely to be incorporated in the classroom if the manager of that room has assisted in their design.

Administrative Preparation

An individual who is often overlooked as a critical element to the successfully mainstreamed hearing impaired child is the school administrator. Familiarization of these persons to the design of the program will have lasting effects of the outcome. Administrators can assist in the commitment to the child and supply confidence to the staff. They can foster the positive attitude of "We can make a difference for this child." They can arrange for the redistribution of duties for teachers serving children who have special needs. And certainly an all-important role is that administrators can support the funding of equipment and materials essential to helping school staff implement teaching strategies necessary for success.[6]

Therefore, professionals working with schools must include administrators in all activities, particularly during the initial stages of program development. They have needs to be addressed just as classroom staff do. Information should be provided that is relevant to their role, strategies should be directed to meeting their needs, and answers should be geared to eliminating their fears. The end result will be a cohesive program with a long-term emotional, professional, and financial commitment.

Team Management

If a hearing impaired child is expected to succeed in a mainstreamed educational environment, it is naive to consider this a "one-man show." It certainly must be a team effort. Members of the team are all individuals concerned with this child's progress. Each member has specific responsibilities and goals, and therefore requires specific strategies and intervention practices.[3]

Recognizing the importance of team management is prerequisite for any program. Identifying the team members and providing them with useful and relevant management information is essential. One individual should be designated team manager.[7] Too often, hearing professionals who are not school staff and are brought in only on a random consultant basis are made to feel as if they are the team managers. However, the role of the team manager is to provide consistency and continuity among members in the implementation of strategies. Is it possible for an individual who visits a school only a few times to serve in this capacity?

Although the hearing consultants are likely the individuals with extensive knowledge and expertise in the area of hearing impaired needs, they are not the individuals who can guarantee daily application of good educational principles. The primary teacher, for example, might be the more appropriate choice for team manager. This individual can assist the school counselor, the speech-language pathologist, the music teacher, the school secretary, etc., in carrying over successful management strategies from the classroom.

The underlying assumption, however, is that this primary teacher has been given the necessary tools for such management to pass on. Here enters the hearing professional. Although these consultants cannot guarantee continuity of daily programming, they can take responsibility for intensive training and education of school staff, particularly the team manager. If adequate staff preparation occurs, the team manager and, subsequently, each team member can take charge of consistent implementation.[4]

Members of the team that professionals often ignore are the parents. Too often, parents are considered a nuisance, a threat, and an intimidation. There are certainly parents who make it difficult to enjoy working with the child because of their pushy, "You work for me" attitude. However, if this aggression were traced back through the child's special service career, we may find it stems from parent needs that were ignored, questions that were unanswered, or concerns that were pushed aside and not addressed.[7]

Most parents want to have an active role in their child's programming, but not to the point of domination like many professionals often think. Parents can be important assistants in the process of identifying strategies that work. Who better to explain successful techniques in communication practices with a child than the individual who uses them most often?

Professionals need to listen carefully and attentively to parents. Information they supply will give insight into the child that educators often miss. Communicating to parents that their input is important and that their suggestions will be incorporated into the child's program is an essential aspect of successful educational programming.

The final essential member of the team is the child. For those children who are old enough to provide meaningful inputs, use it.[5] The child is the only true expert on what facilitates learning. Allow him or her to set the example for strategies that are useful. If the child is of an age that he or she cannot describe these strategies specifically, then observation and manipulation of various procedures will hold the answer.

In-Service Training

No matter what specific information is included for in-service training sessions, or what style or form these sessions take, the intent should be on developing a knowledgeable and accepting attitude toward hearing loss and hearing impaired students. The outcome of such training should be the establishment of a realistic educational environment in which hearing impaired children can function and progress.[8]

In-service training should assist in making school staff comfortable with the management of a hearing impaired child, thus creating that level of motivation and positive attitude necessary for success that was discussed previously. In-service training should not attempt to turn those participating into teachers of the deaf. All school professionals already have established skills as educators that can benefit hearing impaired students. In-service training should simply supply participants with information on how to modify their skills, and how to adapt their professional behavior to better serve the hearing impaired child.[8]

Hearing professionals who may likely be responsible for conducting in-service training must not be dogmatic. Remembering the principles of teacher motivation and team management, it is critical that participants do just that—participate. They must feel that the information presented gives them options for intervention.[3] Preparing staff for working with hearing impaired children should not take away their flexibility or creativity.

When establishing an in-service training program for a school, it is helpful if the information presented can be specific for the hearing impaired children in the school. It is the responsibility of the professional conducting the in-service to know the children in question. Rather than general information on hearing loss, hearing aids, teaching practices, etc., it is much more meaningful to present the topics chosen for discussion as they relate to the hearing impaired children enrolled in that school. Discuss each child's hearing loss and its educational implications. Discuss classroom activities as they relate to that child and trust school. It is helpful to have observed this child in some sort of teaching environment so that specific examples can be given. Know the specific curriculum and textbooks used in the child's class so that modifications necessary to them can be explained in terms of vocabulary, content, etc. If possible, it is certainly meaningful to have the child present during a portion of the in-service so that demonstrations of certain teaching strategies could be given.

There is a wealth of information that hearing professionals feel obliged to convey to school staff during in-service preparation. Table 17-1

Table 17-1 In-Service Training Topics: Teacher, Other School Staff, and Classmates

Definition of hearing loss and nature of problem.
Specific assessment information as it relates to each hearing impaired child (audiologic data, previous academic history, speech/language abilities, etc.).
Orientation to hearing aid, including operation, placement, and maintenance.
Auditory training.
Speech and language activities.
Behavior management.
IEP planning and implementation.
Teaching strategies.
Materials and resources.
Use of an interpreter, tutor, notetaker, or other supportive staff.
Acceptance in the classroom.
Communication needs.
Sign language classes.

contains examples of topics that might be covered. The goal of such training is to instill the attitude that hearing impaired students are a challenge—not a burden—and they can be an asset to the school. Presenters are often over-ambitious and attempt too much during the preparation stage of programming. Certainly our ambition is well meaning in that several areas of need are recognized that warrant discussion. Staff preparation should include information on language, communication, reading, behavior management, peer orientation, speech, hearing aids, classroom techniques, etc.[8]

The timing or scheduling of in-service training can be the variables that dictate the success of the program. School staff are already burdened with many extracurricular assignments, so presenters must guard against lengthy, after-school meetings. Also, brief, frequent meetings are often better received than two- to three-hour workshops. Each session could focus on one particular issue.

Although some initial in-service preparation is certainly necessary before a teacher assumes responsibility for a hearing impaired child, educators will have a much better understanding of a child's needs following direct classroom contact. Therefore, it is critical that in-servicing be an ongoing, continuous process. Staff preparation sessions preceding direct child contact do just that—prepare staff. They do not and certainly cannot acquaint staff with

all situations that may arise. Individuals responsible for staff education should be willing to schedule several meetings throughout the school year.[3]

In addition, professionals should keep in mind that in-service training cannot meet the established goals if it does not keep the interest of its audience. Therefore, a straight lecture format is typically not effective. Demonstrations, visual aids, and open discussion forums are generally excellent techniques to aid in maintaining interest level. Also, although there are many areas that need discussion, some areas are more relevant to certain school staff than others. It is helpful to conduct in-service training on specific topics with specific types of staff. Specialized sessions can be scheduled for speech-language pathologists, school nurses, etc.

Finally, for those professionals who are not comfortable with using the information contained in this chapter to organize the content of an in-service training program, packaged programs are available.[8] A partial listing of these programs and their developers follows in the Appendix at the end of this chapter. It should be noted that a limitation of many prepared training materials is that they are designed for use with regular school personnel. As mentioned previously, special educators also require and are anxious to receive training specific for hearing impaired children. Their needs often take a different direction than other school staff, but are not less important.

INTERVENTION STRATEGIES

General Considerations

Before Public Law 94-142, educational programs met the needs of exceptional children by removing them from the mainstream of regular classrooms, and by serving them in self-contained classes or separate schools. With the shift in emphasis toward the *least restrictive environment* (LRE) of the regular classroom, all teachers are now expected to meet the needs of the exceptional child, unfortunately, with little preparation.[8]

When a regular educator is asked to enroll a hearing impaired child in a school program, it is probably their first contact with such a youngster. For this reason, it is critical that some basic elements of the mainstreamed program be analyzed before specific educational strategies can be addressed.[4] These elements are child, family, class, and teacher centered; the following summarizes essential points for each of these elements:

Child.

(1) The student should be able to participate at or near grade level of the regular class in both academic or communicative areas (regardless of communication type).
(2) The child's social and emotional maturity should be at least equal to that of his or her classmates.
(3) The student should be able to function somewhat independently and exhibit self-confidence.
(4) The child's ability to learn, as measured from standardized testing, should be at least average.
(5) The child should be comfortable with his or her hearing peers, and should be willing to communicate openly regarding his or her hearing loss and not be embarrassed by these handicaps. It is often helpful for the hearing impaired child to teach the class about his or her hearing aid or about sign language.
(6) The student's chronologic age should be within two years of classmates.
(7) The child should have a realistic view of mainstreaming, and be prepared to receive extra help and program modifications.[9]

Family.

(1) The family of the hearing impaired student should show interest in his or her mainstreamed enrollment—helping with assignments, participating in regular school activities, etc.
(2) The family should consistently attend conferences to provide needed input into educational planning.
(3) The family should be aware of the difficulties to be expected in regular class placement, and therefore should not be critical of school staff or place unrealistic demands on the teacher.
(4) The family should be prepared for both success and failure and not become discouraged prematurely.[9]

Class.

(1) The other students in the class should be prepared and ready to accept the hearing impaired child as a member of the class and treat him or her with consideration.
(2) The enrollment of the class should be somewhat smaller than traditional classes, particularly during initial mainstreaming.

(3) It is crucial that the class be informed through an in-service process, just as the teachers are, about the nature of a hearing loss, hearing aids, communication techniques, etc. Classmates and their awareness of the hearing impaired child's needs are as closely linked to the success of mainstreaming as are the specific teaching styles of the teacher.
(4) Classmates should incorporate many of the same techniques the school staff must use that are necessary for improved comprehension for the hearing impaired child.[9]

Teacher.

(1) Teachers must disregard any misconceptions they possibly held previously regarding the hearing impaired child's intelligence, communication, behavior, etc.
(2) Teachers should expect basically the same kind of behavior, responsibility, and dependability from the hearing impaired student as they expect from the rest of the class. A child with a hearing loss is first of all *a child*. What is good for any child is good for the hearing impaired child. Teachers should treat him or her as a normal child.[10]
(3) Teachers should create a climate where experiences of success are frequent, thus encouraging adjustment to the regular class and developing a positive attitude for the child.
(4) Teachers should not overemphasize the hearing loss, but be considerate of the child's special needs.
(5) Teachers should not sympathize, but given assistance.
(6) Teachers should only give those privileges that are absolutely necessary. The hearing impaired child should not be allowed to take advantage of his or her handicap. The child should not be pampered or overprotected.
(7) Teachers should ensure that the hearing impaired child shares in all class experiences and extracurricular activities.
(8) Teachers should try to accept the hearing impaired child positively no matter how impaired his or her comprehension, speech, or vocabulary. Teachers are the role models for the class and set the example. Their reactions or attitudes will generate similar ones from the other children.[10]
(9) Teachers must remember that no two normal-hearing children are alike, so they should not expect every hearing impaired child to be the same. Even those children with identical hearing losses will function very differently. Teaching practices that are successful vary among children.
(10) Teachers should make a consistent effort to communicate frequently with all individuals

involved in the hearing impaired child's program (special educator, speech-language pathologist, etc.).[10]

Now that some of the general educational and attitudinal considerations important to mainstreamed strategies have been reviewed, specific intervention recommendations as they relate to the hearing impaired child in a regular classroom will be discussed.

Classroom Arrangement and Environment

The noise level in the classroom should be kept as low as is practical (see Chapter 11). There is certainly no elementary school class with a noise level of 0 dB SPL. In fact, some studies have found average classroom noise to be as high as 73 dB SPL.[11] However, it is important to remember the limitations of personal hearing aids. All sounds are amplified, prohibiting the hearing impaired child from sorting out the important from the unimportant. Teachers should be aware that these hearing aids do not correct a hearing loss to normal, but only assist in improving awareness or discrimination.[4] The presence of excessive noise often counteracts the benefits of these improvements. As discussed in Chapter 12, the use of FM systems can reduce or eliminate many of the adverse effects of ambient classroom noise.

In addition, the teacher should be aware of classroom acoustics. Although there is usually little that teachers can do to alter the construction of the room, they can control some of the adverse effects. Hard surfaces, such as glass, wood floors, and blackboards, reflect sound and can add to extraneous noise. Increased reverberation results, as speech is repeatedly reflected back and forth from each hard surface, and will cause the hearing impaired child to pick up echoes of several different words at the same time.

There are some materials in the room that can absorb sounds and will assist in decreasing noise. Soft porous materials such as fabrics, paper, carpet, window shades, and cork can be used strategically throughout the room. The rear wall of the classroom can be important for this purpose. Posters or cork bulletin boards arranged on the blackboard and shades or curtains on the windows are certainly helpful. The human body also provides effective dampening of sound. If the teacher can stagger the students' desks instead of arranging them in straight rows, less sound will travel to hard surfaces. Teachers should take care to avoid scheduling verbal presentations or lectures during periods of high activity or noise from either sources in other parts of the classroom or directly outside.

Lighting in the classroom can significantly affect a hearing impaired child's comprehension. There is an obvious correlation between lighting and speechreading ability (see Chapter 15). The best situation is one in which overhead lights and natural lighting are used. They should supply sufficient light, but not be bright enough to cause shadows or a glare. If lighting comes from one of the walls, the teacher should arrange it so that the wall with the lights becomes the back wall. It is best if the light comes from behind the child and falls on the teacher's face. This illuminates the teacher's face, and the child is not blinded by the glare. The teacher should be careful not to stand near a window in bright sunlight, as it often casts a shadow on the face. The teacher should also be aware of the effects of changes of the day on lighting and make appropriate changes.[12]

The importance of preferential seating cannot be underestimated. The hearing impaired child's seating depends in part on the type of hearing loss the child has. If a bilateral loss is present with binaural amplification, placement should be in a central location approximately 3 to 5 feet from the teacher.[13] This allows for optimum use of the hearing aids. The teacher needs to take care not to be too close, so that voice is not directed above the hearing impaired child. Therefore, second-row seating, near the center, is typically most effective. This also eliminates strain at looking up at the teacher. Case History 1 shows how changing the acoustic environment can affect learning for the hearing impaired child.

If a significant asymmetry exists between the ears or a unilateral loss is present, a similar placement in the second row is recommended, but with the child seated off-center so that his or her better ear is angled toward the teacher.

Special seating should not necessarily isolate or further identify the hearing impaired student. The front row is not only a disadvantage for optimum hearing aid use, but also occasionally puts the child on the periphery of the class and causes him or her to stand out.

Preferential seating by itself is not the complete answer to the problems of a child with a

Case history #1.   Adam, 11 years of age, exhibits a moderately severe sensorineural hearing loss in his right ear and a profound, fragmentary loss in his left. Adam uses an ear-level hearing aid on his right ear and no amplification on his left due to its minimal hearing. Adam receives excellent benefit from his monaural aid and responds within the range of normal limits.

Adam entered the fifth grade this school year. He has consistently been placed in regular classrooms throughout his school years, receiving resource room instruction and speech/language services. Adam functions near grade level in all academic areas and has very good communication skills.

Adam's fifth-grade teacher has complained that he often has difficulty following directions and understanding orally presented class material. She finds him a bright student who is quite capable of all work, with minimal resource assistance. However, she is concerned about Adam's auditory comprehension skills and questioned his ability to maintain adequate progress because of this deficit.

Examination of the class by the area's consultant for the hearing impaired found a large room, with wooden floors. One wall was all windows with no shades. Two walls were long blackboards. The back wall of the class was plaster. In addition, the class often divided into groups to complete different activities or projects. Significant background noise is often present caused by the hum of the heating/cooling unit in the rear of the class, pupils' conversations during small group work, and street noise from the unshaded windows.

Several recommendations were made to improve the class signal-to-noise ratio (S/N). Window shades were added. Also, corkboard was placed on the rear plaster wall, which was also used as a class bulletin board. Inexpensive room dividers were used to section off small group work. Also, such a divider was placed around the heating/cooling unit. Portions of each long blackboard, which were seldom used, were used to display class projects, etc., thus assisting with decreasing the amount of hard surface. Student desks were staggered so as to create a body-baffle effect for noise and reverberation.

Further examination also revealed inappropriate seating for Adam. He was seated in the front desk on the far right-hand side of the class. Such a seat placed Adam's unaided, poorer left ear nearer the teacher. It was recommended that he be moved to the second row, off-center to the left. Such placement would provide Adam improved auditory clues, and place his better right ear toward the teacher. Also, such seating would provide Adam better visual access to both blackboards. The teacher was also encouraged to allow Adam flexible seating to be better able to follow orally presented materials from all points in the room.

To monitor Adam's comprehension, his teacher had been asking questions such as "Did you understand what to do?" Adam's response was typically a head nod for yes. It was recommended that the teacher begin asking open-ended questions such as "Which pages in your science book are you to read?"

These simple recommendations were implemented. A nine-week review conference was held to examine Adam's progress. His teacher was quite surprised at the changes in Adam's abilities. She particularly commented on the effectiveness of flexible seating and the use of open-ended questions. In addition, some of her other normal-hearing children had mentioned how much easier it was to concentrate with the decreased noise.

hearing loss. The teacher does not do all the talking in a classroom; typically, a significant amount of information comes from class participation. A child should be allowed some flexibility in seating or orientation, which might mean different seats for different class activities. Or, if such movement attracts too much attention, students should be placed where turning their bodies will assist in comprehension.[10] The teacher may need to cue those hearing impaired students that are unaware of other classmates' participation.

Communication

Speechreading is a skill on which all hearing impaired children exhibit heavy reliance. The success of speechreading is based on the principle of redundancy (the ability to predict the total message after receiving only a part of that message). Speechreading is not absolute. There are many more speech movements per second than the eye is capable of perceiving. In addition, many speech movements are not visible, meaning that the speaker must assist the speechreader with additional cues.

The following are some guidelines to assist in optimum speechreading abilities and to facilitate improved comprehension:

(1) It is critical to make certain that the hearing impaired child is being attentive, and not just listening. However, it is unrealistic to expect continuous attention on the hearing impaired child's part. Afterall, teachers do not expect such a level of attention from normal-hearing children. Some inattention should be tolerated if we are not to wear the child out. Speechreading can be exhausting. Therefore, presenting as many important lessons as possible in the morning hours can help avoid fatigue.[10]

(2) Teachers should speak clearly with moderate speed. The voice should be pleasant and unstrained. Lip movements should be natural and not exaggerated. Raising of the voice or overarticulating will make understanding more difficult for the child.

(3) Teachers should try to speak to the class from a position in the room that allows for adequate light to fall on the face. However, it is nearly impossible to speechread in a glare. Therefore, abundant light should be avoided. Also, teachers should not stand with their backs to the window, because this places the face in a shadow.

(4) Teachers should avoid excess movements during critical speechreading times. They should try to stand as still as practical for their teaching style.

(5) Teachers should try to face the class as much as possible. Writing on the blackboard and talking at the same time should be avoided. In addition, teachers should keep books and papers down from the face when speaking.

(6) Teachers should expect adequate speechreading styles from other students as well. They should be instructed to speak normally. The hearing impaired child should be encouraged to turn and face other children while they are speaking.

(7) Teachers should be aware that many words look alike on the lips. They should, therefore, always put single words into a sentence so that the hearing impaired child can take advantage of the principle of redundancy. Also, teachers

should be patient and understanding with any confusions that occur in comprehension.

(8) Teachers should be aware that it is difficult for the hearing impaired student to speechread a new person who might come into the classroom. Also, although lipstick often assists speechreading abilities, fancy hairstyles, clothes, moustaches, and beards will detract from speechreading.

Although much of the communication success that takes place in a classroom is dependent on visual clues, many hearing impaired students can rely on audition.[13] Therefore, the teacher must employ strategies that ensure adequate comprehension through listening. As mentioned previously, it is important that the teacher makes sure the child is attending. Asking an open-ended question about the subject can often determine if he or she is alert to the content.

Teachers cannot assume that the hearing impaired child understands information presented only one time. These children are notorious for the neutral response technique.[13] Teachers should learn to never trust a nod. It must be emphasized, however, that simply repeating what was said a second time also does not guarantee comprehension. Rephrasing information is helpful, using different vocabulary, less complex sentence structure, and shorter sentences. Such practices are even more important when dealing with new or complex information, or when listening conditions are poor. Again, asking a question can check the child's ability to use or apply what was presented. Hearing impaired children hear in a distorted manner and encounter unfamiliar vocabulary and language structure, as well as new cognitive content, on a daily basis.[12] Teachers will find it necessary to go over verbal instructions or directions given to the child.

In addition, classmates' presentations will also require similar strategies. It is frequently difficult for hearing impaired children to follow discussion when speech is coming from several different directions.[14] Teachers will often need to repeat or rephrase the main points stated by other students during such discussion. The consistent use of repeating and rephrasing provides the hearing impaired child more input and redundancy, thereby aiding comprehension.[12]

Teachers must remember that assignments requiring a very long auditory memory span will be difficult.[13] Hearing impaired children cannot be expected to remember a long list of items presented aurally. The hearing impaired child is never sure if he or she has perceived all the items if they are in list form, rather than as part of a meaningful context. Here is another reason why complete sentences are critical. Teachers must be alert to special auditory learning situations or tasks that may demand skills exceeding the child's auditory-perceptual capabilities.[14]

Finally, the area of listening strategies would not be complete without emphasizing the importance of a clear and natural voice. As described earlier, increased loudness and exaggerated pronunciation only add to the hearing impaired child's distortion and confusion.

Hearing professionals often place so much emphasis on the communication skills of teachers that they forget that certain strategies are specific to the child. Teachers must remember that hearing impaired children have special vocabulary limits. Many words that normal-hearing children use may not be common to the hearing impaired student. Teachers should encourage activities that strengthen vocabulary and enrich communication. Dictionary assignments are helpful. In addition, professionals should develop in the child an interest in reading. Teachers should reinforce and reward attempts to learn or use new vocabulary. And, professionals must remember that the use of slang is important to communication.[10] Hearing impaired children should have the benefit of this exposure as well.

Teachers need to make the hearing impaired child *speech conscious*.[10] Classroom staff can work closely with speech-language pathologists so as to be aware of specific speech goals and targets. Encourage the child to *practice* his or her speech goals in class and correct defective speech appropriately. Naturally, this is not to mean the use of constant interruption or speech nagging. Sometimes, rather than correcting poor speech, the teacher should simply model appropriate production.

Teachers should compliment correct speech as well. Reinforcement and reward are important keys to carry over.[15] Often, hearing impaired children cannot hear improvements, but must depend on the listener to judge his or her accuracy.[13] Educators should not protect hearing impaired children from speaking as-

signments; they should be provided with the same opportunities as the other children.[9]

Many hearing impaired children may exhibit inappropriate volume by either talking too loudly or too softly. Teachers should assist children to work out their own *measuring stick* for monitoring the loudness of their voice.[10] Teachers can help the child recognize the loudness level that should be maintained. Also, on occasion, hearing impaired children vocalize to themselves or make unnecessary noise they may be unaware of. This can be disturbing to the class, so the child should be taught to identify these times through cuing, etc.

It is important that educators instill in hearing impaired children feelings of speech competency. Also, they must learn not to be ashamed or embarrassed if they do not understand. Children should express their confusion immediately, and teachers should watch for signs of poor understanding and not be impatient if the hearing impaired child asks for clarification.[12]

Teaching Methodology— Hints and Recommendations

No amount of in-servicing or chapters in books can prepare classroom teachers for all situations they will encounter with hearing impaired children, or develop in them all of the skills necessary for successful management of these children. Each classroom is different, as is each teacher and each child. However, there are many areas of common ground, and therefore many universal methodologies that should be incorporated in classrooms with hearing impaired children.

Table 17-2 lists ways that school personnel can impact positively on hearing impaired students' learning.[16] In addition to these, teachers must be realistic. No teacher is expected to be all things to all students, particularly those with handicaps. Textbooks often overemphasize how professionals should not frustrate hearing impaired children. They forget to stress, however the frustration of the teacher and its negative effects. Educators cannot reinvent the wheel with every lesson. Instead, they should expect to simply be aware of this population's special needs, be eager to meet them, and do their best. A hearing impaired student's failure to grasp the concept of multiplication is

Table 17-2 Ways to Impact Positively on Hearing Impaired Student Learning

1. Be careful about the assumptions made about the hearing impaired child.
2. Be word and vocabulary conscious. The hearing impaired child encounters new terms daily that other children have had previous exposure to.
3. Be conscious of a student's questioning abilities.
4. Be aware of opportunities to develop word attack abilities, including both phonics and contextual analysis.
5. Keep up with all available resources and materials useful to the hearing impaired.
6. Be aware of the importance of figurative language, syntax, memory, sequencing, inferencing, and comprehension—not only to reading but to all learning areas.
7. Be alert to a student's attitude and motivational level.
8. Develop test-taking abilities of students.
9. Recognize importance of a student's expanding general world knowledge.
10. Expose students to a variety of printed materials.
11. Read to children daily and provide time daily for children to read silently.

not necessarily a reflection of poor teaching or an absence of teacher enthusiasm.

Teachers of hearing impaired students must be aware that the active listening and concentration required of these children will cause them to fatigue more easily than others. Greater effort is necessary for these students; and as a result, they will tire easily.[10] At the end of a school day, they may appear to be not paying attention or to be daydreaming. In actuality, they may be exhausted. This is not to mean, however, that teachers should not expect the hearing impaired student to pay as close attention as others. It is helpful to alternate class activities that require close attention or precise comprehension; listening breaks are useful. Give the class seat work to complete.[12] Teachers should routine their schedule so that hearing impaired children can anticipate subjects, and thereby predict vocabulary, etc.

It is helpful to provide the hearing impaired student with a preview of topics or subjects to come. They could be given assignments to read ahead so that they are familiar with new concepts and vocabulary. Vocabulary lists could be sent home.[16] Early exposure to subjects to be taught can prepare the child for the visual

properties of the new vocabulary and acquaint him or her with contextual clues.

Teachers should include writing as much as is practical in their classroom style. New vocabulary words should be written on the board, as well as spoken. Blackboard outlines of topics being discussed assist in orienting students to the subject matter, and allow them to keep up with the sequence. Homework assignments should also be written on the board as they are given.

Teachers should use natural gestures just as they would during informal conversation. Gestures and cuing assist hearing impaired children with comprehension. When talking about a specific child or object, point to it, walk over to it, or touch it.[16]

Visual aids are very helpful to comprehension. Diagrams, graphs, pictures, maps, etc. are excellent supplements to lecture materials. Overhead projectors are particularly helpful. They assist in reinforcing verbally presented material and increase visual input. Such aids give context and clarify the message.[16] Information may be written on a transparency as the lecture progresses, cuing hearing impaired students to new vocabulary, subject changes, etc. Visual aids increase the number of sensory associations.[5]

Although visual aids are helpful, the use of audiovisual slide presentations and movies are often not as effective. Their sound tracks are frequently poor, and pictures are too small and far away for adequate speechreading. If this type of material is used, it is often beneficial to provide the hearing impaired student with a script or summary before the film or slide presentation is shown.[17]

Instituting a buddy system for the hearing impaired child can be of great benefit for both teacher and child. One or two students in the class can be named as the hearing impaired student's assistant. Such *buddies*, if chosen appropriately, can take some of the demands off the teacher. Buddies can alert the hearing impaired child to critical listening times, and can repeat directions or instructions to ensure comprehension. In addition, notetakers can be assigned to help the hearing impaired student. Not that the hearing impaired child should be excused from notetaking, but teachers must remember that it is very difficult to write and speechread at the same time. Notes supplied by another student can supplement any information missed. Also, in upper grades, many lectures take place in darkened rooms because of the use of slides, etc. The difficulty of this situation for the hearing impaired child is obvious. An important point is that when choosing a buddy for the hearing impaired child, it should be a classmate who is reliable, willing, and an above-average student.[12]

Teachers should recognize that subjects involving numbers or experimentation, such as home economics, math, or science, are more readily understood than those subjects with high language content, such as reading or creative writing.[12] Experimental activities assist in comprehension as well. For example, after discussing farm animals, if possible, a trip to a farm should be scheduled. Pictures can be taken by the students to bring back to class. This helps with carrying over, and provides consistent exposure to new concepts. Also the use of role-playing or dramatic play assists concept development. All children learn best by doing.

Teachers should avoid yes or no questions. This type of response provides no guarantee that the hearing impaired child grasped the material. Teachers can have the child repeat what was said or summarize in his or her own words; if the hearing impaired student did understand the message, he or she will be able to repeat it correctly.

Hearing impaired children sometimes exhibit stubborn or defensive behavior to compensate for their educational problems or inadequacies.[10] Teachers should be prepared for such reactions. As discussed earlier in this chapter, hearing impaired children should be expected to fulfill the same responsibilities as other students. They must adhere to class rules and exhibit appropriate behavior as well. If teachers provide a positive and reinforcing class environment, however, many of the stubborn or defensive behaviors might be avoided. Hearing impaired children need reassurance and feelings of acceptance.[18]

Teachers must find the perfect balance between this reassurance and too much attention paid to the child. As all students get older, they do not want to stand out. This is even more true with hearing impaired students. Teachers must ensure that their teaching style is the same for all students. It is critical to watch for signs of withdrawal on the part of the hearing impaired child.[18] Some failure is to be expected, but educators need to guard against the effects it may have. Hearing impaired chil-

dren must maintain enthusiasm and vigilance for learning. Active participation is the key.

Teachers should avoid introducing new topics without preparing or cuing the hearing impaired child. Verbal and visual connectives and transitions should be used between subjects. Situational clues can be provided that can clue children to what is to come.[10] In lower grades where vocabulary enrichment is a daily event, teachers can label items in the room so that the child is exposed to the vocabulary in printed form.

Often associated with impaired hearing sensitivity is a poor auditory memory. Teachers should break directions down into a step-by-step explanation, so that the child is not required to process multiple components.

Oral tests place the hearing impaired child at an obvious disadvantage. Although written tests are recommended, they cannot always be used. When oral testing is employed, an overhead projector could be used to reveal one question at a time after it is presented orally. This procedure preserves some of the elements of oral testing, and teachers should always be confident that they are testing the hearing impaired student's knowledge, rather than his or her listening skills or language.[17]

Teachers can provide the resource room teacher or the speech-language pathologist with special vocabulary or topics that will be covered in class. These individuals can reinforce classroom instruction or work ahead on certain subjects, providing hearing impaired students with the edge they often require. In addition, it is helpful if the resource room teacher or speech-language pathologist can go into the child's class during key times to assist with instruction, which will also provide them an awareness of the child's group learning style.

Teachers need to encourage hearing impaired students to participate in extracurricular activities. Such involvement fosters acceptance and truly makes them a part of the school. Activities such as scouts, school sports, school clubs, etc. are critical to a successful school experience. Music is an area often thought inappropriate for hearing impaired children. Afterall, how could someone with impaired or distorted hearing succeed in such an auditory area. Most hearing impaired children enjoy music-related activities and gain significantly from them. Music improves listening skills and rhythm, and those hearing impaired children who have enough residual hearing to function with music should not be deprived of this school experience.[12]

Teachers of younger children often speak negatively of comic books. However, these materials can be excellent learning tools, particularly for the hearing impaired child.[10] They employ short, simple sentences, always paired with pictures. This assists the child in language development and reading acquisition, and can assist the hearing impaired child in his or her understanding of idioms—one of the most difficult language structures they will encounter. During the language learning process, hearing impaired children are very literal and concrete.[15] An expression such as "You're pulling my leg" will mean to them just what it says. Comic books can help eliminate the confusion prompted by idioms through their use of pictures.

Teachers should be aware that school announcements over a PA system are very difficult listening situations for the hearing impaired. Not only are they typically distorted and poor quality, they provide no visual clues.[16] Teachers should either repeat such announcements or have the buddy explain them to the hearing impaired child.

Teachers need to be aware of safety hazards in the classroom that may not be as obvious to the hearing impaired child. Precautions need to be taken against such hazards. School crossings and bus loading zones are hazardous areas for all children. Teachers need to be aware of hazardous areas where hearing acts as a signal or warning (fire alarm, cooking timer, traffic, etc.).[16]

Teachers need to recognize that the hearing of all children can fluctuate during the presence of colds or allergies, and that children with documented hearing losses are not immune to the temporary acquisition of additional loss because of these illnesses.[10] Inattentiveness or decreased performance may not be due to conscious behavior on the part of the child, but rather to temporary conductive involvement. Teachers should be alert to such problems, and refer the child for needed evaluation.

To assist in making the child feel a part of the class, and if he or she is not bothered by the attention it may draw, teachers can incorporate the hearing impaired child into an instructional activity. A unit on hearing loss or hearing aids can be taught during science, as demonstrated in Case History 2. A speechreading lesson can be taught to the entire class. An innovative idea is to have the hearing impaired child instruct the class about his or her hearing aid and its use.

Teachers need to communicate frequently with parents. They are, afterall, the *at home* teacher. Teachers need to be willing to discuss both the strengths and weaknesses of the hearing impaired child.[7] They should be encouraged to keep a management diary for the child to take home daily. It could include vocabulary lists, a preview of subjects to come, teaching strategies that work, etc. Using parents to work on topics at home can only improve carry over. Parents can use certain vocabulary introduced at school in different contexts, which certainly facilitates comprehension of multiple meanings.

Special Adaptations

Although many of the teaching strategies previously described are applicable to all children exhibiting impaired hearing, regardless of type or degree, they are often associated only with those children with identified losses in the severe-to-profound range. Children classified as hearing impaired by most educational standards are those requiring special services; that is, those children with academic deficits and more significant impairments.

However, there are many children attending school with hearing losses of varying types and degrees who may be functioning with no difficulty in academic or other school-related areas. They may not require the extent of intervention that the more severely impaired do, but they do require some amount of special classroom adaptation in order for their needs to be met. Table 17-3 lists typical behaviors that hearing impaired children exhibit that teachers should be aware of.

Children exhibiting fluctuating, conductive hearing losses can cause a dilemma for the teacher. On many occasions, the child responds with no difficulty and without problems in comprehension. At other times, the child seems to be "in a dream world" and follows very little of what goes on in the class. These children may be exhibiting fluctuating degrees of hearing loss due to temporary bouts of upper respiratory involvement, middle ear disease, etc. At these times, they may

Case history #2. Emily, 15 years of age, exhibits a bilaterally symmetric, severe sensori-neural hearing loss. She uses binaural ear-level hearing aids, which provide her adequate benefit, improving her acuity to within the borderline mild-to-moderate hearing loss range. For the last three years, Emily has become more self-conscious about her loss and hearing aids. Emily often leaves her aids at home or fails to have spare batteries.

Emily is currently enrolled in the 10th grade. Up until this school year, she received the majority of her academic instruction in a resource room. Emily was mainstreamed into regular classes for math, physical education, and extracurricular activities only.

School staff involved with Emily had observed her motivation to be very high to return to regular classes for more periods. Assessments had shown her abilities to be in the average range. Although Emily was not on grade level for high language-content courses, such as civics, history and English, the staff agreed to attempt increased mainstreaming, with resource/tutoring services cut to one hour daily.

Initial observation of Emily in many of her classes revealed a high level of motivation to succeed. Teachers believed that she was capable of keeping up with the work as long as the resource teacher could review content with her on a one-to-one basis. Teachers were concerned, however, about Emily's reluctance to discuss both her handicap with her peers and her inconsistent use of hearing aids. In addition, Emily's regular teachers had been relying on her to communicate to the resource teacher what material she needed assistance with. At nine-weeks, a conference revealed that Emily was often confused about assignments and had a significant amount of missing material in her classnotes.

In attempts to decrease Emily's self-conscious feelings about her handicap, her science and history teachers approached her with some ideas to introduce her classmates to hearing loss. Although reluctantly, Emily did agree to the teachers' ideas.

An entire unit in Emily's science class was devoted to anatomy of the ear and hearing disorders. Although Emily was initially bothered by the increased attention drawn to her loss, she quickly was pleased to see her classmates were nothing but positive and supportive. Their curiosity and frequent questions about her loss and her hearing aids seemed to improve Emily's self-concept and acceptance of her handicap. Encouraged to bring her aids to school by her peers, so that they could listen to them, prompted Emily's consistent use of her aids.

In addition to the science unit, Emily's history teacher prepared lectures on Alexander Graham Bell and his interest in deafness following his marriage to a deaf woman. This reinforced Emily's improved relation and openness with her classmates.

Once Emily's confidence was enhanced and she appeared more comfortable in her classes, her communication skills improved and her eagerness to participate in class discussion was obvious.

To insure Emily was obtaining all material presented in her classes and comprehending all assignments, a buddy system was implemented. A good student in each class was assigned to make carbon copies of all notes for Emily and to repeat her essential verbal instruction.

Other strategies to assist Emily with keeping up with new material presented in class included each teacher supplying the resource teacher with a weekly preview of new topics and vocabulary.

Preteaching of material, the buddy system, improved self-concept, and consistent use of amplification all contributed to a successful year for Emily. She maintained a B or C average in all classes.

perform and function just as the severely hearing-impaired child does who reveals a permanent sensorineural loss.

Teachers should be alert to changes in responsiveness and understanding. If a history of fluctuating hearing loss is documented and in the child's records, then the teacher might assume such a loss is the cause of the changes and begin incorporating those necessary teaching practices already described. If this is the first indication of poor awareness etc., the teacher should refer the child for testing and consult with the district's specialists on the hearing-impaired.

Table 17-3   Teacher Tips for Identifying a Possible Hearing Impaired Child

1. Inattention.
2. Frequently requests to have a statement or word repeated.
3. Frowning or straining forward when addressed.
4. Easily fatigued.
5. Failure to participate in class discussions.
6. Inability to localize sound.
7. Gives inappropriate answers to simple questions.
8. May isolate him- or herself or be isolated by peer group.
9. Is overly dependent on visual clues.
10. Low tolerance for frustration.
11. Often speaks too loudly.
12. Has poor reading skills.
13. Tends to do better in math than reading.
14. Poor spoken or written language.
15. Sounds distorted or omitted from words.
16. Voice quality harsh, breathy, or nasal or monotone.
17. Pitch rhythm, stress, and inflection inappropriate.
18. History of frequent earaches or ear discharge.
19. Mouth breathing or other nasal symptoms.
20. Complaints of ringing, buzzing or other noises in the head.

For many years, the presence of a unilateral hearing loss was thought to have no effect on the educational achievement of children.[4] As professionals, we now know that is certainly not the case. Unilateral losses (in the presence of one ear with normal hearing) have been found to play a significant role in the abilities of the child exhibiting such disorders. Teachers must be aware when unilateral loss exists; and, if so, they must program for it appropriately. After reading in the child's records that a unilateral loss is present, teachers should not assume that the one normal ear will compensate for that disorder. Obviously, special consideration must be given to seating the child with the better ear directed toward the speaker. Also, as appropriate to the unilateral nature of the loss, modifications should be made to teaching styles, as previously described.

Children with high-frequency losses pose an even greater challenge for the classroom teacher. Similar to those children with fluctuating losses, these children exhibit inconsistent abilities in awareness and comprehension. Special consideration is necessary for high-frequency loss children as well. These students will very often respond normally and comprehend with little difficulty. However, the presence of such a loss will certainly prompt more evident problems when noise occurs, when visual clues are absent, when speech is complex, etc. These children will have greater difficulty processing plurals or other morphologic elements that rely on high frequencies.[13]

Classroom Media

As discussed previously, the use of visual aids can be beneficial to the hearing impaired. However, the equipment used with certain forms of visual aids does have its advantages and disadvantages. The following information may be helpful to teachers planning the use of audiovisual aids:[16]

Overhead Projector.   An overhead projector is an excellent visual aid for students with a hearing loss. Some of the advantages of the overheard projector are:

(1) The teacher is facing the students at all times; the face and lips will therefore be visible for speechreading at all times.
(2) Classroom lights can be left on so students can speechread.
(3) Words that are difficult to speechread can be written on an overhead transparency; the student will therefore not miss them.
(4) Definitions for new class vocabulary can be written on overhead transparencies. If written on a chalkboard, the student's vision is blocked at least part of the time while the teacher is writing on the chalkboard.
(5) Transparencies can be prepared and kept for review. The student with a hearing loss may have more vocabulary problems and therefore more need of review than any other students.
(6) Commercial transparencies can be used when available for the subject matter being taught.

Movies.   Movies are difficult for students with a hearing loss; generally, the more severe the hearing loss, the greater the problem. The students can, of course, see what is happening on the screen and follow the action. They can also follow some of the dialogue in the movie by speechreading. Most movies, however, include things that are heard but not seen. Hearing impaired students will be able to understand the sound track to some degree, but students with a severe-to-profound loss will not. When movies are used as a teaching tool, the following suggestions might help students:

(1) Most helpful would be a teacher-prepared duplicated outline for each student regarding the main points of the movie. The outline would be useful for the student to read before seeing the movies, as well as later for review purposes.
(2) References for reading material containing the same basic information as the film might be provided for the student.
(3) The student should be allowed to choose optional seating for the film. That is, near the speaker, the screen, or both, or wherever the student feels he or she is getting maximum audition, speechreading, or combined cues.

Television (TV).   TV will present the same problems as discussed in the movie section. An additional problem will be that there will usually not be an opportunity to preview the material, and therefore to plan and write an outline. Closed circuit TV is very valuable for the hearing impaired student. Programs can be taped and played over time and time again.

Filmstrips.   Filmstrips that use a record player or tape recorder will present some of the same difficulties as movies for students with a hearing loss.

Tapes.   Information on regular or cassette audiotapes or records will be impossible for students with severe-to-profound losses to follow. All types of listening station materials will fall into this category. Some students may be able to follow tapes and records. If in doubt as to whether a student can understand, it is best to ask the child to indicate what was said on the audiotape or record. Just asking whether he or she understands may well produce a "yes." Questions requiring the student to give specific information will be more adequate in helping to determine what a child can understand. A script or written copy of recorded work will be helpful if the student is unable to follow auditory cues only. If this is not available, an outline will help.

Opaque Projectors.   An opaque projector presents problems for students with hearing losses because the classroom has to be darkened by its use. Most verbal explanations of materials while the room is in such darkness will be missed by the student with a hearing loss when the opaque projector is used. Any explanation given while the lights are out needs to be recapped later.

Captioned Films.   Captioned films are available for free use with students with a severe-to-profound hearing loss. Catalogs of educational and theatrical films are available (see Appendix).

Educational Interpreters

Many hearing impaired students who are served in the mainstreamed environment take advantage of a communication interpreter. School districts employing such professionals use varying titles for this position. These individuals are often classified as tutors, aides, or communication facilitators. Regardless of their official title, if these individuals are held responsible for communicating classroom information to the hearing impaired student, certain guidelines are critical.[17]

Guidelines for interpreters for the hearing impaired are clearly outlined in the Code of Ethics of the National Registry of Interpreters for the Deaf.[19] These guidelines serve the purpose of assuring high-quality interpreting service for hearing impaired individuals. However, as increasing numbers of young hearing impaired students are mainstreamed into public schools, schools are experiencing unique interpreting situations that are not addressed in the above-mentioned guidelines.

Special situations develop for several reasons. One is related to the fact that the very young hearing impaired child does not yet understand how to use an interpreter. In addition, typical early childhood behaviors call for a great deal of flexibility by all people involved, including an interpreter. A further complication is the lack of trained interpreters. The response to this in many schools has been to hire an employee who, in addition to other duties, also facilitates communication with the hearing impaired child by using existing sign language skills.[19]

The following guidelines are designed to assist schools with the unique interpreting problems they may face. Although the following is addressed to the interpreter, the responsibility of the regular classroom teacher and the school administrators should not be overlooked. The use of an interpreter in educational programs truly calls for a team approach by all professionals involved.[19]

Suggested Interpreting Guidelines for Schools That Use Interpreters and/or Communication Facilitators in Classrooms.

(*1*) The interpreter should gather the teacher's lesson plans and check vocabulary prior to class time.

(*2*) The interpreter should maintain good communication with the classroom teacher in all matters related to the child.

(*3*) The interpeter should determine and follow the correct chain of command to resolve problems.

(*4*) The interpreter should refrain from discussing the student or his or her program with people other than school personnel who are directly involved.

(*5*) The interpreter and teacher should privately explain to the child how the interpreting situation will be handled in the classroom.

(*6*) The interpreter should make attempts to regain the student's attention when it is diverted from the lesson. (*Example*: A child who begins to look at the ceiling can be tapped and asked to pay attention.)

(*7*) The interpreter should not take significant disciplinary actions. Major disciplinary responsibility rests with the regular classroom teacher.

(*8*) The interpreter should be free to *pair* other signs or gestures with the signed English version to facilitate understanding. (*Example*: If the interpreter signs the word "TV," she might also point to a nearby TV.)

(*9*) The interpreter should, upon seeing that the student is not understanding, summarize the situation. (*Example*: The interpreter may inform the student that the teacher is now asking each class member for a response; or if the interpreter realizes the child is confused, he or she may summarize information and then resume straight interpreting.)

(*10*) The interpreter should wear reasonably nondistracting clothing or jewelry.

(*11*) The interpreter should use varied and interesting facial expressions, body language, and gestures to accompany signs. These enhance communication with young normal-hearing children, and the same is true for hearing impaired children.

(*12*) The interpreter should use good expressions in signs, including rhythm, smoothness, and directionality. (An example of *directionality* is for the interpreter, when asked to interpret "draw a tree on your paper," to actually sign the phrase near the child's paper.)

(*13*) The interpreter should communicate after class with the classroom teacher to share concepts or vocabulary for which the student may need reinforcement.

SUPPORTIVE SERVICES

Many states have developed a network of consultants to assist public school staff with their management of the hearing impaired student. In addition to the traditional support personnel housed within each specific school district (speech-language pathologist, certified teacher of the deaf, counselor, etc.), many districts or educational regions also have the services of a consultant for hearing impaired management available to them. Although these individuals are not in schools on a daily basis to teach reading or facilitate communication, they can provide an essential service. These professionals can: (*1*) provide the in-service training necessary before embarking on a mainstreamed program; (*2*) educate school staff in successful teaching strategies; (*3*) acquaint personnel in the significance of consistency of amplification; (*4*) assist in due process completion; and (*5*) assist in the guarantee of a least restrictive and successful education.[17]

The following is a summary of the typical role of a hearing consultant. School systems should take advantage of such a service, if established. If such a service is not available in the state, school personnel should pursue the establishment of a statewide hearing consultant.

Identification

(*1*) Assist with hearing screening if needed.

(*2*) Be provided with a list of screening failures, and assist in monitoring of proper medical and audiologic follow-up.

(*3*) Attend referral conferences on screening failures.

(*4*) Secure audiologic/otologic evaluations for screening failures.

(*5*) Provide teachers with information to aid in identification.

Provide In-Service Training to Faculty and Staff, Parent Groups, and Civic Organizations.

(*1*) Identifying students with a possible hearing impairment.

(2) Educational implications of a hearing loss.
(3) Attempting to establish a positive, receptive attitude toward the student with a hearing loss.
(4) Skills and strategies for working with students with a hearing loss.
(5) Teacher observation/identification.
(6) Implications of the fluctuating hearing loss.
(7) Using auditory trainers effectively.
(8) Language and the hearing impaired student.
(9) Speech and the hearing impaired student.
(10) Auditory training with the hearing impaired student.

Due Process.

(1) Attend referral conferences to help determine further assessment.
(2) Attend evaluation conferences:
  Interpret evaluation results.
  Help determine programming needs.
  Assist in development of the individualized educational plan (IEP) long-range goals.
  Assist in placement decisions.
(3) Attend annual review conferences.

Consultation.

(1) Administrators:
  Informing administrators of the consultant program and the role that it can play in the local school.
  Informing administrators regarding educational and social ramifications of a hearing loss.
  Discussing new hearing impaired students with school *principals* and *special education supervisors*.
  Consulting with principals and special education supervisors regarding evaluations, goals and progress of students.
  Consulting with principals and special education supervisors regarding teacher selection.
(2) Teachers:
  Recommending materials.
  Informing and educating teachers regarding the educational effects of a student's hearing loss.
  Assist teachers/speech-language pathologists in developing short-term objectives for the IEP.
  Assist teachers/speech-language pathologists with lesson plans for hearing impaired students.
  Make regular classroom visits as needed.
  Be on call for *emergency* help.

In addition, the hearing consultant can provide the following information:

(1) Information on the severity of the child's hearing impairment and its influence on the child's ability to understand familiar spoken language by hearing alone.
(2) Explanation on how much improvement occurs when the hearing aid is worn and is functioning well.
(3) Examples of the situations in which the child will probably still have difficulty understanding by hearing alone even with the hearing aid.
(4) Explanation of the extent to which being able to see the speaker makes comprehension easier for the child.
(5) Identification of the kinds of classroom activities in which the child will manage well or adequately, and those in which difficulty can be anticipated; indication of specific learning situations (audiotape listening, movies, TV presentations, filmstrips or slide projections, auditorium presentations) that will probably present difficulty.
(6) Indication of the child's receptive vocabulary age, grammatic competence, and ability to understand syntactic constructions appropriate to his or her chronologic age.
(7) Indications of expressive language skills, particularly the child's pragmatic use of language.
(8) Estimation of the extent to which difficulties in comprehension in favorable listening and listening-watching conditions are likely to be due to language deficit.
(9) Indication of the child's areas of greatest need, and explanation of the goals to achieve with the child.

RESOURCE MATERIALS

Information on resource materials useful with hearing impaired children might conclude that there are not many materials available that are appropriate for use with this population.[20] Regular teachers, as well as special educators, then feel abandoned on occasion. Their responsibility is to teach these children, but yet there are no *tools* useful to them.[21]

The theory that curricula materials or resources appropriate to hearing impaired education are limited should be rejected. Not only are there published sources for this population, but most materials designed for *all* students are more than adequate for hearing impaired children, with some modification.[21] Professionals too frequently fall prey to the philosophy that teaching methods and materials must be *laboratory tested* on the designated population before its usefulness can be proven.[22] With the implementation of the strategies previously described in this chapter, many of the traditional or established materials used in the classroom will teach all students, including the hearing impaired child.[22] The Appendix following this chapter lists resource materials that are believed to be appropriate.

In surveying professionals involved with the education of hearing impaired children, many themes emerge in the descriptions of their approaches for organizing activities and content. Emphasis is placed on a natural language approach, strategies that are based on normal developmental information, reliance on teacher judgment and experience to organize content areas, and individualized instruction that best meets the child's needs.[20] There is little difference between these emphasized priorities for hearing impaired programming and those that would be beneficial to *any* student.

Years of experience have assisted this author in exposure to many *tried and tested* curricula and programs. Each of the materials described in this chapter's Appendix are useful tools in the areas they are listed. However, it must be emphasized, that these materials are not intended to be a complete listing of all products beneficial to hearing impaired children. Although this listing only begins to identify helpful materials, readers might become familiar with the publishers or distributors. Many other products offered by these groups are also useful.

SUMMARY

Hopefully, the information contained in this chapter eliminates the need for educators to live under the influence of the self-fulfilling prophecy. Hearing impaired students deserve the chance to prove that they can be successful members of any class. The inclusion of these children can have many positive effects on teachers and the other children in the classroom.

The teacher and class should work together to make the hearing impaired student feel accepted. This cooperative effort results in a class enthusiastic and eager to learn.[16] Also, the experience of getting to know a handicapped child can emphasize the fact that he or she is *a child first*; a child with similar needs, likes, and dislikes. Being hearing impaired certainly requires specific teaching strategies, but it also requires being allowed to be a child.

As detailed in this chapter, teachers need to be more precise and graphic in their teaching style for the hearing impaired child to have a clear understanding of the information presented. Such precision and clarity can only benefit the entire class. Also, since the teacher serves as an example, the class should make an effort to be clear and specific in their communicative endeavors.[16]

Educating a hearing impaired child can certainly be both frightening and overwhelming, but it can also be both dynamic and rewarding. Is this not the case with educating any child?

REFERENCES

1. Ross M, Calvert DR: The semantics of deafness, in Northcott WH, ed: *The Hearing Impaired Child in the Regular Classroom* (Washington, DC: AG Bell Assoc, 1973).
2. Johnson EW: Let's look at the child not the audiogram, in Northcott WH, ed: *The Hearing Impaired Child in the Regular Classroom* (Washington, DC: AG Bell Assoc, 1973).
3. Birch JW: *Hearing Impaired Children in the Mainstream* (Minneapolis, MN: University of Minnesota Press, 1975).
4. Davis J, Hardick E: *Rehabilitative Audiology for Children and Adults* (New York: John Wiley & Sons, 1981).
5. Nix GW: *Mainstream Education for Hearing Impaired Children and Youth* (New York: Grune and Stratton, 1976).
6. Auble LF: The integrated superintendent: Normalization can be a reality, in Northcott WH, ed: *The Hearing Impaired Child in the Regular Classroom* (Washington, DC: AG Bell Assoc, 1973).
7. Freeman RD, Carbin C, Boese RJ: *Can't Your Child Hear? A Guide for Those Who Care About Deaf Children* (Baltimore: University Park Press, 1981).
8. Seltz A: In-service training: Maxi-model, in Northcott WH, ed: *The Hearing Impaired Child in the Regular Classroom* (Washington, DC: AG Bell Assoc, 1973).
9. Schow R, Watkins S: Aural rehabilitation for children, in Schow R, ed: *Introduction to Aural Rehabilitation* (Baltimore: University Park Press, 1980).
10. Gildston P: The hearing impaired child in the classroom, in Northcott WH, ed: *The Hearing Impaired Child in the Regular Classroom* (Washington, DC: AG Bell Assoc, 1973).

11. Olsen W: The effects of noise and reverberation on speech intelligibility, in Bess F, Freeman B, Sinclair JS, eds: *Amplification in Education* (Washington, DC: AG Bell Assoc, 1981).
12. White N: The role of the regular classroom teacher, in Froehlinger V, ed: *Today's Hearing Impaired Child: Into the Mainstream of Education* (Washington, DC: AG Bell Assoc, 1981).
13. Ling D: Auditory coding and recoding: An analysis of training procedures for hearing impaired, in Ross M, Giolas T, eds: *Auditory Management of Hearing Impaired Children* (Baltimore: University Park Press, 1978).
14. Mussen E: Hearing, listening and attending: Techniques and concepts in auditory training, in Roeser R, Downs M, eds: *Auditory Disorders in School Children: The Law, Identification, Remediation* 1st Ed (New York: Thieme-Stratton, Inc, 1981).
15. Kretschmer R, Kretschmer L: *Language Development and Intervention with the Hearing Impaired* (Baltimore: University Park Press, 1978).
16. Orlansky J: *Mainstreaming the Hearing Impaired Child* (Boston: Teaching Resources Corporation, 1977).
17. Brooks N: Educational support services, in Froehlinger V, ed: *Today's Hearing Impaired Child: Into the Mainstream of Education* (Washington, DC: AG Bell Assoc, 1981).
18. Ross M: Mainstreaming: some social considerations. *Volta Review*, 80 (1978), 21–30.
19. Caccamise F, et al: *Introduction to Interpreting* (Silver Spring, MD: Registry of Interpreters for the Deaf, 1980).
20. Cole E, Mischook M: Survey and annotated bibliography of curricula used by oral preschool programs. *Volta Review*, 87 (1985), 139–154.
21. McCarr D, Wisser MW: *Curriculum Materials Useful for the Hearing Impaired* (Beaverton, OR: Dormac, Inc, 1979).
22. Fristoe M: Language intervention systems: Programs published in kit form, in Lloyd L, ed: *Communication Assessment and Intervention Strategies* (Baltimore: University Park Press, 1979).

APPENDIX

Resource Materials and Curricula

Reading

AG Bell Association for the Deaf
3417 Volta Place NW
Washington, DC 20007
  Reading and the Hearing Impaired Individual
  Robert Kretschmer

  Teaching Reading to Deaf Children
  Beatrice Hart
  Guide to the Selection and Use of Reading Instructional Materials
  Freda Brown and Diane Arnell
  Sentences and Other Systems
  Peter Blackwell, Elizabeth Engen, Joseph Fischgrund, Christina Zarcadoolas
  World Traveler Magazine
  The Raindrop

Dormac, Inc.
PO Box 1699
Beaverton, OR 97075-1699
  Simple Language Fairy Tales
  Robert Newby
  Reading Milestones
  Stephen Quigley, Cynthia King
  Many Meanings
  Suzanne Dedrick, James Lattyak
  My Words
  Dorothy McCarr
  Simple English Classic Series
  Elizabeth DiSomma, Mary McTiernan
  Fables/Myths
  Judy Paris, Sandra Tracy
  Building Stories with Julie and Jack

Garrard Publishing Company
Champaign, IL 61820
  Dolch Basic Vocabulary Books
  Dolch First Reading Books

Harper and Row Publishers
10 East 53rd Street
New York, NY 10022
  Design for Reading

McGraw-Hill Book Company
1221 Avenue of the Americas
New York, NY 10020
  Lessons for Self-Instruction in Basic Skills
  New Practice Readers
  Reading for Concepts
  Step Up Your Reading Power

St Johns School for the Deaf
3680 South Kinnickinnic Avenue
Milwaukee, WI 53207
  Basic Vocabulary Worksheets

Continental Press, Inc.
Elizabethtown, PA 17022
  Reading Skills Spirits Masters

Allied Education Council
PO Box 78
Galien, MI 49113
  Mott Basic Language Skills Programs

Scott Foresman & Company
1900 East Lake Avenue
Glenview, IL 60025
  Activity Concept English
  Easy Reading Books

National Association for the Deaf
814 Thayer Avenue
Silver Spring, MD 20910
  Library Classics

Communication Skill Builders
3130 North Dodge Boulevard
PO Box 42050-L
Tucson, Arizona 85733
  Speech, Language and Reading Workbooks
  Margaret Smith

CC Publications
PO Box 23699
Tigard, OR 97223-0108
  Before Reading: A Language Comprehension Program
  Nancy O'Harra

Language

AG Bell Association for the Deaf
3417 Volta Place NW
Washington, DC 20007
  Basic Vocabulary and Language Thesaurus for Hearing Impaired Children
  Daniel Ling, Agnes Ling Phillips
  The Language of Directions
  Mary Lou Rush
  Dictionary of Idioms for the Deaf

Communication Skill Builders
3130 North Dodge Boulevard
PO Box 42050-L
Tucson, AZ 85733
  Communicative Competence: A Functional-Pragmatic Language Program
  Charlann Simon
  TOTAL: Teacher Organized Training for the Acquisition of Language
  Beth Witt, Jeanne Boose
  Teaching Morphology Developmentally
  Kenneth Shipley, Carolyn Banis
  Pictures, Please
  Marcia Abbate, Nancy La Chappelle
  Developing Expressive Language: A Functional Approach for Children 3–8
  Marcia De Palma

Language Remediation and Expansion Series
Shape Up Your Language
Joan Frazer, Cynthia Smith
Natural Language
John Hatten, Pequetti Hatten
Emerging Language 3
John Hatten, Tracy Goman, Carole Lent
UniSet Kits
Elaine Burke-Krassowski
Communicards
Catherine Bush
A Sourcebook of Pragmatic Activities
Elizabeth Johnston, Barbara Weinrich, Ann Johnson
Concept Formation

CC Publications
PO Box 23699
Tigard, OR 97223-0108
  PALS: Developing Social Skills Through Language
  Sharon Vaugn, Linda Levine, Carl Ridley
  Steps Toward Basic Concept Development
  Patricia Collins, Gary Cunningham
  PLUSS—Putting Language to Use in Social Situations
  Thelma Zirkelbach
  Language Rehabilitation
  James Martinoff, Rosemary Martinoff, Virginia Stokke

Reed Education
182 Wakefield Street
Wellington, Australia
  Tate Language Program
  GM Tate

Dormac, Inc.
PO Box 1699
Beaverton, OR 97075-1699
  Apple Tree Language Program
  Marcia Anderson, Norma Jean Boren, Janis Caniglia, Wyman Howard, Emmylou Krohn
  Pronoun Pages
  Paige Townson
  Lessons in Syntax
  James McCarr
  TSA Syntax Program
  Stephen Quigley, Desmond Power
  Imaginative Adjectives/Prepositions
  Dorothy McCarr
  Verbs, Verbs, Verbs
  Beger, McCarr, et al
  Vocabulary Building Exercises for the Young Adult
  Dorothy McCarr

Vocabulary in Context
Suzanne Dedrick, James Lattyak
Idioms
Myra Auslin
Basic Vocabulary Study Cards
Dorothy McCarr
Newby Visual Language Series
Robert Newby
Building Sentences Step by Step

American Guidance Service, Inc.
Publishers Building
Circle Pines, MN 55104
Peabody Language Development Kits

Continental Press
Elizabethtown, PA 17022
Spirit Masters Series

Gallaudet College Press
Gallaudet College
Washington, DC 20002
STEP Series

Teaching Resources Corp.
100 Boylston
Boston, MA 02116
Fokes Sentence Builder

Learning Concepts
2501 North Lamar
Austin, TX 78745
Developmental Concepts

Lingui Systems, Inc.
Suite 806
1630 Fifth Avenue
Moline, IL 61265
HELP—Handbooks of Exercises for Language Processing

Rhythm Productions
Los Angeles, CA 90034
Steps Up to Language
Elizabeth Tabaka-Juedes
In, Out and Round About
Ruth White, Marilyn Rehwald
Mix and Match
Ruth White, Marilyn Rehwald

Council for Exceptional Children
1920 Association Drive
Reston, VA 22091
Helping Young Children Develop Language Skills
Merle Karues

Instructional Industries
Executive Park
Ballston Lake, NY 12019
Project Life Program

Milton Bradley Company
Springfield, MA 01101
GOAL Language Program

Speech

AG Bell Association for the Deaf
3417 Volta Place NW
Washington, DC 20007
Teacher/Clinician Planbook and Guide to the Development of Speech Skills
Daniel Ling
Cumulative Record of Speech Skill Acquisition
Daniel Ling

CC Publications
PO Box 23699
Tigard, OR 97223-0108
Articulation Modification Program
Patricia Collins, Gary Cunningham
Phonemic Context Articulation Program
Joyce Yates, Bridget Chapin

Communication Skill Builders
3130 North Dodge Boulevard
PO Box 42050-L
Tucson, Arizona 85733
Articutales
Catherine Carotta, B. Ruth Hall
Articulation Worksheets
Margaret Smith
Carry-Over Stories for Articulation Therapy
Daniel Zwitman, Judith Thompson
All the Games Kids Like
Dianne Barad
Articulation in Sentences
Harris Winitz
Forming Sounds
Edward Kelly
Speech and Auditory Training: A Program for Adolescents with Hearing Impairments & Language Disorders
JoAnne Subtelny, Ann Lieberth

American Guidance Service
Publishers Building
Circle Pines, MN 55014
Peabody Articulation Cards

Interstate Printers and Publishers
19-27 North Jackson
Danville, IL 61832
The Big Book of Sounds
Speech Activity Card File

St Johns School for the Deaf
3680 South Kinnickinnic Avenue
Milwaukee, WI 53207
Speech Books for the Deaf

Auditory Training

AG Bell Association for the Deaf
3417 Volta Place NW
Washington, DC 20007
The Joy of Listening: An Auditory Training Program
Janice Light
Auditory Training
Norman Erber
I Heard That!
Winifred Northcott

Foreworks
Box 9747
North Hollywood, CA 91609
Auditory Skills Curriculum

Curriculum Skill Builders
3130 North Dodge Boulevard
PO Box 42050-L
Tucson, Arizona 85733
What's That I Hear?
Sam Brown
Sound Investments: Carry-Over Activities for Listening Skills
Elizabeth Wilson
CLAS: Classroom Listening and Speaking
Lynn Plourde
Learn to Listen
Illa Podendorf
Attending
Vickie Simmons

St Joseph Institute for the Deaf
1483 82nd Boulevard
St Louis, MO 63132
ABC of Auditory Training

Interstate Printers and Publishers
19-27 North Jackson
Danville, IL 61832
The Auditory Training Handbook for Good Listeners
Dhyan Cassie

CC Publications
PO Box 23699
Tigard, OR 97223-0108
Auditory Rehabilitation
Rex Prater, Karlene Stefanakos
Auditory Memory for Language
Karlene Stefanakos, Rex Prater
Auditory Discrimination Training Program
Leslie Ehlert

Speechreading

AG Bell Association for the Deaf
3417 Volta Place NW
Washington, DC 20007
Lipreading Made Easy
Audrey Greenwald
Stories and Games for Easy Lipreading Practice
Rose Broberg
Lively Lipreading Lessons
Mae Fisher

Rochester Institute of Technology
NTID
1 Lomb Memorial Drive
PO Box 9887
Rochester, NY 14623-0887
Association Cues
Marjorie Jacobs
Speechreading Strategies
Marjorie Jacobs

Charles C. Thomas Publishers
301–327 East Lawrence Avenue
Springfield, IL
Total Communication Used in Experience Based Speechreading and Auditory Training Lesson Plans
Marta Baucom, Ralph Causby

Other Academic Related Subjects

Dormac, Inc.
PO Box 1699
Beaverton, OR 97075-1699
I Can Write
Dorothy McCarr
HEP—History, Economics, Political Science
Barbara Slater
Time Concept Series
James Lattyak, Suzanne Dedrick
Green Mountain Math

Joy of Learning
Controlled Language Science Series

AG Bell Association for the Deaf
3417 Volta Place NW
Washington, DC 20007
Learning to Write and Writing to Learn
Richard Kretschmer
Science for Deaf Children
Allan Leitman
The Tutor/Notetaker: Providing Academic Support to Mainstreamed Deaf Students
Russell Osguthorpe
Manager's Guide for the Tutor/Notetaker
Russell Osguthorpe, et al.

Rochester Institute of Technology
NTID
1 Lomb Memorial Drive
PO Box 9887
Rochester, NY 14623-0887
The Tutor/Notetaker Comic Book
Tutor/Notetaker Pads

Fearson/Pitman Publishers, Inc.
6 Davis Drive
Belmont, CA 94002
The Pacemaker Arithmetic Program

Continental Press, Inc.
Elizabethtown, PA 17022
Arithmetic Step by Step

Frank E. Richards Publishing Co., Inc.
PO Box 66
Phoenix, NY 13125
Useful Arithmetic
Using Money Series
Science Series

McGraw-Hill Book Company
1221 Avenue of the Americas
New York, NY 10020
Foundations in Mathematics

David C. Cook Publishing Company
850 North Grove Avenue
Elgin, IL 60120
Science Themes
Social Studies Picture Sets

Follet Publishing Company
1010 West Washington Boulevard
Chicago, IL 60607
Beginning Science Books
Beginning Social Studies Books

Milliken Publishing Company
1100 Research Boulevard
St Louis, MO 63132
General Science Series (all levels)
Geography Through Maps
Map Reading Series

Benefic Press
10300 West Roosevelt Road
Westchester, IL 60153
Basic Concept Series
Basic Understanding Series

Note: It should be noted that the following two companies have numerous materials available that are helpful in many readiness and manipulative-oriented areas.

Developmental Learning Materials
7440 Natchez Avenue
Miles, IL 60648

Teaching Resources Corporation
100 Boylston
Boston, MA 02116

Computer Software

AG Bell Association for the Deaf
3417 Volta Place NW
Washington, DC 20007
Natural Language Processing Program with Computerized Language Lessons
Marian Ernst

Dormac, Inc.
PO Box 1699
Beaverton, OR 97075-1699
Lessons in Syntax
James McCarr

Communication Skill Builders
3130 North Dodge Boulevard
PO Box 42050-L
Tucson, AZ 85733
Computer Managed Articulation Treatment
James Fitch
Computer Managed Language Treatment
James Fitch
Idioms in America
Carol Esterreicher
Computer Courseware for the Exceptional Student
Barbara Johnson, Ronald Johnson
Wizard of Words
Anita Neely, Tim Aaronson

First Words I and II
Mary Wilson, Bernard Fox
Twenty Categories
Mary Wilson, Bernard Fox
First Verbs
Mary Wilson, Bernard Fox
Micro—LADS—Microcomputer Language Assessment and Development System
Mary Wilson, Bernard Fox
Stickybear Reading
Richard Hefter, Steve Worthington
Juggles Rainbow Story Machine
Joy Branschreiber, Jeannie Wiegertt
Ship Ahoy Word Scramble
Michael Adler
Gertrude's Secrets
Wendy Beardsley
Tuk Goes to Town
Mercer Mayer
Planning Individualized Speech and Language Intervention Programs
Nickola Nelson

Audiovisual Materials

Captioned Films for the Deaf
5034 Wisconsin Avenue NW
Washington, DC 20016

Association Films, Inc.
866 Third Avenue
New York, NY 10022

National Catalog of Films in Special Education
Ohio State University Press
Columbus, Ohio 43210

AG Bell Association for the Deaf
3417 Volta Place NW
Washington, DC 20007

National Association of the Deaf
814 Thayer Avenue
Silver Spring, MD 20910

In-Service Training

Bono Film Service, Inc.
1042 Wisconsin Avenue NW
Washington, DC 20007
    Lisa, Pay Attention! (Film)

AV Resources
319 15th Avenue SE
Minneapolis, MN 55455
    Hearing Aid Demonstration (Audiotape)

Gorden Stowe Assts.
Custom Records Dept
RCA Victor
Northbrook, IL 60062
    How They Hear (Record)

Anne Seltz
Title III Interdistrict Project for Hearing Impaired Children
Minneapolis Public Schools
807 NE Broadway
Minneapolis, MN 55413
    Team Approach (Slide Tape Program)
    PACT—Procedural Adaptations for Classroom Teachers, Tutors and Therapists (Slide Tape Program)
    Guidelines for Preparing Case Management Conference (Handout Material)
    Questions to Promote Discussion (Handout Material)
    Teacher-Tutor Communication Form (Handout Material)

Instructor Publications, Inc
Dansville, NY 14437
    Hints and Activities for Mainstreaming (Book)

Gallaudet College Press
Washington, DC 20002
    Ear Gear
    Carole Simko

18 | COUNSELING FOR THE PARENT

Caroline J. Mitchell

IMPORTANCE OF PARENT COUNSELING

> "I was confused and the test results made me even more confused.
>
> "For years, I was crying 'Hey, my child has a problem,' but no one would listen to me. I got angry. This is not fair. There are still so many times that you want to scream, to scream out 'Help,' because it is very exasperating, very frustrating, very much a strain on the whole family."

Confusion, anger, frustration, and isolation are just a few of the feelings that parents of hearing-impaired children experience, especially when they are confronted with the initial diagnosis. Confusion over what is wrong with their child, anger without focus, and, many times, frustration in finding answers or services.

Is he deaf? What percent of hearing loss does he have? Will he talk? Can he go to regular school? Why me? Why my child? What caused this problem? The anger is frequently directed at the professional or agency that is seeing the child. *You only spent an hour with him—how could you really know? I've already been here twice—why do I have to come back again? He doesn't like his hearing aid—he cries whenever we put it on him.*

Parent education for a child with a hearing loss involves informing parents about hearing loss, the use of hearing aids, language development, etc. However, the process is frequently muddied with emotional and/or behavioral concerns, mainly because emotional issues have been inadequately addressed prior to the initiation of an educational program. In addition, as awareness of the implications of the hearing loss increases, other emotional reac-

tions are triggered. During the early phase of diagnosis and program planning, professionals must be particularly aware of the emotional state of the parents, so that each professional can effectively communicate with them and establish appropriate expectations as to how recommendations can be implemented.

Communication between the professional and parent can take place through a counseling process. During counseling, the emotional state of the parents can be assessed and questions answered in a way and at a time that they can deal with the information. Also, through this process, support can be provided to sustain parents through the evaluations or until they have settled into an appropriate program. It is to this end—the understanding of the counseling process and parents' need for it—that this chapter is directed.

An underlying assumption of this chapter is that the parents of handicapped children do not present any overt psychopathology or abnormal emotional disturbance. Most parents of hearing-impaired children are normal people undergoing a very stressful situation, who might benefit from a counseling relationship in their eventual adjustment to what will be a long-term or lifetime condition of their child. It is also assumed that counseling is most appropriately performed by a professional with formal training in an area of mental health.

The Mystique of Counseling and Psychotherapy

The terms *counseling, therapy, psychotherapy, parent education*, and *parent support* are all bandied about, used, and frequently abused. The lack of understanding of the above terms and the processes that they represent probably contributes as much to parents' failure to obtain needed services as does the unavailability of the services. Counseling has been variously defined as either "helping clients to accept and understand what they are and realizing their potential,"[1](p4) or a short-term relationship between a person who is skilled in problems of human adjustment and someone who is having a problem in adjustment.[1] Counseling is also frequently defined in terms of what it is not. It is not simply giving information or advice; influencing attitudes, beliefs, or behaviors; or persuading to a point of view. Nor is it synonymous with interviewing, reporting, or educating, although these processes may occur during the counseling process.[2]

Counseling can be distinguished from psychotherapy in that counseling deals with helping "normal" people achieve a healthier or more comfortable life adjustment, whereas psychotherapy deals with psychopathology. However, most people are not aware of this distinction and feel that a referral for counseling indicates a diagnosis, or possibly a suspicion of, psychopathology or emotional disturbance. The term *parent support* has evolved to avoid the suggestion that parents in the counseling process have some form of psychopathology. Used in this way, parent support is a euphemism for counseling.

Stewart[3](p 2) has proposed a definition of counseling specific to parents of handicapped children, which provides not only direction and limits for a counselor, but also describes the process for other disciplines:

Counseling is a helping relationship between a knowledgeable professional and parents of an exceptional child, working toward a better understanding of their unique concerns, problems, or feelings. It is a learning process focusing upon the stimulation and encouragement of personal growth by which parents are assisted in acquiring, developing, and utilizing the skills and attitudes necessary for a satisfactory resolution to their problem or concern. Parents are helped toward becoming fully-functioning individuals who are assets to their child and [who] value harmonious living as members of a well-adjusted family unit.

This definition points out that parents of handicapped children have unique concerns and needs. These special needs demand knowledge of the handicap on the part of the counselor. One unique aspect is that the phases of evaluation and remediation that families experience and the timing of the counseling present different problems during service delivery than in traditional forms of counseling.

Evaluation or diagnosis brings on a period of crisis when parents are, at least temporarily, unable to respond with their usual problem-solving abilities.[4] The demands of remediation activities may preoccupy parents so that they do not work through their mourning or grief. Another aspect of counseling with parents of handicapped children is the sometimes involuntary nature of the counseling. Parents have come to obtain services for their child and do not understand the need to seek services for themselves; yet, "it is widely recognized that the involvement and support of the parents in the management of any handicapped child is critical. . . ."[5](p165)

Crisis in the Life of a Parent

It is difficult for some audiologists, teachers, and other professionals involved with hearing impaired children to understand why a seemingly "normal" set of parents need counseling just because they have been told that their child has a hearing loss. It should be understood that by informing the parents of the handicap, a crisis has been created.

"When I was first told that my child had a hearing loss, I felt the world had dropped out from under me."

"It was kind of like being in shock. It is a physical thing, it's such a shock."

"It hurts. I mean it hurts just as much as if somebody took a knife and stabbed me or shot me."

Many types of crisis situations have conventional social customs that provide support for the persons involved in the crisis. For example, it is customary when someone is ill to send cards or flowers, or to make contact by telephone or to pay a visit. When a natural disaster occurs, human services are quickly mobilized. The rather elaborate ritual of a funeral, when examined for its psychological merits, can be seen as an effective method of maintaining a family through a period of shock, grief, and eventual adjustment to the loss of a family member. Professionals working with parents of handicapped children should be aware of the potential impact of the diagnosis of a hearing loss. Parents of a child who has just been diagnosed as having hearing impairment should be handled in a sympathetic, understanding, and supportive manner, just as if a death had occurred in the family. This comparison may not be as extreme as it sounds, as the emotional reaction to the initial diagnosis of a handicap has been referred to as "the death of the image of the normal child."[6] This concept will be discussed later in this chapter.

Justification of the Need for Counseling

An inverse relationship exists between degree of hearing loss and the age of identification.[7] From birth to about 3 years of age, a hearing impaired child may appear to be very much like a normal hearing child.[8] Gradually, parents may notice unusual or inconsistent responses to sound and become aware of lack of language development. Too often, initiation of action is delayed while the parents wait for the child to "grow out of it" or for the child to "get old enough to test." Also, aggressive action may not be taken as parents feel that the hearing loss will be cured with a hearing aid much like glasses correct impaired vision, or that tubes will correct the hearing loss as they did in the case of the neighbor's child. There are also those who continue to hope for some new discovery that will cure the hearing loss.

These hopes are helpful in that they provide a protection against the traumatic impact of the initial diagnosis. The mechanism of denial serves a positive purpose in protecting parents until they become ready to handle what lies ahead. But when this denial interferes with obtaining appropriate services and making adequate family adjustments, it becomes a negative factor that threatens the well-being of the child. Thus, there is a dilemma. How does one impress parents with the ramifications of the diagnosis of hearing impairment, and yet not overwhelm them before they are ready to hear and understand all that they need to be told?

Many questions that parents ask represent legitimate needs for information, but many are reflections of the feelings, concerns, and frustrations that they experience as they go from pediatrician to audiologist to school and back again. It is not unusual for parents to fail to understand or to not really hear much of the information presented to them at reporting conferences. This lack of understanding results primarily from their level of anxiety rather than their level of intelligence. Parents also do not always follow recommendations or keep appointments. These behaviors are common and should be anticipated and understood by the counselor and other professionals. All too often, professionals are quick to lose patience and criticize parents rather than to adjust their expectations and service delivery to accommodate the parents' needs. It is obvious that parents should keep all of the appointments and follow recommendations, therefore it is important that parents understand the reason for them.

One of the major goals in parent counseling is to keep the lines of communication open with parents so that their children receive needed services as expeditiously as possible. Children fail to get services because parents do not fully understand the importance of an otological examination, the need for early amplification and appropriate educational programs, and because parents do not understand the implications of hearing loss in general. Matkin states that "without professional support, many of the audiologic and educational recommendations will not be followed and as a consequence, primary steps toward habilitation may be delayed during critical periods."[5(p167)] Children also fail to get services because parents cannot emotionally deal with the new demands that are made on them.

> It is a truism that the physical and emotional well-being of the young patient is often directly related to the physical and emotional status of the parent, and that we may seriously impede or harm our therapy for the child if we don't properly enlighten and accommodate the parent.[9(p9)]

The emotional state of the parent should be handled in the context of the counseling process. An experienced, trained counselor is capable of interpreting and handling defenses as well as assessing what parents are ready to hear. When this process is started during the initial evaluations, many negative reactions in potential problem areas, such as feelings of misdirected, debilitating anger, reactions to the initial crisis, and resentment about the referral for involuntary counseling, can be minimized and adequate family adjustment can be facilitated.

Counseling with parents of hearing impaired children is multifaceted and serves several needs:

(1) It provides a supportive cushion for the parents' emotional reaction of the initial diagnosis.
(2) It provides an assessment of the parents' emotional state that should be used to understand their acceptance of the handicap and their ability to follow through with recommendations.
(3) It facilitates the progress of parents through various phases of the adjustment process.
(4) It supplies an accepting atmosphere for the parents' feelings, questions, and concerns.
(5) It establishes a base of rapport and trust with counselors to which parents can turn to as needed.

Many parents plunge into programs with unrealistic hopes, only to be disillusioned. For example, it is not unusual to encounter uninformed parents who expect that a hearing aid will enable their child to talk immediately. When the aid does not produce the expected results, the parents may no longer encourage the child to wear it. Until parents have reached at least a minimum level of understanding and acceptance of the hearing loss, their response to any remediation program may not be positive.[10]

> It is well to keep in mind that a hearing impairment is essentially a hidden handicap only until the time when an individual begins to utilize wearable amplification. Thus, it is not surprising in some instances to find that parents, who seemingly had accepted the fact that their youngster had a hearing handicap, react negatively when the time comes for them to participate actively in a hearing aid orientation program.[5(p167)]

PARENT REACTIONS TO A HANDICAPPED CHILD

Adjustment to Parenting

Most people have some training for the jobs that they hold. Occupations are supported by unions and regulated by licensing laws. The job of being a parent is one of the few jobs that mandates no prior training or experience, does not require a license, and is not sup-

ported by a union. (Perhaps that is fortunate. What would happen if parents went on strike?) Yet, even though it is not always recognized, parenting is one of the most difficult and most important roles that is played in life.

In this age of ready accessibility to birth control, couples can now choose whether to have a child. But how many choose to be the parent of a handicapped child? The meager guidelines that are available for rearing normal children are useless or inadequate for rearing a handicapped child. The complex role of being a parent is compounded with the discovery of a handicapping condition.[11] Dr. Spock doesn't tell when or even if a handicapped child will be toilet-trained. He offers no advice on how to discipline a child who does not hear or understand. The once happy dreams about the long-awaited child become clouded. The future of the child and of the parents is now shrouded with uncertainty. Uncertainty itself is an uncomfortable state.

"Death of the Healthy Child"

Emotionally responding and eventually adjusting to a handicapped child has been compared to experiencing a death; the death of the image of the normal child.[6] This response sometimes can be seen as parents are reunited with their handicapped child following a discussion of the diagnosis. The sight of the child is a very painful reminder of the image of the normal child, and there is a sense of loss and an accompanying sadness.

> "My husband looked like he was going to a funeral for three months—he really did— and everytime he looked at her . . . I could see it. It was just killing him . . . really it was an extremely sad experience, it was a loss . . . a kind of mourning, I guess. It was an extremely sad time."

A primary difference in the life adjustment of the parents of a handicapped child compared to that of normal child's parents is that the handicapped child will require much more care and attention for an indefinite period of time. The realization of this fact can have a serious emotional impact that is sometimes more devastating than the initial shock of discovering the handicap. An additional difference is uncertainty concerning the child's eventual independence and ability to be self-supporting.

Coping with a Handicapped Child

Parents with a handicapped child must, in one way or another, cope with the presence of the handicapped child in their family. Their responses can be healthy and adaptive or destructive and maladaptive. Most responses should be viewed on some kind of continuum. When parents are faced with the prospect of caring for a handicapped child, many experience overwhelming guilt and despair.[6] It is not uncommon for parents to feel that the handicap is in some way their fault. Zealous professionals often add to the stress of the family by implying through their recommendations and expectations that the primary focus and energy of the family be directed entirely on the handicapped child.

Should a family be encouraged to move to a different location in order to obtain services for their child? Should either parent be encouraged to change or give up a job so that they can avail themselves of services? Do service delivery systems accommodate working parents? How much time should a working parent be asked to spend with the child in supplementary tutoring sessions? Should this time vary when there are other children in the home? What provisions or considerations are made for siblings of hearing impaired children? Who deals with their jealousy when all of the attention is paid to the handicapped child?

Parents' guilt usually renders them quite vulnerable to demands made by professionals, and if they can't or don't meet these demands, then guilt increases. "I feel that I must do everything that I can to help [my child]" is an often-heard refrain. By assisting the parent to define the "everything" for their child, a counselor can encourage the parent to set priorities and to keep the other family needs in perspective.

PARENT REACTIONS TO AN INITIAL DIAGNOSIS OF HEARING LOSS

The most common emotional reaction parents have to a diagnosis of hearing impairment is similar to that shown by parents with children having other handicaps, but some circumstances and concerns are unique to a diagnosis of hearing impairment. Deafness is different from many other types of handicap because it is hidden, the implications obscure, and the eventual ramifications slow in coming.

Hearing Loss: The Hidden Handicap

Hearing loss does not fully manifest itself until a child's speech and language is noticeably absent or delayed. There is felt to be a strong relationship between the degree of loss and its effect on language and speech development.[12] The milder the loss, the later the effects, especially if the child is otherwise healthy. Prior to suspicion of hearing loss, parents have grown accustomed to a happy, healthy, normal child. When the child is 3 or 4 years of age, parents have probably begun to think about the child's future in terms of school placement, either in the neighborhood elementary school or at a chosen private school.

Not only is the handicap hidden, but it is also very deceptive. In many cases, the loss may affect only some frequencies and the child may respond to some sounds at normal levels. This may encourage the parents to continue to deny, or at least to doubt, the diagnosis of hearing impairment for an extended period. It may even be deceptive to unsuspecting professionals, who may variously label the child retarded, language-learning disabled, or as having a behavior problem.

In addition to the insidious nature of hearing loss, it is also a difficult concept to explain, because most lay people tend to think in terms of either "hearing" or "deaf," with no middle ground.

> "We did not understand about hearing loss, decibels, frequency, moderate to severe— the news that we understood was 'substantial hearing gone' and that there was nothing to be done about it—it was permanent."

Hearing impairment is confusing to the parent who does not understand the concepts of frequency or intensity but whose child obviously hears some things. How can the parent accept a hearing impairment when his view is either "hearing" or "deaf"? Many parents may also assume that the proposed hearing aid will restore hearing to normal; thus they have no understanding of the need for a remediation program.

"Your Child is Hearing Impaired"

After what may have been months of worry, searching, and confusion, the words "Your child is hearing impaired" are met with various reactions. Some parents are relieved to hear that it is "just a hearing loss," others are devastated because they hoped to hear that their child was normal. Whatever the diagnosis, parents 'hear' very little of it.

> "I remember sitting in the audiologist's office and I can't remember half of what was said. I was sitting there—like in a daze. I could hear, but it just did not soak in."

However calm, understanding, and accepting parents appear to be, one should make the assumption that a strong emotional reaction is occurring, which the parent may be unable or unwilling to share at the moment. For these reasons, a conference in which an initial or confirming diagnosis of hearing loss is given should be a carefully planned process. At this time emotional reactions and defense mechanisms to handle those reactions can be most intense. Skillful handling may contribute to a better lifetime adjustment of those involved.

Parents' Cycle of Reaction to a Diagnosis of Hearing Loss

Table 18-1 illustrates the cycle that parents most often follow in reaction to a diagnosis of a hearing loss in their child. Following the diagnosis, the cycle of shock, disbelief, grief, anger, and frustration, followed by eventual acceptance of the loss is usually seen. This cycle has been well-documented, most notably by Mindel and Vernon.[13] It is well accepted that all parents experience some of the emotions in this cycle to some degree as they go through the process of discovering that their child has a hearing loss. However, it is not well recognized that the cycle is a continuous process that never resolves into complete acceptance. Par-

Table 18-1 Reaction to Diagnosis of a Hearing Loss

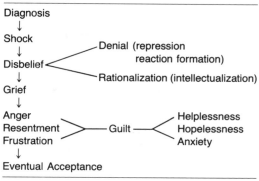

ents will follow different courses as they work through these stages and express themselves in different ways. However, the defense mechanisms used to counter these emotions are much less understood. Professionals dealing with parents interpret superficial or surface responses on the assumption that they represent the parents' basic emotional feelings. But in actuality what they are probably seeing is the parents' defense mechanisms.

A *defense mechanism* is a protective device for dealing with stressful or unexpected occurrences. Defense mechanisms are necessary and healthy unless they interfere with a desired action. Included in the defenses most often used by parents of hearing impaired children are: denial, repression, reaction-formation, and intellectualization.

Denial is a refusal to recognize or acknowledge reality, and is most frequently seen in the early stages of discovery of the hearing loss. Initially, parents deny that there is anything wrong with their child, or insist that there is no hearing loss. The mechanism of denial can be seen in parents who go from clinic to clinic seeking an option that will conform to their wishes for a perfect child. However, other forms of denial may continue for many months as parents deny the implications of the hearing loss. They expect language development and academic achievement to be relatively unaffected.

> "I know he has a hearing loss, but I expect him to be just like any normal child. Once he gets his speech he won't be any different."

Repression is similar to denial, but is potentially more serious. Repression is making unconscious any feeling that is not wanted. Repressed feelings are temporarily forgotten but can return when the source of the feelings can no longer be identified. Our society discourages the display of emotions, especially negative ones. Therefore, people are very reluctant to express themselves openly.

Professionals who have not had some training in this area of mental health are often uncomfortable dealing with these negative emotions, so they strive not to elicit them. These feelings, much to the relief of all, are repressed, but appear later when decisions must be made on critical issues, such as regular or special education, ear-level or body aid, and/or oral or total communication.

> A mother sat quietly through a conference at which time she was told that her child was hearing impaired, and would need a hearing aid and speech therapy. She seemed to understand and accept all of the information presented to her. When she requested services from her local independent school district it was apparent that she had misunderstood the recommendations. When the school did not comply with her request she threatened to take legal action to obtain services.

Reaction formation is a "mechanism in which dangerous desires and impulses are prevented from entering consciousness or from being carried out in action by the fostering of opposed types of behavior and attitudes."[14(p669)] Reaction formation occurs when an attitude is assumed that is counter or opposite to the feared impulse. For example, a parent who is afraid of becoming a child abuser may not discipline the child at all. Reaction formation is frequently seen in parents whose immediate impulse is to reject the handicapped child or the diagnosis. Instead they engage in overprotection, oversolicitation, and overacceptance of the handicap.

> The mother of a child with Treacher-Collins Syndrome and with a moderate conductive hearing loss carried a picture of her child in a locket around her neck to show people what a beautiful child she had. After a very enthusiastic beginning, she quickly dropped out of the parent program.

Parents of handicapped children are much less likely to foster independence and self sufficiency in their children,[15] yet one of their primary sources of anger and frustration is the increased care that the child requires.[13] The desire to relinquish the care of the child is sometimes converted into a devotion of total time to the handicapped child and a neglect of other family members. Parents engage in extreme positive activity, such as becoming advocates for services or service-providers themselves, to avoid dealing with the unwanted feelings.

Intellectualization is the attempt to make everything impersonal, abstract, theoretical, and unemotional. Clinically, it appears that fathers may tend to use intellectualization more than mothers. They challenge the validity of the testing or the credentials of the professional. They request information regarding the efficacy of remedial programs or probability statements about degree of hearing loss and ultimate language development. Yet very few are able to express their sadness at seeing their pert blond child wearing a hearing aid or their fear that their namesake will not be a football star or a partner in the business firm.

> Following a long reporting conference at which time M/M J were told that their 9-month-old daughter was significantly hearing impaired, Mr. J requested a tour of the sound suite and an explanation of the functioning sound equipment. During subsequent appointments Mr. J asked for more and more data regarding testing equipment, efficiency of aids, etc. Fitting his child with an aid became extremely difficult as he never felt that the prescribed aid provided "maximum benefit."

DEVELOPMENTAL MILESTONES

Continuing Crises

> "I haven't completely accepted it. I don't think I ever will."

At every decision point some of the old feelings of anger, grief, and frustration are revived. How parents have worked through the initial adjustment process plays an important part in the handling of each new crisis. A change in the

Table 18-2   Developmental Milestones

Initial diagnosis—Initial shock
└→Entering first grade—Reexperiencing grief
  └→Adolescence-Emotional instability
    └→Adulthood—Able to live independently

hearing loss, particularly for the worse, can be just as traumatic as the original diagnosis. Table 18-2 outlines some significant developmental milestones that can cause additional crises for parents.

Entering the First Grade

Whatever the diagnosis, one of the most frequent questions is, "Will my child be ready for regular first grade?" Entry into a regular first grade is a "landmark" most parents use to confirm that their child is either normal or not normal. Parents and professionals, too, set this as their goal in the child's early education. The emotional need parents have to make their child appear normal influences major decisions involving the child, such as educational placement, hearing aids, and remedial programs. A multidisciplinary team can gather test information and then objectively consider appropriate future educational plans that may or may not involve entering or continuing in an integrated classroom.[16] Even if hearing impaired children appear ready for first grade, there is a contrast between them and normal-hearing children, whose vocabularies grow faster and who obtain more incidental information. Hearing impaired children may stop attending to concepts they don't understand, or fall behind, and/or become behavior problems.[17] As academic demands increase in the third and fourth grades, children with inadequate language development due to hearing impairment who have been placed in integrated classes begin to have difficulty keeping up. When schools report poor grades or progress, parents respond by putting increased pressure on the child or the school, and sometimes both. It is not unusual to find that these children, after a full day of school, have some type of additional tutoring or therapy every afternoon. A counselor with knowledge of the resources available and the abilities of the hearing impaired child can play a vital role in working with the parents to facilitate successful placement and planning.[18]

Adolescence

Unfortunately, successful passage through elementary school can be a minor hurdle compared to the myriad of problems that can arise during adolescence. Adolescence is a crisis in and of itself. When compounded with a hearing loss, the difficulties are geometrically increased. Chess et al[15(p63)] state, "No matter how successful the academic mainstreaming, and no matter how apparently easy the social adaptation was in childhood, with the onset of adolescence the social problem for the handicapped youngster becomes a serious one."

A major goal in adolescence is independence from parents, and a primary means of achieving this is a close alliance with peers. Typically, the communication between adolescents and their parents is, at best, strained. If speech and/or language skills are impaired, communication is even more difficult. These same communication difficulties can interfere with the development of adequate peer relationships. Hearing loss can also have a significant negative effect on the striving for independence, as many parents have probably been overprotective and overindulgent. Parents have arranged and/or endured endless testing sessions, reporting conferences, tutoring sessions, educational programs, etc. They have usually been very involved in their child's development with adolescence. Now they are seen as intrusive and overcontrolling. Adolescents, at times, must take extraordinary measures to break this control.

> One such unusual example was a 14-year-old and her mother, who had been described as the "perfect, cooperative parent." For six years after the diagnosis, she devoted herself entirely to this child's acquisition of speech and success in a regular classroom. She continued to make every decision about what school, what program, and what classes her daughter would take. Concurrently, as the child approached adolescence, she began to have difficulty in school because she wished to hide the fact that she was "different" from her teachers and peers. Thus the mother increased her involvement with the child and the school. Following two years of struggle with rejected hearing aids, failed classes, and truancy, the adolescent was admitted to a psychiatric hospital, weighing 60 pounds with a diagnosis of anorexia nervosa.

Although this example is an extreme one, it brings into focus some of the pitfalls of parenting a hearing impaired child, such as overinvolvement, overprotection, and the unusual emphasis on academic success.

Rejection of hearing aids is one of the most frequent and visible signs of the hearing impaired adolescent's struggle. Entrance into adolescence was once marked by a request for a change from a body aid to an over-the-ear aid. Many more over-the-ear aids are being prescribed for young children, but many teenagers refuse to wear even the most inconspicuous models. The social code requires as much uniformity as possible and a hearing aid is unacceptable, because it makes the teenager too different from peers. The parent may also subtly or unconsciously encourage this rejection, as the hearing aid is a visible sign that their child is handicapped. Typically, this is a time when parents become discouraged about their child's progress toward "normality" and concerned about the future; they also may begin to reject any remedial work because their goal of normality has not been reached.

Finally, successful passage through the stage of adolescence is facilitated by good communication. Many parents of hearing impaired youngsters often think that their child can hear and understand everything that is said. Close scrutiny often reveals that great gaps in language development transform much communication in a sham of nodding and smiling. Again, through counseling parents may be helped to accept and cope with these difficulties. Brill reports[19] a high correlation between parents who participated in a parent counseling program that included basic orientation to hearing loss, communication facilitation, behavior management, and counseling, and the degree of change in the behavior and academic achievement of their children.

WHAT PARENTS NEED FROM PROFESSIONALS

Meadows[20(p23)] states, "Although it is neither feasible nor desirable for these professionals to become qualified counselors or therapists, it would be beneficial if they had an increased understanding of the need of their clients." During the course of diagnosis and educational placement, parents will come in contact with many different professionals. It is not unusual for parents to come to a diagnostic study with an accumulation of months, and even years, of pain and distress.

> "You have to remember that we are sometimes even more anxious and emotional about this [diagnosis and educational placement] than the child, especially if we've been worried and upset about this problem for months, and we've been imaging all sorts of serious defects."[(p8)]

Parents need effective counseling at this crucial time to enable them to work through their feelings and direct their efforts and anxieties toward constructive endeavors for their child. Vernon[21(p30)] has commented, "Unfortunately, instead of professional help toward these ends, parents are generally exposed to the well-intended but often misguided counsel of speech therapists, educators, physicians, and audiologists whose competence and training is often excellent in their respective fields but not in the field of counseling."

The Physician's Role

Typically, parents first discuss their concerns about their child with the family physician, pediatrician, and/or otolaryngologist. The importance of these early contacts cannot be minimized. Parents frequently report dissatisfaction with their physician, and this probably results from two main factors. First, the physician is often the first person to acknowledge to the parents that something is wrong with the child. The initial disbelief, denial, and anger is then directed at the physician. Second, if the physician does not have adequate knowledge about hearing impairment, and its diagnosis and treatment, his/her recommendations may be misguided.

It is difficult to educate all physicians about language development and the importance of early intervention, appropriate diagnostic services, and educational programs, yet many families depend heavily on their physician for diagnosis and prognosis. Therefore, when the physician's report to the family differs from that of other professionals, an additional burden of confusion and stress is placed on the family. Great skill and tact is required from all professionals to guide parents through the maze of conflicting diagnoses, recommendations, and procedures. Increased communication between physicians and other professionals could decrease the amount of misinformation and confusing reports.

The Audiologist's Role

The audiologist plays a critical role in the early diagnostic process, and this professional's skill in managing the family contributes to the initial acceptance of the hearing loss and adjustment. The activities appropriate for the audiologist, according to Stream and Stream,[22] are listed in Table 18-3. These activities may vary considerably given the setting in which the audiologist is employed and the availability of other services. Educational programs are provided through the public schools on a more extensive basis now, so that frequently only an appropriate referral need be made. Care should be taken in describing services provided by other programs, as any misinformation will add confusion. Unless there are no other options available, the audiologist should not bear the entire responsibility for helping parents to deal with their feelings. Audiologists should certainly be aware of and sensitive to these feelings and needs, however parent counseling is performed most appropriately by professionals with training in mental health. The audiologist and counselor, if they are not the same person, should work closely together to provide the needed support.

The Role of a Comprehensive Diagnostic Center

Speech and hearing clinics, or comprehensive diagnostic centers, whether public or private, tend to operate on rigid schedules and sometimes rigid fee arrangements.[23] Clinic styles vary from total and exclusive management of a case to technician-type testing services. Either extreme is undesirable, as this rigidity can be inadequate or impractical in meeting the immediate and ongoing needs of young hearing impaired children and their families.

Audiologists, speech pathologists and/or counselors in a multidisciplinary clinical setting usually have the opportunity to take a more aggressive role in developing compre-

Table 18-3   Activities Appropriate for the Audiologist*

1. Present information on the current status of the child as it relates to factors that affect the child's potential.
2. Develop realistic, supportive educational plans.
3. Support parents in dealing with their feelings.
4. Allow parents to enhance their understanding and acceptance of the hearing disorder.

*Source: Stream and Stream.[2]

hensive services for hearing impaired children than do individual practitioners or school personnel. A clinic staff should define its professional role in regard to case management, extent of services, reporting style, and referral system. Much of the confusion and stress parents encounter results from scattered or piecemeal evaluations. The clinic can act as a coordinator between the physician and any professionals or agencies providing services to the family. The staff of a clinic must also be willing to work cooperatively with the school, but they should not abdicate their professional role by relinquishing total responsibility to the school. Without coordination and cooperation, gaps or overlaps in service will occur. If only a technical service is provided, there may not be an appropriate professional to help the family obtain all of the services that it needs.

Appropriate coordination of services is difficult, time-consuming, and expensive, however ultimate client benefit surely makes the effort worthwhile. The staff of a clinic can serve as a central source for diagnostic evaluations and referral to educational programs. A designated staff member can provide a bridge of support for the parents between the time of initial concern or contact and the time they are enrolled in an appropriate program. The staff member can also be a continuing base of support to which the parents can return as decisions or program changes are made or alternative opinions are sought. A base of support is particularly necessary for parents of hearing impaired children as the decision concerning the appropriate educational program may not be immediately apparent, and several changes in the program, particularly in the preschool and primary years may be needed.

The Role of the Mental Health Professional

Counseling of parents (not education or training) is most effectively accomplished by a professional with formal training in an area of mental health. That is, the counselor should have training in understanding and assessing personality and family dynamics, and should be comfortable and adept at discussing all aspects of emotional concerns.

From the initial contact, parents' feelings and concerns should be considered as important as the correct diagnosis. Sanders[10(pp322–323)] has said, "It must be recognized, therefore, that in these early years in particular, it is not possible to separate our responsibilities for providing help to the hearing impaired child from the need to provide guidance to parents in all aspects of family adjustment. . . . The family members must, therefore, be assisted in their task of dealing with the emotional, social, communicative, cognitive, and educational implications of the child's hearing deficiency."

For this reason, counseling services should be provided to any family during the time of initial diagnosis of a severe handicapping condition such as hearing impairment. However, to engage clients in counseling who have not called to say "I need the services of a counselor" is a different and sometimes difficult task. To establish a relationship and a framework for counseling, a meeting between the parents, the mental health professional providing the counseling, and the audiologist, if they are not the same person, should be conducted *before* any testing is begun. The parents should have an opportunity to express their concerns and to raise any questions that they want answered. This initial session also allows the professionals to assess the emotional state of the parents. Table 18-4 lists some key questions that should be asked during the initial contact. The answers to these questions are then used as a guide for later reporting to the parents, giving the clinician some idea of what the parents are prepared to hear, and how much they already know and can understand. In addition, the answers will provide some clues on how the parents will respond to a diagnosis of hearing loss.

The parents' account of what they have done prior to the interview may predict what they will do in the future. For example, if parents

Table 18-4   Key Questions To Be Asked of Parents During Initial Contact with Audiologist and Counselor

1. How long have you suspected that your child may be hearing impaired?
2. What have you done up to this point?
3. What have you been told?
4. What do you feel about what you have been told?
5. What information and/or services do you want from this center?

indicate that they have been suspicious of hearing loss for a long time, this may indicate that they may not actively seek and use services. For parents who have been told "nothing" about hearing loss, because of the initial shock, it should be assumed that they will hear or understand little of what is told to them in the early stages of the interview process. How they say they feel about the information should not be assumed to be how they feel, but their statements should be used to guide the remediation plan. Through this process, one can determine how to present the information and how the information will confirm or conflict with what the parents have already been told. If they are seeking confirmation, it is important to find out why. If reports are in conflict, information should be presented tentatively, with professional respect for the other source.

Hersch and Amon[24] state that there is no painless way to inform parents that their child is hearing impaired, but a method can be used that will help parents cope most effectively. Initial information should be reported in small doses because it is common for anyone in a state of anxiety to absorb very little. Professionals dealing with parents are all aware of the distortions that occur between what is reported and what is received. Early diagnosis should be tentative, however information should always be presented truthfully. Some professionals tend to skirt issues rather than to present them openly, so as not to evoke emotional responses. Ideally, 45 minutes to one hour should be reserved for the first reporting session, and arrangements should be made for the child and/or siblings to be cared for away from the reporting conference when they accompany the parents. It is almost impossible for a parent to participate in conversation, and for a professional to communicate, while an active 3-year-old is climbing all over them or the office.

Subsequent Interviews

A conference in which an initial diagnosis of hearing loss is made should be followed by a second conference within 24 to 48 hours, although some feel that it should occur in a week. If both parents are unable to attend the first session, every effort should be made to include both of them for the second session. During this time, the parents should be encouraged to review what they have been told so that how much they gained from the previous session can be assessed. The second session can be coordinated with other testing or other interviews, but this procedure should be an accepted format for provision of services, and adequate time must always be scheduled to give a parent the needed information and to listen to questions and concerns.

During both sessions, time should be used to obtain a social history from the parents. The information from this history should be used in planning a remediation program that will meet their needs as well as the child's needs. *In all reporting and planning, there should be an attempt to proceed with deliberate speed*. The counselor should give the parents what they can handle, and not assume that they can effectively function until they have all of the information. Also, during this process, parents should be warned that they may hear conflicting reports and receive opposing recommendations from different professionals. They should be encouraged to ask questions and should be supported in their attempt to reconcile opposing recommendations.

The Role of Schools

Schools have been required to assume more and more of the responsibility for children and parents. In fact, schools have almost been given the exclusive role of providing all things to all handicapped children. Although schools have executed a herculean effort, it is unrealistic to expect that they can or should take over all aspects of the diagnoses, remediation, and counseling needed by hearing impaired children and their parents.

Schools should work closely with private clinics and professionals. Just as the private sector must cooperate with the public schools, schools must be willing to cooperate with private professionals to avoid duplication of services and to ensure that needed services beyond the school's scope or capability are made available to handicapped children. It should be noted that counseling for parents is rarely provided by public schools at this time. In view of the documented need for counseling of parents whose children have handicapping conditions, schools should ensure that this service is appropriately provided through either private or public facilities.

Counseling Needs During the Referral Process

The present educational structure has forced schools to become diagnostic clinics and placement agencies. Although they will vary from district to district, when a handicapped child is referred to a school the following steps are usually required: the child must be on a waiting list for assessment, appropriate medical evaluations must be obtained, various kinds of social history forms must be completed, and a waiting period for assignment to a program must take place. This process can last for weeks or months. Guidelines limiting the maximum waiting time exist, but school personnel are sometimes both overworked and not fully trained to run efficient diagnostic clinics, especially when they are trying to administer ongoing programs at the same time. Parents have increased difficulty with this process, as the delays and the complicated procedures tend to exacerbate all of the negative feelings that have been engendered by the diagnosis. To reduce negative feelings during the referral process, a *contact person* should be assigned to each family upon initial referral to an educational program to provide information and support and to facilitate the parents' progression through the process.

Counseling Needs During the ARD Process*

The admission, review, and dismissal (ARD) procedure is the process by which a child's diagnostic reports are reviewed and appropriate educational placement is recommended. It

---

*For detailed information on procedures used in the referral process for the education of handicapped children, refer to the local guidelines.

is also the time when a child's individual educational plan (IEP) is written. The rationale behind this process is excellent; however, it presents several problems, particularly for parents. Except for larger school districts, diagnostic personnel and members of the ARD committee may have little or no expertise in the area of hearing loss as a handicapping condition. They are poorly equipped to evaluate the child, much less to adequately explain to parents the intricacies of hearing loss and speech and language development. A major drawback is the setting and constitution of the committee. It is intimidating, at best, for parents to sit in a meeting with four to ten professionals and hear their child discussed. No matter how concerned and supportive the committee intends to be, the majority of parents interviewed subsequently relate feelings suggesting that the experience seems to be more of an adversary proceeding than a supportive process.

Parents need information about their child, and it is beneficial for them to play an active role in planning the child's educational program. However, some provisions must be made to meet parents' emotional needs and to respect their feelings before they can be expected to be contributing members of the ARD process.

A reporting conference in which the parents are given a diagnosis should precede an ARD meeting, so that the parent is not presented with significant new information at the ARD. At the reporting conference, new information, progress reports, and new recommendations should be presented by the contact person, a team member who should have good rapport with the parents. The number of personnel at the ARD meeting should be kept to a minimum, and each person should be clearly introduced with the reason for that person's attendance. It must be clearly defined that the goal of the ARD process is to develop the most appropriate program possible for the designated child.

A SUGGESTED PROGRAM

Assumptions:

(1) All parents experience some degree of negative emotional response when their child is diagnosed as hearing impaired.

(2) The successful adjustment to their changed life situation will depend in part on the amount and quality of support that is provided, particularly during the early phase of diagnosis and program planning.

(3) Counseling provided by a mental health professional who is knowledgeable about hearing loss can significantly contribute to the quality of the support provided by other professionals.

Strategies:

(1) Adequate information (records, case history information) should be obtained prior to the first appointment for audiological assessment or confirmation so that appropriate procedures and sufficient time is scheduled.

When a hearing loss is suspected, based on records and case history data, a short, initial conference with the parents, the audiologist, and the counselor should be scheduled immediately prior to the testing session. If a loss is suspected or confirmed based on the testing, an immediate (within 24–48 hours) reappointment should be made both to continue testing and to meet with the parents to provide additional information and to continue assessment.

(2) Depending on the circumstances, some reading material should be provided at either the first or second visit.

Distribution of material would depend on the degree of reliability of the testing and diagnosis, the initial response of the parents, and remedial program availability. Matkin[5] suggests the presentation of slides and other visual aids while the child is being tested. This is a more systematic method of orientation and also allows more time for interaction with the parents.

(3) The counselor should maintain a relationship with the parents until the major steps (diagnosis, obtaining and fitting a hearing aid, program placement, and parent education services) have been taken. In most cases it would be beneficial for the counselor to take a *case manager* role during this time.

(4) Parents should be provided with information regarding their emotional responses and needs, the need for support services, and the programs and services that are available to them. They should be apprised of the laws regulating education of the handicapped, state hearing aid programs, Social Security income

supplements, alternative education programs and services, and sources of information.

(5) All parents who have a hearing impaired child need counseling from the time they are aware of the problem. Garrett and Stoval[25] state, "We must accept that counseling is a necessity, not a luxury. . . . The child's education is the responsibility of both the parents and the schools, and they must work together as a team. Counseling is part and parcel of the whole package."

SUMMARY

It is the consensus of most of the authorities cited in this chapter that parental response to the handicap has a major impact on the child's (and the family's) growth and development. This consensus must now be implemented by all professionals who work with hearing impaired children.

> "I don't know what I would have done without her [the counselor]. Just knowing that she was there, if I needed her, was my source of emotional support. And there are still times that I say 'Help' because I don't yet have all the answers."

REFERENCES

1. McGowan TF, Schmidt LD: *Counseling: Readings in Theory and Practice* (New York: Holt, Rinehart & Winston, 1962).
2. Patterson CH, Stewart LG: Principles of counseling with deaf people, in Sussman AE, Stewart LG, eds: *Counseling with Deaf People* (New York: New York Univ. School of Education, 1971).
3. Stewart TC: *Counseling Parents of Exceptional Children* (Columbus: CE Merrill Publishing, 1978).
4. Drotar D, Baskiewicz A, Ervin N, et al: The adaptation of parents to the birth of an infant with a congenital malformation: A hypothetical model. *Pediatr*, 56 (1975), 710–717.
5. Matkin ND: Hearing aids for children, in Hodgson WR, Sinner PH, eds: *Hearing Aid Assessment and Use in Audiologic Habilitation* (Baltimore: Williams and Wilkins, 1977).
6. Young RK: Chronic sorrow: Parents response to the birth of a child with a defect. *Amer J Matern Child Nurs*, Vol. 2 (January/February 1977), 38–42.
7. Matkin ND: Assessment of hearing sensitivity during the preschool years, in Bess FH, ed: *Childhood Deafness: Causation, Assessment and Management* (New York: Grune and Stratton, 1977).
8. Furth H: *Deafness and Learning: A Psycho-social Approach* (Belmont, CA: Wadsworth Publishing, 1973).
9. Eisenstadt AA: Weakness in clinical procedures. *ASHA*, 14 (January 1972), 7–9.
10. Sanders DA: Educational programming for the older infant, in Bess FH, ed: *Childhood Deafness: Causation, Assessment and Management* (New York: Grune and Stratton, 1977).
11. Mandelbaum A, Wheeler ME: The meaning of a defective child to parents. *Social Casework*, Family Service Association of America (1963), 5–12.
12. Quigley S: Effects of early hearing impairment on normal language development, in Martin FN, ed: *Pediatric Audiology* (Englewood Cliffs, NJ: Prentice-Hall, 1978).
13. Mindel ED, Vernon M: *They Grow in Silence: The Deaf Child and His Family* (Silver Spring, MD: National Assn. of the Deaf, 1971).
14. Coleman JC: *Abnormal Psychology and Modern Life*, ed 3 (Dallas: Scott, Foresman & Co, 1964).
15. Chess S, Fernandez P, Korn S: The handicapped child and his family: Consonance and dissonance. *J Amer Acad Child Psychiat*, 19 (1980), 56–57.
16. Nuernberger J: The role of the psychologist: Evaluating potential for integration, in Northcott WH, ed: *The Hearing Impaired Child in a Regular Classroom: Preschool, Elementary, and Secondary Years* (Washington, DC: AG Bell Assn. for the Deaf, 1973).
17. Frick E: Ensuring successful adjustment to integration, in Northcott WH, ed: *The Hearing Impaired Child in a Regular Classroom: Preschool Elementary, and Secondary Years* (Washington, DC: AG Bell Assn. for the Deaf, 1973).
18. Russell G: The place of the social worker in integration, in Northcott WH, ed: *The Hearing Impaired Child in a Regular Classroom: Preschool, Elementary, and Secondary Years* (Washington, DC: AG Bell Assn. for the Deaf, 1973).
19. Brill RG, Davis F, Lennan RK: *Pilot Program With Emotionally Disturbed Deaf Children*, final report. (Riverside: California School for the Deaf, June 1969).
20. Meadow KP, Meadow L: Changing role perceptions for parents of handicapped children. *Except Child*, 38 (September 1971), 21–27.
21. Vernon M: Current status of counseling with

deaf people, in Sussman AE, Stewart LG, eds: *Counseling with Deaf People* (New York: New York Univ. School of Education, 1971).

22. Stream RW, Stream KS: Counseling the parents of the hearing impaired child, in Martin FN, ed: *Pediatric Audiology* (Englewood Cliffs, NJ: Prentice-Hall, 1978).

23. Horton KB, Hanners BA: Trends in educational programming: The early years of the hearing impaired child, zero to three, in Bess FH, ed: *Childhood Deafness: Causation, Assessment,* *and Management* (New York: Grune and Stratton, 1977).

24. Hersch LB, Amon C: A child has a hearing loss: Reporting the diagnosis of handicaps in children and its impact on parents. *Amer Ann of Deaf,* 120 (December 1975), 568–571.

25. Garrett C, Stoval E: A parent's view on integration, in Northcott WH, ed: *The Hearing Impaired Child in a Regular Classroom: Preschool, Elementary, and Secondary Years* (Washington, DC: AG Bell Assn. for the Deaf, 1973).

INDEX